6/99

Windows NT™ Server

ISBN 0-13-856568-6

90000

9 780138 565688

MICROSOFT BACKOFFICE SERIES

■ Windows NT™ Server: Management and Control,
2nd Edition
Spencer/Goncalves

|| eqn f2 | ↑↓ (home (r690894f = share r690894 f

may be this
doesn't work

Can only try to keep
chatble a otherwise) ?

MICROSOFT BACKOFFICE SERIES

SPENCER/GONCALVES

Windows NT™ Server: Management and Control, 2nd Edition

To join a Prentice Hall PTR Internet mailing list, point to
http://www.prenhall.com/mail_lists/

Prentice Hall PTR, Upper Saddle River, NJ 07458

Library of Congress Cataloging-in-Publication Data

Spencer, Kenneth L., 1951–
  Windows NT server : management and control / Spencer/Goncalves. --
2nd ed.
      p. cm. -- (Microsoft backoffice series)
    Includes index.
    ISBN 0–12–856568–6
    1. Microsoft Windows NT Server. 2. Operating systems (Computers)
3. Windows NT Server. I. Goncalves, Marcus. II. Title.
    III. Series.
    QA76.76.063S675   1998
    005.4'4769--dc21

                                                    97–46924
                                                    CIP

Editorial/Production Supervision: Beth Sturla
Acquisitions Editor: Mike Meehan
Development Editor: Ralph Moore
Cover Design Director: Jerry Votta
Cover Designer: Bruce Kenselaar
Manufacturing Manager: Alexis R. Heydt
Series Design: Maureen Eide
Marketing Manager: Stephen Solomon
Art Director: Gail Cocker-Bogusz
Editorial/Production Supervision: Benchmark Productions, Inc., Boston, MA

 © 1998 by Prentice Hall PTR
Prentice Hall, Inc.
A Simon & Schuster Company
Upper Saddle River, New Jersey 07458

Prentice Hall books are widely used by corporations and government agencies for
training, marketing, and resale. The publisher offers discounts on this book when
ordered in bulk quantities. For more information, contact:

    Corporate Sales Department
    Prentice Hall PTR
    One Lake Street
    Upper Saddle River, NJ 07458
    Phone: 800-382-3419; FAX: 201-236-7141
    E-mail (Internet): corpsales@prenhall.com

Printed in the United States of America

10 9 8 7 6 5 4 3 2

ISBN 0-13-856568-6

Prentice-Hall International (UK) Limited, *London*
Prentice-Hall of Australia Pty. Limited, *Sydney*
Prentice-Hall Canada Inc., *Toronto*
Prentice-Hall Hispanoamericana, S.A., *Mexico*
Prentice-Hall of India Private Limited, *New Delhi*
Prentice-Hall of Japan, Inc., *Tokyo*
Simon & Schuster Asia Pte. Ltd., *Singapore*
Editora Prentice-Hall do Brasil, Ltda., *Rio de Janeiro*

I dedicate this book to my wonderful wife, Trisha, and my great children, Kenny and Jeffrey. They have been an inspiration and motivation to me for many years.

Ken Spencer

I would like to dedicate this book to my beautiful wife, Carla, and my awesome kids, Samir, Andrea, and Joshua. In special, Don Fernando Davalos, for never missing the opportunity to inspire and motivate me. I couldn't have a better father-in-law!

Marcus Goncalves

CONTENTS

PREFACE   XXI
ACKNOWLEDGEMENTS   XXXV

ONE   What Has Changed Since Windows NT 3.5?   1

The Advent of NT 3.51   2

NT 4.0: An Intelligent System   2

Making the Right Choice   6

What About BackOffice?   7

What to Expect in NT 5.0   8

   Individual Domains   8

   Transitive Trusting Relationships   10

What Is Kerberos?   12

Conclusion   16

TWO   Installation of Windows NT Server 4.0   17

General Installation Tips   18

   Installing NT 4.0   19

   Installation Options   19

   Basic Information Before You Install   20

Potential Problems with SCSI Disks and Controllers   23

   What Type of Volume Do I Use for NT System Files?   24

   How NT Handles Installation Media   26

Installation Methods   27
    New Features Affecting the Installation of NT 4.0   28
    Default Versus Custom   28
    Standard Installation   29
General Overview of the Installation Process   29
    Completing a Standard Installation   29
Using an Unattended Answer File for Network Setup   38
Security Considerations for Installing NT 4.0   49
Conclusion   51

THREE   Server Configuration and Management   **53**
Introduction to the NT 4.0 Resource Kit Utilities   54
    Using Programs from the NT Resource Kit   60
Command Prompt Operations   61
    Batch Programs   61
The Registry Database   64
    Editing the Registry Manually with RegEdit and REGEDT32   65
    Editing the Registry with RegKey (NT Resource Kit)   66
NT Server 4.0 License Management   68
Managing Disk Systems   68
Disk Systems and NT   68
    Physical Disk Drives, Partitions, and Volumes   69
    Creating and Deleting Partitions   70
    End Volume Sets   71
    Formatting a Partition   71
    Labeling a Volume   72
    Assigning Drive Letters to a Volume   73
    Saving Disk Configuration Information   74
    Disk Fault Tolerance   75
Device Drivers   81
Services   82
    Managing Services   83
Symmetrical Multiprocessor (SMP) Configurations   86
Control Panel   87

Removing NT Components to Save Space   88

Starting a Server   88

Stopping a Server   89

Configuring Automatic Log-on for NT Server   93

Changing the Log-on Wallpaper for NT Server (and Why?)   95

Connecting to Another System Using IPC$ 96

Management from an NT Workstation   96

Management from Windows 3.x and Windows 95 Systems   97

System Alerts   98

Event Logging   99

  Overview   101

  Event Viewer   101

  DumpEL (NT Resource Kit)   102

  FORFILES.EXE (New in 4.0 NT Resource Kit)   104

  *FTEDIT.EXE: FT Registry Information Editor
    (New on NT 4.0 Resource Kit)   104*

  Kernel Profiler (New NT 4.0 Resource Kit)   105

  Configuring Automatic Restart of a Server   106

Repairing Damaged System Files   108

BOOT.INI Options   109

  Adding a Second Boot Option for NT   109

  BOOT.INI Options for UPS and Other Hardware Devices   110

Stopping an Application on the Server   111

NT Error and Informational Messages   112

Microsoft Diagnostics (WINMSD)   112

Using Multiple Servers with a Single Keyboard/Mouse/Monitor   114

Designing a System for Performance   114

  Server Types   115

  Fast Processor with 256K or Greater CACHE   115

Hardware Notes   121

  Typical Hardware Problems   122

  Preventing Hardware Nightmares   122

  General Hardware Notes   123

Technical Support for Your System   129

Conclusion   131

FOUR Network Configuration and Management 133

Administration Tools 134

Network Client Administrator 134

DHCP Manager 134

WINS Manager 134

Protocols and Related Matters 135

NetBEUI 137

NBF 137

TCP/IP 137

SMB 159

DLC 162

NWLINK, IPX/SPX, and Other NetWare Stuff 162

AppleTalk and EtherTalk 166

Choosing a Protocol 168

Installing or Changing Protocols and Other Network Items 168

General Overview 171

Troubleshooting Programs for TCP/IP 177

Verifying Connections with PING 177

Checking Your DHCP Configuration with IPCONFIG 178

Configuring Browsing on Your Network 180

Browsing Other Domains 181

Monitoring Browsers 182

Shared Resources 184

Special Shares 184

Monitoring Shared Resources in NT 4.0 and NT 3.51 191

Domain Overview 192

Primary Domain Controller 193

Backup Domain Controllers 194

Domain Models 195

Single Domain Model 195

Master Domain Model 196

Multiple Master Domain Model 196

Complete Trust Model 197

Roll Your Own Model 198

Domains and Systems Management Server 199

Domain, Server, User Account, and Group Names and Tips   199

    Domain Names   200

    Computer Names   201

Hints for Managing Your Domain   201

Registry Size and Domains   202

Adding or Removing an NT Workstation or NT Server in a Domain   203

Changing Domains with a Server—Not!   204

Synchronizing Domain Controllers   204

Promoting a Backup Domain Controller to a
    Primary Domain Controller   206

Stopping the Primary Domain Controller   207

Logging On a Backup Domain Controller   207

Trust Relationships   207

    Using Trust Relationships   208

Designing Network Servers   210

Computer Names and NT Server   211

Multiple Network Interface Cards in One Server   211

Mixed Language Networks   212

Coexistence of Windows NT Server with Other Networks   213

    LAN Manager 2.x Servers   213

    Pathworks 5.x   213

    Gateway Services for NetWare   216

    Setting the Search Order for Multiple Network Providers   218

    Binding Network Components   218

Optimizing Memory Utilization on a Server   219

Remote Access Service   219

    Design and Configuration   221

    Installing RAS   223

    Assigning RAS Permissions to Users   224

    Managing the RAS System   224

    Miscellaneous Notes   229

    Accessing an RAS Server and Guest Accounts   229

    RAS with Windows for Workgroups 3.11 and Windows 95   230

    OS/2 RAS Servers   231

Net2Com   231

Replication of Files to Other Systems   232

    Miscellaneous Notes on Replication 234

    Replication Between NT Server and OS/2 Servers 235

    Software Metering and Inventory 235

NET Programs 235

    NET CONFIG 236

    NET ACCOUNTS 237

Synchronizing Time Across a Network with NET TIME 237

Synchronizing NT Time with TimeServ (NT Resource Kit) 238

Sending Messages to Users on a Server 238

Conclusion 240

FIVE User Management **241**

Domain User Accounts 242

    Modifying, Creating, Deleting, and Copying User Accounts 242

    Account Templates 246

    Sorting User Accounts 247

    Controlling Which Workstations a User May Use to Log On 248

    Controlling Log-on Times 248

    Locking Out an Account 251

    Disabling the Default User Name in the Log-on Dialog Box 252

    Disabling and Renaming User Accounts 253

    Restricting an Account for Local Use 254

User Profiles 254

    Potential Problems with Profiles 255

    Types of Profiles 256

    Creating and Assigning Profiles 257

    Controlling Network Connections with Profiles 257

    Storage of Profiles 258

Log-on Script 258

    Client Participation with Log-on and Startup Scripts 259

Groups 265

    Local Groups 265

Logging In from Multiple Workstations   271

Changing Passwords from an OS/2 Server   271

Security Checklist   271

What Will Change in NT 5.0   272

Conclusion   272

SIX   File Systems   275

Overview   276

NT File Types   277

NT File Systems in General   279

    NTFS   279

    FAT   281

    HPFS (for NT 3.51 version only!)   282

DFS   282

Suggested Directory Structures   283

    USERS Directory   284

    Home Directory   284

    Data Directories   285

    Executable Programs   285

    Sharing Directories   286

    Connecting to NT Server Resources   289

Converting File Systems   291

    Compressing Files and Directories   291

    The Repair Disk   293

    Duplicate NT System Files   297

    Replacing a System File   297

    Finding Problems with CHKDSK   299

    Defragmenting a Disk   300

Security Checklist   301

    Volume-Level Security   301

Conclusion   302

SEVEN   NT 4.0 Client Configuration
and Management   303

Clients and Client Tools Included with NT 4.0 Server   304

Using the Client Tools   *304*

Sharing the Client Directory   *306*

Making an Installation Boot Disk   *307*

Using the Installation Boot Disk   *308*

Installing Server Tools   *309*

Configuring Clients   310

Common Features for Clients   *311*

NT Workstations   *313*

Windows 95   *314*

Windows for Workgroups   *315*

Workgroup Add-On for MS-DOS and MS Client   *330*

Remote Boot Option for Clients   335

Adding NTWs to a Domain   335

Logging On a Domain   337

NTW   *337*

Windows for Workgroups   *337*

Windows 95   *337*

Logon Scripts   339

Tracking Network Events on Clients   339

Windows for Workgroups 3.11   *339*

Windows 95   *340*

Microsoft's Zero Administration Kit (ZAK)   341

What You Get with ZAK   *341*

Using ZAK   *342*

System Requirements   *343*

Conclusion   344

EIGHT   Services for Macintosh   345

Services for Macintosh Network Topologies   346

Components of Services for Macintosh   346

Requirements for Services for Macintosh   346

*Requirements for Macintosh Systems Connecting to
   Services for Macintosh   347*

Security   347

File Server Access from Macintosh Clients   349

Installing and Removing Services for Macintosh   349

Installing and Configuring Services for Macintosh   350

Installing the Services for Macintosh Workstation Programs   350

Removing Services for Macintosh   353

Administration of Services for Macintosh   354

Configuring the AppleTalk Protocol   355

Administering Macintosh Users   356

Macintosh Path Lengths   360

File System Issues for Services for Macintosh   360

Making Shared Directories Available to Macintosh Users   360

Disappearing Icons   361

Drop Folders   361

Macintosh Files   361

File and Folder Permissions   362

Mac and NTFS File and Directory Properties   364

Copying a Macintosh File to a FAT Volume   364

Printing with Services for Macintosh   364

Captured Printers   365

Conclusion   365

NINE   Printer Use and Management   367

Architecture   368

Print Manager   371

Printer Security   373

Installing and Configuring Printers   374

Changing Printer Properties   377

Installing and Changing Drivers   377

Other Properties   378

Sharing and Unsharing a Printer   378

Deleting Printers   381

Connecting and Disconnecting to Printers   382

The Print Information Box   383

Using Multiple Printers Connected to One Print Device   384

Printer Pools   384

Considerations for Special Printers   385

   Direct Network Interface Printers   386

   DLC Printers   387

   TCP/IP Printers   387

   PostScript Printer Characteristics   388

Separator Pages   388

Printer Messages   390

Printing from an NT System to a Remote NT Printer   390

Printers on Non-NT Systems   392

Using Printers from Network Clients   393

   Workgroup Add-On for MS-DOS and MS Client   393

   Windows for Workgroups   393

   Windows 95   394

Non-NT Print Servers   396

   Windows for Workgroups   397

   Workgroup Add-On for MS-DOS   397

   NetWare Printers   399

Conclusion   400

TEN   Disaster Preparedness and Management   401

Maintaining Tape Devices   402

Setting Up a Successful Backup Strategy   408

   System Backups   408

   User Backups   409

Tape Backup Programs   410

   NT's Backup Program   410

   Using NTBackup with the NT Scheduler   414

   Other Backup Options   416

Picking the Files to Back Up   418

Other Files   421

Backup Tapes   421

Restoring the System Files (Registry)   421

Backing Up Network Systems   422

Real-Time Backup of Server   423

Octopus   423

Real-Time Fault Tolerance with Clusters   424

Advantages of Clustering   425

Power Backup and Monitoring Systems   426

APC Power Chute   427

Conclusion   428

ELEVEN   Tuning NT Servers and Networks   429

NT Performance Monitoring System   430

Objects and Counters   430

Producing a List of Performance Monitor Counters   432

Performance Monitor   432

General Performance Monitor Tips   434

Setting Alerts with Performance Monitor   434

NT Resource Kit   437

Automating Performance Monitor with DataLog (NT Resource Kit)   437

Monitoring Performance   439

Bottlenecks and Other Problems   439

Creating an Overview Performance Monitor Settings File   440

Steps for Tuning   440

Monitoring and Controlling Server Usage   443

Collecting Statistics with NET STATISTICS   447

Domains   449

Microsoft Network Monitor   455

Tuning Specific NT Subsystems   460

Virtual Memory System   460

System Memory (RAM)   461

Balancing the System Loading   463

Network Performance   464

CPU   466

Disk Subsystems   467

Conclusion   468

TWELVE   Security   471

Validation of Log-ons   473

Security Account Manager (SAM)   475

Security Reference Monitor (SRM)   476

Discretionary Access Controls (DACL)   477

Security and RAS   477

Access to Server Administrative Functions   479

Permissions   479

Securing NT System Files   480

Securing Floppy Disk Drives on a Server   481

File Deletions   482

Computer Accounts   482

Domains and Trust Accounts   482

Guest Accounts   483

Auditing   483

Rights   483

SNMP and Security   484

Passwords   485

Password Tips   486

Changing Passwords   486

Log-on Restrictions   488

Warning Messages at Logon   488

Restricting Access to Certain Programs   488

Automatic NT Log-off   488

Using Profiles for Restricting Users   490

Starting a Screen Saver Before Log-on   490

Finding a User's Permissions with PERMS.EXE (ResKit)   491

Hidden Shares   492

Client Security Issues   492

    Windows for Workgroups   *492*

    Windows 95   *492*

Proxies With NT—Catapult, the Proxy Server   493

Conclusion   494

APPENDIX A   Listing of Products and
  Companies Mentioned   495

American Power Conversion   495

Arcada Systems (Now Owned by Seagate)   495

DigiBoard   496

Consensys Corporation   496

Black Box   496

Digital Equipment Corporation   496

Executive Software   496

Intergraph   497

Microsoft   497

NetManage   497

Network Technologies   497

Octopus Technologies   497

Prentice Hall Technical Reference   497

APPENDIX B   Glossary of Terms and Definitions   499

APPENDIX C   Contacting the Authors   515

APPENDIX D   About the CD-ROM   517

NTMUM   517

BlackBoard Lock   518

Web Trend (30-day Evaluation Copy)   518

DistStat (15-day Evaluation Copy)   519

  Before You Begin   *519*

CodeSafe for Win95/NT V3.0 Version   520

Diskeeper Lite for NT 4.0   521

Commander: A File Utility Tool   522

Dustman File Cleaner   522

INDEX   523

Introduction

This book is the first in the series called "Managing the Enterprise with Microsoft BackOffice" from Prentice Hall. Each book in the series will focus on using a particular piece of BackOffice in a production environment, but will also touch on other parts of BackOffice and other products as we find them useful.

Our approach to this book has been to include anything that is relevant to managing an enterprise NT network, ranging from five clients to thousands of clients. The tools, tips, step-by-step lists, and notes were all designed to provide useful information on taming and managing an NT Server LAN.

Tips on Using This Book

Some commands and program lines in this book show a dash (-) at the end of a line, and a second indented line under the first line. The dash indicates a continued command line or program line that should all be on one line. This syntax is also used on some Registry keys that are too long to fit on one line. A sample command follows,

```
WINNT32 /u:"This is my answer file name" -
    /b
```

Step-by-step lists are used extensively in this book due to a large number of requests from many different readers regarding magazine articles, books, and consulting engagements. Short how-to lists have been the primary request for my magazine columns and previous books. I have also heard from publishers that this type of information is frequently requested. I myself use the material for this book as a handy reference tool when I am consulting or trying to solve a problem.

The book is designed as a reference tool for NT Server managers and administrators, as well as anyone who uses NT Server with more than a passing interest. The preface contains an overview of the NT Server architecture and mentions many of NT's features. Most items in the preface are covered in more detail later in the book. For instance, if you are interested in Network features, check out the notes in the preface and then refer to Chapter 3 on network configuration and management for more details.

There are also many cross references in the book to point you to related material. The page number in the reference should provide a starting point you can use to browse through the related material.

Open Architecture

NT Server and all BackOffice products are members of Microsoft's open architecture, which is defined by the WOSA (Windows Open Systems Architecture) specification. WOSA has long held the promise of a family of operating systems that are open and portable. This promise began to bear fruit in 1993 with the introduction of NT 3.1.

NT Server currently sits at the high end of the WOSA architecture. Other members of the WOSA family include Pen Windows, Windows 3.x, Windows 95, Microsoft's At Work architecture, and Windows NT Workstation 3.5. Future members of the WOSA family include Windows NT 4.0 or Windows NT 96 (97?), which is now known as Cairo.

Evidence of the power of the WOSA architecture is available in many areas. Many of the application programs that ship with both Windows for Workgroups and the NT family are the same for both systems, and they interoperate in a network. These programs include Exchange Server, Schedule +, and many standard Windows utilities such as Write, Notepad, and File Manager. Other features such as the fax capabilities of Windows for Workgroups 3.11 add a new level of integration to the OS. Windows 95 takes the integration one step further, as both it and NT are built on top of the Win32 API. Microsoft has taken a great step with the introduction of Windows NT 3.51 to standardized Win32 between both platforms.

SQL Server is another product that is designed to be a part of WOSA. SQL Server for NT is a full Windows 32-bit database system that uses the full power and features of NT. SQL Server is a powerful database system that can run on a wide variety of NT systems and takes advantage of NT features such as multithreading and multiple processors. SQL Server comes with tools for other 16-bit members of the WOSA family that allow them to administer SQL Server and serve as application front-ends in a true client/server environment. Other Microsoft and third-party tools such as

Visual Basic, Access, and Microsoft Office can also access data stored in an SQL Server database.

The power of the WOSA architecture continues to move forward with the introduction of Windows 95. Windows 95 is a 32-bit operating system that shares many of the features of NT, including the ability to run NT programs. Windows 95 will also be the first Intel-specific version of Windows to run without DOS. This means that memory managers (at least as we know them now) should be history, and you should not see any more EMM386 Exception errors or General Protection Faults. Other unhandled exceptions can occur with NT, but they are usually handled much more gracefully via the Event Log and do not affect other applications.

NT 3.1 Overview

NT 3.1 was the first version of NT introduced. The 3.1 version was used because the NT 3.1 interface was based on the Windows and Windows for Workgroups 3.1. The File Manager and other network features were comparable with Windows for Workgroups, making NT 3.1 feel like Windows's big brother, which is exactly the case.

NT 3.1 was the first operating system designed in WOSA as a high-end platform that would run on a wide variety of hardware platforms including Intel, MIPS, and Alpha processors. NT 3.1 was scaleable and easy to manage because of its many similarities to Windows 3.1.

NT 3.1 introduced a number of utilities such as User Manager for Domains, Disk Administrator, Server Manager, Event Viewer, Performance Monitor, and others for managing the server, workstation, and network features of NT. Third-party vendors began to add to the NT utilities by porting well-known UNIX programs and creating others to NT.

NT's modular architecture provides the foundation for powerful systems such as SQL Server, Systems Management Server, Exchange Server, and others. Powerful solutions using these products and many others have been built on NT 3.1 and have provided many business solutions.

New Features in NT Workstation 3.5 and NT Server 3.51

NT Workstation 3.5 and NT Server 3.51 have several new features. The following list contains the major new features of 3.5, with each list entry followed by the page number of the chapter containing the main reference to the topic. N/A means that particular topic is specific to the NT Workstation version and is not covered in depth in this book.

- Improved performance
- Runs with less stringent system requirements (memory speed, total memory, etc.)
- Automatic restart with memory dump for server crashes
- Integrated PCI bus support
- Account lockout
- TCP/IP performance and management improvements with DHCP and WINS
- TCP/IP and IPX protocols that can be routed over Remote Access Service (RAS)
- Plotter support
- OLE 2.01
- New kernel debugger for building device drivers
- Windows 3.x programs run in multiple virtual DOS machines (VDM)
- OpenGL interface 3D graphics API
- Supports TrueType and Adobe Type 1 fonts
- NetWare client software

Most of the new features and improvements in the 3.51 versions are directly beneficial to NT Server-based networks. The 3.51 versions of NT are generally faster and easier to manage than the original 3.1 version was.

New Features in NT 3.51

Just as I was wrapping up the first version of this book, NT 3.51 was heading into a short beta program. You will find mention of some NT 3.51 features in the book, but only those I was able to test during the beta program. The following list contains a short description of the major new features in NT 3.51.

- File and directory compression features added to NTFS File and Directory compression
- Windows 95 common controls
- Windows 95 help system
- New IPX stack for improved performance
- File input/output performance features
- New command line utilities (PENTNT, NTBOOKS, and COMPACT)
- New licensing options
- New Console applet in Control Panel for configuring DOS command prompt windows
- Support for PCMCIA devices
- New setup features for licensing and detection of the floating point problem in some Pentium processors

- New service API functions
- Replaceable security module for interactive log-on
- All new Win32 API functions for Windows 95 stubbed in NT 3.51

Differences Between NT Server and NT Workstation

NT Server Is a Superset of NT Workstation

NT Server can do anything that NT Workstation can do. NT Server simply adds several new features and utilities to the basic NT system. NT Server also removes the 10-connection maximum that NT provides for network users, opens up the RAS connections to 256, and adds domains and many other network features.

NT Server is designed to perform as a network server and is tuned accordingly. NT Workstation is likewise tuned for higher graphics performance in its role as a high-performance workstation.

Domain Overview

NT Server uses domains for managing users and servers. The concept of domains is familiar to LAN Manager 2.2 managers but may take some getting used to for NetWare administrators.

Domains are groups of NT Server systems in a network. A domain shares the account and security database over the entire domain. A network user logs on a domain, not an individual server. Administration of a domain is much easier because it can be managed as a single entity for most actions.

Domains can also have trust relationships with other domains. A trust relationship between two domains allows the users of one domain to be granted access to resources in another domain without creating additional user accounts for the users in the other domain.

Chapter 3 describes the network configuration (page 133) and has a more detailed discussion of domains and how to implement them.

Central User Profiles User profiles allow users to log on any NT system in the domain and have exactly the same configuration and preferences as when they use their own machine. This feature is also included in Windows 95, further enhancing the WOSA product line and its management capabilities.

Services for Macintosh Services for Macintosh (SFM) allows NT Server to offer file and print services for Macintosh systems in addition to DOS, Windows, and NT clients. Users of these different systems can transparently share files from one system to another.

Extended Remote Access Service Support for up to 256 Ports Remote Access Service provides remote access capabilities for NT and NT Server. RAS supports dial-up, ISDN, and X.25 connection methods. NT Server allows up to 256 RAS ports. This is a major enhancement over Windows NT desktop, which provides support for only one port.

NT Server Specifications

The following list identifies the general specifications for NT Server 3.51. All options shown are included with NT Server. Additional options such as the DECnet protocol can be purchased from other sources.

Maximum connections	Unlimited
Maximum RAM	4GB
Maximum hard-disk storage	408 million terabytes
Minimum hardware requirements	16MB of RAM, 90MB disk, 386/25
RAID support	0,1,2, and 5
Network topologies	Asynchronous, Ethernet, FDDI, ISDN, Token Ring
Transport protocols	AppleTalk, DLC, NetBEUI, OSI, SPX/IPX, TCP/IP

Open Architecture of NT

WOSA is Microsoft's strategy for all the different components of the Windows architecture. WOSA includes not only NT, Windows 3.11, Windows for Workgroups 3.11, and Windows 95, but also other software platforms such as SQL Server and Systems Management Server (SMS).

NT interoperates with WOSA and all the WOSA components in one manner or another. Most WOSA specifications (such as MAPI and ODBC) are published, making it easy for third-party vendors to develop applications that also participate in WOSA.

Protocol Independence

NT provides support for TCP/IP, NetBEUI, IPX/SPX, AppleTalk (SFM), DLC, protocols, and additional protocols (such as DECnet) from third parties. This support allows NT to operate in a wide variety of networks as both a file and print server and an application server.

Standards

Distributed Computing Environment (DCE) compliant Remote Procedure Call (RPC) allows the development of NT programs that can communicate with other NT systems and systems running DCE-compatible systems. RPC is the mechanism that allows NT programs to actually split program tasks across multiple systems over a network.

Application Integration

Dynamic Data Exchange (DDE) and Network Dynamic Data Exchange (NetDDE) allow NT to integrate with any WOSA application that supports one or the other of these two standards. An NT Server can fully participate in both NetDDE and Object Linking and Embedding (OLE) sessions with other systems.

NT also supports Windows Sockets with the TCP/IP protocol. Windows for Workgroups 3.11 and Windows 95 also support Windows Sockets. Windows Sockets is API-compatible with Berkeley-style sockets found on many UNIX and other TCP/IP systems.

Client/Server Design

NT was designed as a client/server system from day one. It uses the client/server model internally and provides an enhanced client/server system for application development. SQL Server under both NT and NT Server has proven to be the easiest and fastest database for creating sophisticated applications.

NT provides many robust features that enhance the ability of SQL Server and other databases to run under NT. It is significant that in porting from OS/2 to NT the code shrank from 50,000+ lines to around 8000 lines and the product runs 10 to 20 times faster, according to many customers.

If you combine NT, SQL Server, and a fast system like a multiprocessor Digital Equipment Corporation Alpha, you have a stable, high-performance system not available with other LAN architectures.

Common Support Structure

Advanced support features of NT include the system Registry, which tracks almost all system configuration information, the event logging system, and the performance monitoring system. These features combine to offer very effective problem tracking and a super support system for applications; each of these features is open to developers for recording application-specific information.

A good example of an application's use of these system features is SQL Server. During installation it installs its own counters in the performance monitoring system and installs an icon that loads Performance Monitor with SQL Server specific counters. This feature allows you to track such things as database performance against overall system utilization.

More and more applications should support these subsystems in the future, because similar features are also included in Windows 95.

Symmetric Multiprocessing

NT Server supports up to four processors in its normal configuration. OEM implementations of NT Server can support 32 processors or more.

SMP support allows NT to use multiple processors actively to improve the performance of a system dramatically. Tests have shown from 60 to 80 percent improvement for each processor added, provided some other subsystem was not creating a bottleneck. I have several clients with Alpha systems, which they tell me really do live up to the speed claims. The Alpha 2100-500 with multiple processors is a joy to run with SQL Server.

SMP is most useful in environments such as SQL Server where there is a heavy application load. Servers that are providing only file and print services usually do not benefit much from adding an additional processor. If you think your system could use another processor, monitor the processor activity using Performance Monitor before you make a decision.

Fault Tolerance

NT Server adds several fault-tolerant features to the server environment over NT Workstation. These options are discussed in more detail on page 75.

Disk Mirroring

Disk mirroring allows a system to automatically keep a second disk in sync with the master disk. Every disk write is completed to both disks. If a disk fails, the system keeps running, using the other disk.

Disk Duplexing

Disk duplexing is essentially the same as disk mirroring except that in addition to the second disk the system uses a second controller for one of the disks. This configuration usually results in a faster system than one with disk mirroring only; the two controllers can read and write to the disks simultaneously and provide for failure of a controller in addition to disk failures.

RAID

Redundant Array of Inexpensive Disks (RAID) is a term used to describe several disks that are configured as a single drive. The levels of fault tolerance are rated from 0 to 5, with 5 providing the highest level of performance and fault tolerance. RAID 5 disks can drastically improve the performance of your system and provide complete fault tolerance at the disk level.

Many RAID systems allow you to hot-swap a bad disk without bringing the system down. The RAID packages usually have a fast RAID controller (like the Digital EISA or PCI controllers) that manage the RAID configuration in the controller. NT sees the entire RAID system as one drive. The physical disk drives usually plug into the RAID cabinet from the front and can be changed while the system is up and running.

NT Server 3.51 provides native support RAID level 0, 1, and 5. Other RAID levels may be used with NT Server if supported by the RAID controller and seen by NT Server as a normal disk. NT-compatible hardware controllers are available from HP, Digital Equipment Corporation, Dell, Compaq, and many other vendors.

Clustering

In the fall of 1997, Microsoft added new fault tolerance features to NT Server with the cluster support in the NT Server Enterprise Edition (NTSE). The cluster feature supports two servers with a shared disk system between them. There are several configurations of the clusters ranging from performance-tuned clusters to pure fault tolerance clusters. This powerful technology will go through several evolutions as it improves in capability and scaleability over time. The first version provides many powerful options and a badly needed feature set for NT.

File Systems

NT Server supports the NTFS, HPFS, FAT, and Macintosh file systems. Macintosh file system compatibility is provided only on NTFS volumes with SFM. NTFS is new with NT and supports many advanced features. HPFS and FAT are supported for compatibility with OS/2 and DOS, respectively. New file systems created with NT can only be NTFS or FAT. For more information on the NT file systems and using the file systems, consult Chapter 5.

NT Server and Memory

Physical Memory

NT and NT Server both use the same memory model and support 4GB of physical memory per system, with up to 2GB for applications and 2GB reserved for system storage. The NT memory system is a flat memory model and provides memory isolation between processes through its protected memory system.

Virtual Memory

NT uses a technique called paging to simulate more memory than may be physically resident in a system. Paging is the mechanism NT uses to address 4GB of memory; most systems that run NT have only between 16 and 512MB of physical memory—a long way from 4GB.

Paging creates "virtual" memory—memory that appears to be in the system but actually is not. In a paging system the operating system moves data from RAM to the hard disk to allow other data to move into RAM as they are needed. This feat is accomplished by dividing all the memory into pages of 4K each.

NT supports multiple page files, each of which may be on a separate disk. If you spread page files across multiple disks on a system with a sophisticated disk controller you can improve performance. See the section on Virtual Memory in Chapter 10 (page 460) for more information.

Interpretability with LAN Manager and Other Servers

NT works well with other LAN Manager systems, including LAN Manager for OS/2, LAN Manager for UNIX, DEC Pathworks, and IBM LAN Server. It also interoperates well with NetWare servers and many other networks. NT is extensible due to its open architecture, so it is likely to be enhanced by other vendors for their networks.

Licensing

NT Server 3.5 changed the license policies, and they have changed once again in version 3.51. NT Server 3.5 introduced the client license requirement; each client accessing an NT server had to have a license. This was a change from NT Advanced Server 3.1, but proved to be cost-effective in the long run, especially for clients with several servers.

NT Server 3.51 has added a license wrinkle designed to lower the cost of network licenses and provide more flexibility to system managers. The Per Seat license option is the same as the license for NT Server 3.5, which required each client that accessed an NT Server to have a license.

The Per Seat option is best when your network clients all must access NT Server(s) at the same time. This license allows you to buy one license for each client and one license per server. You can add all the servers you want and pay only the cost for a server license.

The Per Server license is new and provides some flexibility for small networks or networks in which only some users access NT Server and the specific users vary frequently. If you have a 500-user network with NetWare servers and you want to install an NT Server for use by up to 50 people, these can be any 50 of the total 500 workstations on the network. With the Per Seat license, each workstation on the network would need a license. Using the Per Server license, you can license the server for 50 clients and save lots of money. According to Microsoft's documentation, you do not need client licenses for NT Server when a workstation accesses only an application such as SQL Server. You would, of course, need licenses for the product the clients are accessing.

Licensing has been changing lately, so make sure you read your license agreements and check out the latest options for the software you use. I expect to see more changes in the future, as such vendors as Microsoft and others fine-tune their policies.

Hardware

One of the NT family's most talked-about traits is its ability to run on many different hardware platforms. NT is currently running on everything from Intel PCs to many different RISC processors, including MIPS, PowerPC, and the Digital Equipment Corporation Alpha. Each of these processors has its own strengths and weaknesses.

The portability of NT is accomplished primarily through a layer called HAL (Hardware Abstraction Layer). HAL sits between the rest of NT and the hardware and handles the software/hardware interface to interrupts, I/O, and so forth. The careful design of HAL allows programs to run on different hardware platforms without any changes, except for recompiling with a native mode compiler for the different architectures.

Intel

The Intel platform (286, 386, 486, and Pentium) is the first system that any version of Windows ran on and is still its most popular system. It is almost guaranteed that all future versions of NT will run on Intel processors. The Intel version of NT also finds itself with the widest number of native NT applications. This continues and in fact dramatically increases with the release of Windows 95; all native Windows 95 applications are Win32 and should run on both Windows 95 and NT. Notice I said *should* and not *will*; there is the distinct possibility that some vendors will use specific features and idiosyncrasies of Windows 95 that will preclude them from running on NT.

RISC

The Digital Equipment Corporation Alpha processor is or has been the fastest processor on the planet for running NT (and most other systems).

Versions of the Alpha have been demonstrated running at up to 300-MHz. Systems using the Alpha range from PC-style desktop systems to the powerful Alpha workstation and server series. A particularly powerful series of servers code-named Sable was introduced in late 1994. The Sable server 2100-500 can support up to four 275-MHz processors and supports up to seven front-mounted hot-swappable drives in a built-in StorageWorks shelf. One additional seven-drive shelf can be installed internally. The 2100-500 is a real zinger in performance. The 1000 and 2000 series servers are also powerful and relatively affordable. An AlphaServer 1000 with 2 or 3GB of disk, for example, is less than $20,000 at early 1995 prices.

Digital is constantly upgrading the entire Alpha line with both new models and faster processors for existing models.

Hardware Requirements for NT Server

NT Server can run on a wide variety of systems with many different configurations. Consider the Microsoft recommendations to be the absolute minimum and my recommendations as a realistic minimum. Note that RISC systems may have different minimum requirements than Intel systems do.

The number of users for file and print sharing can be estimated on the basis of average performance reported by some users, and field experience.

The same basic starting point can be used for client/server systems. Remember that a system such as SQL Server places much more demand upon the processor and possibly the memory system of a server than do simple file and print services. You can use a rule of 1.5 times the base server requirements of a file and print server for a database server. For instance, a 90-user client/server system should start out with 96MB of RAM and a Pentium 90 or RISC processor.

NT Resource Kit

You can obtain the NT Resource Kit directly from Microsoft and most Microsoft resellers. If you are running and supporting NT and do not have the kit, order it today.

The NT Resource Kit is the best investment you can make after your purchase of NT. It has low cost (street price of less than $200) and contains a wealth of information as well as many NT utilities for optimizing and troubleshooting your system.

TechNet

TechNet is another tool available from Microsoft that is frequently referred to in this book. This resource is a monthly CD-ROM that is packed with good tips, solutions, and source code. It also includes numerous publications that relate to NT and Windows in general. The cost for the Resource Kit in 1994 was $195 per year. What a deal!

Tips on Using Windows

Here are just a few tips for using Windows. These tips work for Windows 3.x and Windows 95. Windows 3.x includes all versions of Windows NT and Windows NT Server.

Selecting Items in Lists:

1. Click an item to select only that item.
2. Click the first item in a list, hold down the Shift key, and click the last item to select an all-inclusive list.
3. Click the first item in a list, hold down the Ctrl key, and click each item. This allows you to select items that are not contiguous.

Dragging and Dropping:

1. Click an item and hold down the left mouse button.
2. Move the mouse to the drop location, and release the left button. Watch for the mouse cursor to change shape, indicating whether or not it is OK to drop the item.

Starting Programs or Actions with Icons, Menus, and Buttons:

- **Icons**—Double-click an icon in Program Manager or single-click an icon on a toolbar.
- **Menus**—Single-click a menu selection.
- **Buttons**—Single-click a button to trigger its action.

Many applications such as File Manager and Print Manager use toolbars with separate icons to represent different functions. NT 3.51 includes ToolTip help, which was popularized by Microsoft Office and is built in to Windows 95.

Displaying ToolTip Help:

1. Place the mouse pointer over the icon, and do not move it for several seconds.

Starting Help:

2. Press the F1 key whenever you need help. If you have a question on a dialog box, then place the mouse in the field where you need help and press F1.

Disclaimer

All the information included in this book has appeared in print as common knowledge before this book was released from the publisher. Specifically, Windows 95 (Chicago) references pertain to information taken from publications such as *Microsoft TechNet, Windows Magazine, Windows Sources, PC Magazine, PC Week,* and *Information World.*

ACKNOWLEDGEMENTS

From Both of Us

Many people have contributed to this book; many, many people! But we must start somewhere, so we would like to thank Mike Meehan and Ralph Moore for the opportunity and extensive hours of coaching and advising on how to set this book for success.

We also thank the people at Microsoft for their support, especially Dean Leonard and Pradeep Rajurs. Thanks also to Ryan LaPlant, from New Technology Partners, for updates on key information when it was needed the most. As always, we thank the MIS crew at Process Software, as well as Phil Denzer and Dean Goodermote, for allowing Marcus, one more time this year, to share the experiences (good and bad!) they undergo with NT with others.

Marcus Goncalves

I thank my everlasting partner in love and wife, Carla, for her sacrifices coping with me while writing this book. Glory be to God, for the talents He allows me to have and to share with others.

Ken Spencer

I give thanks to my partner and wife of many years, Trisha, for her understanding and support on all my writing projects. I also would like to give God the credit for the talents He has given me and that He allows me to use.

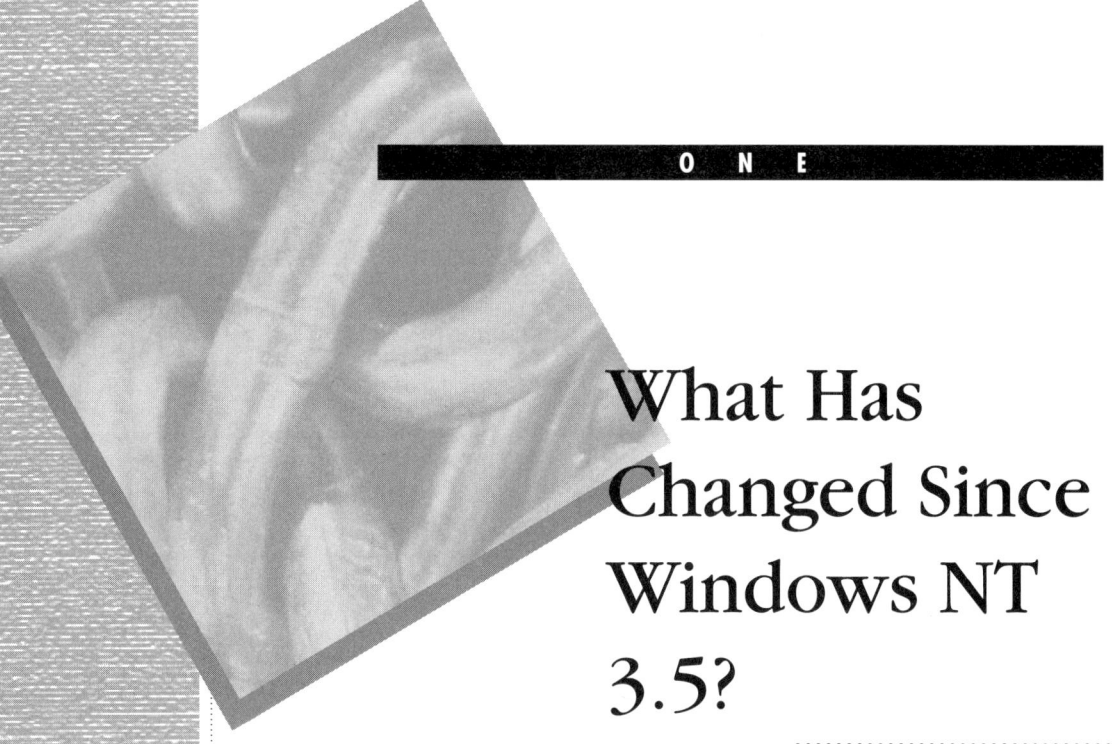

What Has Changed Since Windows NT 3.5?

This chapter helps you sort through a scenario similar to that presented in Scenario 1.1. It is designed to clearly identify and discuss what has changed in NT since version 3.5, outlining the features of version 3.51 and the advantages of upgrading to version 4.0. But, let's start from the beginning, so you can understand the evolution of a complete and robust OS such as NT 4.0, and the challenges that administrators like you deal with in the previous versions.

Scenario 1.1:

Your organization has been using NT version 3.5 since its release in 1994. Some security problems were experienced when your organization first upgraded to 3.5, but those problems have since been ironed out and everything's been working steadily for several years now. Since then, you have been promoted to systems administrator. A colleague at another company has been telling you about the latest release, NT 4.0, and the benefits seem to suit your organization. However, your superiors seem reluctant to change, especially because of security concerns associated with a new organizational system, and they are not too sure about the tangible benefits 4.0 would bring to the organization. What do you do?

One of the major advantages of NT is that it was created as an entirely new product—from scratch. It was not based on any previous code, nor was it adapted from any existing system. NT's development began in 1988 and took almost five years of intensive work to produce a final product.

Its first version was released in July of 1993, under two categories, the Windows NT 3.1 for workstations and the Windows NT Advanced Server 3.1, the server version. Coincidence or not, its graphical interface was very similar to Windows 3.1. However, internally, NT was not only completely different from Windows 3.1, but it was also turbo charged! As a 32-bit application, without any inheritance from DOS, NT was pretty much what its name claimed to be: a New Technology.

Even though Microsoft introduced these two products in a very conservative way, the products attracted the attention of many. The only problem then restraining its success was the hardware requirements. The typical servers were Intel 486, and NT's system requirements were a minimum of 16MB of RAM, while NetWare 3.12 required only 4MB.

Then came the NT 3.5 version, a major evolution, in 1994. The 3.5 version had much better performance then the 3.1, utilizing fewer resources and less memory. Furthermore, it was competing directly with its major opponent, NetWare, as it offered a gateway (NWLink) that permitted both of them to coexist in the same network. Not only that, but this version also offered a NetWare-NT migration tool and support to IPX and TCP/IP protocols, much faster then the previous version. Many more innovations, such as long filenames on the FAT partition and better graphics performance, contributed to the almost immediate success of NT version 3.5. At the same time, Microsoft decided to make the two NT flavors more distinct. You could have the Windows NT Workstation (NTW) or the Windows NT Server (NTS), whichever made much more sense for your environment.

The Advent of NT 3.51

It was in 1995 that Microsoft released its third version of NT, the NT 3.51. This version introduced support to the PowerPC and some of the Windows 95 standard controls and interface, even though the main interface was still like the Program Manager of version 3.1. Only some of the dialog boxes were similar to Windows 95 interface, which allowed for some of the programs written for Windows 95 to run on NT. Another great feature introduced with this version was the ability to compress files in the NTFS partitions.

NT 4.0: an Intelligent System

With version 4.0, released in 1996, the graphical interface of Windows 95 was finally integrated, which made NT much more user friendly, made the administrative tools more accessible, and brought both products, Windows 95 and Windows NT, much closer. It is this version that this book will be discussing. Figure 1.1 shows a screenshot of the Windows NT Server 4.0 logo.

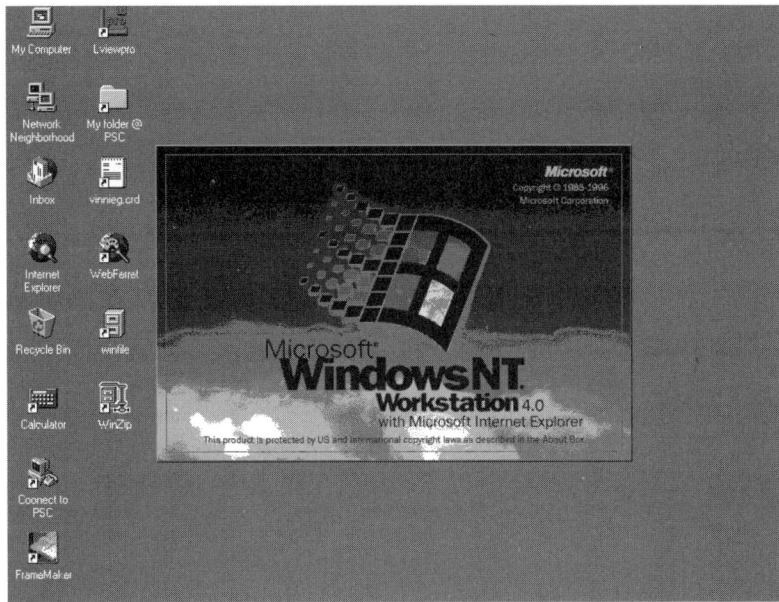

FIGURE 1.1 The Windows NT Server 4.0 Logo appears as wallpaper for this version.

Among the many new features and improvements that NT 4.0 brings are:

- **The Windows 95 graphical interface**–Easier to use; introduction of items such as the Task Bar, Explorer, Network Neighborhood, Recycle Bin, and so forth.
- **Hardware profiles**–Hardware configuration chosen during initialization.
- **MS TAPI (Telephony Application Programming Interface)**–a program interface oriented to telephony, which enables the use of Microsoft Exchange and HyperTerminal, among other applications. Figure 1.2 shows a screenshot of the TAPI configuration window, accessed through Control Panel, via the Telephony applet.
- **Task Manager**–Provides detailed information about the processes being executed. Figure 1.3 shows a graphical view of the systems performance, selected through the Performance tab under Task Manager.

- **Administrative Assistants**–Simplifies some of the administrator's task, by suggesting the most likely device to that particular environment or configuration being set up, for example.
- **New video architecture**–Greater speed when refreshing the screen.
- **DCOM (Distributed Component Object Model)**–Enables objects on remote machines to be executed.
- **IIS 2.0 and IIS 3.0 (Internet Information Server)**–Microsoft's Internet/Intranet server. Its 4.0 version is available as a free download.

- **FrontPage 1.1**–The easy HTML authoring tool from Microsoft.
- **DNS server**–Name resolution using DNS (Internet standard). Figure 1.4 shows the NT 4.0's TCP/IP properties' DNS tab.
- **Multiprotocol routing**–Routing between LANs using IP or IPX.
- **NDS (NetWare 4) support**–The revamped NetWare client.
- **NT Option Pack**–Bundles IIS 4.0, NTS and other tools.

With such a combination of features, very much enterprise-oriented, it is easy to understand the market niche that Microsoft is after: the big companies going through the process of downsizing, eliminating their mainframes, and looking for a cheaper technology that is also more flexible, but with equivalent power and robustness.

To meet various needs of different organizations, Microsoft is also repackaging NT in late 1997. The Small Business Server and Enterprise Server are designed to offer special features to specific business needs.

Also, Windows NTS 4.0 enables Microsoft to offer great benefits for the small LANs, where NetWare had been a standard. The key here is that NetWare users, especially administrators, usually are frustrated with the fact that NetWare will not be able to support a more complex, powerful application (such as SQL servers) running at the server, which NT can do. Besides, NT's ability to coexist with other OS makes it very attractive, as system managers won't need to waste, or replace, the hardware or network strategy already in place.

On the contrary, NT's migration and connection tools, and the fact that it is an open system, make possible its coexistence with not only NetWare, but

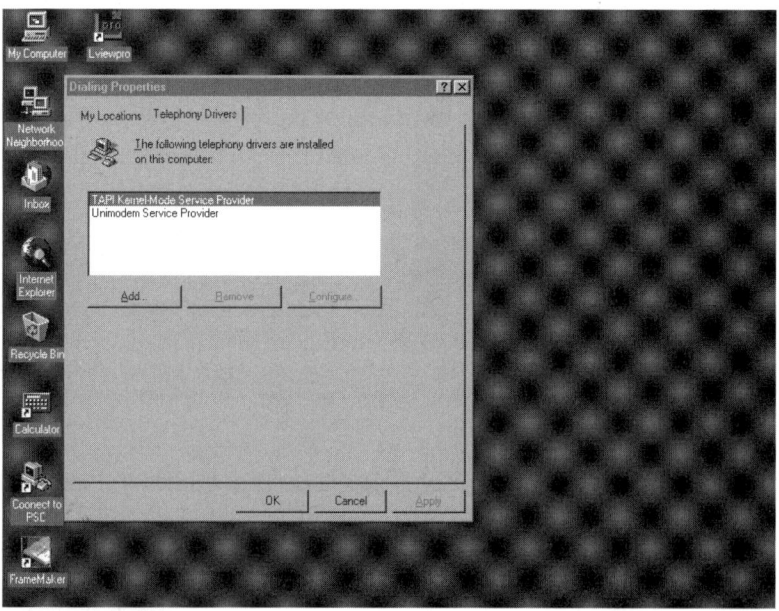

FIGURE 1.2 TAPI configuration window on NT 4.0.

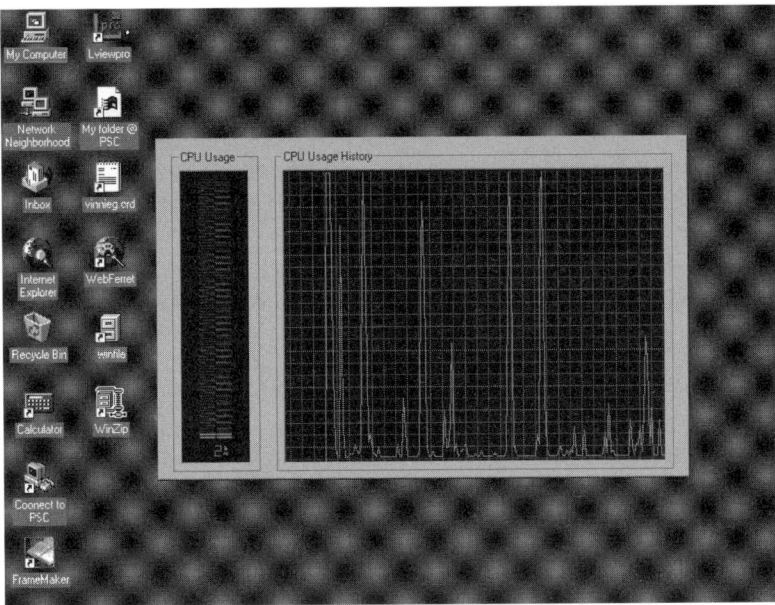

FIGURE 1.3 Task Manager's Performance Window, showing CPU Usage and CPU Usage History.

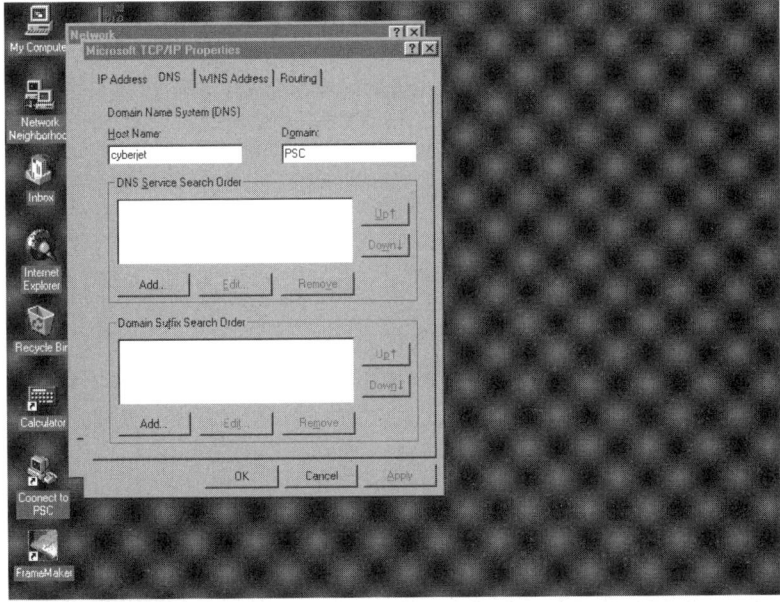

FIGURE 1.4 NT 4.0 TCP/IP Properties windows, showing the DNS configuration tab.

also with Macs and even mainframes (using an SNA server). Thus, the user has the flexibility to gradually make the necessary transition, at his/her own pace, as the benefits of this transition become evident. With NT, the nightmare word of every systems manager—*migration*—became an interesting experience; better yet, it became something very much worth considering.

Making the Right Choice

Now, before we go any further, you must understand that although Windows NTW 4.0, NTS 4.0, and Windows 95 are similar, they are not created equal. So be careful when choosing what to use.

As a rule of thumb, if you need a server for your network, you should use NTS. For high-performance applications, such as CAD, desktop publishing, and modeling, you should use NTW. Finally, if you need a typical workstation, for word processing, running spreadsheets, and even some graphics applications such as PowerPoint, Windows 95 should be fine.

This is a very generic distinction, but these recommendations should not be written in stone. Both Windows 95 and NTW 4.0 can be used for desktop applications as well as a file and printing server for a small LAN. By the same token, you can use very well the NTS 4.0 as a stand-alone system, not even connected to a network. Make sure that you understand your needs so that you can make the right choice.

Nevertheless, the NTS and the NTW are very similar to each other: The operating system is the same, as well as the graphical interface and the API (Application Programs Interface). The main difference is that the server version can be used as a domain controller.

Besides, the NTW version has some limitations, as follows:

- It accepts no more than 10 clients simultaneously connected. NTS has no limit of connections.
- It allows only one user connected through RAS (Remote Access Service). NTS accepts up to 256 connections.
- It does not have any domain administration, trusting relationships, replications, gateways, or NetWare migration tools.

It seems that Microsoft's goal with NT was to include the maximum amount of processing power of the many platforms on the market today without worrying about the hardware minimum requirements. For instance, the 12MB of RAM, which is the minimum requirement for NTW, was not readily available back in 1993, when it was launched. Today we all know that 12MB of RAM is a minimum if we want good performance so it's easy to understand that, although NTW and Windows 95 have similarities, NTW was designed more for the users' running high-performance applications with security and reliability needs.

These examples illustrate what this means: NTW does not work with drivers written for DOS or Windows 3.1 as it is a full 32-bit system, but those can be installed on Windows 95 without any problems because Windows 95 is a "hybrid" system, being 32 bits but also back-compatible with the 16-bit environment. But this is actually a good thing. The 16-bit applications running on Windows 95 are all using the same memory space. In the case of a system freeze or a GPF (General Protection Fault), the corrupted application can thus compromise all the other ones because they share the same space. With NT, this won't happen, because each application has its own memory space.

On the other hand, in its favor, Windows 95 does support Plug and Play and the Power Management (the ability to shut down the monitor automatically, for example), which are functions not yet implemented on NT. If you need these functions or will be working with legacy hardware/software, then Windows 95 may be the best system to use.

What About BackOffice?

BackOffice is a group of Microsoft products designed to act as the backbone environment of all of a company's software applications. While Office (the Microsoft set of front-end applications) works interactively with the users, BackOffice works behind the scenes, guaranteeing good performance and functionality of your network. BackOffice is actually a set of applications for the administrator of the network.

The software components of the BackOffice family are:

- **Windows NT Server 4.0**–Includes Internet Information Server, Index Server, and FrontPage.
- **SQL Server 6.5**–Client-server database manager with scaleability to support large Internet and Intranet databases on a low-cost, standard hardware platform.
- **Proxy Server 1.0**–An Internet proxy server.
- **SNA Server 3.0**–A tool that integrates existing legacy systems and data with modern network systems via the Internet and Intranets. It's also the connectivity manager for PCs and mainframes.
- **Transaction Server**–A network application server that delivers the application "plumbing," including transactions, scaleability services, connection management, and administration.
- **Site Server (and Enterprise Edition)**–A Web-centric server for enhancing, deploying, and managing Intranet sites on Windows NT Server and Internet Information Server. The enterprise edition also provides advanced management of commerce-enabled Web sites.

- **Commercial Internet System**–A set of standards-based, commercial-grade server components that enhance the Internet services and Web sites of commercial service providers (e.g., ISPs, telecommunications carriers, and cable network operators).
- **SMS Server 1.2**–Systems Management Server is a tool that allows for execution of administrative tasks in an automatic and centralized way. These include hardware inventory, software installation, and distribution over the network and remote control of PCs.
- **Exchange Server 5.0**–E-mail server that supports all the Internet standards and extends rich messaging and collaboration to the enterprise.

Needless to say, Windows NT is the key component of this group of applications.

What to Expect in NT 5.0

Although many of you are still considering or busy migrating to NT 4.0, Microsoft is already pushing NT version 5.0. According to Microsoft, as this chapter is written (1997), NT 5.0 should debut somewhere around mid-1998. By then, your NT 4.0 environment should already be stable. You have already noticed some security flaws present and other features absent in 4.0 that you wish you had at your fingertips.

The amount of new features and technology that Microsoft is planning to release with NT 5.0, and BackOffice, is not timid! As a matter of fact, Microsoft is envisioning corporate solutions as being an "Active Platform," as Mark Smith describes it (http://www.winntmag.com/news/pdc96.html) in *Windows Magazine* of November 1996.

Microsoft's Windows NT 5.0 will bring security protocols that are much more safe, flexible, and scaleable than those present on NT 4.0 and earlier versions. Public and secret keys, provided by RSA and Kerberos respectively, will be incorporated into NT 5.0 as well. This will allow private connections between distinct networks in different locations to occur much more securely than they do today. Figure 1.5 outlines this process.

Individual Domains

Individual domains on NT 5.0 also will have the option of establishing transitive trusting relationships, which will allow for greater scaleability for larger enterprises, as smaller domains will not need explicit trust relationships with all other domains in the larger organization. These domains will inherit the trusting relationships established by a parental domain at the root of the organization, thus greatly simplifying the ongoing management of directory and security services. Figure 1.6 shows how the trusting relationships are established in NT 4.0 and what's new with NT 5.0.

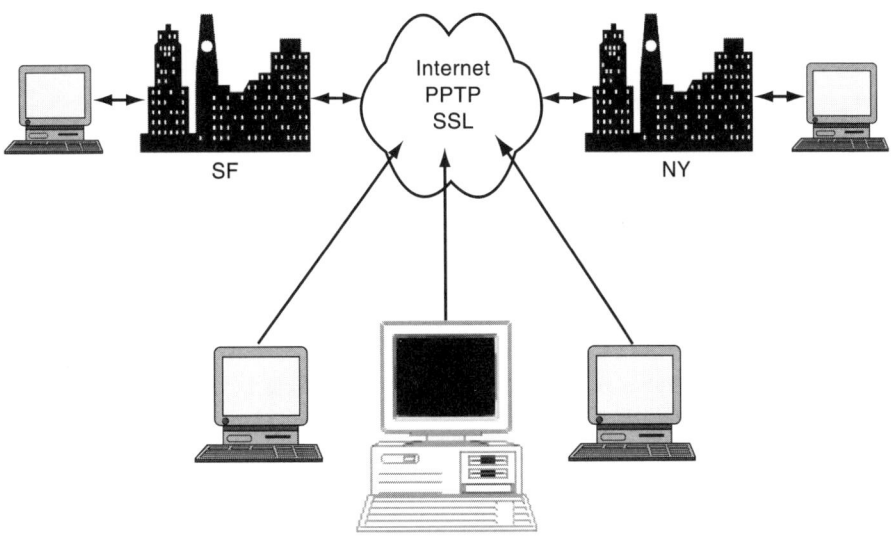

FIGURE 1.5 Businesses will be able to link to private networks securely with NT 5.0.

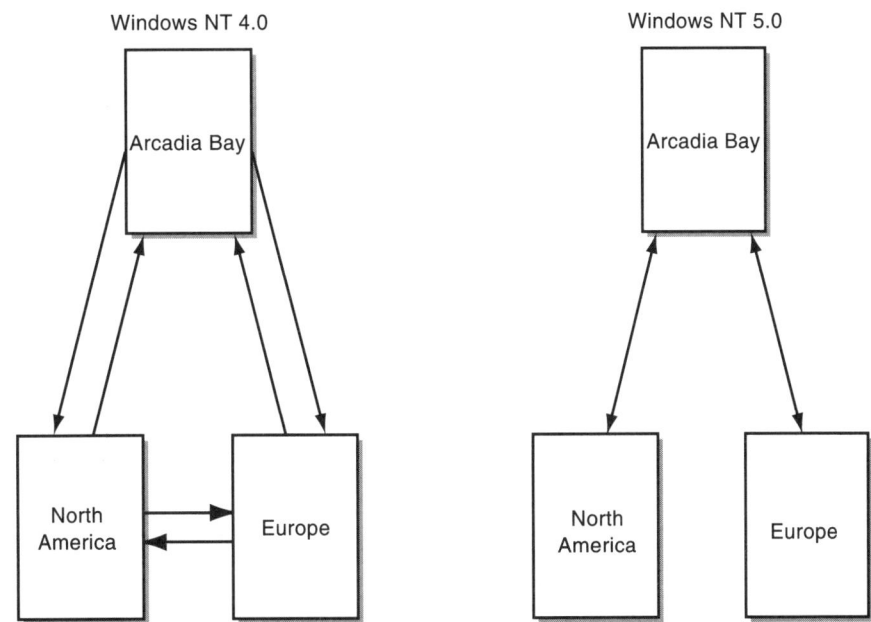

FIGURE 1.6 NT 4.0 requires trusting relationships in all directories. In NT 5.0, trusting relationships will have the capability of being transitive.

Transitive Trusting Relationships

The introduction of transitive trusting relationships will allow a Web server, for example, to be able to act as a user when it accesses other servers on behalf of a user's request. The public encryption key service will make sure the connection is secured and that only the requester gets it. The trusting relationships also will allow an object to be signed, just as in ActiveX objects, so that origin and integrity can be verified.

The base platform for Windows NT 5.0 is to build an Internet security model for full-scale Internet and intranet computing that will be much simpler to use and manage, as well as safer, than in Windows NT 4.0. NT 5.0 infrastructure will support four primary security protocols:

WINDOWS NT LAN MANAGER (NTLM)

This authentication protocol is used already by Windows NT 4.0. It will continue to be used for pass-through network authentication, remote file access, and authenticated Remote Procedure Call (RPC), which enables a distributed application to call services available on various machines in a network, to be connected to earlier versions of Windows NT so that they can be incorporated within NT 5.0 without the need for immediate upgrades or migrations.

THE KERBEROS VERSION 5

In NT 5.0, this authentication protocol will become the primary security protocol, replacing LAN Manager. Needless to say, the Kerberos authentication protocol brings great advantages for the NT 5.0 network authentication system, which includes mutual authentication of both client and server, reduced server load during connection establishment, and support for the delegation of authorization from clients to servers through the use of proxy mechanisms.

DISTRIBUTED PASSWORD AUTHENTICATION (DPA)

This is a shared secret authentication protocol used by some of the largest Internet membership organizations, such as CompuServe. This authentication protocol is specifically designed so that users can use the same Internet membership password to connect to any number of Internet sites that are part of the same membership organization. The Internet content servers use the Microsoft Membership System (MMS) authentication service as a back-end Internet service. Users can connect to multiple sites without reentering their passwords.

PUBLIC-KEY-BASED PROTOCOLS

These protocols will provide privacy and reliability to NT 5.0 users over the Internet. SSL is the de facto standard today for connections between Internet (or Web) browsers and Internet Information Servers. These protocols use public-key certificates to authenticate clients and servers, and depend on a public-key infrastructure for widespread use. NT 4.0 already provides secure channel security services that implement the SSL/PCT (Secure Socket Layer/Private Communication Technology) protocols, but with NT 5.0, the support for public-key protocols is enhanced.

 An IETF standard protocol definition based on SSL3 is forthcoming and is currently known as the Transport Layer Security Protocol (TLS).

The support for multiple network security protocols in NT 5.0 will allow NT workstations and servers to host a variety of network services, in addition to Internet-based technologies. Figure 1.7, taken from Microsoft's TechNet note, shows the architecture support for multiple security protocols implemented in Windows NT using the Security Support Provider Interface (SSPI).

The SSPI is a Win32 system API used by NT to isolate application-level protocols from security protocols used for network authentication. Security providers use different credentials to authenticate the user, either shared-secret or public-key certificates. The security protocols interact with different authentication services and account information stores.

Multiple Authentication Services
Using SSPI

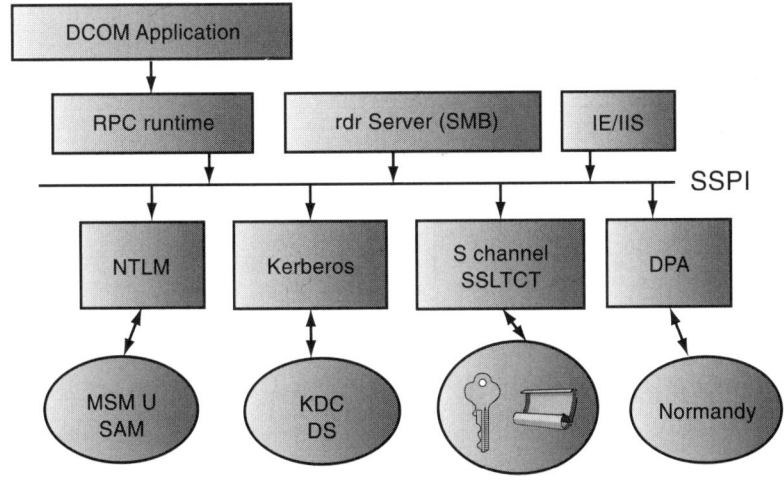

FIGURE 1.7 Architecture for Multiple Authentication Services of NT 5.0.

The NTLM security provider uses the "MSV1_0" authentication and NetLogon services on a Domain Controller for client authentication and authorization information. Now, with NT's Kerberos security model, the security providers will connect to an online Key Distribution Center (KDC) and the Directory Service account store for session tickets.

DPA uses the Microsoft Membership System (MMS) security services for membership authentication and server-specific access information. The secure channel services that are used are based on public-key certificates issued by trusted Certificate Authorities that do not require an online authentication server.

The authentication protocol of Kerberos defines the transactions between a client and network Authentication Service known as a Key Distribution Center (KDC). Microsoft is implementing a KDC as the authentication service of NT 5.0 for each Domain Controller. The NT 5.0 domains will be the equivalent of Kerberos realms.

The NT/Kerberos security implementation is based on the Internet RFC 1510 definition of the Kerberos protocol. The Kerberos user authentication will be integrated with the WinLogon single-log-on architecture. The Kerberos server, or KDC, will be embedded with NT 5.0's security services running on a domain controller and will use the NT Directory Service as the account database for users and groups.

The following is a list of enhancements the Kerberos authentication protocol will bring to NT 5.0:

- The *server authentication* will be much faster at initial log-on, as the application server will not have to connect to a domain controller in order to authenticate a client.
- There will be *delegation of authentication* for multitier client/server application architectures. When a client connects to a server, the server impersonates the client on that system. But if the server needs to make a network connection to another back-end server to complete the client transaction, the Kerberos protocol allows delegation of authentication for the first server to connect on behalf of the client to another server. The delegation allows the second server also to impersonate the client.
- There will be *transitive trust* relationships for interdomain authentication. The user can authenticate to domains anywhere in the domain tree, because the authentication services (KDCs) in each domain trust tickets issued by other KDCs in the tree.

What Is Kerberos?

Kerberos is an authentication protocol. It is called a shared secret protocol because both the user and the authentication services (KDC) know the user's password, or in the case of the KDC, the one-way encrypted password.

The Kerberos protocol defines a series of exchanges between clients, the KDC, and servers to obtain and use Kerberos tickets. To borrow from Microsoft's TechNet notes (March 97), "when a user initiates a log-on to Windows NT (and Windows® 95 clients as well) the Kerberos SSP obtains an initial Kerberos ticket (TGT) based on an encrypted hash of the user's password. Windows NT stores the TGT in a ticket cache on the workstation associated with the user's logon context. When a client program attempts to access a network service, the Kerberos run time checks the ticket cache for a valid session ticket to the server. If a ticket is not available, the TGT is sent in a request to the KDC for a session ticket that allows access to the server." Figure 1.8 describes the authentication protocol used by Kerberos.

As shown in Figure 1.8, extracted from Microsoft's white paper on the Kerberos authentication protocol (`http://www.microsoft.com/msdn/sdk/techinfo/secwp.doc`), the whole Kerberos authentication protocol system is a very dynamic one. It is completely integrated with NT and truly provides a transitive trusting relationship process. Note that NT's domain controller plays an active role in the process, acting as a "clearing house," or key distribution center (KDC). All new connections starting at a client (step 1) need to go through the KDC in order to request a ticket to be admitted in the NT domain, or *realm*, as it is called in Kerberos terms. The ticket the client will receive will take into consideration the client's profile and access

Kerberos Authentication Protocol Overview

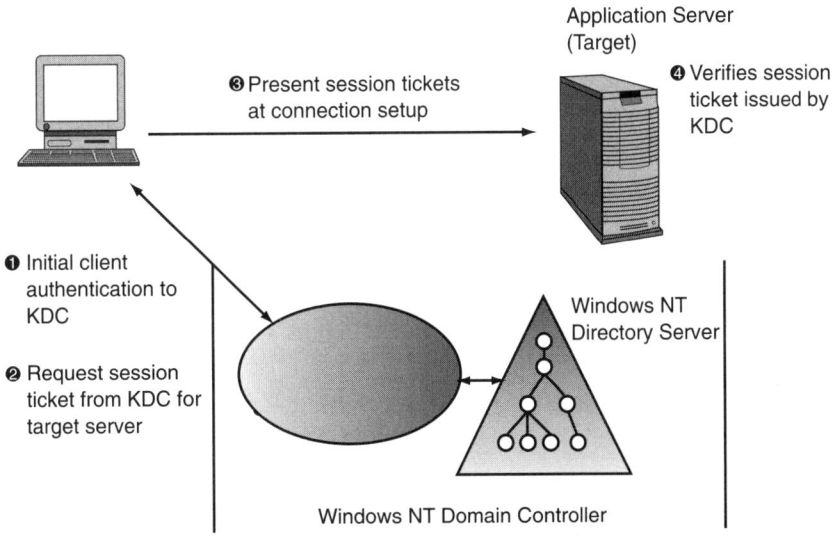

Application Server (Target)

❸ Present session tickets at connection setup

❹ Verifies session ticket issued by KDC

❶ Initial client authentication to KDC

❷ Request session ticket from KDC for target server

Windows NT Directory Server

Windows NT Domain Controller

FIGURE 1.8 Overview of the Kerberos Authentication Protocol in NT 5.0.

permissions to the directory services and domains granted to them (step 2). At connection setup the client will present the ticket to the server it is logging on to (step 3), which in turn will verify the ticket issued by the KDC.

Nevertheless, for the purposes of a discussion of Internet privacy, the "nuts and bolts" of Microsoft's strategy as far as using Kerberos is not our main objective and concern. It is important to know more about the Internet security/privacy issues surrounding NT 5.0/Kerberos and its implementations, so try to search at Microsoft's site for those keywords, as there are a lot of document materials available there.

Microsoft has been developing an Internet Security Framework (ISF) to provide public-key security architecture for all Windows platforms. The security technology enabling strong security on the Internet these days is based on public-key cryptography. Microsoft's ISF utilizes certificate services, a secure channel security provider that implements SSL/PCT protocols, the SET secure payment protocol for credit card transactions and CryptoAPI version 2.0 components for certificate management and administration.

In the same Microsoft white paper mentioned earlier in this chapter, there is a great graphic showing Microsoft's entire Internet Security Framework (ISF). Figure 1.9 shows that graphic, outlining Microsoft's Internet Security Technologies.

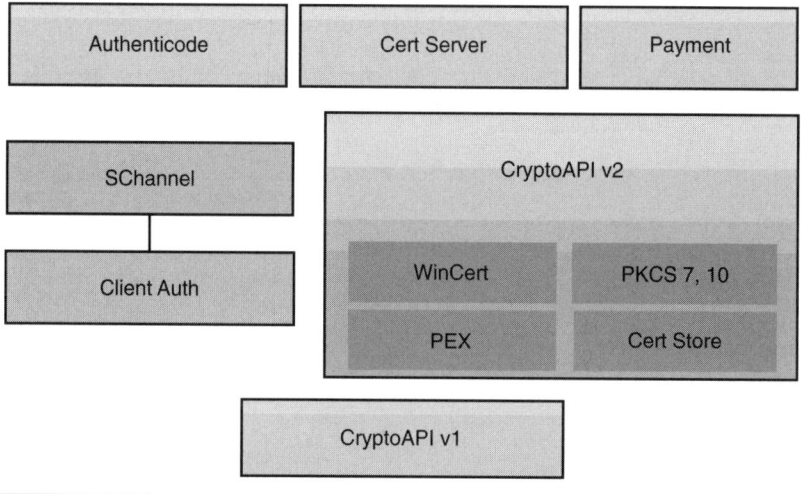

Microsoft's Internet Security Framework

FIGURE 1.9   Microsoft's Adopted Internet Security Framework.

Microsoft's Internet Explorer and Internet Information Server use many of the Internet Security Framework components outlined in Figure 1.9. The new features of Microsoft's ISF, which will be present on NT 5.0, include:

- *Client Authentication* using Secure Socket Layer (SSL) 3.0 and Private Communication Technology (PCT), which are public-key-based security protocols implemented by Secure Channel (which Microsoft calls Schannel) providers.
- *Certificate Services* (CS) providing customizable services for issuing and managing certificates for applications using public-key cryptography. Each request the CS receives coming from RPC, HTTP, or e-mail transmissions is checked against a custom or site-specific security policy and/or properties. CT also will have the capability to allow administrators to customize the certificate revocation list (CRL), as well as publish a signed CRL on a regular basis.
- *CryptoAPI* version 2.0 features with support for X.509 version 3 certificates and X.509 version 2.0 CRL also will be supporting PKCS #10 certificates requests and PKCS #7 for signed enveloped data. Another important feature is the support for digital signatures and verification, as well as data encryption using functions available to applications in HTML, Java, Visual Basic Script, and C/C++.

NT 4.0 already supports CryptoAPI, but only version 1.0, which provides the low-level cryptography support and modular Cryptographic Service Providers.

All of these security tools, some of which are already present on NT 4.0 and most of which will be enhanced for NT 5.0, will provide organizations and Internet users with the option to use Microsoft's Internet Security Framework to solve their Internet security and privacy problems. The ability to issue public-key certificates to specific partners or counterparts, and to use certificates instead of having to create a user account to define a domain trust relationship and identify and authorize access to resources, is a major advantage. It is an effective way to enhance security and try to guarantee secure connections over the Internet.

You should expect a very smooth transition from the present NTLM authentication of NT 4.0 and previous versions to NT 5.0's Kerberos domain authentication. Besides, Windows NT services can support client or server connections using either security protocol. The transition from Enterprise-based services using Kerberos authentication to Internet-based services using public-key authentication is completely transparent to the user.

As most application protocols support multiple authentication, such as LDAP, HTTP/HTTPS, or RPC, which are designed to support multiple authentication services, NT 5.0 will use multiple protocols as well, as they are needed to fit the application requirements and the user community requirements for secure network computing.

Furthermore, because NT 5.0 will continue to support NTLM authentication, NT 4.0 clients that do not use Kerberos authentication will also be able to connect to 5.0 without any problems.

For more information on NT 5.0 see the companion white paper, *Microsoft Windows NT Next Generation Directory Services,* and for additional information on the Internet Security Framework, check Microsoft's paper on security framework. Both are available at Microsoft's URL at http://www.microsoft .com/intdev/security.

To enable developers to take advantage of these technologies as soon as possible, Microsoft announced at the Microsoft Professional Developers Conference, in November of 1996, that they will be shipping these NT 5.0 technologies as they become available. DCOM, for instance, was shipped in Windows NT Server 4.0 last summer. Active Server Pages were shipped in Internet Information Server 3.0 during fall of 1996. Microsoft Management Console was introduced with IIS 4.0. More is to come as the technology becomes available.

Conclusion

You should have a good understanding of some of the improvements that NT 4.0 has introduced and an idea where NT 5 will take us. The future is bright for NT. Sales are up, and people around the world are learning what a great operating system it is. Just today, one of our colleagues was telling us what a great rendering platform it is because of its multitasking abilities and the stability it provides over other platforms.

Chapter 2 will introduce you to the installation process that is required for NT. You will learn how to install NT and how to upgrade to NT, and you will pick up some caveats that will help you with the installation process. Chapter 2 makes it easier to install NT by laying out the ground rules for the installation process.

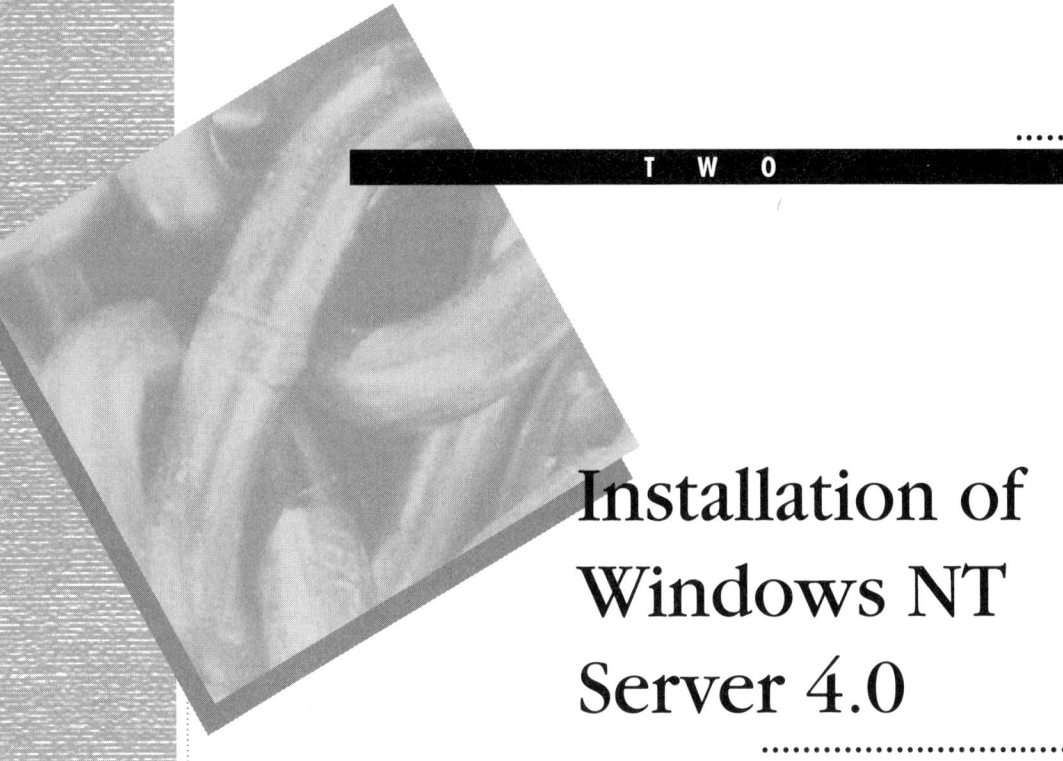

Installation of Windows NT Server 4.0

Installing any application is one of the simplest yet most troublesome aspects of using the software. That problem is compounded when the application is itself an operating system and/or you wish to roll out the operating system over a large number of systems.

Scenario 2.1:

You are a system manager and are faced with rolling out NT 4 workstations and servers on your network. The problem is, there are 250 machines you must upgrade, and you don't want to visit every single workstation.

Scenario 2.2:

Your organization already has several NT Server systems running on Intel processors. You are getting ready to add some power to your network by installing NT Server on an Alpha system. Should work just like installing on Intel—right?

These scenarios show typical situations that system managers run into every day. How do you approach each situation? How do you prepare for the first installation or a large-scale rollout?

This chapter introduces you to many of the issues involved in installing an NT Server or NT Workstation system. We will discuss general issues such as whether or not to use a Custom setup. We will also dive into a few other issues, such as installing NT on an Alpha system and upgrading to NT 4.0.

General Installation Tips

NT Workstation (NTW) and NT Server (NTS) 4.0 are both installed in the same manner. Both NTW and NTS are fairly easy to install: The user-friendly interface, inherited from Windows 95, brings a few assistants that help on the choices you have to make. But don't be deceived into thinking that you only need to answer few questions and you'll be all set. There may be some blocks on the way.

The traditional way to install NT 3.5 and 3.51 was to use the boot floppy shipped with NT to start the Setup process from the CD or continue the installation with the diskettes. Even though the earlier versions of NT are still shipping with several different methods of installation, and the resource kit adds other options, with the NT 4.0 installation can only be done from the CD. Table 2.1 includes the various options.

TABLE 2.1	Installation Options
Method	**Description**
Setup	Setup is the traditional method of installing NT and uses the boot floppy shipped with NT for x86 (Intel) systems. RISC systems use the ARC menu to start the setup process.
WINNT	WINNT is used to install NT over a network or when your system has an unsupported CD-ROM. WINNT is used only on x86 (Intel) systems running DOS. The NT Resource Kit includes the SETUPMGR program, which can create automatic answer files for use with WINNT and WINNT32.
WINNT32	WINNT32 is used to upgrade a system already running NT. It performs the upgrade just like WINNT. The NT Resource Kit includes the SETUPMGR program, which can create automatic answer files for use with WINNT and WINNT32.
CPS	Computer Profile Setup (CPS) is included with the NT Resource Kit and is used to automate the installation of NT and NT Server on Intel platforms. The process is used to build a master copy of NT on a server and then to install the master system to target clients.

NT is a multiplatform operating system. Each processor has different sets of instructions, which requires alterations in the source code of NT. Therefore, you will find on the CD four distinct versions, organized by directories. If you take a look at the root directory of your NT 4.0 CD, you will find the following directories:

- **I386**–Intel version. Because the old versions of NT run on 386 machines, the directory still reflects this.
- **Alpha**–DEC's (Digital Equipment Corporation) chip, present on AlphaServer 2100/8400 and AlphaStation 255/500 (for new and faster

models, check Digital's URL at http://www.dec.com//info.alpha-server).

■ **MIPS**–This processor from MIPS Technologies are mostly used on Silicon Graphics computers. Although NT performance is greater with MIPS than with Pentiums, vendors are not supporting it anymore, so be careful.

■ **PowerPC**–For computers, such as IBM 43P, that use PowerPC.

Installing NT 4.0

There are basically two ways for you to start installing NT: by using the three diskettes (to boot your system so it can access the CD via network), or by using the WINNT command. If you are installing it on a brand-new computer without any OS installed on the hard drive, or you just formatted your hard drive, or even if you already have an OS installed but want to format it with NT and start from ground zero, then you might want to use the three diskettes that come with the software package.

The three diskettes I'm talking about are the Setup Boot Disk, Setup Disk 2, and Setup Disk 3. You will need to boot your computer using the first and insert the CD on your CD-ROM drive and follow the instructions. If you are upgrading from a previous version, then you only need to launch the WINNT32 file from the CD. If you are installing NT on a RISC platform (on an Alpha, MIPS, or PowerPC), you will need to run SETUPLDR in the appropriate directory, in which case the three diskettes won't be utilized.

If you have to re-create the three diskettes for installing NT, take any machine equipped with a CD-ROM drive, running DOS or Windows, access the I386 directory on the CD, and type at the DOS prompt: WINNT /OX. This switch will create the diskettes for you.

Note that if you want to install NT on this same computer, the diskettes you'll insert on the floppy drive should be formatted and empty, and you should insert them in the drive in a reverse order, so that after the system reboot, the first disk will already be in the drive.

Anyhow, setup will present you with the two standard operational methods of installation: Default and Custom. Default is almost always shown as recommended by setup. Nevertheless, choosing the Custom method provides much more control, and you can still take the default answers for any item by pressing the Enter key.

Installation Options

If you use Custom, you also have the option to install specific components such as TCP/IP during the setup process. You must also use Custom if your network supports only TCP/IP (and not NetBEUI) and you are not installing NT Server as a Backup Domain Controller. If you plan to install a Backup

Domain Controller, that system must communicate with the Primary Domain Controller during setup, thus requiring that both systems use the same protocol and are attached to the same network during setup.

Another possibility to take into consideration is if you're installing an upgrade. You may want upgrade your Windows for Workgroups, Windows 95, or most likely Windows NT 3.5/3.51 to NT 4.0. In this case, access the CD and issue the command WINNT /B, which will start the installation without asking to create the three diskettes. The switch /B tells the system to copy all the necessary files to install NT to a temporary directory. The system will find the copy of Windows on the hard drive, and ask you if you want to do an upgrade. If you are doing an upgrade from a previous version of NT (3.1, 3.5, or 3.51), then you should use the command WINNT32 /B.

Now, there is still another option, which can be very interesting, if not useful: setting up your machine with a dual boot! Do this if you want to preserve Windows 95 or even previous versions of NT while having the option to use NT 4.0. In this case, you will be prompted with the choice to boot with the OS previously installed, or with NT 4.0. You will still use the command WINNT /B for upgrades from MS-DOS, Windows for Workgroups, and Windows 95, and WINNT32 /B for a previous version of NT 4.0, but when asked by the system, DO NOT accept to perform an upgrade.

 One more thing: There is no way to install NT on a compressed partition, whether with Stacker or with DriveSpace. You must undo the compression before the installation, unless you're planning to format the disk.

Basic Information Before You Install

It is wise to collect several bits of information before you begin installing NT Server. You will use this information during the installation process or after the system is installed. It is always wise to have a complete picture of the components installed in your server and their configuration. This information will come in handy later when you must change the system's configuration or if you experience a problem.

You should also gather three or four blank formatted disks (depending upon your installation method, as discussed previously, and whether or not you will build an emergency disk), obtain the latest NT Server patches (download them from Microsoft's site at http://www.microsoft.com/NT, or use TechNet), and keep a notepad handy in case you need to take some notes. If you have a newer hardware device (such as a network card) or one that is not on the compatibility list, keep the setup disks and manuals for the device handy during the installation. It's a good idea to have handy the IRQ and I/O configurations of your NIC (Network Interface Card) card to avoid conflicts later on during the installation.

Before you start the installation of your first server, decide on the naming conventions to use for your system:

- NT Server name
- Domain name
- TCP/IP address and subnet mark to use for your system

HARDWARE CONFIGURATION

The first step is to carefully verify the equipment you are planning to install. NT is picky! There is a list called HCL (Hardware Compatibility List) that you will find in the package you get when you buy NT 4.0, that lists all the equipment that was tested and worked properly. The list includes everything from complete computer systems to tape units (DAT) and video cards. If you want to install any component that is not in the HCL list, make sure the vendor provides you with a diskette with the drivers written for NT.

You should keep a list of configurations for your system. This includes, but is not limited to, the items in Table 2.2.

TABLE 2.2	Hardware Configuration Notes
Item	**Description**
BIOS	BIOS (Basic Input Output System) information is normally shown when the system boots. Track the manufacturer (i.e., Phoenix), the version, and the date if shown.
CMOS	CMOS memory is used by Intel systems to keep configuration information such as the system time, memory, disk types and operation, and ROM shadowing methods. The information varies from one hardware vendor to another.
DMA	Many devices such as disk controllers or network cards may use DMA (Direct Memory Address). Record the address for each device in your system that uses DMA.
Memory address	Some network and SCSI controllers use a memory block to interface with the operating system. You should check your card settings to verify if the card uses a memory address and, if so, what the setting is.
I/O Port	Most network cards use input/output ports. Record any port addresses used.
Firmware	Some systems (RISC) use firmware to define features of the system. These systems may require updating to run NT or for enhancements to the hardware.
IRQ	Devices may also use IRQ (Interrupt Request) settings. Examples of devices that use IRQ values are disk controllers, network cards, and communication cards.
SCSI ID	Each device connected to a Small Computer Systems Interface (SCSI) controller must have a unique ID. Unless your system uses a storage system that automatically configures SCSI addresses, you should keep a record of all SCSI devices and their

TABLE 2.2	Hardware Configuration Notes (Continued)
Item	**Description**
	IDs. It is also a good idea to write down which devices have terminators and which ones do not.
Disk Drives	It is a good idea to keep a record of all disk drives in your system. This information is very useful when a problem occurs or when you must plan for an upgrade to the system.
Devices	All cards in your system should be recorded. Note the IRQ and other parameters used by the card.
Network cards	The type of network card and its configuration are used in the installation. Specifically you need the IRQ, base I/O address, and possibly memory address range used. This information should be written in your system manual.
Misc.	Any items that are not explicitly mentioned in this list but that are part of your configuration should also be tracked. This information includes the type and speed of memory and modems.

The minimum system requirement for you to install NT Server 4.0, in the case of an Intel processor, is a 486/33MHz, 16MB of RAM and at least 125MB of free disk space. But in reality, we recommend you to install it on a Pentium, with at least 32MB of RAM.

The information in Table 2.2 will be very useful for maintaining and upgrading your servers. Make sure that you keep a hard copy, and don't rely on a disk file for access to the information. Most managers skip this step because they are in a rush during installation or are happy just to get the system installed and operational. Even though writing down configuration information may be the last thing on your mind, you should take a moment to record it.

WINMSD (the diagnostic tool) and other tools can provide most of the information listed in Table 2.2 and more. It's a good idea to run reports from one of these tools after you modify the configuration of a system or install new software.

If you are running Windows 3.x before you install NT, you can run MSD, which is found in the Windows directory. Winsleuth Gold and other third-party tools can also provide this type of information.

If you are running NT 3.5 or 3.51, then your installation should be much easier, as NT 4.0 will look at your configuration files and keep or adapt all of them.

Another tip is to use Microsoft's SMS (Systems Management Server), part of the BackOffice family, to collect and save the configuration information for each client and server on the network. SMS collects a tremendous

BackOffice

amount of data during its inventory phase and places it in an SQL Server database. You can easily print a copy periodically or even download a view of the data to a local Access database on a client.

Potential Problems with SCSI Disks and Controllers

Here is a summary of the few potential problems you should be aware of when you use SCSI disks and controllers.

DRIVERS

If your system uses non-NT default drives such as those for the NCR chip set, or a nonsupported Ethernet controller, make sure that you have the miniport drivers for NT handy when you begin the installation. Select the Custom install and then use the miniport driver disk when NT complains about not finding your device bus and asks you to insert the disk with the drivers.

SCSI DRIVE ID

If your system has a problem detecting the CD-ROM drive, try setting the SCSI ID for the CD-ROM to anything besides 0 or 1. You should be able to use any ID not used by another device or the SCSI controller itself.

SCSI HARD DRIVES

All hard drives in your system should be on the NT compatibility list. You may still find an unexplained anomaly that can drive you nuts. For example, I ran into a situation while installing NT Server on an Alpha 2100-500 AXP from Digital Equipment Corporation. Time and again the setup process failed after the process started copying files to the hard disk. I also could not run ARCINST from the CD-ROM. If I copied ARCINST to a floppy, it ran fine.

The hard drive was located three connectors away from the CD-ROM on the SCSI cable. I moved the drive over to the connector next to the CD-ROM, and everything worked fine. The experience was very confusing.

The moral of this story is: Make sure that all connectors are tight and that the SCSI bus is terminated correctly. If the problem still occurs, move the drive to another connector on the SCSI cable.

NETWORK CONTROLLERS

Make sure that you know the configuration and type of network card in the system before you start the installation. If you start the installation and NT

Server can't communicate with the network, unless you are installing the Primary Domain Controller or only a server, you are in trouble.

NT Server must be able to communicate with the domain to install a Backup Domain Controller or Server into an existing domain. You cannot change domains with an NT Server after it has been installed. This means that you could install with a bad network card, but you would be forced to reinstall to join the existing domain. Test your network card before installing NT and note the configuration information. This information will be valuable in case there is a problem or NT can't detect the card.

INSTALLING NT OVER A PREVIOUS OS OR WITH UNFORMATTED DISKS

As mentioned previously, replacing another operating system besides MS-DOS with NT should not be a problem. However, NT can fail during the installation procedure and give you a message stating that your system may have a virus. This message usually occurs during the first phase of the installation when NT tries to boot, and it really gets your attention. This symptom can also occur when you install NT on a brand-new system with new disk drives.

The virus message appears because NT sees the other operating system partition and can't recognize it. This message doesn't occur when the system runs MS-DOS or OS/2, but how about VMS or UNIX? NT is vulnerable to attacks during the installation phase, so instead of risking bringing up an infected system, it shuts down.

This problem is solved with a bizarre solution.

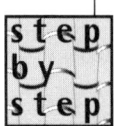

Replacing an OS (Besides MS-DOS) with NT:
1. Unplug all disk drives except for the system drive. If you use a hot-swappable system, simply pop the drives out halfway.
2. Use ARCINST (RISC only) to partition the system disk. If your system is RISC-based, make sure that there is at least a 4MB FAT partition. I always create a 6MB system partition and leave the rest of the drive unpartitioned. NT will partition the drive during installation.
3. Install NT.
4. Reboot and test.
5. Plug the drives back in. You may need to shut down the system before plugging the drives back in.

We have tested this process on an Alpha 2100-500 and Alpha 2000, and it works fine.

What Type of Volume Do I Use for NT System Files?

NT Server can be installed on a brand-new system or a system that is currently running another operating system. As shipped, NT 4.0 supports two file system types: the MS-DOS File Allocation Table (FAT) and the NT File System (NTFS). Unlike previous versions, NT 4.0 no longer supports OS/2s' HPFS file system. You will be prompted to choose the file system you want to use or rebuild it during installation. The benefits and drawbacks to both approaches are listed in Table 2.3. NT cannot install its system files on a drive larger than 4GB.

Along with the considerations outlined in Table 2.3, NT offers you four options when choosing the file system. You can choose to format the drive using FAT, using NTFS, convert an already FAT formatted drive onto NTFS, or just leave it intact ("No Changes," option). Simply choose whether to leave the file system in place or to reformat the file system. The entire setup process can still be accomplished in less than 1 hour.

Installing on a Virgin Partition (Intel (Only):

1. Repartition the system drive using FDISK. You should make a bootable floppy disk and copy FDISK, FORMAT, EDIT, and any other programs you may need to the floppy. Make sure that you also save any startup files such as CONFIG.SYS and AUTOEXEC.BAT and any drivers or such that may be required by the SCSI systems or other devices. The partition size for the boot partition should be around 100–120 MB.

2. Install NT on the drive. Select the option to reformat the existing file system to NTFS during installation.

3. Format the other partitions and drives on your system for NTFS or FAT.

4. Run Control Panel and select the System applet. Make sure NT is the default operating system, and change the time before it automatically boots to five seconds.

TABLE 2.3   Installation Considerations for File Systems

Replacing the file system	Replacing the file system when installing NT is the best option because it places NT on its own file system with no other operating systems.
Leaving the existing file system	Leaving the current file system in place leaves your system with the original files in place and NT installed on top of the existing file system. This may be a problem if your system was running Windows 3.x because NT will be installed in the Windows directory. I recommend this option only when you must upgrade Windows to NT Server, which is rarely the case. See installing on a virgin DOS system below.
Installing on a virgin DOS system	Installing NT on a FAT partition allows you to access the NT system files via DOS if the system becomes unbootable with NT. This approach creates a security problem because the NT system files can be accessed by booting with a DOS diskette.
Compressed drives	Never place NT system files on a compressed drive created within DOS or Windows 95. Make sure that the partition that is used for NT is not compressed and does not have the UNDELETE SENTRY enabled.

After NT is up and running, you can reboot the system using DOS at any time by restarting the system and selecting DOS within five seconds. If an NT file gets corrupted and NT will not boot, you can replace the file from DOS if the Repair Disk option does not repair the file.

Installing a clean copy of NT on a RISC system is similar to the process for Intel systems. You may need to run ARCINST in step 1 to delete any existing partitions on the system disk and create a new system partition.

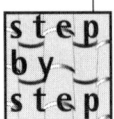

Installing on a Virgin Partition (RISC Only):

1. Delete all partitions on the system disk using ARCINST.

2. Create a new system partition (6MB) on the system disk.

3. Install NT using the ARC menu options (Supplementary menu "Install NT from CD-ROM"). Select the remaining free space on the system disk for the NT system files and select the option to reformat to NTFS. An NTFS partition for the system files is created during the installation process.

4. Format the other partitions and drives on your system for NTFS, or FAT.

You can use a redirector, called NTFSDOS, to have DOS and Win 3.1 users use network-mounted NTFS file system. However, users won't be able to use the long filename NT access permission features.

How NT Handles Installation Media

As mentioned previously, NT can be installed from several different types of media, including CD-ROM, floppy disks, and network resources. The major problem with installing NT is that it will always look for upgrades and new drivers from the original installation media, which is inconvenient, to say the least. This is a drastic change from Windows 3.x, but it takes off in the wrong direction!

There is a work-around for solving this problem. NT looks for the setup media in two places: POINTER.INF in the SYSTEM32 directory and the SourcePath value in the Registry. After you make these changes, Setup looks for any updates on the correct device.

Table 2.4 includes the major INF files used by NT during installation. Each file has an INF extension when uncompressed. Additional information on modifying the setup files can be found in the NT Resource Kit book.

TABLE 2.4	INF Files Used by NT During Installation

File Name	Description
DOSNET	Used by text-mode Windows NT Setup. Also used by WINNT and WINNT32 to determine which files are copied to the hard disk during installation. Used during all setup modes (Setup, WINNT, WINNT32).
INITIAL	Windows NT Setup script file for additional NT components. Used during all setup modes (Setup, WINNT, WINNT32).
PARTIAL	Windows NT Setup script file for optional NT components and to create Program Manager groups. Used during all setup modes (Setup, WINNT, WINNT32).
TXTSETUP	Text mode setup script for core NT components. Used during all setup modes (Setup, WINNT, WINNT32). Changes made to this file must be made on the first floppy disk or on the distribution share.

Changing the Installation Path for the NT Distribution:

1. Expand the POINTER.IN_ file from the media you wish to use to the SYSTEM32 directory. The syntax for a pointer device is

   ```
   EXPAND A:\POINTER.IN_ POINTER.INF
   ```

   This command assumes that you are using a floppy disk as the new media. If you are switching to a CD-ROM or network, you must supply the correct drive and directory for that resource.

2. Use REGEDIT32 and change the SourcePath under the following key to point to the new source:

   ```
   HKEY_LOCAL_MACHINE\SOFTWARE\Microsoft\
   Windows NT\CurrentVersion
   ```

Installation Methods

To tell you the truth, this should be the shortest part of this book. Microsoft really did a great job ensuring an easy and straightforward installation process for NT 4.0. Nevertheless, Murphy's Law always applies, and you should assume that *easy* and *straightforward* doesn't always mean "peachy!" Therefore, before moving forward, let's take a look at some of the changes that the maturing process that NT has gone through.

New Features Affecting the Installation of NT 4.0

As outlined in Chapter 1, "What Has Changed Since Windows NT 3.5?", the changes in NT 4.0 are substantial and do affect its installation:

- To begin with, the initial screen is different! If your computer has a BIOS that allows booting from a CD, which in the past was exclusive to a RISC option, the NT 4.0 installation CD is an auto-run CD.
- You now have wizards. These are applets that were added to the installation process to make the use of the server more friendly. They provide fast and automated access to standard setup and administrative chores, such as adding users and changing security.
- Many device drivers are no longer supported directly by Microsoft. Look for them in the driver library (the DRVLIB directory on the NT distribution CD).
- All the drivers for the IDE components are now controlled by ATAPI.sys, and not Atdisk. So, if you're upgrading from a NT 3.50/51, make sure to disable Atdisk in the Control Panel, under the Service applet after installation.
- Hardware profiles exist. You can now set specific profiles for booting onto NT.
- You can now log-on an NT domain through RAs by enabling the Logon Via Dial Up Networking option in the Logon dialog box.
- The User and Graphics heaps have been moved to the kernel, which eliminates one layer of client/server complexity but requires drivers to be reconfigured and recompiled. That also means that many drivers from NT 3.51 won't work on version 4.0, such as printers and video drivers.
- As mentioned earlier, NT 4.0 no longer supports HPFS. You must convert it to NTFS.
- You no longer specify a printer on setup as you did with NT 3.51. All printers are set up later, once the setup procedure is successfully finished.
- NT 4.0 won't install on Intel 386 computers. You must have at least a 486 and a minimum of 12MB of RAM for an Intel computer or 16MB of RAM for a RISC.

Default Versus Custom

Microsoft recommends using the Default mode of setup unless you have any problems or peculiarities with your system. We heartily agree with this approach unless you have installed NT successfully before. If you use Custom, it is assumed that you have installed NT before or are planning to change a particular feature during setup.

During the Default mode, NT automates the process as much as possible, including asking the minimal number of questions during the installation and automatically detecting all the devices in your system.

If you try Default mode and have problems, you may have to use Custom mode and manually specify the location of device drivers that are not standard with NT. This may be the case if you have a new controller or other device that was produced after your NT kit was shipped. The manufacturer or another source may have the drivers available. You must use the Custom mode to tell NT to use the manufacturer's drivers.

Setup also detects only one network adapter during installation if you are using Default mode. You can install other adapters after installation by using the Network applet in the Control Panel. You can also install multiple network adapters during setup by choosing the Custom option.

Standard Installation

The normal procedure for installing NT is to run the setup program from either a CD-ROM or the three floppy installation media. But remember, you will need the CD anyway, as there is no way for you to install NT 4.0 from a floppy, as NT 3.51 users could. Setup is similar to the installation program of the same name for most installation programs (besides the fancier and more user-friendly Windows 95 interface!) and makes the entire process painless. Running WINNT or WINNT32 across a network is also very convenient, especially if you have created an automatic answer file that helps to automate the entire process.

General Overview of the Installation Process

As mentioned earlier, the installation of NT 4.0 is much easier than that of 3.51. Nevertheless, regardless of the platform on which you're installing NT, there are some issues you should watch for so that your installation can be successful.

Completing a Standard Installation

Installing NT on a RISC-based computer is a little different from installing it on a Intel-box. On an Alpha computer, you will install NT directly from the CD and will not use the /B switch we were talking about earlier in this chapter when you want to avoid the creation of the three diskettes with the Intel systems.

Also, by default on an Intel system, the setup will attempt to run automatically if you boot from the CD, and if you are using the diskettes, the setup will abort the installation after Disk 3, unless the CD is available for use. But assuming you're installing NT on an Intel-based computer, let's do a dry run.

Installing NT on an Intel-based Computer:

1. Start setup (WINNT or WINNT32, with or without the /B switch) or boot with the Setup disk or CD.

2. Choose Custom or Default. For this installation, we suggest that you choose Custom, as it enables you to see and select the applications that are being installed.

3. Verify the system components summarized for you by the detection procedure. If any components listed are incorrect, restart setup and when the system displays the message "Setup is inspecting your computer's hardware configuration," press F6 to bypass auto-detection and indicate the components you know are present (such as legacy SCSI drivers, for example).

4. Select the partition, file system, and directory for NT Server system files (remember that you will need to convert any HPFS partitions onto NTFS). If you are going to keep a small FAT partition on drive C: (for file maintenance via DOS), keep in mind that this will be violating C2 security. Our suggestion is to use NTFS as much as possible, especially if you're using large drives (greater than 1GB).

5. Fill in your user name, computer name, and so on.

6. Enter the security role for the server, and the administrator's password. Be wise! Make sure to enter a password of at least eight characters, and stick a nonsense symbol in it!

7. Choose the local language for the system.

8. Enter the domain name the server will participate in.

9. Verify or enter the parameters for the network card, and choose the default network protocol. Here, if you are familiar with previous NT installations, you will find a major change from previous setups as you encounter the new wizard. You are given the choice of not connecting the computer to the network at this time or of having the computer participating on the network (default), which allows you to choose it via a direct wire by an ISDN or a standard network cable or via remote access through a standard modem.

10. Decide if this server will be a Primary Domain Controller (PDC), which is the default, or a Backup Domain Controller (BDC), which assumes there is already a PDC on the network, or choose a standalone server. Spend some time here deciding what your server will be. A server can't be promoted to a PDC later, so you will need to reinstall it!

11. Enter your local time zone.

12. Select video adapter settings. This is much easier in NT 4.0 than it used to be on earlier versions. You simply select the resolution you want. Once you reboot, you will be able to change the resolution without having to reboot, but if you decide to change the size of the font, then you'll need to reboot your system.

13. Finally, create the emergency disk.

Custom setup enables you to override a number of defaults for the installation process. Default setup automates the process by asking only a minimal number of questions and using defaults for everything else, and it is recommended for most users. One particular option you may need to override using Custom setup is the automatic hardware detection feature. This should only be turned off if setup fails on a system for some reason during setup.

In general, it is best to install NT with the suggested video display options because picking an incorrect mode or option may cause the installation to fail. Once NT has booted after installation, you can change the display settings. Any problems can be recovered gracefully by using the Last Known Good option during startup.

If you are installing NT Server into an existing domain, make sure that the network connection used for the new server is working and that the domain can be accessed from that connection. If you install the new server and it cannot reach the Primary Domain Controller (PDC), you must reinstall the server.

Checking the network connectivity and the accessibility of the domain is very important! Failure to do this results in lots of lost time as you continue to reinstall the server because the system cannot communicate with the PDC.

FLOPPY DISK

Floppy disk installations are the most time-consuming option for NT Server and used to be performed only on x86 architecture systems, up to the NT 3.51 version. With NT 4.0, you must use the CD.

As discussed earlier, the setup of NT 4.0 automatically searches for a CD-ROM drive when it is started from the setup boot floppy. If it doesn't find the CD-ROM, it will abort the installation, so make sure to have it available on the drive or on a directory on the network.

Installing an NT 3.51 Version from Floppy Disks:

1. Insert the first Setup floppy disk in the drive.

2. Reboot the system.

3. Follow the general setup instructions to complete the installation.

If you're installing from a CD-ROM, the steps are very similar to those for NT 4.0 installation, only that NT 3.51 won't have the installation wizards we mentioned previously, nor the Windows 95 interface present in NT 4.0, aside from a few little updates.

CD-ROM (X86 SYSTEMS ONLY)

Installing from CD-ROM is one of the fastest and simplest methods for installing NT Server, and the only way to install NT 4.0, unless you do it through the network. This process is simple and can be accomplished in thirty minutes to an hour, if you don't encounter any problems. Be sure to read the first sections of this chapter and follow all the steps.

Installing from CD-ROM:

1. Insert the first Setup floppy disk in the drive.
2. Reboot the system.
3. Insert the Setup CD in the CD-ROM drive when you are prompted.
4. Follow the general setup instructions to complete the installation.

RISC SYSTEMS ONLY

RISC systems can install NT only from CD-ROM. Upgrades can be performed over the network using WINNT32 or the CD-ROM.

The first thing you must do to install NT on a RISC system is to determine the steps for starting a program from CD-ROM on your system. Use these instructions to start the Windows NT Setup program. Most RISC systems that can run NT use the ARC menu and have a menu option for installing NT under the Supplementary menu.

The system partition used for NT should have at least 5 MB of free space, but we always use 6MB to 10MB for a little free space. The hidden files OSLOADER.EXE and HAL.DLL must reside in the \OS\WINNT directory on this partition. The balance of NT Server can be placed on this partition or another partition formatted as FAT or NTFS. Use NTFS because it provides the best performance and security.

The following steps work on a Digital Equipment Corporation Alpha system. Systems used for testing this procedure were AlphaServer 2100 and AlphaServer 2000 servers with varying configurations. If you have problems with these steps, consult your system manuals to determine the steps for installing on your particular model.

After the system partition is created, you are ready to install NT. Make sure that the remaining space on the system drive is not partitioned.

When the NT Setup screen appears, complete the installation in the normal manner.

ALPHA AXP EXAMPLES

There are several things you can do to configure an Alpha AXP RISC system for NT. These steps involve setting system parameters or upgrading firmware

Creating a System Partition for NT:

1. Load the NT Server CD-ROM.
2. Restart the system.
3. From the Boot menu, choose Run a Program.
4. Enter cd:\alpha\arcinst and press Enter.
5. Select Configure Partitions from the menu.
6. Delete any existing partitions on the system disk. WARNING: This step deletes all files on the disk.
7. Choose Create Partition.
8. Select the disk to use for the system disk.
9. Enter the size for the partition (should be 6) and press Enter.
10. Select Make Existing Partition into a System Partition.
11. Answer Y to the prompt to overwrite any existing system partition.
12. If you receive a message that Boot Selections already exist, then return to step 5 and complete the procedure again. Make sure all partitions on the system disk are deleted before step 7.
13. Exit ARCINST.

Installing NT on a RISC system:

1. Load the NT Server CD-ROM.
2. Restart the system.
3. From the ARC menu, choose Supplementary menu.
4. Select Install NT from CD-ROM.
5. If the last option is not available, choose Run a Program. Enter

    ```
    cd:\system\setupldr
    ```

    and press Enter. cd: is the device specification for the CD-ROM, which may vary on different systems. You may need to use the full ARC specification for your CD, such as scsi(0)cdrom(4)fdisk(0).

to work with newer versions of NT. Most of these steps should work with your RISC system, because most RISC systems that work with NT use the ARC menu for system configuration. Commands issued at the >>> prompt are specific to certain versions of Alpha systems.

Some RISC systems that run NT come with NT installed so that these steps won't be necessary. If you have a system running another operating system like VMS, you may need to take some or all of these steps.

During installation, you may encounter a message that NT cannot continue with the installation because a possible virus has been detected. This message usually occurs when you have several unformatted drives on the system or when a disk is installed that has had another operating system installed that NT does not recognize (such as VMS). The work-around is to disconnect all disks except the system disk and finish the installation. When the installation is complete, reconnect and configure the other disks.

If you still encounter the error, make sure that the system has been powered down completely and restarted. Repowering will absolutely reset everything in the system and should allow you to continue.

If the system you are installing will be a Backup Domain Controller or Primary Domain Controller, you must reinstall NT. You cannot change an NT PDC or BDC from one domain to another

SETTING THE SYSTEM TO BOOT NT AND STARTING THE ARC MENU • Make sure that your RISC system is set to boot NT automatically if NT is the default operating system. The steps in this section work on the AlphaServer 2000 and 2100 systems, but vary on other Alpha versions, which you may have to download firmware updates from Digital's URL.

If the system was running either VMS or OSF/1, you need to change the operating system mode to NT. At the boot prompt, enter

>>> Set os_type NT

After using this command, the system automatically starts the ARC menu system and boots NT when it boots. Enter the INIT command to change the setting permanently and reboot the system using

>>> Init

The ARC menu now displays as the default, and NT boots automatically using its BOOT menu.

You can also invoke the ARC menu at the boot prompt by entering

>>>ARC

When the ARC menu starts, you can access configuration commands by choosing options from the menu. Use the arrow keys to move up or down the menu and then press enter to select an option.

DEVICE DEFINITIONS AND SUCH • The startup instructions for operating systems in the BOOT.INI file (Intel only) can give you a glimpse of the device descriptions for disk drives and other devices. This arcane format actually describes the type of bus and device and the actual device numbers.

The CD-ROM in an AXP system has a description like scsi(0)cdrom(4) fdisk(0), which describes the type of bus (SCSI), the bus number (0), and the

SCSI number of the device (4). The description also shows that this device is a CD-ROM.

Devices on the system can be listed with the Show Hardware Configuration option on the Supplementary menu. Most systems will use CD: as a shorthand environment variable for the CD-ROM drive.

You may also need to configure EISA devices using the ECU (EISA Configuration Utility) program and RAID controllers using the SWXCRMGR or other vendor-supplied program. The documentation for your system should be consulted for the latest information on both of these programs.

DOS SYSTEMS WITH UNSUPPORTED CD-ROM • NT includes the WINNT and WINNT32 procedures for installing NT from a network or an unsupported CD-ROM drive. This process starts from DOS and copies the NT installation files to the local hard drive. This means that you must have an extra 70MB or so of storage to be used during the installation. The installation files are deleted automatically when the installation is complete. This process may take much longer than the normal installation from CD-ROM. The extended time is required mainly because the files must be copied to the hard disk before the installation process starts.

Installing from an Unsupported CD-ROM (Intel Only):

1. Boot the system from DOS.
2. Change to the drive and directory containing the NT installation files:

   ```
   E: CD \I386
   ```

3. Have at least four blank, formatted floppy disks handy.
4. Label the blank unformatted floppy disks—Disk 1, Disk 2, and so forth. See your NT manual for the exact number of disks for your version of NT.
5. Start the installation process by running WINNT.
6. Follow the normal NT setup directions.
7. Enter the name of the directory from which you started WINNT (e.g., Z:\I386) when you are prompted for the directory that contains the Windows NT Source.
8. Insert the blank disks when you are prompted (unless you use the /b parameter, in which case this step is skipped). Make sure you correctly label each disk as the files are copied to the disk.
9. Follow the instructions to complete the setup process.

If your CD is not supported under NT, you can get around some things by copying the installation images from the CD to the system's hard disk via DOS. Boot the system with a floppy disk that includes the CD drivers. Copy the directory structures to an NT hard disk that you can access. Note that this disk can only be a FAT disk. Then run the installation steps from the files on the hard disk using the WINNT command.

Even though this last procedure does work, you should get a CD that works with NT. Most NT software is available on CD, and many PC vendors are also moving most applications to CD.

NETWORK-BASED INSTALLATION • You can automate the installation process by placing the NT distribution on a network drive that is accessible to the new machines or sharing the CD-ROM drive from an available network system. The only restriction to this procedure is that the clients that install over the network must be DOS, Windows 95, or NT based and have access to the shared network hard disk or CD-ROM.

Loading NT Server Files on a Server:

1. Connect to the shared directory that will contain the NT files.
2. Use XCOPY, or File Manager, or Explorer to copy the NT Server files from the CD-ROM to the server.
3. Disconnect the connection to the share.

Make sure to copy the files to the appropriate area on the share. For instance, the files for Alpha systems should be copied to a directory named the same as the Alpha files on the CD-ROM (typically \ALPHA).

We usually create a share called DistDisk$ that has subdirectories for all network installation files. DistDisk$ points to the Distribution Disks directory. The NT files are placed in the WINNT35 subdirectory with individual directories of ALPHA, MIPS, and I386. These directories should match the corresponding CD directories. With this structure, you can add places for PowerPC or any other architecture files in the appropriate subdirectory. This structure will help when you are trying to remember which files are in what directory.

After you move the files to the server, modify any configuration files to your standards. For instance, you can specify the network protocols and the product ID in different INI files on the server. The easiest way to modify the setup files is to use the SETUPMGR.EXE program in the NT Resource Kit. SETUPMGR allows you to create or modify an answer file for installing NT. The answer file can be used with WINNT or WINNT32 to perform an unattended setup.

The answer file is one of the best approaches to installing multiple NT systems because it is easy to build and doesn't take up much space on the server. The answer file ensures that questions are answered the same each time it is used.

The next step in the installation process is to install NT on the target machines. The target machine must be running DOS or NT and connected to the network drive that contains the NT distribution. You can use any compatible network (MSClient, Windows for Workgroups, or NT) that allows you to access the files. When you are connected to the network, change the current drive and directory containing the NT distribution.

Next, start the DOS-based NT installation by executing the following command on a DOS system:

```
x:\WINNT35\i386\>WINNT
```

or the following command from an NT system:

```
x:\WINNT35\i386\>WINNT32
```

Use WINNT from a DOS system and WINNT32 from an NT system. The WINNT command will perform several steps during the installation process:

1. Create an NT Setup boot floppy disk plus several additional Setup floppy disks. The Setup boot floppy disk is used to start NT for the final stage of the installation process, and the additional two floppy disks are used during that process. You can skip this step by using the /b parameter.

2. Copy the entire NT distribution to the local hard disk. The directory on the local disk is WIN_NT.~LS.

3. Reboot when WINNT instructs you to reboot the PC with the Setup boot floppy disk still in the drive. NT boots from the floppy and completes the installation. The NT files are moved from the WIN_NT.~LS to the NT boot directory (usually WINNT).

This procedure works very well and can be used with either NT or NT Server. This process is very efficient because it enables you to copy the files from the network instead of either a floppy disk or a CD-ROM. You can start multiple installations at the same time from the same source.

INSTALLING WITHOUT FLOPPY DISKS (X86 ONLY)

You can cause WINNT or WINNT32 to complete the setup without building the floppy disks if you do not need to reformat the system partition during the installation process. This procedure simplifies and improves the performance of the installation process. The system partition can always be converted to NTFS after installation. The following command starts the installation process without building setup floppy disks:

```
WINNT /b
```

or the next command from an NT system:

```
WINNT32 /b
```

Using an Unattended Answer File for Network Setup

NT 3.51 introduced a new method for installation with both WINNT and WINNT32, using an automated answer file to supply the setup answers. The answer file could be created and then used with WINNT or WINNT32 to install multiple systems quickly over the network.

NT 4.0 allows you to use the same command to run the unattended (unattended.txt) installation. To start the unattended setup in NT 4.0, you must issue the following command

```
winnt[32] /u:<unattended.txt> /s:<install source>
```

where <answer file> is a file containing information to automate the installation process and <install source> is the location of the Windows NT 4.0 installation files.

Normally, the syntax for issuing the command in an NT 3.51 install would be

```
{driveletter}:\I386\WINNT /u:[answer_file_name]
```

or the next command from an NT system:

```
WINNT32 /u:[answer_file_name]
```

Running this command without specifying an answer file causes setup to run and use all default answers. The user name and/or organization name and license prompts must be answered, because there is no default for these options. You can create an answer file with defaults for these options, which can totally automate the process. This default file is valuable in organizations in which a standard user name and company name are used.

The answer file is created with a neat little utility included with the NT Resource Kit called SETUPMGR.EXE. This program takes the pain out of building and managing existing answer files. The following steps show how to use the program.

Creating and Editing Setup Answer Files for NT 3.51 Setup:

1. Start the Setup Manager (SETUPMGR.EXE).
2. Click the Open button to edit an existing answer file or skip this step to create a new one.
3. Specify the settings for the file.
4. Specify the file name for the answer file.
5. Click OK.

Before using the file created in this process, you should add license information to the file if you are using 3.51. Edit the answer file and add information on the license options. The format for the license information for a PerSeat license follows:

```
[LicenseFilePrintData]

AutoMode = PerSeat

AutoUsers = 0

If you are using PerServer licensing, then use

[LicenseFilePrintData]

AutoMode = PerServer

;Change 100 in the following line to the number of licenses for

;your server.

AutoUsers = 100
```

If you make a mistake in the license information, WINNT displays the normal setup dialog box and stops the unattended mode of setup.

If your organization has slightly different configurations for different NT systems, you may need to create multiple answer files. The basic idea is to first create generic files that match the most popular configuration options (system, video, network, etc.) and then use these files to build the new configuration files.

You will find an example of the unattended.txt file on the NT 4.0 distribution CD. You can also review Microsoft's TechNet article ID: Q155197, from April 30, 1997, which covers all the setup parameters that your file should include. The following is the sample file we've used when using unattended.txt in the past:

```
[Unattended]

OemPreinstall = no

ConfirmHardware = no

NtUpgrade = yes

Win31Upgrade = no

TargetPath = WINNT

OverwriteOemFilesOnUpgrade = no


[UserData]

FullName = "Process Software"

OrgName = "PSC"
```

```
ComputerName = ORLANDO
ProductId = "xxxxxxxxx"

[GuiUnattended]
TimeZone = "(GMT-05:00) Eastern Time (US & Canada)"

[Display]
ConfigureAtLogon = 0
BitsPerPel = 16
XResolution = 1024
YResolution = 768
VRefresh = 75
AutoConfirm = 1

[Network]
DetectAdapters = ""
InstallProtocols = ProtocolsSection
InstallServices = ServicesSection
JoinDomain = PSC
CreateComputerAccount = administrator, uotemsomdeu

[ProtocolsSection]
TC = TCParamSection

[TCParamSection]
DHCP = no
IPAddress = 197.048.035.51
Subnet = 255.255.255.0
Gateway = 192.042.95.126
DNSServer = 192.42.95.1

[ServicesSection]
```

The following steps enable you to create generic answer files for configurations (see Figure 2.1 for a screenshot of its interface).

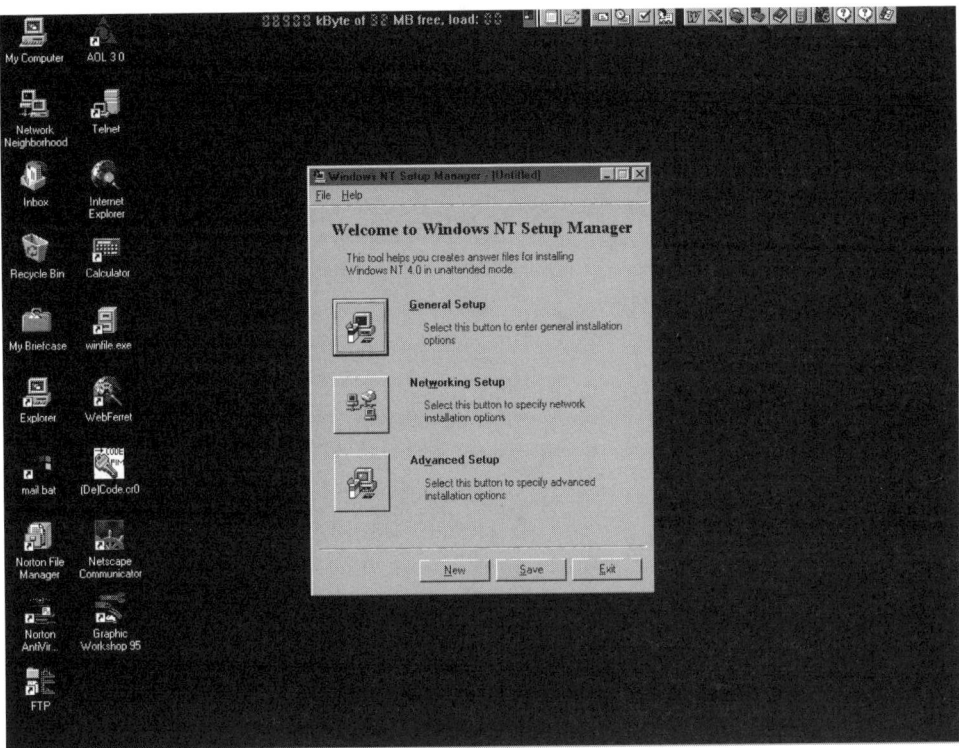

FIGURE 2.1   SETUPMGR, a tool for unattended Windows NT setup.

Creating Generic Answer Files for Configurations:

1. Start Setup Manager (SETUPMGR.EXE).

2. Decide what kind of installation you're going to use (General, Networking, or Advanced) and create a new answer file. Specify the default values for the most-often-used options.

3. Specify settings for the nearest configuration that matches most systems.

4. Save the file.

5. Create a similar file for each major configuration.

Now that you have created generic files, you can follow the next set of steps to create custom answer files.

Creating Custom Answer Files:

1. Copy the generic files to the new answer file name.
2. Start Setup Manager.
3. Open the new answer file created in step 1.
4. Change the settings.
5. Save the file.

Don't forget that we can use our old friend the DOS prompt and its batch files to further automate this step.

UPGRADING NT SERVER

Upgrading to NT 4.0 from a previous version of NT is simple, especially with your computer has a CD-ROM. The following is a detailed list explaining how to upgrade a workstation and a server.

NT WORKSTATION • You must consider carefully whether an NT system that will be upgraded to NT Server will be a stand-alone system or will serve as a controller on a domain. You must perform a new installation if the server will be used as a Backup Domain Controller (BDC) or Primary Domain Controller (PDC) on an existing domain. Performing a new installation is the only way to upgrade a system to a controller and have the domain tools installed on the system. Performing an upgrade switches the tools on the workstation to the new version, but it does not upgrade the tools to NT Server tools.

NT SERVER • There are several methods that can be used to upgrade NT Server. You can use any of the methods for installing NT Server as long as the NT installation media can be accessed by the server before the installation starts.

If you are upgrading from NT 3.1 to NT Server 3.5 and up, you will need to perform a new installation of NT Server.

A special version of the installation program (WINNT32) is included for running from within NT Server. WINNT32 runs on both Intel and RISC systems.

The upgrades are usually painless because they use the information in the NT Registry to answer questions during the upgrade process. The only questions that must be answered relate to new features such as TCP/IP, where Setup cannot find the information to perform the upgrade. Setup also asks you for a new disk for the emergency repair information.

COMPUTER PROFILE SETUP INSTALLATION (NT RESOURCE KIT FOR NT 3.51) •
The Computer Profile Setup (CPS) installation is another alternative to the

WINNT-based setup. The CPS option is available as part of the NT Resource Kit from Microsoft.

Upgrading NT Server Versions with WINNT32:

1. Connect to the network share or insert the NT Server CD.
2. Change to the appropriate directory on the installation share or CD (e.g., Alpha, MIPS, Intel).
3. Run the WINNT32 program in the appropriate directory.
4. Follow the instructions.

Upgrading NT Server Versions with Setup:

1. Shut down the system.
2. Place the NT Server CD in the CD-ROM drive.
3. Insert the first Setup floppy disk.
4. Reboot the system.
5. Follow the instructions.

Computer Profile Setup has two big caveats:

- It can be used only for machines that are almost exactly the same. In other words, the same hardware drivers, program manager groups, and so forth, must be used on every system and the systems can only have Intel processors. The installation does allow for different-size hard disks and larger memory, but that is about all. You can create several different profiles for different types of systems to work around this problem.
- It works only on Intel systems.

The CPS files are located in the \I386\CPS directory on the NT Resource Kit CD. Copy the files to a directory on a server or to a directory on the system that will be used to create the master system. This system must be running NT or NT Server.

The Computer Profile Setup is composed of three parts:

1. Set up an NT System that will be used to build the profile for the master server.
2. Run Create Profile to create the .CPS template file or files that will be used for the installation. This step must be run from an NT machine with the configuration that you want to record.
3. Run Install Profile, which takes the information from the template file and installs NT with the correct settings.

The second part must be run from within NT. This means that NT must be able to connect to the network resource that contains the NT template file.

Creating the CPS Profile on a Server:

1. Install and configure the NT Master system. This system must be configured exactly like the target systems to be installed. For instance, network functions, NT options, accessories, approximate disk space, and custom programs should be installed and working.

2. Create a directory to hold the profile on the distribution server and share the directory. This directory will hold the entire NT setup from the machine used to create the profile.

3. Upload the files from the master server to the distribution server by executing the uplodprf command with the following syntax:

```
uplodprf -s:x:\master\cpq1 -i:profile.
ini [\dir1 dir2 ...]
```

where

-s   Directory where the master files will be stored.

-i   Name of the PROFILE.INI file to use.

dir1 dir2 Additional directories on the master system that you wish to preinstall on target systems.

After you have completed these steps, edit the DEFAULTS.INF file in the SYSTEM32 subdirectory of the new master installation on the server. You may want to change values in the [DefaultValues] section to automate the installation process completely.

All options except for /S, /T, and /I accept a trailing - (as in /B-) to override any default value or to negate the action of the original option (for instance /B reboots immediately, while /B- cancels this action and pauses before rebooting, which is the default action).

Installing a New Machine Using the Master Installation:

1. Create a bootable floppy disk that can access the network share or access the master installation files copied to a hard disk.

2. Execute the installation command WINNTP. This command is located in the Resource Kit directory and may be moved to another commonly accessible directory. The syntax is

```
WINNTP /S:\\server1\mastercpq1 /T: c:
options
```

where

/S   The \\server1\mastercpq1 specification points to the share name of the directory you used to install the profile to.

/T	c:\nttmp specifies the temporary file location for the installation. Setup does this automatically if this option is left out.
/I:inf	Can be used to specify another INF file besides DOS-NET.INF.
/B	Causes the installation to reboot automatically without pausing after the files have been copied to the temporary drive.
/U:	Specifies the user name for the system.
/O:	Specifies the organization name for the system. This name appears in the same dialog box as the user name during a normal setup.
/M:	Specifies the machine name (computer name) for the system.
/N:	Specifies the domain name for the system.
/Z:	Specifies the time zone for the system. See the CPSREAD.TXT file included with the NT Resource Kit for details on this option.
/E:	/E:NO causes the installation to not prompt to build a repair disk. The default is /E:YES.

CPS installations can be much more sophisticated than this illustration. For instance, you can create difference profiles that are the same except for certain items. Consult the end of Chapter 3 in the NT Resource Kit for NT 3.51, Volume 1.

WINDOWS NT 4.0 SYSDIFF.EXE

Windows NT 4.0 does not use CPS. Instead, it uses a tool called SYSDIFF.EXE. This utility enables you to preinstall applications, including those that do not support scripted installation, as part of an automated setup.

With SYSDIFF, you first create a "snapshot" of Windows NT system after it has been installed on a reference computer. Then you install the desired applications on the reference computer and create a difference file with information on the applications. Finally, you apply the difference file to new installations on other computers, as part of an unattended setup or at any later time after installation is complete.

If many applications must be installed, the difference file can become unmanageably large, as it contains the files and settings for all the applications. In this case, SYSDIFF allows you to create an information (.INF) file, containing only Registry and initialization file directives, from the difference file and to use this to install the applications.

To use Sysdiff:

1. Install Windows NT Server on the reference computer.
2. Run sysdiff /snap on the reference computer.
3. Install the applications you want onto the reference computer.
4. Run sysdiff /diff on the reference computer to create the difference file.
5. Apply the difference file using sysdiff /apply (during end-user setup) or sysdiff /inf (to the installation source).

UPGRADING NT 3.51 TO NT 4.0 SERVER

Although an upgrade from NT 3.51 to NT 4.0 should be smooth, as a rule of thumb you should always remove (or disable) all the old device drivers, especially third-party services and devices, before beginning the installation of NT 4.0.

If you don't, there may be a risk of these devices or services trying to start during the reboot between the character-based and GUI-based portions of your setup, which could cause your server to display a debug screen yes—the blue one!—such as "STOP 0x0000050" or "STOP 0x0000001E") and halt, or even become so unstable that setup wouldn't be able to continue.

If a driver or service is not required for system operation, it should always be disabled before upgrading to Windows NT4.0. If you will need a driver or service (such as a SCSI controller or network card), then you should obtain a driver for Windows NT 4.0 from the third-party provider and have the driver available on a floppy disk for use during the upgrade process.

To Disable a Driver:

1. In Control Panel, double-click Devices.
2. Click the third-party driver you want to disable, and then click Startup.
3. In the Device dialog box, click Disabled, and then restart the computer.
4. In Control Panel, double-click Devices, and verify that the device did not start.

To Disable a Service:

1. In Control Panel, double-click Services.
2. Click the third-party service you want to disable, and then click Startup.
3. In the Service dialog box, click Disabled, and then restart the computer.
4. In Control Panel, double-click Services, and then verify that the service did not start.

If you have PCAnyWhere installed on your NT 3.51 server and are going to upgrade it to NT 4.0, watch for the "blues" again. There are certain steps you must take before performing the upgrade, otherwise you may end up with a "STOP 0x1E in Win32K.sys!"

The actual exception error that is usually displayed is "STOP: 0x0000001E (C00000005, 0xA0036FC2, 0x00000000, 0x00000004) ...KMODE_EXCEPTION_NOT_HANDLED address 0xA0036FC2 in Win32K.sys."

This may occur if the following registry key, installed by PCAnyWhere, exists:

```
\\HKEY_LOCAL_MACHINE\SOFTWARE\Microsoft\
    Windows NT   \Current Version\Winlogon\Ginadll
```

where Ginadll has a value of <Drive>\PCAnyWhere\Awgina.dll : REG_SZ.

To resolve this problem, try to restore your previous version of Windows NT 3.51 and delete the Gina.dll key or install a second instance of Windows NT 3.51 and run the previous copy of Regedt32.exe to delete the Gina.dll key.

REINSTALLING NT

You can reinstall NT Server over an existing installation of NT or NT Server if you have at least 80MB of free disk space on the boot drive. The installation process requires a minimum of 80MB and does not consider whether or not you already have NT installed. This means that if your system has less than 80MB free on the boot drive, you will have to remove part of or all your configuration before performing the reinstallation.

Before you take off and reinstall NT Server, let's take a look at several precautions. They are necessary because of the way NT manages security and files. The following list contains several things you should watch out for before starting the reinstallation process.

- You cannot move a computer to a new domain without reinstalling NT.
- The computer account for an NT system in a domain must be deleted before the reinstallation starts.
- Be sure to back up the NT Registry files before starting the reinstallation.

AUTOMATING THE CONFIGURATION OF A NEW SERVER

This is probably a good time to interject our opinion on automating things. We prefer to automate everything possible, both to save time and to cut down on the possibility of errors entering the process.

Fortunately, NT includes command-line options for most of its configuration commands. These commands allow us to build an automated script that will configure most of our options on new NT systems. You may want to build two different scripts—one for servers and one for workstations. You may also build logic into your script to have common setup options on all systems and only certain options on servers.

The code example in Listing 2.1 shows a simple batch command that can be tailored for your tasks.

This little command is very useful for configuring servers. In this example, insert your commands in one of the three locations: Common, Server, and NT Workstation. Common items for both servers and workstations go in the common area. Server-only options go in the server area, while the workstation area gets only workstation commands.

There are many options you may want to place in this little command. Likely candidates are not only NET commands but also commands to build

LISTING 2.1 NTCONFIG.BAT example program

```
@echo off
Echo NT Configuration Script
rem kls 12/13/94


rem ------------------------Common Area----------------------------
Echo Executing Common commands
rem Common Commands go here
rem --------------------------------------------------------------
rem Check for Server or Workstation (default)
if "%1" == "SERVER" GoTo SERVER
if "%1" == "Server" GoTo SERVER
GoToWORKSTATION
rem --------------------------------------------------------------
:SERVER
rem --------------------- Server Only Area -----------------------
Echo Executing Server Only commands
rem Server Commands go here
GoTo EXIT


rem --------------------------------------------------------------
:WORKSTATION
rem ------------------ NT Workstation Only Area ------------------
Echo Executing Workstation Only commands
rem Workstation Commands go here
rem --------------------------------------------------------------

:EXIT
```

common directory structures, connect to a shared directory service and download certain files to the new system, enter user accounts that are standard for all systems, start or stop services, and so on.

Table 2.5 lists several options that you may want to include in this command.

The command is executed using the following syntax:

```
NTCONFIG [SERVER]
```

Specifying SERVER or server after the command will run only the common and server options, while executing only NTCONFIG will execute the common and workstation options.

TABLE 2.5	Options for NTCONFIG.BAT Example
Command	**Description**
MD dirname	Creates a directory
NET USE x: \\server\share /y	Connects to a shared directory
COPY file file	Copies files from a network share to the local system
NET SHARE name=path /y	Shares a directory on the network

UPGRADING AN EXISTING INSTALLATION OF NT

The normal upgrade process for a system already running NT Server is the same as a system running another operating system. You have the option of directly running WINNT32 instead of Setup or WINNT.

You should review the compatibility list for your hardware before you blast in and install any new major version. New versions usually support the same hardware as older versions, but this observation is not always true, especially in areas such as network cards, video monitors, and SCSI controllers. If you are using a popular and standard model from companies like 3Com (say an EtherLink III) or Intel, it will most likely be supported. Models such as ArcNet cards from an unheard of vendor may drop off the list. I have also heard of network cards from a large vendor (HP) that were supported in NT 3.1 but not in NT Server 3.5.

Security Considerations for Installing NT 4.0

You must deploy and install Windows NT using one of the several methods Microsoft provides. Otherwise, you can be compromising the security of the systems running NT.

For instance, never copy the hard disk from one computer to another as a way of deploying NT on several servers. One of the important features of Windows NT is its security. Each computer is assigned a unique Security ID (SID) during Setup at the time the machine name is entered; this ensures that it can be identified on the network. Almost all of the network services have this security information encoded in their entries in the registry during Setup or subsequent installation. If you simply copy the contents of one hard disk (through Xcopy, LapLink, or any other similar means) to another one, you would be giving the same SID from the first machine to that second one as well, making security impossible to maintain.

This SID is computed to contain a statistically unique 96-bit number. For a Windows NT backup domain controller (BDC), that SID is identical to the SID of the PDC for the domain. The primary SID is generated during the installation of Windows NT and is the prefix of the SIDs for all the user accounts and group accounts created on the computer. The SID is concatenated with the RID of the account to create the account's unique identifier.

Therefore, by copying the hard drive of one machine to another, you not only will be duplicating the SID, but the first user account generated (and so forth) on each machine will be the same because the SID on both computers is the same.

Another problem relates to getting support. Because the SID identifies the computer or domain, as well as the user, it is critical that it be unique to maintain support for current and future applications. Microsoft does not provide support for systems that have been installed by duplicating fully installed copies of either Windows NT Workstation, Server or Windows 95.

This does not include the use of NT 3.51 CPS and Windows NT 4.0 Deployment Tools, while unattended, which are not simple copies and do configure the operating system correctly.

For more information on NT 4.0 Deployment Tools, check the Microsoft Knowledge Base at http://www.microsoft.com or the the Windows NT 4.0 Resource Kit.

You can also download the following file to get the latest information on Windows NT deployment: http://www.microsoft.com/ntworkstation/deploy.exe.

Finally, you should know that Windows NT has a uniform security architecture that was designed to provide a safe environment to run mission-critical applications as judged by government security standards.

For Windows NT version 3.5, Microsoft submitted NT for a security evaluation by the United States National Computer Security Center, and since then, NT has met the requirements of C2-level security. Windows NT 4.0 with networking is currently undergoing this evaluation. Windows NT 3.51 is being evaluated in the UK and Germany for a F-C2/E3 security rating. Windows NT 4.0 will be subject to the same standards.

Conclusion

This chapter has introduced you to many of the issues you will face when you install NT. After reading this chapter, you should be cautious about installing NT, especially on any system that is not a plain vanilla Intel processor. You should also be aware of problems that may arise if you have certain applications such as PC AnyWhere installed on NT and you try to upgrade to a new version of NT.

Chapter 3 will introduce you to many of the management tools that NT provides. We will take a look at using batch files, using the NT Resource Kit, and using standard NT tools, and we will discuss some of the other tricks you can do with NT from a management perspective. For instance, would you like to set up NT so it will automatically log on when it boots? We'll show you how in Chapter 3.

Server Configuration and Management

Managing any network or corporate system is an experience, to say the least. The experience seems to be full of potholes, hidden traps, and many nuisances. Working with NT over the last few years, we have had our fair share of experiences with management and with finding ways to dig out of the mess.

Scenario 3.1:

You have a new software application that runs on NT, and it installs just fine. Then you discover that the package only works when NT has a user logged in—the package does not run as an NT service. The package is installed on a secure server in your computer room, so security would not be breached if the machine were continually logged on. How do you make NT log-on automatically when it boots?

Scenario 3.2:

It's 11p.m. on Thursday night, and one of your NT servers dies with the dreaded "blue" screen. You can't afford to have this system down the next day, so what do you do? This is where planning comes in.

Windows NT 4.0 Server contains several utilities for managing your NT Servers and other NT systems on the network.

Other sources of management utilities come with the NT Resource Kit from Microsoft, the Microsoft Systems Management Server system, third-party tools in general, and Simple Network Management Protocol (SNMP)-compliant systems from other vendors. There are also other utilities on the Web at sites such as www.microsoft.com and www.ntinternals.com.

This chapter and others in the book cover the NT utilities, some of the NT Resource Kit utilities, and some other programs that were available when we wrote this book. We do not intend, nor would it be possible, to cover every possible management program thoroughly. Use the management section as a guide to tools and hints; then survey the market and see how the utilities mentioned in this book compare with others on the market.

Introduction to the NT 4.0 Resource Kit Utilities

The NT 4.0 Resource Kit contains a number of programs that are extremely useful for any system manager. Some of the programs, such as the Command Scheduler, are useful for administrators to schedule processes or tasks to be deployed on the server or even another workstation, while many others, such as the Shutdown workstation utility, can come in handy to every system manager.

Table 3.1 lists the tools that we view as administrative programs in the 4.0 version of the NT Resource Kit. Not every program in the NT Resource Kit is covered in this book. Not all the programs contribute to managing a system like NT Server, and some are outside the scope of the book. See the NT Resource Kit for more information on all programs.

note Please note that while TechNet includes the full document set for the BackOffice and NT Server 4.0 Resource Kit, the utilities CDs are available separately from your local ordering center or subsidiary. This is due to the size of these utilities. You should obtain a copy of the new NT Resource Kit at your first opportunity. Patches with the most current corrections to the utilities and their documentation, as well as the POSIX and Perl public domain source code files, are available on the Internet at URL ftp://ftp.microsoft.com/ bussys/winnt-public/reskit/nt40/.

The NT Resource Kit comes in a version for NT Workstation and NT Server. We suggest that you get both kits. The hard-copy documentation alone is worth the price.

TABLE 3.1	Administrative Programs in NT Resource Kit

Program Name	Description
ADDUSERS.EXE	AddUsers was updated from previous versions. It is a 32-bit administrative tool that uses a comma-delimited file to create, write, and delete user accounts. AddUsers is most beneficial when the file is maintained in a spreadsheet, such as Microsoft Excel, that will work with comma-delimited files.
ATANLYZR.EXE	This GUI utility performs an AppleTalk lookup for registered AppleTalk devices on an AppleTalk network. You can perform a lookup of all AppleTalk devices, specific Net, Name, Type, or partial Name, and Types in the selected zone(s).
BROWMON.EXE	Monitors the status of the browser service
C2CONFIG.EXE	This is a Windows NT C2 Configuration Manager that can be used to compare the current security configuration on your Windows NT Workstation with C2-level security requirements of the United States government's National Computer Security Center.
CHOICE.EXE	Provides input facility for batch files.
COMPREG.EXE	A Win32 character-based/command-line "Registry DIFF" that enables you to compare any two local and/or remote Registry keys in both Windows NT and Windows 95.
QSLICE.EXE	Quick Slice is a program that shows the percentage of total CPU usage for each process in the system.
dbWeb	This is a gateway between Microsoft Open Database Connectivity (ODBC) data sources and the Internet Information Server (IIS) that allows you to publish data from an ODBC data source and provide familiar World Wide Web (WWW) hypertext navigation.
DELPROF.EXE	Utility to delete user profiles on computers running Windows NT
DELSRV.EXE	This command-line utility unregisters a service with the service control manager
DH.EXE*	This command-line utility enables you to lock heaps, tags, stacks, and objects.
DHCPCMD.EXE	The command-line DHCP Administrator's Tool provides an auxiliary method of administering DHCP servers.

TABLE 3.1	Administrative Programs in NT Resource Kit (Continued)
Program Name	**Description**
DNSSTAT.EXE*	This utility provides a dump of DNS server statistics (queries and responses, database size, caching, memory consumption) on a computer running Microsoft DNS Server.
DRIVERS.EXE	Displays a list of the current drivers on a system.
DUMPEL.EXE	Dumps the Event Viewer log to a file.
EM2MS.EXE	Converts verbose descriptions of files stored on NT-based EMWAC (European Microsoft Windows NT Academic Centre) Gopher Servers to the Microsoft Internet Information Gopher Server content format.
EMWAC	EMWAC Internet services for NT.
ENUMPRN.EXE	This is a new GUI version, that enumerates installed printer drivers.
EXCTRLST.EXE	Provides information on the Extensible Performance Counter DLLs that have been installed on a computer running Windows NT, listing the services and applications that provide performance information via the Windows NT Registry.
EXETYPE.EXE	Determines what type of operating system and processor is required to run a program.
FINDGRP.EXE	Displays global and local groups that a user belongs to (works in the current domain or across domains).
FLOPLOCK.EXE*	Restricts access to the floppy disk drive on an NT system.
FORFILES.EXE	Enables you to run a command on or pass arguments to multiple files.
FREEDISK.EXE	This command-line utility checks for free disk space.
FTEDIT.EXE	FTEDIT.EXE allows you to create, edit, and delete fault-tolerance sets for disk drives and partitions of local and remote computers.
GETSID.EXE	Displays and matches SIDs for two-user accounts.
GLOBAL.EXE	Displays members of global groups on remote servers or domains.
GRPCPY.EXE	Enables users to copy the usernames in an existing group to another group in the same or another domain or on a computer running Windows NT.

TABLE 3.1	Administrative Programs in NT Resource Kit (Continued)
Program Name	**Description**
HEAPMON.EXE	This command-line tool enables the user to view system heap information.
KERNPROF.EXE	This command-line utility provides counters for and profiles of various functions of the Windows NT operating system Kernel.
KILL.EXE	Terminates a task.
KIX32.EXE	A logon script processor and/or enhanced batch language for Windows NT and Windows 95 workstations in a Windows Networking environment.
LOGTIME.EXE	Logs the start or finish of command-line programs from a batch file.
Mail Server	Enables you to configure a computer running Windows NT Server as an e-mail provider for intranet or Internet users.
MIBCC.EXE	MIBCC compiles SNMP MIB files.
MUNGE.EXE	Allows you to search for and replace strings in a file.
NETSVC.EXE	Controls services from the command line.
NETWATCH.EXE	Shows which users are connected to resources.
NTCARD.HLP	Network card help file.
NTDETECT.COM1	Same as NTDETECT.COM shipped with NT but has debug switch turned on to display hardware detected during startup.
NLMON.EXE	This command-line utility can be used to list and test many aspects of Trust relationships.
PERFMTR.EXE	Displays performance statistics.
PERMS.EXE	Shows what access a user has to specific files.
PERMCOPY.EXE	Copies share-level permissions (ACLs) from one share to another.
PMON.EXE	Displays running tasks programs and some statistics.
POSIX Utilities*	Miscellaneous utilities that run under the POSIX subsystem.

* This program or system requires an additonal installation step beyond copying the files to the server or a workstation or running the NT Resource Kit installation program.

TABLE 3.1 Administrative Programs in NT Resource Kit (Continued)

Program Name	Description
PSTAT.EXE	Displays running programs and their tasks, along with the status of each task.
PULIST.EXE	Tracks what processes are running on local or remote computers.
PVIEWER.EXE	This is a Windows-based tool that displays information about a running process and allows you to stop (kill) processes.
PUTINGRP.EXE	Command-line utility to place program(s) into Program Manager groups.
QSLICE.EXE	Displays the amount of CPU usage used by each running process.
RASUSERS.EXE	Enumerates RAS users.
RCMD.EXE	Remote Command Line Service for secure command-line operations with remote systems.
REGBACK.EXE	Performs a backup of Registry files.
REGENTRY.HLP	Help file with information on Registry entries.
REGINI.EXE	Changes Registry via a script.
REGKEY.EXE	Displays and changes certain Registry entries for Logon and FAT file system settings.
REGREST.EXE	Restores the Registry files from the backup files created with REGBACK.
REGTOGRP.EXE	Creates *.GRP files for Program Manager groups (These files are placed in the current directory and can be used only by GRPTOREG.EXE.).
REMOTE.EXE	Provides a remote command line to an NT system.
RMTSHARE.EXE	Creates or deletes a remote share.
SCOPY.EXE	Copies or moves NTFS files while preserving security.
SETUPMGR.EXE	Utility for assisting in automating the process of installing NT on multiple systems by creating an answer file for use with the WINNT and WINNT32 setup programs.
SHUTDOWN.EXE	Allows remote or local shutdown of a system.
SLEEP.EXE	Pauses execution of a batch file for a certain period of time.
SMBTRACE.EXE	Traces SMB packets.

TABLE 3.1	Administrative Programs in NT Resource Kit (Continued)
Program Name	**Description**
SMI.MIB	MIB Source file for SNMP.
SNMPUTIL.EXE	SNMP Browse utility.
SNMPUTIL.EXE	Provides SNMP information from an SNMP host located on the network.
SRVANY.EXE	Allows you to run almost any application as a service.
SRVMRG.EXE	Server Manager for Domains for NT Workstation.
SYSDIFF.EXE	Enables you to preinstall applications, including those that do not support scripted installation, as part of an automated setup for NT 4.0 systems.
TAPE.EXE	Tape drive utility.
TIMESERV.EXE	Service to synchronize the time on NT with a certified and/or nationally provided time service over either serial connections or the Internet.
TROUBLE.HLP	Help file complete with troubleshooting flow charts.
TZEDIT.EXE	Time Zone editor.
UPEDIT.EXE	Enables you to change the system and default profiles on NT Workstation.
UPTOMP.EXE	Upgrades a single processor NT system to a multi-processor system.
USMGR.EXE	User Manager for Domains for NT Workstation.
USRSTAT.EXE	This command-line utility displays username, fullname, and last login date and time for each user in a given domain.
USRTOGRP.EXE	Adds users to groups.
WINAT.EXE	Graphical interface to the Command Scheduler (AT command).
WINCIM.EXE	WinCim utility for accessing CompuServe.
WINDIFF.EXE	Displays the differences between two files or directories.
WINEXIT.SCR	Screen saver that logs user out after time expires (shows up as Logoff Screen Saver in Control Panel).
WINVTP.EXE	Communications tool that works with Net2Com utility.
WNBSTAT.EXE	Displays NetBIOS statistics.
WNTIPCFG.EXE	Graphical version of the IPCONFIG utility for configuring TCP/IP.

The following list contains tools that are part of a supplement to the NT Server 4.0 Resource Kit that were introduced in mid-July 1997. You should upgrade the NT Server 4.0 Resource Kit with this update to obtain the latest tools and information. You can find out more information at the following URL:

```
http://mspress.microsoft.com/mspress/Books/Abs/1358.HTM
```

Following are the updated utilities in the supplement:

- **Reg.Exe**–A consolidated command-line registry manipulation utility that replaces and improves on eight of the current registry utilities.
- **SrvMon.Exe**–A tool that monitors any service on any machine and sends e-mail and/or a paging signal when the service stops or starts.
- **FileWise.Exe**–A GUI-based file version extraction tool. Operates on single files and entire folders and provides more file information than any current tool.
- **NetDom.Exe**–A full-featured command-line domain management utility.
- **AuditPol.Exe**–A command-line tool for modifying the audit policies on local or remote machines
- **Waitfor.Exe**–A batch command, with easy-to-use syntax, for synchronizing batch processes between remote machines over the network.
- **Translate.Exe**–A highly useful command-line tool that simply translates obscure return codes from Win32 to error messages that are readable by humans.

Using Programs from the NT Resource Kit

The NT Resource Kit contains versions of most of its programs for the Intel, MIPS, Power PC, and the Digital Alpha processors. These programs are stored in subdirectories of the program that are named: I386 (Intel), MIPS (MIPS), PPC (PowerPC), and ALPHA (Digital Alpha). Make sure that you use the proper version for your system.

Running the install program in the root directory of the NT Resource Kit CD normally installs the correct version of the utilities for each system.

Most NT Resource Kit programs can be used by copying the program to a directory on the PATH or placing the program's directory on your PATH. The default directory is \RESKIT35 for the 3.5 Resource Kit, which is located on the WINNT boot drive, unless you selected a different drive and/or directory during installation. We normally place the programs in a utility directory located on the PATH if they are programs that we will use frequently. The NT Resource Kit installation program places the \RESKIT35\RESKIT directory in the path.

Check the documentation for the commands you need to install the components of the Resource Kit. There are normally several setup commands to install all the utilities.

Command Prompt Operations

Many of the NT Command Prompt commands are useful for network environments where NT Server is used. Some of these commands perform tasks that the graphical commands can't (to list contents of a directory to a file in File Manager, use DIR), while others are somewhat quicker to use. This last point is especially true if you build batch programs that contain your commands.

The command prompt uses the command interpreter (CMD.EXE) to manage the command line, run programs, and so on. CMD.EXE is the NT equivalent of COMMAND.COM in MS-DOS. The command interpreter supports several internal command prompt commands such as DIR and COPY. Other features, such as redirection (> and >>) and pipes (|), are also supported by the command interpreter.

Normally, you won't be concerned with CMD.EXE because the command prompt and other features of NT that use DOS-type programs make its use transparent. You may find that you occasionally need to run a program explicitly using the command interpreter. You will usually notice this in NT Server 3.51 or greater with the AT command because it no longer loads the command interpreter by default. Batch files using DIR or COPY or the redirection or pipe features fail when they are run using the scheduler.

There is a simple fix for this problem with the command interpreter and AT. Simply prefix all your commands in the batch files with **cmd /c**. The /c causes the command interpreter to terminate at the completion of the command. This prefix tells the command interpreter to execute your command and then terminate. The following example shows how it works:

```
cmd /c dir c:\logfiles > c:\logfiles\errorlogs.txt

cmd /c copy c:\logfiles\errorlogs.txt n:\errorlogs\
thisserver.log
```

Batch Programs

Except for a few differences, NT batch programs are built the same way as DOS batch programs. NT batch programs can end in a suffix of .BAT or .CMD. The program names must also conform to the file system that you are using (NTFS, FAT, or HPFS). For instance, if you are using NTFS or have long FAT names enabled, the following command name would be legal:

```
"Show Scheduled Accounting Jobs"
```

The quotes around the name allow you to use spaces in the name. Chapter 6 contains more information on file systems used by NT and the allowable characters for the file system. Be aware that some programs such as EDIT or WINNT do not work with long file names, even on NTFSP.

PASSING PARAMETERS

Parameters can be used in NT batch commands just as those in DOS are used. The % character is used as the variable indicator both for parameters passed from the command line and for environment variables. Parameters passed from the command line start at %0 and go to %9; %0 contains the name of the batch program while %1 through %9 contain the options specified after the name. If you intend to specify more than nine parameters after the program name, check out the SHIFT command later in this chapter.

Accessing and using the parameters in your program are fairly easy. Simply substitute the name of the parameter each time you want to access its value. For instance, if you want to use the first variable, enter **%1**. The following batch program uses the ECHO command to display the first parameter:

ECHO %1

It is highly recommended that you check a variable before using it, especially if your program will be used by many people. You can check a variable with the IF command:

IF NOT "%1" == "" ECHO %1

NT provides several default environment variables that are useful in NT batch file. These variables are useful for certain tasks on NT, such as determining which processor is used on a system. For instance, let's say you have several NT systems with a mix of Intel, Alpha, or MIPS processors. The following example determines which processor type is used and changes to a directory for that particular processor before executing a command. This type of logic is used by SMS and many other NT packages to determine which version of software to install or execute.

```
REM %PROCESSOR_ARCHITECTURE% test file
REM
if "%PROCESSOR_ARCHITECTURE%" == "x86" cd I386
if "%PROCESSOR_ARCHITECTURE%" == "X86" cd I386
if "%PROCESSOR_ARCHITECTURE%" == "mips" cd MIPS
if "%PROCESSOR_ARCHITECTURE%" == "MIPS" cd MIPS
if "%PROCESSOR_ARCHITECTURE%" == "alpha" cd Alpha
if "%PROCESSOR_ARCHITECTURE%" == "ALPHA" cd Alpha
INSTALL
```

An actual batch program typically has more logic to detect such errors as trying to run the program on Windows for Workgroups or Windows 95.

DISPLAYING CHOICES (NT RESOURCE KIT)

The Choice command that is included in the NT Resource Kit is useful for displaying choices and allowing users to choose a command. The syntax for Choice is

```
choice /C:12 /S /T:1,nn text
```

- /C:12—The items after the /C: determine what options are displayed. The default is Y,N./S Treats choices as case-sensitive./T:1,nnDefaults to choice 1 after nn seconds.

The Choice command is very useful in batch commands for obtaining information from a user. The following example shows a command that is used to query the user for a yes or no choice:

```
Choice "Please enter Y or N for your choice"
if errorlevel 1 GoTo YES
:NO
Echo No was selected
GoTo Exit
:YES
Echo Yes was selected
:EXIT
```

NOTES ON BATCH FILE IF COMMANDS

The DOS batch language has been around for a long time and has many little idiosyncrasies. The following notes provide some samples, and demonstrate how to use this powerful command.

- Do not use "then" in an "if" statement:

```
if %1 == 5 GoTo to YES
```

- Use == when you wish to compare something:

```
if "%PROCESSOR_ARCHITECTURE%" == "x86" cd I386
```

- Check for both upper- and lowercase names:

```
if "%PROCESSOR_ARCHITECTURE%" == "alpha" cd I386
if "%PROCESSOR_ARCHITECTURE%" == "ALPHA" cd I386
```

- Use "" around both sides of the comparison operator to allow the command to work correctly when one side of the comparison is empty:

```
if "%PROCESSOR_ARCHITECTURE%" == "ALPHA" cd I386
```

- Use the Errorlevel option for checking return values from programs:

```
if errorlevel 1 GoTo YES
```

The Registry Database

The Registry is the NT database in which almost all configuration and performance information is stored. The database is broken up into major and minor keys. Each major key is called a *hive*. REGEDT32 displays the keys in an outline format, making traversing the keys easy. The four major keys are shown in Table 3.2.

Each hive is stored in the %SystemRoot%\SYSTEM32\CONFIG directory.

Each value in the Registry is tagged with the type of data it can contain. Each data type supported by the registry provides not only a certain type of value but also other attributes of the data such as whether the item is a multiple or single string. The registry data types are described in Table 3.3.

For more information on the structure of the Registry, consult the NT Resource Kit for version 4.0.

TABLE 3.2 Major Registry Keys

Registry Key	Description
HKEY_USERS	This key contains all the actively loaded user profiles. HKEY_CURRENT_USER is a subkey of this key.
HKEY_CURRENT_USER	This key is a subkey of HKEY_USERS and contains the current profile of the user currently logged on interactively.
HKEY_CLASSES_ROOT	This key contains Object Linking and Embedding (OLE) and other file-class-related information.
HKEY_LOCAL_MACHINE	This key is the most frequently accessed by administrators and contains information about the local system. It includes hardware and software information such as types of hardware devices, device drivers, and startup data.

TABLE 3.3	Registry Data Types	
Data Type	**Format**	**Description**
REG_BINARY	Hexadecimal	Normally used for raw data. Most hardware information uses this format.
REG_DWORD	4-byte number: Hexadecimal, Decimal, or Binary	Represents a number that is 4 bytes long. Used for parameters for device drivers and services.
REG_EXPAND_SZ	Expandable string	Used for values that require a single string definition and allow for a variable to be expanded when called by an application. For instance, %SystemRoot% is an environment variable that is stored in the registry.
REG_MULTI_SZ	Multiple string	Used for values that require multiple strings. Most of these values are used for human-readable text. Each entry in the string is separated by NULL characters.
REG_SZ	String	Used for a single string in human readable form.

Editing the Registry Manually with RegEdit and REGEDT32

REGEDT32 and RegEdit are used for manually editing the NT Registry. Normally the registry is changed by management and administrative programs within NT or from application programs that automatically change entries relative to the program. These changes take place behind the scenes and are normally invisible to users and administrators.

Occasionally it may be necessary to change something in the Registry manually. This could be as simple as configuring NT to log on automatically at startup or to fix a device driver entry that cannot be fixed any other way. When this type of manual change is required, REGEDT32 and RegEdit are the tools to use.

You can wreak havoc with your system by manually changing the Registry. At worst, your system will fail to boot. Please backup the Registry files before making any changes. Use RDISK to perform the backup.

The Registry editors are actually easy to use and provide a nice front end into the Registry. Figure 3.1 shows REGEDT32 with the HKEY_LOCAL _MACHINE key expanded.

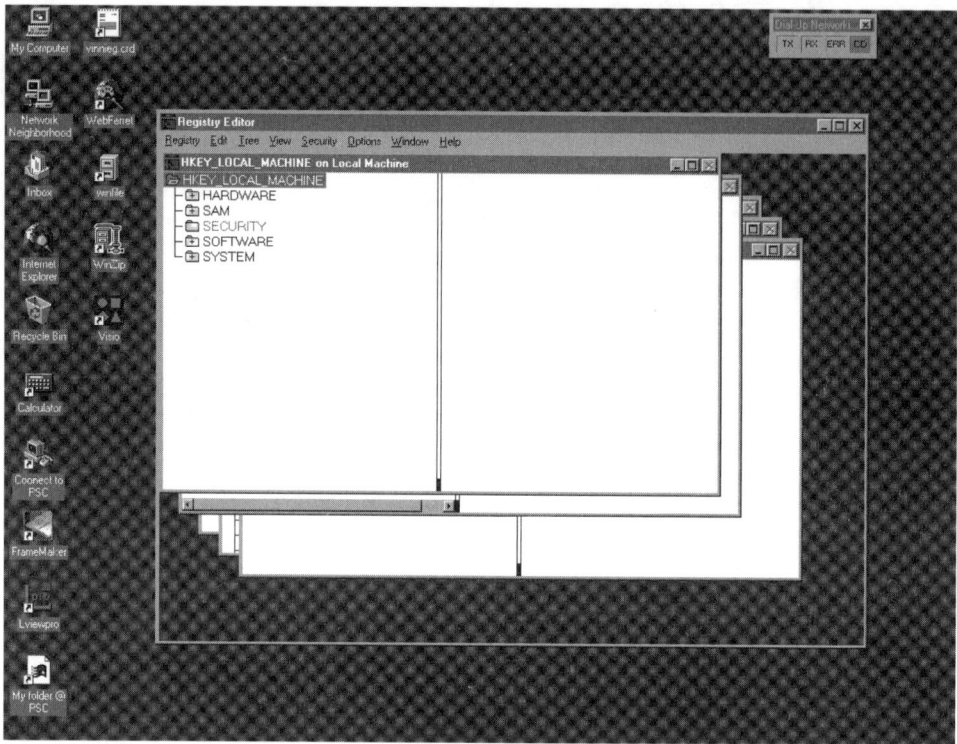

FIGURE 3.1 REGEDT32 showing the HKEY_LOCAL_MACHINE key.

These tools work much like File Manager. Double-click a key to expand or collapse the subkeys, and then click an entry to select it. Various task menus appear across the top of the screen. The File and Edit menus contain the commands to actually change the database.

You can create an icon for both tools to be placed in the desktop of Windows NT 4.0 to provide quick access to the program. You can also place the icon in a personal group to keep other users from seeing the program's icon. REGEDT32 has more features, while RegEdit has the Find command, which searches for specific values.

Editing the Registry with RegKey (NT Resource Kit)

REGKEY.EXE provides another way to edit certain options in the Registry without your having to slog through the different keys and such. This is another of those NT Resource Kit tools that are handy for performing a task quickly.

Figure 3.2 shows the REGKEY.EXE dialog box.

Table 3.4 explains the options available on the dialog box.

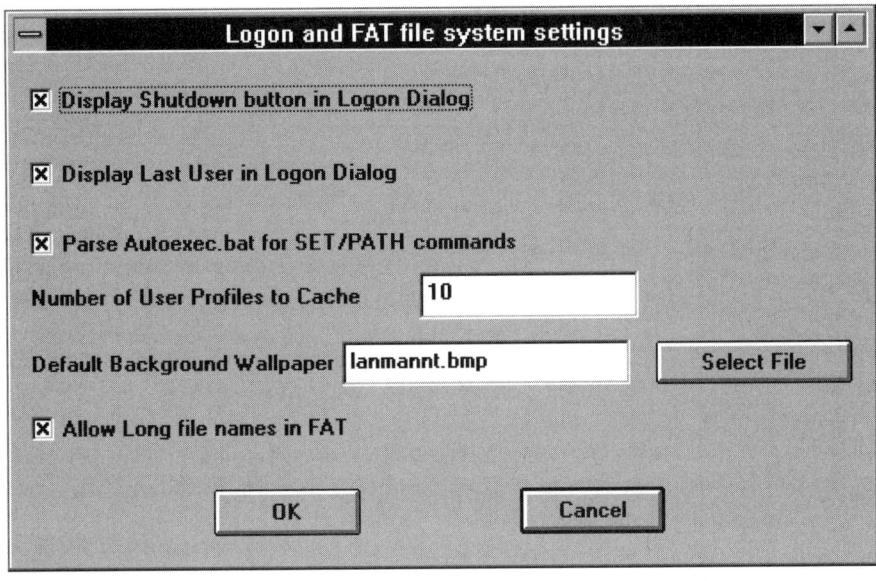

FIGURE 3.2   RegKey allows you to set a number of configuration options quickly without having to use REDEDT32.

TABLE 3.4   REGKEY Settings Options

Option	Description
Display Shutdown button in Logon Dialog	This option displays the Shutdown button on the Logon dialog box, allowing you to stop the system without logging on. Use only when the system is secure such as in a computer room.
Display Last User in Logon Dialog	Turning off this option removes the last user name from the Logon dialog.
Parse Autoexec.bat for SET/PATH commands	Checking this option will cause NT to pick up SET and PATH commands from the AUTOEXEC.BAT file.
Number of User Profiles in Cache	Determines the number of User Profiles in Cache memory.
Default Background Wallpaper	Sets the default background wallpaper for the desktop.
Allow Long file names in FAT	Turning on this option allows long file names in FAT file systems.

NT Server 4.0 License Management

NT Server license options are maintained by the License applet in Control Panel. This simple application currently allows you to change only the following options:

- Change from a Per Server license to a Per Seat license (one time only). Per Server licensing basically forces you to purchase a server license for each NT Server you install. This is the mode pre 3.5 versions used. This option is best when you have only one server or a light load of users who frequently log on and off. Per Seat licensing requires a client license for every system connecting to the server. This license option is preferred for any networks with more than a few users and multiple NT servers.
- Change the number of licenses if you are using Per Server licensing. we leave the exploration of this application to you. It is extremely simple, and it is likely to change in a future version of NT Server. If you have questions about this applet, start it and select help (F1).

Managing Disk Systems

Disk Administrator is the primary tool for managing many aspects of the disk systems under NT. It is augmented by many of the standard commands such as FORMAT, DIR, DELETE, and File Manager. Most of these tools are used for user-type management chores and are not what are normally called management tools except perhaps for the FORMAT command.

Disk Administrator is used to

- Create and delete partitions, stripe sets (including Stripe Sets with Parity—RAID 5), volume sets, and mirrored drive arrangements.
- Format logical disk drives.
- Assign drive letters.

Table 3.5 shows a number of other programs that are useful for managing disk or systems related to disks.

Disk Systems and NT

Disk systems are the heart of any OS, and there are many things to consider for managing them.

TABLE 3.5	Other Programs That Manage Disks

Program Name	Description
File Manager (WINFILE.EXE)	Can be used for many file-system-related tasks. It is also useful for formatting floppy disks, setting NTFS security, and setting audit parameters.
Performance Monitor (PERFMON.EXE)	Can display many useful statistics for both the physical and logical disks in a system or on other systems.
Event Viewer (EVENTVWR.EXE)	Displays system event messages that are generated regarding the disk system.
Format (FORMAT.COM)	Useful for formatting disks, both floppy and hard.
Label (LABEL.EXE)	Can be used for assigning or changing the label for a volume.
Convert (CONVERT.EXE)	Can convert a FAT or HPFS partition to an NTFS partition.

Physical Disk Drives, Partitions, and Volumes

A physical disk is actually a device you can hold in your hand. Physical disks are known as disks, drives, and, for some systems managers who have been around a while, platters. The NT documentation simply calls any disk drive a physical disk.

The term *physical disk* is mainly used in reference to installing disk drives into a system and reviewing Performance Monitor counters. The Physical Disk object in Performance Monitor collects statistics related to the entire disk. When you use a hardware RAID controller, NT sees all drives in a single array as a single disk.

NT writes a unique signature on each physical disk that uniquely identifies the disk to NT. Disks may be moved on controllers or within an SCSI chain and will still show up correctly because of the signature used by NT. The signatures are stored in the Registry.

A disk partition is part of a physical disk that has been set aside for a logical drive. All application software treats a partition as a separate entity. A single disk will have at least one and possibly more partitions.

A primary partition is one that may be used by an operating system. A physical disk can have up to four primary partitions.

An extended partition can be created on a physical disk. Extended partitions can be subpartitioned to contain multiple logical drives. Only one of the partitions on a physical disk can be an extended partition.

Once you have partitioned a disk, you must format the partition and assign a drive letter to the formatted volume.

Drive letters are logical because they point to a formatted volume that represents a partition. If you do not assign drive letters, they may change as you add disks or remove them from a system. The best way to look at logical drive letters is to think in terms of network shares. We can connect M: to one share today and another tomorrow; M: is a logical letter that may be used for different connections. Drive letters may also be useful for different connections for local volumes.

NT includes two special types of partitions:

- The system partition is the disk partition pointed to by the ROM BIOS and is used to boot NT. On RISC systems, this is the small (6MB or so) FAT partition that contains a few files.
- The boot partition is the disk partition that contains the NT system files.

The boot and system partitions can be duplexed or mirrored but may not be striped, parity striped, or put on a volume set.

Creating and Deleting Partitions

You can use Disk Administrator to create, remove, or change how a disk partition is used. Disk Administrator is an improvement over FDISK, which we became familiar with from MS-DOS. Disk Administrator graphically displays information about a partition and tells whether or not the partition is used. Partitions are color coded, with keys showing the used space on a partition and the unused space.

At the time of the 3.5 version of Disk Administrator, a new wrinkle was introduced into its operation by forcing you to commit changes before they become final. This option is still present in 3.51 and 4.0. The Commit Changes Now option is on the Partition menu.

Creating a Primary Partition:

1. Run Disk Administrator.
2. Select an area of free space on a drive in the main window.
3. Choose Create from the Partition menu.
4. Enter the size of the primary partition that you are going to create.
5. Click OK.

Creating an Extended Partition:

1. Run Disk Administrator.
2. Select an area of free space on a drive in the main window.
3. Choose Create Extended from the Partition menu.
4. Enter the size of the partition that you are going to create.
5. Click OK.
6. Select the Commit Changes Now option from the Partition menu. After the changes are committed, you can format the partition.

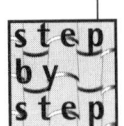

Deleting a Partition:

Warning: This option deletes all data on a partition.

1. Run Disk Administrator.
2. Select the partition, volume, or logical drive to delete in the main window.
3. Choose Delete from the Partition menu.
4. Choose Yes in the confirmation box.

End Volume Sets

Volume sets are a collection of volumes that are referred to by a single logical drive letter. A volume set is a collection of more than one partition that is treated as a single unit. The entire volume set receives the drive letter. A user sees only the total space from a volume, not the individual partitions that make up the set.

Volume sets may be useful if you have many physical disk drives and would like to treat groups of them as one. We would recommend using one of the RAID implementations over volume sets, unless you have fewer disks than are required for a minimal RAID configuration.

Formatting a Partition

Before you can use a partition, it must be formatted. If you are installing NT on a DOS system, NT will use the existing FAT partitions. A new unformatted disk or a new partition created with Disk Administrator must be formatted before it can be used.

NT 3.5 had a couple of new options that were added to Disk Administrator and that were sorely needed in the 3.1 version. The first option is Format, which allows you to format a partition in Disk Administrator, which remained in versions 3.51 and 4.0 of Disk Administrator. With this option, you can create and format a partition and assign the label for the logical drive within the same tool. Format is located on the Tools menu.

Formatting a Partition with Disk Administrator:

1. Run Disk Administrator.
2. Select the partition you wish to format in the main window.
3. Select the Format option from the Tools menu.
4. Choose the file system type from the drop-down list.
5. Enter a label.
6. Select Quick Format if the partition has been used before.
7. Click OK to start the format process.

You cannot use the Format option of Disk Administrator to format a volume that contains Windows NT system files.

The DOS Prompt FORMAT command can also be used to format disk volumes. This command is just like the old FORMAT command except that it now takes a switch for formatting different types of file systems. The following example shows how to format an NTFS drive using FORMAT.

```
FORMAT D: /fs:NTFS /v:LABEL
```

This command formats volume D: with the NTFS file system and assigns a volume label of LABEL to the new volume.

The FORMAT command is most useful for formatting floppy disks. Another useful option of FORMAT is for formatting NTFS partitions when you wish to override the allocation unit size that NT automatically sets. The allocation unit size default is based upon the size of the volume. The allocation unit size is set with the /a: switch and can be: 512, 1024, 2048, or 4096. The size of the allocation unit size value is the number of bytes per cluster.

You can also use File Manager to format floppy disks by choosing Format from the Disk menu. Make sure that the floppy disk is in the disk drive before you select the command, because Format goes out and retrieves information from the disk before it displays the Format dialog box.

Labeling a Volume

Volume labels show up in such places as File Manager and the DOS prompt. Many application programs also display volume labels when they refer to a drive list box. We suggest using descriptive names for labels, such as

- **SYSTEM**–volume containing the NT system files
- **DATA**–RAID volume used for data
- **DB01**–RAID volume used for a database

Disk Administrator allows you to modify the label of a volume using the Label option on the Tools menu.

Labeling a Drive with Disk Administrator:

1. Run Disk Administrator.
2. Select the volume you wish to label in the main window.
3. Select the Label option from the Tools menu.
4. Enter the new label.
5. Click OK.

You can also use the Label command to perform this task at the DOS prompt, as follows:

LABEL D: LABEL

This command labels volume D: and assigns the name of LABEL to the volume.

Assigning Drive Letters to a Volume

Disk Administrator allows you to assign drive letters to a volume or volume set, change a drive letter, or specify that a volume does not have a letter assigned to it. The latter option is useful if you wish to create more than twenty-four volumes. Any partition or logical drive that does not have a drive letter cannot be accessed until a letter is assigned to it.

Disk Administrator is useful for assigning drive letters when you move a drive from one system to another. Simply run Disk Administrator after adding the drive and restarting the system; then select the new partition/logical drive and change the drive letter. This trick is especially useful when you move a drive that has references to its drive letter (such as in INI files, batch files, programs, or SQL scripts).

Assigning or Changing the Drive Letter for a Volume:

1. Run Disk Administrator.
2. Select the volume or volume set you wish to change the letter for in the main window.
3. Select the Drive Letter option from the Tools menu.
4. Select the drive letter to assign to the current volume from the drop-down list.
5. Click OK.

Another feature of Disk Administrator is the addition of "sticky" drive letters for CD-ROM drives. This feature allows you to assign a drive letter to a CD-ROM that will stay with the drive across boots of the system and changes to your other drive configurations. This feature is also accessed from the Tools menu.

Assigning Sticky CD-ROM Drive Letters:

1. Run Disk Administrator.
2. Select the CD-ROM Drive Letters option from the Tools menu.
3. Select the CD-ROM you wish to change the driver letter for in the list on the left of the dialog box.
4. Select the Drive Letter from the drop-down list on the right.
5. Click Change.

Disk Administrator is used for manipulating most aspects of your disk systems.

Saving Disk Configuration Information

You should save the disk configuration information before and after you add or move a disk on an NT system. Saving the configuration information copies the disk information from the Registry to a diskette. The diskette can be used later to restore the configuration in the event that you must reinstall NT or upgrade to a new version of NT.

Saving the Disk Configuration to a Floppy Disk:

1. Start Disk Administrator.
2. Choose the Configuration option under the Partition menu.
3. Choose the Save option under the Configuration submenu.
4. Place a formatted blank diskette in the first floppy disk drive (usually A:).
5. Create a label for the diskette. Make sure that it includes the date, a header such as Disk Configuration Backup, and your initials.
6. Click OK to start the save operation.

The Restore option enables you to load the disk configuration from the diskette and update the Registry. This step is dangerous, because you must make sure that the diskette is current as of the last time you added or moved a disk. A Restore performed from the wrong diskette could result in lost data.

Restoring the Disk Configuration from a Floppy Disk:

1. Start Disk Administrator.
2. Choose the Configuration option under the Partition menu.
3. Choose the Restore option under the Configuration submenu.
4. Place diskette with the previously saved configuration in the first floppy disk drive (usually A:).
5. Click Yes to start the save operation.

Disk Administrator also includes the Migrate menu option on the Configuration menu. You can use Migrate if there is a previous version of NT on your system.

Disk Fault Tolerance

The disk fault tolerance features of NT Server are a big improvement over those of older network servers. NT Server provides support for mirrored disks, duplexed disks, and stripe sets with parity (RAID 5). These fault tolerance features are part of NT and are managed totally by NT. RAID (Redundant Array of Inexpensive Disks) consists of levels 0 through 5. Higher and more complex RAID levels will probably be added to NT in the future. NT does not support all RAID levels via software.

DISK MIRRORING

Disk mirroring is the same as RAID 1. This technique uses a second disk to mirror the primary partition. Every write to the primary partition also goes to the mirror partition. Mirroring is a good technique to use for your system and boot partitions to make them fault-tolerant.

DISK DUPLEXING

Disk duplexing is disk mirroring on steroids! This technique is exactly like disk mirroring, except that a second disk controller is used for the mirror disk.

This configuration enables NT to improve performance, because there are separate data paths to each drive. NT can read or write to each drive independently of the other, allowing NT to maximize system performance. This is especially true on reads in which NT will read from the drive that can provide the data the fastest.

RAID IN DETAIL

RAID is a term used to define the method of combining several inexpensive disks into what appears to be a single large disk. RAID replaces the older method normally referred to as SLED (Single Large Expensive Disk) that we have traditionally been using for most systems. NT systems can mix both methods in one system.

RAID can be implemented in either a hardware or software configuration, and NT supports both methods. Hardware RAID implementations are usually the preferred method. See "Hardware RAID Solutions."

RAID is described in terms of levels from 0 to 5. Table 3.6 describes the RAID levels. RAID levels 0, 1, and 5 are supported in the NT Server 4.0 software implementation, while hardware implementations may support all six or more levels.

Several RAID levels implement *disk striping,* which is a technique for improving disk performance, redundancy, or both. Striping basically creates one logical disk from a group of disks. Data are written across all disks

TABLE 3.6 RAID Levels

Level	Advantages	Description
0	Performance only	RAID 0 is normally known simply as disk striping. Striping is used to improve performance of the drives but contains no fault tolerance. RAID 0 is actually less reliable than unstriped drives because the entire array will go down if a failure occurs, and you must restore the entire array from a backup.
1	Fault tolerance only	RAID 1 is disk mirroring. Every time a write occurs to the primary disk, it is also written to the mirror disk.
2	Fault tolerance Improved performance	RAID 2 uses additional disks as check disks. Performance can be good if the system reads and writes large data blocks. Microsoft notes that RAID 2 is normally beneficial only in large systems.
3	Fault tolerance Improved performance	RAID 3 uses a single check disk for a drive array. The check disk receives the backup information for all drives in the array.
4	Fault tolerance Improved performance	RAID 4 uses a single check disk for a drive array like RAID 3. The check disk receives the backup information for all drives in the array. Data are written to the drives using block or sector striping instead of bit striping as used in RAID 3. Performance is improved over RAID 3 because data are transferred in larger blocks. Write operations are bottle-necked in both RAID 3 and 4 because all backup information must be written to the same drive.
5	Fault tolerance Improved performance	RAID 5 is the preferred fault tolerance method for NT systems because it provides fault tolerance and optimal performance (theoretically). RAID 5 dedicates the equivalent of one disk to storing backup information but splits the backup data over the entire array. Spreading the backup data over the entire array allows the RAID system to write to only two disk drives in any write operation. Multiple read operations can take place simultaneously, as can multiple write operations.

in "stripes" instead of to one disk at a time. Performance improve because reads and writes are split over multiple disks and can usually occur concurrently.

See the section in this chapter on "Hardware RAID Solutions" for more information on using hardware RAID options with NT Server. Hardware options can dramatically improve the performance of your system by handling the management of the RAID system at the hardware controller and relieving NT of this management task.

Creating a Mirror Set with NT:

1. Click the partition you wish to mirror.
2. Ctrl+Click the second partition on a different disk with at least as much free space as the first partition.
3. Click Establish Mirror from the Fault Tolerance menu. NT creates the mirror using a partition size on the mirror partition that matches the original partition.
4. Answer Yes to the confirmation prompt.

CREATING MIRROR SETS • Mirror sets are created like other fault tolerance options, with Disk Administrator.

The size of member partitions may vary by up to 1MB when drives with different geometry are used in a mirror or stripe set, because Disk Administrator rounds the size of the secondary members up to the next cylinder. Any extra space in a partition is not used. When a mirror set is built, the second partition, which will become the mirror, should not be formatted.

A mirror set can be disabled if the set is broken. Once the set is broken, each volume becomes an independent member.

Breaking a Mirror Set:

1. Click the mirror set you wish to break.
2. Click Break Mirror from the Fault Tolerance menu.

The original drive, or working drive if one drive is orphaned, retains the drive letter previously assigned to the mirror set. If both drives are working, the mirror drive will receive the next available drive letter.

CREATING STRIPE SETS • Stripe sets are created in the same manner as mirror sets. Disk Administrator is used to create the set and for other functions such as deleting a stripe set. A software implementation of striping can use from 2 to 32 drives in a stripe set. Stripe sets with parity (RAID 5) must use a minimum of three disks.

Creating Stripe Sets:

1. Run Disk Administrator.
2. Click first partition in the set.
3. Ctrl+Click each additional partition.
4. Select Fault Tolerance and click on Create Stripe Set.
5. Enter the size of the new stripe set.
6. Click OK.

Creating Stripe Sets with Parity:

1. Run Disk Administrator.
2. Click first partition in the set.
3. Ctrl+Click each additional partition.
4. Select Fault Tolerance and click on Create Stripe Set with Parity.
5. Enter the size of the new stripe set.
6. Click OK.

Deleting Stripe Sets of Either Type:

Warning: This option deletes all data on the stripe set.

1. Run Disk Administrator.
2. Select the stripe set to delete.
3. Select the Partition menu and click Delete.

WHEN A DRIVE FAILS • When a disk failure occurs on a system using RAID 1 or RAID 5, the RAID system continues to operate. There is no fault tolerance on the array until the failed member is replaced. Disk failures show up in the System log in Event Viewer.

DISK RECOVERY USING NT SOFTWARE SOLUTIONS • NT supports disk recovery with RAID 1 and 5. When a mirror or stripe member fails, it is called an *orphaned drive*. All new reads and writes are directed to the other disks in a set when a drive is orphaned.

Once a drive is orphaned, it must be replaced before the fault-tolerance features are restored to the system. The procedures for recovering a drive are different between the two RAID fault-tolerance levels. Hardware RAID systems also vary in how a bad member is replaced. A hardware RAID controller should ship with a monitor program that monitors the RAID system and feeds any problem reports to the NT Event Viewer System log when an error occurs.

Rebuilding a Damaged Mirror Disk. RAID 1 is disk mirroring and has a separate "mirror" volume for each volume you mirror. When you install a new disk to replace the failed member, NT rebuilds the new volume to match the existing member.

Steps for Rebuilding a Mirrored Member:

1. Run Disk Administrator.
2. Break the mirror set.
3. Replace the orphaned disk.
4. Reestablish a mirror set.

Rebuilding a Damaged Stripe Disk. RAID 5 is slightly different because it uses disk striping. NT updates the new disk by rebuilding it from the back-up information (Parity data) stored across the rest of the array.

Rebuilding a Stripe Set with Parity Member (Disk):

1. Replace the orphaned disk.
2. Run Disk Administrator.
3. Select the recoverable stripe set.
4. Select the replacement disk free space.
5. Select Fault Tolerance and click on the Regenerate command.
6. Quit Disk Administrator and restart the system.

This process uses the parity information to re-create the data that were stored on the disk that failed. The set will once again be fault tolerant.

You may experience a problem when a member is orphaned due to some problem other than a physical disk problem, for example, are cable, controller, or power problems. When these problems occur, you should select the orphaned disk in step 4 and continue the process from there. NT will re-create the data on the member using the parity information and once again include the former member in the set.

DISK RECOVERY USING HARDWARE SOLUTIONS • Most hardware implementations of RAID provide for quick disk recovery when a problem occurs. These systems normally use a *hot-swap* method, which allows you to pull a disk from the drive array and replace it while the system is running. This form of disk replacement is the coolest ever.

Many hardware systems automatically rebuild a failed member disk when it is replaced. You simply pull the bad disk and insert the new disk. The hardware controller takes care of the rest.

Some systems, such as the Digital StorageWorks controllers, take this procedure a step further by providing capabilities for a *hot spare*. A hot spare is a disk inserted in the RAID array that is not used but is designated as the spare disk. When a failure occurs, the new disk is generated, the old disk is failed by the controller, and the system continues to run with complete fault tolerance. This is the ultimate in disaster preparation at the disk level.

Many hardware RAID solutions also provide software that can be used to determine the status of the RAID system and control certain aspects of the system. For instance, the Digital StorageWorks includes software that graphically displays each drive in the array. You can selectively touch each drive. One of the nice features of this software is that it enables you to select a drive and manually fail the drive. This feature effectively takes the drive out of the set. Using this technique, you can pull a drive and replace it gracefully without ever shutting down the system.

CONVERTING A FAT PARTITION TO NTFS

The Convert utility can convert a FAT partition to NTFS. The utility must run from the command prompt. The syntax is

```
CONVERT d: /FS:NTFS
```

This is a one-way process. You can't convert from NTFS to FAT, and remember, NT 4.0 no longer supports HPFS.

When you run this command on the boot volume, you receive a notice that NT can't run the command because the volume can't be locked. This notice occurs because the volume contains the NT system files that are in use. You will be asked if you wish to run the command the next time the system boots. Simply answer yes, and the Convert command is scheduled to run the next time the system boots.

ADDING DISKS

NT automatically determines when a new disk has been added, unless you are using a hardware RAID controller. The number of disks that a system may use is determined by the hardware configuration. For instance, some RAID systems may allow 32 disks, while others may use only 8.

Hardware controllers typically require you to bring down the system, reconfigure the RAID system with a custom utility, and then restart the system.

APPLICATIONS AND STRIPE SETS

Many applications can benefit from using stripe sets on your disk drives. Stripe sets usually outperform the same disks with traditional formatted volumes on each disk. This outperformance is especially true if you are using the new controllers that support striping in hardware. NT and applications see the entire stripe set as one huge disk, while the hardware handles the physical access to the disk drives.

Adding a Disk Drive:

1. Install the new disk.

2. Run Disk Administrator.

3. Click OK when Disk Administrator notifies you that it needs to update its configuration.

4. Select the new disk and perform any operations necessary to put the disk in service (partition creation, formatting, and so forth).

5. Choose the Configuration menu from the Partition menu; then choose the Save submenu option to save the disk configuration. Make sure to label the disk correctly.

The more drives you add, the better the performance should be—theoretically. This increase in performance occurs because each write to the stripe set is simultaneously split over the entire set of striped disks, with the read or write operation happening simultaneously on multiple disks.

Stripe sets are particularly nice for systems running a large database program such as SQL Server. SQL Server and most major databases have for years provided the ability to split the database over different disks using a variety of methods to balance the Input/Output (I/O) load. None of the methods were easy, and usually someone had to spend a lot of time fiddling with device names and other fun things while continuously monitoring database performance. Make another change, monitor, make another change, monitor, and so on. You can't imagine what a pain this is until you have tried it.

Now the system administrator can simply take a fair-sized disk array, create a stripe set, and then place the entire database on the resulting volume. Microsoft engineers indicate that stripe sets almost always outperform traditional optimization methods for physical disk layout.

Device Drivers

NT controls, and interfaces to, many different parts of a computer with device drivers. Device drivers normally provide the interface between NT and a hardware device such as a tape drive or disk controller.

Most device drivers are installed and configured automatically during the installation of NT or when a new device is added. For instance, adding a new adapter or tape device with Windows Setup will most likely install a new driver unless a compatible one is already on the system.

Devices can be manually started and stopped using the Devices applet in Control Panel. This applet is almost identical to the Services applet, which is also in Control Panel.

Starting a Stopped Device:

1. Start Control Panel.
2. Select the Devices applet.
3. Select the device to start.
4. Click the Start button.

Stopping a Device:

1. Start Control Panel.
2. Select the Devices applet.
3. Select the device to stop.
4. Click the Stop button.

Most devices are set up correctly when they are installed, and you never have to mess with the startup configuration. When the time comes to change these parameters, the Devices applet comes to the rescue.

Configuring Startup Options for a Device:

1. Start Control Panel.
2. Select the Devices applet.
3. Select the device to setup.
4. Click the Startup button.
5. Select the desired startup option and close the dialog box.

Services

NT uses services for a variety of tasks, ranging from operating system tasks such as NetLogon to network services like NetDDE or RPC (Remote Procedure Call) and numerous other tasks. Application and other add-on software can also install services for use with that particular application.

Services are similar to a device driver in the way they are managed and the tasks they perform. Most services can be considered part of the operating system or an operating system support feature for an application. For instance, SQL Server and Systems Management Server both install services that provide various functions for the particular application. Other services included things like the Scheduler service that provides the AT functionality for batch routines, the messenger service that provides messaging support, and the various network services such as NetLogon, Server, and Workstation.

Services provide an efficient behind-the-scenes mechanism for both NT and NT applications. Services don't show up in the task list and there is no icon for a service, but the services are running and performing their allotted tasks.

Services can be set to start up automatically when NT comes up. Services also do not terminate when a user logs out from the NT console. Most services for systems such as SQL Server and Systems Management Server are set to start automatically when NT boots. Services must be configured for automatic startup to provide continuous support for a particular function across log-ons at the console.

Managing Services

The Services applet in Control Panel is the primary interface for managing services. Server Manager and the Net command also provide access to managing services. Server Manager is particularly useful because you can use it to remotely manage services on any NT system on the network or over RAS.

Server Manager provides direct access to the Services applet that is used in Control Panel. Once you have displayed the Services applet with Server Manager, managing services is the same as in Control Panel. One helpful feature of Server Manager is that not only can you access lots of other server features but you can also access services on other systems and access services from a Windows 3.x or 95 client via the client tools edition of Server Manager.

Accessing the Services Applet from Server Manager:

1. Start Server Manager.
2. Select the NT system to manage from the list of computers.
3. Choose the Services option from the Computer menu.

Either Net Start or the Services applet can be used to view the status of all running services quickly. These tools are frequently used to check on the status of currently running services.

Displaying Running Services with the Services Applet:

1. Start Control Panel or Server Manager.
2. Start the Services Applet.

Displaying Running Services with Net Start:

1. Access the DOS Command prompt.

2. Enter the following command:

   ```
   net start
   ```

The best way to start a service that is used frequently is automatically at boot time. The following steps describe how to set this up.

Configuring a Service to Start Automatically:

1. Run Control Panel and run the Services Applet or run Server Manager and select the Services command from the Computer menu.

2. Select the service.

3. Click Startup.

4. Click the Automatic button.

5. Click the System Account button or click This Account and select the user account for that service. If you select a user account, you must enter and confirm the password.

You may need to start a service manually from time to time, for example when you set a service to start automatically but do not want to reboot the server to use the service. Simply set the startup options to start the service automatically the next time NT is booted, and then manually start the service for the current session.

You will most likely run into another instance when a service fails to start at boot time. This failure is often caused by something like two systems trying to be the domain controller, or an incorrect network setting. Simply use one of the following techniques to start the service after you have corrected the problem.

Starting a Service with Control Panel:

1. Run Control Panel and run the Services Applet or run Server Manager and select the Services command from the Computer menu.

2. Select the service.

3. Click the Start button.

A service can start automatically or manually depending upon the settings in the Services applet. You can also disable a service and interactively start or stop a service. You may also Pause or Continue a service if there is a need to stop the service for a period of time.

Starting a Service with Net Start:

1. Access the DOS Command Prompt.
2. Enter the following command:

    `net start SERVICE`

SERVICE is the name for the service.

For instance, to start the workstation service, enter

`net start workstation`

Stopping a Service:

1. Run Control Panel and start the Services applet, or run Server Manager and select the Services command from the Computer menu.
2. Select the service.
3. Click the Stop button.

Pausing or Continuing a Service:

1. Run Control Panel and start the Services applet, or run Server Manager and select the Services command from the Computer menu.
2. Select the service.
3. Click Pause or Continue. The Pause button stops other users from connecting to the service until it is restarted or continued.

You may when you need to use these commands at odd times. Sometimes a service fails to start when NT boots for one reason or another, and you must manually start it. Maybe you need to perform some type of maintenance and wish to stop the service manually, perform the task, and then restart the service.

Wouldn't it be great if we could create our own services? Imagine your own program starting automatically when the system boots, and performing some magic in the background with no user intervention.

The NT Resource Kit provides a tool called SRVANY.EXE that performs this task. SRVANY.EXE allows you to run almost any application in the background as a service. Most programs behave properly in this manner, even as users log in and out. The documentation for SRVANY.EXE mentions that some 16-bit programs will not survive a log-out, so test your program carefully by installing and configuring the service. Then start the service, log out, log back in, and make sure the service is still running. The best way to test an automatic starting service is to log out and reboot the system and then make sure that the service is running.

You can also write services in C++ and Visual Basic. Visual Basic developers can purchase SpyWorks 5.0 or later from Desaware (www .desaware.com). SpyWorks lets you create both NT services and Control Panel applets.

Symmetrical Multiprocessor (SMP) Configurations

Symmetrical MultiProcessor (SMP) systems can add real bang to certain NT Servers. The biggest effect occurs when your system is processor-bound. A processor-bound system is typically performing lots of application tasks or working as a heavily used application server. File servers are rarely processor-bound but rather bottlenecked at the disk or network subsystems (I/O). Performance Monitor can provide lots of information on how heavily your system is taxing the processor subsystem.

NT schedules the highest priority thread first to ensure that the top-priority thread is always running. In an SMP system, NT schedules the highest priority threads on all processors in the system. The low-priority threads always share a single processor. For instance, if your system has four processors, the three highest-priority threads run on three of the processors, while the remaining threads run on the fourth processor.

SMP systems such as the Compaq and Digital Equipment lines can add lots of power to file and application servers. We had the chance to install NT Server on a Digital 2100-500 AXP (Alpha) system. The particular system had 640MB of RAM, 18GB of disk, and a 190-MHz processor. As you can imagine, this system ran NT so fast that everything except for some disk activities seemed to happen instantly. The 2100-500 design is elegant; up to four processors can be installed in the same box. A few months later, another client purchased a 2100-500 with 128MB of RAM and two 275-MHz processors. Now this was a screamer. When processor performance becomes an issue on this type of system, it will scream again if you add a new processor. Imagine up to four 275-MHz processors in a system configuration like this.

Compaq and many other vendors have come out with high-performance SMP systems that are designed to run NT. As more and more systems come out, the price will drop for all of us. Watch the trends, and when the price is right, pull an SMP system into your network.

NT will automatically recognize multiple processors during installation. If you add a processor to a system once NT has been installed, you need to notify NT of the change. The NT Resource Kit has a utility to upgrade your system with an additional processor. This step must be performed before NT can use the additional processor.

Adding an Additional Processor to an SMP System:
1. Run UpToMP.
2. Specify the drive that contains the NT distribution files.
3. Choose your processor (HAL) from the list box.
4. Click OK.

Control Panel

Control Panel is one of the key management tools for NT. Control Panel uses tool files for each major function or group of functions in Control Panel. Each tool file has a CPL extension. Table 3.7 lists the major tools included with NT Server 4.0.

Additional tools can be added to Control Panel by simply placing the tool file in the appropriate directory (%SystemRoot%\SYSTEM32). New tools are often provided by third-party vendors or with network applications that provide specific functions. Notice that all the program file names for Control Panel end in .CPL.

TABLE 3.7   Control Panel Support Files

File Name	Description
CURSORS.CPL	Allows you to customize the cursors used by NT.
DISPLAY.CPL	Manages the display settings for NT.
FTPMGR.CPL	Manages the FTP Server options.
MAIN.CPL	Provides functions for managing color, fonts, ports, mouse, desktop, keyboard, printers, international, system, and date/time.
MULTIMED.CPL	Manages multimedia options: Sound, MIDI Mapper, and Drivers.
NCPA.CPL	Manages the network settings for NT.
NWC.CPL	Manages the NetWare Services.
SFMMGR.CPL	Manages the Services for Macintosh.
SRVRMGR.CPL	Manages the following options: Server, Services, and Devices. Provides the same functions as Server Manager in the Administrative Tools group.
UPS.CPL	Manages the UPS service.

Removing NT Components to Save Space

Many NT components can be removed to conserve disk space and usage of system resources. Removing NT components also precludes users from accessing the programs, and it can cause problems.

The best way to remove NT components is with the Windows NT Setup tab under Add/Remove Programs Properties applet in Control Panel. You can remove items such as readme files, games, accessories, tools, and others. Removing a component deletes the files from the server and makes the services unavailable. Proceed with caution. Of course, you can always add it again in the future, but since NT 4.0 comes on CD only, unless your machine has a CD-ROM drive, you may have to connect to a machine over the network that has it your simply won't be able to do it.

Removing NT 4.0 Components:

1. Click Start in your Taskbar.
2. Select Settings and choose Control Panel.
3. Click over the Add/Remove Programs applet icon.
4. Select the tab Windows Setup.
5. Unselect the boxes corresponding to the applications, tools and accessories you would like to remove.
6. Click OK.

Removing NT 3.51 Components:

1. Start NT Setup.
2. Add/Remove Windows Components.
3. Select the components to remove.
4. Click Continue.
5. Click OK.

Starting a Server

NT Server starts automatically, including the startup of services set to start automatically. Always check Event Viewer for details on any service that does not seem to be working. You may occasionally get a message on the Domain Controller or another server stating, "At Least One Service or Driver Failed During System Startup. Use Event Viewer to Examine the Event Log for Details." This message occurs when one or more services fail to start.

When you consult Event Viewer, you should see an error at the top of the list if the list is sorted by Newest First (the default sort order). You can identify the event because the date and time should be close to the time the server started.

You may find a message in the Event Log noting that "Browser service forced an election on...." This message occurs because the Domain Controller always comes up with a higher priority because it is the browsemaster for the network; there is no other browsemaster available. This message is usually harmless. It simply indicates that there was no browsemaster available when the server started; it can be ignored. A *browsemaster* is the NT Server that maintains a list of browseable systems and services. You should consult the Event Log anytime there is a problem at startup, either when this is indicated by a message or when a service is not available.

Stopping a Server

The normal procedure for stopping an NT system is to choose Shutdown from the File menu in Program Manager or select the Shutdown button on the Windows NT Security dialog box after you press Ctrl+Alt+Del. Of course, to do this you must be an Administrator on NT Server or have explicit rights to shut down the server.

Another option for shutting down a system is to place a Shutdown button on the Welcome dialog box. This button enables anyone to shut down the system without logging on. This button can be useful in situations in which the server or workstation is locked in a secure room or in a very low-risk environment.

The Shutdown button in the Welcome dialog box is enabled by making a small change to the Registry.

Adding a Shutdown Button to the Welcome Dialog Box:
1. Run REGEDT32.
2. Change the value of ShutDownWithoutLogon value to a 1 for the following key: HKEY_LOCAL_MACHINE\SOFTWARE\Microsoft\Windows -   NT\CurrentVersion\Winlogon

After this change is made, NT displays the Shutdown button on the Welcome dialog box. Remember this change before you move this system into a nonsecure environment. You can remove the Shutdown button by changing the WinLogon value to 0.

You can add the Shutdown button to the dialog box using REGKEY.EXE from the NT Resource Kit. This program provides one-click access to the change and is therefore much easier than using REGEDT32.

The NT Resource Kit provides another option for stopping a server with the Shutdown command. This command runs from the command prompt and works on both the current server and remote servers. The command can also be included in a batch program.

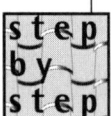

Stopping an NT System with Shutdown (NT Resource Kit):

1. Execute the following command:

   `shutdown \\computername /L /A /R /T:n /Y /C "Msg"`

   Where

`\\computername`	Specifies the system to shut down. If not specified, the local system will be shut down if the /L switch is used.
`/L`	Specifies a local shutdown. This switch must be used to force a local shutdown.
`/A`	Aborts a shutdown in progress that has not reached time 0.
`/R`	Specifies an auto reboot after shutdown.
`/T:n`	Determines the amount of time (n) in seconds before the server shuts down. Default time is 20 seconds.
`/Y`	Automatically answers Yes to all questions.
`/C`	Automatically forces all applications to close without prompting to save any open files.
`"Msg"`	Specifies the shutdown message to display on the system going down.

The Shutdown command is extremely useful in production situations in which you wish to perform several tasks before the system goes down. NT provides the standard DOS batch language to handle these types of tasks in conjunction with Shutdown. Systems managers from VMS installations will like this batch command called SHUTDOWN.BAT (remember SHUTDOWN.COM?).

```
@echo off
rem
rem ShutDown.bat
rem Ken Spencer
rem
```

```
Echo Do you wish to reboot after shutdown?
choice
echo .
if errorlevel == 1 set options=/R
echo Run site specific shutdown procedures?
choice
echo .
set RunSpec=n
if errorlevel == 1 set runspec=y
echo Select time in minutes until shutdown
choice /C02
if errorlevel == 2 set options=%options% /T:99
echo .
echo Force all applications to close?
choice
if errorlevel == 1 set options=%options% /C
echo .
echo Shutdown All Systems (N = only the local sys-
tem) choice
set AllSystems=n
if errorlevel == 1 set AllSystems=y
if %runspec% == y GoTo RunSpec
GoTo SkipRun
:RunSpec
Rem
Rem Place site specific options here
Rem
Echo Executing Site Specific Shutdown options at
this time
:SkipRun
Rem Place actual shutdown commands at this point
Rem ---------------------
Rem
Rem Sample Local shutdown command
```

```
\reskit35\shutdown /L /Y %options% "System is
Shutting Down" /Y
Rem
if %AllSystems% == y GoTo RunAll
GoTo SkipAll
Rem
Rem
:RunAll
Rem
Echo Shutting down all remote systems
Rem Sample Remote shutdown command
Rem \reskit35\shutdown \\Server /Y %options%
"System is Shutting Down" /Y
:SkipAll
```

SHUTDOWN.BAT should be placed in a directory on the PATH that is located ahead of the RESKIT35/3.51 or 4.0 directory where SHUTDOWN.EXE is located. This position forces SHUTDOWN.BAT to execute first when you enter the command. The following example shows the correct way to set up the PATH if SHUTDOWN.BAT is in the C:\U directory.

```
PATH=C:\WINNT\system32;C:\WINNT;D:\SQL\BINN; -
D:\SQL\DLL;C:\u;E:\RESKIT35\;m:\sql\bin;C:\WINNT; -
C:\DOS;E:\MDIABLTZ;e:\CONTROLS;
```

The next example shows the prompts and output from SHUTDOWN.BAT.

```
Do you wish to reboot after shutdown?
[Y,N]?Y

.

Run site specific shutdown procedures?
[Y,N]?Y

.

Select time in minutes until shutdown
[0,2]?2

.
```

```
Force all applications to close?
[Y,N]?N


Shutdown All Systems (N = only the local system)
[Y,N]?N
```

Specific programs that should run each time you shut down the system can be placed in the section under the ":RunAll" label. These commands are executed each time you run SHUTDOWN.BAT and answer **Y** to the prompt "Run site specific shutdown procedures?"

Multiple NT systems can be shut down with one command. Simply add the other systems in the section of SHUTDOWN.BAT labeled "Sample Remote shutdown command." Copy the sample command, remove REM at the start of the line, and edit the computer name.

Answering **Y** to the "Force all applications to close?" prompt immediately closes all running applications. Any unsaved data are lost. Answering **N** allows each application to prompt to save any open files.

The handiest way to run this program is to create an icon in Program Manager that points to it.

Configuring Automatic Log-on for NT Server

You may find it useful to have a server automatically log on to a user account when it boots. Reasons for this may be to start Performance Monitor or Event Viewer or some other program at startup. The automatic logon process is fairly simple to set up using of the Registry editors.

Setting up an Automatic Log-on at Startup:

1. Run REGEDT32 or RegEdit.

2. Enter values for DefaultDomainName, DefaultUserName, and DefaultPassword under the key:

   HKEY_LOCAL_MACHINE\SOFTWARE\Microsoft\Windows-
   NT\CurrentVersion\WinLogon

3. If the password entry does not exist, make an entry for DefaultPassword with a type of REG_SZ and the value equal to the password for the DefaultUserName.

4. Add an entry for AutoAdminLogon = 1 with a type of REG_SZ.

5. Restart the system after you have changed the values and exited REGEDT32.

You may encounter one problem with automating the log-on process. This problem exists because the log-on may finish before some services have had time to start. For instance, NT 4.0 may try to connect to network services before the required network services have started, or an application in the Startup group may try to start before a required service it depends on starts.

We ran across this problem when we tried to load both the OS/2 External and Dispatch utilities for Microsoft Mail during the automatic log-on process when NT Server started. The batch file we created to run the programs from the Startup group started before the OS/2 subsystem started. We solved the problem by creating a small Visual Basic (VB) program that runs in place of the original log-on batch file.

This VB program works by asking the system for the time when it starts. The time is reformatted and has 10 minutes added to it. This time is then fed to the AT scheduler for each command in a small batch file. At the conclusion of the process, the batch file is executed by the Shell command.

We also developed another way to solve the same problem, also using VB. This time, we just created a small application with a form, one text box, and a timer control. The timer interval was set to 60,000 (1 minute), tracked the total number of minutes with a global counter, and then started the correct program using the Shell command when 10 minutes were up. This program takes about 10 minutes to write and debug. You can add any number of programs to start or even use an INI file to list programs to start. We also placed a loop in the timer event that beeps the number of minutes remaining as the program counts down. This way, there is an audible and visual indicator of when programs will start after NT boots and logs on. The following code sample shows the entire Visual Basic code for the application.

Listing 3.1 VB Application to execute a program on a time delay

```
Dim MinuteCounter As Integer

Sub Form_Load ()
      MinuteCounter = 0
      Text1.Text = MinuteCounter
End Sub
Sub Timer1_Timer ()
Dim x As Integer
      If MinuteCounter = 9 Then
         x = Shell("E:\WGPO\EXTEROS2.BAT")
      Else
      MinuteCounter = MinuteCounter + 1
        Text1.Text = MinuteCounter
```

Listing 3.1 VB Application to execute a program on a time delay (Continued)

```
        For x = 1 To MinuteCounter
            Beep
        Next x
      End If
End Sub
```

The "`Dim MinuteCounter As Integer`" statement should be placed in the global declarations statement of the form. To add more programs to the startup list, copy the SHELL line in the TIMER1_TIMER subroutine and change the program name between the double quotes (" ").

Changing the Log-on Wallpaper for NT Server (and Why?)

You are probably wondering why we would want to change the wallpaper used during the log-on process for an NT Server. This task is usually reserved for workstation users who spend much of their time tweaking the colors and other appearance items of their systems.

Changing the wallpaper actually has one good use: identifying the name and purpose of the server. Displaying the name and purpose (File Server, DB Server, and so forth) makes it easy to see which server is which or which server you have connected to via a switch such as those marketed by Black Box, Network Technologies, and other vendors that allow you to set up several servers that use the same monitor, keyboard, and mouse.

The secret in setting up different wallpaper for the log-on screen is using REGEDT32 or RegEditto change the default setting.

Changing the Default Wallpaper for the Log-on Screen:

1. Create the new BMP file.
2. Copy the file to the Windows NT system directory (WINNT32 by default).
3. Start REGEDT32.
4. Find the key:

   `HKEY_USERS\DEFAULT\Control Panel\Desktop\Wallpaper`
5. Change the string from LANMANNT.BMP to your new BMP file.

You can also use REGKEY from the NT Resource Kit to perform this change quickly.

Connecting to Another System Using IPC$

Sometimes you may want to manage a system remotely but do not have an account on that system with the same user name and password, or the machine is in another domain that does not have a trust relationship with your domain. Simply execute the following command:

```
NET USE \\servername\IPC$ /USER: domainname\username *
```

Replace servername with the server you wish to connect to. Replace domainname\username with the domain and user name where the system you are connecting to is located. The * causes NET USE to prompt you for your password. Once the command completes, you can access the system from the Administrative tools by entering the server name in the Select Computer dialog boxes.

When you create a trust relationship using the IPC$ connection, NT will not confirm the creation of a trust relationship as long as the IPC$ connection exists. This is most likely because a computer cannot be logged in to a domain from two sources such as RAS and a network connection at the same time. The trust relationship works as soon as the IPC$ share is disconnected.

Management from an NT Workstation

You can manage most features of your NT Server from any NT Workstation. This includes running most of the NT Server administrative tools from the client workstation. The utilities for NT Server are also included with the NT Resource Kit. The Resource Kit includes a license allowing you to use the utilities from NT Workstations.

This license can be slightly confusing because many of the NT Server tools look and/or sound like an NT Workstation tool. Examples of these tools are NT's User Manager (MUSRMGR.EXE), NT Server User Manager for Domains (USRMGR.EXE), and the NT Server "Server Manager" program (SRVMGR. EXE). The NT Server Server Manager program adds a new front end and a few features to the standard NT "Server" applet in Control Panel (SRVMGR.CPL), which is also included with NT Server.

Other NT Server tools such as Performance Monitor (PERFMON.EXE), Disk Administrator (WINDISK.EXE), and Event Viewer (EVENTVWR.EXE) are the same on both NT and NT Server. Performance Monitor and other standard NT tools can access the same features on an NT Server as on a regular NT machine. You do not need to do anything special other than to select the server name when you use the tool.

Using NT Server-specific tools from an NT workstation is slightly more interesting, because you must access the tools over the network or move the tools to your local machine. The easiest way to access these tools is to create a share of the SYSTEM32 directory on the NT Server and access this share from your workstation. I set up a connection from drive Z: to this directory on my system to provide permanent access to the resources in NT Server, and then created a Program Manager icon for each of the NT Server tools I needed.

The easiest way to place a program icon in Program Manager is to connect to your shared connection in File Manager and move the File Manager window until you can see both the File Manager window with the new drive and Program Manager at the same time. You can do the same thing in NT 4.0 by putting a shortcut on your desktop with Explorer. Then click on the file you wish to set up in Program Manager, drag it over the Program Manager group, and release the mouse button. Program Manager warns you that this file may not be available later because it is on a network drive. Select OK and you are through. Repeat this process for each application you wish to set up.

Setting up Program Manager icons with Drag and Drop from File Manager is much quicker than using the File New method from Program Manager.

There is one caveat to setting up the tools this way: The NT Server license allows you to use the Administrative tools from only one machine at a time. Microsoft has solved this by placing the NT Server tools in the NT Resource Kit. You can install the programs on any NT or NT Server system. The Resource Kit comes with a site license for all the programs, making it necessary to buy only one copy of the kit per site.

Management from Windows 3.x and Windows 95 Systems

Many of the NT 3.50/3.51 management tools have been ported to Windows 3.x via the WIN32s API, but no longer for 4.0. As a matter of fact, you can't even manage an NT 3.5/3.51 server from an NT 4.0 workstation. But there are tools (User Manager for Domains, Server Manager, and so forth) that allow a Windows for Workgroup 3.x , or Windows 3.x client to be used to manage the NT desktop and NT Server machines on the network.

Several programs for 16-bit versions of Windows ship with NT Server. These programs include

- User Manager for Domains
- Server Manager
- Event Viewer
- Print Manager for Windows NT Server
- Tools for File Manager that add the Security menu, allowing you to change security settings on an NTFS volume

You must install a new redirector (VREDIR.386) for Windows for Workgroups 3.11 or LAN Manager systems before using these tools. Check the readme file contained with the server tools to determine if this applies to your system, and check the procedure for installing the redirector. If you're working with NT 3.5/3.51, this file and others for Windows for Workgroups are located in the \Clients directory on the NT Server CD. For NT 4.0, you will only find Win95 for client.

Each of the Win16 tools works just about like its counterpart under NT Server. The most notable difference occurs during startup, when you must select a server. This prompt doesn't occur when you run the tools on NT Server, because they default to the current system. The exceptions are Server Manager—because it focuses on the current domain, and File Manager—because its focus is on whatever drive you are using.

Installing NT Server Tools for Windows 3.11:

1. Share the CD-ROM or hard disk that contains the distribution files. The files are stored in the directory tree (\Clients\SrvTools\Windows) on the distribution CD.

2. Connect to the share from the Windows for Workgroups system you wish to install on.

3. Run the Setup program under the \Clients\SrvTools\Windows directory on the share.

System Alerts

NT generates a number of different alerts for system events. These alerts are separate from the alerts that can be set on counters in Performance Monitor. Alerts are generated by various subsystems of NT as events occur. Alerts are generated for security problems, access problems, server problems, potential power outages reported by the UPS subsystem, and printer problems.

Alerts can be triggered by any NT Workstation and NT Server system. Any system that generates alerts must be running the Alerter and Messenger services. Systems that receive the alert message must be running the Messenger service. Figure 3.3 shows the Services applet with the Alerter and Messenger services started. Note that the Startup parameter is set to Automatic. For more information on configuring services, see "Services."

You can determine the user and systems that receive alerts by using the Server applet in Control Panel. This applet provides a way for you to enter either a user name or system name to receive alerts. Multiple alert targets can be entered on one system.

Checking the Services Required for Alerts:

1. Make sure the Alerter and Messenger services are running on the server.
2. Start Control Panel/Services or Server Manager and select Services from the Computer menu.
3. Verify that the correct services are running. Figure 3.4 shows both the Alerter and Messenger services running with the Startup option set to Automatic.

Assigning Systems and Users to Receive Alerts on NT 4.0:

1. Click Start at the Taskbar and choose Settings.
2. Select Control Panel.
3. Click on Server.
4. Click the Alerts button and select the usernames or computer names you want to be alerted and click the Add button.
5. Click OK.

Assigning Systems and Users to Receive Alerts on NT 3.51:

1. Start Server Manager.
2. Click Alerts button.
3. Enter the user names and computer names that you wish to be notified when alerts occur.
4. Click Add button or press Enter.
5. Repeat steps 3 and 4 until you have entered all the names.
6. Close the dialog box.

For more information on other alerts, check the section in Chapter 10 on performance monitor alerts.

Event Logging

NT includes a superb event-logging system that is similar to the performance-monitoring system. Both the event-logging and performance-monitoring

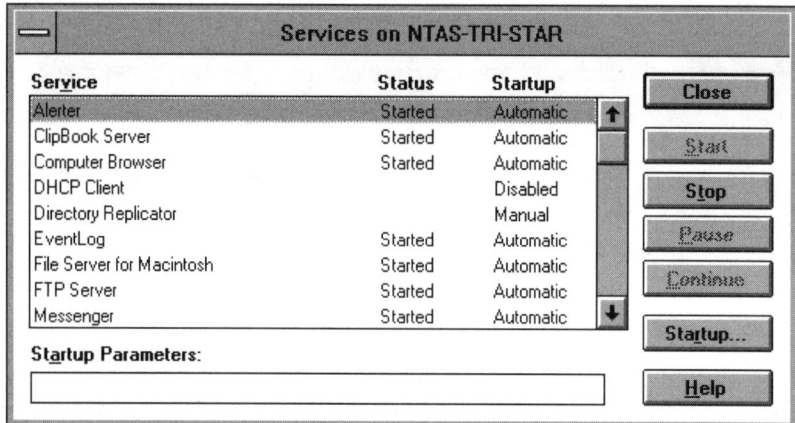

FIGURE 3.3 The Services dialog box shows the services running on a particular system.

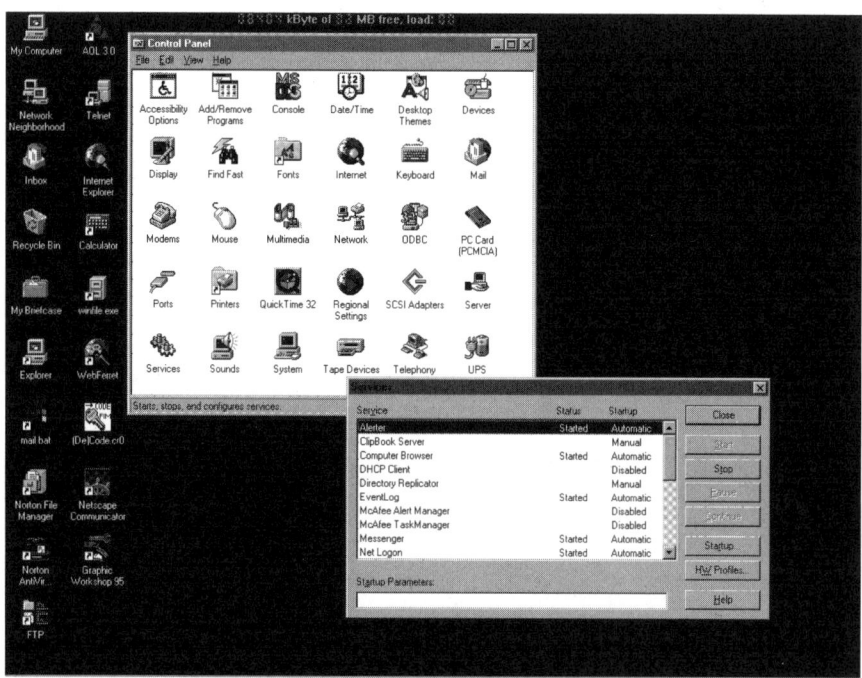

FIGURE 3.4 Alerter and Messenger services running with the Startup option on NT 4.0.

systems serve as a central place for recording events and performance counters for applications, security systems, and the operating system. The event-
logging system allows third-party systems to plug into the central system
instead of each application's implementing its own log files.

Overview

This centralized event tracking makes it much easier for a systems manager
to review any type of occurrence on the system: Start Event Viewer and
review each of the logs. Event Viewer is in fact the primary place to look for
information on almost any type of event in the system. You will be amazed
at the wealth and detail of information included in the various event logs.
Everything from a notification (print job completion), security event (log-on
attempt fails), potential problem (server disk is nearing capacity), to startup
problems (a service fails to start) is recorded.
    NT supports three types of event logs:

- System records events from the operating system.
- Application records events from application programs.
- Security records security and audit events.

Event Viewer

Event Viewer is the central tool for manipulating event logs. Event Viewer's
interface is clean and straightforward, as shown in Figure 3.5.
    Event Viewer is a powerful and simple tool to use. Simply start Event
Viewer and you are in the network management business. You can perform
a number of other tasks using Event Viewer.

Displaying Details on a Log Event:

1. Start Event Viewer.
2. Double-click the event, or select the event and press Enter.

    Make sure you have set the log options to limit the event logs to a rea-
sonable size. "Reasonable" in this case must be small enough not to choke
your system but large enough to display adequate event information. You
should also use care when performing operations that may quickly load up
the log. For instance, running CACLS from a batch file to reset permissions

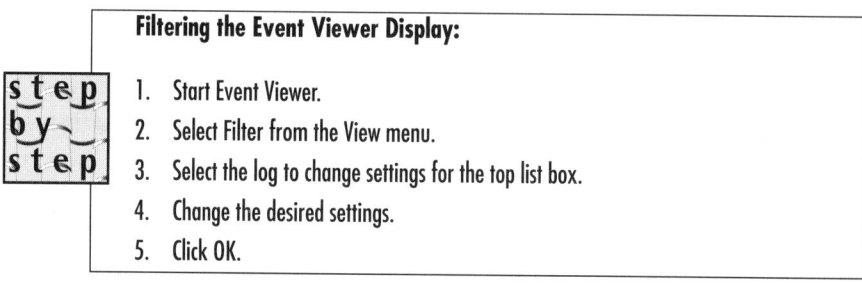

FIGURE 3.3   Event Viewer lists the events from the most recent to oldest. You can change the sort order in the View menu.

on a bunch of user directories is one command that may fill up the security log in a hurry.

Filtering the Event Viewer Display:

1. Start Event Viewer.
2. Select Filter from the View menu.
3. Select the log to change settings for the top list box.
4. Change the desired settings.
5. Click OK.

DumpEL (NT Resource Kit)

DumpEL is a tool from the NT Resource Kit for dumping Event Logs. DumpEL dumps an event log from one system and log at a time into a delimited text file. Once the data is in the delimited file, you can manipulate it easily with many different tools. The nice thing about DumpEL is that it can be easily automated with a batch program.

DumpEL can be used to dump the log on the local system or on a remote system. Selection filters can be used to limit the information extracted. The syntax is

```
dumpel -s ServerName -f OutPutFile -l LogName -m -r
```

-s   Server name, not including leading backslashes (\\). Defaults to the current server.

-f   Output file name. Defaults to the screen (stdout). This option over-writes any file existing with the same name.

-l   Log file name.

-m   Source of the records to dump (e.g., Serial, TCP/IP). Only one source at a time can be used.

-e   Event id to filter for. The format is -e n1 n2 n3 ... n10, with up to 10 event ids specified at once. Can be used only with the -m switch. The -r switch can be used to reverse the action of -e, in which case all events specified by -e will be ignored and everything else will be dumped.

-r   Reverses the filter action. When -r is used, it excludes any events selected with the -m and -e options.

-t   Separates strings in the output with tabs. Spaces are the default.

The ability to dump by event id is neat because you can filter the event log for certain problems. Every event logged has some type of event id such as 2000 or 2010. Determining the suspect event ID can be as easy as finding a few suspect events in the event log using Event Viewer and writing down the event ID numbers. Then use DUMPEL to pull all suspect events out of the log.

Some examples of how to use this command are in order. To dump the SYSTEM log on the current system to the event.out file:

```
dumpel -l system -f event.out
```

To dump the APPLICATION log on the current system:

```
dumpel -l application -f event.out
```

To dump the SECURITY log on the current system:

```
dumpel -l security -f event.out
```

To dump the SYSTEM log on the server FS01:

```
dumpel -s FS01 -l system -f event.out
```

To dump the SYSTEM log on the current system for only TCP/IP events:

```
dumpel -l system -f event.out -m tcpip
```

To dump the SYSTEM log on the current system for everything but TCP/IP events:

```
dumpel -l system -f event.out -m tcpip -r
```

FORFILES.EXE (New in 4.0 NT Resource Kit)

This utility can be used in a batch file to select files in a folder or tree for batch processing. It enables you to run a command on or pass arguments to multiple files. You could, for example, run the TYPE command on all files in a tree with the *.TXT extension. Or you could execute every batch file (*.BAT) on the C:\ drive with the filename "MYINPUT.TXT" as the first argument.

FORFILES works by implementing the "recourse subdirectories" flag on tools designed to process only a single file. Here it is the syntax:

```
forfiles [-ppath] [-msearchmask] [-ccommand]
[-dddmmyy] [-s] [-v] [-?]
```

Where:

-ppath

should be the path on which to start searching. The default folder is the current one from which FORFILES is run.

-msearchmask

searches files according to your entered searchmask. The default searchmask is *.*

-ccommand

indicates a command you want executed on each file. The default command is "cmd /c echo @FILE"

-dddmmyy

selects files with a date greater than or equal to ddmmyy.

-s

provides to FORFILES to recourse into subdirectories.

-v

runs FORFILES in verbose mode.

FTEDIT.EXE: FT Registry Information Editor (New on NT 4.0 Resource Kit)

This is a new GUI utility that allows you to create, edit, and delete fault-tolerance sets for disk drives and partitions of local and remote computers. It improves on the functionality of the command-line utility SHOWDISK.EXE.

The great thing about this utility is that it allows the information on disks, as well as fault tolerance, to be stored as disk keys in the Registry. To read it, you only need guest access (by default), but to change it, you must have the permissions necessary to write to the SYSTEM hive of the Registry.

Kernel Profiler (New NT 4.0 Resource Kit)

This is a command-line utility that provides counters for and profiles of various functions of NT's Kernel.

The Kernel Profiler (KERNPROF.EXE) allows you to monitor details and frequency for each function the Kernel calls, how often a process switches from User mode to Kernel mode, and, on a multiprocessor computer, display information for each processor.

Here it is the syntax:

```
kernprof [-a] [-d] [-c] [-w waittime] [-x] [-p] [-v]
[-s source] [sampletime] [lowthreshold]
```

Where:

-a

displays all function address, length and bucket size of the actual functions being called by the Kernel.

-d

computes hit density for each of the functions, telling you how many times each function is being called, which can be helpful in determining what the majority of the Kernel calls are.

-c

displays individual counters per call.

-w waittime

establishes a wait time of waittime before starting sampling (collection).

-x

displays context switch counter, which tracks how many times a process switches from User mode to Kernel mode.

-p

displays per-processor profile objects.

-v

displays verbose symbol information.

-s source

specifies a source to use instead of the clock as profile source.

sampletime

specifies, in seconds, how long to collect profile information. The default is to sample until CTRL + C is pressed.

`lowthreshold`

specifies a minimum number of counts to report. The default is 100.

Configuring Automatic Restart of a Server

A useful feature of the 3.5 version of NT Server that extended through versions 3.51 and 4.0 is System Recovery, which provides the ability to configure automatic reboot of the server when a fatal error occurs and the option of reporting the failure. The System applet in Control Panel is used to configure the System Recovery feature, as shown in the Figure 3.6 in the Startup/Shutdown tab.

The standard configuration for error recovery is for the server to write event log data to the system log, send an alert to Administrators, dump system memory to a file, and then automatically reboot the server. This recovery happens when a fatal error occurs and NT cannot recover gracefully.

You can change the following items using the System applet:

- write an event to the system log,
- send administrative alerts,
- insert options for the log file, and
- automatically reboot or shut down and wait to be rebooted

Setting System Recovery Options with NT 4.0:

1. Click the Start button in the Taskbar.
2. Select Settings and Control Panel.
3. Click System applet icon.
4. Click Startup/Shutdown tab.
5. Change the appropriate options.
6. Click OK.

Setting System Recovery Options with NT 3.51:

1. Start Control Panel.
2. Run the System applet.
3. Choose the Recovery button on the System dialog box.
4. Change the appropriate options.
5. Click OK.

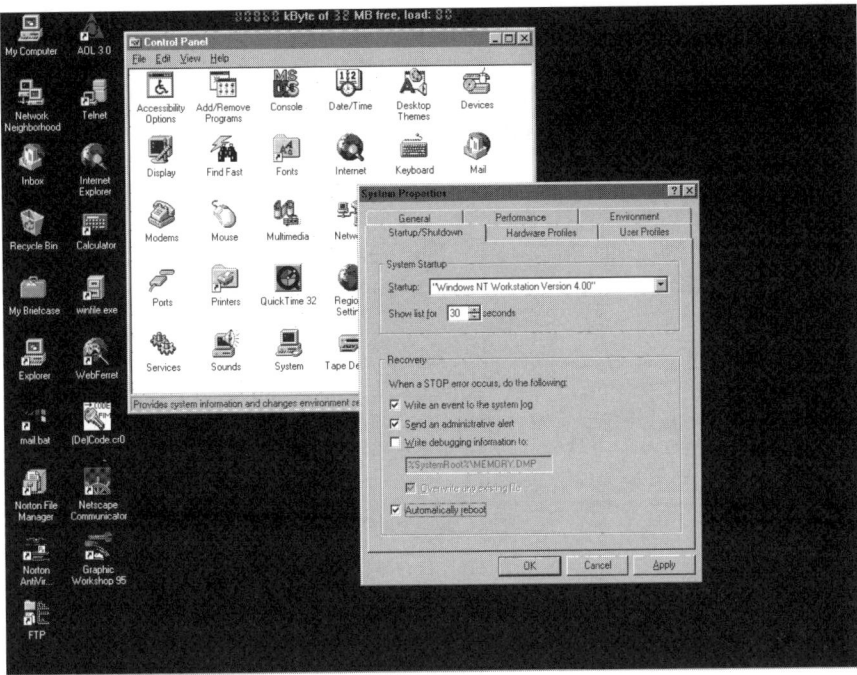

FIGURE 3.6 Configuring Startup and Shutdown on NT 4.0's Systems Recovery feature.

The server may need to be rebooted for some of these changes to take effect. If rebooting is required, NT will prompt you.

Notice that the default log file is MEMORY.DMP and is in the system root directory (WINNT by default).

Why should you use any of these features of NT 4.0? With NT Advanced Server 3.1, the system would stop automatically when it bumped onto certain errors. This reaction is similar in many systems when they are hit with a "fatal" error. Have you ever seen a parity error on a PC or a PC lockup for another hardware problem such as a General Protection Fault (GPF) or the dreaded "black screen" when Windows 3.x goes away? It's the same thing. This reaction can be aggravating under certain circumstances, such as when you have lots of users on a system and can't afford extended downtime. It is much better to have the system reboot after writing the exception data to a log file.

This type of behavior is exactly what the new shutdown features are designed for. Simply set NT Server to auto reboot, write an entry to the event log, and write the memory dump to the log file. If the system ever hits a "fatal" STOP error, it will recover, and you can use the memory dump to debug the problem.

Repairing Damaged System Files

NT stores information to repair the system on the Emergency Repair disk created during the installation and in the \SystemRoot\REPAIR directory.

The REPAIR information can be used when your system files become corrupted for some reason. It can also be useful when you have toasted your system files and need to replace them quickly. Make sure that the Repair disk is up to date before you start the repair process to avoid losing information added since installation. (See Chapter 9 on tips for the Registry.)

Using the Repair Process:

1. Start the NT Server Setup program in the same manner used to install the system.
2. Press R during the DOS part of Setup when Setup asks if you want to install NT or repair files.
3. Follow the instructions, inserting the Repair disk when prompted.
4. Restart your system at the completion of the process by following the instructions given by Setup.

The Repair process can replace a number of files and perform verification checks on the system. Table 3.8 lists the items that NT Server can check and repair.

TABLE 3.8 Options That Repair Process Checks and Repairs

Option Checked	Description
System files	All NT Server files on the system partition and the \SystemRoot tree are checked to verify that all files are present and that none are corrupt. Any corrupt or missing files are updated. Setup automatically removes and restores permissions during the repair process if the files are on an NTFS partition.
Default system configuration	All Registry files are checked for errors. If any are corrupt, they are replaced. Setup prompts you to replace them with files from the installation media. Note: Unless you have updated the Emergency Disk recently, you will lose all user accounts and file security plus other Registry changes.
Boot variables	Boot variables are checked and replaced from the Repair disk if necessary.
Boot sector for x86 systems	Setup checks the boot sector and repairs it by updating any files and writing a new boot sector on the partition.

See the section on using Rdisk in Chapter 9 for information on updating the Repair disk. This step should be performed on a regular basis.

BOOT.INI Options

BOOT.INI is stored in the root directory of the boot drive for Intel systems and in memory for RISC systems. The boot loader reads BOOT.INI during the startup process to determine the options displayed in the startup list. BOOT.INI is maintained by the System applet in Control Panel.

You may find it useful to add or change the options in BOOT.INI (Intel only) manually in certain instances. Options that are useful are multiple boot options for NT, special debug options for NT, setting the startup options for NT, and, if you are running NT on an Intel processor, an MS-DOS boot option.

```
[boot loader]
timeout=30
default=multi(0)disk(0)rdisk(0)partition(1)\WINNT35
[operating systems]
multi(0)disk(0)rdisk(0)partition(1)\WINNT35="Windows
NT Server -Version 3.51"
multi(0)disk(0)rdisk(0)partition(1)\WINNT35="Windows
NT Server -Version 3.51 - [VGA mode]" /basevideo
C:\ = "MS-DOS"
```

Options for NT are specified on the same line as the desired NT boot option, after the description, and are preceded by a /. Table 3.9 contains the boot.ini options. Notice the /basevideo option in the last example for a boot.ini file.

Adding a Second Boot Option for NT

One of the options you should consider for management purposes is adding a second entry for NT to BOOT.INI. This entry should include the /DEBUG and /BAUDATE=9600 switches to the end of the line. This setting turns on the DEBUG option for NT and sets the speed to 9600. The debug option allows Microsoft support engineers to dial into your NT system if it dies due to a hardware exception error. Note that we said *if it dies*. This means that when the system dies with the big blue screen, they can still dial in and debug the memory dump. Pretty cool!

TABLE 3.9   BOOT.INI Options

Option	Description
/NODEBUG	Default: No debugging information is collected or transmitted during startup.
/DEBUG	Enables debugging information to be sent and collected during startup. The COM port used is the last one detected during startup unless a port is specified with the DEBUGPORT option.
/DEBUGPORT=COMx	Specifies the specific COM port to use for debugging. Specify the one used for your modem connection.
/BAUDRATE=xxxx	Specifies the speed at which data are sent through the debug COM port. Default is 19200.
/CRASHDEBUG	Enables an amount of stack pages to be accessible via the debugger. These stack pages are made available only after the system encounters a FATAL error. The default amount is 9600 for debugging via a modem.
/SOS	Turns on the display of drivers as they are loaded during NT startup.
/NoSerialMice=x	Turns off serial mouse detection during startup. If x is specified, checking is turned off only on that COM port. If no port is specified, then checking is turned off on all COM ports. Multiple ports can be specified as: /NoSerialMice=COM1,COM3....

Adding a Second Boot Option for NT 4.0 and or NT 3.51:

1. Change the attribute for BOOT.INI from "Read Only," to allow editing the file, using the ATTRIB -R command:

   ```
   ATTRIB -R C:\BOOT.INI
   ```

2. Edit BOOT.INI:

   ```
   EDIT BOOT.INI
   ```

3. Copy the boot entry for NT and add the following to the end of the line:

   ```
   /DEBUG /BAUDRATE=9600
   ```

4. Change the attribute for BOOT.INI back to "Read Only," using the ATTRIB + command:

   ```
   ATTRIB +R C:\BOOT.INI
   ```

BOOT.INI Options for UPS and Other Hardware Devices

UPS and some other devices may require turning off mouse detection on the COM port used for the UPS signal line. Each time NT starts, it tries to detect all devices attached to the system, including any mice attached to a COM port. This detection has the possibility to turn the UPS off during the detection process when the UPS picks up the signal and thinks it should shut down. Of course, this situation is undesirable.

Turning off Mouse Detection (Intel Only):

1. Change the attribute for BOOT.INI from "Read Only," to allow editing the file, using the ATTRIB -R command:

```
ATTRIB -R C:\BOOT.INI
```

2. Edit BOOT.INI:

```
EDIT BOOT.INI
```

3. Edit the boot entry for NT and add the following to the end of the line:

```
/NoSerialMice=COMx
```

where x equals the COM port used for the UPS device

4. Change the attribute for BOOT.INI back to "Read Only" using the ATTRIB + command:

```
ATTRIB +R C:\BOOT.INI
```

Stopping an Application on the Server

You can normally use the Task Manager (CTRL+ALT+DEL and click Task Manager select the application you want to terminate) in NT 4.0 or the Task List in NT 3.51 to kill a program that is executing on the server. In NT 3.51, simply press Ctrl+Esc to display the task list, select the program by clicking the name, and then click Terminate.

KILL (NT Resource Kit) is another way to stop a program. KILL is a utility that allows you to stop a program by specifying the name of the application or the name of its executable or by its Process ID.

You can determine the Process ID from TLIST or PVIEW or Performance Monitor. If you specify the name of the executable and more than one instance of the application is running, all instances are killed.

As you can guess, this is one of those extremely useful applications that must be carefully guarded. A user with access to a privileged account could create some interesting problems with KILL.

```
KILL { PID | programname } /f
```

- **PID**–PID Indicates either the process ID for a process or the task ID for a task.
- **programname**–You can optionally specify the program's name or its window title.
- **/f**–Causes the process to terminate immediately without waiting for the process to kill itself.

TLIST is another NT Resource Kit utility useful when you need to kill a process. If you don't know the name of a process or want to specify its process ID, simply type **TLIST** and press Enter. You will be presented with a nice list of all the running processes and tasks on the system.

NT Error and Informational Messages

NT Server 3.51 comes with the Messages database and NT 4.0 extends and updates the books available in the 3.51 version. This handy tool provides information on the many messages that NT displays. The Messages database is built using Microsoft Access and can be a ready reference once it is installed. It is not installed during the NT Server installation.

Installing the Messages Database:

1. Obtain access to the installation media (only on the CD-ROM).
2. Run the following command:

   cd_rom:\SUPPORT\WINNTMSG\SETUP

3. Enter your name and organization.
4. Click Continue.
5. Answer Yes to the Multiuser Installation.
6. Enter the directory to install the messages.

Double-click the Windows NT Messages icon to start the application.

After the Microsoft Windows NT Messages program starts, click the Find button to search the messages database. The program allows you to search the database on message ID, message text, and Notes.

Microsoft Diagnostics (WINMSD)

The WINMSD utility is the NT counterpart of the MSD utility that shipped with Windows 3.x and Windows 95. WINMSD is useful for determining a variety of configuration information concerning an NT system without your having to resort to digging through the Registry.

WINMSD provides a GUI interface into many configuration parameters and gives you access to several other tools as well. You can use WINMSD to view any file (including EXE files) and display many configuration settings for your system. These include settings for Network, IRQs, memory, operating system version, processor, and ports, among others. As you can gather from this list, WINMSD is a very powerful tool for determining system settings and for diagnosing problems. It is also useful for determining the current settings before you install any new hardware in your system.

The first step in using WINMSD is to create an icon for the program in a Program Manager group. The executable for the program is WINMSD.EXE and is located in the SYSTEM32 directory.

WINMSD uses another program called WINMSDP.EXE when you use the Tools menu and request a report. The WINMSDP program can be called independently of WINMSD with command-line options to specify the program's action. The options are listed in Table 3.10.

Two of the options are what we call wildcard options. The /A switch reports on all settings, while /N reports on only those settings that affect network activities.

The report is always saved in the file MSDRPT.TXT. If a previous report file exists, it will be saved as MSDRPT00.TXT. The 00 will be incremented, depending upon how many preexisting files exist.

You may want to set the WINMSDP.EXE program up as a batch job to automatically dump all settings for your systems at regular intervals. The batch program could also copy the report file to a shared directory, making the file accessible to the system managers over the network. This will be especially useful if you create a program that picks up all changes from all NT machines and updates a management database on the network. This program will ensure that you have up-to-date information on all your systems as of the last time the batch jobs ran.

TABLE 3.10	WINMSD Command-Line Options		
Option	**Description**	**Option**	**Description**
/A	All Settings	/Y	Memory resources
/D	Drives	/P	Port resources
/S	Services	/U	DMA resources
/R	Drivers	/W	Hardware
/M	Memory	/E	Environment
/I	Interrupts resources	/N	Network-related settings

Using Multiple Servers with a Single Keyboard/Mouse/Monitor

You will most likely end up with several NT servers in your computer room if your system is of any size and/or performs many tasks such as File and Print servers plus a Database server, plus a Systems Management Server (SMS), and so forth. Several servers soon create a mess of cables, monitors, and keyboards (not to mention mice) that must be managed. The easiest solution is to use an automated switch that handles all three devices and shares them among multiple servers.

A number of vendors make suitable switches for servers. Some vendors also build cabinets with switches included. There are potential problems with implementing a switch that may preclude choosing the most cost-effective switch from a catalog:

- System uses workstation-style monitors with coax connectors. Systems such as Alpha and other RISC systems may use coax connectors that have specific cable-length requirements and that do not work with standard VGA switches. Network Technologies (800-RGB-TECH) provides standard cables, custom cables, and switches that work with either coax-style connectors or standard VGA monitors.
- Keyboard fun and games. You may encounter keyboard problems with a fast system (such as a Pentium 60 or faster) and some switches. Call the switch vendor and request updated firmware to resolve the problem.
- Fuzzy monitor. This is the same type problem as the keyboard, except the monitor just looks "fuzzy." The problem may be with either switch firmware or the type of cables used to connect the monitor and switch.

Designing a System for Performance

There are many parameters to consider when you design the hardware platform for NT Server. This section is not meant to be an all-inclusive guide to hardware but rather to provide suggestions on major issues for your server.

One important factor in deciding upon your choice of hardware is the service provided by the hardware vendor. Make sure that your vendor can support not only the hardware but also NT. Its support for NT should include knowledge of possible failure codes for NT and how they relate to the particular platform you will use as a server. We have seen problems occur with NT that Microsoft could not solve but that the hardware vendor technical support could resolve in less than five minutes. The vendor could break down the error code to point to a specific problem on the machine.

Make sure that your choice of server is not from a company that is experiencing customer support problems or that has a poor track record in the industry.

Server Types

NT supports many different types of general-purpose and specialty servers. The common nature of operations performed on certain types of servers leads to general conclusions about the loading of different types of servers. This information can be extremely valuable for designing the servers and choosing the hardware for each server. Table 3.11 lists some general parameters to consider as you plan new servers and upgrades for existing servers. Table 3.11 can also be used as a guideline for items to monitor for particular servers.

TABLE 3.11 General Server Parameters

Primary Server Function	Most Important Subsystems	Notes
File and print	Disk, disk controllers, network cards	Most activity on File and Print servers takes place on the disk subsystems and the network interface.
Application (DB)	CPU, memory	Application servers typically run systems such as SQL Server, Systems Management Server, SNA Server, and Exchange Server. The stress points of an application server typically involve CPU and memory. Database servers also place high demands on the disk and network systems and thus may also experience a heavy load, depending upon the particular application and data requirements.
Communications (RAS)	Communications, network cards, memory, CPU	Communications servers typically stress the communications subsystems (serial, X.25, etc.) and network. Memory and CPU are increasingly important as the load on the server increases.

Fast Processor with 256K or Greater CACHE

Viable processors for NT systems range from Pentium systems to MIPS and Alpha-based RISC systems. NT has leveled the playing field for computer hardware, turning most systems into commodity items. It has also given users a distinct advantage, because you can protect your investment in software and freely upgrade hardware to more powerful platforms without being locked into a single vendor's solutions.

INTEL

Intel servers for NT Server should have a Pentium or Pentium Pro or faster processor. Given mid-1997 prices, we would suggest buying a high-end Pentium system as the server. Some of the new systems from Digital, Dell, and Compaq (not to mention others) are sporting multiple processors that make an ideal server for NT. Remember that the faster the processor(s), the better.

RISC

The Alpha and Power PC systems provide outstanding price/performance benefits for most organizations. These systems are usually better built than most of the PC clones on the market. In particular, the new 4000 server from Digital is a screamer. It can house from one to four 275-MHz processors with up to 2GB of memory (1GB with four processors) and 200GB of disk. If the PCI disk controllers are used, the disk throughput is 132MB/sec. The 2100 also has sophisticated fault management software and a built-in maintenance processor and diagnostics control bus. It is an outstanding system for NT Server. Digital has also added the AlphaServer 1000 and 2000 to its line of servers. These systems follow the same architecture as the 2100.

LOTS OF MEMORY

NT is very sensitive to the amount of memory in a system. Memory is used by applications and the operating system, for caching the disk drives, and for other functions. The more memory your system has, the better NT is able to use the available memory dynamically.

There are no set benchmarks for servers and the amount of memory they should have, but we would make the suggestions outlined in Table 3.12.

We suggest adding more memory than you think will be required. If you need 32MB, start with 64MB. This built-in expansion factor provides good performance and allows usage of your system to grow over time with no system changes.

TABLE 3.12 Optimal Server Memory

Number of File/Print Server Clients	Server Memory
25 or less	48MB or more
26–50	64MB or more
51–100	128MB or more
101 and up	Over 128MB

Database servers do not fall into the same general categories as file and print servers because of the varied nature of the application and database design for these systems. The database software itself varies greatly in efficiency, depending upon the overhead it places on the server operating system and the degree to which it integrates with and uses features of the server.

Database servers should typically start out with more memory than a file and print server for the same number of users. For instance, a database server for 40 clients should start with 64MB of memory or more. A 100-user system should probably start at 256MB. These RAM sizes are extremely reasonable in the late 1990s due to current prices. You should also consider a platform that can handle multiple processors (SMP) for your database server. SMP systems can usually handle more physical memory and have higher-capacity we/O systems, providing a much nicer incremental growth path for your system.

Make sure that any NT system can support adding memory without throwing away the existing memory. For instance, purchase a 32MB system with 16MB SIMMS instead of 8MB SIMMS to save open memory banks for future expansion; 32MB using 8MB SIMMS requires four banks, while using 16MB SIMMS requires only two.

NETWORK CARDS

Use the fastest network cards you can get. This usually means a 16-bit smart card such as a 3C509 (EtherLink III) from 3Com. Network cards are available now for the high-speed PCI bus, EISA bus, and ISA bus, with options to 100-bits.

Adding additional network cards can also improve the performance of your system. Multiple cards can segment the network and reduce the traffic on each segment while allowing each network card to process half as many packets. This type of configuration must be carefully established and balanced with the needs of users to access resources on each segment.

VIDEO SYSTEMS

Servers may or may not need a high-speed video system, depending upon the amount of time you use the monitor attached to the server and the type of applications you run on the server. The price of video systems has come down, so that it makes sense to put a high-priced video system on the server, because most standard components supply adequate power.

DISK DRIVES AND CONTROLLERS

Disk systems are dependent upon a number of factors. The disk system is like a chain; It is only as strong as its weakest and slowest link (component).

CONTROLLERS • NT supports many different types and styles of disk controllers. Some of the most popular controllers in recent systems, such as the PCI ones, are the local bus variety that are built onto the motherboard. These controllers are usually very fast and provide different levels of functionality, depending upon the vendor. Check out the speeds and features for your particular system. For instance, the Alpha 4100 and 8100 from Digital comes with a built-in controller and RAID system with hot-swap drives. Other systems may have similar features that include controllers or controllers and disk systems. Systems with built-in components are normally easier to set up and manage and are more reliable.

CACHING DRIVES AND CONTROLLERS • Caching drives and controllers are a great way to add performance to a system. The controller or drive usually carries a large memory cache, which drastically enhances the performance of the drive.

There is one large caveat to these types of drives: Do not use them for storing a SQL Server database unless the drive has write-through assurance. SQL Server guarantees that data were written to the physical disk but it cannot do so when it uses a caching drive unless write caching on the drive, is turned off.

You should carefully weigh the use of caching controllers or any other device that uses memory. NT does a good job using its memory to the maximum extent possible, so spending your money on more RAM for NT may make more sense than using a high-priced caching controller. This decision must be made based on a particular controller, the BUS architecture of the system you are using for your server, and other factors such as the amount of RAM your system can handle. For instance, older systems that use the ISA bus may benefit from a caching controller, because less data must be moved over the bus into RAM at one time. A server using a fast disk controller on a PCI bus may make better use of system RAM than a caching controller. Caveat emptor! Don't believe everything you hear from a vendor or read in the press. Evaluate carefully, and then make a decision.

RAID SYSTEMS ARE USUALLY FAST • RAID systems can usually improve the performance of your system because they can write to more than one disk at a time. NT supports both a software solution (set up with Disk Administrator) and hardware implementations.

A hardware implementation of RAID 5 provides the best possible performance and gives you the highest level of fault tolerance.

Hardware implementations of RAID handle the entire striping process in the controllers and drives and do not cause any overhead on the server, because NT sees the entire RAID system as one drive. This allows NT to function at an optimal level.

Choose carefully when you pick a hardware implementation, because these drives are usually very expensive and can vary in performance levels from one vendor to another.

One caveat for RAID systems: Make sure that you have good tape backups of all RAID drives. We have seen a RAID controller die and take the entire array with it. There is no substitute for good backups!

Bus Architecture • Bus architecture is a prime concern for any system that will be used as a server. The bus is the primary channel that all I/O flows through to the disk drives and network. The PCI (Peripheral Component Interconnect) local bus standard is our favorite of the PC buses circa 1997. The PCI bus is fast (80MB/sec of sustainable throughput), processor-independent (PCI is used in PC, PowerPC, Alpha, and other systems), and autoconfiguring.

The next bus we would use would be EISA (Extended Industry Standard Architecture). EISA is sort of fast (33MB/sec) and is software-configurable through a special setup program (normally called ECU–EISA Configuration Utility). An ECU cannot run unless the system is shut down and restarted.

CONFIGURATION ISSUES

Like the components in a system, its configuration will also have an impact on its performance and reliability.

Multiple Paging Files • NT uses page files to simulate memory using the hard disk system by moving data and programs from physical memory to the page file(s) when memory demand is high. NT does this by using a sophisticated algorithm to determine what to move. If your demands on memory outgrow the physical memory available, NT begins using the page files. Remember that page files are slow compared to physical memory. High usage of page files drastically slows down your system.

You can spread the page files over multiple disks and controllers to allow NT to access multiple-page files at the same time. This is especially good for fast drives and smart controllers that handle disks very efficiently. The System applet in Control Panel is the tool for managing page files. Click on the Performance tab, then the Change button (or the Virtual Memory button on NT 3.51) to make changes or to review current settings. Look for newer industry-standard controllers from leading vendors, and check their features.

Correctly Size the Paging Files • Paging files automatically grow up to the maximum allowed in the Virtual Memory dialog box. This maximum allows NT to adjust the size of the file as needed, due to demands of the system. Any time a page file is extended, it usually slows down the system during the extension process and results in a more fragmented disk, which will adversely affect performance.

You can monitor page file fragmentation by setting a large maximum page file size and watching the actual size of the page file(s). If the file(s) grows beyond the initial setting, defragment the disk and create a larger page file. Continue to monitor the page file(s) until it does not grow.

Use some common sense when you plan your page file size and configuration. If your system has lots of RAM (256MB or more) and is never using the page file, you don't need a very large page file. However, the cost of disk is relatively low these days, so a good-sized page file that can account for future growth should not be a high-cost item.

DISABLE UNUSED NETWORK CARDS • Disabling unused cards reduces the amount of overhead on the server, because every network card that is enabled processes packets from the network, even when the server is not using anything on that particular segment.

CAREFULLY CHOOSE YOUR PROTOCOL • NetBEUI is a small fast protocol but cannot be used for WAN connections. TCP/IP is much more robust because of its routing features and management tools, but was significantly slower than NetBEUI. But back when NT 3.5 was released, Microsoft introduced a completely rewritten TCP/IP stack. This new TCP/IP stack was able to perform almost as well as or better than NetBEUI on a LAN, as it was designed to incorporate many of the advances in performance and ease of administration made over the past decade. The stack is a high-performance, portable, 32-bit implementation of the industry standard TCP/IP protocol. With the release of NT 3.51, and again with the NT 4.0 release, the stack has been updated with new features. This was very good news, because now we can use only TCP/IP and still have the best performance on LAN and a WAN.

New features and changes were introduced to the TCP/IP stack that comes with Windows NT version 4.0. The stack released with NT 4.0 also includes changes made to the one released with NT 3.51 version and its various service packs. Below are the changes and new features introduced to the TCP/IP stack you'll find with NT Server 4.0.

Additional or changed TCP/IP registry parameters include:

- **ArpCacheLife**–Introduced on NT 3.51 with Service Pack (SP) 4
- **ArpTRSingleRoute**–Introduced on NT 3.51 with SP 5 and included with NT 4.0
- **DefaultTTL**–Updated on NT 4.0 release, the IP changed from 32 to 128
- **DontAddDefaultGateway**–Introduced in NT 4.0
- **MaxForwardBufferMemory**–Introduced in NT 3.51 SP 2
- **MaxForwardPending**–Introduced in NT 3.51 SP 2
- **MaxNumForwardPackets**–Introduced in NT 3.51 SP 2

- **EnableSecurityFilters**–Released in NT 4.0
- **RawIpAllowedProtocols**–Released in NT 4.0)
- **TcpAllowedPorts**–Released in NT 4.0
- **UdpAllowedPorts**–Released in NT 4.0
- **PPTPFiltering**–Released in NT 4.0
- **PPTPTcpMaxDataRetransmissions**–Released in NT 4.0
- **MaxUserPort**–Released in Windows NT 3.51 SP 5 and included with NT 4.0
- **TcpTimedWaitDelay**–Released in Windows NT 3.51 SP 5 and included with NT 4.0
- **PersistentRoutes**–This key was added as the fourth parameter in NT 3.51 SP 2

There was also a change in the **IgnorePushBitOnReceives** key of the AFD.SYS registry parameters, which was released in NT 3.51 SP 5 and included in NT 4.0.

Some other significant additions and changes released in NT 4.0 include:

- **NetBIOS** name resolution on multihomed computers, which is now better documented
- **DNS** (Domain Name Server) added
- **nslookup** DNS/resolver troubleshooting tool added
- **NetBT** Internet/DNS Enhancements added
- **MPR** (MultiProtocol Router) support, which was originally released with NT 3.51 on SP 2
- **TCP/IP printing** support enhancements added
- **PPTP** (Point-To-Point Tunneling Protocol) added

Don't forget that you can also install multiple protocols such as TCP/IP and NetBEUI with NT. This is often the optimal situation for certain networks when you need both protocols for some reason. For instance, in mid-1995 we were working with a development tool that relied on a network protocol (TCP/IP or NetBEUI) for its communications. There was supposed to be no difference in using either protocol, but the package would not perform one particular function using TCP/IP (the default). After many hours of work, we changed the protocol used by the package to NetBEUI, and it worked. This was an easy step, because both the server and the client were running NetBEUI and TCP/IP.

Hardware Notes

It used to be that 90 percent of the problems with a system were hardware related. That situation has improved drastically as our industry has matured, but there are still many issues that must be addressed.

Typical Hardware Problems

Sooner or later, your server will crash. It is almost inevitable, with the sophistication we have today, that eventually a system will go down. This is especially true of some clones or other name-brand systems that use cheaper parts such as memory, I/O cards, controllers, and disks.

Microsoft and other support groups can remotely diagnose your NT system if you have a modem. This is very important to remember, because not all Microsoft Product Support technicians offer this service. If you have a machine down and other solutions to the problem don't work, they can transfer the problem to another team that can remotely dial in and diagnose the system.

You should also keep a copy of tools like the NT Resource Kit, Microsoft TechNet, the messages database, and others around to use for research when an error occurs. You may also find that we have covered the error in this book, although that is not guaranteed.

Another good source of information is the TechNet CD from Microsoft. This gem ships each month and contains the Microsoft Knowledgebase and all kinds of useful information on NT and almost every other Microsoft product. Microsoft publishes several CDs with TechNet that include driver updates and patches for NT as well as many other Microsoft products. You can obtain TechNet directly from Microsoft for a nominal fee (as we go to press with the second edition of this book, the fee is currently $299 for a single user in the United States or $329 for international users) by calling 1-800-344-2121, Dept. 3092..

Preventing Hardware Nightmares

Many hardware problems can be prevented if you buy the right kind of hardware for your server and keep spare parts. We strongly recommend that all servers use hardware that is on the Microsoft NT compatibility list.

Compatible hardware ensures that at least the system has been tested with NT and that the support engineers for the component should have some NT knowledge. They may even know what the hardware-specific error codes mean. The sophistication of NT and current hardware trends means that choosing a vendor like Digital or Dell over some other manufacturers makes sense. We mention these two because we have had great success with the support staffs of both. We also like the new Compaq machines, but we have had disappointing luck with their support staffs on DOS and Windows systems, as well as NT.

NT is a very robust operating system and places a great deal of stress on its hardware components, which include all components in the system. Other operating systems, such as DOS, may run fine on a system using RAM of a different speed, while NT may fail on that same box. NT may also fail on systems that use inexpensive components that usually have marginal performance and quality standards. We have seen a cheap monochrome card cause a NetWare network to go crazy. The hardware used for a server must be of top quality, as NT puts as much or more strain on a server as does NetWare. Network clients running Windows for Workgroups or Windows 95 should also be first-class, to prevent your having to raise support requirements.

Another good tip for saving yourself some headaches is to keep spare parts around. When one of us managed a large NetWare LAN, he kept a spare server in running condition and several other spare parts. When a server died, he would move the disks (unless it was a disk problem) over to the spare system and fire it up. The network was usually back up in 10 to 15 minutes. Then he could take his time to debug the problem system. Hot-swap drives and storage systems make this solution even easier to accomplish than older systems using internal drives and cables.

General Hardware Notes

There are a number of things you can do to improve your hardware platforms and their reliability. Choosing the correct system from a reliable vendor is a head start. See Appendix A, "Listing of Products and Companies Mentioned," for more information on the vendors mentioned in this book.

STANDARD HARDWARE RECOMMENDATIONS

We strongly recommend that NT Server systems have the following minimum configuration:

- Pentium 133-MHz or faster processor for Intel systems; RISC systems should be based on a processor equivalent to a DEC Alpha.
- A multiprocessor machine with two or more CPUs. More process-intensive systems such as Application and Database servers will benefit more from multiple processors than a traditional File and Print server. NT Server supports up to 4 CPUs out of the box, while OEM systems can support a much greater number of CPUs such as 8 to 12.

DIGITAL EQUIPMENT CORPORATION

The newest Alpha systems from Digital (circa mid-1997) are the AlphaStation and AlphaServer line. These systems are powerhouses. They come with a built-in StorageWorks cabinet with hot-swappable drives.

Two of the most cost-effective systems are the AlphaServer 4000 and 8000 series. The 4000, characterized by the Digital Prioris models as a departmental server, are fault-tolerant servers, powered with fast 5/466 processor option, with VLM64 (Very Large Memory) power and symmetric multiprocessing (SMP). The 8000 models, characterized as enterprise servers, providing better-than-mainframe and supercomputer performance at a fraction of the cost. They come with the 437MHz Alpha processors, 64-bit RISC architecture, symmetric multiprocessing (SMP) and VLM64, as well as the ability to add up to 14 processors, 28GB of memory and 39TB of disk storage.

Digital also has a remote management package for most of its servers, called Remote Server Manager. This package works over standard phone lines and can even dial into a dead system. The client software runs on NT and can manage multiple systems at once.

COMPAQ PROSIGNIA AND PROLIANT

The first level of Compaq servers is the ProSignia 200s. For small to medium enterprises, they are affordable, dependable, and deliver real server features at a desktop price. They come with a 166 MHz Pentium processor and 16 MB of EDO RAM that can grow to 128 MB, providing capacity and performance to run databases and other demanding applications.

The top level, Compaq Proliant series, offers a powerful option for servers. They have very good hardware components, lots of horsepower due to the multiprocessor options, and many other options for peripherals. They are perfect workgroup servers, with breakthrough price/performance ratio, large storage capacity, and dual processing option.

Compaq systems have first-rate quality and support and are usually rated as fast as anything else.

The COMPAQ INSIGHT Manager links in to the low-level hardware of the Proliant server to provide diagnostics, configuration, firmware updates, and reboots. The system can be managed both locally and remotely.

The package is SNMP-compliant and supports NT and NT Server.

DELL AND HP

The other vendors we would consider using to run NT Server in a production environment are Dell and HP. Both vendors have a long track record of quality in both production and design. They also have good support groups that understand NT.

The 1997 servers, from both vendors promise to be both powerful and solid. Both vendors are proactive in providing management software for their products to ease the support crunch. Check with the vendors for information on specific models and features.

DISK DRIVES

The disk configuration of your server will have a big impact on performance and maintenance. A little extra money goes a long way here.

STORAGE ARRAYS AND OTHER CUSTOM DISK SYSTEMS • One of the most interesting things to come along for network managers is the new breed of storage systems coming from a number of vendors. Most of these systems support multiple disk drives, tape drives, and power supplies in one cabinet.

Typically, the cabinets are modular and enable you to plug the drives and devices in via a front panel. Most of these systems are hot-swappable, which means that you can pull a drive or power supply from the system and replace it without turning off the system.

Some of these systems have also simplified the problem of installing SCSI devices and trying to get the correct match of device numbers for your system. Simply plug the drives into the storage cabinet, and it sets the correct SCSI number. In reality, the SCSI number is set for the cabinet slot and passed to the drive.

HARDWARE RAID SOLUTIONS • RAID systems implemented in hardware provide the best performance. Hardware RAID systems off-load NT from managing the RAID system, removing any overhead associated with managing RAID from the operating system. NT sees the entire RAID volume as one volume, regardless of the number of disks.

Another benefit of hardware solutions is the hot-swap capability provided by most top-line systems. Because hot-swap systems allow you to remove or insert a drive in the array without stopping the system, you may never need to shut down your system to swap a disk if you keep an extra drive on hand!

Hardware RAID systems use the controller to handle creation and regeneration of the RAID methodology. Hardware implementations are normally the preferred method of implementing RAID, because the hardware handles control of the entire RAID device.

Some hardware implementations can mix two or more levels of RAID at the same time. For instance, some systems can combine both 0 (striping) and 1 (mirroring) to obtain maximum performance and reliability.

Performance and functionality can vary greatly with RAID systems from different vendors. For instance, as shown in Figure 3.7, one of the Digital Equipment storage works controllers has three channels on the controller. This enables you to have three separate RAID arrays from this one controller, or to spread the three channels across one RAID array. Imagine a RAID system with eight disks, with a separate channel for each with three disks except the last two. This is high-performance RAID at its best.

SCSI DEVICES

Small Computer Systems Interface (SCSI) devices have been around for many years and have proven to be some of the most reliable disk architectures available. SCSI devices are also very flexible; many different drives work with a variety of manufacturers' controllers, and vice versa. SCSI devices are ideal for NT because of their robust architecture and the common availability

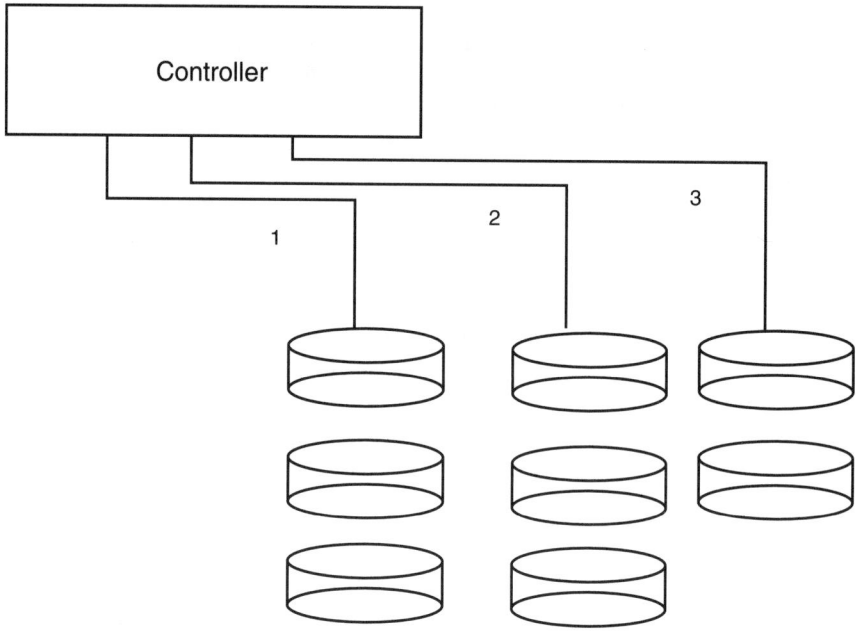

FIGURE 3.7 The controller card is an EISA StorageWorks card produced by Digital Equipment Corporation.

of different drives and controllers. SCSI drives in particular are also available in many different sizes ranging from less than 100MB to 4GB or greater. NT uses the disk drives in a much more aggressive manner than DOS and many other systems, placing much more stress on the entire disk system. NT transfers larger blocks of data and uses faster disk transfer modes than DOS.

CABLING • SCSI cables vary in quality from supplier to supplier. The SCSI-II standard defines the following characteristics for cables:

- 100% shielded round cables with 25 twisted pairs of wires
- impedance between 90 and 110 ohms for each pair
- wire gauge of 26 or 28

Systems with only one or two devices may work fine with a cable that does not meet these specifications, but when another drive is added, the devices fail. You may also have SCSI devices that worked fine with another operating system and no longer work with NT. Either of these situations can be caused by an improper cable.

The following vendors make SCSI cables available to end users:

- **Digital Equipment Corporation**–800-DIGITAL
- **Amphenol Interconnect Products (better known as AMP)–** 607-786-4221

■ **Icontec**–408-945-7766
■ **Black Box**–412-746-5500

Also contact your system vendor.

The Microsoft Technet CD lists the following publications for those of you who would like to explore SCSI more fully:

■ Title: *Building Fast SCSI Subsystems*
  Available from: Technology Focus
  Distributed Processing Technology
  140 Candace Drive
  Maitland, FL 32571
  Phone: 407-830-5522
■ Title: The SCSI Bench Reference (copyright 1989)
  Author: Jeffrey D. Stai
  Available from: ENDL Publications
  14426 Black Walnut Court
  Saratoga, CA 95070
  Phone: 408-867-6642
■ Title: SCSI: Understanding the Small Computer System Interface
  Author: John B. Lohmeyer (Chairman, X3T9.2) NCR Corporation
  Publisher: Prentice-Hall, New Jersey
  ISBN: 0-1 3.796855-8
■ Title: Fast Track to SCSI: A Product Guide (copyright 1991)
  Author: Fujitsu Microelectronics, Inc.
  Publisher: Prentice-Hall, New Jersey
  ISBN: 0-1 3.307018-2

CONNECTING SCSI DEVICES • SCSI devices that are not part of a storage system are typically connected on a daisy-chain cable. The cable runs from the SCSI controller to each device, continuing on to the next device. Each SCSI controller supports up to seven devices.

SCSI devices use a terminator to prevent signal reflections. Proper use of terminators ensures faster and more reliable operation from your system. A SCSI system requires that only the devices on the ends of the SCSI bus have terminators. Terminators come in several types. External terminators look like an external SCSI cable connector with no cable attached. They are used on external SCSI devices that have two cable ports. The terminator goes on the unused port when the device is the last one on the SCSI bus.

Internal terminators usually consist of two or three resistor SIPs (single in-line packages) that look like small circuit boards with connectors along the side. Internal terminators are normally located on or at the end of the circuit board that attaches to the device. Switched or jumped terminators use a switch or jumper setting to enable or disable the termination.

Automatic termination is found on many of the new disk subsystems that are sold by different vendors. For instance, the Digital StorageWorks system can automatically set the correct termination for the bus.

SCSI devices each have a unique ID for all devices on the system. The ID numbers range from 0 to 6. Internal SCSI devices require you to set the SCSI ID of the device manually. The difficulty of performing this task varies with your device. Automatic configuration is found on many of the new disk subsystems. For instance, the Digital StorageWorks system can automatically set the correct SCSI ID for a drive when it is plugged into the subsystem. You can actually move devices around in the subsystem, and their ID will change with the slot they are plugged into. You should consult your device documentation for instructions on setting the ID for the device.

 Do not configure your CD-ROM with a SCSI ID of 0 or 1. Doing so may cause problems with NT and its ability to detect the CD-ROM drive, because ID 0 and 1 are normally used for hard disks.

SERIAL COMMUNICATIONS

NT supports many different types of serial interfaces ranging from the standard COM1 and COM2 capabilities of most PCs to add-in boards that have powerful processors and provide a number of enhancements for your serial communications. Up to 256 serial ports are supported by NT.

The Control Panel Ports applet is normally used for configuring serial port parameters. This applet can be used for ports from 3 through 256 but not for ports 1 and 2. If you wish to change the IRQ, we/O Address, COM port number, and FIFO-enabled parameters, you must use REGEDT32.EXE.

CHANGING HARDWARE

When you change the hardware configuration, you may need to reconfigure NT.

ADDING A CD-ROM DRIVE • When you add a CD-ROM drive to a system running NT, you must make sure that the SCSICDRM service is set to start automatically when NT starts. This procedure forces it to start when the system starts.

Automatically Starting the SCSICDRM Service:

1. Run Control Panel.
2. Select the Services applet.
3. Select the SCSICDRM service.

> 4. Click Startup.
>
> 5. Check the Automatic button.
>
> 6. Click the System Account button.

ADDING A VIDEO DISPLAY • Video cards are simple to install if you follow a few basic steps. If you don't, you will have to choose a VGA boot option and reset the card. It is much simpler to do it right from the start.

Installing a New Video Card:

1. Choose the Display option in Control Panel and configure the system for the new card.

2. Shut down the system.

3. Install the new card.

4. Restart the system.

If the system fails to start, select the VGA boot option to allow the system to restart. Change the settings with the Display/Settings option in Control Panel and check it out with the Test button. You must always use the Test button when you make a video change to ensure that the change is correct, or Control Panel will not let you make the change. Incorrect changes can also damage your monitor, so proceed with caution when you make changes to refresh rates or things other than resolution.

HARDWARE ISSUES ON PERFORMANCE

Some Intel systems may experience a performance loss when you upgrade from 8 to 16MB of RAM. This is found primarily on early 90s systems. This loss could be because the hardware cache is specifically designed for a certain amount of memory and is not capable of managing larger amounts. If this occurs, try disabling the hardware cache. Be sure to measure the performance before and after the changes using Performance Monitor or another tool. You should also check with your hardware manufacturer for more information on improving performance and possibly upgrading the cache.

Technical Support for Your System

The best plans and preparations sometimes go awry and require that you use some type of technical support. This support may be in the form of a phone call or access to an information source such as CompuServe, the Internet, or the Microsoft Network. There are a variety of other sources that you may choose from. Table 3.13 lists several sources and the access method for each source.

TABLE 3.12   Sources of NT Technical Support

Source	Description	Access/Contact
Microsoft Web Site	The definitive site for NT information. Also visit www.microsoft.com/NT	www.microsoft.com
Microsoft Fast Tips	Fast tips over phone—recorded information	206-635-7245.
CompuServe	On-line service	GO WINNT or GO MSKB. Lots of other useful sources and support areas. (800) 848-8199 for introductory kit.
Microsoft Down Load Service	BBS with latest patches and stuff from Microsoft	206-936-6735 (1200,2400,9600, no parity, 8 data bits , 1 stop bit). Also available on CompuServe (GO MSL), Internet ftp.microsoft.com with anonymous log-in.
Internet	The Information SuperHighway.	Lots of stuff related to NT and NT net works works. Look under BUSSYS on ftp.microsoft.com. Microsoft also supports a World Web server: www.microsoft.com.
Microsoft Solution providers	Third-party vendors with direct links to Microsoft. Provide support, training, consulting, and development.	Computer Technologies Inc. 910-547-1407 ask for Ken Spencer. Microsoft can provide names of other solution providers at 800-227-4679 and on the TechNet CD. All Solution Providers charge for support services.
Microsoft	Microsoft Technical Support	206-635-7022 @ $195 per call on your credit card. A faxback service is also available. Check the MS documentation for the current number or call one of the numbers above. Annual support plans are also available from MS or Solution Providers. Microsoft no longer supports 900 numbers for Developers and NT support.

TABLE 3.12	Sources of NT Technical Support (Continued)	
Source	**Description**	**Access/Contact**
Technet	Monthly CD from Microsoft	Contact Microsoft.
Developers Network	Quarterly CD for developers	Contact Microsoft.
NT Resource Kit	Books and CD packed with useful stuff and utilities	Order from your NT vendor.

Conclusion

This chapter covered many of the tools and issues that you will face when managing NT systems on a day-to-day basis. It provided an overview of the system management tools that come with NT and the NT Resource Kits, and introduced you to some of the general management issues you might run into.

Some of the tips and techniques in this chapter are things we learned from beating our heads against the wall. For instance, why do we cover NT's DOS language here? Its important to use when automating management tasks on NT. Why the long discussion on disk systems? The disks are the foundation of your NT system and must be correctly configured for your system to perform correctly. Other tips like volume label names are included to help you create an easily manageable configuration.

Chapter 4 picks up on the network and introduces network management with NT. We take a look at protocol issues such as TCP/IP, NT management issues for the network, and Remote Access Services (RAS). There are lots of other things that you can do in a network environment that will make your life much easier. The hardware and management topics that we discussed in this chapter are vitally important to network management. Remember the analogy of a chain? One weak component, and your entire network comes down!

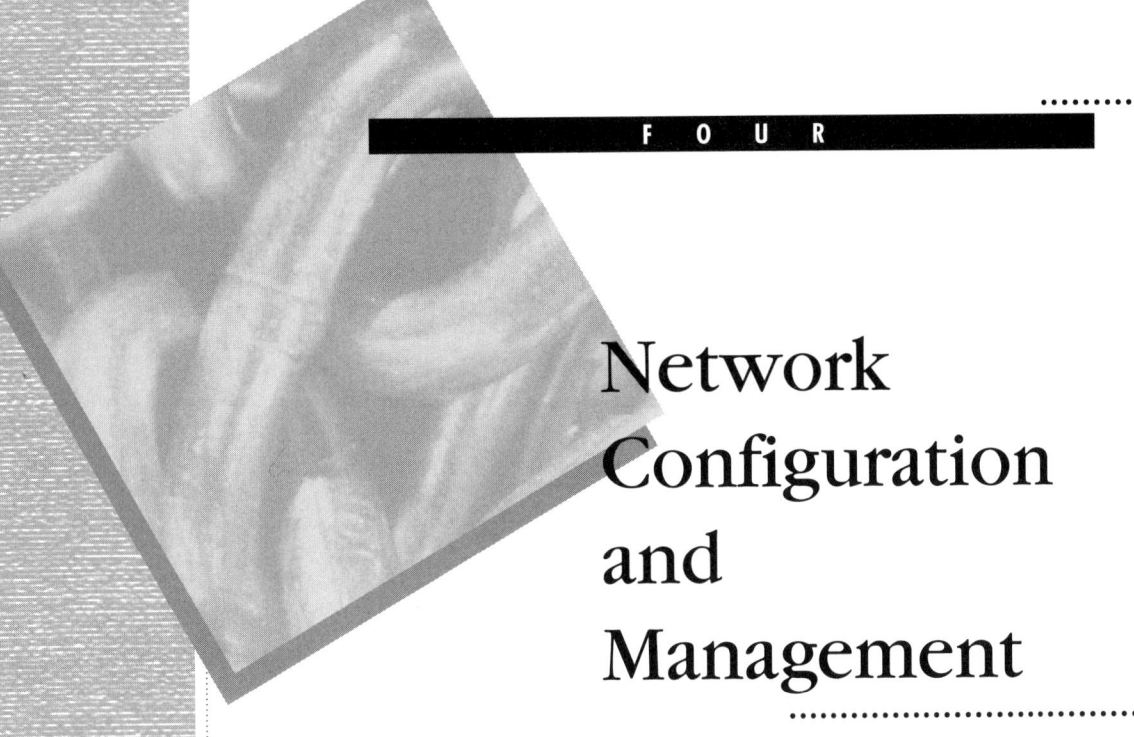

Network Configuration and Management

NT and the various client operating systems and utilities provide many of the tools we need to manage our systems from day to day and to solve problems when they occur. Many problems can be solved by proper planning and implementation on the front end, which turns out to be the best approach almost every time. This chapter focuses on some of the typical tasks, tools, and techniques you can use to both plan and manage your network.

Scenario 4.1:

Network management takes on many different forms. Today it's printer problems, while tomorrow it's a problem with Microsoft Office on someone's system. Maybe it appears to be a Microsoft Office problem, but it's really a network problem. How do you determine the source of the problem and fix it?

Scenario 4.2:

You start installing NT Server and the installation process asks for a Domain name. Any old name will suffice—right? Not necessarily. Same thing occurs with computer names. Why does it matter what you name a system? How many support calls has your staff fielded in which users asked, "Is that marketing file on the system called Snoopy, or is it on Spock?"

The first thing you must consider is that a network should not be viewed as a network with servers and clients but as a single system or entity. We like to refer to a network as "the system" and view it as a single entity made up of modular components such as servers, clients, bridges, routers, and network cards.

If you view the entire network as a system, you develop a managerial mind-set that enables you to understand fully the available power. This approach also provides us with a good understanding of the different components and how they fit together, because we must develop this knowledge in order to manage the system.

Administration Tools

NT has several utilities that are useful for managing various components of a network. At one time or another in this book each of these tools is discussed as it relates to certain tasks. This chapter mentions them for completeness and discusses several things that you should consider about the tools from a management perspective.

There is one thing to keep in mind about almost all NT management tools: They can be used to remotely manage other servers and/or clients. Remote management can make the manager's life much easier. Always look on the left-most menu in each application for the Connect or Select Computer or Domain option. Many of the command-line utilities with the NT Resource Kit also support remote management.

Network Client Administrator

The Network Client Administrator is used to install and update client workstation components (such as network drivers and components like the redirector). Check the client directory on the NT Server CD and review the readme files to determine which updates are on your CD. Remember that, based on the date you purchase NT Server, you may get additional updated components and clients from the current CD. With the Network Client Administrator, you can build installation disks, copy client network administration tools, and view Remoteboot Client information.

DHCP Manager

DHCP Manager is used to manage the DHCP system within NT Server. It is used to initialize the DHCP system and for management once the system is in use. DHCP fortunately does not require very much in the way of management if it is set up correctly.

WINS Manager

WINS Manager manages the Windows Internet Naming System for NT Server 3.51. WINS Manager is similar to DHCP manager in that it is used both to configure the WINS system and to manage the system. WINS may be used on an ongoing basis·to add and manage static TCP/IP nodes that do not participate in DHCP.

TELNET AND TERMINAL

What are Telnet and Terminal doing in a network management section? They are satisfactory tools for managing some TCP/IP devices such as network print servers and hubs. Many of these devices have a character mode setup feature that is accessible via the Telnet service over TCP/IP. Telnet and Terminal are great choices because they are included with NT.

When a client uses the Telnet utility to connect to port 135 of a computer running NT Server 3.51 and 4.0, and then types more than 10 random characters and disconnects, the server CPU usage jumps to 100 percent and does not come back down until the server is restarted.

You should be aware of this, as it points to a problem with the remote procedure call (RPC) components in Windows NT. Fortunately, Microsoft was quick to fix the problem by creating a hotfix for it. You can download the fix for NT 3.51 from the FTP site at the following URL:

```
ftp://ftp.microsoft.com/bussys/winnt/winnt-
public/fixes/usa/NT351/hotfixes-postSP5/rpc-fix
```

For NT 4.0, you can download the fix from the following URL:

```
ftp://ftp.microsoft.com/bussys/winnt/winnt-
public/fixes/usa/NT40/hotfixes-postSP2/rpc-fix
```

NETWORK TOPOLOGIES SUPPORTED

NT supports different types of network architectures for connecting your NT system to the network. The most popular options by far are Ethernet and Token Ring. We do not intend to try to solve the war between all the fans of either; instead, we cover how they play with NT Server environments. Both work with NT Server, depending upon the environment that you are using. We personally prefer Ethernet because of the diversity and ease of use it offers. Ethernet is generally more cost effective than Token Ring, especially with the explosion at the low end of the component market in recent years.

Protocols and Related Matters

NT supports several major protocols out of the box: TCP/IP, NWLINK IPX/SPX, DLC, and NetBEUI. IPX/SPX is the default protocol installed by NT. Your choice of protocol depends upon your background and what you plan to accomplish with your network. Most users with a UNIX or minicomputer background will probably choose TCP/IP. New network managers will probably opt for NetBEUI, because it installs with virtually no interaction with the system, while users with NetWare networks will use IPX/SPX.

NetBEUI is useful for LANs with from 1 to 200 workstations that don't need to communicate over a Wide Area Network (WAN). The new TCP/IP drivers for both Windows and Windows NT are about as fast as NetBEUI and can be used in larger systems and over a WAN. TCP/IP requires more expert knowledge of the protocol, and the LAN but provides many benefits over the other protocols because of its ability to connect to the Internet, to provide SNMP (Simple Network Management Protocol) support for NT and other SNMP-compliant systems, and to support the wide availability of tools and programming tool kits.

If you are planning on using your NT system in a WAN, you should choose TCP/IP or another protocol that is routable. NetBEUI cannot be routed and is not useful for a WAN. NT 5.0 and many applications will rely heavily on TCP/IP, making it the protocol of choice. Other protocols, such as DECnet, can be used on NT and are routable, which makes them valuable on a WAN. The problem with choosing a protocol is making sure that the protocol is usable by all systems on your network that need access over the LAN or WAN.

Let's look at a network that has 20 Windows for Workgroups workstations and an NT Server. This LAN must communicate with another LAN that consists of 150 Windows for Workgroups, an NT Server, and a VAX. If you choose to run DECnet on the local NT Server, you will be able to communicate with the VAX over the WAN, but the Windows for Workgroups workstations will not be able to communicate over the WAN. NT supports multiple simultaneous protocols that allow the NT systems to communicate over both NetBEUI (for the LAN Windows for Workgroups workstations) and DECnet (for the WAN access to the VAX).

Another option is to run TCP/IP on both the NT Server and all other systems on both sides of the WAN. This allows all workstations to communicate over the WAN as well as the LAN. Installing TCP/IP in this manner can be effective but may also raise the cost of your systems. TCP/IP comes with NT, and you have a free TCP/IP driver for Windows for Workgroups on the NT Server CD, but you usually must pay for TCP/IP on systems like VMS. You must carefully choose a protocol when your system will be part of a larger system or when there is potential for your system to grow beyond a LAN.

You also need a protocol such as IPX/SPX or DECnet if your NT Server must participate in a NetWare or other network that uses only a particular protocol.

It is beyond the scope of this book to present an exhaustive discussion of which protocol to use, but it is our goal to emphasize that you should choose with care. While choosing wrong is a minor problem, its consequences are multiplied greatly when you must update a vast number of workstations and servers after they have been running only a few months.

NetBEUI

NetBIOS Extended User Interface (NetBEUI) is a transport protocol used by Microsoft and other networks. NetBEUI is small and fast, making it ideal for small networks. It is also easy to configure because it requires only a computer name. NetBEUI is also self-tuning, which makes it ideal for small networks without a support staff.

Table 4.5 in the "Choosing a Protocol" section later in this chapter provides a quick list showing which protocol to use when.

NBF

NetBEUI Frame (NBF) is the protocol driver used by NT to implement NetBEUI. NBF provides support for other systems running NetBIOS or NetBEUI. For instance, Windows for Workgroups works with NT systems using the NetBEUI protocol.

The biggest problem with NBF and any other version of NetBIOS is its inability to be routed. This means that you can't use NBF across a WAN, as noted earlier.

This section on NetBEUI is much shorter than the section on TCP/IP, because NBF is very easy to set up. It is automatic when you install NT. You simply give your system a unique computer name, and voilà, your system is part of the network. TCP/IP and other protocols such as DECnet are much more difficult, because you must manage a node address and node name for each workstation.

TCP/IP

NT includes the TCP/IP protocol and a number of TCP/IP utilities. NT also supports SNMP, which allows an NT system to participate in an SNMP management system. This feature is very important because, with SNMP, you can monitor NT systems along with hardware devices such as routers and bridges using the same tools. NT also supports other standards or pseudo-standards such as the Dynamic Host Configuration Protocol (DHCP) and the Windows Internet Name Service (WINS), both of which automate most of the management of TCP/IP (more on this later in this chapter). Other features such as FTP (File Transfer Protocol) are also included in the standard NT kit. NT also includes the TCP/IP stack for Windows for Workgroups. TCP/IP is not a standard but is guided by approved RFCs (Request For Comments) that define the many different elements of the protocol and its utilities.

TCP/IP is a much more complex protocol than NetBEUI, but it is also more powerful. NT includes a number of tools that may actually make it easier for you to manage your system. All the standard NT utilities work over

TCP/IP as well as NetBEUI. The TCP/IP-specific utilities allow you to run a number of connection-type tests over the network as well as to perform traditional TCP/IP services over the network.

This book is not intended to be a tome on TCP/IP, so we refer you to other sources of information for a more in-depth discussion of TCP/IP. The Windows NT Resource Guide from the NT Resource Kit has an excellent section on TCP/IP. The NT documentation also has a good description of TCP/IP, terms, concepts, and overall operations. Bookstores like Borders also carry many TCP/IP titles.

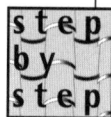

> **Successfully Installing TCP/IP on NT 4.0:**
>
> 1. Open the Network Control application by either right-clicking the Network Neighborhood icon and selecting Properties, or clicking the Start button, select Settings, Control Panel, then double-clicking on the Network icon.
> 2. In the Network settings, click the Adapters tab. You should have at least one Network Adapter installed. To add a Network Adapter, click Add, and from the adapter list select MS Loopback Adapter. This is a software-only driver. You do not need an actual network adapter for this to work.
> 3. Insert the NT 4.0 CD in the drive, and click OK.
> 4. Select the default for Frame Type. Then, if you are prompted, provide the CD drive letter and the appropriate path.
> 5. Select the Protocols tab, click Add, and select TCP/IP Protocol.
> 6. Insert the NT 4.0 CD in the drive, and click OK. Then, if you are prompted, enter the proper path as above. Add the protocol and click OK.
> 7. Setup will go through a number of binding processes, and eventually will prompt you for TCP/IP configuration information. If your machine is connected to a network, you should obtain TCP/IP configuration information from your System Administrator (that is, you should use DHCP, a TCP/IP address, and so forth).
> 8. Click the DNS tab, and make sure the Host Name matches your Computer Name.
> 9. Reboot when you are prompted to do so.

The TCP/IP protocol is composed of two major parts:

- TCP is the Transmission Control Protocol, which is the high-level part of TCP/IP.
- IP is the Internet Protocol and is the low-level part that actually delivers the network packets.

TCP/IP NODE ADDRESSES

Now for the fun part! Remember when we said that TCP/IP was more complex than NetBEUI? Welcome to the concept of IP addressing. Every node (host in TCP/IP parlance) on your network must have a unique IP address. Hosts include every device that attaches to the network and uses TCP/IP. Examples of different types of hosts are computers (both clients and servers), routers, gateways, 10Base T hubs, and network print servers that use TCP/IP.

If your network plugs into the Internet, it must be assigned a unique network address from the Defense Data Network—Network Information Center (DDN—NIC) or an Internet access provider. It is not a bad idea to obtain a unique network number anytime you build a new network to ensure that your network is unique.

The IP address is a long string (32 bits) of numbers separated by periods. The IP address consists of three parts: a class descriptor, a network ID, and a host ID. The network ID uniquely identifies the network class, the unique network ID, and a particular host (workstation or server). Let's look at a sample IP address:

145.201.102.33

IP addresses are currently broken into three different classes. Each class describes the number of possible addresses by specifying a range for the class number. For instance, class A starts with 1 and goes through 126. In addition to determining a range for the first number of IP addresses, the class defines the default subnet mask. Table 4.1 describes these basic elements of the current three classes.

A typical class A IP network might have the first part of its address as 123. Notice that in the world of valid IP addresses there are only 126 class A networks. A typical class B address might be **133.128**. IP addresses are handed out by the sanctioning body of the IP world for those who want to participate in the Internet. The easiest way to obtain a block of addresses is to work with your Internet provider.

If your network is not going to be part of the Internet, you can pick any address range you want as long as the subnet mask you use matches the range from the table. For instance, a network address of **201.123.3.1** cannot have a subnet mask of **255.255.0.0** because our IP address in this example can be used only on a class C network. Take care in choosing your network numbers because you can start out easily and end up with a mess. For instance, let's say that you start with an address range of **201.123.3.x** for your first systems. if you choose this range you can't have more than 254 hosts on a given subnet, because 201 is a class C network, and can't use a subnet mask other than **255.255.255.0**. If you change the network range to **132.x.x.x**, you can use different subnet masks to split up your network.

TABLE 4.1	IP Address Classes	
Class Descriptor	**Address Range**	**Default Subnet Mask**
A	1–126	255.0.0.0
B	128–191	255.255.0.0
C	192–223	255.255.255.0

Subnets can be useful for splitting up a network into smaller logical networks. Typically, all nodes physically connected on a LAN should have the same network and subnet ID. The exception to this occurs when you intentionally use subnet masks to subdivide your network and manage the traffic.

Our example assumes that the subnet mask for this network is **255.255.0.0**. The subnet mask is used to break the IP address into its network and host ID. The subnet mask works by converting the subnet mask to binary (ouch!) and using it with the full IP address to determine which parts to use for the network and which to use for the host. The actual operation performs a bitwise AND with the IP address, and the subnet mask splits out the host and network components.

Notice from Table 4.1 that the default subnet masks always use 255 in the first one, two, or three positions of the mask. This cleanly breaks the network and host portions of the IP address into two components separated at one of the decimal points. There is no need for any binary mess here.

If you wish to delve beyond the normal subnet masks (**255.255.255.0** and the like), the Microsoft Technet CD has a good description of the process in article PSS ID Number: Q96683, title: Subnet Masks in TCP/IP.

The values 0 and 255 are used for broadcast purposes by all nodes and must not be used for a any part of a host IP address.

The NT documentation has reasonably good coverage of TCP/IP concepts and addressing. We suggest reading this section of the documentation thoroughly.

IP ROUTERS AND GATEWAYS

IP gateways or IP routers are used to connect multiple subnets, which are connected to an internet. Notice the lowercase *i* for *internet* this time? Any time multiple subnets are connected, they constitute an internet. The IP gateway (we use the term *gateway* generically to indicate either a router or gateway in this TCP/IP section) handles all packets that move from one subnet to another.

Every router or gateway must have an IP address. If it has more than one channel (such as two WAN ports), then each channel must have its own address.

IP routers can be devices that perform only routing services, or they may be more general-purpose systems that have routing capabilities such as

NT or UNIX systems. NT can be used as a router if you install two or more network cards that create subnets and use NT as a router between the two subnets. When NT is configured with more than one network adapter, each adapter that will use TCP/IP must have its own IP address.

HOW TCP/IP MANAGEMENT WORKS WITH NT

NT 3.5's most notable improvement besides performance improvements centers around TCP/IP. TCP/IP and its various utilities and components have continued to evolve with NT 4. Microsoft has developed technology that is compliant with the RFC for the DHCP. This specification calls for management tools that handle both the client and server administration of TCP/IP. The new tools provide for easy administration of the entire process when clients that are compliant with DHCP are used on an NT network. Windows for Workgroups 3.11 clients are compliant with DHCP when the new TCP/IP stack that Microsoft has included with NT Server 3.51 is used.

Microsoft has also developed a service called the Windows Internet Name Service. WINS maintains an Access database of TCP/IP addresses and computer names on the WINS server. WINS can run on any NT server on the network and also supports backup WINS servers. WINS is an invaluable service because it provides name resolution for TCP/IP hosts. Name resolution occurs when a request is made to access a TCP/IP host using its name instead of the TCP/IP address. For instance, entering **PING MySystem** (see the section entitled "Verifying Connections with PING" later in this chapter for more information on using PING) triggers a WINS name resolution to provide the TCP/IP address for MySystem. See the later section entitled "WINS" for more information on WINS.

The DHCP and WINS specifications are implemented by a number of tools that are still evolving from different vendors. What is important about these tools is the functionality they provide. A system manager can use the management tools to specify the parameters for the network. These parameters include the allowable IP address range, the network subnet number, and other global parameters that affect the entire network. You can also specify excluded addresses that are used by routers or other devices. Another feature is used to specify static address numbers for non-DHCP workstations and servers.

DHCP and WINS automate almost the entire TCP/IP management process for administrators. Each DHCP client system checks with the DHCP server each time the system boots. If the system does not have a valid TCP/IP address, it requests one from the DHCP server. The DHCP server sends down a potential set of configurations that works for the client. The client chooses one set and the DHCP server then provides all the configuration information for the client. A DHCP client also communicates with a DHCP server from time to time when it needs an updated lease on its address.

When the client obtains the IP address, it actually gets a lease for the address from the DHCP server. This lease runs for the time specified by the system administrator on the DHCP server. Just as a normal lease on a house or car, the IP address lease must be renewed on a set schedule. The lease schedule is set by the administrator and is suggested to vary according to the dynamics of your network. Setting the lease renewal time to less than a week means that you can make drastic changes to your network structure, reboot all the machines, and the network will come back up. The only problem with this approach to a very short lease is that the DHCP server must be up just about every time a client boots. A backup DHCP server is a necessity here. If your network configuration is less dynamic and does not have computers moving around from segment to segment, you can get by with a longer lease time, such as 30 days. Long leases of a month or longer work well in this type of network in which changes are rare.

In planning your DHCP strategy, also consider notebooks and laptops that connect to the network and how many users you have per segment. Lots of notebooks and laptops indicate that a shorter lease should be used. Short lease times are also useful when a network segment has a high percentage of users to IP addresses. For instance, if you have 254 available addresses and 240 active users, then use a short lease time. For the same network, 40 active users could get by with a long lease time because the demand for the IP addresses is low.

If you have a router implementing the DHCP/BOOTP relay agent (as specified by RFC 1542), you can have it used for routing traffic between your DHCP server and clients located on different subnets. The relay agent on your router will forward requests from your DHCP clients to your remote DHCP server and subsequently relay the DHCP server responses back to the DHCP clients. Figure 4.1 shows an example of a routed network with DHCP server and DHCP clients.

With NT Server 4.0, you have Multi-Protocol Router (MPR), which is included with the package. MPR is a routing software that can be configured on a general-purpose computer to provide DHCP/BOOTP relay agent support. MPR includes:

- BOOTP relay agent for DHCP
- Routing Information Protocol (RIP) for TCP/IP
- Routing Information Protocol for IPX

warning   NT does not support BOOTP. Therefore, you find no problems in using Microsoft DHCP server on the same network with clients and servers running BOOTP. NT's DHCP servers will ignore any BOOTP client packets received from the network. You must make sure, however, that the BOOTP server and the DHCP server do not manage leases for the same IP addresses.

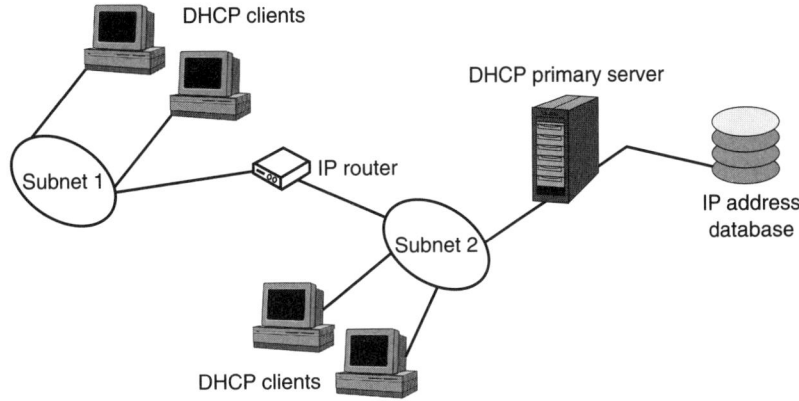

FIGURE 4.1 Using Automatic TCP/IP Configuration with DHCP for setting up TCP/IP on NT 4.0.

By supplying the IP address with a lease, the DHCP server can actually give the same IP number to another system. For instance, a system gets turned off for a week while the user is on vacation. During the same time, 10 new systems are added to the network. It's very possible that the lease expires on the system that is off for a week, thereby freeing the address for use by one of the new machines. Now one of the new machines has the address that the machine that is off had when it was turned off. What happens when the machine that was turned off for a week comes back up? The machine asks the DHCP server if the IP address is OK, receives a reply that it is not, and is then supplied with a new IP address. The WINS server is notified, and the system continues its boot process without any problems. This is a simplified version of what happens during the boot process but basically explains the functionality that DHCP and WINS provide. The two services work together to maintain the address list (of TCP/IP address and computer name) on the WINS server.

NT 3.51 also had TCP/IP services enhanced to include a new feature that allows a host to find out the computer name (host name) that matches a TCP/IP address, regardless of whether DHCP is being used to dynamically assign TCP/IP addresses or not.

The Windows Sockets programs that comes with NT 3.51 uses the GetHostByAddr() call to resolve a TCP/IP address to a computer name by having it attempting to look up the computer name by contacting a domain name server (DNS), if one is configured. If the DNS lookup does not return a host name, then GetHostByAddr() attempts to resolve the TCP/IP address to a computer name by using a NetBIOS Node Status Request (as defined in RFC1001/1002).

NAME RESOLUTION

Name resolution denotes what happens when one system tries to access a service or send information to another system on the network using the target system's name. The original method for talking to another system was to use only the TCP/IP address to target the other system. For instance, a user could use the PING command to test for the existence of another system by entering the following command to find out if Joe's system was alive and well:

```
PING 198.84.8.10
```

This example tries to determine if the system with address 198.84.8.10 is actually running on the network. This method was fine when there were two or three systems and you had memorized the addresses. What happens when there are hundreds or thousands or more hosts on the network, and all you know is the system's name? This dilemma long ago led to the concept of name resolution. For example, you want to access the other system by name and have your system automatically determine and use the TCP/IP address. Using some type of name resolution, you should be able to enter the following PING command if Joe's computer is known by the name JOEMKTG:

```
PING JOEMKTG
```

This command works if your system can successfully determine the address for JOEMKTG and reach the other system. How does this name resolution happen? NT and most other Microsoft systems support several different methods of name resolution. Each of these methods is fully described in the Windows NT Networking Guide in the NT Resource Kit, Chapter 12. The following list provides a brief overview of each method used by NT:

- **Windows Internet Name Service**—The WINS server maintains a list of the hosts TCP/IP addresses on the network and the respective name for each host. Whenever a request is made for a host from a WINS-compliant client, the WINS server supplies the IP address for the server. WINS provides the preferred method for network hosts (clients, servers, and other devices) to obtain the address of another system. It is typically faster and more reliable than other methods of address resolution. See "WINS," later in this chapter, for more information on WINS. The method used by WINS is also known as p-node name resolution and is defined in RFC 1001/1002. WINS provides support for NetBIOS over TCP/IP (NBT) systems.

- **Broadcast Name Resolution**—Broadcast name resolution requires each host to broadcast its name over the network for resolution. All systems on the network area targeted by the host must interact to challenge duplicate name registrations. Each system must also respond to a name query for its registered name. Broadcast name resolution is defined in RFC 1001/1002 as b-node.

■ **Domain Name System (DNS)**–DNS is a name resolution system that is similar to WINS. DNS is available on many different systems including UNIX, VMS, and NT (in the NT Resource Kit). DNS provides support for NetBIOS over TCP/IP (NBT) and Windows Sockets applications. DNS traditionally maps domain names to TCP/IP addresses. Many systems use the Windows for Workgroups or NT computer name for the host part of the domain name. DNS also does not provide automatic name registration as WINS does for DHCP systems.

■ **HOSTS and LMHOSTS files**–HOSTS files provide support for name resolution requests using the domain name used by Windows Sockets applications. LMHOSTS provides support for NetBIOS over TCP/IP (NBT) systems. Both HOSTS and LMHOSTS files are simple text files that map TCP/IP addresses to computer names, as described in the next section.

■ **Combination Modes**–NetBIOS over TCP/IP (NBT) is defined in RFC 1001 and 1002. NBT provides support for several of the preceding methods (b-node and p-node). NBT also has two combination modes that use more than one method of name resolution:

  m-node uses b-node first and then, if name resolution fails, p-node.
  h-node uses p-node first and then, if name resolution fails, b-node.

■ NT defaults to h-node name resolution when WINS servers are specified (see "WINS"); b-node name resolution is the default mode if there are no WINS servers specified. You can enable DNS and LMHOSTS lookups using the Network applet in Control Panel and configuring the TCP/IP protocol.

TCP/IP NAME RESOLUTION AND THE HOSTS FILES

TCP/IP has traditionally used a HOSTS file to define the name and TCP/IP address of each host on the network. This file is a simple ASCII file that lists both the address and the name for each host. We consider the HOSTS file simple until it's time to maintain one with names and addresses for every host on the network; then the HOSTS file becomes a nightmare.

Windows Sockets applications on a Microsoft network uses the HOSTS file for name resolution. A HOSTS file is roughly equivalent to having a DNS server on the network. When a system using a HOSTS file must resolve a TCP/IP name request, it looks up the name in the HOSTS file and determines the corresponding TCP/IP address. Other software such as terminal emulators or any TCP/IP application may also use the HOSTS file to look up the TCP/IP addresses of target systems.

You may want to consider augmenting WINS with a HOSTS file to provide these types of lookups (see "WINS"). If you have legacy hosts (such as a VMS or UNIX system) that do not use DHCP or any other kind of host for which you must supply addresses, it makes sense to maintain the addresses in a central HOSTS file. This file can be maintained with the addition of each static system (this does not happen often) and can be used to load the addressees for WINS, because WINS can import static addresses from a HOSTS file.

Both NT 4.0 and 3.51 provide name resolution services for both NetBIOS computer names and Domain Name System (DNS) host names on TCP/IP networks. The LMHOSTS file is one method of name resolution for NetBIOS name resolution for TCP/IP networks. The other NetBIOS over TCP/IP (NetBT) name resolution methods that are used, depending on the computer's configuration, are:

- NetBIOS name cache
- IP subnet broadcasts
- WINS NetBIOS name server

By default, if your computer is running NT and is not configured as a WINS client or WINS server, this computer is called a *b-node* computer, which is one that uses IP broadcasts for NetBIOS name resolution.

Although IP broadcast name resolution can provide dynamic name resolution, it does increase the network traffic and the level of ineffectiveness of routed networks. Moreover, any resources located outside the local subnet will not receive IP broadcast name query requests because the router won't pass IP-level broadcasts to remote subnets on the local subnet.

What you can do, as an alternative, is to manually provide NetBIOS name and IP address mappings for remote computers by using the LMHOSTS file. Selected mappings from the LMHOSTS file are maintained in a limited cache of NetBIOS computer names and IP address mappings. This memory cache is initialized when a computer is started. When the computer needs to resolve a name, the cache is examined first and, if there is no match in the cache, Windows NT uses b-node IP broadcasts to try to find the NetBIOS computer.

The LMHOSTS file can be used to map computer names and IP addresses for computers outside the local subnet. You can also use the LMHOSTS file to find remote computers for network file, print, and remote procedure services and for domain services such as log-ons, browsing, replication, and so on. The biggest restriction in the format of a HOSTS file is that white space (space or tab) must be included between the address and the name. NT includes a sample HOSTS file (HOSTS.SAM) in the \WINNT35\SYSTEM32\DRIVERS\ETC directory.

Creating a HOSTS File:

1. Copy the HOSTS.SAM file to HOSTS.
2. Edit HOSTS, and replace the sample entries with your own.

This is an example of a working HOSTS file:

```
199.10.5.1      MyServer      #Master Server
199.10.5.2      NewServer     #Last Server purchased
199.10.5.88     Joe           #Joe's PC
```

NT reads the HOSTS file when it cannot resolve the name any other way. If you must use a HOSTS file, create an icon for the file in the Administrative Tools group (File/New/Program Item) in Program Manager to provide double-click access to the file for editing/reviewing.

Another HOSTS file that was added by Microsoft for LAN Manager systems is LMHOSTS. This file provides name resolution for NetBIOS over TCP/IP in a similar manner to WINS. LMHOSTS is still used for small networks that do not use WINS and in large networks to specify hosts that are beyond the local subnet.

LMHOSTS is also a simple ASCII file and NT includes a sample in the \WINNT35\SYSTEM32\DRIVERS\ETC (LMHOSTS.SAM) directory. This file can be modified for your network.

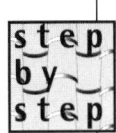

Creating a LMHOSTS File:

1. Copy the LMHOSTS.SAM file to LMHOSTS.
2. Edit LMHOSTS, and replace the sample entries with your own.

An example of a working LMHOSTS file follows:

```
199.10.5.1      MyServer      #DOM:MasterDOM      #PDC
199.10.5.2      NewServer     #Last Server purchased
199.10.5.88     Joe           #Joe's PC
#source server
#
#BEGIN_INCLUDE
#INCLUDE \\localsrv\public\lmhosts
#INCLUDE \\rhino\public\lmhosts
#END_INCLUDE
```

The # indicates a comment in this file and is also used as the prefix for special keywords like #DOM and #BEGIN_INCLUDE. LMHOSTS is much more sophisticated than HOSTS and has many options. Consult the Windows NT Networking Guide from the NT Resource Kit (Chapter 12) for more information.

If you use either HOSTS or LMHOSTS, it is handy to keep a master on a server and simply update the master, then copy it to other systems when changes occur. This procedure also reduces inaccuracies and potential problems from occurring.

Beware that if you upgraded from NT 3.51 to NT 4.0, the SNA Server Admin may no longer be able to locate a primary SNA Server 2.1/2.11 configuration present in your network. This problem will occur if your SNA Server "server" computer is separated by TCP/IP routers, and consequently no LMHOSTS files are being used to define NT's domain controllers where the SNA Servers is running.

For more information on troubleshooting SNA Server 2.1 or 2.11 communication across TCP/IP routers, check the article Q148969 in TechNet.

WINS

WINS servers provide many benefits to a network, including

- Replacing the need for HOSTS and LMHOSTS files
- Replacing the need for DNS servers
- Reducing IP broadcast traffic by replacing b-node name resolution
- Increasing browsing capabilities for NT, Windows for Workgroups, and LAN Manager 2.x clients in large networks
- Providing built-in scaleability and redundancy
- Providing automatic name registration for DHCP clients and servers

Installing WINS removes the need for having a HOSTS or LMHOSTS file on every system in the network (except in certain instances. Installing WINS on an NT server and enabling WINS name resolution on your clients allows your systems to perform name resolution automatically using WINS. WINS is used automatically after it is configured and resolves the need for each client to have a HOSTS or LMHOSTS file. The WINS database is updated automatically via DHCP when a DHCP client obtains a new address. Performing name resolution on DHCP client systems would be an almost impossible task without the use of WINS because of the dynamic changes in TCP/IP addresses with DHCP clients over time.

WINS is also the desired choice for name resolution in large networks. WINS uses a distributed database that can support multiple WINS servers. Each server can be a partner with another server. The partner relationship supports both pull (server1 requests an update from server2) and push (server1 sends an update to server2) relationships. Microsoft suggests that all partners support both a push and a pull relationship with other partners. You can have more than one partner for a server. Using multiple servers spreads the WINS load across multiple systems and provides redundancy when one WINS server goes down.

There is a known problem that usually happens when you log in to NT Workstation 4.0 with TCP/IP. Right after loggin in, you may get the following message:

```
At least one service or driver failed during system
startup.

Use Event Viewer to examine the event log for
details.
```

And, checking the Event Viewer, you have an Event ID: 7001 logged, with the description

```
The WINS Client TCP/IP Service depends on the
TCP/IP. Service and failed to load due to the
following error:

The specified service is disabled and cannot be
started.
```

This error is usually caused if the TCP/IP service is not started in the Devices tool in Control Panel. You can even confirm that by trying to PING it, which would generate the message

```
Unable to connect to IP driver. Error code 2
```

If this ever happens to you, make sure the TCP/IP service was started. To do this, you will need to

1. Go to Control Panel and double-click Devices.

2. Click TCP/IP Service, and then click Start.

Always make sure that the TCP/IP service is set to start automatically. Click TCP/IP Service, and then click Startup. Click the Automatic option, and then click OK to make sure it will start automatically. Don't forget to restart the computer.

Another concept supported by WINS is the use of a proxy system to listen for UDP name queries from non-WINS systems. A WINS proxy can be any NT system that is not running WINS server but has enabled WINS for name resolution.

WINS can also work with DNS servers if you use the DNS server shipped with the NT Resource Kit. See Chapter 21 of the Windows NT Networking Guide from the NT Resource Kit.

You may not need to install the WINS server if you installed it along with the TCP/IP protocol earlier. Check the Services applet and Control Panel and look for the Windows Internet Name Service. If it is installed, then WINS is already installed and may require configuration only.

Installing a WINS Server:

1. Start the Network applet in Control Panel.
2. Click the Add Software button.
3. Select the TCP/IP Protocol and Related Components in the Network Software box.
4. Select the options to install the WINS Server Service.
5. Optionally select the option to install the SNMP Service.
6. Click OK.
7. Enter the path to the distribution files and click Continue.
8. Configure the TCP/IP service.
9. Click the Close button, and allow the system to reboot.

Make sure the Windows Internet Name Service is started before you continue. Use the Services applet in Control Panel or Server Manager to verify the status of the service.

Network clients must be configured to use WINS before they can use it for name resolution. The following steps show you how to configure WINS on both Windows for Workgroups and Windows 95 clients. You can make sure WINS is working by performing the test following the client configuration options.

Watch for multihomed computers when you run NT 4.0. A multihomed system contains two network cards. When one of the network interfaces of a multihomed computer running 4.0 is out of service, you won't be able to establish a NetBIOS-over-TCP/IP connection to the multihomed computer. That will happen because when you load NetBIOS over TCP, it only binds to one IP address per physical network interface.

To understand why this happens, you will have to look at the issue from the TCP/IP viewpoint: It will consider a computer as multihomed only when it has more than one network interface card (NIC) installed. When a name registration packet is sent from a multihomed computer, it is flagged as a multihomed name registration so that it will not conflict with the same name being registered by another interface in the same computer.

If a broadcast name query is received by a multihomed computer, all TCP/IP interface bindings receiving the query will respond with their addresses, and by default the client will choose the first response and connect to the address supplied by it. This behavior can be controlled by the RandomAdapter registry parameter.

When a directed name query is sent to WINS, the WINS server responds with a list of all IP addresses that were registered with WINS by the multihomed computer.

However, if you are running NT 4.0 without the Service Pack 2 (SP2), if the IP address chosen from the list does not respond, the connection attempt will fail. In some cases, you may succeed your second or third attempt to connect the resource; however, the user or application may receive an error, and the retries may need to be instigated manually.

Therefore, you must upgrade to NT 4.0 SP2, which includes an enhancement to NetBT (TCP/IP). Although NetBT still uses an algorithm to choose a the best IP address to connect to on a multihomed computer, with SP2 it retains the list of addresses and orders them by preference.

Configuring a Windows for Workgroups Client to Use WINS:

1. Start the Network applet in Control Panel.
2. Click the Drivers button.
3. Select the TCP/IP protocol and click the Setup button or double-click the TCP/IP protocol.
4. Enter the TCP/IP address of the preferred WINS server in the Primary WINS Server box.
5. Enter the TCP/IP address of the secondary (optional) WINS server in the Secondary WINS Server box.
6. Click OK.
7. Close the Network applet and reboot the system.

Configuring a Windows 95 Client to Use WINS:

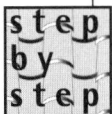

1. Select Network from Control Panel.
2. Select Microsoft TCP/IP.
3. Click the Properties button.
4. Click the WINS Configuration tab.
5. Select Enable WINS Resolution.
6. Enter the TCP/IP address of the preferred WINS server in the Primary WINS Server box.

7. Enter the TCP/IP address of the secondary (optional) WINS server in the Secondary WINS Server box.

8. If a DHCP server is available, select Use DHCP for WINS Resolution instead of entering the addresses for the WINS server. Selecting the DHCP option enables automatic detection of a WINS server over DHCP, removing the need to maintain a specific IP address on each client for a WINS server.

9. Click OK to close the TCP/IP Properties form.

10. Close the Network form.

11. Reboot the system if prompted.

As with any network options, it is a good idea to test any configuration changes, especially when it is an action that may affect a large portion of your network. The following steps provide a quick check of the operation of WINS. You should also get to know PING well, because it is a powerful tool for troubleshooting.

Testing WINS from a Client:

1. Start a DOS prompt session.

2. Make sure that there is not a HOSTS or LMHOSTS file present in the Windows directory or the PATH.

3. Execute a PING (see the later section entitled "Verifying Connections with PING") command using the name of a host on your network that is defined in the WINS database.

PING should receive a reply from the host almost instantly. If you do not receive a reply, try using PING with the IP address of the host. If using the IP address works, make sure WINS is enabled and running on the server and that the system you are trying to PING is in the WINS database. You should also verify that the WINS settings of the client system are pointing to the correct WINS server or using automatic detection with DHCP (Windows 95).

PLANNING WINS SERVERS

The NT Resource Kit contains a great deal of information on configuring and planning for WINS servers in the Windows NT Networking Guide. The book also has detailed suggestions on implementing systems to optimize performance. The information on planning and performance is summarized in Table 4.2.

TABLE 4.2	WINS Server Planning Summary

Topic	Description
Number of systems per WINS server	Plan for one WINS server and at least one backup WINS server for every 10,000 systems on the network. This figure is based on a performance ratio of 1500 name registrations per minute and 760 name queries per minute. You should include at least one WINS server on each LAN segment.
File system for WINS database	Use NTFS for the system drive and any WINS files. This improves performance because NTFS is much more robust and faster than the other available file systems.
Processors	WINS runs about 25% faster on a system with two processors.
Renewal time	Adjust the renewal time of the WINS server after the system is up and running. Lengthening the renewal time decreases the name registration traffic.
WINS proxy systems	Limit the number of WINS proxy systems on the network to limit the resources used for name query responses.
Replication time	Change the replication time between WINS partners to match your needs. WINS servers across a WAN should have a longer replication time than servers on a LAN.
Logging	Setting the Logging Enabled and Log Detailed Events options on the WINS Server Configuration dialog box turns on logging of changes to the WINS database. The Log Detailed Events option should be turned off unless you are troubleshooting to conserve system resources.

CONFIGURING A WINS SERVER

A number of tasks must be considered for managing and configuring a WINS server. This section does not provide exhaustive coverage of each option but touches on the main parameters necessary for efficient operation of WINS. For a more detailed look at any option of WINS, consult any of the following resources:

- Windows NT Networking Guide from the NT Resource Kit
- NT System Documentation and help files
- Microsoft TechNet

STATIC ADDRESSES • Static addresses are TCP/IP addresses that are manually entered on a given host system—in other words, non-DHCP systems. Typical systems that have manual addresses are DHCP servers, non-DHCP-compliant systems such as many hubs, print servers, older systems (UNIX, VMS), and anything else attached to your network that requires a manually entered TCP/IP address. DHCP servers are the exception to the rule because, even though you must enter the address for the server manually, DHCP will send its name and address to the WINS server.

Before you can use WINS to resolve a static address, you must add the mappings manually to WINS. The "WINS" section has more information on combining the HOSTS and LMHOSTS files with WINS to address this issue. You can also enter the static mappings in WINS manually.

Adding a Static Mapping to WINS Manually:

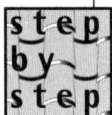

1. Start the WINS Administrator program.
2. Select the WINS server to modify.
3. Select Static Mappings from the Mappings menu.
4. Click the Add Mappings button.
5. Enter the host name.
6. Enter the host TCP/IP address
7. Click the Add button.
8. Continue steps 5–7 for all static mappings.
9. Click the Close button.
10. Close the WINS Administrator.

Adding a Static Mapping to WINS by Importing a File (HOSTS or LMHOSTS):

1. Start the WINS Administrator program.
2. Select the WINS server to modify.
3. Select Static Mappings from the Mappings menu.
4. Click the Import Mappings button.
5. Select the import file.
6. Click OK.
7. Click the Close button.
8. Close the WINS Administrator.

MISCELLANEOUS OPTIONS FOR WINS IN NT 3.51 • The WINS Server Configuration dialog box provides quick access to many of the WINS options.

Setting WINS Options (General) in NT 3.51:

1. Start the WINS Administrator program.
2. Select the WINS server to modify.
3. Select Configuration from the Server menu.
4. Change the desired options.
5. Click OK to close the configuration dialog box.

One of the options that should be set on every WINS system is the backup database path. Setting this option triggers WINS to perform a backup of the WINS database every 24 hours. If the WINS database becomes corrupted, WINS restores the database automatically from the backup.

Setting WINS Backup Options in NT 3.51:

1. Start the WINS Administrator program.
2. Select the WINS server to modify.
3. Select Configuration from the Server menu.
4. Click the Advanced >> button.
5. Enter the path for the backup database, or click the Browse button and select the directory.
6. Click OK to close the configuration dialog box.

As mentioned earlier, WINS servers maintain a database that maps computer names to IP addresses, allowing users to easily communicate with other computers while gaining all of the benefits of using TCP/IP.

The installation of WINS server in NT 4.0 is a little different than in NT 3.51, mainly due to its Windows 95 interface. In NT 4.0, the installation of WINS server is an integrated part of the process of installing TCP/IP in your NT server. Assuming that you already installed NT server, these are the steps you'll need to take in order to install WINS on NT 4.0 (make sure to be logged on as a member of the Administrators group!).

Installing WINS on an NT 4.0 System:

1. Click Start, Settings, and click Control Panel.
2. Double-click Network.
3. Click the Services tab.
4. Click Server, and then click Add.

> 5. In the Select Network Service dialog box, click Windows Internet Name Service (as shown in Figure 4.2).
>
> 6. Click Have Disk if you are loading the software from disks or a CD-ROM, or click OK if you are loading from the network.
>
> 7. In the Windows NT Setup dialog box, type the full path to the Windows NT Server WINS files, and then click Continue.

Make sure to reboot the computer so that the new settings will take effect. The WINS Manager will appear on the Administrative Tools (Common) menu on the desktop.

Your server will use WINS Manager to complete the configuration of WINS. To start it, just click Start, point to Programs, point to Administrative Tools (Common), and click WINS Manager. You should see a configuration window as shown in Figure 4.3.

Now, before you are able to administer/manage WINS servers, you need to add the WINS servers to the Server List of your NT 4.0 server by using the WINS Manager graphical interface of 4.0. Unless you add the WINS server, no WINS features will be available. Once the servers are added to the list, administration of any computer running Windows NT Server WINS Service can take place from any other computer running Windows NT Server WINS Manager.

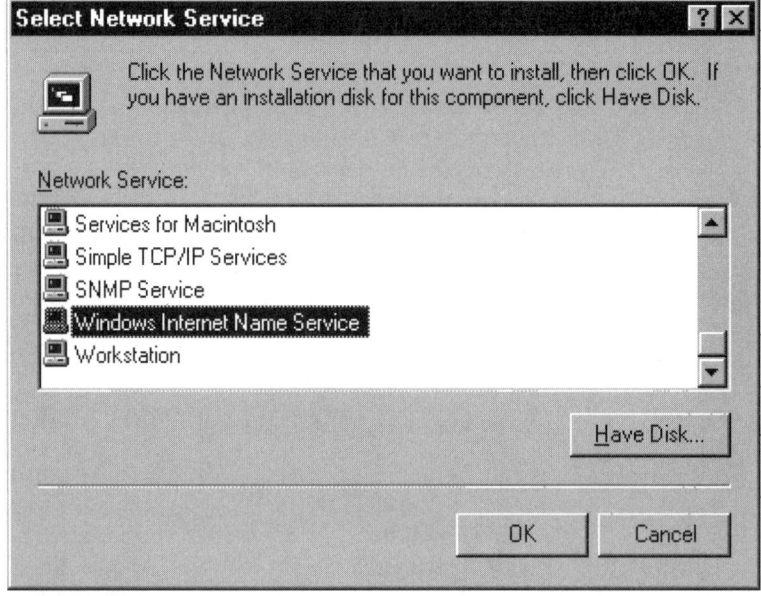

FIGURE 4.2 Network Service Configuration Window of NT 4.0.

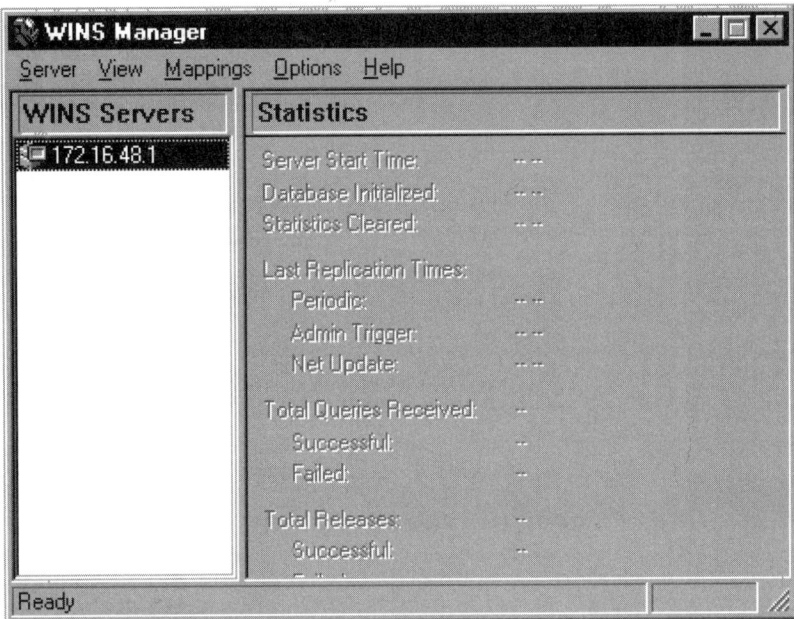

FIGURE 4.3 WINS Manager configuration made easier in Windows NT 4.0.

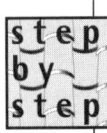

Adding WINS to Your Server List:

1. From the WINS Manager Server menu, click Add. The Add WINS Server to Server List dialog box will appear, as shown in Figure 4.4.

2. In WINS Server, type the IP address of the DHCP server to be added to the list, and then click OK.

3. Now you can configure your WINS server.

Usually, you will want to configure WINS server to increase the availability and balance the load among servers.

Configuring WINS Server:

1. From the WINS Manager, click the server you want to configure.

2. From the Server menu, click Configuration. The WINS Server Configuration dialog box will appear, as shown in Figure 4.5.

3. Select the configuration options you want.

   Type a value in Renewal Interval.

   Type a value in Extinction Interval (the interval between the time an entry in the WINS database is marked as *released*, or no longer registered, and when it is marked as *extinct*).

Type a value in Extinction Time-out (the interval between the time an entry is marked extinct and when the entry is scavenged, or removed).

Type a value in Verify Interval.

To specify pull parameters, select the Initial Replication check box under Pull.

Type a value in Retry Count (the number of times that the WINS server will attempt to contact a replication partner for pulling new WINS database entries).

To have the WINS server notify its replication partners of the status of its WINS database when the system is initialized, select the Initial Replication check box under Push Parameters.

To notify the replication partners of the WINS server when a name registration changes the WINS database status, select the Replicate on Address Change check box.

4. Click Advanced to configure other options.

To specify logging of database changes to Changes.log, select the Logging Enabled check box.

Select the Log Detailed Events check box if necessary.

To replicate only WINS push or pull partners, select the Replicate Only With Partners check box.

To automatically back up the database when WINS Manager stops, select the Backup On Termination check box.

The database backup path must have a directory specified.

To treat static unique and static multihomed records in the database as dynamic when they conflict with a new registration or replica, select the Migrate On/Off check box.

To set the highest-version ID number for the database, enter that number in Starting Version Count.

To specify the directory where the WINS database backups will be stored, type the path in Database Backup Path.

5. When you have completed all changes in the WINS Server Configuration dialog box, click OK.

TCP/IP UTILITIES OVERVIEW

NT Server comes with several utilities that are useful for TCP/IP management. These programs range from utilities providing access to other systems to others that are useful for managing TCP/IP systems and networks. Table 4.3 lists

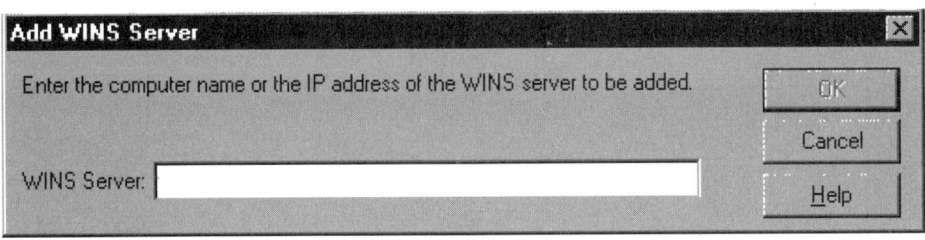

FIGURE 4.4 Add WINS Server to Server List dialog box of NT 4.0.

several of the programs and provides a short description of their use. The TCP-32 column indicates which programs have comparable versions in the MSTCP-32 driver set for Windows for Workgroups and Windows.

TCP/IP OPTIONS

The TCP/IP options for NT have many different components. You do not need to install all TCP/IP components to use TCP/IP or some of its options. Table 4.4 lists the TCP/IP options available during the installation process or when configuring TCP/IP.

SMB

Server Message Block (SMB) is a high-level protocol used by Microsoft systems to make file and print service requests over a network. SMB commands are embedded in transport protocols such as TCP/IP or NetBEUI.

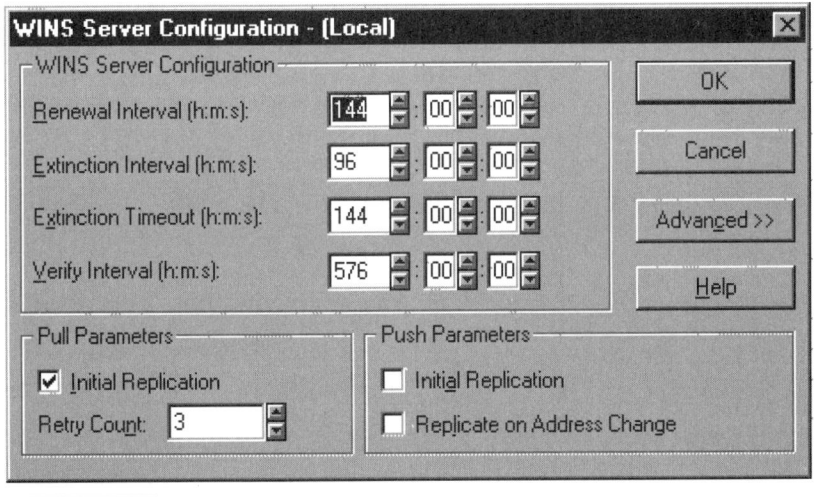

FIGURE 4.5 WINS Server Configuration dialog box in NT 4.0.

TABLE 4.3 MT Server Programs for TCP/IP Management

Program	Description
ARP	Used to display or modify the IP-to-Ethernet or Token Ring address translations tables used by the Address Resolution Protocol (ARP).
DHCP Manager	Used to configure and manage the DHCP server. An icon for this program (DHCPADMN.EXE) is in the Network Administration group.
FINGER	Displays information about a user or users on another system.
FTP	Used to transfer files to and from another system. The other system must be running an FTP service. FTP has a complete command set, which is covered in the NT documentation.
HOSTNAME	Displays the name of the current host.
IPCONFIG	Used to display information about the TCP/IP configuration of the current system. Can also be used to disable TCP/IP on the current system and release the DHCP configuration for that system.
NBTSTAT	Displays protocol statistics and current TCP/IP connections. It uses the NBT (NetBIOS over TCP/IP) protocol.
NETSTAT	Displays protocol statistics and current TCP/IP connections.
PING	Used to check the TCP/IP connection between two systems. It is one of the most-used utilities for TCP/IP.
RCP	The Remote Copy command, used to copy information between systems. The remote system must be running rshd (remote shell daemon), which is available on UNIX systems.
REXEC	The remote execution utility, used to run commands on remote systems. The REXEC service must be running on the remote system.
ROUTE	Used to display and change routing tables on an NT system.
RSH	Used to run commands on remote systems running the RSH service.
TELNET	A terminal emulator that runs over TCP/IP. TELNET uses the Telnet service.
TFTP	Transfers files with systems running the Trivial File Transfer Protocol (TFTP).

TABLE 4.3	MT Server Programs for TCP/IP Management (Continued)
Program	**Description**
TRACERT	Traces the route to a destination system through each router on the network.
WINS Manager	Used to configure and manage the DHCP server. An icon for this program (WINSADMN.EXE) is found in the Network Administration group.

Beware of another small bug with NT 4.0! Sometimes applications will try to locate a file with no extension, and the operation may fail. Microsoft's article # Q159972, found on TechNet, gives an example of a simple Qbasic application, which uses the Qbasic Kill command, which will report Error 53, computer name not found, when it tries to delete a file with no extension located on a Windows NT 4.0 server.

The problem here is that when NT 4.0 server receives an SMB search command for a file name with no extension, the server returns an SMB search response in which the file name field is not correctly populated. This will happen only if the filename doesn't have an extension. In order to resolve this problem, you should update your NT 4.0 server with SP2.

TABLE 4.4	Windows NT TCP/IP Services
Option	**Description of Facilities Installed**
TCP/IP internetworking	TCP/IP protocols, NetBIOS, Windows Sockets, and diagnostic utilities for TCP/IP.
Connectivity utilities	Connectivity utilities: finger, ftp, rcp, rexec, rsh, telnet, and tftp.
SNMP service	SNMP agent and other support utilities.
TCP/IP network printing	Support for TCP/IP printers directly connected to the network (such as the NetQue from Emulex) or UNIX systems.
FTP server service	Allows sharing files on an NT system with other systems that support FTP. This option is not required if you share files only with systems running Windows for Workgroups or DOS.
Simple TCP/IP services	Provides the TCP/IP Character Generator, Daytime, Discard, Echo, and Quote of the Day.
DHCP server service	Software to support DHCP for TCP/IP management.
WINS server service	Software to support WINS.
Automatic DHCP configuration	Enables automatic configuration of TCP/IP parameters from a DHCP server. Not available if this computer will be a DHCP or WINS server.

DLC

The Data Link Control (DLC) protocol is another built-in protocol that allows NT to communicate with IBM systems or any other device that uses the DLC protocol. Because of the complexity of communicating with the various IBM systems, we do not cover it in depth here. If you are using NT in such an environment, you should purchase the NT Resource Kit from Microsoft and take a hard look at SNA Server from Microsoft. There are also many third-party tools for use in an IBM environment.

The DLC protocol is not installed during NT 4.0 setup. However, you do have an option to install the DLC driver when you're installing NT 4.0 or later versions.

Installing the DLC Driver When You're Installing NT 4.0 or Later:

1. Click Start, Settings, and Control Panel.
2. Double-click Network.
3. Click the Protocols tab, and then click Add.

If you want to configure the network bindings for DLC (connections between network cards, protocols, and services) you can do it because the order of the bindings is significant to DLC (as an adapter is specified at the DLC interface as a number—typically 0 or 1, although Windows NT DLC can support up to 16 physical adapters). DLC applications use a value of 0 to refer to a NIC adapter, so if you have only one card, this won't make any difference, but if you have more then one, then you might want to modify the bindings.

Manually changing DLC Bindings:

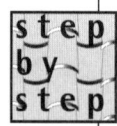

1. Click on Network in Control Panel.
2. Select the Bindings tab and make the changes to:
   Enable a binding
   Disable a binding
   Move the order (priority) of the bindings up or down

NWLINK, IPX/SPX, and Other NetWare Stuff

NWLINK is a NetWare-compatible transport used by NT to allow NetWare workstations to communicate with NT application servers.

NWLINK is a 32-bit implementation of IPX/SPX that supports full SMB networking. It supports sockets, RPC, Novell NetBIOS, and the NetWare

IPX/SPX API. NWLINK supports a wide variety of network cards through the NDIS 3.x interface. NWLINK is supported on all NT platforms, including both Intel and RISC systems. It also supports SMP systems.

Several different frame types are supported to allow you to configure your system for different types of networks. You must set the frame type using the Network Control Panel applet to configure the NWLINK frame type to match that of your NetWare Server.

NWLINK is used as the protocol for both application servers in a NetWare environment and for supporting NetWare Core Protocol (NCP) for NT and Windows clients accessing a NetWare Server.

NT systems can also run the Microsoft Compatible Workstation Service (MCWS) that allows NT systems to access file and print services on a NetWare Server.

The NetWare Compatible Gateway is also included with NT Server and allows NT Server clients to access file and print services on NetWare servers. The gateway translates between the SMB protocol used by Microsoft networks and the Novell NetWare Core Protocol.

What all this means is that with the use of NWLINK and NWCS, an NT system can function both as an application server and client, and as a file and print system client in a mixed network using both NT and NetWare systems.

You should need only the NWLink protocol in the following situations:

■ Your NetWare client/server applications work only with IPX/SPX.
■ Routers in your network work only with IPX/SPX.
■ Network clients that must talk to NT are running only IPX/SPX.

If you have any installation of Novell NetWare in your company, which usually are used for file and print services, NWLink can help you integrate the two OSs, Novell and NT. Because Novell uses the IPX/SPX protocol as its primary network protocol, Microsoft developed NWLink, an IPX/SPX-compatible protocol, to enable NT servers and workstations to talk to Novell. With NWLink, NetWare-compatible services become available for the NT platform as well as allowing connectivity for database access to databases running as NetWare Loadable Modules (NLMs) on NetWare servers.

With the Client Service for NetWare (CSNW), a computer running NT Workstation is able to share basic file and print connectivity with a NetWare 3.x server, or a NetWare 4.x server. In case of running an NT server, the Gateway Service for NetWare (GSNW) provides access to NetWare Servers.

Adding CSNW in NT 4.0:

1. Click Start, Settings, and Control Panel.
2. Double-click on Network.
3. Click the Services tab.

4. Click Add.

5. Click Client Services for NetWare, and click OK.

6. Type the path to the CSNW files, and click Continue.

7. In the Client Services for NetWare Dialog box, type the name of the NetWare Server that will be used for authentication, click OK, and then click Close.

You will have to reboot your workstation to complete the installation.

You now have to configuration CSNW to enable NT workstation to connect to the NetWare server.

Configuring CSNW:

1. Click Start, Settings, and Control Panel.

2. Double-click CSNW.

3. In the Current Preferred Server dialog box, select a server, if necessary, as shown in Figure 4.6, and then click OK.

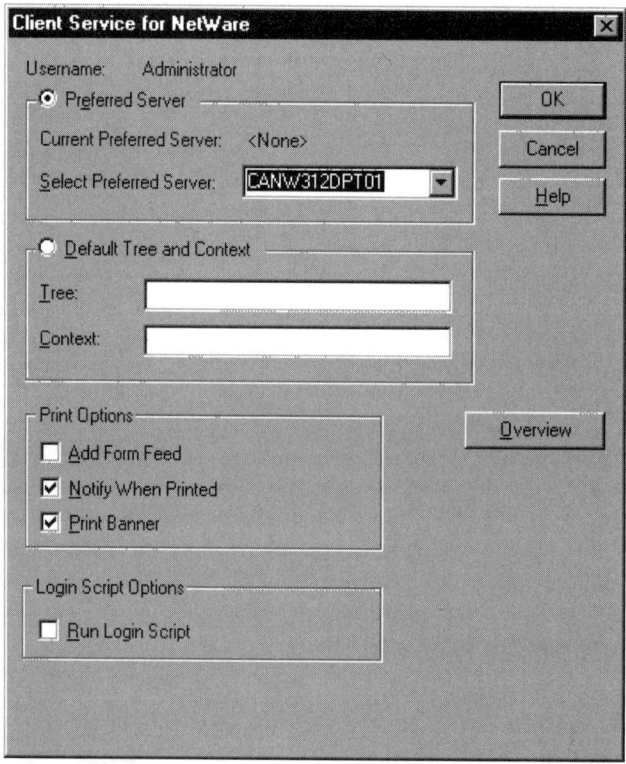

FIGURE 4.6 Current Preferred Server dialog box of NT 4.0.

The Gateway Service for NetWare (GSNW), as discussed previously, enables your NT 4.0 server to access the NetWare servers as if they were just another client and, in addition, allows the network clients to access files on a NetWare server without having to have a NetWare client redirector on an IPX/SPX protocol stack loaded.

To install the Gateway Service on NT 4.0 Server, you must be logged on as a member of the Administrators group. The NWLink transport protocol will be automatically installed when you install the gateway.

Installing the Gateway:

1. Click Start, Settings, and Control Panel.

2. Double-click Network.

3. Click the Services tab.

4. Click Server, and then click Add.

5. Click Gateway Services for NetWare, and click OK.

6. Type the path to the source files, and click Continue.

7. In the Gateway Services for NetWare dialog box (Figure 4.7), enter the name of the NetWare server to which the computer running Windows NT Server will connect.

8. Click Gateway.

9. Select the Enable Gateway check box, as shown in Figure 4.8.

10. Type the NetWare user account created to log-on the NetWare server from a computer running Windows NT Server, and click Add.

11. In the New Share dialog box, as show in Figure 4.9, type the Share name of the gateway on the NetWare server.

12. Type the full path to the new share on the NetWare server.

13. Type an entry in Comment, if you want one.

14. Enter a letter for the drive on which the new share will reside.

15. If necessary, enter a value to limit the number of users.

16. Click OK.

The GSNW option is added to Control Panel and is used to activate the gateway.

Another great feature available in NT 4.0 to integrate NetWare services is the File and Print Services for NetWare (FPNW), which allows users of NetWare 2.x/3.x (and 4.x in bindery mode only) to utilize the multipurpose features of Windows NT Server 4.0 by enabling the seamless integration of Windows NT Server into an existing NetWare network.

This is an add-on product, does not come with NT 4.0, and must be licensed separately. File and Print Services for NetWare enables a standard

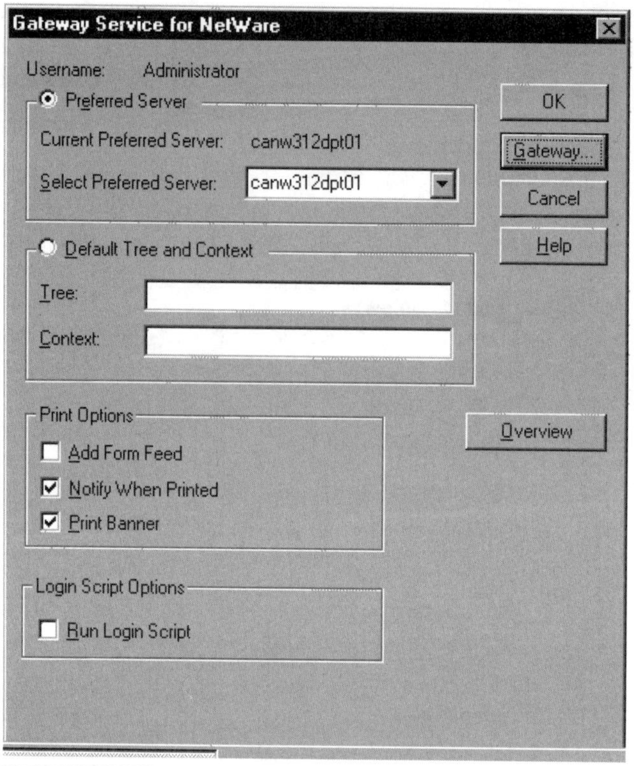

FIGURE 4.7 Netware dialog box in NT 4.0 for setting up Gateway services.

NetWare client to access file and print resources on a Windows NT Server-based computer.

NT 4.0 also has the Directory Service Manager for NetWare (DSMN), which provides administrators with features that will ease on network tasks and enables NetWare clients to access NT servers.

AppleTalk and EtherTalk

NT Server can use AppleTalk as a protocol with Services for Macintosh (SFM). This capability enables Macintosh clients to participate in an NT Server network using either the standard AppleTalk network included with Macintosh systems or Ethernet. AppleTalk is slow and should be used only as a last resort.

EtherTalk can also be used with SFM. EtherTalk runs over Ethernet and is much faster than AppleTalk. EtherTalk also takes advantage of the wide variety of standard devices in the Ethernet market. Using EtherTalk can also

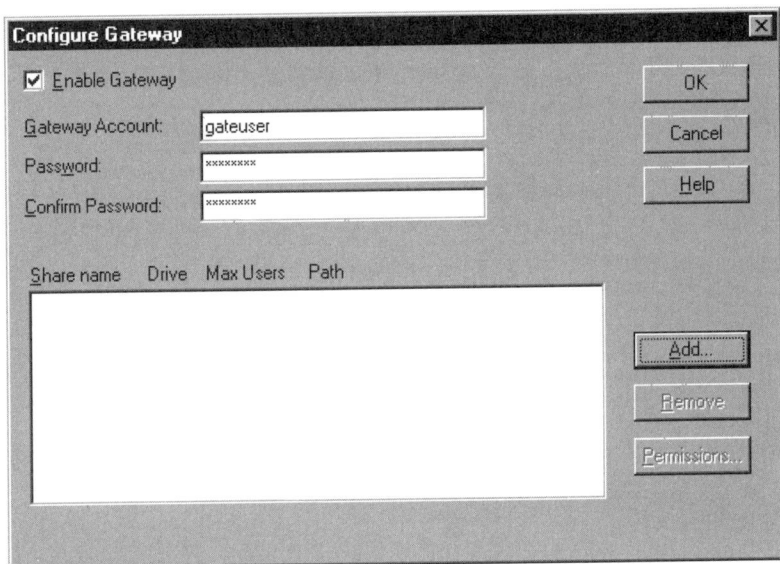

FIGURE 4.8 This option in NT 4.0 enables Gateway services by your simply checking the box.

simplify your life as a network manager because you can standardize on Ethernet for all your network clients. Maintaining two network protocols that use different network topologies and devices is expensive and a real pain.

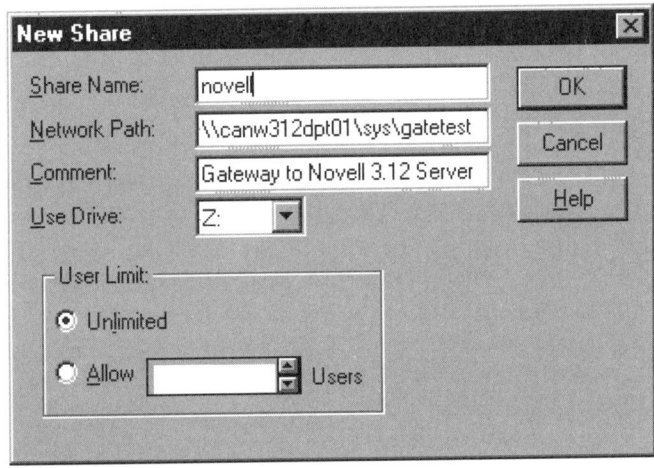

FIGURE 4.9 Setting up a new share is also easy through the dialog box of NT 4.0.

Choosing a Protocol

Choosing a protocol is similar to choosing a network architecture like Ethernet—everyone has his or her own idea. The choices are becoming easier now because of the move toward the Information SuperHighway and the spread of TCP/IP in the networking field. TCP/IP is the one protocol that is moving toward a de facto standard.

More networks are moving from proprietary networks such as SNA or DECnet to TCP/IP. Reasons for this movement are varied, but several important factors should influence your decision. Table 4.5 covers TCP/IP, IPX/SPX, and NetBEUI and offers suggestions for deciding which to use.

Installing or Changing Protocols and Other Network Items

Protocols are installed and managed using the Network applet in Control Panel, which is shown in Figure 4.10 (for NT 3.51) and 4.11 (for NT 4.0).

Using the Network applet, you can change settings for a protocol and add or remove a protocol, among other things. Other sections of this book contain information on changing other options.

TABLE 4.5	Protocol Summary
Protocol	**Notes**
TCP/IP	TCP/IP is widely used and connects to most systems via standard or third-party protocol stacks. Microsoft includes an NT TCP/IP stack with NT and NT Server. NT Server also includes DHCP, WINS, and MSTCP-32 for Windows and Windows for Workgroups 3.x. TCP/IP can be used on small, medium, and large networks.
NetBEUI	NetBEUI is a small and fast protocol that is best used on small to medium networks up to 200 clients. It is the easiest protocol to install, configure, and manage, but it is not routable.
IPX/SPX	IPX/SPX is useful for networks that include a NetWare server or applications that require this protocol. Microsoft is recommending IPX/SPX as the default protocol on Microsoft networks.
Other	Vendors such as Digital Equipment offer protocol stacks that allow NT and NT Server to access systems with proprietary protocols (that is, DECnet).

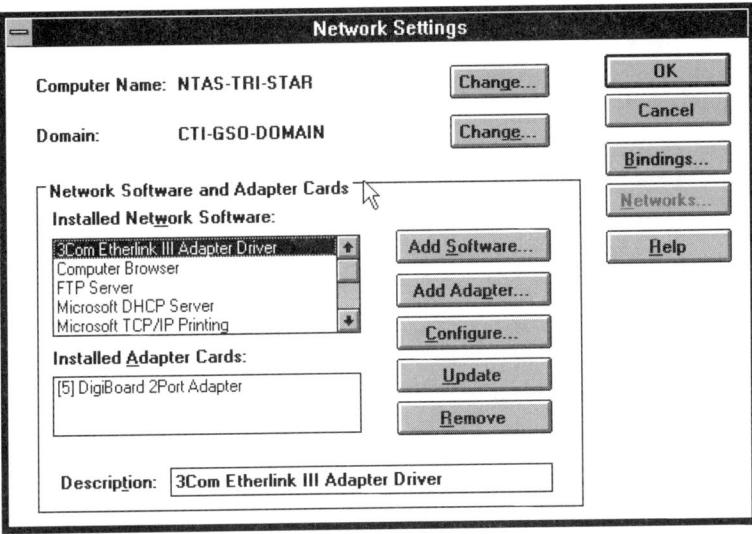

FIGURE 4.10 The Network applet in Control Panel provides an interface for changing most network parameters.

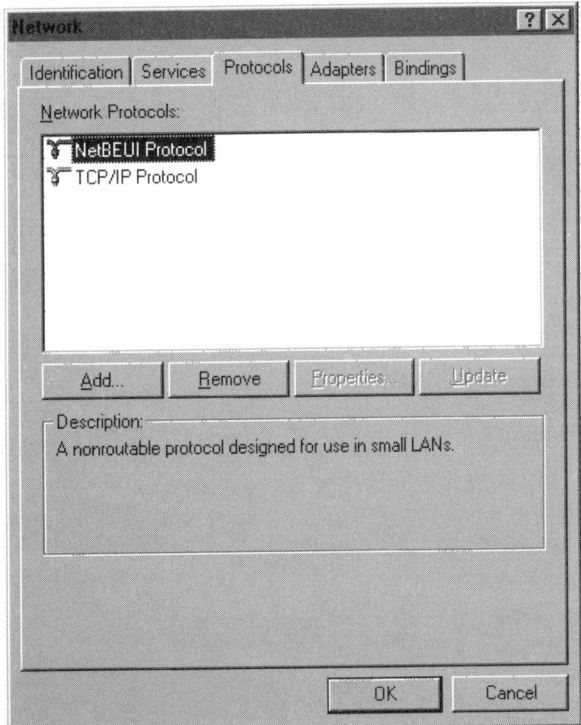

FIGURE 4.11 Screen shot of the Network setup applet in NT 4.0.

Notice how you choose which components to work on from the list, and then click the corresponding button to perform an action.

Adding a Protocol in NT 4.0:

1. Click on Network from Control Panel
2. Click on Protocol Tab, and click Add to add protocol.

Adding a Protocol or Other Network Software in NT 3.51:

1. Start the Network applet in Control Panel.
2. Click the Add Software button.
3. Select the new protocol from the list in the Add Network Software dialog box.
4. Choose configuration options, and close the Network applet.
5. Reboot the system if you are requested to do so.

You may need to change parameters for a protocol or other network software option, such as TCP/IP. The configuration dialog box functions exactly as it does during installation in most cases.

Changing a Protocol or Other Network Software:

1. Start the Network applet in Control Panel.
2. Select the protocol from the list.
3. Click the Configure button.
4. Choose your configuration options, and click OK.
5. Close the Network applet.
6. Reboot the system if requested.

The Network applet also provides a way to remove a protocol or other network software.

Be careful with this step, because you may lose network functions or other abilities if you delete the wrong software.

If problems occur after one of these steps, see the instructions on recovering a system configuration at boot time, using the last known good system configuration.

Removing a Protocol or Other Network Software:

1. Start the Network applet in Control Panel.
2. Select the protocol or software from the list.
3. Click the Remove button.
4. Answer Yes to the confirmation question.
5. Reboot the system if requested.

General Overview

Now we can dig into practically configuring TCP/IP on NT. This section covers the current version of TCP/IP on NT 3.51 and NT 4.0.

In 1998, our NT 5.0 book will look into the new network features, especially TCP/IP. We expect to see major changes in NT's TCP/IP support. In particular, NTS will *probably* incorporate TCP/IP v6.

CONFIGURING TCP/IP

TCP/IP provides lots of utilities for managing and configuring the protocol and its related components. Many of the utilities are needed only when a problem occurs on the network or you must change a TCP/IP parameter manually. Both DHCP and WINS have removed much of the management load from using TCP/IP.

TCP/IP can be configured using the Network applet in Control Panel. You can use this process to turn on DHCP or manually enter the IP address and subnet mask. If you use manual entry of the IP address, you must track the IP addresses for each system on your network. This is a real pain in the neck and requires detailed records for each system. If you miss or incorrectly list one address, you are set for future (maybe quite soon) problems with duplicate addresses. Most systems such as Windows for Workgroups, Windows 95, and Windows NT provide a duplicate address error message, but debugging can still be a pain.

The dialog boxes in Figure 4.12 (NT 3.51 version) and 4.13 (NT 4.0 version) are used for TCP/IP configuration, including manually setting the IP address and enabling DHCP.

Configuring TCP/IP in NT 4.0:

1. In the Network option in Control Panel, double-click Microsoft TCP/IP in the list of installed components. Note that if you have more then one network adapter on your computer, then list will include an instance of TCP/IP for each network adapter. Make sure to configure each adapter with its own IP address, subnet mask, and gateway.
2. In Microsoft TCP/IP properties, click the IP Address tab.

3. Click Specify An IP Address.

4. Type an IP address and subnet mask in the respective boxes.

5. To view or specify which network clients are bound to the TCP/IP protocol, click the Bindings tab.

6. Click the Gateway tab, as shown in Figure 4.14. Type at least one IP address for the default gateway (IP router) on the network, and then click Add.

7. Type an additional IP address, if necessary, in the New Gateway box, and then click the Add button. If this is the first gateway in the list, NT will consider it the default gateway. If you need to prioritize your gateway address, you can drag the IP address in the list of installed gateways.

8. Click OK, and then restart the computer for changes to take effect.

Configuring TCP/IP in NT 3.51:

1. Start the Network applet in Control Panel.

2. Select the TCP/IP protocol.

3. Click the Configure button.

4. Enter the parameters for TCP/IP.

5. Click OK.

6. Restart the system if prompted.

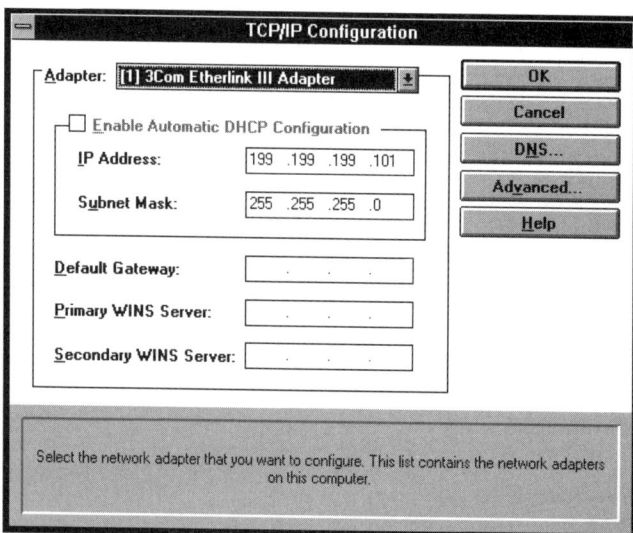

FIGURE 4.12 The TCP/IP Configuration dialog box for NT 3.51 is used for accessing the numerous TCP/IP options.

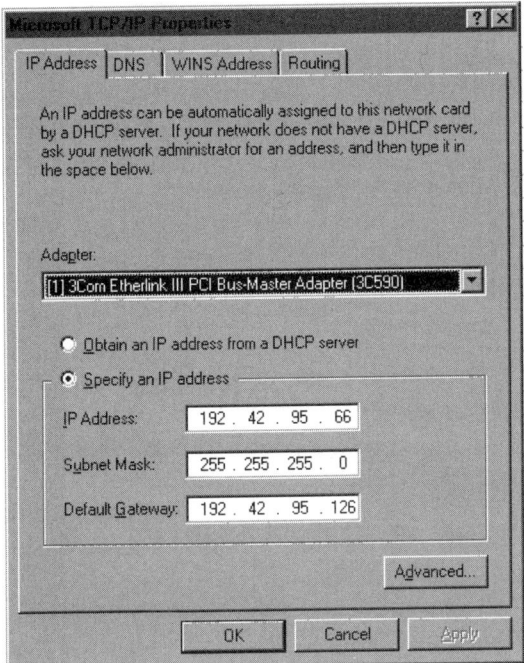

FIGURE 4.13 TCP/IP configuration in NT 4.0.

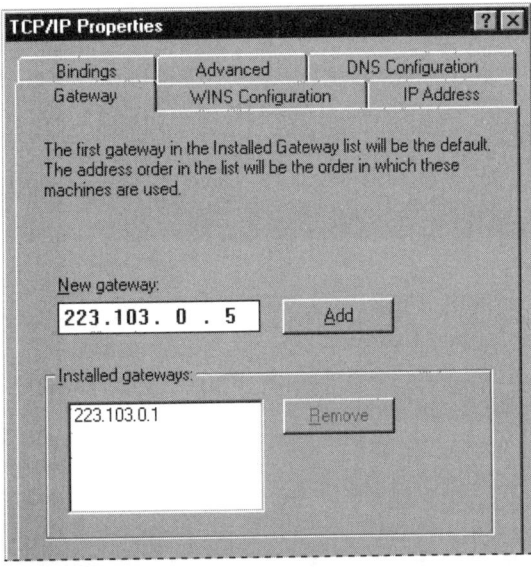

FIGURE 4.14 The TCP/IP Properties and Gateway settings dialog box.

MULTIPLE NETWORK ADAPTERS AND TCP/IP

Systems using multiple network adapters with TCP/IP are termed *multi-homed systems*. Each network adapter in this type of system actually creates its own network segment and requires a separate IP address.

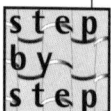

Configuring Multiple Adapters for TCP/IP:

1. Start the Network applet in Control Panel.
2. Select the TCP/IP protocol.
3. Click the Configure button.
4. Select the adapter to configure from the list at the top of the dialog box.
5. Enter the parameters for the adapter.
6. Repeat steps 4 and 5 for each adapter that will use TCP/IP.
7. Click OK.
8. Restart the system if you are prompted to do so.

ENABLING DHCP

DHCP services must be enabled before you can access a DHCP server from other systems. This process is actually very simple and involves one step on the server and one on each client. Control Panel contains most of the tools for installing and configuring services. Other tools for administering DHCP and WINS are located in the Network Administrative Tools groups.

Enabling DHCP service on NT 4.0 is simple. In order for a client computer to obtain an address from a computer running the DHCP service, the client must be able to locate the server responsible for leasing it an IP address. You need to make sure that the IP address of the server leasing the Ips—the one running DHCP service—won't change, which means that it must have an static IP address.

Configure a Static Server Address:

1. Go to the Microsoft TCP/IP Properties dialog box.
2. Click the IP Address tab.
3. In Adapter, select the network adapter for which you wish to specify an IP address, and then click OK.
4. Click Specify an IP address.
5. The settings in your dialog box will be similar to the one shown in Figure 4.15.

Make sure to reboot the server so that the changes can take effect.

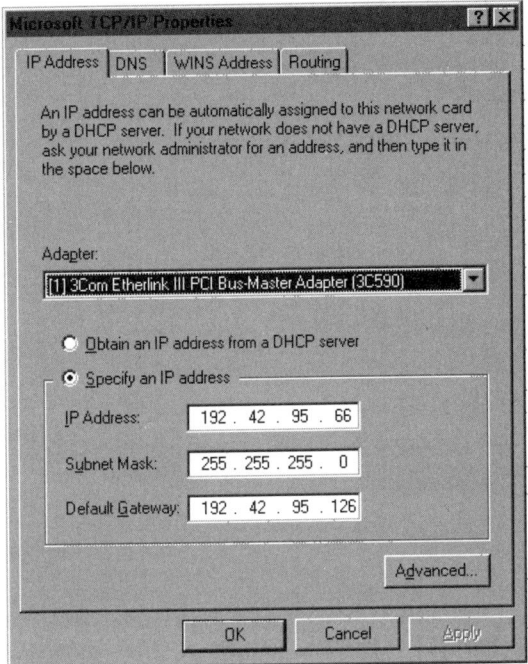

FIGURE 4.15 The Microsoft TCP/IP Properties dialog box for setting up the service on NT 4.0.

Enabling DHCP Servers and Clients Overview (NT 3.51 Version):

1. Configure DHCP on the Server(s).
2. Enable DHCP on the client.

The first step must be taken on each system that will be a DHCP server using DHCP Manager.

Enabling DHCP on NT Server:

1. Run the DHCP Manager.
2. Click on Local Machine.
3. Select Create from the Scope menu.
4. Enter the address range for the scope.
5. Enter the subnet mask for the scope.

6. Enter the scope name.

7. Enter a description for the scope in the comment field.

8. Click OK.

You can enter any excluded address ranges for the scope on the same form. Fill in the Start Address and End Address under the Exclusion range and click the Add button. This procedure excludes that range of addresses from use by DHCP. Most likely, you will exclude the same addresses as those listed as static addresses in WIN5.

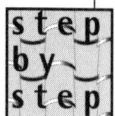

Enabling DHCP Client Services on Windows for Workgroups Clients:

1. Run the Network Setup program in the Network group.

2. Click the Drivers button.

3. Select the TCP/IP protocol and click the Setup button.

4. Click the check box to enable DHCP.

5. Close all the Network Setup dialog boxes and reboot.

Enabling DHCP Client Services on Windows NT and NT Server:

1. Run Control Panel and start the Network applet.

2. Select the TCP/IP protocol.

3. Click the Configure button.

4. Click the check box to enable DHCP.

5. Click OK.

6. Restart the system if you are prompted to do so.

Enabling DHCP Client Services on Windows 95:

1. Start the Network applet in Control Panel.

2. Select TCP/IP from the list. Make sure it is the correct TCP/IP item as you may see one bound to a dial-up adapter, whereas another is bound to a network adapter.

3. Double-click the TCP/IP item in the list, or click the Properties button.

4. Click the Obtain an Address from a DHCP Server option.

5. Click OK.

Figure 4.16 shows the properties dialog box for the TCP/IP settings.

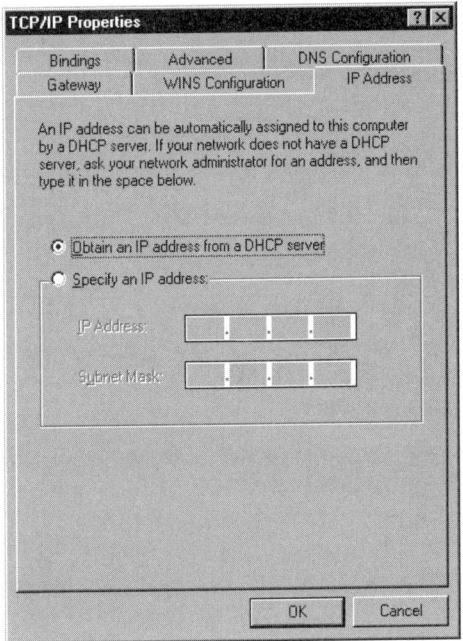

FIGURE 4.16 The TCP/IP Properties dialog box where the tabs for other options provide one-click access to major settings options.

Troubleshooting Programs for TCP/IP

NT Server TCP/IP provides by far more tools for troubleshooting your network than any of the standard NT protocols. This is partly because of the long history of TCP/IP and the outgrowth of tools for troubleshooting the protocol and the implementation of some new tools such as DHCP and WINS support by Microsoft. You will find many of these tools by the same name or a slightly different name on other Microsoft systems such as Windows for Workgroups, Windows 95, and the DOS network products. Some tools such as PING are also standard on almost all TCP/IP network systems.

Verifying Connections with PING

PING is the simplest and best known of the TCP/IP utilities. It is also possibly the most useful when you can't communicate from or to a particular system.

The first step we use when we diagnose a communication problem with a server or workstation is to fire up PING and see if the problem system is alive. It is also a good idea to run PING from the problem system and see if it can talk to any other systems.

The syntax for PING is

```
PING name | address
```

name   The name of the target system.

address   The address of the target system.

The following example uses PING to try to connect to a system called JOHNS:

```
PING JOHNS
```

If you receive a reply from the other system, you know the connection is OK. If the other system does not answer, there is a problem somewhere between the two systems. Try using PING against several systems to determine the source of the problem.

You may experience problems with accessing a shared print or file resource on a host system such as VMS (Pathworks) or UNIX. Sometimes when this occurs PING returns a reply indicating that the target system is alive and well. The problem may be in the security the TCP/IP vendor uses for TCP/IP. TGV's MultiNet product can restrict access by IP address. We have seen a case in which an NT system could not access a file service but PING worked fine. If this problem occurs, try using another system to connect to the resource. If the other system works, look at the security settings for your IP address or DHCP range on the server. If you can't access the system from another system, then check the security settings for all addresses on the system.

Instead of specifying the name of the other system, you can also use the TCP/IP address. This is very useful when there may be a problem with name resolution such as an error in a HOSTS or LMHOSTS file or a problem with the WINS server or database. Let's assume that our PING test to JOHNS failed, and we are curious about the next step. Try this PING command, where 198.84.8.10 is the TCP/IP address for JOHNS.

```
PING 198.84.8.10
```

A reply from this command would indicate that JOHNS is alive and well and that a problem exists in resolving the name JOHNS with the TCP/IP address 198.84.8.10. The next step is to check your name resolution setup. You should also try using PING from more than one system when you can't contact a target system. For instance, in our test if PING JOHNS worked from another system and failed on ours, then the problem must be in name resolution for our system. Check the WINS configuration, HOSTS or LMHOSTS files, or DNS, depending upon your network configuration.

Checking Your DHCP Configuration with IPCONFIG

IPCONFIG is useful for checking the TCP/IP configuration of a system. The following command and output uses the default IPCONFIG options and displays only addressing information for a client workstation:

```
IPCONFIG
    Windows IP Configuration Version 1.0


Ethernet adapter EtherLink III:


        IP Address. . . . . . . : 199.199.199.110
        Subnet Mask . . . . . . : 255.255.255.0
        Default Gateway . . . . :
```

This is convenient, because if the system is using DHCP, how else do you find out its IP address?

What happens if we want a full breakdown of configuration information? Use the /ALL switch on IPCONFIG.

```
IPCONFIG /ALL
    Windows IP Configuration Version 1.0


        Host Name . . . . . . . : DEC-P5-KENS
        DNS Servers . . . . . . :
        Node Type . . . . . . . : Hybrid
        NetBIOS Scope ID. . . . :
        IP Routing Enabled. . . : No
        WINS Proxy Enabled. . . : No
        DNS Resolution For Windows Networking
        Applications Enabled: No


Ethernet adapter EtherLink III:


        Physical Address. . . . : 00-60-8C-CC-F1-1F
        DHCP Enabled. . . . . . : Yes
        IP Address. . . . . . . : 199.199.199.110
        Subnet Mask . . . . . . : 255.255.255.0
        Default Gateway . . . . :
        DHCP Server . . . . . . : 199.199.199.101
        Primary WINS Server . . : 199.199.199.101
        Secondary WINS Server . :
```

```
                            Lease Obtained. . . . . : Wed 2nd. Nov
                            1994 10:38:18 pm
                            Lease Expires . . . . . : Sat 26th. Nov
                            1994 10:38:18 pm
```

This option provides some useful information. We have the physical address of the workstation, the IP address, and even lease information for DHCP. This information is useful if you are having trouble with a workstation and need to verify that it has a valid lease. It is also useful for verifying routing information for the workstation or server.

IPCONFIG can also release the current DHCP lease, effectively shutting down TCP/IP. The following command shows the syntax:

```
                    IPCONFIG /Release
```

You can also use this command to renew the DHCP lease. This command is useful when you need to make sure the lease is updated or want to verify whether a system is connecting with the DHCP server.

```
                    IPCONFIG /Renew
```

You should use WINIPCFG on Windows 95 systems.

These are few other TCP/IP diagnostic utilities that you should be aware of, as follows:

- **arp**–View the ARP (address resolution protocol) table on the local computer to detect invalid entries.
- **hostname**–Print the name of the current host.
- **ipconfig**–Display current TCP/IP network configuration values, and update or release TCP/IP network configuration values.
- **nbtstat**–Check the state of current NetBIOS over TCP/IP connections, update the LMHOSTS cache, and determine the registered name and scope ID.
- **netstat**–Display protocol statistics and the state of current TCP/IP connections.
- **ping**–Verify whether TCP/IP is configured correctly and that a remote TCP/IP system is available.
- **tracert**–Check the route to a remote system.

Configuring Browsing on Your Network

Windows for Workgroups systems must have the new redirector (VREDIR.386), which ships with NT Server 3.5x installed to participate in browsing with an NT server across a router. Windows 95 includes the features of this redirector by default.

Windows for Workgroups systems should be set up in different workgroups of 25 or so workstations. Each workgroup should have a name that is different from the domain. This organization breaks up browsing among the different workgroups and provides the optimal performance.

You can improve performance of specific Windows for Workgroups workstations by making the workstation ineligible to be a browsemaster. Set the value of MaintainServerList to no in the SYSTEM.INI Network section.

```
[Network]

MaintainServerList=no
```

Browsing Other Domains

NT Server must be told in certain instances to show other domains when a user browses the network. This instruction usually occurs for LAN Manager 2.2 domains (such as Digital Equipment's Pathworks 5.x). You may also need to issue this instruction when you have domains separated by a router and you have not set up WINS.

You can add and remove domains from the browse list using the Network applet in Control Panel. Figure 4.17 shows the Computer Browser from the NT Control Panel Network applet.

Adding a Domain to the Browser:

1. Run Control Panel.
2. Start the Network applet.
3. Click Computer Browser.
4. Enter the domain name in the box, and click Add.
5. Click OK.

Removing a Domain from the Browser:

1. Run Control Panel.
2. Start the Network applet.
3. Click Computer Browser.
4. Click on the domain name to remove.
5. Click the Remove button.
6. Click OK.

It may take up to 15 minutes or more for the browse lists to be updated after you make a change, due to the time lag between updates to the browse list.

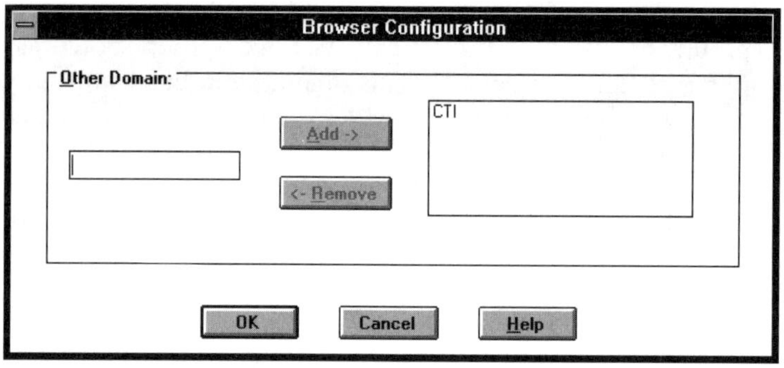

FIGURE 4.17 The Browser Configuration dialog box is used to alter the browse list for the current domain.

Monitoring Browsers

Two tools that come with the NT Resource Kit are handy for monitoring and troubleshooting browser services: Browser Monitor and BrowStat. Browser Monitor is a GUI tool; BrowStat is character-based.

Browser Monitor displays a lot of information on browsers and their status. You can tell at a glance which system is the browsemaster for a domain or workgroup and whether or not there is a problem. Figure 4.18 shows a simple network (one domain and one workgroup) viewed from the Browser Monitor main window.

You can double-click an entry for any transport to display the Browser Status window for that system, as shown in Figure 4.19. The details window provides useful information such as the number of servers currently in the domain or workgroup, the domains and workgroups visible to the browsemaster you are viewing, and several summary statistics and details in the top frame.

The Info button provides access to detailed statistics on the browser. Systems such as NT may provide more detailed statistics than Windows 95 or Windows for Workgroups 3.11.

Browser Monitor is a good tool for troubleshooting browsing services. The details provided by the tool do not necessarily give you an instant solution to a problem, but they do point you in the right direction. The Browser Status window provides a helpful summary for a quick check on a server. The main Browser Monitor window is also a good place to check because of the graphical overview.

The status on all systems is updated every 900 seconds (15 minutes) by default. The default refresh rate can be changed using the Intervals option on the Options menu.

You can also set Browser Monitor to alert you when an error condition occurs. Click the Alarm on Error option on the Options menu.

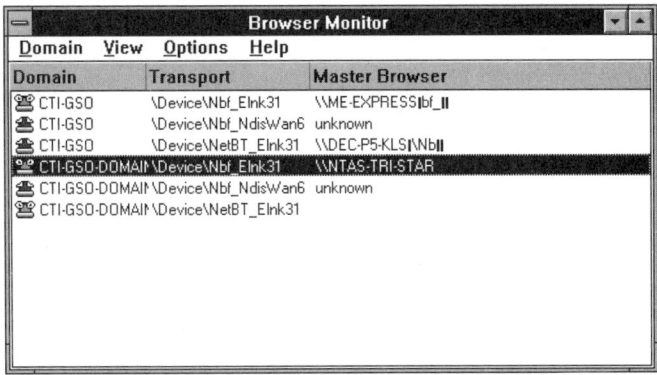

FIGURE 4.18 Notice the different shapes of the icons to the left of the domain name. The top, fourth, and sixth icons are actually blue and indicate a well system. The second, third, and fifth icons show systems that indicate some type of problem. A separate entry is shown for each transport used by a system.

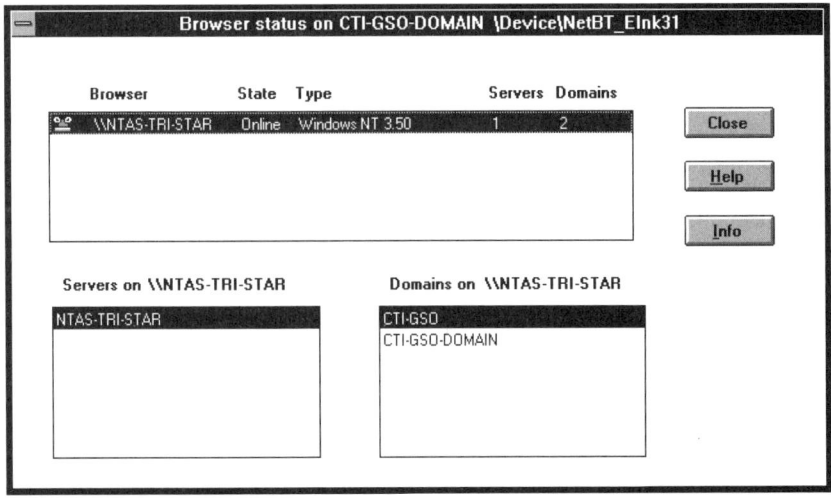

FIGURE 4.19 The top frame in this window shows a blue icon for \\NTAS-TRI-STAR, indicating that the system is currently online. You can see at a glance the type of software on the system, number of servers, and domains.

Shared Resources

NT resources that can be connected to over the network consist of printers and directories that have been explicitly shared or are special shares that are automatically created by NT. The ClipBook and applications can also share resources, but they are not covered in detail in this book. Shared resources can be used by any supported client or server on the network as if they are local resources. Shared resources are subject to the NT security established on both the share and any directories and files in the shared directory path.

All NT shares are referred to using the UNC (Universal Naming Convention). UNC names are specified by the use of the server name and the resource name:

$$\backslash\backslash \text{SERVER } \backslash \text{RESOURCE}$$

SERVER   Name of server with the resource.

RESOURCE Name of the shared resource.

Any system can connect to the device by the direct use of the UNC name or by the use of a browse dialog box to build the UNC name by selecting first the server and then the shared resource name. Many systems can use the UNC name to point to a shared resource without explicitly mapping a drive letter to the share. For instance, Microsoft Word can use the following command line in its icon to specify the location of Word:

$$\backslash\backslash \text{Server1}\backslash\text{WINWORD}\backslash\text{WINWORD.EXE}$$

This example uses a server named SERVER1 and a share named WIN-WORD. The use of the UNC name allows the client to find the Word files even if the shared resource containing the files is not currently mapped to a drive letter. Also notice that direct connect network printers show up in Print Browse dialog boxes using UNC. UNC names are also used by the NET USE command and many network API functions.

Special Shares

NT creates several special shares for specific purposes. As shown in Table 4.6, these shares are automatically created and managed by the system and should not be deleted or modified.

Adding a $ to the end of any share name turns that share into a hidden share that does not display in any browse list. This is a handy trick to use on those shares that you don't want anyone to mess with (such as the MSMAIL share, or all users' home directories). We use this on all shares that users do not need to browse. This trick works in NT, Windows for Workgroups, and Windows 95.

TABLE 4.6	Special NT Shares
Share Name	**Description**
driveletter$	All drives on an NT system are shared with a share name of the drive letter and a $. The shares are considered administrative shares and can be accessed by only administrators, server operators, and backup operator accounts.
ADMIN$	The ADMIN$ share points to the Windows NT root directory (usually C:\WINNT) and can be accessed only by administrators, server operators, and backup operator accounts. This share is used during remote administration of NT.
IPC$	The IPC$ share is used to communicate between systems. It is used by named pipes.
PRINT$	This resource is used to support shared printers.
REPL$	This share is required for export replication servers and is created by the system.
NETLOGON	The NETLOGON share is used by other NT servers when processing log-on requests.
ShareName$	Any directory shared with a $ after the share name will not be listed in any browse list on the network.

Creating a Shared Directory in NT 3.51 with File Manager:

1. Start File Manager.
2. Select the directory to share in the file window.
3. Select the Share As command from the menu or toolbar.
4. Enter the share name.
5. Enter permissions for the share.
6. Click OK.

Figure 4.20 shows the New Share dialog box creating a share named BOOKS.

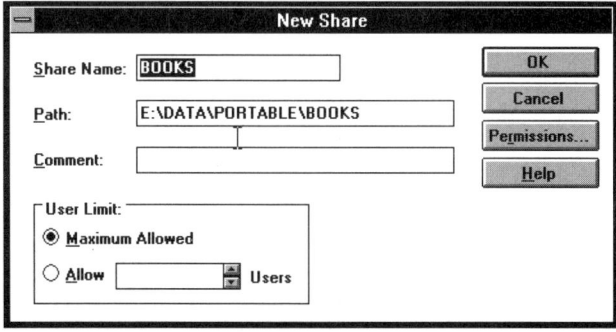

FIGURE 4.20 The New Share dialog box in File Manager can be used to create a new shared directory.

Creating a Shared Directory in NT 4.0 Using File Manager:

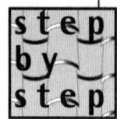

1. From File Manager, click on the create share icon, as shown on Figure 4.21 (note the selected icon). The Map Network Drive window will show up, as shown in Figure 4.22.

2. In the Path field, type two backslashes, the name of the computer, and the shared directory that you want to connect to, as shown in Figure 4.23. If you're not sure of the name of the computer or directory you want to connect to, you can browse through the list and select the computer and that share you wish to attach to, as shown on Figure 4.24. Browsing will show you only the computers in your workgroup or domain, unless your domain has a trusting relationship with other domains, in which case you will have the option to browse computers and shares in other domains, as shown in Figure 4.25.

3. To assign a drive letter to the shared directory, click the little arrow pointing down in the Drive field and select the letter you want to use, and then press ENTER, or click OK. If you do not specify a drive letter for the shared directory, Network Client assigns the first available drive letter.

4. If you want to connect your computer to the shared directory every time you log on, make sure an X appears in the Reconnect at Logon check box, as shown in Figures 4.21 through 4.25.

Creating a Shared Directory with Server Manager:

1. Start Server Manager.
2. Select the server you want to manage.
3. Select Shared Directories from the Computer menu.
4. Click the New Share button.
5. Enter the share name, path, and optionally comments.
6. Enter permissions for the share.
7. Click OK.

The Shared Directories dialog box in Figure 4.26 is handy for resolving share problems or reviewing all shares on a server.

One advantage of using Server Manager is its ability to create new shares on remote servers. This is convenient because it enables you to manage shares from any remote computer running Server Manager. Remember that you can do this in the Windows 3.1 client version of Server Manager also.

You can also create new directories with the NetShare command:

```
NET SHARE sharename=path
```

sharename   The name for the new share.

path   Description of the complete path of the share
             (C:\MDIR).

After you have created a share, users can connect to the share with File Manager or the Net Use command.

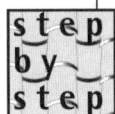

Connecting to a Shared Directory with File Manager in NT 3.51:

1. Start File Manager.
2. Select the Connect Network Drive command from the menu or toolbar.
3. Select the drive letter to use for the resource.
4. Enter the UNC name, or select the resource from the browse box.
5. Click OK.

The Connect Network Drive dialog box shows up in many places. As shown in Figure 4.27, it is a common dialog box within Windows and can be used by virtually any application. When you click the Network button in a file open or save dialog box, you get this dialog box.

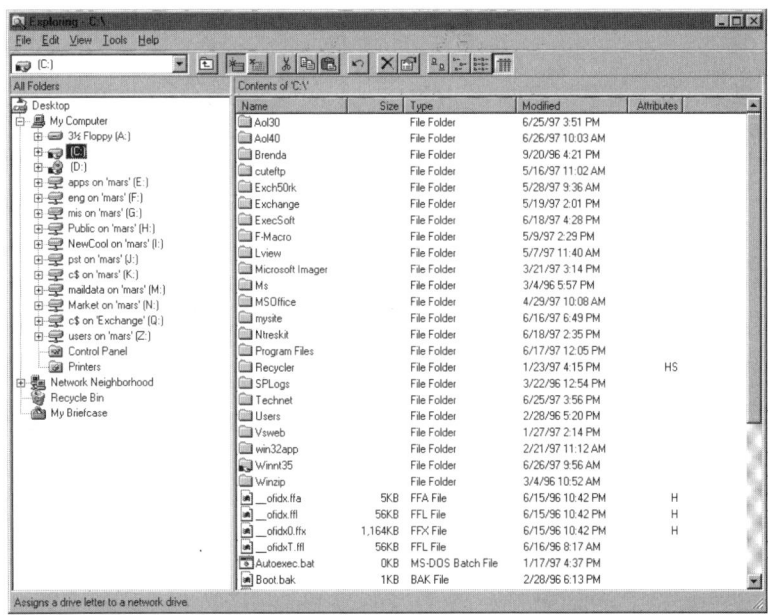

FIGURE 4.21 Assigning a drive letter to a network drive, notice the hard drive icon selected on the figure.

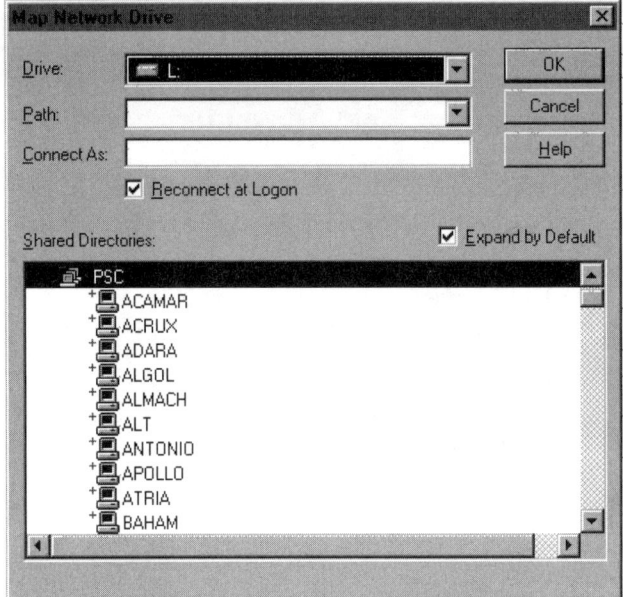

FIGURE 4.22 In Map Network Drive window, choose the machine you want to connect and the letter you want to assign to the drive.

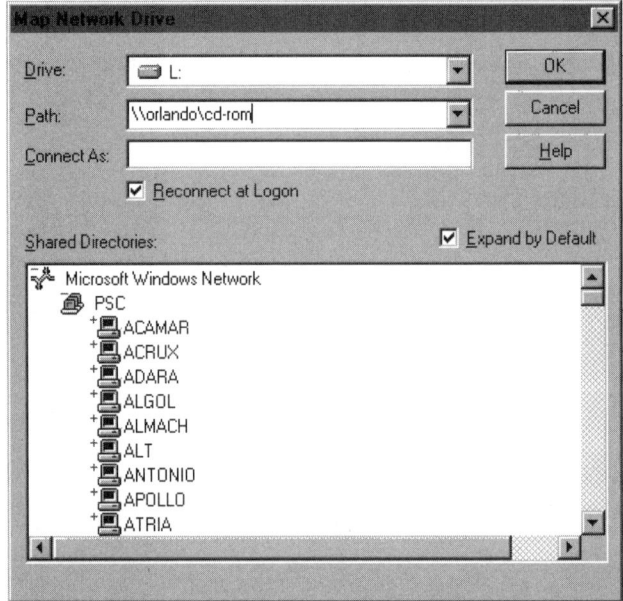

FIGURE 4.23 You can also type in the path field the name of the computer and share to which you want to attach.

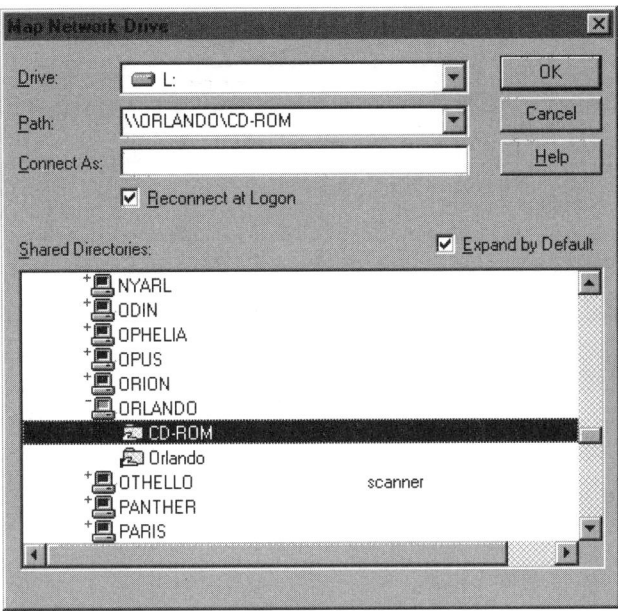

FIGURE 4.24 You can select the computer and share from the network list.

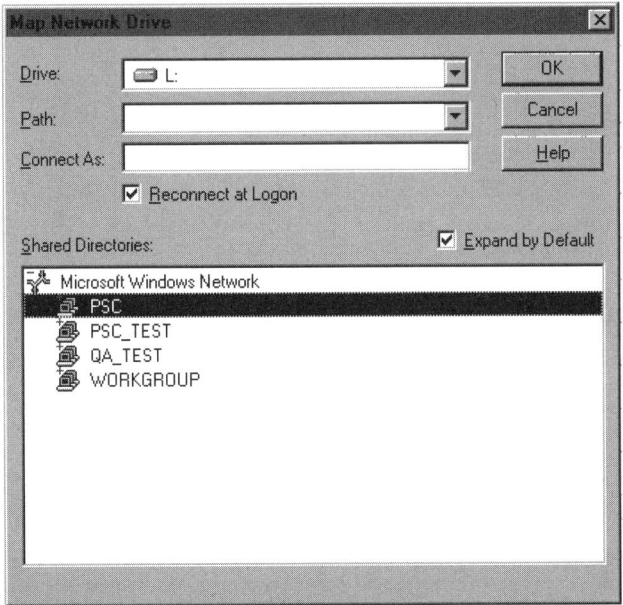

FIGURE 4.25 The global network list also show you the domains you can attach to and the computers part of that domain.

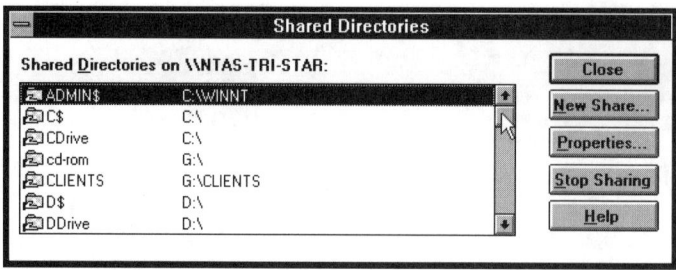

FIGURE 4.26 The Shared Directories dialog box from Server Manager provides quick access to a number of options for shares.

Click the Reconnect at Logon box if you want to connect to this share automatically each time you log on.

Turning off the Expand by Default check box speeds the display of this dialog box because it does not automatically expand the workgroups and domains when the dialog box opens. This action allows you to immediately enter the path manually or to select it from the history list without waiting for the browse list to return.

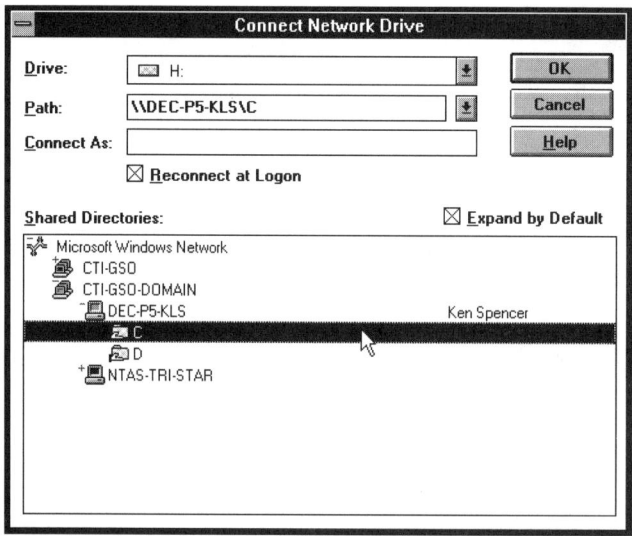

FIGURE 4.27 The Connect Network Drive dialog box from File Manager in Windows for Workgroups works basically the same way in both Windows for Workgroups and NT.

Monitoring Shared Resources in NT 4.0 and NT 3.51

There are several ways to monitor shared resources in NT Server using both standard server tools and NT Resource Kit tools. Server Manager is the most obvious tool to use and is located in the Administrative Tools group in Program Manager. Net Watch is another useful tool and comes with the NT Resource Kit.

Figure 4.28 shows Net Watch running on NT Server 3.51, and Figure 4.29 shows Net Watch running on NT Server 4.0.

Double-clicking a share connection displays details on the connection including the number of files that are currently open on the connection. Double-clicking a share displays information on the share itself and the number of connections to the share. You can stop sharing a resource by clicking on the share name and pressing Delete or selecting Stop Sharing from the connection menu.

Using NetWatch to Monitor Shared Resources:

1. Double-click Net Watch in the NT Resource Kit group to start NetWatch.
2. Select the server to monitor.
3. Double-click any share to see the details of the current usage.

We personally like NetWatch because it presents a nice graphical interface showing the shares and any users of a share. Because it monitors only shares, it is designed with great efficiency in mind for performing that task. Any task can be performed with only a few clicks of the mouse.

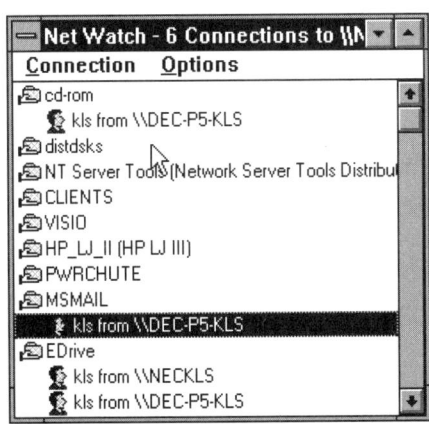

FIGURE 4.28 Net Watch monitors the shares on the PDC in this sample.

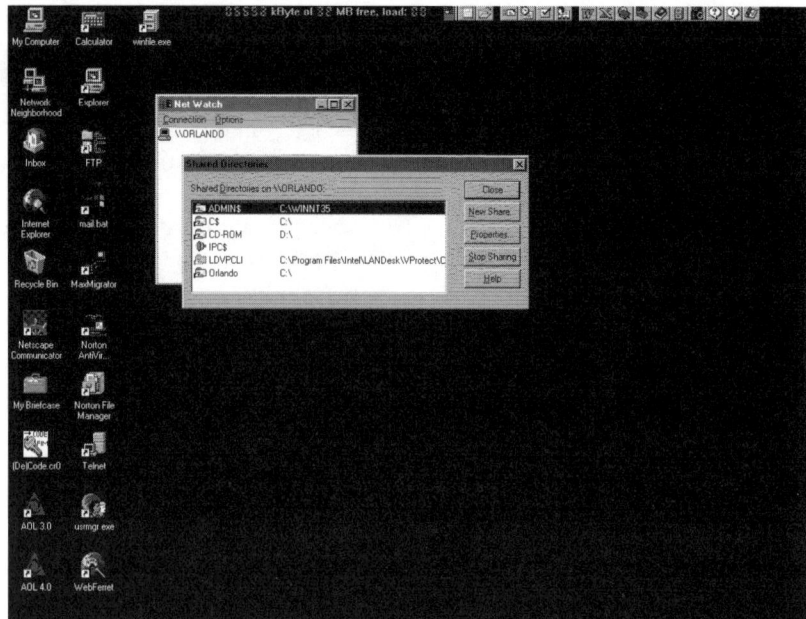

FIGURE 4.29 Net Watch running on NT Server 4.0.

Server Manager is another tool that is useful for managing shared resources. Server Manager is useful because it not only shows the shares but also provides quick access to other information on current users, files in use, and other server-related options.

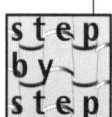

Monitoring Shares in Use with Server Manager:

1. Start Server Manager.
2. Click the Shares button.
3. Select the resource in question.
4. Review the bottom window, which shows all users connected to the resource. Pay attention to the In Use column. In Use indicates when a user has a file open on the resource by displaying a value of Yes by the file. A No value indicates that the user has a connection to the resource but is not actively using the resource. A quick look down this list should show which users are placing the load on the resource.

Domain Overview

A domain is a domain is a domain. A domain in this sense is Microsoft's terminology for a grouping of NT servers and other LAN manager servers. The key thing to remember about a domain is that you can treat a domain of servers as a single unit for management and security purposes. Systems are added to a domain by assigning the domain name to a new system during installation or from an NT Server, which is a Backup Domain Controller (BDC) or a Primary Domain Controller (PDC) in the domain (more on this later).

Domains are really neat because all the servers in the domain share the same user account and security database. Users log in to the domain once and have access to resources throughout the domain. This access makes using and managing a domain much simpler than a network that has several individual servers (such as NetWare 3.x). There are no multiple servers to manage account and security databases for and no myriad of server names for users to remember. What a dream!

Domains also segregate the workstations in a network when a user browses the network for file or print resources. All servers and workstations in a domain appear indented under the domain in a browse list. You also see workstations in a workgroup listed under the workgroup name in the list. Both workgroups and domain workstations can appear in a browse list at the same time.

Primary Domain Controller

The key to the successful implementation of the domain concept is the organization of the servers in the domain. NT Server uses one server in each domain to serve as the Primary Domain Controller (PDC).

The PDC maintains the master copy of the account and security database. Currently only NT servers can serve as PDCs, because they are the only servers that fully support trusted domains and other features of the NT Server network.

The PDC is the system that makes all changes to the account and security database. NT Server allows you to manage the account and security database easily with User Manager for Domains. User Manager for Domains allows you to choose which domain to manage by selecting the domain from a list. User Manager for Domains automatically updates the database on the PDC as changes are made.

In addition to the PDC, you should have at least one Backup Domain Controllers (BDC) per domain. If the PDC becomes unavailable, a BDC can be promoted to primary domain controller, and the domain continues to function.The user account and security database is copied from the PDC every five minutes to all BDCs in the domain. All other NT Server BDCs in the network ask the PDC if any changes to the database have been made. Changes are then sent to each NT Server BDC in the network. The entire database is not sent, only the changes are sent.

In case of a BDC being promoted to a PDC (PDC crashes, for example), an up-to-date copy of the domain's directory database is replicated from the old PDC to the new one, and the old PDC is demoted to a BDC or if there was only one BDC and the PDC crashed, then there won't be a back-up for the new PDC!

In this case, if the former PDC later returns to service, you will need to demote the former PDC to BDC. Until it is demoted to a BDC, it will not run the Net Logon service nor participate in authentication of user log-ons, and its icon in the Server Manager window will be dimmed.

Microsoft uses the term *replication* to indicate the copying of anything from one system to another system. See "Replication of Files to Other Systems" for more information on copying files to other systems.

The PDC is a very busy system because of all the tasks that it performs. The larger the network, the busier the PDC. The PDC validates most of the network log-on requests, performing replication of the SAM database, maintaining the browse list for domain resources, and attending to other tasks related to the domain.

Here are some tips for successful use of a PDC:

- For networks larger than a few workstations (say 100), install a separate NT Server as the PDC. This server doesn't need much disk (500MB) or RAM (32MB).

- Don't share any printers or file resources on the PDC.

- Don't run SQL Server or any other intensive software on the PDC.

- If you do run SQL Server on the PDC, don't check the Boost SQL Server Priority box in the SQL Server Setup program.

- Run the latest version of NT Server on the PDC. If you run higher versions of NT Server on a BDC than on the PDC, newer features (such as account lockout in 3.5) are disabled. If you run the new version on the PDC, NT Server usually enables the features for the entire network.

Backup Domain Controllers

Every NT Server BDC in a domain can serve as a backup to the PDC by maintaining a copy of the domain database. Any NT Server BDC can be promoted to the PDC with the assurance that the domain database is no more than five minutes out of date.

The NT Server BDC in a domain also improves the performance of the network. Each NT Server BDC can process a log-on request by any workstation in the domain. This capability drastically improves the performance of the domain when a large number of users log on the domain at one time, for instance, first thing in the morning after they get to work.

This discussion of other NT servers in a domain becomes more important in our discussion on tips for managing your domain later in this chapter.

Domain Models

The Microsoft NT Server documentation (Concepts and Planning Guide) lists four different domain models. We have added our own to the end of the list.

- **Single Domain Model**–This type of domain consists of a single domain for all servers. This model is best for organizations that have small networks (with only a few servers in one location) or do not need to split their network into multiple domains for organizational purposes.
- **Master Domain Model**–This model uses a single Master domain that is trusted by all other domains. The master domain contains all user accounts and global groups that are recognized by the other domains.
- **Multiple Master Domain Model**–This model is built on the master domain model and primarily adds scaleability to the concept. A small number of master domains are used as the account domains, which are trusted by all other domains. This flexible model works well with large organizations and large networks.
- **Complete Trust Model**–This model is well suited to organizations that are decentralized and want local departments to manage their own domains. Each domain in this model trusts every other domain in order for each user account to be available on every system. This model is very flexible but requires managing lots of trust relationships [no of servers * (no of servers − 1)]. This task may not be too monumental, because a trust relationship is usually established once and left alone.
- **Roll Your Own**–The best model to use may be your own variation of one of these models. Most networks do not require all users to have access to all domains in a network. This is especially true for typical organizations in industries such as manufacturing, banking, insurance, or any other organization in which people are locally based and do not travel extensively.

The documentation mentions briefly the concept of an account domain. This is a domain that contains the accounts for other domains that do not have their own accounts. The master domain models use account domains for the master domains.

Single Domain Model

The single domain model consists of one or more NT servers in a single domain. The domain is very easy to manage and establish. The single domain model can consist of any number of workstations and servers but has only one domain. This model is easy to manage, because there are no trust relationships or multiple domains, but it will suffer in performance if the domain grows too large.

Master Domain Model

The master domain model has one domain that contains all user accounts and groups. All other domains in the network trust this domain and use the accounts and groups from the master domain. A network based on this model is still very easy to manage, because all user accounts and groups are located in the master domain.

The ease of management of the master domain model is one reason that this model is used in Microsoft's own networks. Networks based on this model have one domain that contains all user accounts for the company while each office typically has its own domain. The local domains in each office have groups that reference the user accounts in the master domain. Using this model, which is shown in Figure 4.30, a user can move to any office in the company while keeping the same user account.

Multiple Master Domain Model

The multiple master domain model uses several master domains to manage the domain databases for the network. Each domain trusts all the master

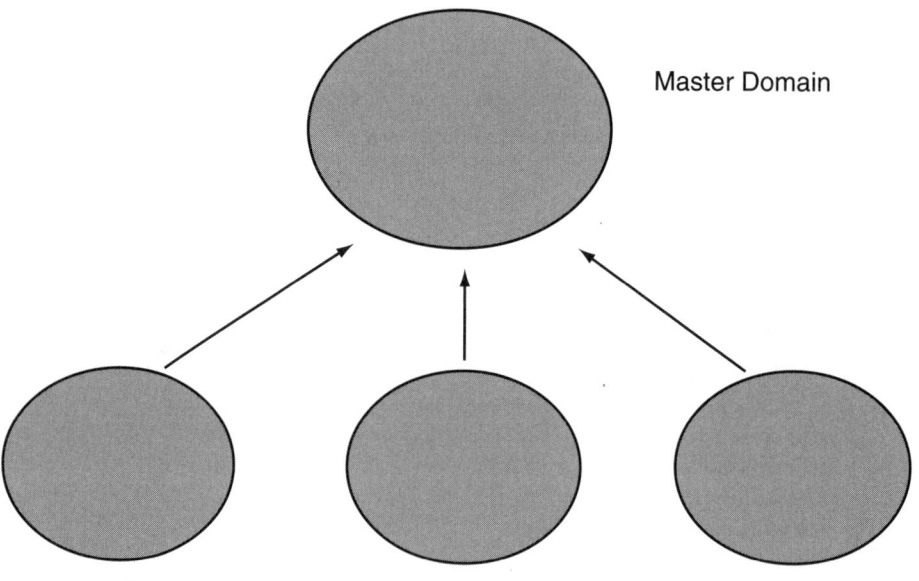

Master Domain

Other Domains

FIGURE 4.30   Organization of a master domain model. Notice how all the other domains trust the master domain, which allows them to use the account database from the master domain.

domains, and the master domains trust each other. This relationship makes all user accounts in the master domain available to all other domains.

In Microsoft's multiple master domain model, domains other than the master domains are not trusted by any other domains, as shown in Figure 4.31. You may want to establish a trust relationship between other domains if you have added users to those domains that are not in the master domains. This would also apply to the master domain model.

Microsoft uses the master domain model for its own networks. According to an internal Microsoft NT product manager, Microsoft has more than 9,000 user accounts on the master domain. It has trust relationships with all other domains in the different offices and locations around the world. Personnel can move from one location to another within the entire organization simply log on, and go to work.

Complete Trust Model

The complete trust model (see Figure 4.32) is the most flexible of all the domain models and also the most difficult to set up. This model is built by establishing a trust relationship with every other domain in the network. This means that an account can be added to any domain in the system and instantly used on any other domain.

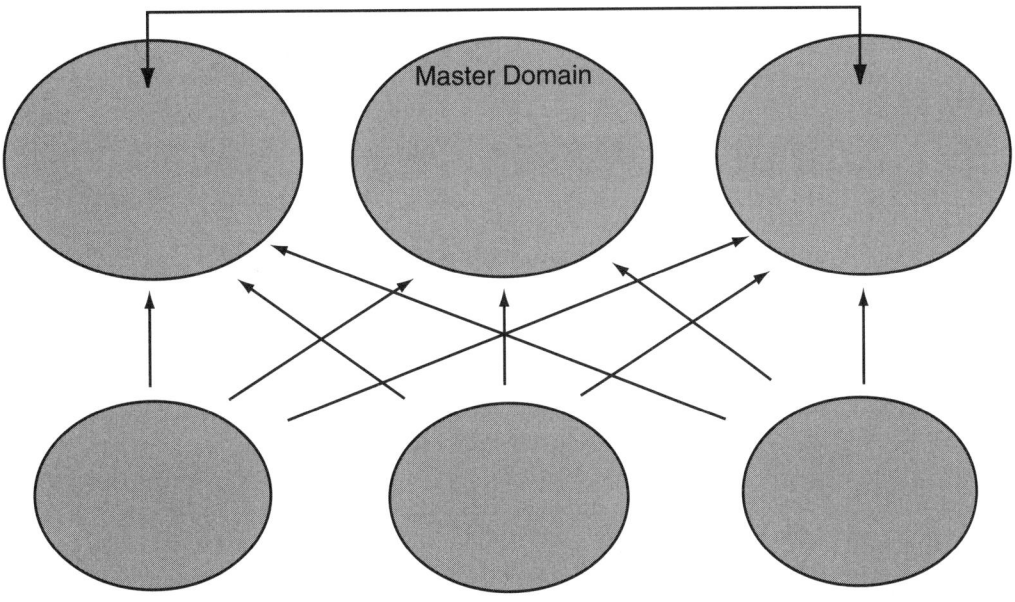

Master Domain

Other Domains

FIGURE 4.31 Organizations of a multiple master domain model. Notice how all the other domains trust all the master domains, allowing the user accounts from the master domains to be used on all other domains.

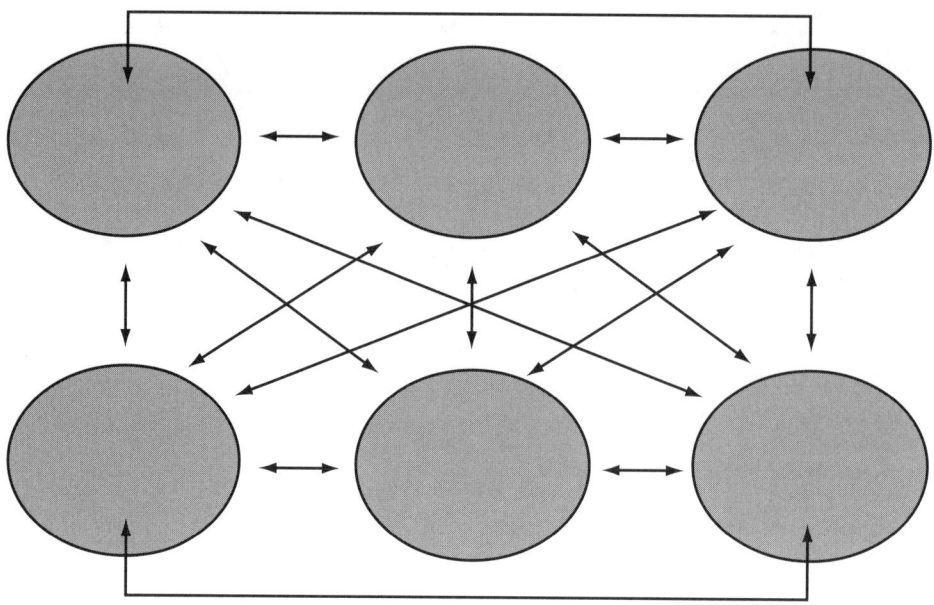

FIGURE 4.32 Organization of a complete trust model. Notice how all domains trust all other domains.

The only problem with this model is the overhead of creating the trust relationships. The number of trust relationships is [no of servers * (no of servers − 1)]. As mentioned earlier, this number does not seem so bad when you consider that once the relationships are created, you do not have to manage them further except when you add a new domain.

The complete trust model may add to your management chores because of the number of security databases that must be backed up or restored and managed. You should be backing up all servers in your network anyway, but this model means that a lost connection to the servers in a domain or the loss of a domain with no BDC disables all accounts that are in that domain.

Roll Your Own Model

The flexibility of the domain architecture makes it easy to design your own model. You may need a network that has only two domains with some type of trust relationship between them. This type of architecture would be ideal for local management by the department that owns the domain.

On the other hand, you may have a large organization that requires several diverse networks, each with its own domain and domain database. A Wide Area Network could be used to link the domains and allow both local and remote administration of each domain.

Another organization may have part of a network that works on the complete trust model with other parts of the network based on the master model, or a combination of one or the other. The key thing to remember for your network is to spend the time to plan its architecture and maintenance. You should include your cable plants, network components, backup plans, and common sense in your plans. Remember: If it can fail, it will fail.

Domains and Systems Management Server

Systems Management Server depends upon the domain structure for many of its operations and power. The SMS site model consists of one or more domains for managing systems. The logical ordering of sites and domains can make life much easier if the domains and sites are built carefully.

The master domain model fits nicely with the site model when the master domain is the central site. This grouping is a natural because, with this model, all information collected by SMS will roll up to the central site.

Networks using SMS should install multiple servers for the best performance. SQL Server runs best when it is running on a dedicated or lightly loaded server. You can install SMS on any system running NT Server. You can also set up other NT Servers as helper servers. The only requirement is that every site must have its own SMS server.

More information on SMS and other Back Office products can be found in other books in this Prentice Hall series.

Domain, Server, User Account, and Group Names and Tips

Naming conventions are a very important part of your planning process for the system design. Domain, server, and user account and group names are used in every NT Server network. Many users in the past have not placed much significance on naming conventions as their systems have grown over time. This often leads to problems with confusing names, as more and more users are added to the system. We have seen many networks where servers are named after comic strip characters, TV shows, and the like. Even worse, some systems have servers named SERVER1, SERVER2, and so forth. The same problem occurs with domain, server, and group names as system managers become more familiar with the concepts.

We prefer to use a more formal system that makes creating the names easy and to some extent prevents problems with duplicate names. Every name should be meaningful and related to the operations it supports. For instance, a server that provides file and print services may have a prefix of FSPS or FP. The entire name could be FPSHIPPING. A file server might be FSHIPPING. Likewise domain and group names should relate to what they are used for. You may have a domain called Manufacturing or Shipping. This is much better than DOMAIN1 or DOMAIN. I also like to add _DM as a suffix to domain names to distinguish them from workgroup names.

Table 4.7 lists several items to consider.

The major point of all the naming conventions is to decide on a format and stick to it. Avoid using names that are cute but meaningless because this practice can lead to confusion when users browse the network.

Domain Names

Domain names can be from 1 to 15 characters in length and must be unique from all other domains. A domain name is only a descriptive name as in the case of a user name. The domain name is linked to a security ID that is never visible and is used by NT as the internal ID for the domain name.

Changing a Domain Name:

1. Start the Network applet in Control Panel.
2. Click the Change button beside the current domain name.
3. Enter the new domain name.
4. Close the Network applet.
5. Reboot the system if you are requested to do so.

TABLE 4.7	Domain Naming Conventions
Name	**Description**
Domains	Domain names should describe the function of the domain. If you have only one domain and it will never grow, you may choose to give it the name of your company. If you have a much larger system, the domain names may be the location or function of the domain. The major point is to establish a format and stick to it.
Users	User names are required for people to access the network. User names may be very simple (users' initials) or very complex (5+2+1 format—first 5 characters of last name + first two characters of the first name + a single digit starting at 1).
Shares	Share names for servers should be descriptive and simple. Share names are used for both file and print services.
Computers	Computer names should describe the function of the server. You may want to prefix server names if your servers are used for different functions. For instance, the application server in shipping would be APSHIPPING while the file server in shipping would be FSSHIPPING. Naming systems this way sorts the servers by type in any browse list they appear in. Other conventions can be used depending upon your needs.

Computer Names

Computer names can be from 1 to 15 characters in length and must be different from all other computers on the domain. Each NT computer must also have an account on the domain server.

Computer names must be entered during the installation of NT Server but may be changed later. The Network applet in Control Panel is used to make the change.

Changing a Computer Name:

1. Start the Network applet in Control Panel.
2. Click the Change button beside the current computer name.
3. Enter the new computer name.
4. Close the Network applet.
5. Reboot the system when you are requested to do so.

Use care when changing the computer name of a production server, as workstations, servers, and many applications may have the computer name stored in password lists, program INI files, and so on. Even though the system ID for the server does not change, the simple name change can be trouble. This can create havoc when you change a computer name and users can't access the system.

Hints for Managing Your Domain

Domains are both the easiest and most difficult to maintain of all the network features of NT Server. Properly managed domains are easy to set up and manage as long as you follow the rules. These things differentiate a good domain practice from a bad practice:

- Make sure that a backup server can communicate with the domain controller during the installation process. If it complains when you supply the domain name, then check out the network connections (cable, card, repeater, and so on) before continuing. If you install a backup server with the same domain name as a new domain, you must reinstall NT Server before you can use the server on the original domain!
- Plan your domain strategy before you install the servers and create domains.
- Don't duplicate user names within different domains.
- Plan the naming architecture for domains, user accounts, and groups.
- Plan the network topologies and protocol(s) to be used for your network.

Registry Size and Domains

The Registry can grow as needed as your system changes and grows. There is one possible scenario that you may run into if you have a large network. The Registry has a default size limit of 15MB for the SAM database, which can be exceeded if you have many user accounts. Fortunately, it is easy to change the size limit.

The size limit for the SAM database is controlled by the Registry key

```
HKEY_LOCAL_MACHINE\SYSTEM\CurrentControlSet\
Control\RegistrySizeLimit
```

This key controls the overall size of the Registry, which is 25% of the default Paged Pool Size default 32MB. The minimum the Registry Size Limit can be is 4MB and the maximum is 102MB. The size of the Registry Size Limit value can't be greater than 80% of the Paged Pool Size, which can be a maximum of 128MB. The value for Paged Pool Size is under the key

```
E\SYSTEM\CurrentControlSet\Control\SessionManager -\
Memory Management\PagedPoolSize
```

A Registry Size Limit of 8MB can support a user accounts database of 5000 users. The maximum size of 128MB can support 80,000 users, but Microsoft does not recommend using this value. If you change the Registry Size Limit on the PDC to allow for more user accounts, you must also update all BDCs to use the same size limit.

Changing the Registry Size Limit and the Paged Pool Size:

1. Calculate the size of the new Registry Size Limit. Total the value of the Registry Hives in the \WINNT\SYSTEM32\CONFIG directory and multiply by at least 1.3 to provide a 30% buffer. You can set the Registry Size Limit to 0xffffffff to force the size limit to 80% of the current Paged Pool Size.

2. Calculate the new size of the Paged Pool. Multiply the new Registry Size Limit by 1.2.

3. Start REGEDT32.

4. Edit the value for the Registry Size Limit key, and replace it with your new entry.

5. Edit the value for the Paged Pool Size key, and replace it with your new entry.

6. Exit REGEDT32.

7. Restart the system.

NT Server 3.51 introduced a change to the System applet in Control Panel that allows you to change the maximum Registry size quickly. The bottom of the Virtual Memory dialog box now contains a frame titled Registry Size. The Maximum Registry Size (MB) box contains the new size, while the current size is displayed just above the maximum.

Changing the Registry Size Limit with Control Panel:

1. Start the System applet in Control Panel.
2. Click the Virtual Memory button.
3. Enter the new Registry size in the Maximum Registry Size (MB) box.
4. Click OK.
5. Close the System applet.
6. Restart the system when you are prompted to do so.

Adding or Removing an NT Workstation or NT Server in a Domain

An NT system must be added to a domain before it can use any resources on the domain. During the process, a user account is created for the new system on the domain. The user account is used by the system each time it logs on the domain and is transparent to the user of the NT system.

There are several ways for an Administrator to add a system to a domain.

Adding an NT System During Installation:

1. Choose to join an existing domain, and enter the domain name when prompted.

Adding an NT System Using Server Manager:

1. Start Server Manager.
2. Choose Add to Domain from the Computer menu.
3. Click the button for NT Workstation or NT Server.
4. Enter the system's name in the Computer Name box.
5. Click Add.
6. Click the Close button when you are finished adding systems.

You can also remove an NT workstation or server from a domain. Removing an NT system from the domain does not allow that system to participate in domain security. There are two ways to remove an NT system.

Removing an NT System Using Server Manager:

1. Start Server Manager.
2. Select the system to remove.
3. Choose Remove from Domain from the Computer menu or press Del.
4. Click the Yes button on the confirmation box.
5. Click OK on the information box.

Removing an NT System Using Net Computer:

1. From the command prompt, enter the following command:

    ```
    NET COMPUTER \\computername /DEL
    ```

You may find that you must remove a computer account if you are reinstalling NT Server or another server on the domain. I have seen the installation fail because the account for the system already existed on the domain. This problem usually occurs when you do a reinstall, not an upgrade. If it occurs, just follow the steps for removing the account from a domain, and then perform the reinstall.

Changing Domains with a Server—Not!

An NT Server, which is a PDC or a BDC, cannot be moved from one domain to another without reinstalling the NT Server software. This limitation makes NT Server servers as secure as possible.

The only way to bring up the server on the new domain is to do a complete reinstall on the server after it is connected to the new domain. All security information on the system is replaced. This is actually not too bad when you consider that the security information will be updated within five minutes or so from the PDC.

Synchronizing Domain Controllers

All servers on a domain are automatically synchronized every few minutes (five minutes is the default). There is usually no need for any intervention by a system manager except for special circumstances. One such circumstance could be when you need to down the domain controller for maintenance or some other reason. You may want to do an immediate synchronization to make sure that the backup server you use to replace the PDC is in synch with the current PDC. Immediate synchronization may also be required when you change a user parameter (say the log-on script name) and then try to test the change. If the log-on server that processes your log-on is the PDC, you are okay. However, if a BDC processes the log-on, it probably will not have received the replicated change when you perform your log-on. The solution is to perform an immediate synchronization with the PDC.

The normal synchronizing process updates the security database of all BDCs with the PDC. Once the process takes place, the security database on all backup servers should be the same as the PDC until a change is made to it. Any backup server can be promoted to the domain controller with no problems immediately after the synchronization is completed.

What happens when you need to make absolutely sure that a backup server is synchronized with the domain controller? You can take one of the following steps, depending upon whether or not you want to update only one system or all the backup servers on the network.

Synchronizing All Backup Servers (Server Manager):

1. Start Server Manager.
2. Select the Primary Domain Controller from the computer list.
3. Choose Synchronize Entire Domain from the Computer menu.

Synchronizing One Particular Backup Domain Controller (Server Manager):

1. Start Server Manager.
2. Select the server to be updated from the computer list.
3. Choose Synchronize with Domain Controller from the Computer menu.

Synchronizing One Particular Backup Domain Controller (Net Accounts):

1. Enter the following command on the BDC to synchronize:

   NET ACCOUNTS /sync

Synchronizing All Backup Domain Controllers (Net Accounts):

1. Enter the following command on the PDC:

    NET ACCOUNTS /sync

The more servers and users you have in a domain, the longer the synchronization takes. For several hundred users and fewer than five servers, the process normally occurs in seconds. Just be aware that it can vary with your particular configuration.

Promoting a Backup Domain Controller to a Primary Domain Controller

It is sometimes desirable to switch the role of PDC to another system. Shutting down the PDC, performing maintenance on the PDC, and testing a BDC are just a few possible reasons. Fortunately, the process is simple using Server Manager.

Promoting a Backup Domain Controller to a Primary Domain Controller:

1. Start Server Manager.
2. Synchronize the server to be the new PDC with the current PDC if possible.
3. Select the Server to be the new domain controller from the computer list.
4. Choose Promote to Domain Controller from the Computer menu.

You normally will not need to demote a PDC to a server unless the domain controller is offline for some reason when the new PDC is promoted. When this situation occurs, the old domain controller must be demoted before it can be placed back online. If it is not demoted, the Net Logon service will not start on the original domain controller.

This situation is actually not too rare, it can easily occur when the PDC goes down, after which a BDC is promoted to PDC. When the old PDC is rebooted, it still thinks it is the PDC.

Demoting a Primary Domain Controller to a Backup Domain Controller:

1. Boot the original domain controller without connecting it to the network.
2. Log on as Administrator.
3. Start Server Manager.

> 4. Select the server to be demoted from domain controller.
>
> 5. Choose Demote to Server from the Computer menu.

Stopping the Primary Domain Controller

Whenever the domain controller must be taken offline for any reason, you should promote another BDC to be the PDC to ensure that the network still functions correctly. During the promotion process the security database of the new server will be synchronized with the PDC, then the BDC can be safely promoted to PDC.

The only time you should take down the PDC without promoting another BDC first is if the PDC is unstable and the promotion cannot be performed.

Logging On a Backup Domain Controller

You should not log on immediately after reboot to a system that has just been set up as a BDC because attempting to log on immediately may cause the log-on process to complete before the account database has been replicated to that system. Because the replication of the database occurs every five minutes, you should have to wait no longer than five minutes to log on. You can be sure that this is the case if you cannot log on with a valid account but can successfully log on with the default Administrator account with no password.

Trust Relationships

The idea of computers trusting computers is scary! *Trust relationship* is a term Microsoft came up with to describe how one domain interacts with another domain. Most networks require a user on one area of the network to have an account on another server in order to access resources on the other system. The trust relationship between any two NT Server domains removes this restriction by allowing user accounts and global groups in one domain to be granted privileges in another domain.

The trust relationship is implemented by treating the two domains that will have the trust relationship as different entities. One domain becomes the trusting domain, which recognizes the user accounts and global groups of the trusted domain. The split trust distinction allows one domain to access another domain, while users in the second domain cannot access the first domain. This split trust relationship can allow you to build a hierarchy of domains with different types of access between each pair of domains.

Every trust relationship is between two domains only and represents a one-way relationship between them. You must implement a two-way trust relationship as two separate trust relationships.

The trust concept brings a tremendous flexibility to the management of your network, but it also adds a lot of responsibility. When you give permission to a global group or add a global group to a local group in a domain, the administrator of the other domain can add other users to your domain automatically by adding them to the global group. See Chapter 12 for more on security issues in domains.

The Concepts and Planning Guide has a good discussion of trust relationships and their inner workings with other domains.

 For information about planning and managing trust relationships, see the *Windows NT Server Resource Kit* version 4.0.

Using Trust Relationships

A trust relationship is created between two domains with User Manager for Domains.

Creating a Trust Relationship:

1. The trusted domain administrator chooses the trusting domain with User Manager and enters the trust password.

2. The trusting domain administrator establishes the other side of the relationship with User Manager.

Trust relationships are secured by the servers in a domain by an automatically changing password that is hidden by NT Server. Whenever a new trust relationship is added, the server immediately changes the password. This password is then changed regularly by NT Server to further secure the trust relationship. When a trust relationship is broken, it cannot be reestablished by simply restoring one end of the relationship, because there is no way to know the trust password. The relationship must be removed completely from both ends and reestablished.

The Microsoft Knowledge Base mentions a caveat that can occur when you create a domain. After the relationship is set up on the trusted domain, the administrator of the trusting domain has only one chance to enter the password correctly. As soon as the password is entered on the trusting domain, the NT Server changes it. If the password was entered incorrectly, it will not match. The only resolution to this problem is to totally remove the trust relationship on the trusted domain and add it again. The administrator of the trusting domain can then complete the trust relationship.

CREATING TRUST RELATIONSHIPS

Trust relationships are managed with User Manager for Domains. The process is simple and usually takes only a few minutes.

Creating Trust Relationships:

1. Start User Manager for Domains.
2. Select Trust Relationships on the Policies menu.
3. Click the Add button for the appropriate relationship.
4. Enter the domain name and password.
5. Close the dialog box.

You must go through this procedure once for each relationship. For instance, if you want to have a trusted and trusting relationship with another domain, you must run the procedure twice on each system. Figure 4.33 shows the Trust Relationships dialog box used for this process.

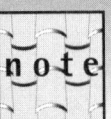

You may encounter a message that the trust relationship cannot be confirmed on the domain. This error usually occurs when your domains are separated over a WAN. After you have set up the trust relationship, test it by trying to access a public service with an account on your domain. If it works, the relationship should be okay.

Trust Relationships

Domain: CTI-GSO-DOMAIN

Trusted Domains:

Permitted to Trust this Domain:

Cancel

Help

Add...

Remove

Add...

Remove

FIGURE 4.33 The Trust Relationships dialog box enables you to establish a trust relationship with other systems.

Duplicate user accounts on different domains can cause problems when the two domains trust each other. Make sure that users have an account on only one domain and that they use that account for assigning permissions. This assignment will clear up any problem, because only one account with that user name will exist.

Designing Network Servers

NT was designed for distributed computing environments. Many traditional mainframe and network systems embraced distributed environments only when they had to, resulting in patches to existing systems to facilitate the new requirements. Because of the modular design in NT and the support for client/server architecture in the NT internals, NT is most at home when it is used in a distributed environment.

Table 4.8 lists several types of suggested servers and describes why each should be used.

Don't be constrained by the suggestions in Table 4.8. You may find that you need one or more dedicated or shared servers for specific tasks, such as controlling factory machines or managing specific application functions. It is not unusual to have several dedicated database servers on one network, each handling a particular application or set of applications.

TABLE 4.8 Types of Common Servers

Server Type	Description
Primary Domain Controller	The PDC handles most log-on requests, and lots of other overhead. For systems other than small networks, this server should be a separate system.
Backup Domain Controller	Normally every NT Server should be a BDC. A BDC provides assistance during answering log-on requests and takes over as PDC only if the PDC goes down.
Database server	A system such as SQL Server or Oracle running on NT should be on its own server. A dedicated database server can be tuned for performance and will not be bogged down by other requests.
File and print server	Heavy demand for file and print servers often suggests a dedicated server or at least a combination file and print server.
Systems Management Server	Large sites should have a dedicated server for SMS if there are frequent log-on/log-out occurrences and many packages being distributed. Remember that SMS must have access to SQL server.
Communications Server	A dedicated communications server is a good idea when there will be sizable numbers of frequent RAS users and possibly heavy demand for fax services.

Computer Names and NT Server

Every NT Workstation or NT Server on the network must have an account name for the system. The account entry is normally generated automatically when a system is added to a domain. Users and system managers do not have to be concerned with the account name unless the computer name is changed.

Changing a Computer Name:

1. Log on with an Administrator account to the machine on which you are going to change the name.
2. Start the Network applet in Control Panel.
3. Click the Change button beside the computer name.
4. Enter the new name and click OK.
5. Log on the domain as a Domain Admin user, and start Server Manager from the Administrator Tools group.
6. Select the system on which you changed the name.
7. Select Remove from Domain from the Computer menu, or press Del.
8. Resynchronize the domain with all BDCs.
9. Select Add to Domain from the Computer menu.
10. Select Windows NT Workstation or Windows NT Server for Computer Type.
11. Enter the computer's name.
12. Click the Add button.
13. Resynchronize the domain with all BDCs.
14. Click Close.
15. Reboot the system on which you changed the name.
16. Change any user specifications that referenced the old server name, including any UNC names in the command line of icons, startup files, INI files, and so on.

Multiple Network Interface Cards in One Server

NT Server enables you to install multiple Network Interface Cards (NICs) in one server to improve the performance of the network. Each card must be installed on a different network segment (Ethernet) or ring (Token Ring or FDDI). Figure 4.34 illustrates a sample of how *not* to hook up multiple network cards. The problem with this figure is that NIC 1 and NIC 2 are both connected to the same logical network through the router. In this

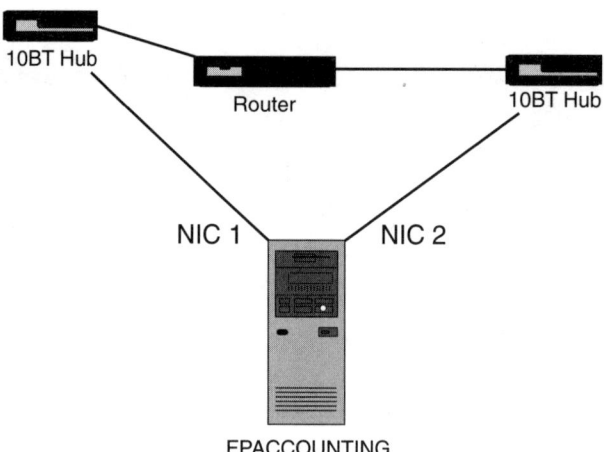

10BT Hub

Router

10BT Hub

NIC 1   NIC 2

FPACCOUNTING

FIGURE 4.34 How not to configure multiple NICs in one server.

example, the router routes all traffic on the network segments to all other segments. This setup can cause a variety of problems, from duplicate name found messages to machines that won't boot.

One resolution to this situation is to disconnect one or the other NIC from the network. In our example, either NIC 1 or NIC 2 would be disconnected. Another option is to use the router to filter traffic where the two segments do not see the same packets.

The best approach is to separate the two networks and make the only place they come together at the server via NIC 1 and NIC 2. This is actually how a system with multiple network cards is designed to work. Network traffic is segregated across the two networks, improving performance, and there are two paths in and out of the server, again improving performance.

Mixed Language Networks

NT Server works well in networks that use foreign languages because of its support for UNICODE and other features supporting multiple languages, Particularly those using domains with mixed languages. When an NT server is added to a domain with another language, the Administrator account on the new server changes its spelling to match the Administrator account from the domain. This change occurs because the domain account database is replicated to the new server shortly after it is added to the domain.

The Knowledge Base suggests two possible resolutions to the problem:

- Creating accounts on the domain for all possible spellings of Administrator that could be applicable on your network.
- Adding separate accounts for user management and placing them in the Administrators group for the domain.

Coexistence of Windows NT Server with Other Networks

NT works well in a network with multiple types of operating systems. LAN Manager networks work particularly well, as NT was originally based on LAN Manager.

LAN Manager 2.x Servers

LAN Manager 2.x Servers can validate logons for LAN Manager 2.x, Windows for Workgroups, and other clients, but it cannot validate log-ons for any Windows NT workstations or servers. For this reason, we recommend that LAN Manager 2.x servers not be used to validate log-ons in your network. Intel servers running LAN Manager 2.x should be upgraded to NT Servers so that they can be full members in the domain.

Users cannot access LAN Manager resources on a remote domain with both NT servers and LAN Manager servers unless the user has an account on the domain controlled by the NT server, because LAN Manager Servers do not recognize global groups or trust relationships between domains. To gain access to LAN Manager resources, the user must explicitly log on the domain containing the LAN Manager server resources.

Pathworks 5.x

Pathworks 5.x from Digital Equipment Corporation is a LAN Manager 2.2 server and includes support for LAN Manager 2.2-style domains. A Pathworks server can participate in a domain managed by NT Server but cannot be promoted to the PDC.

The easiest way to use NT Server with Pathworks 5.x is to install NT Server before installing Pathworks. If you have already installed Pathworks, continue as follows: Install NT Server in the normal manner, and make the NT Server the domain controller during the installation. Once NT Server is installed, make sure that you can connect to resources on the new server from somewhere on the network. The first connection should be to a shared directory that has permissions set for the share. Log on the domain with the user name with permission to access the share, then try to connect to the share. Once you can log on successfully and connect to a share, you can proceed to the next step. If you cannot log on or access the share, do not try to install other servers (either NT or Pathworks) until you have resolved the problems.

Now that NT Server is up and running, you can integrate Pathworks with NT Server. This process is actually fairly simple, but it must be performed in the right sequence.

Integrating Pathworks 5.x and NT Server from the NT Server:

1. Make sure that both NT Server and Pathworks are using the same protocol (NetBEUI and/or TCP/IP).
2. Make sure that an NT Server is the PDC.

    Run Server Manager.

    Select the NT server.

    Select Promote to Domain Controller from the Computer menu.

3. Enable the Guest account on the NT Server, and make sure that the password is null. The password should also be set to never expire.
4. Enable browsing of LAN Manager 2.x clients on NT.

    Run Network applet in Control Panel.

    Choose Computer Browser in the Installed Network Software box.

    Click the Configure button.

    Add LANMAN domains.

5. Enable browsing of NT servers by LAN Manager 2.x servers.

    Run Network applet in Control Panel.

    Choose Server in the Installed Network Software box.

    Click the Configure button.

    Check the Make Browser Broadcasts to LAN Manager 2.x Clients check box.

6. Synchronize the time between the two servers (NT Server and Pathworks).

Integrating Pathworks 5.x and NT Server from the Pathworks Server:

1. Log on an administration account.
2. Edit the LANMAIN.INI file and change the following lines:

    ```
    applyhostmapcomment = yes

    hostmapmode = if_exist_else_default

    hostpaswordsync = yes
    ```

3. Set the server's role to stand alone:

   `$ NET ACCOUNTS /ROLE:STANDALONE`

4. Create an Administrator account that exactly matches the Administrator account on the NT server.

5. Log on the Pathworks server using the new Administrator account.

6. Change the server's role to member or backup:

   `$ NET ACCOUNTS /ROLE:BACKUP`

7. Synchronize the time between the two servers again.

Integrating Pathworks 5.x and NT Server—Final Steps from the NT Server:

1. Make sure the Administrator accounts use the same password on both NT and Pathworks.
2. Start Server Manager.
3. Select the NT server.
4. Select Synchronize with Primary Domain Controller from the Computer menu.

Moving Pathworks 5.x Users to NT Server:

1. Log on an administrator account on the Pathworks server.
2. Run @SYS$UPDATE:PWRK$CONFIG.
3. Answer Yes to the question: Is this server joining an existing domain?
4. Enter the NT Server domain name when you are prompted for the name of the existing domain.
5. Select the Additional Utilities option and select the Merge UAS option. This option merges the Pathworks Users with the NT Server security database. You have the option of doing a complete merge or using the Upgrade Reports option. For more information on using Upgrade Reports, see your Pathworks documentation. The upgrade process should provide you with status information as it updates the NT Server database.
6. Start the Pathworks server.

The Merge UAS option should have populated the NT Server domain security database with the Pathworks users and groups. Log on the NT Server domain, and run User Manager to check the security database. If the Pathworks users are not in the database, you may need to rerun the upgrade process on the Pathworks server.

After the upgrade process, the Pathworks server should restart. Run the Admin utility and make the Pathworks server a Member Server using the Accounts menu—Security option. Make sure that the time on both the domain controller (NT Server) and Pathworks server have the time set within five minutes of each other. The domain controller updates the Pathworks server account database every five minutes (default time).

Once the Pathworks server is a member of the domain, clients can access both Pathworks and NT Server resources with a single log-on. The log-on will be processed and validated by the NT Server(s).

Gateway Services for NetWare

For an overview of the NWLINK transport and other NetWare utilities, see "Protocols and Related Stuff," earlier in this chapter.?

The NWLINK protocol is installed by default along with NetBEUI during the NT Server installation process.

Preparing for Installing (GSNW) Gateway Services for NetWare on NT Server:

1. Create an account to use as the gateway account on the NetWare server.
2. Create a group with the name NTGATEWAY on the NetWare server.
3. Add the gateway account created in step 1 to the NTGATEWAY group.
4. Add the proper file permissions to the NTGATEWAY group.

Installing GSNW:

1. Start the Network applet in Control Panel.
2. Click the Add Software button.
3. Select the Gate Service for NetWare from the list.
4. Click the Continue button.
5. Click OK.
6. Reboot the system when you are prompted to do so.

Configuring GSNW:

1. Start the GSNW applet in Control Panel.
2. Select the preferred NetWare server from the drop-down list.
3. Configure the required print options.
4. Click the Gateway button to access the configuration dialog box.

5. Check the Enable Gateway button.

6. Enter the NetWare account to use for access by NT Server.

7. Add or remove NT shares to NetWare services in the lower box. Use the Add and Remove buttons to manage the shares. The Permissions button allows you to set NT permissions on the shares.

GSNW creates and maps NetWare server shares and printers to make them accessible to NT clients, such as Windows for Workgroups and Windows 95. Users can access the NetWare services and have no idea that they are connected to anything but NT resources.

Sharing NetWare Print Resources to NT Server Clients:

1. Start Print Manager.

2. Click on the Connect to Printer button.

3. Select the NetWare printer to use in the browse list.

4. Follow the prompts to complete the installation. NT will most likely prompt to load a driver for the printer.

5. Choose the Properties option on the Printer menu.

6. Click the Share this Printer on the Network check box.

7. Enter a share name.

8. Enter the printer's location.

9. Close the Properties dialog box.

Users from any client of the NT server will now see this printer as an NT printer.

Sharing NetWare Print Resources to NT Server Clients:

1. Start the GSNW Control Panel applet.

2. Click the Gateway button.

3. Enter the user account.

4. Click the Add button to select the NetWare volumes to share as NT shares.

5. Enter the network path to the NetWare volume (that is, \\ServerName\ VOL1).

6. Enter the NT share name.

7. Enter a comment for the share.

8. Close the GSNW dialog boxes.

Once these steps are complete, users can access the NetWare volumes as if they are NT shares. The performance will be slightly slower, because all file requests are going through NT to get to the NetWare server.

Setting the Search Order for Multiple Network Providers

Installing multiple networks on an NT system can cause performance problems if the network used the most frequently is not specified first in the search order. NT uses a specific search order based on the settings in the Network applet.

The current search order can be displayed by selecting the Network button in the Network applet. The search order is displayed in the list box, starting at the top. You can change the order by clicking on the network you wish to change and then clicking the Up or Down button to change its order in the list. Move the network that is used most frequently to the top of the list.

Binding Network Components

The Network applet in Control Panel is used to configure network services such as protocols, the workstation and server services, and others related to the network. The normal process for configuring a network service is to select a service (that is, TCP/IP) and then click the Configure button.

All network components perform specific tasks related to the network. Each component must be "bound" to other system components to form a working group before it can be used. For instance, NetBEUI must be bound to a network adapter before you can use the NetBEUI protocol.

Normally you will find groups of two or more components bound together. For instance, you will normally find the Workstation service bound to a protocol such as NetBEUI, and NetBEUI will in turn be bound to a network adapter. This component packaging allows a system manager total flexibility in configuring the components and determining how they are used.

The Network Bindings dialog box can be used for several tasks, such as determining how the network components are bound together, removing a component from other components, and specifying the order that the system uses the transports bound to an adapter.

The Network Bindings dialog box is especially useful in the latter two cases. For instance, if you have both Token Ring and Ethernet cards in a system, you can use this dialog box to bind certain protocols to each adapter, improving the performance of your system. The default is to bind all protocols to all adapters.

You should change the order of network bindings to reflect the real world your systems are used in. If you use TCP/IP for most connections, move TCP/IP to first in the bindings order. Taking this small step can make network connections much faster.

To Change a Binding:

1. Start Control Panel.
2. Start the Network applet.
3. Select the Bindings button.
4. Select the Binding to Change.
5. Click the Enable or Disable button to change a binding.

You can change which bindings are shown in the list by clicking on the drop-down list at the top of the dialog box and selecting the object to display.

Optimizing Memory Utilization on a Server

The Network applet enables you to control how much memory to use for network operations. This option can be used to tailor NT for the manner in which your system is used. You have the option of selecting only four settings. Table 4.9 shows the settings suggested by Microsoft in the NT documentation.

The steps for changing the memory usage settings are simple.

Changing the Server Memory Settings:

1. Start Control Panel.
2. Start the Network applet.
3. Select the Network Settings button.
4. Select the Server button.
5. Select the desired setting.

If you design your network using distributed servers for different tasks, it will be easy to determine which setting to use. Dedicated file and print servers are usually set to Maximize Throughput for File Sharing. Dedicated database servers use Maximize Throughput for Network Applications. Both Minimize Memory Used and Balance are adequate for small networks only and are not suitable for NT Server, as a server should never be used for much interactive work.

Remote Access Service

Remote access is a very powerful and important tool that is included with both NT and NT Server. The difference in the NT Server version of Remote

TABLE 4.9	Suggested Settings for Server Memory Utilization

Option	Normal System Loading or Usage
Minimize Memory Used	Places the minimum memory load on the server and is usually adequate for up to 10 network connections.
Balance	Attempts to balance the memory used for network operations and server operations. This option is adequate for approximately 64 connections. Default setting.
Maximize Throughput for File Sharing	Provides the best performance for network servers, especially systems with over 64 simultaneous connections. Network File Sharing operations are given priority in using system memory.
Maximize Throughput for Network Applications	Maximizes memory for network applications that perform their own memory caching. The System Guide mentions SQL server as an example of these types of programs. I recommend checking with your application manuals for the settings suggested for specific applications and then testing the application to make sure it performs in the manner desired.

Access Service (RAS) is the support for up to 256 connections instead of the single connection in NT Workstation.

RAS is composed of two services and several applications for administering and using RAS. Table 4.10 lists the major components.

TABLE 4.10	Major Components of RAS

Name	Description
Remote Access Server	RAS service
Remote Access Connection Manager	RAS service
Remote Access	User program for connecting to a RAS system. This program includes the phone book and dialing tools for RAS.
Remote Access Monitor	Monitor program for RAS. This program monitors the communications line used for RAS and contains four indicators that show the status of each modem signal.
Remote Access Admin	Administrator's program for RAS. Remote Access Admin is used to set up permissions for RAS users and start and stop the RAS Server. It can also be used to view users who are currently accessing the system via RAS and view the status of the RAS system.

NT Server RAS supports the following features:

- Open access to all file and print services on the RAS server and systems accessible over the RAS server's network. This is the most important feature of RAS and allows access to any server accessible with a protocol common to the NT server running RAS.
- RAS clients can access remote network services using any combination of NetBEUI, TCP/IP, and IPX.
- Point-To-Point (PPP) and Serial Line Internet Protocol (SLIP) have been added to RAS. PPP also supports IPX for NetWare support. PPP is the newest and preferred of the two protocols for accessing the Internet (SLIP and PPP).
- Automatic modem detection during installation of RAS.
- Access to resources such as SNA Server for Windows NT, SQL Server, and numerous others.
- Numerous RAS access methods: ISDN, X.25, serial (modem and with a NULL-modem cable).
- Integration with NT security system.
- IP (for TCP/IP protocols) and IPX (for NetWare protocols) routing on the NT server.
- Modem pools.
- The NT Option Pack adds support for Virtual Private Networks (VPN) on RAs.

Design and Configuration

RAS offers many features to NT networks, but requires correct care and feeding for it to work effectively.

HARDWARE

RAS systems perform much better with a faster serial interface than a standard serial port can provide. Intelligent adapters are the best choice for RAS because they off-load the processing of serial services to the adapter. Off-loading frees the NT system from handling the details of the serial system. Check the NT hardware compatibility list under the heading Multiport Serial Adapters for the latest versions. The NT HCL in included with Windows NT Server and an up-to-date copy can be found in the Microsoft Software Library. I have used the 2Port adapter from DigiBoard and can certify that it works fine. The ChiliPorts product from Consensys also looks like a great product.

The ISDN Adapters heading contains a list of certified ISDN adapters for use with RAS. ISDN is usually much faster than a standard line but is not as widely available. You should check with your local telephone suppliers for availability in both areas that will be used in an ISDN connection. Some devices do provide ISDN support for dialing in from a standard phone connection. ISDN configuration is not covered in this book because of the wide variation in availability and the disparity in supporting ISDN at local phone companies. I view ISDN as an emerging technology that is starting to take off. Consult the various NT newsletters and magazine articles, as well as TechNet, for more information on ISDN.

Your choice of modems and other RAS support equipment is also critical but has less impact on the server than the serial adapter to use for RAS. One point to keep in mind is the new series of high-speed modems. All the current crop require a high-speed serial interface such as a DigiBoard, ChiliPort, or some other adapter. The standard RS-232 interfaces in a PC do not provide a fast enough throughput for these high-speed modems, except for some systems from late 1994 and later that have high-speed modem support built in.

Another issue regarding modems is compatibility between an RAS client and an RAS server. We recommend using modems from the same manufacturer on both ends of the connection, if possible. Using the same model modem on each end of the connection is also a good idea. The faster the modem, the more likely you will experience problems if the modems are not from the same manufacturer. This is especially true if the modems are V.35 or V.42 compatible or even more so if the modems are one of the new fast modems.

This suggestion is not just a repeat of the Microsoft documentation. We have experienced the problems with both RAS and mail servers. We have also had problems using PC Anywhere with some modems, so choose your vendors carefully. Remember that if you have both modems from the same vendor, they are easier to manage and replace when a modem fails. This also includes having to learn the peculiarities of only one set of modem commands.

FITTING IN WITH DOMAINS

What does RAS have to do with domains? The overall configuration of your network is important for users and administrators of RAS for several reasons. The Security Account database is used by RAS when a user attempts to connect. RAS checks the local domain for the RAS user's account, and, if it is not found, it simultaneously checks all trusted domains for the account. The first response for that username from a domain is used by RAS for the authentication. This response seems to do the job most of the time.

If the user has more than one account in the domain and in any of the trusted domains, all the passwords must be the same. The user who has an account on a trusted domain but does not have an account on the local domain may or may not be able to log on with RAS. The best policy is to create only one account for a user on all domains and to make sure that there are no duplicate user accounts. Considering the implications of the user account issues, it may be best to use the master domain model for your network.

Use of the master domain model does not require that the RAS servers all be in the master domain. You should locate the RAS servers in a domain that is local to a log-on server. In other words, don't place an RAS server in a domain where the log-on server is accessed over a low-speed connection such as a modem.

Installing RAS

The installation of RAS is a simple process and can be accomplished in a short period of time, if it is done correctly. The entire process should take somewhere between 15 minutes to an hour, depending upon your hardware setup. ISDN may require a little longer to set up (it will take quite a bit longer until the phone and equipment vendors get their act together).

Installing RAS for Serial Communications:

1. Install the hardware to be used with RAS.
2. Restart the Server if necessary.
3. Start the Network applet in Control Panel.
4. Click the Add Software button.
5. Select the Remote Access Service from the list.
6. Click continue.
7. Enter the path to the NT distribution files if you are asked to do so, then click Continue.
8. Select the COM port to use for RAS.
9. Allow Setup to detect your modem, or click Cancel to select the modem from a list.
10. Click Network to access the Network Configuration dialog box.
11. Check the box for each protocol to use over RAS. Make sure to check both dial-out and dial-in boxes. Check the box for either dial-in or dial-out or both, depending upon how you are planning to use RAS.
12. Click the Configure button beside each protocol in the Server Settings section to set the parameters for that protocol—for example, whether to use DHCP to assign addresses or to use static addresses for TCP/IP.
13. Click OK when you are finished with the Network Configuration dialog box.
14. Choose whether or not to allow remote users to access only the current computer or the entire network, then click OK. This setting is by protocol.
15. Click OK after reading the note on the Remote Access Service Setup dialog box.

16. Click OK in the Network dialog box to complete the installation. This step takes a few minutes, because it involves configuration programs for all the network software, including RAS.

17. Reboot the system by clicking Restart Now when prompted. RAS will not work until the system has been rebooted.

Assigning RAS Permissions to Users

The Remote Access Service Administrator program is used for managing many features of RAS, including assigning permissions to users. Before a user can access the system using RAS, he or she must be granted permission to do so.

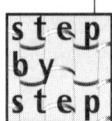

Assigning RAS Permissions:

1. Start Remote Access Service Administrator.

2. Select the Users menu.

3. Select Permissions.

4. Set the desired options from this dialog box. Table 4.11 outlines the options available.

5. Click OK on the Permissions dialog box.

Remember that a user must have both RAS permissions to access RAS and NT permissions to do anything on the network or server. A user who has permission from RAS to access the server can not necessarily do anything.

Managing the RAS System

RAS is managed in a number of ways, including using the standard administrative tools for NT such as Event Viewer, Control Panel, User Manager, and so forth. One of the primary tools is Remote Access Service Administrator. This tool can be used for a number of different tasks:

- Control permissions for RAS users
- Start, stop, and pause RAS
- View and manage RAS activity by user and server
- Perform all the preceding activities on other servers

RAS Administrator is located in the Remote Access Service group, as are all the other RAS tools. The other RAS specific tools are the RAS Monitor and the Remote Access programs. Table 4.11 provides an overview of each of the RAS components.

TABLE 4.11	RAS Permission Options
Option	**Description**
Revoke All	Revokes RAS permission for all users in the user account database.
Grant All	Grants RAS permission to all users in the user account database.
Grant Dial-in Permission to User	Grants permission to the user or selected users. If you grant permission to all users, make sure you revoke permission for the GUEST account, or add a password for this account.
Call Back	Button group to determine call-back options for the selected user.
No Call Back	Does not enable call-back for the user.
Set By Caller	Allows the user to enter the number for the return call.
Preset To	Presets the call-back number. Enter the number to call back for this user in the box below this button.

CONFIGURING RAS HARDWARE—MODEMS

RAS supports a number of different modems, which are listed on the NT hardware compatibility list, and provides a mechanism for configuring unsupported modems. The following steps outline the process for setting up your modem to use with RAS.

Configuring a Modem:

1. Start the Network applet in Control Panel.
2. Select Remote Access Service from the list.
3. Click Configure.
4. Select the port you wish to configure on the Remote Access Service dialog box. If the port you wish to configure is not listed, click the Add button and choose the new port from the list.
5. Click Configure.
6. Select your modem from the list or select a modem that is close to yours.
7. Choose the port usage option for the port to determine its allowable actions for dial-in.
8. Click OK.
9. Click Continue.
10. Click OK on the Network dialog box.
11. Reboot your system if you configured a port that was not in use.

warning If your modem is not on the list in step 6 of the previous steps and you do not have a driver from the vendor, you may be in for bigger problems.

You may need to use the Ports applet in Control Panel to configure a port for RAS to use. RAS can use only ports that are defined in the Ports applet. If your port is not shown, you can select the Add option and define the port. Make sure the IRQ and memory options are set correctly.

We like to test the ports in a clean manner before we configure RAS, or if RAS has a problem. The easiest way to do this is to make sure that the port is defined correctly, attach a modem to the port, access the MS-DOS prompt, and run the following command:

```
echo ATDT12213 > COM2:
```

This example is testing COM2:. The command tells the modem to dial (ATDT) the phone number 12212. If the command works, the modem dials and the lights flash. If this does not happen, the port is probably not defined correctly, or some other problem is preventing the modem from receiving the command. There is no sense in fooling with RAS until this step works.

Hardware devices such as DigiBoard adapters may need other types of configuration. For instance, the DigiBoard adapter is installed and configured using the Network applet in Control Panel. The hardware vendor should provide the documentation for installation and configuration of any devices not supported directly from the NT distribution.

STARTING, STOPPING, AND PAUSING RAS

RAS can be started, stopped, and paused in several different ways. The RAS Admin utility has options for all three options on the Server menu.

One way to start RAS is to use the Services applet in Control Panel or from Server Manager. The Services applet allows you to start and stop RAS and to configure RAS to start automatically when NT starts.

Automatically Starting the RAS Service:

1. Start the Services applet in Control Panel.
2. Select the RAS service.
3. Click the Startup button.
4. Select the Automatic button for Startup Type.
5. Select System Account for the Log On As option.
6. Click OK.
7. Click Close.

When you must start and stop the RAS service for maintenance, the Remote Access Administrator is the most convenient method. It not only provides access to start and stop the service, but also provides management services for most of the RAS features as well.

Starting the RAS Service (Remote Access Administrator):

1. Start the RAS Admin program in the Administrative Tools group.
2. Select the Start Remote Access Service command from the Server menu.
3. Enter the name of the Server on which you wish to start RAS.
4. Click OK.

Stopping the RAS Service (Remote Access Administrator):

1. Start the RAS Admin program in the Administrative Tools group.
2. Select the Stop Remote Access Service command from the Server menu.
3. Click Yes.

Pausing the RAS Service (Remote Access Administrator):

1. Start the RAS Admin program in the Administrative Tools group.
2. Select the Pause Remote Access Service command from the Server menu.

Occasionally you need to stop or start a service at the command prompt or in a batch program. The NET commands are normally the best resource for accessing services. The following steps show you how to start the Remote Access Service using Net Start.

Continuing and Starting the RAS Service (Net Command):

1. Start the RAS Admin program in the Administrative Tools group.
2. Select the Continue Remote Access Service command from the Server menu.

You can also use Net Start to start the Remote Access Service:

```
Net Start Remote Access Server
```

MANAGING THE RAS PHONEBOOK

Rasphone is the utility used to manage the phonebook for RAS. This utility is straightforward and has several useful options in addition to entering phone numbers and dialing RAS servers. You can configure each phone number for a different port and type of service such as ISDN, X.25, Modem, or switched.

The following outlines cover the steps for entering entries in the phonebook and configuring them to use a certain type of service.

Entering New Phonebook Entries:

1. Start Remote Access.
2. Click the Add button.
3. Enter the following fields for this phone book entry.

   > Entry Name

   > Phone Number

   > Description

4. If you wish to use the user's current user name and password to authenticate them on the remote system, make sure that the Authenticate Using Current User Name and Password box is checked.

Assigning Modem Parameters to Entries:

1. Start Remote Access.
2. Select the entry to change.
3. Click the Edit button.
4. Click the Advanced button.
5. Click OK.

Connecting to an RAS Server:

Just as there are several options for starting RAS, there are also several options for dialing.

- Start RASPHONE, and double-click the entry to call.
- Start RASPHONE, select the entry to call, and click DIAL.
- Enter the following command at the DOS prompt or as the command line for an icon:

```
RASDIAL entryname
```

Windows for Workgroups supports RAS connections to NT systems. The procedure is the same as using NT because the RASPHONE utility is included with Windows for Workgroups.

You must be logged on a domain to use any resources on the NT system once you are connected with RAS. This step is not necessary if you are connected to a network that has a trust relationship with the NT domain you wish to access. When you connect to the domain, you will be prompted if you must log in. Answering **Yes** will display the log-on dialog box asking you for user name and password.

There is a potential problem when you are logged in one domain and use RAS to connect to another domain with which the current domain does not have a trust relationship. You must log out of the first domain and then log on the new domain before you can use any services on the domain.

Miscellaneous Notes

You should always close the Network applet in Control Panel before you try to start RAS or any other network service. If the Network applet is open when you attempt to start the service you may receive an error.

Remote Access Service supports 256 simultaneous connections on an NT server. This limit was raised in NT Server 3.5x from 64 in NT Advanced Server 3.1.

The DSR (Data Set Ready) and DCD (Data Carrier Detect) signals should be set to function normally on your modem. RAS requires these signals to be operating to function properly. These signals are used to determine when the phone line has been hung up. When a hangup occurs RAS resets the modem by sending the modem initialization string.

If your system is remaining connected until the time-out occurs (default is 20 minutes), you should check the cable to your modem and the switch settings for DCD and DSR. You can tell if RAS has not hung up, because RAS Admin shows a port status of "Connected, user authenticated" after the line has been hung up.

You can change the time-out value by editing the Registry. The key is

```
\\HKEY_LOCAL_MACHINE\SYSTEM\CurrentControlSet\
Services -

\RemoteAccess\Parameters\AutoDisconnect
```

Change the value from 20 (hex 0x14) to whatever you like. A value of 0 disables the automatic time-out.

Accessing an RAS Server and Guest Accounts

NT does not automatically use a guest account when someone tries to connect to the server with an unknown account. The user is denied access to the network, even though a valid Guest account exists on the server. If a user does not have an account on the server or domain, they must specify **GUEST** as their log-on name in order to connect to the system.

You will notice an anomaly if you check out the Event Log after a user has tried to access the network with an unknown account. The log shows a successful log-on for the user, followed by a log-out, because NT actually logs the user in through RAS, checks the user's log-on name and password, and then logs the user out. During the time the user is logged on for this check, NT does not allow any access to system resources.

IRQ AND ADD-ON CARDS

Some cards may cause problems if they require an IRQ for each port configured on the card. The DigiBoard series is nice because the IRQs are usually turned off when using NT. This configuration allows you to use a card and set the ports for COM3 and COM4 with no conflicts with COM1 and COM2.

LIMITING ACCESS TO SYSTEM RESOURCES

You can set NT to limit access to selected network protocols or the entire network except for the RAS server. This setting is useful when you wish to restrict access to the entire network for remote users or want to supply only selected information to remote users via the RAS server. For instance, you can disable all access to the network for RAS clients and routinely import to the RAS server the information the RAS clients should access. NT server is ideally suited to this task by using its replication feature. You could, of course, perform this manually on an NT Workstation system with a simple program.

Access to the LAN can be restricted by setting the NETBIOSGATE-WAYENABLED parameter to **0**. It is normally enabled with a setting of 1. This value is located under the key

```
SYSTEM\CurrentControlSet\Services\RemoteAccess\
Parameters
```

RAS with Windows for Workgroups 3.11 and Windows 95

Windows for Workgroups 3.11 includes RAS client software that works with both the Windows for Workgroups Point-to-Point RAS software and RAS for NT. The Windows for Workgroups RAS client is similar to the NT RAS client software.

Before trying to install RAS, check out the CompuServe or Internet conferences or Microsoft Technical Support for any updates to the software. You should always run the latest copy of RAS, because it contains enhancements to the software.

The RAS software is simple to install, depending upon your system configuration and types of modems that you are using. Check out the system documentation for Windows for Workgroups for more information on installing the software.

Windows 95 uses dial-up networking to connect to NT over RAS. Simply start the dial-up networking application, and follow the prompts.

OS/2 RAS Servers

When an NT server is added to a network with an OS/2 RAS server, it can no longer be administered from any OS/2 server on the network, including the RAS server. All administration must be done from an NT system using RAS Administrator.

Net2Com

Net2Com is a utility that provides network support for NT modems, enabling Windows 3.x, Windows for Workgroups 3.11, and MS-DOS clients to use the modems for outbound calls. NT clients can also use Net2Com to access modems via Windows or MS-DOS-based terminal programs. NT clients may also use the WINVTP.EXE terminal program that comes with the NT Resource Kit.

Net2Com can be downloaded from CompuServe. The file name is TECHNE.ZIP and is located in the WINNT forum, library 1. We have not tested this program, but for completeness we have included the installation steps from the release notes.

Installing Net2Com:

1. Copy the files to a directory.
2. Extract the files using a PKZIP-compatible tool. Use the -d switch to retain the directories. The file contains files for Intel, Alpha, and MIPS, each in its own directory.
3. Run the Net2Set program from the appropriate directory.

Starting Net2Com:

1. Start the Services applet in Control Panel.
2. Select Net2Com and click the Start button. You should use the Startup button at this point to have the service automatically start each time.

The only configuration options available for Net2Com are the COM port and the name of the NetBIOS service. The default COM port for the service is COM2. These values are stored under the Registry key

```
HKEY_LOCAL_MACHINE\SYSTEM\CurrentControlSet\
Services\ -

Net2Com\ComMechDLL
```

This key has two entries: The fifth line under the first entry is normally blank and defaults the COM port to COM2. The fifth line under the second entry is set to LIONHEART by default.

Replication of Files to Other Systems

NT supports replication of files to synchronize files from one system to another. NT uses a system called the *export server* that contains the files to replicate, whereas an *import server* is any NT or LAN Manager system that receives the files. The export server must always be an NT server. NT server supports both import and export replication of files. The Workstation version of NT supports only import replication.

The replication process works by the following process:

1. The import server establishes a connection to the export server at regular intervals.

2. Any files or directories subject to replication that have changed on the export server are replicated to the import server, and the directories of the import server are synchronized with the export server.

The default directories are shown in Table 4.12.

Replication can work between computers in a domain and across domains. If an export server exports to a domain, all import servers in the domain receive the export data. If an import server is configured without specifying an export server, the import server automatically replicates files

TABLE 4.12 NT Replication Default Directories

Directory	Description
C:\WINNT\SYSTEM32\REPL\EXPORT	The default export directory tree. Up to 32 subdirectories, with 1000 files each, can be exported.
C:\WINNT\SYSTEM32\REPL\IMPORT	The default import directory tree.

from the export server in its domain. Replication can also take place between two computers in different domains, if the domains have a trust relationship.

Configuring an Export Server:

1. Start User Manager.
2. Create an account for the replication process. It is a good idea to name the account ReplicatorAccount or something similar to identify the account. Remove the check mark from the User Must Change Password at Next Logon check box. Make sure that the account has the right Log On As a Service by placing it in the Replicator group.
3. Run the Services applet in Control Panel.
4. Select the Directory Replicator service and click Startup. Make the Startup Type Automatic.
5. Click the button for This Account in the Log On As box and select the account you created in step 2 for replication from the account list. You can access the account list by clicking the ... button beside the account box. Be sure to enter the password if you entered one for the account.
6. Run Server Manager.
7. Select the system you have chosen as the export replicator, and choose Properties from the Computer menu.
8. Click the Replication button.
9. Click the Manage button to configure the directories you wish to export. The default directory path is \WINNT\SYSTEM32\REPL\EXPORT. The Manage button allows you to configure the subdirectories under the tree that you wish to export. The default directory to replicate is SCRIPTS. Checking the Entire Subtree box causes the selected directory and all of its subdirectories to be exported. The Add Lock button locks a directory from replication until all the locks have been removed. This button is useful when you wish to make some changes to a directory and you need to make sure that the directory is not exported until you are finished. The Wait Until Stabilized box is also useful because it forces NT to wait for two minutes after the last file has changed before it replicates the directory again.
10. Close the Manage dialog box.
11. Click the Add button to add systems that you wish to export to. You can enter the name of a computer or domain when prompted. If you specify a domain, the replication is to any system in the domain that is configured as an import server.
12. Close the Directory Replication dialog box. NT attempts to start the Replicator service if it is not already started. If it does not start, use Event Viewer to review the error log for details.

Configuring an Import Server:

1. Run the Services applet in Control Panel.

2. Select the Directory Replicator service and click Startup. Make the Startup Type Automatic.

3. Click the button for This Account in the Log On As box and select the account you created for replication on the domain from the account list. You can access the account list by clicking the ... button beside the account box. Be sure to enter the password if you entered one for the account.

4. Run Server Manager.

5. Select the system you have chosen as the Import Replicator, and choose Properties from the Computer menu.

6. Click the Replication button.

7. Select Import Directories. The default path is \WINNT\SYSTEM32\REPL\IMPORT.

8. If you wish to restrict replication to a specific system, click Add, and add the system that will be exporting to your system. By default, the list of export servers is blank, and the system imports from the local domain. Adding any entries to the list of export servers overrides the default operation and causes NT to replicate files only from the systems on the list.

9. Click Manage to display the directory management dialog box. The Add Lock button can be used on an import server to temporarily stop a directory from receiving updates. The Status field can contain any one of the following indicators:

OK	The subdirectory receives regular updates from an export server.
No Master	The subdirectory is not receiving regular updates.
No Sync	The subdirectory has received updates, but its data are not up to date.
Blank	The subdirectory has never been updated.

Miscellaneous Notes on Replication

- NT supports replication across domains with trust relationships. You should make sure that the same replication account and password are used in all domains. Microsoft strongly recommends using the default import and export paths, due to the complex permissions that are established on both paths.
- You can make an NT Server both an import and export replicator, but NT Workstation can only be an import server.

- An import replicator that uses a FAT drive for its import drive and receives files from an NTFS system receives only the 8.3 file names.
- NT adds the Replicator account to the Backup Operators and Domain Users groups.

Replication Between NT Server and OS/2 Servers

NT Server can import and export files from and to an OS/2 LAN manager server. Files that are exported to an OS/2 LAN manager server must meet the criteria for the OS/2 server file system. In other words, if the OS/2 Server is using a FAT system, then the exported files must meet the requirements for a FAT system. If the OS/2 server is using HPFS, then the exported files must meet the requirements for an HPFS file system. For exact details on the naming requirements for each system, see Chapter 6.

Software Metering and Inventory

System Management Server can perform software metering to some extent. SMS basically performs metering by checking for the installed software on a client workstation with the SMS inventory agent.

If you want to perform actual software metering as applications are running, then you need a product that works with SMS or provides stand-alone software metering.

SMS includes help desk support for remote control and inspection of a client system, automated software delivery, running programs on client systems, performing tests on clients, and all kinds of other interesting things. Also included is a killer sniffer called Network Monitor.

NET Programs

The NET programs are a set of commands that run from the NT command prompt. The programs are all prefixed with the word NET when the command is executed. NET is actually the program (NET.EXE) that executes each of the 60 or so separate commands. This is a simple execution of the NET CONFIG command:

```
NET CONFIG
```

Most NET commands are similar in usage to the NET commands from LAN Manager, Windows for Workgroups, Windows 95, and the Microsoft MS-DOS clients. The following sections cover some of the more useful NET commands for managing servers. Other chapters have similar information on NET commands for other tasks.

NET CONFIG

NET CONFIG is a useful command for several tasks. You can add a comment to a server name using the following syntax:

```
NET CONFIG SERVER /SRVCOMMENT:"Master Server"
```

This comment is displayed in most applications that display information about the server such as NET VIEW and File Manager. You can also enter and edit the comment via the Server applet in Control Panel. The comment works identically to the one that you set up with the Network applet in Windows for Workgroups.

Another useful NET CONFIG option is its ability to display information about the NT server or workstation. The syntax for displaying information about a server is

```
NET CONFIG SERVER
```

This command displays the following information:

```
Server Name \\CTI-MEXP-NTAS

Server Comment CTI Master Server

Software version Windows NT 3.51

Server is active on Nbf_Elnk301 (00608ce98f1b)

Server hidden No

Maximum Logged On Users Unlimited

Maximum open files per session 2048

Idle session time (min) 15

The command completed successfully.
```

As you can see, this information is valuable for a quick look at the status of the server. Among other things, this view shows you the number of users the system supports, the current server version, the protocols and network card the server is running on, the maximum files that may be open per session, and the idle time that can expire before the user session is disconnected.

The syntax for displaying information about a workstation is

```
NET CONFIG WORKSTATION

    Computer name \\CTI-MEXP-NTAS

    User name ken

    Workstation active on Nbf_Elnk301
    (00608CE98F1B)
```

```
Software version Windows NT 3.51

Workstation domain DOM-KEN

Logon domain DOM-KEN

COM Open Timeout (sec) 3600

COM Send Count (byte) 16

COM Send Timeout (msec) 250

The command completed successfully.
```

NET ACCOUNTS

Entering NET ACCOUNTS with no options displays several bits of policy information for a domain, as follows:

```
NET ACCOUNTS
Force user logoff how long after time
expires? 0

Minimum password age (days) 0

Maximum password age (days) Unlimited

Minimum password length 0

Length of password history maintained None

Lockout threshold Never

Lockout duration (minutes) 30

Lockout observation window (minutes) 30

Computer role BACKUP

Primary Domain controller for workstation
domain \\MyServer

The command completed successfully.
```

Synchronizing Time Across a Network with NET TIME

NET TIME is available with Windows NT, Windows 95, and Windows for Workgroups. It can be used to display the time from another system on the network and set the system clock on the current system with that of another system. It can be used to obtain the time from Windows for Workgroups, NT, NT Server, or LAN Manager systems.

NET TIME is useful in log-on scripts and by itself.

The format is

```
NET TIME [\\computer | /WORKGROUP:wgname] [/SET]
[/YES]
```

computer	The name of the computer (time server) whose time you want to check or synchronize your computer's clock with.
/WORKGROUP	Specifies that you want to use the clock on a computer (time server) in another workgroup.
wgname	The name of the workgroup containing a computer whose clock you want to check, or with which synchronize your computer's clock. If there are multiple time servers in that workgroup, NET TIME uses the first one it finds.
/SET	Synchronizes your computer's clock with the clock on the computer or workgroup you specify.
/YES	Carries out the NET TIME command without first prompting you to provide information or confirm actions.

Synchronizing NT Time with TimeServ (NT Resource Kit)

You can further automate this program and make it much more accurate by using one of your NT servers to run the TimeServ application included in the NT Resource Kit. TimeServ can use a dial-up line via modem or the Internet to access a host of time services around the world. This application is documented in the NT Resource Kit, which provides both tips on setup and configuration and the time services available.

Using an application like TimeServ makes synchronizing workstation times easy with our little VB program. Just have the program fire every half hour or hour (depending upon your requirements), and reset the time from the updated time server. It is simple but elegant.

Sending Messages to Users on a Server

Before you take a server down for maintenance or begin an upgrade, it is often useful to send a message to the users connected to the server. This process is very easy if you use Server Manager.

> **Sending Messages to All Users on a Server:**
>
> 1. Start Server Manager.
> 2. Select the server from the list.
> 3. Select the Send Message command from the Computer menu.
> 4. Enter the message, and click OK.

You may also sometimes like to communicate with specific users via a message instead of using mail. Messages are processed immediately and displayed immediately, instead of arriving in a queue and sitting until the user takes action to read the message.

The NET SEND command provides a quick way to send a message to one user or all users on a server. This command must be run from the DOS prompt because there is not a GUI equivalent yet. The syntax is

```
NET SEND name | /domain:name | /users "message"
```

name   User, message name, or computer name to receive the message. If a user name is used, the user must be logged in.

/domain:name   User name in another domain to receive the message.

/users   Send the message to all users on this system.

"message"   Text of message to send.

NET SEND is useful by itself and in a batch file. The following command shows an example of a message sent to Administrator:

```
NET SEND administrator "Lets take the system down
at 5:00pm"
```

This command also works nicely in various batch files. For instance, in a shutdown batch file, you could include a NET SEND command to notify users that the system is going down in a certain period of time. Other batch files could be maintained to send messages to certain groups of users. For example, if you have a stored procedure in SQL Server, use NET SEND to notify a user that the procedure is completed. There are many uses for this command.

You should be aware of several points when you send messages:

- Windows for Workgroups and Windows users must have WinPopUp running to detect and display messages.
- NT and NT Server must have the messenger service running to send and receive messages.

- Windows 95 must use WinPopUp just like Windows and Windows for Workgroups. Place WINPOPUP.EXE in the Startup folder to start messaging services at startup. Because Windows 95 enables you to run Windows programs from the DOS prompt, you can execute WinPopUp when a user logs on in the log-on script for the user. Starting WinPopUp a second time simply places the focus on the currently running copy.

Conclusion

You should have a good grasp of some of the network management issues that you will face with NT networks. Understanding protocols, naming conventions, network components such as network adapters, and other related issues are critical for managing complex networks. Seemingly small decisions during installation can come back to haunt you over and over again if you don't make them with the proper design considerations. You can always change a server or domain name after installation, but what happens to the 1,500 workstations that have connection information to that server or domain stored locally?

Chapter 5 brings us to User Management. User Management centers around user accounts and user groups. How do you add users? How do you add 500 users at one time? How do you migrate users from one system to another? In this chapter we discussed naming conventions for servers and domains. How can we apply logical naming conventions to user and group accounts in the same fashion?

User Management

User management is another of the most critical management tasks that you face with any network or operating system. Properly creating and managing account names, group names, log-on scripts, password and user restrictions and such will make your hair turn gray or fall out—check out the picture on www.32nt.com if you don't believe it.

Scenario 5.1:

You own a large network with 5,000 users. As you upgrade to NT, you are thinking about implementing a clean, new user account naming convention. Do you want 5,000 people to call you at 8 a.m. when they can't log on?

Scenario 5.2:

Today security is at the forefront of everyone's plans. Actually, things have been like that for as long as humans have been able to use the written word. How does NT help or hinder us in managing security from the user perspective?

This chapter will show you how to correctly building user accounts and groups. We point out not only how to accomplish this, but why it is important in the first place. We also delve into building log-on scripts and what you can accomplish with them. Along the way, we will touch on other user issues, such as setting account parameters and working with multiple accounts at one time.

Domain User Accounts

A domain user account is the magic account by which anyone gains access to resources on an NT Server network. Domain user accounts are exactly the same as an NT workstation user account, but they are valid across the domain in which the account is created. Domain accounts may be used to access other domains via a trust relationship to the domain.

A user account consists of an account name and the full name for the account. Many other properties are tied to the account (for example, log-on times and groups).

An account can be from 1 to 20 characters in length and may consist of all the characters except for

$$ " \ / \ \backslash \ [\ ] \ : \ ; \ | \ = \ , \ + \ * \ ? \ < \ > $$

User accounts may be both uppercase and lowercase, and must be unique for the domain. User accounts are not case-sensitive. For example, if you creat an account named Smith, you could log on using either SMITH or smith.

Each account also has a password that can be up to 14 characters in length. Passwords can also use either lower- or uppercase characters, but passwords are case-sensitive! This means that the password JoeBlow is different from the password joeblow.

Chapter 12, "Security," has more information on passwords.

GUEST ACCOUNTS

Guest accounts should not be disabled on domains that have Windows for Workgroups clients. If security is a concern, you should remove the access rights and privileges for the guest account.

ACCOUNT DUPLICATION

User accounts should not be duplicated on different domains that have trust relationships with each other. This can cause problems when a log-on is attempted using an account name from a Windows for Workgroups workstation on a domain with a duplicate account name.

Modifying, Creating, Deleting, and Copying User Accounts

User Manager for Domains is the primary tool used for managing accounts, groups, and policies. You can also perform many of these tasks from the DOS prompt using various NET commands. Figure 5.1 shows User Manager.

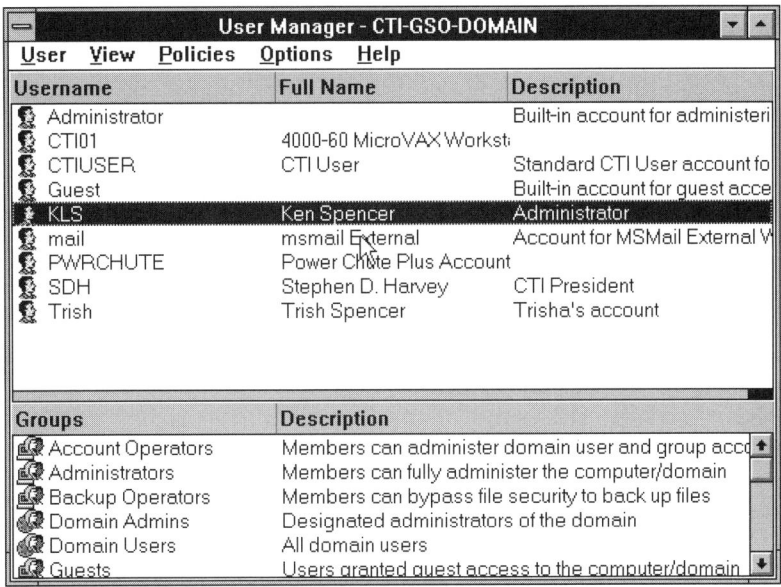

FIGURE 5.1 Accounts are listed in the top pane, and groups are listed in the bottom. The two panes are not linked. Clicking on a user account does not show the groups the user belongs to in the bottom pane.

Creating a User Account:

1. Start User Manager from the Start menu, choose Programs, and the Administrative Tools folder in the Taskbar.
2. Choose the New User command from the User menu.
3. Fill in the New User dialog box.
4. Click OK to add the new user.
5. Click the X at the upper right corner to close the dialog box.

Figure 5.2 shows the User Properties dialog box from User Manager.

Deleting a User Account:

1. Start User Manager for Domains as you did previously.
2. Select the user accounts to delete.
3. Choose Delete from the User menu, or press the Delete key.
4. Confirm the deletion when you are prompted to do so.

User Properties

Username:	KLS
Full **N**ame:	Ken Spencer
Description:	Administrator
Password:	**************
Confirm Password:	**************

- [ ] User **M**ust Change Password at Next Logon
- [ ] U**s**er Cannot Change Password
- [x] Pass**w**ord Never Expires
- [ ] Account Disa**b**led
- [ ] Account Loc**k**ed Out

OK   Cancel   Help

Groups   **Profile**   **Hours**   **Logon To**   **Account**

FIGURE 5.2   The User Properties dialog box contains user information and access to most user properties.

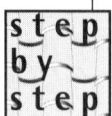

Copying a User Account:

1. Start User Manager for Domains.
2. Select the user account to copy from.
3. Choose Copy from the User menu.
4. Modify the properties of the account.
5. Click the OK button to add the account.
6. Modify the properties, and click OK for all additional new accounts from the original.
7. Click X at the upper right corner when you finish with the copy process.

Don't start User Manager for Domains in the Startup group of an NT workstation or NT server. This may cause User Manager for Domains to focus on the machine name instead of the current domain name. This shift in focus occurs because User Manager for Domains can start before the NetLog-on service is completely up and running. You can start User Manager and other programs in this manner if you create a program to start the programs in a specific group after a certain delay.

ADDING MANY USERS AT A TIME

What happens when you have many user accounts to add at one time? This is a good place to use the NET commands for performing the operations. The following code example shows a batch file that uses NET USER to add many users at once.

```
NET USER ADAMS password /ADD/FullName:"Joe
Adams"

NET USER ADAMSD password /ADD/FullName:"David
Adams"

NET USER GRAND password /ADD/FullName:"Jack
Grand"

NET USER JONES password /ADD/FullName:"Nancy
Jones"

NET USER SMITHJ password /ADD/FullName:"Joe
R.Smith"

NET USER AMAB password /ADD/FullName:"Tom Amab"
```

This example adds each user, sets the initial password to "password," and enters the user's full name in the FullName field. This short example is part of a file created by a Visual Basic program that converts a VMS user list into NT users. The actual file contains about 300 account names. We also split out users for different sites into separate files, generate files for adding users to groups, add shares for each user, and so on. This organization takes the pain out of upgrading to NT from systems such as Pathworks 4.x or VMS that don't have conversion tools on the market. Computer Technologies, Inc., uses this tool and many others during conversions for many of their clients.

Another option for loading many users at one time is ADDUSERS from the NT Resource Kit. ADDUSERS is also useful for dumping the user list from NT. ADDUSERS either writes the user list to a comma-delimited file (CSV) or loads new users from a file with the same format.

ADDUSERS is preferred for many environments because it can add users to a group and specify their home directory and log-on script at the same time the users are added. This is a convenience. There is one caveat: A group must exist before the group is referenced with this command.

The format for ADDUSERS is

```
addusers [\\computername] /C | /D filename

\\computername Specifies the system to perform the
operation on.

/CCreate accounts.

/DDump accounts.
```

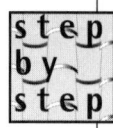

Creating an ADDUSERS Template File:

1. Dump users to a file:

   ```
   addusers /D filename
   ```

2. Edit the file and delete all accounts but leave the header.

This process generates a file with only a header. The file is easily used for creating new users at any point in the future. The format of the template file is

```
Name, Full Name, Password, Comment, Home drive,
Home Path, Profile, Script
```

Adding Accounts with ADDUSERS and a Template File:

1. Copy the template file to a new name.
2. Edit the file and add the new users to the file under the header.
3. Add users with

   ```
   addusers /C filename
   ```

PERFORMING OPERATIONS ON MULTIPLE EXISTING ACCOUNTS

Many times, you will need to work on many accounts at once. This can be accomplished to some extent with User Managers. Beyond the GUI tools, various DOS utilities come to the rescue.

Performing Operations on Multiple Accounts:

1. Select the accounts by clicking the first account; then hold down the Control key and click each additional account. You can also select a range of accounts by clicking on the first account and then holding down the Shift key while clicking the last account in the range.
2. Press Enter or Select Properties from the User menu, and make your changes. Changes made affect all user accounts.

Account Templates

Account templates are a handy trick for managing different types of user accounts where the accounts have certain types of properties for different users.

For instance, manufacturing users may have different log-on times by shift or department. This schedule can be managed very easily by creating a template account for each type of user. Creating a new user account is simply a matter of copying the template account and changing the User Name and Full Name fields.

Another handy trick for account templates is to create a short prefix for the User Name or Full Name fields. A good prefix might be PS01 for Plant Shift 01. With the prefix in place, you can sort the accounts by either field to provide quick access to the group of accounts. For instance, if you need to change the log-on hours for all PS01 accounts, simply sort the accounts by the field you use the prefix in, select all the accounts with the PS01 prefix, select Properties from the User menu, and make your changes. The total time is four minutes or less.

Creating a Template Account:

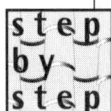

1. Start User Manager for Domains.
2. Create a new user account.
3. Name the account with a generic name for the type of user it represents. For instance, a special account for the Marketing Department might be called TEMP_Marketing.
4. Modify the properties for the template account.
5. Click OK to add the account.
6. Click the X at the upper right corner of the screen to close the New Account Properties dialog box.

Creating an Account from a Template Account:

1. Start User Manager for Domains.
2. Select the template account from the account list.
3. Press F8 or select Copy from the User menu.
4. Name the account with a specific name for the user it represents.
5. Modify the properties for the new account.
6. Click OK to add the account.
7. Click the X at the upper right corner of the screen to close the New Account Properties dialog box.

Sorting User Accounts

User Accounts can be sorted by user name or full name. The View menu commands Sort by Full Name and Sort by User Name will switch the User Manager for Domains display to the new order.

Sorting the User Accounts display:

1. Start User Manager for Domains.
2. Select Sort by User Name or Sort by Full Name from the View menu.

Controlling Which Workstations a User May Use to Log On

Controlling which workstations and servers a user can log on from is useful in environments where a high level of security is required or where a selected group of users needs to be restricted to only certain workstations. For instance, you can restrict assistants to only the workstations located at assistants' desks.

A Windows for Workgroups workstation generates a Network Error 2240 when a user attempts to log on but the workstation is not a valid log-on workstation for that user.

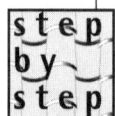

Restricting Workstations Users Can Use to Log On:

1. Start User Manager for Domains.
2. Select the accounts to modify.
3. Select Properties from the User menu or press Enter.
4. Click the Log-on To button.
5. Click the Users May Log On To These Workstations button.
6. Enter computer names for each system the user can log on in boxes 1 to 8.
7. Click OK to close the dialog box.

The Logon Workstations dialog box is shown in Figure 5.3.

Controlling Log-on Times

The Logon Hours in Users Rights control when a user can access the domain. The user is allowed to log on only during the allowable times and can optionally be forcefully logged off when the time expires and he or she is still logged on. Forced log-off is set in the Account Policy dialog box.

Restricting hours a user can log on a system is a useful technique for two purposes. One, you can prevent people from logging on at times when no one should be using the system. This is useful if you have an 8–5 type operation and are certain that users, or at least certain users, do not need access to the system after hours or on weekends. Simply set their log-on times to 8–5 or 7–6 during normal working days (M–F). You can do this selectively by user or for several accounts at once. It's typical to set the log-on times for users to exclude the period when the backup runs. Most backups are run at 2 or 3 A.M. when

```
┌─────────────────────────────────────────────────────────────┐
│ ▬                    Logon Workstations                       │
├─────────────────────────────────────────────────────────────┤
│                                              ┌──────────┐     │
│  User:  KLS (Ken Spencer)                    │    OK    │     │
│                                              └──────────┘     │
│                                              ┌──────────┐     │
│                                              │  Cancel  │     │
│                                              └──────────┘     │
│      ○ User May Log On To All Workstations   ┌──────────┐     │
│      ⦿ User May Log On To These Workstations:│   Help   │     │
│    ┌─────────────────────────────────────────└──────────┘──┐ │
│    │ 1. ┌──────────────┐    5. ┌──────────────┐            │ │
│    │    │ PC0002       │       │              │            │ │
│    │    └──────────────┘       └──────────────┘            │ │
│    │ 2. ┌──────────────┐    6. ┌──────────────┐            │ │
│    │    │ PC0003       │       │              │            │ │
│    │    └──────────────┘       └──────────────┘            │ │
│    │ 3. ┌──────────────┐    7. ┌──────────────┐            │ │
│    │    │ PC0004       │       │              │            │ │
│    │    └──────────────┘       └──────────────┘            │ │
│    │ 4. ┌──────────────┐    8. ┌──────────────┐            │ │
│    │    │       ▷      │       │              │            │ │
│    │    └──────────────┘       └──────────────┘            │ │
│    └───────────────────────────────────────────────────────┘ │
└─────────────────────────────────────────────────────────────┘
```

FIGURE 5.3   Boxes 1 through 3 have computer names. Clicking OK at this point allows only the user KLS to log on these workstations.

there should be no users on the system unless your system is in an environment where users work 24-hour days or is used by people in many time zones.

CONTROLLING LOG-ON TIMES AND FORCING USERS OFF WHEN LOG-ON TIME EXPIRES

Log-on times are set with the Logon Hours dialog box. This dialog box is very graphical, enabling you to easily select log-on hours by highlighting a block of hours across several days. This makes setting log-on times very easy. We also like to set the log-on hours on a dummy account and copy the account so that the log-on hours are established correctly by default.

Figure 5.4 shows the graphical design of the Logon Hours dialog box.

Restricting Hours of Access:

1. Start User Manager for Domains.
2. Select the accounts to modify.
3. Select Properties from the User menu or press Enter.
4. Click the Hours button.
5. Using the mouse, select the hours when the user can log on or the hours he or she cannot log on.
6. Click the Allow or Disallow button.
7. Click OK to close the dialog box.

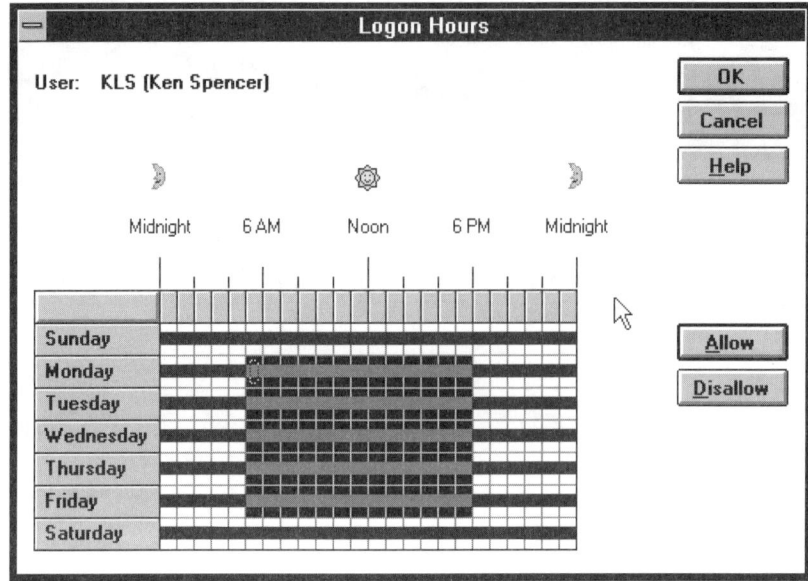

FIGURE 5.4 The Log-on Hours dialog box from User Manager. Notice that only one user (KLS) is selected.

Setting the Forcibly Disconnect Remote Users from Servers When Logon Time Expires option on the Account Policy dialog box (see Figure 5.5) does exactly what the name implies. When the user's log-on time expires, any open files the user has open will be closed, and the user will be logged off. This feature is very useful along with the Logon Hours dialog box to control when users can access the server.

Before the log-on times can be used to force users off, you must set the account policy option to force users off. This setting needs to be made only once on a domain because it affects the entire domain account database.

Changing the Policy for Forcing Users to Log Off When Time Expires (User Manager):

1. Start User Manager for Domains.
2. Select Account from the Policies menu.
3. Click the Forcibly Disconnect Remote Users from Server when Log-on Hours Expire box.
4. Click OK on the Account Policy dialog box.

The Net Accounts command can also be used to change the Account Policy for forcing users off.

Forcing Users to Log Off When Time Expires (Net Accounts):

1. Enter the following command at the command prompt:

   NET ACCOUNTS /forcelogoff:minutes /DOMAIN

---

where minutes is the number of minutes to notify the user before forcing the log-off to occur.

Turning Off Forcing Users to Log Off When Time Expires (Net Accounts):

1. Enter the following command at the command prompt:

   NET ACCOUNTS /forcelogoff:NO /DOMAIN

The /DOMAIN option is needed only if you execute this command from an NT Workstation. NT servers automatically update only the domain security database.

Locking Out an Account

Accounts can be set to lock out automatically when a certain number of failed log-on attempts occur for that account. This option is set on the Account Policy form.

Setting Account Lockout Policies:

1. Select Account from the Policies menu.
2. Click the Account Lockout button.
3. Change the defaults as needed.

Figure 5.5 shows the Account Policy dialog box.

This is a key part of your security system, because it controls what happens when an intruder is trying to guess a password. Many intruders are smart enough to know the default accounts for NT and NT Server and will try to log on when they suspect that the system is running NT. Setting the Account

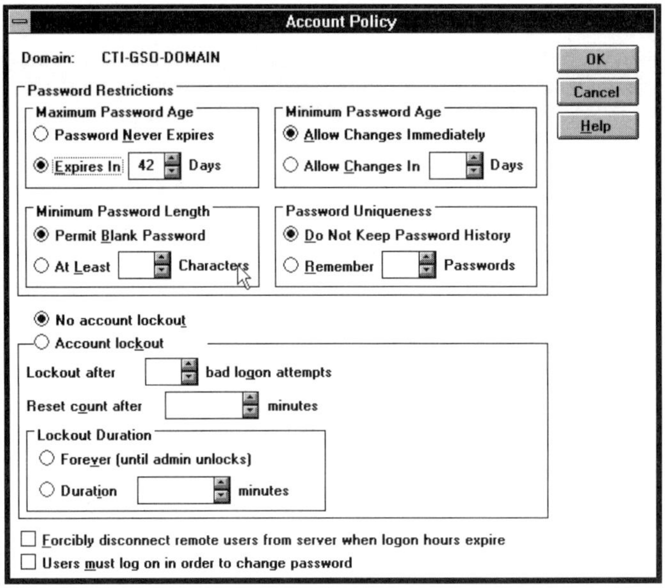

FIGURE 5.5 This account policy has been set to automatically lock out an account when five bad log-on attempts occur. Notice that you can force an account to be totally locked out until it is cleared, using the Forever button.

Lockout parameters can force an account to stay locked out for a period of time or until it is reset. Locking out accounts until they are manually reset may be a reasonable approach to take on the default accounts.

Disabling the Default User Name in the Log-on Dialog Box

Another trick is to disable the display of the default user name displayed in the log-on dialog box. A simple Registry key change makes it disappear. You can also disable the display in Windows for Workgroups by using a small program to periodically wipe out the UserName= value in SYSTEM.INI. Good times to wipe this out are just after a log-on (when it gets set) and when the system boots.

The user name can be removed from the NT log-on dialog box much more easily. Simply create the following entry with a value of 1:

```
HKEY_LOCAL_MACHINE\SOFTWARE\Microsoft\WindowsNT\ -

CurrentVersion\WinLogon\DontDisplayLastUserName
```

Disabling and Renaming User Accounts

You can disable a user account in order to prevent anyone from using the account. This method is preferred for handling accounts for users who have left the company or are out of the office and have sensitive accounts. Disabling the account allows you to reactivate the account and all its privileges simply by unchecking the Account Disabled box.

If you remove the account, it will be impossible to re-create the account and its associated permissions without manually performing each step. An account cannot be re-created and have the same access privileges and group membership, because the Security ID (SID) is used to link the user account to all items in the Security database. Re-creating an account with the same name will have a different SID. Disabling an account leaves the SID for the account intact, so that it can be restored to full status very easily.

Disabling an Account:

1. Start User Manager for Domains.
2. Double-click the account to modify or select multiple accounts, and choose Properties from the User menu.
3. Check the Accounts Disabled box.
4. Click the OK button to close the dialog box.

Reenabling a Disabled Account:

1. Start User Manager for Domains.
2. Double-click the account to modify or select multiple accounts, and choose Properties from the User menu.
3. Uncheck the Accounts Disabled box.
4. Click the OK button to close the dialog box.

You can also rename an account, retaining all the account's properties for the new user. This is very useful for a user who assumes the position of the former owner of the account, because it immediately gives the new user access to everything the former account owner had access to.

Renaming a User Account:

1. Start User Manager for Domains.
2. Double-click the account to modify.
3. Enter the new user name.
4. Click the OK button to close the dialog box.

Restricting an Account for Local Use

You can restrict an account for local use in User Manager for Domains. This setting is on the Account Information dialog box. Selecting the Local Account button restricts the account for use on the local NT system only and does not allow the user to participate in a domain. The default is set to Global Account, which allows domain access, as shown in Figure 5.6.

SPECIAL USER ACCOUNTS

Every access to an NT system must take place via a user account, as discussed in Chapter 12, "Security." Even programs that are started by the NT Scheduler (AT Command) must run using a user account to log on the NT system.

Several services require special consideration for the user account assigned to the service.

Services use the default system account as the log-on account unless you change it. The change can be made using the Services applet in Control Panel.

Changing the Log-on Account for a Service:

1. Start the Services applet in Control Panel or run Server Manager, select a server, and then select the Services command from the Computer menu.
2. Select the service you wish to change the account for.
3. Click the Startup button.
4. Click the This Account button.
5. Enter the account name or click the button beside the text box to select the account name from a list.
6. Enter and confirm the password for the account.

If you later change the password for the account, you must change the password for the service on every server that uses the account for the service.

Accounts that are used for services should be set up for passwords that never expire.

User Profiles

User profiles store information about a user's desktop environment in a separate file for each user or a group of users. The types of information

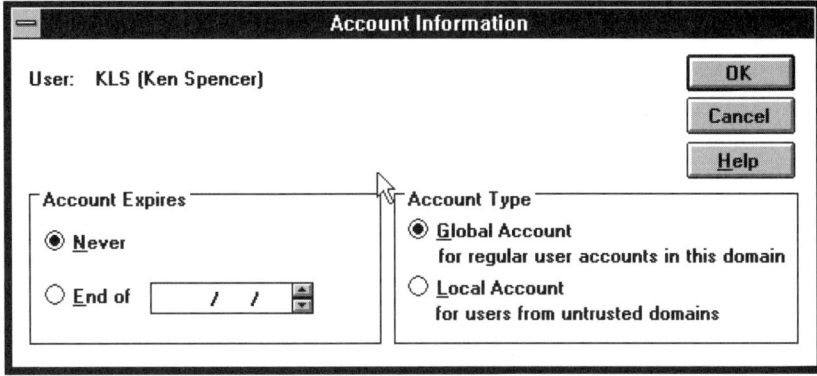

FIGURE 5.6 The Account Information dialog box is used for setting an expiration date on an account or forcing the account to be used locally on the current domain.

stored are Program Manager groups, program items in groups, printer connections, and window characteristics and colors. Profiles provide system managers with a great deal of control by enabling the manager to restrict users from modifying the information in the profiles. Profiles can be created for a specific user, and other profiles can be created and shared for multiple users. The User Profile Editor provides complete control over creating and managing profiles. User Manager for Domains is used to assign a profile to a user or group of users.

User profiles perform the same functions as log-on scripts but are much more powerful, because of their ability to store information about preferences, control a user's configuration capabilities, and specify which Program Manager group is used as the startup group.

NT maintains a default profile for each user who has logged on an NT workstation except for guest accounts.

Be careful with the Administrator's account. This account is very powerful, and you should have a good password set for it.

Settings made in the User Profile Editor have no effect on Administrator accounts, except for the Startup group setting.

Potential Problems with Profiles

The biggest problem with user profiles is that they work only on NT systems, which limits their usefulness on a network that is using NT Server as a server and has many MS-DOS, Windows for Workgroups, and Windows 95 clients. The MS-DOS and Windows for Workgroups clients must use log-on scripts. Windows 95 supports user profiles, but the Windows 95 profiles are not compatible with NT profiles.

Profiles are device-dependent regarding screen resolution and possibly other settings. Profiles should be created on the lowest resolution device for users who share the profile. Ideally, you should create separate profiles for users with high-resolution monitors, so that they can take full advantage of the screen resolution.

Profile changes may not appear to take effect immediately after the change is made on domains with more than one server. This change takes some time, because the profile must be replicated to all the servers in the domain before it is totally effective. You can force this to happen by using Server Manager, selecting the PDC from the servers list, and then selecting Synchronize Entire Domain from the Computer menu. This selection causes all the servers in the domain to be immediately updated with all replication changes.

Types of Profiles

The following sections outline the four types of user profiles and how to create them.

INDIVIDUAL OR GROUP

The individual or group profile is created by logging on as the user and selecting File/Save To Current Profile. You can also create an Individual or Group profile by selecting File/Save As File. This choice will save the profile settings as a file, which can then be specified for a user or group of users.

USER DEFAULT

A User Default profile is the one used when a new user is created. You can create this type of profile by selecting File/Save As User Default.

SYSTEM DEFAULT

The System Default profile is used by a system when there is no user logged on to the system. This type of profile is created by selecting File/Save As System Default.

MANDATORY

Mandatory profiles allow you to control a user's ability to change their environment. A Mandatory profile can also be edited to allow users to have access to new applications.

Creating and Assigning Profiles

Profiles are created and modified with the User Profile Editor, which is usually located in the Administrative Tools group. Figure 5.7 shows the NT 3.51 version.

When you enter the location for the User Profile, make sure that you use the UNC definition for the file location. Using the UNC definition causes NT to connect to the designated server and service to find the profile. If you use a typical FAT designation such as C:\USERS\PROFILE, NT always looks on C: for the location of the profile. The UNC designation is always the preferred method for specifying a file location because it forces NT to connect to the correct server even if no connection exists.

Controlling Network Connections with Profiles

User profiles store information about current printer and file connections. The user profile causes the connections to be reestablished at log-on time. These new connections take the place of persistent connections in both Print Manager and File Manager because these two programs are available only on a local machine when a person logs on again on the same machine.

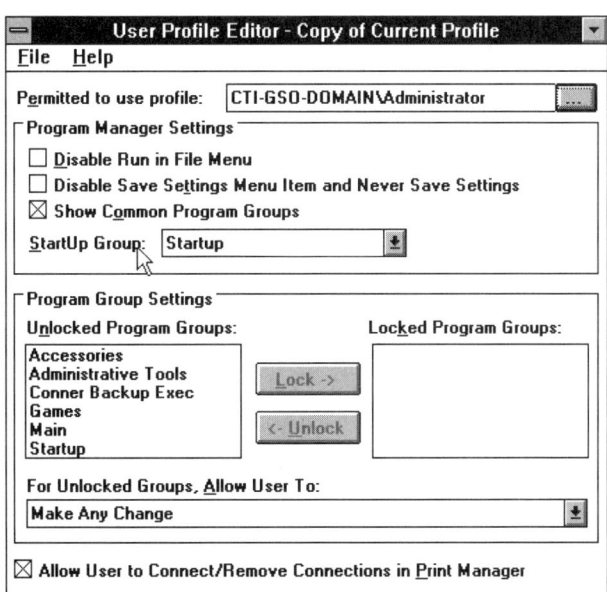

FIGURE 5.7 The User Profile Editor is used to create profiles for different users. A profile automatically configures an NT workstation or server when the user logs on.

Server-based user profiles make persistent connections available to a user at any workstation they use to log in to the network.

Storage of Profiles

Profiles that are stored on a server should be stored on a high-availability server. This server should be up all the time to make sure that profiles are available to users.

Unlike NT 3.51, which stores profiles in a single file, NT 4.0 stores them in a directory. Therefore, if you have a mixed NT 3.51 and NT 4.0 environment and want your users to keep their profiles when logging in to a 3.51 and a 4.0 computer, then you will need to specify a profile.man or .dat (where "profile" can be the users' last name or login name). However, if your environment only supports NT 4.0, then you only will need to specify the profile directory (no filenames or extensions to play with!).

You can store a master copy of the profile on the server and use directory replication to move a copy of the profiles to each individual system. This structuring probably works fine for department-level or group-level profiles. The overhead in replicating a large number of individual profiles to all the workstations on the LAN might be too high in larger networks.

You can make an user's profile mandatory by renaming it to Ntuser.man. This way, no user will be able to change it.

Replicated files should be located in the IMPORT/SCRIPTS directory of the import server. These files are automatically shared as NETLOGON and are accessed during log-on to find log-on scripts and profiles.

Log-on Script

In the simple days of NetWare 2.0a and all-DOS clients, Logon scripts were very simple. You simply used NetWare's famous (infamous) SysCon to create the script, and you were in business. NT Server brings a tremendous amount of flexibility to the good old log-on script, while at the same time adding complexity to the process (flexibility and complexity always seem to go together).

By the way, NT 4.0 has a NetWare Migration Tool that will convert NetWare 3.x and 4.x log-on scripts for use on NT.

Windows for Workgroups, Workgroup Add-On for MS-DOS, MSClient, Windows 95, NT, and NT Server all inherit the same basic log-on script capabilities. The only problem with NT and log-on scripts is determining which log-on script to run on which machine. This problem occurs because NT downloads the log-on script to the client workstation for processing. If you specify a batch file using NT batch commands for a user and then log on that account from a DOS machine, the log-on script fails. If you log on the account from an NT workstation, the log-on script works fine.

Special environment variables are provided for log-on scripts under NT or NT Server systems at log-on time. These variables are documented on Chapter 6, in the NT documentation.

NT restores persistent connections before running your log-on script.

Log-on scripts and their associated files should be stored in the \WINNT35 \SYSTEM32\REPL\IMPORT\SCRIPTS directory. This directory automatically shares as NETLOG-ON.

Computer Technologies, Inc., has developed a tool called NTLOG-ON that works with Windows for Workgroups clients logging in to an NT Domain. This program uses the standard Windows for Workgroups log-on routines and allows you to have customizable toolbars based on the user (using another CTI product called FloatBar), connect to specific services for each user during log-on, and numerous other tasks.

Client Participation with Log-on and Startup Scripts

Another part of client configuration is what happens on your client workstations when they boot or when the user interface comes up, such as when Program Manager starts with Windows for Workgroups. You can accomplish a lot with these small VB programs and pave the way for further interaction with your server via the log-on script. These programs can also save the user time when they are run as the workstation boots. Users seem to be more patient when a workstation takes a while to boot versus a workstation that boots quickly and then takes forever to log on after log-on IDs have been entered.

The following list contains some of the more interesting things you can do with these programs.

- **Client Configuration Data**–With a little ingenuity, you can create a program to collect information on your clients with little effort. Your NT and

Windows for Workgroups clients in particular can benefit from Visual Basic programs that execute when Windows starts. A neat little VB program can grab the configuration data for your machine and stuff it on a server drive. Then it's easy for NT to pick up the data and update your configuration database. The types of data you can collect include memory configuration, processor type, math coprocessor, and applications listed in the WIN.INI file or Registry. You can tweak your CONFIG.SYS or AUTOEXEC.BAT files to include SET statements for other important pieces of data such as the number for the workstations network cable.

■ **Starting Other Programs**–You may have certain programs that must be started when a user logs in. Examples of these programs are Schedule+ and a mail-monitoring program. You might ask: "Why not start these programs in the Startup group of the user's workstation?" Starting the programs in the log-on script allows users to have access to them wherever they log on and not just from their normal workstations. You must check with individual programs to determine their idiosyncrasies for running from different locations for a single user. For instance, Microsoft Mail requires that the mail files be kept on the Post Office if the user accesses mail from different places or if more than one user logs on mail from a workstation.

■ **Connecting to Network Resources**–Another useful trick is using the log-on program to connect to standard services during the log-on process. This process removes the need to rely on the system to reconnect to all services that were connected when the user shut down the client or logged out. You can use the NET commands—such as NET USE—to connect or disconnect any network resources during the log-on process.

LOG-ON SCRIPT EXAMPLES

This section contains two example log-on scripts that you can use, depending on your needs. Log-on scripts are handy for lots of network management tasks.

SAMPLE DOS/WINDOWS/WINDOWS FOR WORKGROUPS LOG-ON SCRIPT • This sample script was born of a need to solve a problem involving SMS.INI when developing a procedure to install new PC workstations at a client site. SMS.INI is installed automatically using several defaults for users to fill in regarding whether the PC can be remotely monitored and controlled. This client—as is the case with many others—did not want to give the users the option but force the user to allow remote control. This problem was solved using a small batch program and a little VB-DOS program. The following code sample shows the batch program.

```
Echo Log-on Script for NewPCs
Echo.
```

```
Echo Execute standard SMS log-on script
net use x: \\server1\netlog-on
net use w: \\server1\sms_shr
set oldpath=%path%
path=%path%;x:\;
w:
call smsls
Echo
Echo Reset SMS.INI variables
x:SETSMS
c:
net use x: /d /y
net use w: /d /y
path=%oldpath%
```

This routine performs the following tasks:

1. Connect to the NetLog-on and SMS_SHR shared resources.
2. Save the current Path in the variable old path.
3. Change to the W: drive (SMS_SHR).
4. Run the SMSLS.BAT log-on script.
5. Run the SETSMS.EXE program on drive X: (NetLog-on).
6. Change to the C: drive.
7. Disconnect both shared resources.
8. Restore the path.

SETSMS.EXE is actually a small VB-DOS program that edits the SMS.INI file and changes several settings.

This little routine saves lots of time by

■ Logging on the new system using the NEWPC account
■ Installing and reconfiguring SMS on the fly

warning You should be able to take this example and configure it for your needs. A word of caution: If a log-on script does not terminate normally, it will hang the log-on process. If you experience a log-on script that is hanging, try using a simple script that does nothing to verify that the PC can log on successfully. More complex log-on scripts such as those used by SMS can run into this problem frequently if there is a logic or other problem that hangs the log-on script.

SMS Log-on Script • SMSLS.BAT is the standard LOG-ON script for Systems Management Server and runs the standard SMS items for inventory and the like.

The following files must be on the NetLog-on share for SMS to find them during a normal log-on:

CHOICE.COM

CLRLEVEL.COM

DOSVER.COM

NETSPEED.COM

NETSPEED.DAT

SETLS16.EXE

SETLS32I.EXE

SMSLS.BAT

You can also use NET USE in a log-on script to connect to the SMS_SHR and then run SMSLS. This procedure removes the need to copy the files to the NetLog-on share and also resolves a problem that occurs when SMSLS.BAT runs on the`NetLog-on share and finds itself there. It then tries to run as if it were running from the SMS_SHR.

Most of these files can be found in the SMS\LOGON.SRV directory. The SETLS16.EXE file can be found in the X86.BIN subdirectory of LOGON.SRV, while versions of SETLS321.EXE are found in the appropriate subdirectory for the server (ALPHA.BIN or X86.BIN). A SETLSOS2.EXE program is in the X86.BIN directory for OS/2 clients.

There are also two other SMSLS programs: an SMSLS.CMD for OS/2 and a SMSLS.SCR for NetWare. The NetWare version should be included in the system log-in script.

NTLOGON AND FLOATBAR

NTLog-on is a log-on script designed specifically to work with NT clients such as Windows for Workgroups. It was enhanced to work with Windows 95.

NTLog-on disconnects users if they are connected when the program runs. Before the disconnection takes place, File Manager and MSMail are disconnected if they are running.

NTLog-on enables a system manager to have more control during the log-on process. A user file (USER.INI) that is located in the user's home directory controls the shares connected during log-on. Shared directories and printers are simply listed in USER.INI, and the connections take place automatically. All other shares are disconnected regardless of whether or not the shares are persistent. The default server is listed in NTLOGON.INI in the U: directory on the SiteSys$ share, along with any shared resources that all users should connect to. A sample NTLOGON.INI is shown in the following code sample:

```
[SERVER]

ServerName1

[FILEPUBLIC]

z:\\ ServerName1\distdsk$

[PRINT]
```

Both NTLOG-ON.INI and USER.INI share the same format.

The next to the last thing NTLog-on does is set the workstation time from the default server listed in NTLOG-ON.INI in the U: directory on the SiteSys$ share. If you simply keep the server time set correctly, every workstation follows as long as it logs on each day. If you set the Force Users Off When Logon Time Expires option, each user must log on if you limit their log-on time to every 23.75 hours per day.

You can download a simple version of NTLog-on from www.32nt.com.

WINDOWS NTLOGON SCRIPTS ONLY

Windows NT and NT Server both use a flexible format for log-on scripts. You can call any executable program as a log-on script from either system. This flexibility enables you to use a mixture of batch programs and executable programs, depending upon the requirements of your network. This flexibility also means that you don't have to learn a new log-on script language to take advantage of this powerful tool.

We like using a tool like Visual Basic or Visual C++ for log-on scripts because they provide speed. They also are compiled to EXE files and the source code is hidden from the user. Maintaining source code versions is easier with these tools, because you can be sure that no one has tweaked a file at a remote server and forgotten to update the master copy on the server.

The only problem with using Visual Basic for a log-on script is that NT does not support it. A log-on script must be a batch file (BAT or CMD) or a true executable such as those created by C++ or Visual C++. You can get around this restriction with a little ingenuity, such as calling the log-on functions from a VB log-on utility like NTLog-on.

DEFAULT VARIABLES • Table 5.1 defines special variables that may be used within log-on script programs but only when logging on from an NT system. A similar table can be found in the Concepts and Planning Guide manual.

These parameters are useful for determining special options at log-on time, depending upon the user's operating system, machine type, domain,

TABLE 5.1	Special Environment Variables for Log-on Script Programs
Parameter	**Description**
%HOMEDRIVE%	Specifies the drive letter that points to the drive containing the user's home directory. When no home directory is used, the default is the drive NT is installed on.
%HOMEPATH%	Specifies the full path name for the user's home directory. When no home directory is used, the default is \Users\Default.
%HOMESHARE%	Specifies the share name for the service containing the user's home directory. When no home directory is used, the default is the blank.
%OS%	Specifies the operating system for the user's workstation.
%PROCESSOR_ ARCHITECTURE%	Indicates the processor architecture for the system. It is used with the %PROCESSOR_LEVEL% variable to identify the exact type of processor. This option returns ALPHA, MIPS, or X86 depending upon the system.
%PROCESSOR_LEVEL%	Specifies the processor level for the user's workstation. Examples for this variable are 21064 for Alpha systems and 5 for an Intel Pentium system.
%USERDOMAIN%	Specifies the domain containing the user's account.
%USERNAME%	The user name for the user running the log-on script.

and so forth. You access these parameters by specifying its name in a command. The method of access is slightly different for each language you may use for a log-on script.

LOG-ON SCRIPT TIPS • Some useful tips for log-on scripts follow:

- Connect to specific resources.
- Most networks require that certain file and print resources are available when a user logs in to the network.
- Make sure that specific resources are not connected.
- Run specific application programs.
- Run update programs.

Preferences and last-shared connections are set and reconnected before log-on scripts are executed.

The path to a log-on script is built by adding the NetLog-on path to the log-on script name.

HOME DIRECTORIES

A home directory is typically a location on a server where a user stores personnel files. All users should have a default home directory that is connected each time they log on. Every user's connection to the home directory should also use the same letter.

As you know, every user has an account under the USERS directory. This account should be shared with the user name followed by a $ (to make it a hidden share). When each user logs on, each user should connect the same drive letter to its own share. If your user name is KENS, for example, you should connect to the KENS$ share. You normally use the drive letter specified on most Pathworks networks—M:. This is a good choice because users think of M: as MY drive.

You can specify a home directory for users using User Manager. Select the Properties for a user, and then click the Profile button. Include either a local path or a UNC name. The UNC name is a favorite because it works for both interactive and network log-ons over the LAN.

One problem with home directories is that Windows for Workgroups and DOS clients do not see their home directories unless you connect them in the log-on script. You should either use a log-on script to connect to the user's home directory or use the NTLOGON program or one similar. This setup makes sure that a user is always connected to his or her own home directory with the same drive letter. It cuts down on a lot of confusion.

The NET USE command supports an option for attaching to home directories (/HOME). This command only works during the execution of your log-on script.

Groups

NT provides local and global user groups to assist in managing user actions. Groups are handy for setting permissions, setting management chores, and soon.

Local Groups

NT and NT Server include several default local groups. Table 5.2 lists the default groups and indicates whether or not the group is for NT or NT Server only.

Local groups are represented by an icon with two faces superimposed over a computer. A local group is useful only on the NT workstation or NT Server domain on which it was created. Local groups can contain user accounts from the workstations, user accounts, and global groups from the domain and trusted domains.

warning Watch your Guest accounts. They can allow untrusted users to access your system, so unless you have a use for them, you should disable them. Avoid setting up Guest accounts for anonymous users accessing your network.

| TABLE 5.2 | Default User Groups |

Group	Description
Administrators	Members have more control over managing systems than any other group.
Backup Operators	Members of this group can back up and restore files on primary and backup domain controllers. They also have the ability to log on the servers interactively and shut them down.
Server Operators	Members of this group can manage the domain's PDC and BDC for tasks such as backup, printer management, share management, backup chores, formatting the server's disk, miscellaneous tasks, and shutting down the servers.
Account Operators	The Account Operators local group is designed for managers that need to manage user accounts. Account Operators can use User Manager for Domains for most tasks but cannot modify or delete the following groups, users, or policies: groups (Administrators, Domain Admins, Account Operators, Backup Operators, Print Operators, or Server Operators), users (administrators), and policies (security).
Print Operators	The Print Operators group is designed for users who must have full management over printers.
Users	The Users local group lists all users of an NT system. Users normally contains the Domain Users group.
Guests	The Guests local group is for users who require minimal access to the network. Guests usually contains the Domain Guests global group.
Replicator	The Replicator group is designed to provide support for Replicator functions. The only account that should be in this group is the domain user account used to log on the Replicator services.

Local groups are useful for maintaining security permissions on a domain because a local group can contain global groups and users from trusted domains. For instance, you can create a group on a domain that contains both users on the current domain and users on trusted domains, as well as global groups.

Local groups with the same name can be created in different servers and/or domains, but can cause confusion.

SPECIAL GROUPS

NT Server also includes other default groups that contain no members. These groups are used only to specify how a particular user is using the NT system at a certain point in time. These groups are listed in Table 5.3.

TABLE 5.3	Default Groups That Contain No Members
Group	**Description**
Interactive	Users who log-on the system interactively.
Everyone	Every user who accesses the system in any manner.
Creator/Owner	The user who creates or takes ownership of a resource.
Network Users	Users who access a resource through the network.
System	The operating system.

The special groups are useful when NT Server presents a list of users for tasks such as setting permissions. These generic groups enable you to assign permissions by type of user instead of only by the local or global groups or user account. For instance, if you want to prevent access to a particular directory or file over the network, simply assign no access permission to the Network Users group.

GLOBAL GROUPS

Global groups are represented by an icon with two faces superimposed over a globe. They are used only on NT Server domains. A global group can contain only user accounts from the domain and global groups from trusted domains.

Global groups can pass through trust relationships, while local groups cannot. In other words, a global group can be accessed anywhere you can see groups and users, such as in the Permissions dialog box in File Manager. NT Server creates three global groups at installation: Domain Admins, Domain Users, and Domain Guests.

If a global group is created with the same name as a local group, they will be treated as two separate entities. Any permissions assigned to one group will not carry over to the other group because both groups have separate security identifiers.

It is a good idea to add a special identifier to the front of a global group name to make it readily identifiable even though the icon for global groups is different from the icon for local groups. A prefix such as Domain at the front of a global group name provides instant recognition for your global groups wherever they are used or viewed. Notice that this prefix is the same prefix used by Microsoft for the built-in global groups.

Table 5.4 includes the built-in global groups with NT Server.

MANAGING GROUPS

Global and local groups are managed in the same manner. The main difference in creating a new group is whether you choose New Local Group or New Global Group from the User menu in User Manager.

TABLE 5.4	NT Server Built-in Global Groups
Group	**Description**
Domain Admins	Members have more control over managing systems than any other group.
Domain Users	The Domain Users group is (by default) a member of all NT and NT Server local users, groups, extending membership in the users, group to all domain users. New domain users are automatically added to Domain Users.
Domain Guests	The Domain Guests group contains the built-in guest account on NT Servers. Domain Guests is a member of the Guests local group on the domain.

Creating a New Group:

1. Start User Manager for Domains.
2. Select the initial users for the group.
3. Choose New Local Group or New Global Group from the User menu.
4. Enter the name of the group in the Group Name box.
5. Enter a description for the group in the Description box.
6. Add any new members not selected to the group by clicking the Add button and selecting the users.
7. Choose the OK button to close the dialog box.

Copying a Group:

1. Start User Manager for Domains.
2. Select the group to copy.
3. Choose the Copy command from the User menu.
4. Enter the name of the group in the Group Name box.
5. Change the description for the group (recommended) in the Description box.
6. Add any new members not selected to the group by clicking the Add button and selecting the users.
7. Remove any users not desired in the new group.
8. Choose the OK button to close the dialog box.

Groups can be deleted quickly with User Manager.

Deleting a Group:

1. Start User Manager for Domains.
2. Select the group to delete.
3. Choose the Delete command from the User menu or press Del.
4. Confirm the deletion by choosing OK and then Yes.

Removing Users from a Group:

1. Start User Manager for Domains.
2. Double-click the group to modify.
3. Select the user(s) to remove.
4. Drag the users to the Not Members box or click the Remove button.
5. Click the OK button to close the dialog box.

Users gain access to all permissions and rights given to a group when they become a member of the group.

Adding Users to a Local Group:

1. Start User Manager for Domains.
2. Double-click the local group to modify.
3. Click the Add button to display the Add Users and Groups dialog box.
4. Select the users.
5. Click the Add button.
6. Click the OK button to close the dialog box.

Adding Users to a Global Group:

1. Start User Manager for Domains.
2. Double-click the global group to modify.
3. Select the users.
4. Click the Add button.
5. Click the OK button to close the dialog box.

Modifying Properties of a Group:

1. Start User Manager for Domains.
2. Double-click the group to modify.
3. Modify the desired properties (description and users).
4. Click the OK button to close the dialog box.

A neat future that can be obscured in the steps to create a group is the ability to automatically add users to a new group.

Creating a New Group and Automatically Adding Users:

1. Start User Manager.
2. Select the users from the user list.
3. Choose New Local Group or New Global Group from the User menu.
4. Enter the name of the group in the Group Name box.
5. Enter an optional description for the group (recommended) in the Description box.
6. Add any new members not selected to the group by clicking the Add button and selecting the users.
7. Click the OK button to close the dialog box.

The NT Resource Kit for NT 4.0 (and 3.51) includes a utility that is useful for managing groups. USRTOGRP.EXE can add many users to a group at one time. The specifications for the users to add are supplied from a text file. This command is especially useful because a group will be created, if it does not exist. User accounts must exist before they are referenced in this command.

The command also works well in a trusted domain environment because it searches all trusted domains for users that are added to local groups. USRTOGRP checks only the current domain for user accounts added to a global group.

The format for the input file is

```
domain: domainname
localgroup(or globalgroup): groupname
Username1
Username2

...
```

Adding Many Users to Groups with USRTOGRP.EXE (NT Resource Kit):
1. Edit or create the input file.
2. Execute the command:
`usrtogrp filename`

Logging In from Multiple Workstations

A user may not receive pop-up messages correctly when they are logged on to multiple machines simultaneously with the same user name. This message occurs when the user has logged in to several machines with the same user name, and a network pop-up message is sent to the user account and not a machine name. The message is sent to the user account because the first workstation the user logs in to registers the user name and subsequently captures the pop-up message when it is sent.

Changing Passwords from an OS/2 Server

Administrators should not change their passwords from an OS/2 server, because doing so will cause the rights associated with the account to be last.

Security Checklist

As you have probably realized, Windows NT 4.0 is not only a revision of NT 3.51, but it is nearly a complete overhaul. With NT 4.0, Microsoft changed almost every aspect of the NT environment, from several updates to enhancements and alterations.

Most of the changes were for the good, but Microsoft changed so many things in NT 4.0 that mastering all of it is not a piece of cake. Don't expect to know everything about NT 4.0 too soon, or expect this book to bring you there! There is a lot to learn, whether you are only doing an upgrade from NT 3.51, 3.5 or even Windows 95, or whether you are installing it for the first time.

You should keep your eyes open for security issues that could jeopardize your systems' integrity or the safety of your users. Even if you were to be a NT guru, just attend one of those Internet security conferences and hear what they have to say about hackers, crackers, and other whackers, all trying to gain access to your system.

An intruder usually will try to gain access to your system by targeting your administrator's account. Not only does this account have unlimited privileges to the system, but unless you went to the NT 4.0 Resource Kit and used the PASSPROP.EXE file, the network access to the administrator's account is not locked! If you can protect the administrator's account, you will be preventing many other attacks to your system.

As a first item of your security checklist, you should change the name of the administrator's account to a long string of alphanumeric characters, making sure it's not in any dictionary. The password should also be of at least 10 characters, alphanumeric, and not part of any dictionary. You can even have an account named Administrator to be used as a decoy. Make sure to set an alarm in the Event Log for anyone trying to log in as the Administrator. At least you'll be able to know from which workstation the individual was trying to log in and check it out.

In addition, you should go to the Account Policy option in User Manager and set lockouts on all other accounts. You may be surprised, but there is a large percentage of intruders attacking servers that are originated from inside the company.

One more precaution when setting up accounts is to disable Remote Services Administration. Although a feature, we can't really see why an administrator would log on a server from a remote location! It's like opening the company's system's gate wide, as security is dangerously compromised.

What Will Change in NT 5.0

As Ben Heskett wrote for C|Net (April 18, 1997), the Windows NT camp at Microsoft (MSFT) says that "Windows NT is becoming the victim of its own success."

As discussed in Chapter 1, Microsoft plans to incorporate Kerberos security methods, but to date it has not yet done so, preferring to develop its own security solutions. Although NT 4.0 offers C2-level security, Microsoft will be including Kerberos security architecture among the new features of Windows NT 5.0, scheduled for the first quarter of 1998.

Conclusion

You should have a good understanding at this point of what administering an NT network is all about. This chapter has covered the basics of practical user management. You should also spend some time reviewing Microsoft TechNet on a regular basis and picking up any new information and problem resolutions that are provided there. The NT Resource Kit is also a good source of information that can add to your understanding how accounts work on NT.

Chapter 6 will introduce you to the NT file systems and tell you what you can and should do with them. You will learn the basics and some of the not-so-basic things you should be aware of. We will also introduce you to things like the Repair disk and how it can affect your systems.

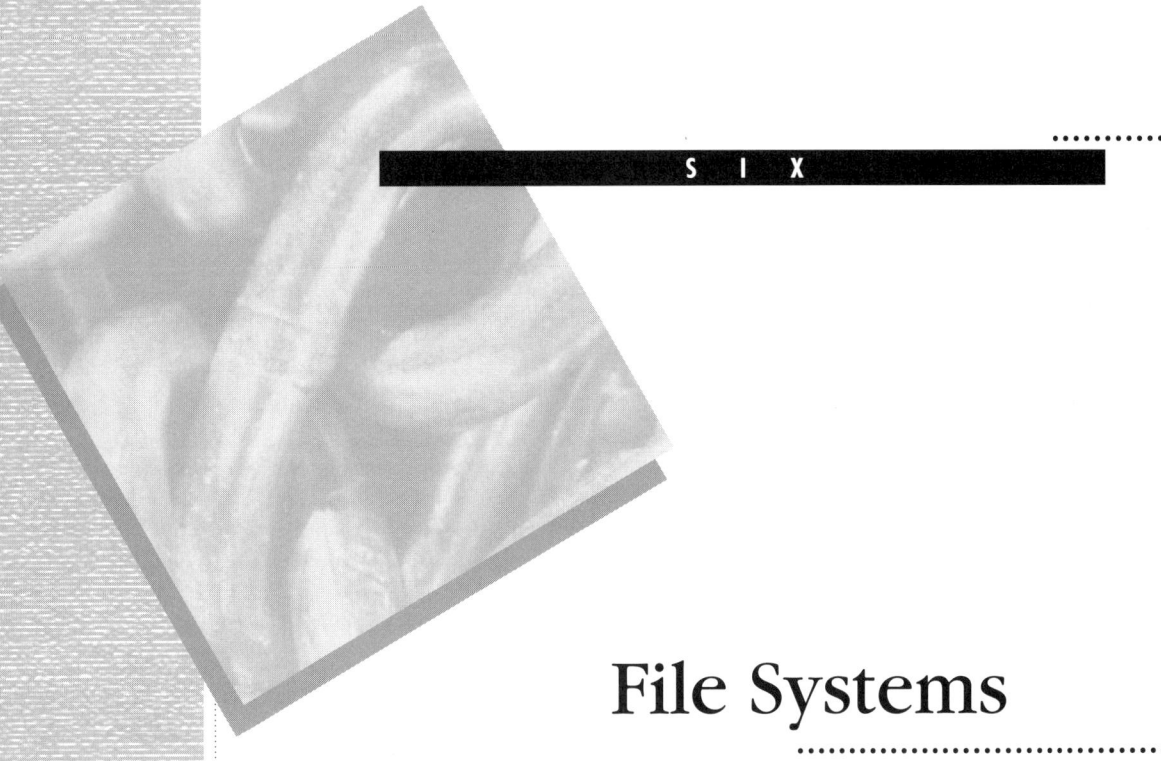

File Systems

File system management with NT is as simple as managing files with Windows 95 or Windows 3.x, and as complex as managing files for thousands of users at a time. NT is mostly used in network environments and, as such, is responsible for serving files to many users at once.

Scenario 6.1:

You are a Systems Manager responsible for rolling out NT Server in your company. You are faced with doing this quickly. How can you automate the creation of network share points on the servers? How do you effectively set up the file systems on the servers so they can be easily managed?

Scenario 6.2:

When you built your NT Server, you were rushed and did not build the Repair disk. Should you care about the repair disk and, if so, how do you go back and create it after the fact?

This chapter introduces you to file systems on NT. We cover not only the various file systems you can use, but also take a look at how to manage the file systems. Suggestions are included for using the various management tools, choosing to compress files or not, and how to use the Repair disk. We also touch on security at the file level.

Overview

Like any good operating system, NT must support some type of file system. NT 3.51 used to go beyond this simple requirement by containing native support for several different file systems, as follows:

- NTFS is the NT File System and contains the most advanced features of any file system supported by NT.
- FAT is the File Allocation Table file system that is carried over from DOS.
- HPFS is the High-Performance File System first introduced with OS/2. HPFS has support for extended file names and other features that the FAT system does not support. HPFS is not supported by NT 4.0.
- The CDFS file system supports the industry standard CD-ROM devices that are typically used in PCs today.
- MAC-NT supports the Macintosh via the Services for Macintosh subsystem. SFM must be installed as an option and only works with NTFS.
- DFS is the Distributed File System available for NT Server 4.0 (with Service Pack 3).

Each of these file systems is designed for a specific purpose and may be mixed and matched in NT to support your particular environment. For instance, many Intel systems run a small FAT partition (200MB) to hold the NT operating system and then use NTFS on the remaining disk space. Other users may use NTFS, FAT, and HPFS (for NT 3.51 and earlier only) on the same system if they are supporting DOS and OS/2 users.

However, with NT 4.0 Server, only two file systems can be chosen: FAT or NTFS (and CDFS and MAC NT). With 4.0, NT no longer supports HPFS.

All diskettes formatted with NT use FAT.

One of the main advantages of the NTFS file system, besides security, is its reliability. Every activity is registered on NTFS. If there is a power surge while you're saving or moving files from one directory to another, for example, the NTFS system can recover from the point where it stopped and continue the process. Sounds incredible, right? But it's true. It's happened that we've been remotely transferring files from one directory to another when the modem lost the connection. As soon as the modem reconnected to the shared volume, NT continued to transfer the files as if nothing had happened.

Another advantage is that NTFS executes "hot fixing," which is the act of immediately marking bad sectors as it finds them on the disk. Do you remember the famous SCANDISK from DOS? With NT, you no longer need it, with the advantage that NT does it automatically on every writing operation. For administrators, NTFS has yet another advantage: file compression.

 **note** If you are going to keep a dual boot system on your computer, such as Windows 95 and NT, make sure to use FAT instead of NTFS; otherwise, your Windows 95 won't be able to see the NTFS volumes.

Although you can have a FAT partition with NT, unlike with DOS the FAT partition does not allow for undelete or defragmentation. Unfortunately, the Recycle Bin only works locally and does not undelete files over the network. If you delete a file on the network, unless you use third-party software such as Diskeeper, from Executive Software (`http://www.execsoft.com`), which defragments and undeletes files on your NT partitions, you're dead in the water! Rather than a weakness in the system, this is a C2 requirement.

NT File Types

NT has quite a number of files that are used as part of the system or by different applications. Table 6.1 contains a useful list of most of the file types used on NT sorted by file extension and also includes short descriptions.

TABLE 6.1 NT File Types (Extensions)

Extension*	Description
none	Some Registry files and others have no extension
ALT	Registry files for alternate configuration
ANI	Animated cursors
BAS	Basic programs
BAT	Batch programs
BMP	Bit-mapped picture—graphic file
CMD	Batch programs for OS/2
COM	Executable programs
CPI	Font files
CPL	Control Panel tool files
CUR	Cursor files
DLL	Dynamic Link Library
DRV	Drivers

TABLE 6.1	NT File Types (Extensions) (Continued)
Extension*	**Description**
DRV	Drivers
EVT	Event Viewer files
EXE	Executable programs
FNT	Font files
FON	Font files
FOT	Font files
HLP	Help files
IND	Full text search index for help files
INF	Setup files
LEX	Spelling lexicon files
LOG	Log files for Registry and other applications
NLS	National language files
PCD	Plotter Driver files
PMA	Performance Monitor Alert settings file
PMC	Performance Monitor Chart settings file
PML	Performance Monitor Log settings file
PMR	Performance Monitor Report settings file
PMW	Performance Monitor Workspace settings file
PPD	Adobe PostScript printer description files
SCR	Screen savers
SEP	Separator page files
SEQ	Introduction to NT sequence files
SYS	Drivers
TIF	Tagged Image Format graphic file
TTF	Font files
TXT	Text files
WAV	Sound WAV files
WRI	Windows Write file
Other	Miscellaneous files

Table 6.1 is certainly not a complete list of every NT file type, but it covers most programs, applications, and support files.

NT File Systems in General

NT supports huge file systems up to 408 million terabytes in size. For many people, that number is beyond comprehension. The importance of the number is that it will be a long time before your NT system runs out of disk space capability. In fact, you will probably bump up against the physical limit of disk space on your server before the NT limit comes into play.

NT also supports large volume sizes for your disks, enabling you to have a partition that uses the entire disk instead of having to split the disk across several partitions, as was the case in some versions of DOS. We have installed NT Server on systems with as little as 1GB of total space to 20GB systems using mirrored volumes for the system disks and RAID 5 storage for data. NT scales beautifully with its wide support of file systems and storage types.

NTFS

NT File System (NTFS) is a new file system designed explicitly for NT. It has extended features such as transaction processing for file system metadata, advanced security, and long file names. It also supports short file names for any program or system that does not support long file names. The following list covers the main features of NTFS:

- NTFS supports cluster sizes of 512, 1024, 2048, and 4096 bytes.
- Names can be up to 256 characters.
- Paths can be up to 259 characters.
- Blanks and periods can occur anywhere in a file or directory name.
- The following characters cannot be used in a file or directory name:
  < > : " / \ | * ?.
- Case can be upper, lower, or mixed in a file or directory name.
- It is fast—very fast.

You must use quotes (" ") around a file name that contains spaces to force NT to parse the file name properly. Luckily, you can access most files from File Manager and programs that use directory list boxes to provide access to the file system. This type of graphical interface makes accessing files with long file names easy and removes the need to remember or to type a 200-character file name.

When you create an association for a file in File Manager, be sure to use quotes around the file name parameter to enable the application to open a file with spaces in the name.

Creating File Associations for File with Spaces in the Name (File Manager) in NT 3.51:

1. Start File Manager.
2. Select the Associate option from the File menu.
3. Select the file type to change from the list.
4. Click the Change Type button.
5. Click in the Command box and press the End key to move the cursor to the end of the command.
6. Change the parameter from %1 to "%1".
7. If the file type has more than one Action property (Open, Print, and so forth), make the changes in steps 5 and 6 for each action in the Action list.

Creating or Modifying File Associations in Windows NT 4.0:

1. Double-click My Computer.
2. On the View menu, click Options.
3. Click the File Types tab.
4. To create a file association, click New Type.
5. To modify an association, click the file type in the Registered File Types bos, and the click Edit.
6. To remove an association, click the file type, and the click Remove.

When you double-click a file type without an association, Windows NT 4.0, just like 95, opens a dialog box so you can create an association if you want.

Using spaces in names is a common approach once you get used to NT, so this option is very useful, especially for programs like Performance Monitor or Microsoft Word. Any time you have a problem accessing a file name with spaces, check out the syntax and make sure that you have included the quotes.

NT automatically creates short file names for all NTFS files, unless the short file name feature is turned off. NT uses the following rules for creating DOS file names from NTFS names:

- All spaces and UNICODE characters are removed.
- Periods are removed except for the last period that precedes a character.
- The first three characters after the period become the DOS extension.
- All NTFS characters that are illegal in the FAT system (. " / \ [ ] : ; = ,) are converted to underscores (_).

- The prefix for the DOS file becomes the first six characters of the NTFS file name plus a tilde (~) and a single digit number from 1 to 4. NT increments the number until the short file name is unique. If the resulting name is not unique after the number reaches 4, then the first characters of the name are used followed by four characters generated from the long file name. A ~5 or other number is appended to the resulting six-character name to guarantee uniqueness.
- All characters in the file name are translated to uppercase.

The exception to these rules is when the NTFS file name is less than eight characters long and contains a space. To work around this problem, anytime you have an NTFS name that is less than eight characters long, use another character (such as _ or -) to replace the space.

You should plan on disabling short-file-name generation at some point in the future when all users have upgraded to NT, Windows 95, and use only programs that can handle long file names. Turning off short-file-name generation will improve file system performance.

Disabling Short-File-Name Generation:

1. Start REGEDT32.

2. Change the DWORD value for the following entry to 1:

   ```
   HKEY_LOCAL_MACHINE\SYSTEM\CurrentControlSet\
   Control\ -
   ```

   ```
   Filesystem\NtfsDisable8dot3NameCreation
   ```

FAT

The File Allocation Table (FAT) system has been around for years on systems using MS-DOS. NTFS continues support for FAT to maintain compatibility with the many millions of systems still using DOS.

The FAT file system generally uses more space to store files than do HPFS or NTFS. Files require more storage space because FAT uses fixed 4K clusters to allocate disk space for files. For instance, when a file is created to hold 256 bytes of data and the cluster size for the partition is 4K, the file requires 4K of disk for the 256 bytes. The more files you store that are smaller than the cluster size, the more wasted space will occur.

The following list shows the parameters for FAT file systems on NT:

- Names up to 8.3 characters long. Version 3.5x or higher NT workstations and NT servers can both handle FAT names up to 255 characters. This limit is also true for Windows 95.
- Full path names can be up to 64 characters long.
- Blanks cannot occur anywhere in the file or directory name.

- A period can be used only to separate the name from the extension.
- The following special characters can be used in a file or directory name: - ( ) ! @ # $ % ^ & _ ~ '.
- All other special characters cannot be used in a file or directory name.
- File or directory names will always be uppercase, except on version 3.5x or higher NT workstations and NT servers, which can use mixed-case file names. This is also true of Windows 95 and NT 4.0.
- NT 3.5x automatically generates short file names in the 8.3 format using the same short-file-name generation method as NTFS.

HPFS (for NT 3.51 version only!)

The High Performance File System (HPFS) is a carryover from OS/2. It is included primarily for compatibility with OS/2 systems that share a network with NT. NT 3.51 and later versions allow you to use an existing HPFS volume but do not provide support for creating one. The following list covers the parameters for HPFS:

- HPFS supports cluster sizes of 1024 bytes.
- Names can be up to 254 characters.
- Paths can be up to 259 characters.
- Blanks and periods can occur anywhere in the file or directory name.
- The following characters can be used in a file or directory name: [ ] , + = ;.
- The following characters cannot be used in a file or directory name: < > : " / \ | * ? &.
- Case can be upper, lower, or mixed in a file or directory name.

DFS

DFS is a powerful new feature for NT Server. DFS basically enables you to create a master server that offers a directory tree as a network share. The DFS tree can contain directories on any server on the network, making the distributed directory an easy-to-use entity for accessing network files. For instance, suppose you have a network with the following servers:

- Marketing
- Production
- HumanResources

The DFS tree can have entries for directories on each one of these servers. Instead of users traversing each server looking for a particular directory, the user need only access the DFS tree and perform a search with Explorer or any other tool that performs file searches. The DFS tree presents a logical browse point into the entire set of resources provided by the servers.

DFS also improves network browsing. A user needs only one persistent connection to the DSF tree to browse anywhere in the tree. You no longer need to have 15 different connections for each user to get to common files.

The DFS administrative tool is used to build and maintain the DFS directories. The administration tool is also scriptable, enabling you to automate many management tasks.

The DFS root volume must be hosted on NT Server 4.0 running the DFS software. Leaf volumes can be hosted on any type of Microsoft server, or other server that is an NT-based client. This includes:

- Any version of NT Server or Windows NT Workstation
- NetWare
- Windows 95
- Windows for Workgroups
- LAN Manager
- NFS

Banyan Vines volumes can not be added to Dfs trees, however.
The DFS Admin Guide is located at this URL:

> http://www.microsoft.com/ntserver/dfs/dfsdocdl.htm

You can download DFS from the following URL:

> http://www.microsoft.com/ntserver/info/dfsdl.htm

Suggested Directory Structures

NT's default directory structure is laid out with the systems manager in mind. The structure supports the NT system and provides an initial directory tree for user directories.

Microsoft Windows NT Directory Service (NTDS) has been available since the first release of Windows NT Server in 1993, but in Windows NT Server 4.0, NTDS offers enhancements, such as increased maximum number of directory service objects, to extend the number of trusted domains that can be set up. This makes NTDS even more scaleable and flexible. NTDS is a secure, reliable architecture, with graphical and ease administration, and open interoperability with Novell NetWare 2.x and 3.x.

NTDS enhancements in NT 4.0 accommodate a larger number of objects. The recommended maximum number of trusted domains was increased from 128 to an unlimited number of trusting domains. The Local Security Authority component has been enhanced in NT 4.0 to allow a greater number of trusted domains, and to allow that number to scale with server memory.

Also, in NT Server 4.0, the maximum recommended trusted domains scales with server RAM and is now based on the size of the nonpaged pool (NPP).

The default size of the nonpaged pool is based on server RAM, as follows:

- 32MB server RAM results in 1.2MB NPP for a maximum of 140 TRUSTED domains
- 64MB server RAM results in 2.125MB NPP for a maximum of 250 TRUSTED domains
- 128MB server RAM results in 4.125MB NPP for a maximum of 500 TRUSTED domains

These NPP sizes are now adjustable by the administrator, so servers with 64MB could be adjusted to support 500 trusted domains via resizing of the NPP. This way, you have a more scaleable and flexible directory service in Windows NT Server 4.0 than you had with NT 3.51.

USERS Directory

The USERS directory is the default directory for user directories. This directory should be on an NTFS partition and should have restrictions placed on it clarifying who can do what. This setup stops prying users who have access to the server from getting into other people's files.

Another benefit of hanging all users' directories from the USERS directory is that it makes backup much easier. If you want to back up all the user files, for instance, just back up the entire USERS tree. This approach gets all users, directories at one time. The use of this structure also makes restoring directories easier.

Home Directory

The Home directory is the default directory for users when they log in. Administrators should create standard drive letters for all users' home directories such as M: for Mine. During the log-on process, the M: drive should automatically be connected to this directory and should be made the default drive.

The Home directory is very important to users because it is the directory they should use for their personal files. This directory should be protected from other users via the NT file permissions. This setup enables you to tailor the permissions to a particular user for his or her directory only. You could also use permissions to grant others access to a particular subtree. For instance, you could grant a manager access to his or her files and to the files of everyone else in the department. We suggest that you give the Domain Admins group full control access to all users' home directories, if possible. This access gives you the ability to manage setup files and other important user files easily.

Data Directories

The user directory concept of a master directory and separate subdirectories for data can be used for shared data directories for applications such as word processors and spreadsheets. You can also use the same concept for database files. We generally create a directory called DATA that contains the subdirectories for different types of data. Table 6.2 shows some samples of the subdirectories we usually place under DATA and their descriptions.

So far, we have discussed only one data directory on one disk. What happens when you have two or more disk drives and you want to spread the data over all the drives? The solution is to create a data directory off the root of each drive. This directory becomes the backup point for both drives and enables you to have a common structure for each drive. Spreading the data over multiple drives also improves the performance of your system if you have the drives on separate controllers, or if the controller handling both drives can gain simultaneous access to each drive.

Executable Programs

We have found that the best way to handle executable programs is to separate them by application in their own directory. Most applications such as Word or Excel insist on having their own directory anyway. Place these directories on your server in an area that can be shared for groups of applications. For instance, you can create a directory called MSOFFICE and install all Microsoft

TABLE 6.2	Suggested Data Subdirectories
Subdirectory	**Description**
DataBase	Contains all the database files for the server. This may include application-specific directory names for different projects.
Clients	Contains a separate subdirectory for each client my firm deals with. This allows us to track correspondence and spreadsheet files for this client. Under the Clients subdirectory, I have other subdirectories for general items and specific projects.
Vendors	Same as the Clients subdirectory, except that it contains a subdirectory for each vendor.
Projects	Allows me to track project-related items that are not related to a vendor or client. These could be programming projects or a manufacturing project for a new product.
Other	Takes into account any other type of information that your users may track. For instance, under my DATA directory there is a directory for Articles, another for Books, and so forth. I also have a directory called Products for information on products that my firm carries.

Office applications under this directory. Then you can share the MSOFFICE directory, and users will have access to all MSOFFICE applications.

What about utilities and in-house programs? Create a directory called U site specific on the server. Place all utilities that are used by everyone on the server U subdirectory. Share this directory as SiteSys$ or something similar. Then make sure that all users connect to this share at startup, and place the directory in their path. This connection gives them access to all files in the U directory or the SiteSys$ share. I also place DLLs for programs such as Visual Basic, third-party controls (VBX, OCX, and DLL), and other support programs on the U directory, where all workstations will find them, because U is located close to the front of the PATH.

You may want to create other directories under the SiteSys$ share for different applications.

NT treats programs with the following extensions as executable files: COM, EXE, BAT, and CMD. Other files with the extension DLL, VBX, or something else may contain code libraries (such as DLLs or VBX files). The search order for a program is specific to the program that launches it. For instance, all programs that use the NT API function CreateProcess look for an EXE file if the extension is not specified. Programs that use other methods to execute a file must create their own order of precedence for executing a program if the order is important.

Most executable programs are found by NT, and all versions of Windows and DOS occur if they are located in a directory on the PATH or if the program is in the current directory when the attempt to execute the program occurs.

Sharing Directories

Establishing shared directories under NT is simplicity itself. The same process is used for both NT 3.5 Workstation and NT 3.51 Server. The same or a similar process is also shared by Windows for Workgroups and to some extent Windows 95 and NT 4.0. The heart of the share process is File Manager.

Sharing a Directory with File Manager:
1. Start File Manager.
2. Select the directory you wish to share.
3. Click the Share As icon or select Share Directory As from the Disk menu.
4. Enter the share name.

You can assign security permissions to the share when it is created or after its creation.

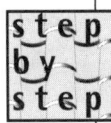

Sharing a Directory with Explorer (NT 4 and Windows 95):

1. Start Explorer.
2. Right-click the directory you wish to share.
3. Choose the Sharing command from context menu.
4. Enter the share name and parameters directory you wish to share.

Sharing a Directory from the Command Prompt:

1. Start a Command Prompt session.
2. Enter the following command:

```
NET SHARE sharename=path
```

Net Share has four different uses, as follows:

■ Create a new share:

```
NET SHARE sharename=path /users /unlimited /remark
```

sharename   Name for the new share.

path   Path for the directory to share.

/users:n   Specifies the maximum number of users as n (/users=10).

/unlimited   Specifies an unlimited number of users.

/remark   Specifies a description for the share (/remark "Kens share").

■ Display current shares:

```
NET SHARE
```

■ Change parameters of a share:

```
NET SHARE /users /unlimited /remark
```

■ Removing a share:

```
NET SHARE sharename /delete
```

/delete   Removes a share definition.

The following example shows how to create a share for the directory DATA on the D: drive:

```
NET SHARE MyData=D:\DATA
```

The next example shows how to obtain a listing of all shares on a server with Net Share:

```
NET SHARE

Share Name        Resource        Remark

-------------------------------------

ADMIN$      C:\WINNT35      Remote Admin

C$ C:\      Default share

IPC$        Remote IPC

mirror      C:\OCTOPUS\mirror

NETLOGON    C:\WINNT35\System32\repl\imp... Logon
server share

The command completed successfully.
```

NET SHARE is most useful in batch files or other automated operations. A batch file can be created very quickly with several NET SHARE commands. This is a useful trick for setting up a new server.

What happens when you wish to share a directory on a remote system? This can be a frequent occurrence when you have several NT systems on a network, especially if they are located across a WAN and are not readily accessible. Fortunately, there are two options for remotely creating shares:

- Use Server Manager.
- Use RMTSHARE.EXE from the NT Resource Kit.

Creating a Share with Server Manager:

1. Start Server Manager.
2. Select the server on which to create the share from the list.
3. Select Shared Directories from the Computer menu.
4. Click the New Share button.
5. Enter the share name.
6. Enter the full path (UNC name) for the share.
7. Enter a comment for the share.
8. Set the concurrent user limit.
9. Optionally add permissions for the share.
10. Click OK.

Another handy way to create a share is with the RMTSHARE command from the NT Resource Kit. This command is useful in a batch program, when you wish to create a number of shares at once.

Creating a Share with RMTSHARE.EXE (NT Resource Kit):

1. Execute the following command:

    ```
    rmtshare \\name /users /unlimited /remark /delete
    ```

    where

\\name	UNC Name for the share and the directory specification for the share. The following example illustrates the format to share the C:\TEMP\KEN directory on the server named SERVER1 \\Server1\ThisShare =c:\TEMP\KEN.
/users:n	Specifies the maximum number (n) of users for the share.
/unlimited	Allows an unlimited number of users to simultaneously access the share.
/remark:text	Specifies the comments (in "quotes") for the share.
/delete	Used with only the share name.

Connecting to NT Server Resources

Users can connect to NT Server resources using several methods. Windows for Workgroups and NT 3.51 systems can use either File Manager or the NET USE command to connect to resources. Workgroup Add-On for MS-DOS clients must use the pop-up interface or the NET USE command. Windows NT 4.0 (and Windows 95) users can connect to shared resources using Explorer, File Manager, the NET USE command, and many other applications that support the connect functions.

FILE MANAGER

The steps to connect to a shared resource with File Manager are the same for both NT and Windows for Workgroups systems.

Connecting to a Shared Resource (File Manager):

1. Start File Manager.
2. Click the Connect button or select Connect Network Drive option on the Disk menu.
3. Select the drive letter to connect to the resource.
4. Enter the path to the service in the Path box, or select the path from the browse list.
5. Click OK. You can also double-click the share name in the browse box.

Checking the Reconnect at Startup box or Reconnect at Logon box (Windows NT 4.0 and 95) causes Windows for Workgroups, Windows 95, or NT to reconnect to the resource when Windows restarts. This is the default configuration.

If the resource you select requires a password, a dialog box appears requesting the password, unless you have connected to this resource before and have used a valid password. NT and Windows for Workgroups can remember passwords for resources by user name, and will automatically supply them when you connect to the resource.

You must explicitly enter the share name when you connect to a hidden share, because the share will not be displayed in the browse list. The following steps should work well. Remember that you can also use the NET USE command to connect to hidden shares.

Connecting to a Hidden Shared Resource (File Manager):

1. Start File Manager.
2. Click the Connect button or select Connect Network Drive option on the Disk menu.
3. Select the drive letter to connect to the resource.
4. Enter the path to the service in the Path box.
5. Click OK.

NET USE

NT, Workgroup Add-On for MS-DOS, Windows NT 4.0, Windows 95, and Windows for Workgroups clients can use the NET USE command from the command prompt to connect to shared resources. This command is useful because it can be used in batch programs or accessed from icons in Program Manager or the Windows NT 4.0 (or Windows 95) desktop. The command is also useful in log-on scripts to connect to various resources during log-on via a batch program.

The format for NET USE is

```
NET USE drv \\srvr\share /USER:Domain\UserName -PWD
```

drv	Drive letter for the connected drive.
srvr	Server name of the NT Server.
share	Share name of the shared resource.
Domain	Domain name for the desired domain.
UserName	Account name for the user.
PWD	Password for the user account.
/Y	Carries out the command with no prompting.

The following command connects the P: drive letter to the FILES resource on server CTI-NT SERVER. The domain name is CTI.

```
NET USE P: \\CTI-NT SERVER\files /USER:CTI \ken
```

The USER option is used to pass the domain name to the NT server. This is necessary only when the NT system is not logged in to the domain but is logged in to an NT workgroup. Normally NT passes the domain name to the NT Server except when the machine is not logged in to the domain.

NET USE has an undocumented switch (*) that enables you to use the next available drive letter to connect to a resource. For instance, the following command connects the next free drive letter to the resource KEN:

```
NET USE * \\CTI-NT SERVER\files /USER:DOM-KEN\ken
```

You can also use the * in place of the password.

Converting File Systems

In NT 3.51, HPFS and FAT file systems can be converted to NTFS by the use of the Convert command. With NT 4.0, only FAT can be converted. You can also convert a file system to NTFS during the installation of NT.

Once a file system is converted to NTFS, you cannot convert the system back to FAT or HPFS (HPFS only with NT 3.51 version!) without backing up the partition, reformatting the partition, and restoring the files.

The syntax for Convert is

```
Convert /NTFS C:
```

/NTFS   Convert the file system to NTFS.

C: Drive to convert.

If Convert cannot lock the file system, it will ask if you wish to convert at the next boot. Answer **Y**, and reboot the system at your convenience.

Compressing Files and Directories

Both NT 3.51 and NT 4.0 include a nice compression feature for NTFS volumes. Both files and directories can be compressed. The compression feature is conveniently integrated into NT and is not implemented as separate utilities like DriveSpace in Windows 95 or MS-DOS. For instance, you can compress an entire directory tree with three clicks of the mouse, using File Manager (File menu/Compress/Yes). Not only are the current directories and files compressed, but any new files are also compressed added to a compressed directory. Individual files can also be compressed in the same manner—select the files in File Manager and then choose File menu/Compress. You can also compress or uncompress files and directories by selecting the Properties option in File Manager and changing the Compressed check box.

In keeping with the improving graphical nature of many programs, File Manager shows all compressed files and directories in a different color (currently blue). Make sure that you don't set your background to this color, or you will not see any compressed files or directories in File Manager.

NT actually places a compress attribute on compressed files and directories. The attribute is visible in the Properties dialog box in File Manager. If you change the Compress attribute on a directory or file, it accomplishes the same thing as using Compress and Uncompress from the File menu.

UNCOMPRESSING A FILE(S)

The COMPACT utility is included to provide access to file compression from the command prompt. COMPACT is very useful for batch file operations in which you wish to perform many compression operations on a group of specific files or directories. The next two steps illustrate how to use the command.

COMPRESSING A DIRECTORY USING COMPACT

The following command compresses the current directory and all subdirectories:

```
COMPACT /C /S
```

The compress attribute is also set on the directory and all subdirectories to compress automatically any new files added to one of the directories.

COMPRESS A FILE USING COMPACT

This command compresses all *.TXT and *.DOC files in the current directory.

```
COMPACT /C *.TXT *.DOC
```

UNCOMPRESSING A DIRECTORY USING COMPACT

This command removes the compress attribute from the D:\DATA directory and all subdirectories.

```
COMPACT /U /S D:\DATA
```

It does not uncompress any files in the directory tree.

UNCOMPRESSING A FILE USING COMPACT

This command uncompresses all files in the D:\DATA directory.

```
COMPACT /U D:\DATA\*.*
```

- The /F switch can be used to recompress a file that was in the process of being compressed when the system crashed.
- /A causes COMPACT to also include hidden and system files.
- The /I option is useful in batch files to cause COMPACT to continue even if errors are encountered.
- /Q is also useful in batch files to suppress some of the output generated during the compression process.

Checking the Compression Status of a File or Directory:

1. Select the file or directory in File Manager.
2. Press Alt+Enter or select Properties from the File menu.

You can also enter **COMPACT** with no parameters to display the compression status for a file or directory.

What happens when you move or copy a compressed file to a noncompressed directory or copy a file from a FAT disk to a compressed directory? The following list illustrates the simple concepts for several actions involving a compressed file or directory:

- **Move a compressed file within an NTFS partition**–All compressed files moved to a target on an NTFS partition retain the file's compressed state and attribute.
- **Copy a compressed file within an NTFS partition**–All compressed files copied to a target on an NTFS partition receive the compression attribute of the target directory and are automatically compressed or uncompressed.
- **Move or copy a compressed file to a non-NTFS partition**–All compressed files moved to a target not on an NTFS partition lose the compression attribute and are uncompressed.
- **Move or copy a file from a non-NTFS partition to a target on an NTFS partition**–All files copied to a target on an NTFS partition receive the compression attribute of the target directory and are automatically compressed or uncompressed.

The Repair Disk

The repair disk created during the installation of NT is both a valuable tool and a potential hazard. The repair disk can be used to correct system problems or to recover configuration information if it is kept up to date. The information stored on the repair disk includes the system configuration and security information.

POTENTIAL REPAIR DISK PROBLEMS

The NT repair disk process is often confusing to new administrators and can lead to problems if it is not handled correctly. If the repair disk is used wisely, it can be a source of help when your system breaks.

One source of trouble that can occur with a repair disk revolves around Primary Domain Controllers and Backup Domain Controllers. If you build a new server and designate it as a PDC at setup time, the repair disk contains the designation for that server as the PDC. If you later make the server a BDC and then use the repair disk to recover the Security Accounts Manager and security files, the server becomes the PDC again.

If you ever have a missing or corrupted file, the emergency repair disk can be used to install a new version of the file for you. The emergency repair disk can also help you in identifying those corrupted or missing files. If the file in question is a Registry hive, the Emergency Repair disk can be used to restore the hive as well.

If you must use a repair disk to recover the security and SAM files in this type of situation, take the server off the network until it has been rebooted and downgraded to a PDC again.

UPDATING THE REPAIR DISK

RDISK.EXE is a handy utility shipped with NT that enables you to update the repair disk created when NT was installed. You can also copy the repair information to a local or network disk instead of to a floppy disk.

The solution to many problems around the repair disk is to use the RDISK.EXE utility shipped with NT 3.5x. This utility is located in the SYSTEM32 directory and is most useful if you create an icon for it in Program Manager.

RDISK.EXE can manipulate the NT Registry in several ways. The Emergency Information for a system can be saved to a hard drive/directory and restored later. RDISK stores the information in the REPAIR directory under the WINNT boot directory. After you have updated the repair information with RDISK.EXE, you can rebuild the repair disk for the system.

The best way to run RDISK.EXE is to create an icon for it in Program Manager or, in NT 4.0, to place it on the desktop.

Creating an Icon for RDISK:

1. Select the group to contain RDISK.
2. Select New from the File menu.
3. Enter the following information for the command line:

   `C:\WINNT\SYSTEM32\RDISK.EXE`

4. Enter the following information for the working directory:

   `C:\WINNT\SYSTEM32`

5. Replace C:\WINNT in both lines with the Windows NT root directory for the system on which you are creating the icon.

Figure 6.1 shows the simple RDISK form from NT 3.51, and Figure 6.2 shows the same for NT 4.0.

RDISK performs two tasks you can access via the command buttons:

■ Update Repair Info updates the repair information in the REPAIR directory. It can also create a new repair disk.
■ Create Repair Disk builds a new repair disk from Emergency Information you have previously saved.

Updating the Repair Information:

1. Start RDISK.
2. Click the Update Repair Info button.
3. Answer Yes to the prompt.
4. Optionally allow RDISK to build a new repair disk.

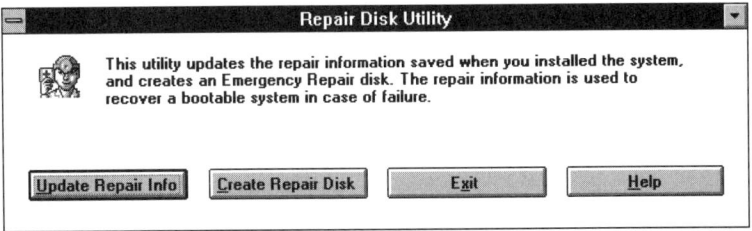

FIGURE 6.1 The Repair Disk Utility (RDISK.EXE) can be used to update the repair information for an NT system and to create a new repair disk.

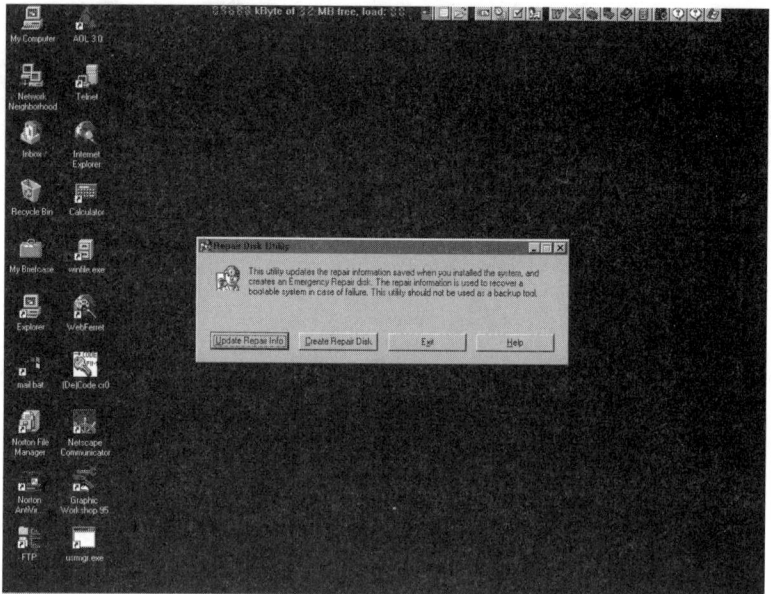

FIGURE 6.2 The interface of RDISK hasn't changed much between 3.51 and 4.0.

Creating a New Repair Disk Only:

1. Start RDISK.

2. Click the Create Repair Disk button.

3. Place a floppy disk in the drive and answer Yes.

PROBLEMS WITH THE REPAIR DISK AND PATCHES

One problem that may occur on your system happens when you have applied patches to NT using either the Microsoft Down Load service, the service packs on TechNet, or patches from another source. Once a patch has been applied, the repair disk is no longer valid for the system. Even if you update the repair disk, the patches are not updated because NT does not have information about the new files in the setup files.

One solution to this problem is to create a list of any patches that have been applied to your system(s). Make sure that the patches are readily available on a network share (that is backed up routinely). If you have to use the repair disk to recover a system, it is easy to reapply the patches by reapplying the patches or restoring a backup of the system files. The latter option is the best if you have performed routine backups of the boot volume.

Duplicate NT System Files

NT installs several files in two places. The exact files and their location depend upon whether or not you installed NT over an existing Windows 3.x system.

All NT-executable files are stored in \WINNT\SYSTEM32 for security purposes. The SYSTEM32 directory is also first on the search path ensuring that files in that directory are the first to be executed even if a file with the same name exists somewhere else on the system. The SYSTEM32 directory is also secured on NTFS partitions.

The duplicate files from SYSTEM32 and their alternate locations are shown in Table 6.3.

The following files in the SYSTEM directory share the same name as files in SYSTEM32, but the contents of the files are different: SHELL.DLL, SYSTEM, and VER.DLL.

Replacing a System File

There may be times when your system experiences a problem that is traced to a corrupted NT system file or when an existing file must be replaced with a new version. This problem can be corrected if you know the file that is corrupted and can access the system either from that particular machine or from the network.

A likely scenario is when the system is reachable from the network but you cannot log in interactively. In this case, you can perform the following steps to fix the problem, if it occurs because SHELL32.DLL is corrupt. These

TABLE 6.3	Duplicate NT Files
Executable File	**Alternate Directory**
NOTEPAD.EXE	\WINNT
TASKMAN.EXE	\WINNT
WRITE.EXE	\WINNT
COMMDLG.DLL	SYSTEM
MMSYSTEM.DLL	SYSTEM
MMTASK.TSK	SYSTEM
OLECLI.DLL	SYSTEM
OLESVR.DLL	SYSTEM
SETUP.INF	SYSTEM

steps also work from an interactive NT session if you can successfully log in. Either log in to the machine with an Administrator account, or access the machine over the network by connecting with an Administrator account.

There are two possible ways of resolving this problem. The first and most obvious way is to rename the old file and copy the new file to the correct directory. We have used this step to replace the NTFS.SYS file, which controls the NT File System.

Replacing NTFS.SYS or Other Drivers:

1. At the Windows NT command line, type the letter of the drive where Windows NT is installed and then change to the Windows NT drivers subdirectory.

   ```
   CD %windir%\SYSTEM32\DRIVERS
   ```

2. Rename NTFS.SYS.

   ```
   REN NTFS.SYS NTFS.001
   ```

3. Copy the new NTFS.SYS from this Update.

   ```
   COPY NTFS.SYS %windir%\SYSTEM32\DRIVERS
   ```

4. Reboot the computer. The new NTFS driver is now in effect.

When this procedure won't work, you may need to resort to fooling NT with the following procedure.

Replacing a System File Normally Locked:

1. Copy a new version of the file to the same location in the system with the problem and give the file a new name. For instance, change the last two characters of the file name (not the suffix) (that is, SHELL32.DLL becomes SHELL-NEW.DLL). Run REDEDT32.EXE and select the machine with the problem.

2. Locate the section HKEY_LOCAL_MACHINE.

   ```
   SYSTEM\CurrentControlSet\Control\SessionManager\
   KnownDLLs
   ```

   A key under this section points to the affected file. The key should have the same name as the file, and the value for the key is the name of the file.

3. Change the value of the key to point to the new file (SHELLNEW.DLL).

4. Exit REGEDT32.EXE and reboot the machine with the problem.

5. Log on the machine as Administrator.

6. Replace the problem file (SHELL32.DLL) by deleting the original file and copying the new file to the original file name (COPY SHELLNEW.DLL SHELL32.DLL).

---

7. Run REDEDT32.EXE on the machine with the problem.
8. Locate the section HKEY_LOCAL_MACHINE.

   ```
   SYSTEM\CurrentControlSet\Control\SessionManager\
   KnownDLLs
   ```

   A key under this section points to the affected file. The key should have the same name as the file, and the value for the key is the name of the file.
9. Change the value of the key to point to the original file (that is, SHELL32.DLL).
10. Exit REGEDT32.EXE and reboot the machine with the problem.
11. Delete the new file (SHELLNEW.DLL).

These steps are necessary because NT usually locks its system files when they are in use. If you use this method, you are simply pointing NT to a new file name, allowing it to free the affected file the next time it boots. Then you can replace the file and reset the pointer to the file.

Finding Problems with CHKDSK

CHKDSK can be used to find problems on a disk volume. It will check any NT file system and report on any problems it finds. CHKDSK is a DOS prompt command that tests a disk volume for a variety of ills. The /F option causes CHKDSK to also attempt to repair the file system of the disk by turning any mismatched file data (known as cross-linked files) into a group of files with the name FILEXXXX and the extension CHK. The XXXX in the name is replaced with 0001 through 9999, depending upon how many files CHKDSK must create. Once CHKDSK has completed, you can delete these files and recover the space they were using. You may want to browse through the *.CHK files and look for anything that resembles useful data, before you delete the files. The files are in ASCII format and can be copied or otherwise manipulated to save the data.

You may encounter a problem with CHKDSK /F for several reasons. One is when CHKDSK is started from the volume you wish to check. This problem most likely generates the message "Cannot lock the current volume." This message may be easily fixed if you make another volume current before you execute the command. For instance, suppose that you change to the D: volume, run CHKDSK, then receive this error message. Simply enter **C:** and reenter the Chkdsk command with Dial the last parameter. This procedure should allow the message to continue.

The second problem occurs when someone has files open on the volume you wish to check. This problem generates the message "Cannot lock the volume for single user." After this message, you have two options: If the volume you wish to check does not contain the NT operating system, make sure all files are closed on this volume. If the volume is used for paging, you will have to remove the page file on the volume before you continue or allow NT to run CHKDSK when it reboots.

Another option occurs when the volume to be checked contains NT system files. NT always prompts you when it cannot run CHKDSK and asks if you wish to run CHKDSK /F the next time the system boots. This is the only option for running CHKDSK /F on the volume that contains NT. Simply answer **Y** to the prompt and reboot the system.

Repairing Files with CHKDSK:

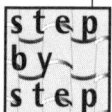

1. Change to the volume to check.
2. Run the following command

   ```
   CHKDSK /F
   ```

3. If any errors are reported, look at all FILE***.CHK files and make sure that they don't contain any valuable data.
4. Delete all *.CHK files.

Defragmenting a Disk

A physical disk becomes less efficient over time because blank spots of different size occur as files are added and removed. This process is called *fragmentation*, because files become fragmented when they are stored on disk and there is not a single block of space large enough to hold the entire file. New files are then "split" over several blank chunks of free space instead of being placed in one contiguous chunk. When a program tries to read the file, the data must be retrieved in several cycles of the disk as the data is read from each chunk and returned to the program.

Fragmentation is a problem, because a disk that becomes fragmented continually becomes less efficient over time as the problem becomes worse. Most PC network managers have had to use different utilities from third parties to defragment a disk. Defragmenting a disk is usually a manual process , and it must be performed from time to time.

Executive Software, mentioned earlier, has a product called Diskeeper LiteTM for Windows NT 4.0 that claims to be one of the best NT defragmenters on the market. This high-speed, manual defragmenter is the first and only one of its kind, designed exclusively for Windows NT 4.0 (build 1381 or higher).

As this book goes to press (September 1997), Executive Software (http://www.execsoft.com/dklite/) is making Diskeeper Lite available for free download without time-out. You can use it for as long as you want.

Security Checklist

If you have a large network, and especially if you have a connection to the Internet or even an FTP server, you definitely should use NTFS security settings to control specific access to files and directories and to configure the behavior of files and directories. You will need to format your disk or partition as NTFS.

Make sure to use File Manager/Explorer to set permissions for the various groups and users on NTFS partitions. If you want additional information to the one discussed in this chapter, a good source to check is the Windows NT *System Guide* for information about setting file permissions with File Manager.

If you have Internet users accessing any portion of your server, you should create a read-only directory for that purpose, so users will not be able to change files. However, NTFS security is flexible and can be used for creative problem solving.

One example of using file system security to control the behavior of directories is creating a drop box for your Internet customers to leave files in. By setting the permissions on the income directory to write only, Internet users can place files in the income directory, but cannot see or copy any of the files left there by other customers. Only internal users with appropriate permissions can access the files.

You cannot use Windows NT with any compression or partitioning software that requires disk device drivers to be loaded by MS-DOS. Therefore, you cannot use MS-DOS 6.0 DoubleSpace or MS-DOS 6.22 DiskSpace on a FAT primary partition or logical drive that you want to access when you run Windows NT.

File system security can also be used with other Internet server services for additional security, although the inherent nature of most other Internet server services provide more security than an FTP server.

One issue to watch out for is that when you use Windows NT 4.0 as your HyperText Transfer Protocol (HTTP) Server, you cannot effectively use Windows NT file system (NTFS) permissions to secure access to files when they are accessed from a World Wide Web browser, unless users are authenticated by authentication systems. Make sure to remember that before you open the doors of your Web server to the Wild Internet.

Volume-Level Security

First of all, do not confuse volume-level security with the file- and directory-level security provided by the NTFS system!

Microsoft Windows NT provides auditing and access control facilities for physical and logical volumes called volume-level security, which was designed to control volume-level access, such as formatting operations. It does not act at the file and directory-level operations. Also, you should know that unless your volume is formatted with NTFS, volume-level security will not protect your logical volumes as well as it will with an NTFS volume.

Windows NT was designed to have security descriptors applied to volumes control and audit volume-level access such as formatting a disk or reading raw disk sectors. The file system with which the logical volume is formatted is responsible for control and auditing of access to files and directories.

You can have two types of volume-level operations: physical drive access and logical volume access. Physical drive access enables Win32-based applications to manage hard disk partition tables and logical volumes. Logical volume access enables Win32-based applications to manage the contents of a partition below the file system level. Logical volume access is most often used to format a partition with a particular file system, such as FAT or NTFS.

Conclusion

This chapter introduced you to the various file systems you can use with NT. You should have learned which file systems to use in various situations and how to manage them. You should also take away a general understanding of the security NT provides on its file systems.

The NT File System (NTFS) was a major advance in file system technology when it was introduced. Microsoft created this advanced file system as an extensible architecture that can grow with future advances, such as those that the Object File System NT may support someday. NTFS is also flexible, as shown by its ability to natively support the Applet File System.

Chapter 7 deals with network client configuration and management for NT networks. We discuss various aspects that affect the client workstations—from logging in to the NT network to using the NT management tools on the client. We also introduce you to some of the day-to-day things users must do, such as changing their domain password.

NT 4.0 Client Configuration and Management

One of the talked-about things in the 1990s is the management of client workstations and the problems associated with it and with the cost of ownership. The news is full of talk about the Network Computer (NC) and how that device will reduce the cost of ownership and be some type of panacea for all of us. We think many of these discussions are inaccurate.

Here are some typical problems that come up:

Scenario 7.1:

You manage a network with 1,000 PCs and must manage users and determine how they work on the PC. How do you handle this?

Scenario 7.2:

You need to manage NT from a variety of workstations, including both NT and Windows 95. What can you do, and what can't you do?

Cost of ownership is not about what type of workstation you use. It is rather a combination of using the right workstation and using the right approach to managing the workstation. In this chapter, we introduce you to a number of issues related to client workstations, including managing NT from Windows 95, configuring client workstations, adding NT workstations to an NT domain, and the Zero Admin Kit from Microsoft.

Clients and Client Tools Included with NT 4.0 Server

After choosing Windows NT 4.0 as your server, you now have to face another decision: Which system are you going to use as a client?

If your network is fairly new and you have the flexibility to use faster computers (at least Intel-based 486 DX2-66 with 8MB of RAM), then your choices should be either Windows 95 or NT Workstation (NTW). In Chapter 1, we described the differences between the two, so you should be able to decide which one best suits your needs.

However, if your network comes from a Netware environment, where the hardware requirements are minimum, some of your computers may not be able to handle Windows 95 or NTW without some investment in hardware upgrades. Otherwise, you might have to settle for either Windows for Workgroups or MS-DOS. Yes, it is possible to log on NT through the RIP DOS. Fear not—NT will do almost all the work!

Actually, NT 4.0 includes not only Windows 95, Windows for Workgroups, and MS-DOS, but also Remote Access Server (RAS), LAN Manager 2.2, and LAN Manager OS/2 network clients, which are included in the NT Server distribution. Also included in the same directory structure are the new TCP/IP software for Windows for Workgroups, RAS for MS-DOS, and network administration tools for Windows 3.x.

You may install the client packages using a special boot disk that connects the client to the network and performs the installation, or you may use an installation disk set for some clients (except for Windows for Workgroups). Some of the kits can be installed over the network if you create a special share and perform the installation using the share.

NT Server does not include a client license for Windows for Workgroups or Windows 95. We suggest that you either get an operating system with your clients or purchase an MLP (Microsoft License Pack) or MOLP (Microsoft Open License Pack) for your total projected number of clients. The MLP or MOLP lowers your client cost drastically.

Using the Client Tools

If you plan to use the client installation kits, you should copy the installation sets to the server or share the clients directory on the NT server CD-ROM. If you are going to use the client installations infrequently, you can share a CD-ROM on the server and run the installation from that device. Keeping the NTCD loaded in a drive is a great idea if you house an extra CD online. You may want to copy only certain clients to the server, or you may want to copy the entire set of files, then remove the ones you don't need.

The Network Client Administrator (NCA) in the program Manager Network Administration group is used to perform most of the tasks related to the client kits and utilities. Figure 7.1 shows the main window for the NCA.

With the NCA, you can create a directory on the hard drive of the server with various software to be installed on a client, and then create a boot disk to automate the installation.

If this is the first time you're installing NT, make sure to insert the NT 4.0 CD into the computer CD-ROM drive before you continue. If you click Continue on the window shown in Figure 7.1, it will bring you to another configuration window, as shown in Figure 7.2.

The other option for installing the files on a server is to use File Manager (or DOS) to copy the files. We like using File Manager because it affords more control over the process.

 If you want to keep an administrative copy of Windows 95, Workgroups, NT server, or NTW in the directory, just create the respective directories under the \CLIENT directory, then copy them from the installation CD onto those directories. The README.TXT file under \CLIENT\SUPPORT directory on the CD explains in more details how to accomplish this.

Copying the Client Tools to the Server with the Network Client Administrator, NT 3.51:

1. Start the Network Client Administrator.
2. Select Copy Client-based Network Administration Tools.
3. Follow the instructions on the next dialog box.
4. Start File Manager and delete all subdirectories that you will not use. Do not delete the \CLIENTS\MSCLIENT\NETSETUP directory, or you will not be able to install Windows for Workgroups or the Microsoft Network Client for MS-DOS.

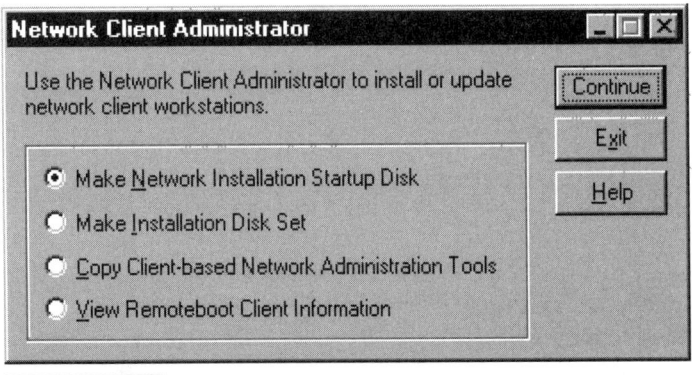

FIGURE 7.1 The Network Client Administrator presents a simple interface for assisting in installing client tools.

Share Network Client Installation Files _ □ ✕

Path: [   ] [...] [OK]

○ Use Existing Path [Cancel]

⦿ Share Files [Help]

  (No server hard disk space required)

  Share Name: [Clients]

○ Copy Files to a New Directory, and then Share

  0 MB server hard disk space required

  Destination Path: [   ]

  Share Name: [   ]

○ Use Existing Shared Directory

  Server Name: [   ]

  Share Name: [   ]

FIGURE 7.2 The Network Client Administrator presents a simple interface for assisting in installing client tools.

Copying the Client Tools to the Server with the File Manager or Explorer:

1. Start File Manager.

2. Select the directory tree to copy (Clients or subtree).

3. Drag and drop the directory tree onto the destination hard drive, or select the File/Copy command and enter the target drive and directory.

4. Start File Manager and delete all subdirectories that you will not use. Do not delete the \CLIENTS\MSCLIENT\NETSETUP directory, or you will not be able to install Windows for Workgroups or the Microsoft Network Client for MS-DOS.

Sharing the Client Directory

You should share the clients directory to provide network access to all the installation files.

In the window shown in Figure 7.2, Share Network Client Installation Files, you should indicate where the clients files are located. If this is the first time you're running the NCA, the client files only exist in the NT 4.0 Server CD, in the path box (\\yourCDpath\CLIENTS). Use Share Files, specifying the name of the share, and the system will share the directory \CLIENTS of the CD-ROM, which will avoid using unnecessary hard disk space.

The best option is really to use the option Copy Files to a New Directory, and then Share, which will copy the whole directory from the CD to the hard drive, making it unnecessary for you to have the CD available in the CD-ROM drive during installations. Note that when you choose this option, it will indicate how much space you will need on the hard drive (28MB).

The last option, Use Existing Shared Directory, enables you to use a shared directory created previously, or in another server. You just need to provide the names of the server and the share.

Sharing the Clients Directory:

1. Select the Clients directory in File Manager or Explorer.

2. Use the Share As command from the toolbar or Disk menu to complete the share or if using Explorer, right-click the directory and select Sharing.

3. Add a $ to the end of the share name to force the share to be hidden from all browse lists.

4. Set permissions on the share to allow only the appropriate accounts (for example, Administrator) to access the accounts.

Making an Installation Boot Disk

One of the best things included with NT Server 4.0, as well as with 3.5x, is the ability to make an installation boot disk for a new client system. This process automates the client installation process. You need to perform this procedure once for each client, or use another little installation trick.

Recall from Figure 7.1 that the first option of the NCA is to Make Network Installation Startup Disk. This option is the "spirit" of the whole process. It creates a diskette ready to be used. The diskette will boot the new client, load the network drives, connect to NT, and start the installation of the chosen software via the network.

The following steps show how to create the boot disk for Windows for Workgroups 3.11.

Creating a Windows for Workgroups 3.11 Installation Boot Disk:

1. Start the Network Client Administrator.

2. Select Make Network Installation Startup Disk.

3. Select the type of system to install and the network adapter card on the Target Workstation Configuration dialog box.

> 4. On the Network Startup Disk Configuration dialog box (shown in Figure 7.3) enter the following criteria:
>
>   Computer name for the new system
>
>   User name for the installation process
>
>   Domain name for the target domain
>
>   Network protocol to use for the installation
>
>   Other parameters as necessary (that is, TCP/IP)
>
> 5. Click OK.
>
> 6. Click OK on the next dialog box to begin building the disk.

 The easiest way to use this technique is to assign a unique computer name for the client installation process and then to use this disk only for installations. This technique allows you to create the disk one time and then to use it over and over.

Using the Installation Boot Disk

As discussed previously, the boot disk built by the Network Client Administrator is just a DOS boot disk that automatically connects to the network using the MSClient for DOS, and runs the appropriate setup program.

```
┌──────────────────────────────────────────────────────────┐
│ ═            Network Startup Disk Configuration        ▼  │
├──────────────────────────────────────────────────────────┤
│ Select the options to be used by the network startup disk. │
│ These options only apply during the startup process.  ┌──────┐ │
│                                                       │  OK  │ │
│ Computer Name:  │KENTEST                    │         └──────┘ │
│                                                     ┌────────┐ │
│ User Name:      │Administrator              │       │ Cancel │ │
│                                                     └────────┘ │
│ Domain:         │CTI-GSO-DOMAIN             │       ┌────────┐ │
│                                                     │  Help  │ │
│ Network Protocol: │TCP/IP Protocol      ▼ │         └────────┘ │
│  ┌ TCP/IP Settings ─────────────────────────┐              │
│  │  ⊠ Enable Automatic DHCP Configuration    │              │
│  │  IP Address:      │0.0.0.0        ▶       │              │
│  │  Subnet Mask:     │0.0.0.0        │       │              │
│  │  Default Gateway: │0.0.0.0        │       │              │
│  └──────────────────────────────────────────┘              │
│ Destination Path:  │A:\           │    │...│               │
└──────────────────────────────────────────────────────────┘
```

FIGURE 7.3 The Network Disk Configuration dialog box is used to enter the parameters for the installation startup disk.

This is the AUTOEXEC.BAT from a sample Windows for Workgroups 3.11 startup disk:

```
path=a:\net
a:\net\net initialize
a:\net\netbind.com
a:\net\umb.com
a:\net\tcptsr.exe
a:\net\tinyrfc.exe
a:\net\nmtsr.exe
a:\net\emsbfr.exe
a:\net\net start
net use z: \\FPMASTER\CLIENTS
echo Running Setup...
z:\wfw\netsetup\setup.exe /#
```

The installation boot disk uses the MS-DOS client software to boot and make the connection. Notice how the connection to the CLIENTS directory is made with the NET USE command? It is pretty simple. The /# switch on the Setup command is not documented when you run SETUP /?, but causes Setup to start a network installation of the software.

Place the disk in the boot drive of the new system and reboot. Follow the prompts on the screen to complete the installation. The new system retains the computer name from the installation diskette. After the installation is complete, change the computer name and other related items (user name, comment, TCP/IP parameters), and reboot the system.

You can also use the /H:filename switch to initiate a total batch mode installation. The /H switch enables you to specify the installation parameters in a file. Setup processes the file and answers the questions with no interaction. You can leave out options that vary from the setup file, and Setup uses defaults where possible and performs automatic detection of hardware devices such as mice and hard disks. The setup file should have an SHH extension. The Windows 3.1 Resource Kit contains complete descriptions of the options for the /H switch.

Installing Server Tools

The server tools can be installed by connecting to the CLIENTS share and running the appropriate setup program. The server tools are located in the SRV-TOOLS directory. \Clients\Srvtools\Windows contains the Win32s versions for Windows 3.x, whereas \Clients\Srvtools\WINNT contains the NT version.

Installing Server Management Tools on a Client:

1. Connect to the Clients share.
2. Start SETUP.EXE in the appropriate directory (..\Windows or ..\WINNT).
3. Complete the instructions displayed by Setup.

If you are installing the tools on a Windows for Workgroups worksta-tion, a new redirector is installed and you must reboot the workstation before using the tools. Setup installs Win32s if it is not already installed for Windows or Windows for Workgroups workstations.

Configuring Clients

As discussed earlier, NT Server 4.0, as well as 3.51, supports many different types of clients. You can build a network with DOS, Windows 3.x, Windows 95, Windows NT, and Macintosh machines for clients. Client and servers can be mixed and matched to improve network availability and performance. Even within these systems, there are several different methods of connecting to the NT server.

DOS machines can use LAN Manager client software, MS Client, and the Microsoft Workgroup Add-On for MS-DOS to connect to an NT server. The Microsoft Workgroup Add-On for MS-DOS provides the most advanced fea-tures and is identical to the MS Client included with NT Server in most respects. You can also use almost any old LAN Manager client, including Digital Pathworks, as an NT Server client. Make sure that you are using a sup-ported protocol when using a non-Microsoft client. For instance, you can't connect to NT Server over DECnet if NT Server is running only NetBEUI or TCP/IP. Load TCP/IP on both the client and server, and voilà, it works.

Windows NT, Windows 95, and Windows for Workgroups can connect to NT Server out of the box. If you answer the network, user name, and work group/domain questions correctly when you install Windows for Workgroups, the workstation connects to NT Server with minor changes to the startup parameters in Control Panel. We suggest that you upgrade to Windows for Workgroups 3.11 for all clients. The 3.11 version adds special features for NT Server networks and works much more nicely in the NT Server environment than the 3.1 version does. The preferred clients in an NT or other LAN environment are NTW 3.51 or later, Windows for Workgroups 3.11 or later, and Windows 95 or later. Other clients work fine but may not provide as many features as the preferred clients do. Windows 95 adds many network and management features and places it as the future client operating system for most LANs. A detailed discussion on configuring Windows for Workgroups 3.11, and Windows 95 for use with NT Server, follows below.

The references in this chapter to Windows for Workgroups refer to version 3.11, unless another version is specifically cited. Some of the information in this section repeats information from the Windows for Workgroups manual or accompanying documentation and is included here for those of you who may not have Windows for Workgroups or who may have an earlier version (3.1). This information also is useful for others because it is contained in a single source with the other client information. Windows 95 shares many features with Windows for Workgroups 3.11. As a matter of fact, we suggest that you upgrade your Windows client to Windows 95, or use NTW.

NT desktop systems can connect to an NT server and/or domain with very little trouble. If you install NT and answer the network-related questions correctly, it works just about like Windows for Workgroups clients. The main exceptions are the support for NTFS on the workstation and the advanced security for the workstation. NTWs can also use the enhanced preference management of NT and NT Server.

Macintosh systems also work well in an NT Server environment because of NT Server's Macintosh support using Services for Macintosh. Macintosh systems all support AppleTalk and can use this protocol to communicate with NT Server. For information on configuring NT Server for use with SFM, see Chapter 8.

The most common methods, and an explanation of how to configure each client system, follows.

Common Features for Clients

The following features are common for Windows 95, Windows for Workgroups, NT, and NT Server systems. Small variations may exist between different versions of the same tools. For instance, the connect dialog box in Windows for Workgroups may look slightly different from the Connect dialog box in NT, while the connect box in Windows 95 takes on an entirely new look. NT 3.51 inherited many of the user interface features of Windows 95 and began the migration toward making the two interfaces consistent. In mid-1995, Microsoft made available a Windows 95 interface for NT. Now, with NT 4.0 server, the interface is much the same.

The workgroup and computer names identify the computer workstation, whereas the user name and password identify the user of the workstation. NT and Windows 95 use the user name and password of the server for validating all actions (if user level security is set on Windows 95).

WORKGROUP NAME

The workgroup name can be up to 15 characters long and can include all characters except:

$$! \# \$ \% ( ) - . @ ^{\wedge} \_ ' \sim$$

If the workgroup name is the same as the Domain Name, the workstation shows up under the domain in the browse list. Figure 7.4 shows the Connect Network Drive dialog box from Windows for Workgroups and Figure 7.5 shows the NT 4.0 interface of the dialog box so that you can see the difference on the interface.

The workgroup name should be set to a separate workgroup name that does not conflict with a domain name. If the workgroup name is different from the domain name, the workgroup can access systems in the domain but will appear in its own workgroup for browsing purposes. We suggest breaking the workgroups into groups of 20 to 25 workstations to improve browsing performance. See Chapter 4 for more information on browsing.

COMPUTER NAME

A computer name should clearly identify the computer on the network. How you identify the machines is dependent upon how you structure and name the systems in your network. You may use the user's name for the computer name or possibly use a code that is linked to another aspect of the network, such as a node address. If you use something other than the user's name, you should use a comment to identify the user or the location of the system.

One nice feature of using a node address for the computer name and the comment for the user name is the ease with which you can move a system or upgrade a system after someone has left the company. If you have used a node address or other unique identifier for the computer name, you must change only the comment on the workstation when the user changes. This is especially important if you have built programs that depend upon

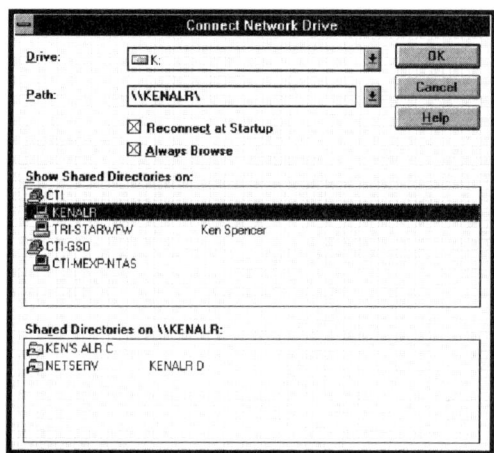

FIGURE 7.4   The Connect Network Drive dialog box from Windows for Workgroups.

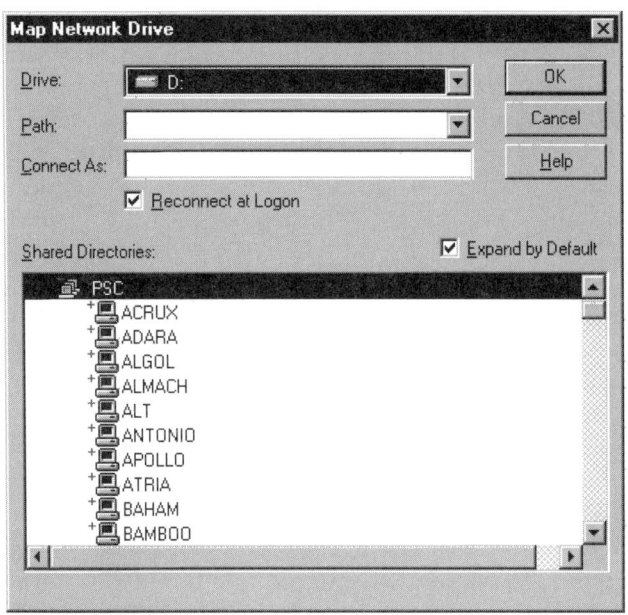

FIGURE 7.5 The NT 4.0 Map Network Drive dialog box illustrates the interface differences between Windows for Workgroups and NT 4.0.

certain computer names on the network. This approach also works well with SMS because the computer name along with almost every other detail of the workstation is stored in the SMS database.

The Comment for a computer name may be up to 48 characters long and may contain all characters except a comma (,). The comment is displayed by the NT, Windows 95, and Windows for Workgroups Browse command whenever a user attempts to connect to a resource from within File Manager, Print Manager, or any other program that uses the Windows API (such as WinPopUp) to show available resources. Figure 7.4 shows the connect to network resource dialog box from File Manager.

USER NAME AND PASSWORD

User names and passwords are discussed in Chapter 5. A user name and password is the key to a user's access to NT Server resources and also unlocks access to the domain for the user.

NT Workstations

NT 4.0 workstations and NT Server 4.0 systems are by far the easiest and most secure workstations to add to an NT Server domain. Any NT system contains the same security, network, and file features as NT Server, except for domains and some disk fault tolerance features. Because of their common base with NT Server, NTWs are a natural for your network. NTWs also work well with other types of clients on the network, including sharing resources. In fact, an NTW can serve as a high-powered print server right out of the box, as long as you do not need more than ten connections to its resources.

Windows 95

Windows 95 is the best client operating system, along with NTWs, for use on an NT Server network. Windows 95 was designed from the start as a networked workstation with extensible management features. Windows 95 is built on top of Win32 and uses a Registry that is somewhat similar to the NT Registry.

Windows 95 can also use the NT Domain security system for pass-through security. Pass-through security validates everything on the client against the master security database (Domain). For instance, if you set permissions on a share using Windows 95, you can set permissions for users in the Domain database. Every log-on and security check also validates against the Domain database. This integrated security management from a single Domain database is an incredible benefit for the systems manager.

Windows 95 supports sophisticated features such as policies and profiles to simplify management tasks. These features are similar to the ones by the same name in NT but are implemented in a different manner, to provide easier management for client systems. Remote Procedure Call (RPC) is supported by Windows 95, providing a mechanism for running programs on remote systems and allowing most Windows 95 management tools to access any Windows 95 system on the network.

THE REGISTRY

The Windows 95 Registry is composed of two files: USER.DAT and SYSTEM.DAT. Both of these files are stored by default in the Windows directory. The Registry replaces the myriad of INI files that are found with Windows 3.x and, like those INI files, is extensible by application programs.

The Registry is managed by many Windows applications such as Control Panel and Setup. REGEDIT.EXE can also be used to manage the Registry directly. RegEdit can take advantage of RPC to manage the Registry on another Windows 95 system remotely. As with the NT Registry, an incorrect change to the Windows 95 Registry can be hazardous.

As with NT, the Windows 95 Registry not only stores software settings but also is the complete database for system hardware, software, configuration, and user information. If all this information is in one database, it is easy to manage and provides much greater security control for controlling access to system and user configuration options.

AGENTS

Agents are basically a snap-in component that provides some level of capabilities. For instance, many systems (including NT) use an agent to provide Simple Network Management Protocol (SNMP) data to management systems. Windows 95 includes built-in agents for several tasks:

- Backup agents for Arcada and Cheyenne backup products provide the ability to centrally back up client systems.
- An SNMP agent provides SNMP capabilities for the myriad of tools that support the SNMP standard.

USER PROFILES

User profiles track preferences for user settings such as colors and desktop appearance for each user of a Windows 95 system. A user profile also tracks settings such as the desktop configuration, network settings, and application specific settings.

User profiles can be maintained on a server to allow a user to log on the network from any Windows 95 system and obtain the exact same configuration, including icons on a toolbar. User profiles are a powerful tool for customizing the Windows 95 interface as users log on. Windows 95 processes the user's profile as the log-on occurs and automatically sets the desktop and everything else in the profile for the user.

The best way to use profiles is to store them on a network server in the user's home directory. This way, Windows 95 finds the profile during log-on and makes the correct changes.

Windows for Workgroups

Microsoft Windows for Workgroups (WFW) is basically a self-contained version of Windows 3.1 that includes all the network software necessary for sharing files, printers, OLE objects, and DDE data with other WFW-equipped computers or with Microsoft LAN Manager-compatible network clients or servers. For that reason, WFW is the idea client for Windows NT Server in the 16-bits realm. It contains an improved user interface, including configuration options for use with LAN Manager or NetWare servers (in case your network also has NetWare and OS/2 servers), as well as its own server functionality available on an Intel 80386-based or later processor. Although Windows 95 is really your best choice, as discussed previously, if you must remain on a full 16-bit environment due to memory limitations, for example, you should consider WFW.

INSTALLATION

Windows for Workgroups is the next easiest system to add to a domain, after Windows 95. The steps for installing Windows for Workgroups are very similar to those for installing NT and normal Windows. Windows for Workgroups has several switches that can be used with the Setup program. Each switch is documented in Table 7.1.

Creating a Windows for Workgroups Server Installation:

1. Create a directory on the server for Windows for Workgroups (I use \WFW311, the default).
2. Share the directory using File Manager or the NET SHARE command.
3. Install Windows for Workgroups to the directory. Select the CD-ROM directory containing Windows for Workgroups, and run the command SETUP /A. When Setup asks for the location of the installation directory, enter the directory created in the first step. This command copies all the Windows for Workgroups files into the directory just created.

Installing Windows for Workgroups from the Shared Directory (WFW311):

1. From the new client, connect to the share for the Windows for Workgroups installation (WFW311). The connection can be from a prior version of Windows for Workgroups, a LAN Manager client, Workgroup Add-On for MS-DOS, or other client software.
2. Change to the Windows for Workgroups shared directory.
3. Run Setup by entering

   `F:\WFW311>SETUP`

4. Answer the prompts, and reboot the workstation.

You can also install Windows for Workgroups directly from the CD-ROM containing NT Server 3.5x or from the network location where you placed the files. This process is the one we use most often. It saves space on the server and does not require using SETUP /A to expand the files to the network.

Installing from the NT Server CD-ROM or the Server:

1. From the new client, connect to the share for the clients directory for Windows for Workgroups. This may be the CLIENTS directory on the CD-ROM, or the location of the files on the server, if you copied them to a network drive. The

TABLE 7.1	Windows for Workgroups Setup Switches
Switch	**Description**
/A	Copies and expands all Windows for Workgroups files to the specified location. This switch is normally used to place the entire distribution on a network drive for later access and automated installation.
/B	Forces Setup to use monochrome display attributes.
/H:filename	Forces Setup to operate in batch mode. The file name of the driver file for the setup is specified after /H:.
/I	Turns off automatic hardware detection.
/O:filename	Use this option to specify the location and name of the INF file used for the installation.
/S:filename	Allows you to specify the location of the Windows for Workgroups installation files.
/T	Forces a check for known software that is incompatible with Windows.

> connection can be from a prior version of Windows for Workgroups, a LAN Manager client, Workgroup Add-On for MS-DOS, or other client software.
>
> 2. Run Setup by entering
>
>   `F:\WFW311>SETUP`
>
> 3. Answer the prompts, and reboot the workstation.

CONFIGURING A WORKSTATION

Setting up a workstation requires careful planning for your system. Minor things such as comments and network names can be extremely helpful if you make the right choice, or they can cause you lots of grief if you don't.

Comments indicating the full name of a workstation and information on the workstation's location are very useful. The computer name, comment, and other network-related information are stored in the SYSTEM.INI file on each Windows for Workgroups workstation. The [Network] section of the file contains entries for the computer name, workgroup, user name, and comment. Notice that there are a number of other options in this section as well. A typical [network] section from SYSTEM.INI follows:

```
[Network]
winnet=wfwnet/00025100
multinet=nonet
```

```
FileSharing=Yes

PrintSharing=Yes

LogonDisconnected=Yes

EnableSharing=Yes

UserName=KEN

Workgroup=CTI

ComputerName=TRI-STARWFW

Comment=Ken Spencer

logonvalidated=yes

MaintainServerList=NO

SlowLanas=3

SessTimeout=600

reconnect=yes

reshare=yes

cachethispassword=yes

LogonDomain=DOM-KEN

AutoLogon=Yes

StartMessaging=Yes

LoadNetDDE=Yes

LMLogon=1
```

Table 7.2 lists the options for the [Network] section of SYSTEM.INI that we consider relevant for using on an enterprise network. Table 7.2 does not list specific settings for Windows for Workgroups that are useful only for a Windows for Workgroups workstation or a workgroup network. Most of these options can be set via the Control Panel Network applet, while a few must be manually changed.

The SYSTEM.INI file also has information for shares and password lists in the section titled [Password Lists]. A sample of this section (Windows For Workgroups 3.11) follows:

```
[Password Lists]

*Shares=C:\Windows\Shares.PWL

TRI-STAR=C:\Windows\TRI-STAR.PWL

KEN=C:\WINDOWS\KEN.PWL
```

The PWL files contain the passwords and associated shares that Windows for Workgroups uses when it connects to a network resource. If you delete the PWL files, be sure to remove the entries for them under the [Password Lists] header in SYSTEM.INI.

| TABLE 7.2 | Options for Enterprise Network Settings in Windows for Workgroups |

Parameter	Default	Description
AutoLogon	Yes	AutoLogon causes Windows for Workgroups to log you in to the network automatically when the system is booted. If you have set a non-blank password for your user name, the log-on dialog box is displayed. Changed in the Network applet.
Comment	None	Comment is used for a comment (maximum 48 characters, and cannot contain commas) for the workstation. This comment appears next to the ComputerName in browse boxes. Changed in the Network applet.
Computer	None	ComputerName contains the name Name for the workstation (maximum 15 characters, consisting of all but !#$%()-.@{}~). It is set during the installation of Windows for Workgroups and can be changed with the Network applet of Control Panel. Changed in the Network applet.
Enable	Yes	Setting this parameter to Yes enables sharing of resources, whereas a setting of No disables sharing. Changed in the Network applet.
FileSharing	Yes	A Yes for this parameter turns on file sharing. Changed in the Network applet.
KeepConn	600	This entry controls the time in seconds that Windows for Workgroups 3.11 waits before disconnecting an implicit network connection. It is useful for applications that are slow or heavily used, namely pipes. It must be changed manually.
LMAnnounce	No	This entry controls whether a system announces its presence to LAN Manager systems on the network. The default of No disables this feature. To enable the feature, edit the SYSTEM.INI file, and change the value to

| TABLE 7.2 | Options for Enterprise Network Settings in Windows for Workgroups (Continued) |

Parameter	Default	Description
		Yes. Note: Network traffic and workstation overhead increases slightly when this value is Yes.
LMLogon	1	LMLogon determines whether you automatically log on (1) an LM Domain when Windows for Workgroups starts. It is set to 1 by checking the Logon to Windows NT or LAN Manager Domain check box on the Startup Settings dialog box in the Network applet. Setting LMLogon to No (0) causes Windows for Workgroups to not log you in to the domain at startup. For proper interaction between Windows for Workgroups and domains, this value must be set to Yes (1) unless you are using a product like NTLogon.Changed in the Network applet by clicking the Logon to Windows NT or LAN Manager Domain box.
LoadHigh	Yes	A setting of Yes tries to load all conventional network drivers loaded by Windows for Workgroups into the upper memory area (UMA). Setting LoadHigh to No turns off this feature.
LoadNetDDE	Yes	Turns on NetDDE. Set by checking the Enable NetDDE box in the Network applet of Control Panel.
Logon Disconnected	No	A setting of Yes allows Windows to boot without connection to previous network services. This option is set by checking the Ghosted Connections box in the Network applet from Control Panel.
LogonDomain	Workgroup Name	LogonDomain contains the domain name for the domain that you wish to log in to from Windows for Workgroups. Changed in the Network applet Enterprise Startup dialog box.
LogonValidated	No	This parameter is not user-maintainable. It is used to ensure that you are correctly logged off the domain if the LMLogon parameter is set

TABLE 7.2	Options for Enterprise Network Settings in Windows for Workgroups (Continued)	
Parameter	**Default**	**Description**
		to 1. It is set each time you successfully log on a domain.
MaintainServerList	Auto	This entry specifies whether your system can ever maintain the list of servers in your workgroup. If the setting is Auto, Windows for Workgroups decides when to use your system as the browsemaster. A setting of Yes gives the system a higher priority as the browsemaster, whereas a No means that the system will never be the browsemaster. Each workgroup needs at least one Windows for Workgroups system with a setting of Auto or Yes.
MultiNet	(blank)	This value specifies any secondary networks that are installed for Windows for Workgroups.
NumBigBuf	No Entry	This value contains the number of cache buffers used for the 32-bit redirector. Each cache buffer is 4096 bytes in size and is enabled by choosing 32-Bit File Access in the 386 Enhanced Enhanced applet in Control Panel. The default memory used for the cache is one eighth of the available physical memory at the time the cache is loaded. It can be manually edited to a larger value to improve performance.
PrintSharing	Yes	A Yes for this parameter turns on printer sharing. Changed in the Network applet.
Priority	80	Sets the priority for sharing resources over local usage. The higher the number, the greater the priority. Changed, using the Performance Priority slider in the Network applet in Control Panel.
SlowLanas	none	Specifies which LANA numbers are used for slow network connections. This option typically identifies the RAS LANA and any other slow-speed network adapter. Among other things, it prevents the Windows for Workgroups system

TABLE 7.2 Options for Enterprise Network Settings in Windows for Workgroups (Continued)

Parameter	Default	Description
		from being a browsemaster for systems across a slow speed connection. Set manually or by installing a slow service.
StartMessaging	No	A setting of Yes turns on the WinPopUp application for sending and receiving messages. It is set using the Network applet in Control Panel. When messaging is enabled, Print Manager automatically sends messages on completed print jobs. Changed in the Network applet.
UserName	Computer Name	The UserName (maximum of 20 characters) is set to the Computer Name until your first log-on to Windows for Workgroups and then reflects the last user name used during a successful log-on.
WinNet	wfwnet	Defines the primary Windows network driver. The primary network driver can be changed using the Network Setup program.
Workgroup	Workgroup Name from Setup	This parameter (maximum of 15 characters) contains the Workgroup from name for the Windows for Workgroups workgroup. It also sets the default LogonDomain parameter when Windows for Workgroups is installed. Changed in the Network applet.

Figure 7.6 shows the dialog box from Control Panel Network applet, and as a comparison, you can see the same Control Panel Network interface on NT 4.0 in Figure 7.7. This dialog box enables you to configure the network setup for the workstation and provides access to the event log for the workstation. In the 4.0 version, the applet also allows you to configure the services, the protocols, and bindings by clicking on the respective Tabs, which makes it very functional and easy to setup.

Clicking the Startup button brings up the Startup Settings dialog box shown in Figure 7.8. Windows 95 does not have a Startup button like Windows for Workgroups. In both Windows 95 and NT 4.0, the startup options are found in the Network applet in Control Panel under the ? options. Figure 7.9 demonstrates how different the interface looks under Windows 95.

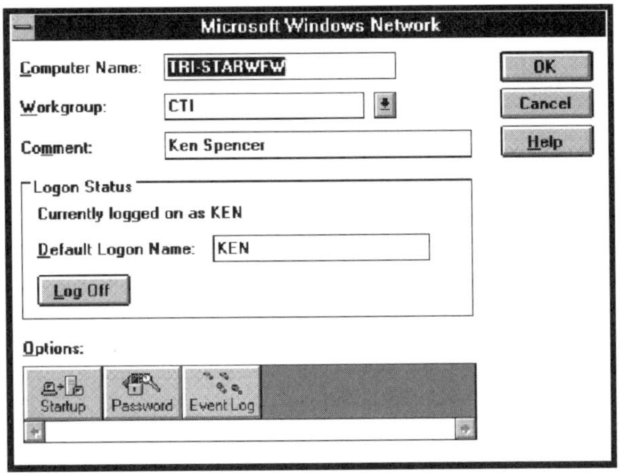

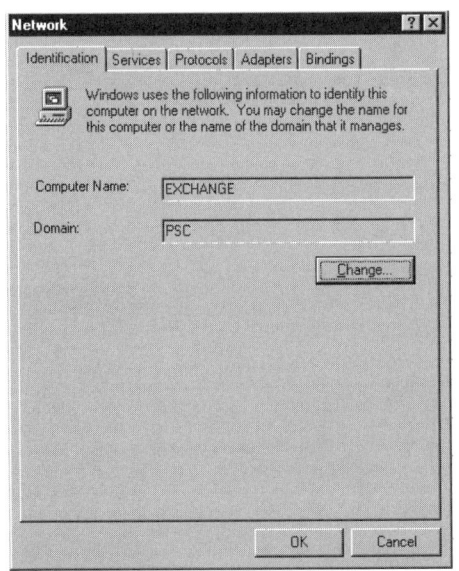

FIGURE 7.6 The Windows for Workgroups 3.11 Control Panel Network applet is the starting place for most network-related configuration options.

The key parameter in the Startup Settings dialog box is contained in the Options for Enterprise Networking frame. The Logon to Windows NT or LAN Manager Domain check box must be checked to access resources on a

FIGURE 7.7 The NT 4.0 Control Panel Network interface for comparison.

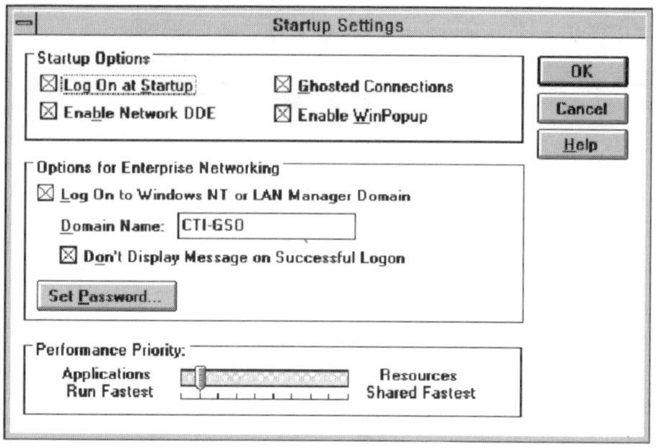

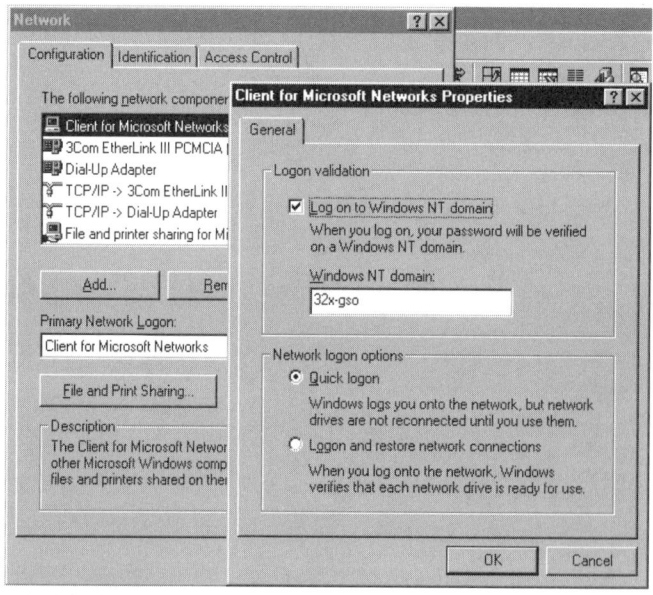

FIGURE 7.8 The Startup configuration dialog box is used to set or change the options discussed in SYSTEM.INI.

domain properly. The Domain Name box is enabled by clicking the Logon to Windows NT or LAN Manager Domain check box. The default Domain Name is the Workgroup name for the system.

You may also want to check the box below the Domain Name box. Checking this box prevents the Successful Logon message from displaying each time the Windows for Workgroups user logs in.

FIGURE 7.9 The Windows 95 startup options must be set for the Client for Microsoft Networks component.

We like to check the other parameters in the Startup Options box. These options turn on log-on at startup to display the Logon dialog box when Windows for Workgroups boots, turn on messaging (WinPopUp), enable NetDDE, and set up ghosted connections, which bring up network connections unconnected, but enables them to connect when they are first used.

The Set Password button enables users to change their domain passwords. Clicking the button brings up a dialog box asking the user for both the old password and the new password, and asking the user to confirm the new password.

Windows for Workgroups has another configuration file that is very important: WFWSYS.CFG. This file is created the first time Windows for Workgroups starts, and it contains settings for resource sharing and password maintenance (see the following discussion of ADMINCFG.EXE). This file is encrypted, and it is uniquely identified to the workstation that creates the file. The Workgroup Add-On for MS-DOS from Microsoft also uses the WFWSYS.CFG file.

BROWSING FUNCTIONS FOR WORKGROUPS • The workgroup name should be different from all domain names. Each group of 20 to 25 workstations should have its own workgroup to segment the browsing functions of the network. This grouping improves browsing performance of both the workgroups and the domains by reducing the number of workstations in each workgroup and domain.

You can set the value **MaintainServerList = no** in the SYSTEM.INI for all Windows for Workgroups workstations that you wish to protect from the performance impact of serving as a browsemaster. This setting forces the Windows for Workgroups system to not act as a browsemaster for the network. At least one NT, Windows for Workgroups, or Windows 95 machine must be running in the network and be available to be a browsemaster at all times to support browsing for a workgroup.

32-BIT FILE ACCESS

Windows for Workgroups 3.11 includes 32-bit disk and file access modes that can drastically improve the performance of a Windows for Workgroups system. Of special interest in this section on clients is the 32-bit file access mode.

Enabling 32-bit file access not only improves local disk performance but enables a fast 32-bit cache. This cache is used by both the file access routines and the protected-mode redirector (VREDIR.386).

The cache is a read-ahead routine that reads ahead by file and not by sector, as most caches do. Reading ahead in this way makes the cache much more effective in reading the information most likely to be requested next.

The 386 Enhanced applet in Control Panel turns on the 32-bit File Access. Figure 7.10 shows the Virtual Memory dialog box from 3.51. Compare it to the VM dialog from 4.0, shown in Figure 7.11.

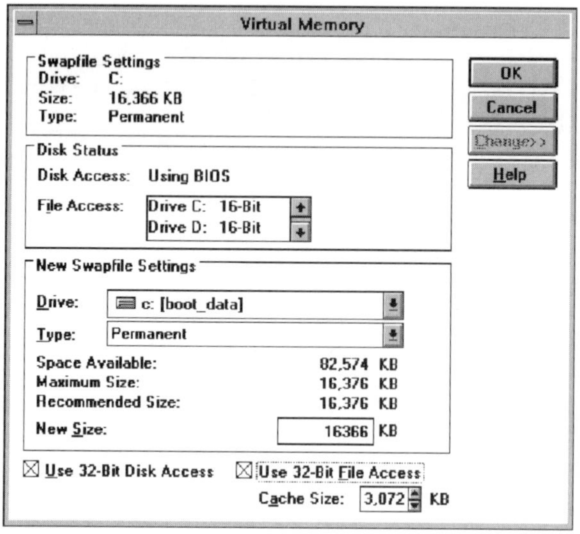

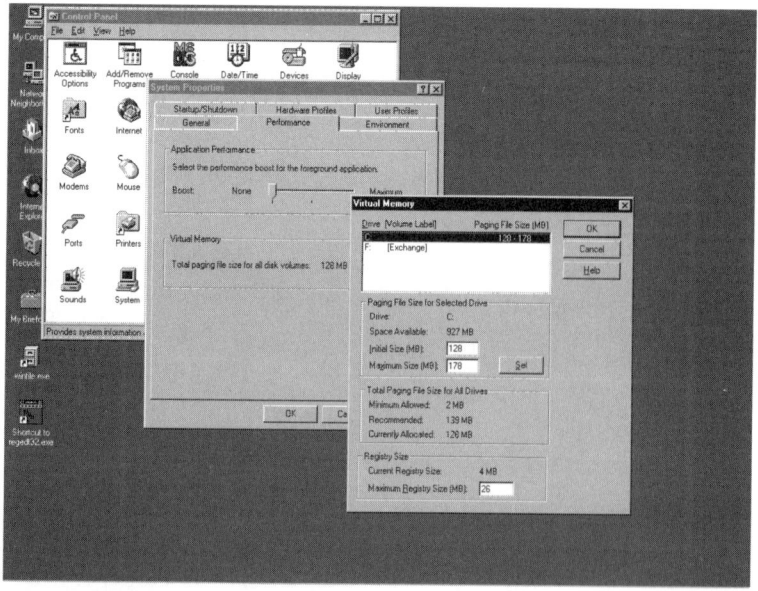

FIGURE 7.10 Turn on both 32-bit Disk Access and 32-bit File Access in the Virtual Memory dialog box, if your system supports them.

FIGURE 7.11 NT 4.0's Virtual Memory dialog box.

Configuring 32-bit File Access:

1. Start Control Panel.
2. Double-click the 386 Enhanced applets icon.
3. Click the Virtual memory button.
4. Click the Change>> button.
5. Check the 32-Bit File Access box.
6. Answer Yes to the question "Change Virtual Memory?"
7. Restart Windows.

ADMINISTRATION CONFIGURATION PROGRAM (ADMINCFG.EXE)

Windows for Workgroups 3.11 introduced a new program for managing Windows for Workgroups clients: ADMINCFG.EXE. This program is located on the last diskette of your Windows for Workgroups distribution disk set, and it is not installed by default. The following items are controlled by ADMINCFG:

- **Disable Resource Sharing (File, Print, and Net DDE)**–These options enable you to selectively disable either File, Print, or Net DDE sharing from a workstation. The workstation still can access shared resources from other servers.
- **Extended Password Management**–The password management options of ADMINCFG allow you to tailor how a workstation's passwords are managed. This control includes both options for the local workstation and one option that affects how the workstation interacts with an NT Server or LAN Manager domain.
- **Administrative Options**–ADMINCFG has some powerful options for controlling clients from your server. These options include creating groups of workstations that share common features and having the workstation configuration file (WFWSYS.CFG) updated from the server each time the workstation is booted.

ADMINCFG must be manually installed either on a workstation or onto the server. We prefer to install the program and then copy it onto a secure area of a server that will be available across the network.

Installing ADMINCFG:

1. Load the last disk from your Windows for Workgroups disks into a local drive or make sure that you have access to the Windows for Workgroups distribution over the network.
2. Change your current directory to the directory you wish to install the program into (usually the Windows directory).
3. Install the program with the EXPAND utility:

```
EXPAND A:EXPAND ADMINCFG.EXE
```

Expand can be run either from the DOS prompt or from File/Run within Program Manager or File Manager.

After you install the program, create a Program Manager icon by selecting File/New or drag ADMINCFG.EXE to a Program Manager group from File Manager. Next double-click the icon, and you are ready to roll.

ADMINCFG is very simple to use and has a very simple layout (see Figure 7.12).

It is possible to use ADMINCFG and configure your workstations for optimum management ease while saving yourself lots of future hassles.

MANAGING THE WFWSYS.CFG FILE • You can configure your Windows for Workgroups workstation with ADMINCFG and save yourself some headaches.

The first concern for the configuration file is choosing how to create the initial file. This is not a concern for networks that already have Windows for Workgroups installed, because the file already is installed on the workstation. You can create a preconfigured WFWSYS.CFG file and place it in the directory with the Windows for Workgroups distribution. The Setup program then copies this file to each Windows for Workgroups system as part of the installation process. The workstation automatically associates the file with that particular workstation the first time it boots. This is the preferred option for systems that do not have Windows for Workgroups clients in place already.

The Windows for Workgroups documentation mentions that the WFWSYS.CFG file can be updated from the workstation if the settings do not change very often, or from a server if you expect the settings to change frequently. We suggest that you use the server option regardless of how often you think they will change. If you set up a remote update when you install or configure the workstation, you can update all your machines at once as new options become available or when the need arises. Remember that

FIGURE 7.12 The Security Settings dialog box enables you to change the sharing settings for a workstation immediately.

Windows 95 expands upon the configuration options of Windows for Workgroups. Another nice feature of Windows for Workgroups and the Workgroup Add-On for MS-DOS is that they can both use the same network location and configuration to update from.

Remote configuration works this way: Each time Windows for Workgroups boots on a workstation configured for remote configuration, Windows for Workgroups opens the configuration file from the server and, if necessary, updates the settings of the local file. This update ensures that the workstation's file is updated to match the server's file each time the workstation boots.

The only caveat to this feature is that you must make sure that your users do not have access to ADMINCFG.EXE. Smart users who have access to this file can change their settings file. You can and should set a password on your configuration files, to make sure that the files cannot be updated except by the proper people.

The update process is also very flexible because of its support for exceptions to standard remote updates. When Windows for Workgroups starts, it looks for a directory on the configuration share that has the same name as the workstation. This procedure enables you to build a standard configuration for all users and then allow certain workstations to be treated differently by name. The Windows for Workgroups manual also suggests creating groups of workstations that have different configuration shares with different settings. To be honest, the limited settings available in WFWSYS.CFG probably do not require grouping workstations in most installations.

Remote updating of the configuration file is enabled by the selection of the Admin option from ADMINCFG, which displays the Administrator Settings dialog box.

Enabling Remote Updating of the Security File:

1. Start ADMINCFG.

2. Click the Update Security Configuration from Server box.

3. Enter the network path to the configuration share. This can be a drive letter and path (G:\CONFIG) or a UNC name (\\ADMINSRV\CONFIG). Click the Use Root Directory Only box to force the update from the master configuration even if a subdirectory for the workstation exists.

The following directory structure is an example of a configuration file system that treats all users as the same except for the workstation named TRI-STAR:

```
WFWCFG

TRI-STAR
```

Other directories contain a copy of WFWSYS.CFG, which is configured for the appropriate user. All users except for the workstation TRI-STAR get the standard configuration file from WFWCFG. TRI-STAR picks up the file from the TRI-STAR directory. The WFWCFG directory should be shared read-only to give all workstations access to the directory.

You may want to set two other configuration options with ADMINCFG: The Display Error Messages box and the Require Validated Logon to Windows NT or LAN Manager Domain. The first option causes Windows for Workgroups to display an error message on the workstation if it is not able to update the security settings remotely. Reasons for Windows for Workgroups to not update the settings could be a network problem or a server that is down. You may or may not want your users to be aware that the settings were not updated. Unless you have recently changed the settings, it will not matter that they were not updated, because they should already be the same as the ones on the server.

The other option is used to force Windows for Workgroups to validate your log-on with a Windows NT or LAN Manager domain. If the log-on is not successful, the user is denied access to network resources, which include resources on the domain and other Windows for Workgroups systems.

Workgroup Add-On for MS-DOS and MS Client

The Workgroup Add-On for MS-DOS is a neat little package for systems that are still running MS-DOS. It allows the MS-DOS workstations to connect and participate in a LAN with both Windows for Workgroups and/or NT Server systems. It is also useful for Windows systems to participate in the network without upgrading to Windows for Workgroups. The retail price for the package is $49.95, but the product can probably be obtained for less from retail sources.

The MS Client included on the NT Server kit is similar to the Workgroup Add-On for MS-DOS except that it cannot be used to share file or print services. Both products are used and installed in the same way, and they function identically, other than the sharing restriction.

Commands for the Workgroup Add-On for MS-DOS and the MS Client can be abbreviated to the shortest length that does not conflict with other commands. The next section describes the most important commands.

INSTALLING THE WORKGROUP ADD-ON FOR MS-DOS AND THE MS CLIENT

Both the Workgroup Add-On for MS-DOS and the MS Client included with NT Server 3.5x are installed with the SETUP.EXE program.

STARTING THE CLIENT SOFTWARE

Most of Microsoft's PC networks now start using the NET START command in AUTOEXEC.BAT. This is true for the Workgroup Add-On for MS-DOS, the MS Client, and Windows for Workgroups 3.11 when it is running in real mode.

The syntax for Net Start is

```
NET START
```

The full redirector can be started by using

```
NET START FULL
```

There are several other qualifiers that you can use for NET START to control its operation. Enter **/?** after the command for a description.

USING THE WORKGROUP ADD-ON FOR MS-DOS

When you use the Workgroups Add-on, you must have a previous version of Windows already installed. The program will search your hard drive for it. If it doesn't find it, then you'll be in trouble, as the system will refuse to load. This doesn't mean that you have to install Windows 3.1 on a PC to then install Workgroups. You can just insert disk 1 in your floppy drive when Workgroups asks you for it.

LOGGING ON • The NET LOGON command is used log on to the network. It is similar to other log-on commands or methods in that it requires you to provide the domain name, user name, and password if you are accessing an NT domain. Along with logging you on the domain, Net Logon also restores your persistent connections just like Windows for Workgroups.

The format for the command is

```
NET LOGON [user name [password | ?]]
[/domain:domainname /savepw:no -
/disconnected]
```

NET LOGON prompts for your user name and password if you enter the command with no options. The ? causes NET LOGON to prompt for the password and echoes the password with * in place of the characters.

The domain name must be entered if you are logging on an NT Server domain. The following example shows the command syntax for accessing the server DOM-KEN:

```
NET LOGON kens ? /domain:dom-ken
```

NET LOGON can save your passwords in a password list file. The password file is named with your user name and a PWL extension: KENS.PWL. Each user of a Workgroup Add-On for MS-DOS has a password list file unless they have always logged on and answered **No** to the create password list prompt or have used the following syntax for NET LOGON:

```
NET LOGON kens ? /domain:dom-ken /savepw:no
```

The password list file is protected by your password. The file is encrypted and can be accessed only by your user name and password through the Workgroup Add-On for MS-DOS utilities. The file holds the UNC definitions and passwords for remote connections you have made in the past. This cache allows the connections to be restored automatically when you log on. The only problem with persistent connections is that they can cause the log-on process to take a long time if you have many connections. The /disconnected option can be specified as in the next example to log on and restore the connections in a disconnected state. This process makes the log-on proceed very quickly. The connections are connected automatically the first time they are accessed. After the first access, the connection remains just like a normal connection.

```
NET LOGON kens ? /domain:dom-ken /disconnected
```

LOGGING OFF • NET LOGOFF performs the opposite of NET LOGON and disconnects you from the remote systems you are connected to. The next command logs off the current system and prompts you to confirm the process.

```
NET LOGOFF

You have these connections:

     G:   \\KEN\SYS

     Z:   \\KEN\APPS

Continuing will cancel the connections.

Do you want to continue this operation? (Y/N) [N]
```

The /yes option can be used to force the command to log off immediately without prompting:

```
NET LOGOFF /y

You have these connections:

     G:   \\KEN\SYS

     Z:   \\KEN\APPS

Continuing will cancel the connections.

KENS was logged off successfully.
```

CHANGING YOUR DOMAIN PASSWORD

The Workgroup Add-On for MS-DOS allows you to change your domain password with the NET PASSWORD command. NET PASSWORD allows you to change both your local Workgroup Add-On for MS-DOS password, which controls your password file and your domain password. The syntax for changing your password for the password file is

```
NET PASSWORD [oldpassword [newpassword]]
```

Entering the command with no parameters causes NET PASSWORD to prompt for both passwords. You can enter the old password with the command and NET PASSWORD prompts only for the new password.

The following syntax shows the Net Password syntax for changing your domain password:

```
NET PASSWORD \\computer | domain:domainname
[user oldpassword [newpassword]]
```

Notice that NET PASSWORD allows you to change your password on a domain or a single system in the NT or LAN Manager server on your network. Specifying the following syntax allows you to change your password on the server named KEN:

```
NET PASSWORD \\KEN kens junk
```

This command causes NET PASSWORD to prompt for the new password because the user name and old password are specified on the command line. If you do not specify the user name or either password, the command prompts for all three.

The following command changes the password on the domain DOM-KEN:

```
NET PASSWORD domain:DOM-KEN kens junk
```

OTHER USEFUL COMMANDS • Table 7.3 lists several other commands that should prove useful in a network environment. Consult your documentation for more information.

PRINTING • What about setting up a cheap print server or controlling print jobs on the curreNTW or a remote system? The Workgroup Add-On for MS-DOS can handle both situations. NET USE is the command for connecting to or disconnecting from a remote printer. NET PRINT is used to manage print jobs on a local workstation and remote systems, and NET SHARE is used to share a local printer as a network resource.

The Workgroup Add-On for MS-DOS should be more than adequate for a print server for most low-end dot matrix printers. It should also work well as a print server for laser printers. You should expect a degradation in performance if you are attempting to share a printer and use the system as a

TABLE 7.3	Useful Network Commands
Command	**Description**
NET	Loads the pop-up interface into memory.
NET CONFIG	Displays configuration information for the workstation. The display includes the user name, computer name, and software versions.
NET DIAGNOSTICS	Displays information about the status of your workstation and can be used to test the connection between two workstations.
NET FILE	Displays the files from your system that other users have open. The command shows the file path, how many systems have the file open, and the number of locks on the file.
NET HELP	Displays information about specific Workgroup Add-On for MS-DOS commands and error messages.
NET INITIALIZE	Used to load the protocol and network adapter drivers into memory without binding them to the Protocol Manager. This command is primarily used when third-party network protocols are used.
NET SESSION	Allows you to monitor connections to your system and optionally disconnect sessions.
NET SHARE	Displays information about current shared resources on your system and is used to connect to shared resources.
NET VER	Displays the current version of the redirector. See the NET CONFIG command.

workstation at the same time. Chapter 9 contains more information on using the Workgroup Add-On for MS-DOS as a print server and on using NET PRINT in general.

STOPPING THE CLIENT SOFTWARE

NET STOP shuts down the network client components and removes them from memory.

NET TIME

NET TIME displays the time on the client system. It can also be used to set the time on the client from an NT, LAN Manager, or Windows for Workgroups system.

CONNECTING TO NETWORK RESOURCES

The NET USE command is used to connect to remote shared resources. This is the same command used by all Microsoft network products including the Windows and DOS versions.

SHARING RESOURCES

The NET SHARE command is useful for sharing printers for other users. The format follows:

```
Net Share sharename=portname [/remark:"text"]
[/saveshare:no] – [/full:password]
```

sharename	Name of the shared printer.
portname	Printer port to which the printer to share is attached.
/remark	Comment for the share.
/saveshare	No specifies that the share will not be saved. Yes causes the share to be restored automatically.

VIEWING NETWORK RESOURCES

NET VIEW displays a list of shared resources on other systems.

Remote Boot Option for Clients

MS-DOS clients can use the Remote Program Load (RPL) protocol to allow the systems to boot over the network. This protocol provides support for diskless systems that remote boot and obtain all services from an NT Server.

Remote boot is not covered in detail in this book because we had many bad experiences with remote boot client systems many years ago, but we know there are few environments that are still "locked" with old technologies. Keep in mind that local boot workstations with adequate disk space always outperform remote boot systems. We prefer to spend more time getting the clients up to current technology, such as NTW, Windows 95, or the upcoming Memphis (the new version of Windows 95) than working on management techniques that allow them to effectively use those systems and upgrade them remotely. Windows 95 and NTW both come with remote setup facilities (native!) designed for networks. See the information throughout this book on tools such as Systems Management Server that make the task of managing remote systems much easier.

Adding NTWs to a Domain

Before an NT 4.0 workstation or server can be used in the domain or access resources on domains with trust relationships, it must be added to the domain.

Systems can be added to a domain by any one of three methods:

- By using Server Manager
- During the installation process of an NT or NT Server system or
- By using the Networks applet in Control Panel on the NTW

The following procedure must be used from an NT server in the domain or from an NT or Windows for Workgroups system running Server Manager. You must log on with an account that has Administrator privileges to perform this process.

Adding a Workstation to a Domain with Server Manager:

1. Start Server Manager from the Administrative Tools group.
2. Choose Add To Domain from the Computer menu.
3. Select either the server or workstation option to add the system to the domain.
4. Enter the system's computer name in the Computer Name field and click Add. After Add has completed, click Close.
5. Verify that the system has been added correctly by running Networks applet in Control Panel on the system you added and verify that the list of domains includes the domain you added the system to.

Another option that is slightly easier is to add the system to the domain at the time of installation. This step can be performed only if your system has a connection to the domain network during the installation. This option not only simplifies the process of adding the system to the domain, but it also prevents the system from installing an initial user account on the system.

Adding a Workstation to a Domain During Installation:

1. Enter the domain name when you are prompted to do so during the installation process for a BDC. This system should not be configured as the PDC during installation, unless the domain does not exist.
2. If an account for the system you are adding is not already in the domain, select an administrator name and password.
3. NT displays a message confirming that the system has been added to the domain.

The following steps add an NTW to the domain and must be performed from the workstation.

Adding a Workstation to a Domain with Control Panel:

1. Start the Networks applet in Control Panel.
2. Click Change to change/add the system to a domain or workgroup.

> 3. If an account for the system you are adding is not already in the domain, select an administrator name and password.
>
> 4. NT displays a message confirming that the system has been added to the domain.

Logging On a Domain

One of the more interesting problems you may encounter is how to log in to your NT server from workstations running different operating systems. This section addresses those issues.

NTW

The easiest workstation to use in a domain is another NT system. Logging on or off your domain is the same as logging on or off the workstation, except that you specify the domain name in the list box on the Logon dialog box. When you log on from an NTW, the log-on server in the domain sets your preferences from your profile (if a profile is specified) and then downloads your log-on script to the workstation (if a log-on script is specified).

After you have logged in, you are set. You can connect to any resources in the domain that you have access to or perform any other tasks that have been authorized for your account.

You must select the domain name in the From list box on the Welcome dialog box. If you select your local machine (which shows up in the list), you are logged in to the local machine if your user name and password match. When you log in to a local machine instead of a domain, your domain log-on script (if any) is not run, and you are not logged in to the domain. You can, however, still connect to resources in the domain even though you are not logged in.

Windows for Workgroups

Logging in from Windows for Workgroups is slightly more challenging than logging in from an NTW. Windows for Workgroups is the preferred 16-bit client for an NT network, and version 3.11 is the preferred Windows for Workgroups version.

Windows for Workgroups 3.11 introduced a log-on/log-off utility in the Network group (LOGONOFF.EXE). Version 3.11 also has an enhanced Control Panel Network applet that understands the difference between domains and workgroups. Figure 7.13 shows the successful Logon dialog box.

You must log on the Windows for Workgroups machine with a user name and password that are recognized by the domain before you can gain access to any network resources. Figure 7.14 shows the Domain Logon dialog box.

Windows 95

Windows 95 presents the user with a log-on dialog box similar to that for Windows for Workgroups, except for the Domain text box at the bottom.

FIGURE 7.13 Notice that the Logon message box in Windows for Workgroups 3.11 contains the domain name, user account, and privileges granted.

This dialog box enables you to log on the same domain as last time (the last domain name is filled in by default) or to enter a different domain. With Windows for Workgroups, you were forced to change the domain in Control Panel or come up with another work-around to easily change domains each time you logged in.

Logging Off from Windows 95:

1. Click the Start button.
2. Select the Shutdown option.
3. Highlight the Close all programs and log on as a different user? option.
4. Click Yes.

You may have noticed that Windows 95 shuts down all programs during the log-off process. This feature eliminates many support calls for programs that are running when a log-off occurs and the program can no longer find its network connection.

Logging On from Windows 95:

1. Click the Start button.
2. Select the Shutdown option.
3. Highlight the Close all programs and log on as a different user? option.
4. Click Yes.
5. Enter your user name (if different from the default).
6. Enter your password.
7. Enter your domain name (if different from the default).
8. Click OK.

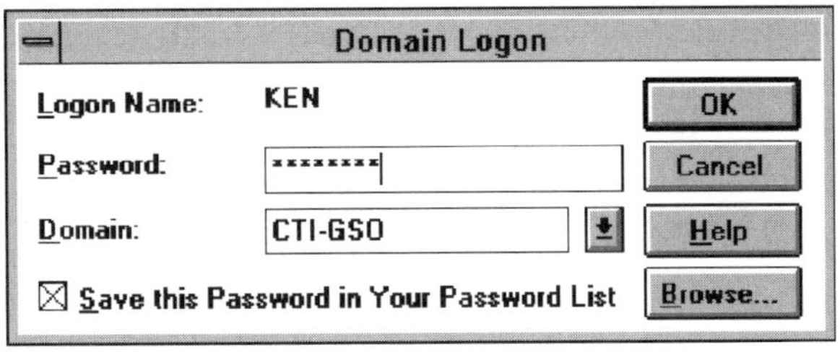

FIGURE 7.14 The Domain Logon box is presented the first time you log on a domain from Windows for Workgroups 3.11 with a new user name or one that does not have a password list.

Logon Scripts

Chapter 5 provides details and examples of log-on scripts for DOS, Windows, and NT clients.

Tracking Network Events on Clients

One of the problems that system managers face is tracking the performance of workstations on the network. It's usually a daily or weekly task to monitor what's going on and decide how to deal with it. Not only is this time consuming, but each different OS used for a workstation usually has its own tools for the task.

Windows for Workgroups 3.11

Windows for Workgroups 3.11 is the first DOS version of Windows to implement any type of network event-logging for clients. The event-logging capabilities are configured in the Control Panel Network applet. The Event Log button brings up the Event Log Settings dialog box shown in Figure 7.14.

The events tracked in the event log follow:

- Connect to Server
- Unsuccessful Connect Attempt
- Server Startup
- Server Shutdown
- Pause Print Job
- Resume Print Job
- Delete Print Job
- Complete Print Job

Note that all these events are triggered by things that happen on the Windows for Workgroups system as a server, and not on an NT server on the domain where the workstation may be using resources.

Windows 95

Windows 95 includes many tools for monitoring the client system and network components. Most of these tools are being enhanced with Memphis. You should look at these things for your Windows 95 clients:

- System Monitor (SYSMON.EXE) provides a tool that is slightly similar to Performance Monitor under NT. System Monitor provides a nice graphical interface, remote monitoring capabilities, an extensible monitoring system using counters like Performance Monitor, and the standard Windows 95 look and feel.
- An SNMP agent that ships with Windows 95 provides hooks into most SNMP management systems.
- The System Policy Editor (POLEDIT.EXE) provides control over users and computers. You can use this tool to set access privileges by user, group, or computer name. The policy file (*.POL) can be placed on a domain controller and automatically downloaded when a user logs in.

Figure 7.15 shows the Policy Editor. Notice the icons and tree list format common to Windows 95.

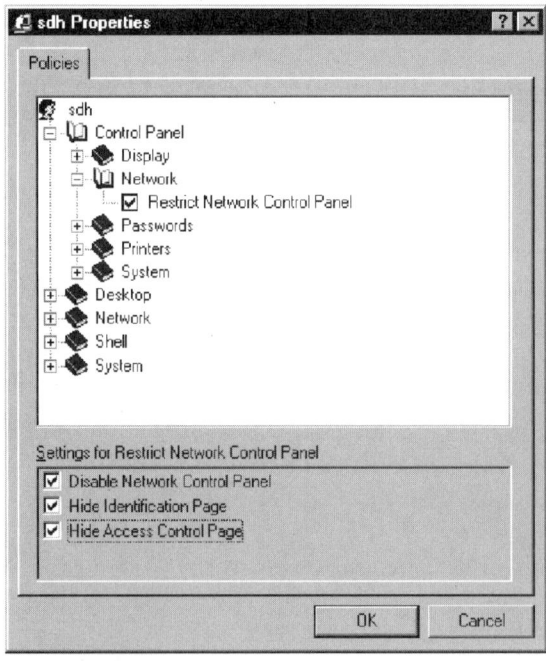

FIGURE 7.15 The System Policy Editor controls the type of access and control that a user has over a system.

Microsoft's Zero Administration Kit (ZAK)

Microsoft's Zero Administration Kit (ZAK) Windows NT Workstation 4.0 and Windows 95 is a set of tools, methodologies, and guidelines for MIS managers and systems and network administrators that allows for simplified implementation of a centralized and/or policy-based management of NT and Windows 95-based networks through a series of existing Windows technologies that were bundled together with this kit.

ZAK for Windows NT Workstation is a bit different from its Windows 95 version, as it takes advantage of the security and reliability of the Windows NT file system (NTFS).

With ZAK, there are now two new modes that can be set up to a workstation:

- **The Taskstation Mode**–This mode is geared toward the worker who needs streamlined access to a single line of business application or to a browser-based application.
- **The Appstation Mode**–This mode is perfect for the employee who needs access to multiple applications but may not have the experience to take advantage of the flexibility of a complex system.

What You Get with ZAK

First and foremost, ZAK limits your end-users from accessing system files and unauthorized applications, which will reduce the amount of support you need to give them. Also, ZAK allows you to:

- Simplify your users' environment throughout the company
- Centralize your desktops configuration for easy administration
- Increase your control over your desktop users
- Allow applications and data to be accessed from the server

If you want to learn more details about ZAK, youi can download a full demo from Microsoft's site at:

`http://www.microsoft.com/windows/platform/info/zakdemo.htm`

One of the main goals of ZAK is to reduce the cost of managing the PCs, or workstations, at the workplace. This may sound like a hostile takeover by IS managers of users' autonomy over their PCs, but if you take a look at the costs of managing a distributed Windows environment, you will find out that much of it is spent fixing changes or consequences caused by users who made changes to the application software running on their systems.

In a sense, you are returning to the old Mainframe model by establishing some control over these end-user operation costs, which usually involve two main areas:

1. Wasted time due to self-induced system problems

2. Unproductive activities

However, you're still allocating computing power to these workstations and allowing a controlled freedom for the user to work at his or her environment. What you're really after is not control over users; but rather control over unproductive activities performed by them, such as:

- Unintentional deletion of necessary system-files from a hard drive
- Incorrect changes in the control panel or registry
- Introduction of incompatible applications or even viruses through the unauthorized installation of software
- Playing "Mr. Admin" with the workstation, playing with systems settings such as colors, backgrounds, and desktop arrangement
- Installing and using unapproved and/or non-job-related software such as games, personal accounting software (especially during tax season!), and the like

It is to control these costs that managers like you need tools like ZAK, so you can prevent your users from making changes to your system.

Using ZAK

Using ZAK is simple. ZAK comes with a setup tool that installs itself onto the Windows NT Server 4.0. This setup tool will configure the system so it is ready for the Zero Administration Kit, and it even provides configuration samples for you to use.

On the Windows NT Workstation, you will just need to set up a clean installation of Windows NT Workstation, and then log into the Windows NT Server. All of the desktop configuration information is created centrally on the server, so there is no need to go to each desktop and do any user setup. Because ZAK is typically loaded onto the server, it gives you the advantage of providing centralized management, and all of the tools that are normally run from there. From the client side, the user just gets a controlled, secure desktop.

Further, ZAK uses the power and flexibility of system policies and user profiles, which:

- Enables you to lock down desktops and prevent end-user operations that result in support time, downtime, or help desk calls
- Provides centralized configuration of the desktop
- Eliminates end-user access to system files and features
- Removes the ability to install unapproved applications

System Requirements

According to Microsoft, the following are the systems requirements for implementing ZAK.

MINIMUM NETWORK CONFIGURATION

Microsoft recommends for an NT-based network the following minimum network configuration:

- One computer running Microsoft Windows NT Server version 4.0
- Two computers capable of running Microsoft Windows NT Workstation version 4.0
- All computers capable of running TCP/IP

MINIMUM SERVER REQUIREMENTS

Microsoft recommends for a NT-based network the following minimum server configuration:

- A Primary Domain Controller (PDC)
- At least 1 GB of free hard drive space
- At least 32 MB RAM (at least 64 MB if using Microsoft Exchange)
- CD-ROM drive
- Windows NT Server version 4.0
- File system should be NTFS

MINIMUM WORKSTATION REQUIREMENTS

Microsoft recommends for a NT-based network the following minimum workstation configuration:
- Hardware configurations should be as similar as possible
- Network cards must be unattendable. (Refer to the Windows NT Deployment Guide "Automating Windows NT Setup" for a list of unattendable network cards)
- 486 or later processor (recommended Pentium 90 or later)
- 16 MB RAM or later (recommended 32 MB or later)
- Clean hard drive with at least 300 MB of free space
- MS-DOS network boot disk
- ZAK compatible workstation (NTW, Windows 95, Windows 3.1, Macintosh)

OTHER REQUIREMENTS

In addition, Microsoft recommends that you have:

- Zero Administration Kit compact disc
- Service Pack 3 (SP3) or later for Windows NT Server version 4.0. You can download SP3 from Microsoft's site at URL
  `http://www.microsoft.com/ntserver/info/servicepack3.htm.`

- Windows NT Workstation version 4.0
- Microsoft Office 97 (for AppStation only)
- Microsoft Windows NT Workstation Deployment Guide "Automating Windows NT Setup." You can download this guide from Microsoft's URL at `http://www.microsoft.com/ntworkstation/info/aadeploy-guide.htm`
- Windows NT Workstation Resource Kit
- Microsoft Office 97 Resource Kit. You can download this kit from Microsoft's site at URL http://www.microsoft.com/office/ork/
- Microsoft Exchange Server 5.0, if you want to test the Microsoft Outlook client with Exchange

Conclusion

This chapter should give you some thoughts on managing client workstations. In particular, the Zero Admin Kit and Windows 95 / NT 4.0 policies can drastically reduce your management load.

There are many more things you can do that are outside the scope of this chapter. For instance, you can use the Win32 API and VB to get a handle on your workstations. Using VB to create log-on scripts and to control what the user can and can't do will take you a long way toward a manageable NT network. See Spencer's Web site (`www.32nt.com`), and check out Desaware (`www.desaware.com`) for more information on using the Win32 API and some of their tools and books.

Services for Macintosh

Services for Macintosh (SFM) is the NT feature that smoothly integrates Macintosh services with an NT network. The NT Server administrator needs to manage only one set of users and groups for all NT users, regardless of whether they log on from a PC or a Macintosh. The same NT Server security system treats all access to the domain the same..

Services for Macintosh can convert LAN Manager Services for Macintosh 1.0 to NT Server Services for Macintosh.

Scenario 8.1: ....

Your organization has a group of users in the Marketing department who love their Macs and will not give them up. At the same time, you must provide a way to enable the Mac and PC users to share files and communicate.

Scenario 8.2: ....

For several years you have been using SFM to support your Mac users. Now you have finally moved all the users from Macs to a PC platform running either Windows 95 or Windows NT. How do you remove SFM and safely move the remaining Mac files to a PC format?

Macintosh clients must be running System 6.0.8 or later. Users on DOS, Windows, or NT systems can share files with Macintosh users and let NT handle the duties of translating the files. NT Server is also a high-performance file and print server for Macintosh clients. Macintosh clients can use NT printers as if they were LaserWriters, and other clients can use Macintosh printers.

Services for Macintosh Network Topologies

LocalTalk (Phase 2), Ethernet, Token Ring, and FDDI are supported by SFM. Ethernet and Token Ring are the most popular topologies for PC networks for integration of SFM. FDDI is typically used for a network backbone or other high-speed interface.

LocalTalk networks are by far slower than any of the others. If you are using LocalTalk, we recommend that you upgrade to Ethernet or Token Ring to improve the performance of your network. You can do this over time, because Services for Macintosh can use LocalTalk as well as the other topologies. You can use a router or a LocalTalk card in your NT server to allow the LocalTalk machines to participate in the network until they are upgraded to a faster network.

For more details on setting up networks for use with SFM, you should consult the SFM documentation that comes with NT Server. This documentation has lots of details, including information on Macintosh networks, routing, and seeding routers.

Components of Services for Macintosh

Services for Macintosh has two major components that you will see running as Services.

- File Server for Macintosh is the service that handles file sharing for all Macintosh users.
- Print Server for Macintosh is another service that handles the printing for Macintosh users and handles printing for PC users that are printing to Apple LaserWriters on the Macintosh network.

Requirements for Services for Macintosh

Services for Macintosh does not require many additional resources on your system. The official Microsoft guidelines are

- 2MB of free disk space
- NTFS partition for Macintosh volumes

We suggest adding more memory to your server to support the extra overhead that SFM will add, unless your server has lots of free RAM. NT is always happier when you add extra memory as your system grows.

You can easily create an NTFS volume from a FAT volume by using the CONVERT command. This command converts the directory structure from HPFS (for NT 3.51 versions) or FAT to NTFS. The format for the command is:

```
CONVERT /FS:NTFS E:
```

CONVERT converts only a partition to NTFS; it will not go back the other way. The only way to get back from an NTFS partition is to back up the entire file structure to another disk or tape, reformat the partition, and copy the files back.

If you are starting with a unformatted partition for a Macintosh volume, you can use the FORMAT command. FORMAT creates an NTFS volume from scratch. The syntax is:

```
FORMAT /FS:NTFS E:
```

Notice that the syntax is exactly the same as CONVERT. Remember that FORMAT cannot be used on an existing drive because it will destroy the contents of the drive. If you are adding a new disk for use with SFM, you must use Disk Administrator to partition the disk before you use the FOR-MAT command.

Requirements for Macintosh Systems Connecting to Services for Macintosh

Macintosh workstations must be able to use AppleShare in order to connect to a Services for Macintosh server. The Microsoft SFM manual states that all Macintosh systems except the Macintosh XL and Macintosh 128K can use SFM. Macintosh workstations must be running System 6.0.8 or higher.

Security

Services for Macintosh uses the same security system as the standard NT Server, including the user accounts and other security features of NT Server. Services for Macintosh introduces some peculiarities because of the way the Macintosh operating system handles security; which is different from what NT Server and Windows do.

LOG-ON METHODS FOR MACINTOSH USERS

Macintosh users can log on using a user name and password or via a guest log-on. The guest log-on must be enabled through SFM. Guest log-ons are enabled by choosing the Guest account in User Manager and clearing the Account Disabled check box on the User Properties dialog box.

Guest log-ons provide the lowest level of security, but they also provide the least hassle for your users, because they allow users to access services on the server without having to remember a password.

Using passwords allows SFM to function just like NT Server in the way it handles other clients when it validates user accounts. The Macintosh complicates the issue slightly because it normally uses what are called Cleartext passwords. A Cleartext password is nothing more than the text representation of the password being sent over the network. This can cause problems in a secure environment, where someone may have access to a protocol sniffer such as Network Monitor or to another device that can capture network information. Capturing information in this manner is more difficult than it sounds, because the snooping user must capture several pieces of information to gain any useful information.

The Macintosh Cleartext password presents one problem: The password is limited to eight characters. This can be a problem for users of both PC and Macintosh workstations, who use the same account for both workstations, because the NT Server passwords can be 14 characters in length.

One way to solve both of these password problems is to install the Microsoft UAM that comes with NT Server. The installation of the UAM is covered in later in this chapter, in "Installing the Services for Macintosh Workstation Programs."

The Microsoft UAM enables the user to use passwords up to 14 characters in length. It also encrypts the passwords at the Macintosh workstation before they are sent over the network. You can also set SFM to force Macintosh users to use the Microsoft UAM when they log on the SFM server.

The UAM also enables the user to specify another domain than the current domain of which the NT Server running SFM is a member. The domain the user wishes to log on must be a trusted domain of the current NT Server domain. The syntax for logging on another domain is

```
Domainname\Username
```

The Domainname\Username should be entered in the Name text box.

GROUPS

Each SFM user must be assigned to a global group. This group becomes the default SFM group when you assign permissions under SFM. If you do not have a global group assigned, you will get the error: "This operation is not allowed on this special group. ID 2234."

Each time a Macintosh user creates a new folder, the primary group is the group associated with the folder. The files owner or a system administrator can change the primary group.

File Server Access from Macintosh Clients

SFM enables you to use an NT Server to provide file and print services to both PC and Macintosh clients. NT Server allows up to 255 Macintosh clients to connect to a single server at one time. The Macintosh users see the NT file system as an AppleShare volume. PC users can connect to the same server and share files with Macintosh users. SFM provides the mechanism to share most files transparently between PC and Macintosh users.

Some tricks are necessary when files are shared simultaneously between a PC user and a Macintosh user. For instance, when a PC user has a file open in Excel and a Macintosh user tries to open the file, the Macintosh user will get an "access denied" message. This problem can be solved on the Macintosh if you click the Read-only button on the File Open dialog box. This problem occurs because the Macintosh defaults to read-write access when it opens a file and encounters an error when the Macintosh user tries to open the file.

The interface between the PC and Macintosh works well because NT Server manages the differences in the file systems behind the scenes. The PC user sees the file as a DOS file, whereas a Macintosh user sees the file as a Mac icon, complete with the appropriate icon image. NT Server can also launch Macintosh applications that are stored on the server and associated with a file.

AppleShare volumes can be located only on an NTFS volume. NTFS supports storing the resource fork and Finder information directly in the file. NTFS also supports 31-character file names that are compatible with the Mac file system. File names are automatically translated between different client types.

The system administrator can require Macintosh users to use Windows NT Encryption when they log in to a server, to provide enhanced password and network security. See the section in this chapter on the Microsoft User Authentication Method for more information.

Services for Macintosh allows you to create AppleShare volumes on NT or NT Server from both File Manager and Control Panel.

NT Server automatically translates NT file and directory permissions to and from Macintosh permissions.

Installing and Removing Services for Macintosh

SFM is installed in a similar manner to other NT options. The installation process is quite simple, especially if you have already created the NTFS volume. You configure SFM in a slightly different manner than you would configure other NT options.

Installing and Configuring Services for Macintosh

SFM can be installed during the installation of NT Server, or it can be installed after you have installed NT Server. You must log in as a member of the Administrators group to perform the installation. The installation steps are very simple and can be completed in 10 to 20 minutes, assuming that everything works as planned and there are no problems with your server.

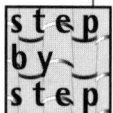

Installing Services for Macintosh:

1. Start Control Panel and select the Network applet.
2. Click the Services tab.
3. Click the Add button.
4. On Network Services, click Services for Macintosh.
5. Click OK.
6. Type the full path of the Services for Macintosh and click continue.
7. In the Apple Talk Protocol Configuration dialog box enter the changes to suite your environment.
8. Choose OK.

The computer will have to be restarted before the service is started.

Configuring Services for Macintosh:

1. Start Control Panel and select the Network applet.
2. Click the Services tab, select Services for Macintosh.
3. Click Properties. The Microsoft AppleTalk Protocol Properties dialog box, as shown in Figure 8.1, opens.
4. Select the default network from a list of adapter cards bound to the AppleTalk protocol.
5. Click OK.

Installing the Services for Macintosh Workstation Programs

You can easily install the Microsoft user authentication software on each Macintosh workstation. The workstation software is installed on the NT Server in a volume called Microsoft UAM Volume. This makes the UAM software accessible to all Macintosh workstations on the network.

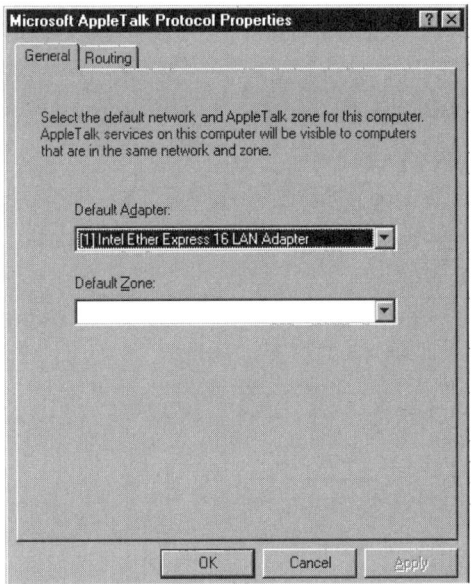

FIGURE 8.1 The Microsoft AppleTalk
Protocol Properties dialog box.

The first step in this process is to require workstations using the NT Server to use the Microsoft UAM. This step forces all System 7 or later Macintosh workstations to use the Microsoft UAM, and not the AppleShare UAM, to log on the NT domain.

Because Apple System software prior to version 7.1 did not fully support custom user authentication modules, Microsoft recommends the installation of Microsoft Authentication (MS UAM) only if increased security is necessary on the network computers running Windows NT Server.

Turning On Forced Authentication:

1. Run Server Manager on the NT Server.
2. Select Properties from the MacFile menu.
3. Select the Attributes button.
4. Click the check box for Require Microsoft Authentication.

The UAM must be installed on each Macintosh client before it can be used.

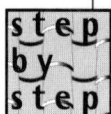

Installing the UAM Software on a Macintosh Workstation:

1. Select the Chooser from the Apple menu. The Chooser dialog box opens, as shown of Figure 8.2.

2. Select the AppleShare icon.

3. Select the zone that the NT Server running SFM resides in.

4. Select the NT Server name from the list of servers and click OK.

5. Log in to the NT Server when the sign-in dialog box appears.

6. Select the Microsoft UAM Volume from the list of volumes on the server, as shown in Figure 8.3, and click OK.

Once you have installed the UAM, the user will have the option of using the standard Macintosh authentication or the Microsoft UAM when he or she logs on the SFM server, unless you have performed the first set of steps in this section to force users through the Microsoft UAM.

If your system requires that you use the UAM to provide extended security services for Macintosh clients, you should protect the UAM from the users. Leaving the UAM unprotected allows users to move the UAM or delete it from the Macintosh client.

Microsoft suggests two methods for protecting the UAM from users. You can use one or both of these methods. The use of both methods provides the

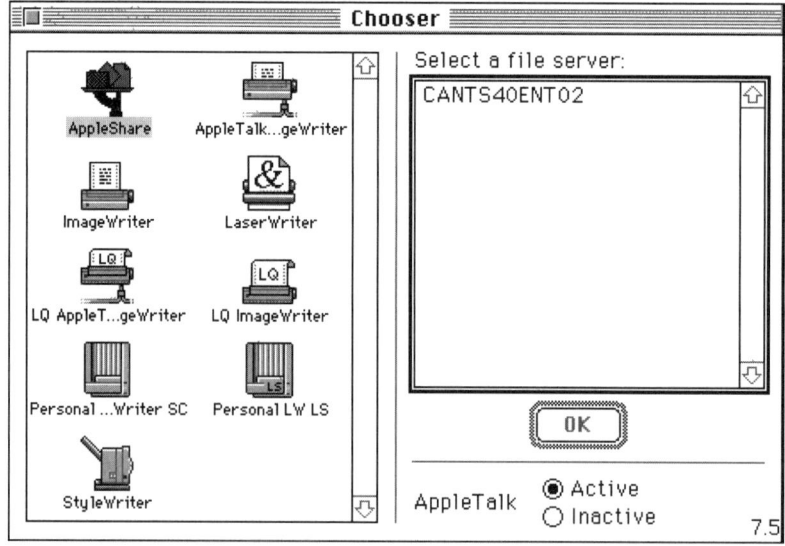

FIGURE 8.2 The Chooser dialog box of a Macintosh Workstation.

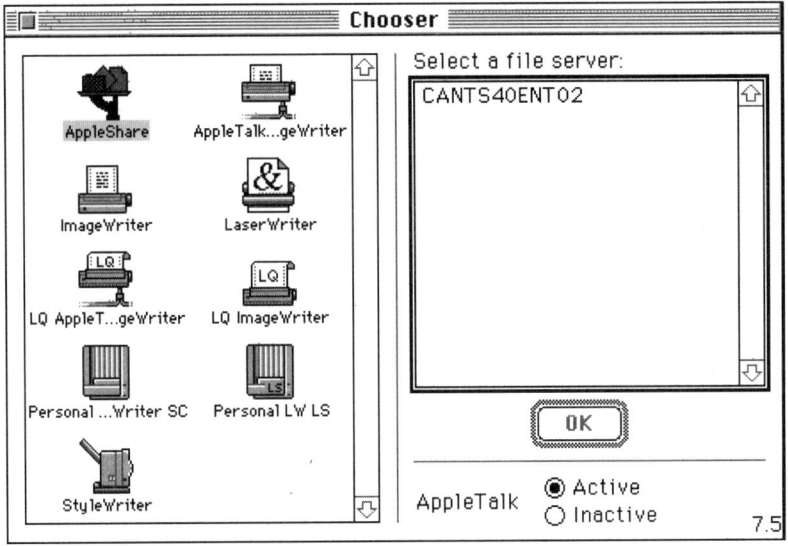

FIGURE 8.3 Selecting the MS UAM Volume.

greatest security but still does not keep a sophisticated user from creating problems with the UAM.

Protecting the UAM:

Method 1

1. Set the AppleShare folder in the Macintosh's System Folder to invisible, using ResEdit or a similar program.

Method 2

1. Select the UAM file in the AppleShare Folder, as shown in Figure 8.4, using Finder.

2. Choose Get Info from the File menu.

3. Select the Locked check box.

Removing Services for Macintosh

SFM can be removed very easily. This process takes only a few minutes. As with other administrative-type tasks, you must be logged in as a member of the Administrators group to perform these tasks.

Removing Services for Macintosh:

1. Start Control Panel.

2. Select the Devices applet.

3. Select the AppleTalk Protocol from the list, and click the Stop button. Click OK when the Stopping dialog box appears. This step stops the AppleTalk protocol and related services.

4. Close the Devices application, and select the Network applet.

5. Select Services for Macintosh in the Installed Network Software box.

6. Select the Remove button, and answer Yes to the prompt to confirm the removal.

7. Select OK to complete the process.

All SFM files are deleted from this process. Any directories used as Macintosh volumes will become unavailable to Macintosh users, although the files will not be deleted.

Administration of Services for Macintosh

SFM adds a number of tools for administering Macintosh services. Most of these tools are integrated into normal NT Server programs by the addition of a MacFile menu or option. Other SFM features may show up as standard NT

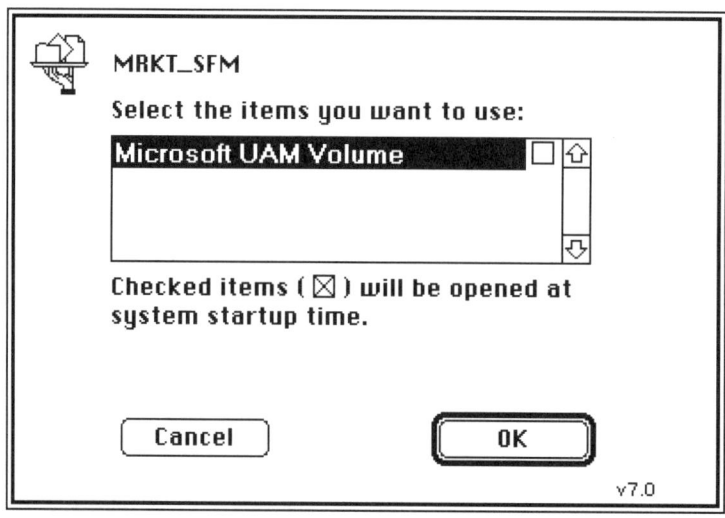

FIGURE 8.4 The AppleShare Folder in the MS UAM Volume.

options. The various management options for Services for Macintosh and can be integrated into the standard NT options.

Configuring the AppleTalk Protocol

Several features of the AppleTalk protocol can be configured using the Network applet in Control Panel, as discussed previously. You can select which network adapter to use for the default, select which zone the NT Server should be in, enable NT Server as a router for the Macintosh network, and configure the routing features of SFM.

Stopping the AppleTalk Protocol:

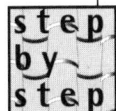

1. Start Control Panel.
2. Select the Devices applet.
3. Select the AppleTalk Protocol from the list.
4. Click the Stop button. Click OK when the Stopping dialog box appears. This step stops the AppleTalk protocol and related services.

Starting the AppleTalk Protocol:

1. Start Control Panel.
2. Select the Devices applet.
3. Select the AppleTalk Protocol from the list, and click the Start button. This step starts the AppleTalk protocol and related services.

ROUTING PARAMETERS

You can enable NT Server as a Macintosh router by using the Network applet. Care must be used when you set up routing services because, if you configure the router seeding incorrectly, the other routers on the network may fail.

Setting Up Your Server as an AppleTalk Router:

1. Select the Network icon in Control Panel.
2. Select Services for Macintosh from the list of services.
3. Click the check box beside Enable Routing.

To allow the server to be a seed router, select the Advanced button in the AppleTalk Routing box.

To enable the server as a seed router, click the Seed this Network check box. You should make sure that the network you wish to seed is specified in the Networks list box. This list contains all the to which that the AppleTalk protocol is bound. If the correct adapter is not shown, select the correct adapter from the list.

After you have checked the Seed this Network box, you can select the network range and add or remove any zones to the current list. When you enter network ranges or zones on this dialog box, remember that you are actually changing the settings for the network.

The Zone Information and Network Range, along with the Seed this Network check box, all apply to the network shown in the list box. Once you have made your choices, click OK to complete the process.

Administering Macintosh Users

The primary tool for administering Macintosh users is the MacFile applet in Control Panel. Luckily for managers, Microsoft made this applet almost identical to Server Manager.

MacFile enables you to monitor users, volumes, files, and Services for Macintosh attributes. Figure 8.5 shows the interface for MacFile.

MacFile works the same as Server Manager. Click the appropriate button, and the attributes are displayed. You can perform most actions with one or two clicks of the mouse.

FIGURE 8.5   The MacFile Properties dialog box is similar to Server Manager.

Displaying the Users on a Services for Macintosh Server:

1. Start the MacFile applet in Control Panel.
2. Click the Users button.

Disconnecting a User on a Services for Macintosh Server:

1. Start the MacFile applet in Control Panel.
2. Click the Users button.
3. Select the user to disconnect.
4. Click the Disconnect button. You can disconnect all users by clicking Disconnect All.

Sending a Message to Services for Macintosh Users:

1. Start the MacFile applet in Control Panel.
2. Click the Users button.
3. Select the user(s) to which to send the message.
4. Click the Send Message button.
5. Enter the text of the message, and follow the prompts.

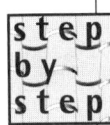

Displaying the Volumes in Use on a Services for Macintosh Server:

1. Start the MacFile applet in Control Panel.
2. Click the Volumes button.

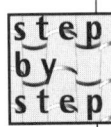

Breaking a Connection to a Volume on a Services for Macintosh Server:

1. Start the MacFile applet in Control Panel.
2. Click the Volumes button.
3. Select the user to disconnect.
4. Click the Disconnect button. You can disconnect users from a volume by clicking Disconnect All with a volume selected.

Figure 8.6 shows the Macintosh-Accessible Volumes window in NT 3.51 version.

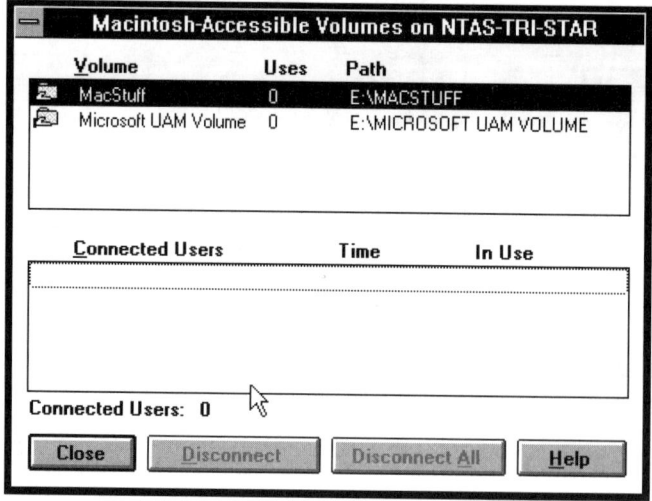

FIGURE 8.6 Notice how closely this dialog box matches the corresponding dialog box for shares in Server Manager. It takes only two clicks of the mouse to disconnect a user from a volume using this tool.

Displaying the Files in Use on a Services for Macintosh Server:

1. Start the MacFile applet in Control Panel.
2. Click the Files button.

Closing a File in Use on a Services for Macintosh Server:

1. Start the MacFile applet in Control Panel.
2. Select the file to close.
3. Click the Close Fork button. You can close all Macintosh files on the selected server by clicking Close All Forks.

The attributes option of MacFile is a little more involved than point and click. This tool changes the settings for the SFM server and can cause you problems if you do not handle it with care and plan your changes carefully. The following options can be changed:

- Server name as seen by AppleTalk workstations. I suggest leaving this set to the same name as the server name to avoid the confusion of having two names for the same server: one for Macintosh users and one for all others. Besides, it is nice for users who use both systems to be able to identify the server with the same name.
- The Logon message seen by Macintosh users.
- Security settings change the personality of the server. Secure environments want to turn off the first two options and turn on the last option:
    - Allow Guests to Logon allows user to log in to the server via guest accounts.
    - Allow Workstations to Save Password allows the user to save his/her password locally.
    - Require Microsoft Authentication requires the more secure logon authenticator.
- The Sessions box allows you to limit the number of concurrent sessions on the SFM server. The default is unlimited.

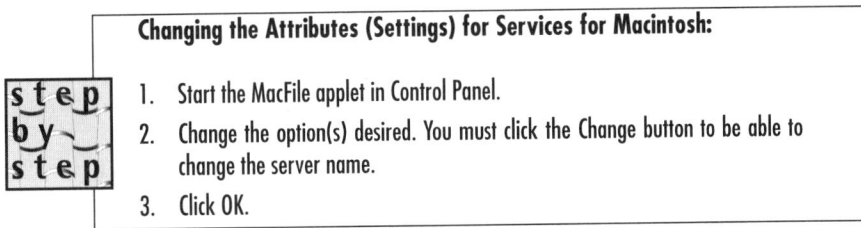

Changing the Attributes (Settings) for Services for Macintosh:

1. Start the MacFile applet in Control Panel.
2. Change the option(s) desired. You must click the Change button to be able to change the server name.
3. Click OK.

Figure 8.7 shows the MacFile Attributes dialog box of NT 3.51.

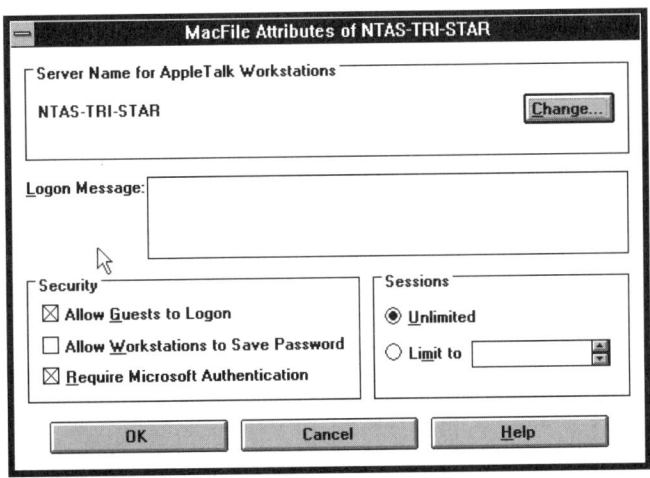

FIGURE 8.7 The MacFile Attributes dialog box provides access to a number of server parameters.

Macintosh Path Lengths

NT cannot handle path names longer than 260 characters, whereas Macintosh can. You should not create directory names longer than 260 characters because of this problem. This is a potential problem area because NT cannot access files in directory paths longer than 260 characters, causing problems for backup operations and other operations that must access files in these directories.

Macintosh file names are allowed to contain a trailing space, although NT does not support this for NT and DOS users. You will most likely receive a message from NT stating that it cannot find the file when you try to access the file. The only resolution to this problem is to rename the file from the Macintosh and remove the trailing space.

Macintosh file names are mapped to UNICODE as files are created on an NTFS volume. File Manager cannot access files that use UNICODE characters that do not have a corresponding ANSI character. The UNICODE characters problem shows up when you try to access the files in NT from either File Manager, the NT Backup program, or the command prompt. The files can be accessed from a Macintosh with no problems.

File System Issues for Services for Macintosh

Making Shared Directories Available to Macintosh Users

An administrator must designate a directory as a Macintosh-accessible volume before it can be accessed by Macintosh users. The Macintosh user sees the directory as a Macintosh volume, whereas PC users see the directory as a standard shared directory. Macintosh users see the volume and its files as if it were a standard Macintosh volume, whereas PC users see the directory structure and its files as a normal DOS directory tree.

For starters, all Macintosh volumes must be created on an NTFS volume. HPFS (up to Windows NT 3.51 only) and FAT volumes do not support the extended features required for the Macintosh file system.

You can create only one Macintosh volume in a subdirectory tree. This means that one and only one Macintosh volume can exist down any one directory path. For instance, if you make a top-level directory a Macintosh volume, no other subdirectory in that tree can be a Macintosh volume. If you make a subdirectory a Macintosh volume, you can make other subdirectories at the same level a Macintosh volume.

However, it is not possible to configure one directory as multiple volumes. For example, once E:\MACVOL has been made a Macintosh-accessible volume called MACVOL, it is not possible to create another Macintosh-accessible volume called MACVOL2 from the E:\MACVOL directory.

Also, you cannot nest volumes. For example, if you create a Macintosh-accessible volume called MACVOL, you will not be able to create volumes for \SCAN, \GRAPHICS, or \GAMES because these directories are in the MACVOL directory tree.

But you can create another individual volume for each of the sub-directories and not create the MACVOL volume at the parent directory level.

The maximum number of volumes is 255 (this is an AppleTalk limitation), although the number that can be seen by Macintosh workstations is determined by the length of the volume names.

Volume names can be from 1 to 27 characters in length. The AppleTalk protocol places a limit on the number of Macintosh volume names that can be displayed to Macintosh users. This limitation is based on the length of the volume names and the number of volumes. The exact formula is

```
(Number of Volumes) * (Average Length of Volume
Names + 2) <= 4624
```

Disappearing Icons

You may occasionally copy a Macintosh file on a PC and notice that the icon for the new file disappears when the file is accessed from a Macintosh. This error usually occurs when the file has a custom icon. Custom icons are stored as hidden files and cannot be copied correctly if the file name has a UNICODE character in the name. When you lose an icon, File Manager has used the short name to copy the file, resulting in a lost association to the icon. There is currently no work-around to this problem.

Drop Folders

Drop folders are a handy tool that allows users to "drop" files that cannot be changed after they are dropped. A drop folder is created by making a directory that gives the dropping users only Make Changes permission. NT Server supports drop folder permissions only for the immediate contents of the folder.

You should manually add drop folder permissions to all subdirectories under the main drop folder. Use the MacFile menu from File Manager and select Directory Permissions or use the Sharing dialog box on a Macintosh client. You must manually update these permissions if you add a directory to the main drop folder.

Macintosh Files

Macintosh files are bound by the same restrictions as they would be on a normal Macintosh system with a few additional restrictions. The restrictions occur because it is possible for a user to create a file with a file name that contains illegal NTFS characters. SFM checks each file name as it is created and changes any invalid characters to NTFS characters. Macintosh users see the unaltered name as they entered it, whereas other users see the name with the replaced characters.

File names that are too long for FAT names will have a short name created using the same process as any other NTFS name. Macintosh file names can have up to 31 characters, whereas NTFS file names can be up to 255 characters.

The diversity in file names does make for some potential confusion for systems with mixed DOS, NT, and Macintosh users. The problem comes about because of the diversity in file name lengths, as shown in Table 8.1.

What does this mean to us as users? Any file that is over 8.3 characters in length will look different to users on different Macintosh and Windows 3.x or DOS systems. For instance, any file over 8.3 and up to 31 characters will look fine to Macintosh users and NT users but not DOS users because DOS users will see only the short 8.3 name created by NTFS or SFM. Any file longer than 31 characters will look okay to NTFS users but not Macintosh or DOS users, both of whom will see the short 8.3 name. For more information on file systems in general and how the NTFS short name is created, see Chapter 6.

File and Folder Permissions

NT Server and SFM resolve the differences in the way the Macintosh and NTFS handle permissions on files, and directories/folders. Even though NTFS provides the ability to fine-tune the permissions on a file and/or directory, the Macintosh operating system provides only four types of permissions for a folder. SFM automatically translates between the Macintosh and NTFS permissions on the fly. Table 8.2 shows the Macintosh permissions and the corresponding NTFS permission.

The Macintosh permissions are much more restrictive than NTFS permissions. Permissions cannot be assigned to multiple users or groups as in NTFS. The Macintosh allows permissions to be assigned to the owner of the folder, a single user or group, and a special classification called Everyone, which includes all users on the system.

Comparing the security features of Macintosh versus this or that system is like comparing Ethernet to Token Ring—it's a religious war. The practical side of the limitations on the Macintosh for permissions means that you must

TABLE 8.1	File Name Lengths
File System	**Characteristics**
FAT	8.3 (eight characters + . + 3 characters), 255 on Windows 95 or NT
NTFS	255
Macintosh	31

TABLE 8.2	Macintosh and NTFS Permissions	
Macintosh	**NTFS**	**Description**
Cannot move, rename, or delete	N/A	User cannot move, rename, or delete the folder.
Make Changes	Write, Delete	User can perform any action on files within the folder.
See Files	Read	User can see folders contained within the folder.
See Folders	Read	User can see and read files within the folder.

create more groups on the server if you have security requirements that involve intricate sharing of files or folders. For more information on how the Macintosh deals with permissions, see the SFM documentation or your Macintosh documentation.

The SFM manual points out one interesting caveat regarding the translating of NTFS and Macintosh permissions: permissions assigned to Everyone on the Macintosh overrides any other rights assigned to the Owner or a group. Permissions set to the group Everyone on NTFS do not override any other permissions for users or groups.

NTFS also has file permissions that can be applied directly to any file on the system. The Macintosh has no corresponding file permissions, only folder permissions. What SFM does when it encounters file permissions is to give the appropriate access to the Macintosh user transparently. The Macintosh user never sees the permission but is affected by the permission. For instance, if a file has read-only access for a user, no Macintosh permission on the parent folder can override the specific file permission. In this instance, the user could read the file but not modify or delete the file.

SETTING FOLDER PERMISSIONS

Setting permissions on folders applies to almost the same restrictions that NTFS uses for NTFS files and directories. Only a file's owner or an administrator can change the permissions on the folder. A Macintosh, a PC, or an NT can be used to change the permissions. File Manager can actually set Macintosh-type permissions using the MacFile menu.

VOLUME PASSWORDS

Volume passwords are case-sensitive and can be assigned to a volume when it is created. These passwords apply only to access to the volume from a Macintosh and not from a DOS or NT system. Macintosh users must always supply the password when mounting the volume.

A volume with a password cannot be automatically mounted because of a limitation with System 6 and System 7.

Mac and NTFS File and Directory Properties

NTFS and the Macintosh file system both use different attributes for files and directories (folders on the Mac). As you can imagine, there must be some mechanism for Services for Macintosh to map NTFS attributes to Macintosh attributes. Table 8.3 shows how this is done. If an attribute from one system is not listed, it does not have an equivalent on the other platform and is not mapped.

Copying a Macintosh File to a FAT Volume

Users must be careful when copying a file from an SFM volume to a DOS floppy disk. A Macintosh file has two parts: a data fork and a resource fork. NTFS tracks both of these forks, which allows the file to reside in its native format on the NTFS volume by using an extended attribute to track the resource fork.

Most systems that copy Macintosh files to a FAT disk split the file into two different pieces representing the data and resource forks. When the file is copied back to a Macintosh, the two pieces are put back together. These two parts are not required with SFM because NTFS treats the two parts as a single unit just like the Macintosh.

Copying a Macintosh file to a FAT diskette results in the loss of the extended attribute that represents the resource fork. When an application needs the resource fork, the operation fails because the attribute is not present.

Printing with Services for Macintosh

SFM provides printing services for both Macintosh and PC users on the same printers. Macintosh users can use both PostScript and many non-PostScript printers, while PC users can print to a LaserWriter that is connected to the Macintosh network.

NT Server supports all printers through its printing system. This support makes management easy because each printer can be managed by Print Manager. The spooling system improves printing for Macintosh users by

TABLE 8.3 Macintosh and NTFS File Attributes	
Macintosh Attribute	**Windows NT Server Attribute**
File Locked	Read Only
Invisible	Hidden

allowing Macintosh users to print a document and return quickly to their applications, whereas NT Server spools the print job to the printer. The spooling takes place on the server and does not use disk space on the Macintosh client.

SFM has an integrated PostScript-compatible print engine that allows a Macintosh user to print to almost any printer connected to the NT network as if that printer were a LaserWriter. The print engine translates the PostScript file to the appropriate format for the target printer, allowing your Macintosh and PC users to share easily the printer investment on your network.

Captured Printers

SFM has the ability to capture a Macintosh printer such as a LaserWriter that is connected to the Macintosh network and not directly to the NT server. Capturing allows SFM to maintain complete control over the printer and not allow the printer to accept print jobs from any other source but the SFM server.

Failing to capture a printer may cause interference between the printer and the SFM server. When another system tries to print, either that system or NT sees the printer as busy.

Conclusion

SFM offers a new dimension to NT Server networks. You should now be ready to install SFM and configure it for your Mac systems. As you can see from this chapter, there are still several issues you should be aware of. This is certainly true when you have Mac and PC users sharing files created with sophisticated applications such as Microsoft Word and other Microsoft Office tools.

The next chapter takes us into the NT printer system and the many options that it offers. Understanding printers is certainly important to almost every organization due to the heavy printing demand placed on the networks by the user population. This chapter will introduce you to the NT printer management tools and to the variety of things you can do with them.

Printer Use
and
Management

Windows NT introduces a new printing system to the Windows and LAN environments. This system works with and looks like the printing system in Windows 3.x and Windows 95 (NT 4), but is a very different and powerful animal. The significant thing about this new printing system is that it is designed to work with future systems and is able to work with existing systems until and after these newer systems come along.

Scenario 9.1:

Your organization has a number of printers that are services by NT Server, and these printers have become vital to the success of the organization on a day-to-day basis. How do you manage those printers to keep them running and finally tuned? What do you do when a problem occurs?

Scenario 9.2:

You need to add a high-performance printer to your network for a specific group of users. The printer must be high speed but cost effective, and will be responsible for delivering output for many small print jobs. Should you purchase an expensive printer, or just use NT's printing services by pooling several existing printers?

Evidently, printing is a very important aspect in any network. NT 4.0's configuration, as you will see, is very similar to the one used on Windows 95. If you are already familiar with it, you won't find any difficulties configuring the printers on NT 4.0. It is not the configuration of the printer that will be the challenge, but planning the load of each one of the printers on the network in such a way that none will be overloaded while others are seldom used.

The printing performance of NT 4.0 has been greatly improved over NT 3.51 through server-based rendering of print jobs. This allows for a much quicker return of control of your desktop and applications. Another change is that printer drivers for shared printers are located on the server for what Microsoft called "point and print" automatic client driver installation. Remote drivers were also benefited by the creation of printer folders, which enable easier browsing of shared printers.

Architecture

The NT printing architecture is a giant step into new technology for managing printers and printer resources. NT's printing architecture is modular and supports an easy management scheme for printers. For instance, you do not need to install a printer driver on every NT system that will use a printer. The driver needs to be resident only on the server to which every NT workstation or server has access. This is a far cry from Windows 3.x in which you have many different printer drivers spread over your workstations. Storing only one copy of all your drivers on a server makes managing updates much easier than having a copy on each workstation, although having a locally stored copy improves performance slightly.

One of the innovations of NT is the way it handles printing batches. A document sent by a user to a printer is considered a print job. It doesn't matter if it is a graphic, text, or a Web page that is being printed. This print job is sent to a local printer (connected to the computer itself) or to a printer on the network, connected through the printer server.

NT uses several special terms that relate to printers. Some of these terms are new, some are used differently than on other systems, and the rest are generic terms for the industry. Table 9.1 lists the most important terms for NT's printer systems.

Print Manager is used to create and manage NT printers. You must specify a printer port and a printer driver for each new printer. The entire process of creating a new printer usually takes about two minutes to complete. You also use Print Manager to create printers for print devices that are connected to the network and managed by an NT Server. Print Manager can also connect a printer to a network queue on another system.

TABLE 9.1	Vocabulary for NT's Printer Subsystems
Term	**Description**
Print Device	The physical printer, such as a LaserJet IV.
Printer	The printer name and the software that controls the printer. This is what users see as the printer name in browse lists and other places.
Queue	The software that users see as the printer. The term *printer* in NT refers to the same thing as a *queue* in other systems.
Network-Interface Printer	A printer that interfaces directly to the network.
Dots Per Inch	DPI. The most frequent term used for printer resolution. *DPI* refers to the number of dots per inch that are used to make up the characters and graphics on a printer. The higher the DPI, the better the print quality.
Pixel	The resolution of a screen. Pixels are similar to DPI.
Graphical Device Interface	GDI. The command set that applications output defining the print job. The GDI output contains both content and formatting information for the print job. The GDI is the boundary between the application and the graphics engine.
Graphics Engine	The print processor that takes the GDI output from an application.
Device Driver Interface	DDI. The interface between the graphics engine and the print processor and print driver.
Journal File	Files that contain the commands and data to print. Journal files are very precise and are tuned to the target printer.
Halftoning	A method of providing higher-quality output and improved color accuracy on a print device or monitor. Halftoning support is provided by the graphics engine.
Print Processor	A DLL that interprets data types passed from the spooler. NT comes with two print processors: ■ WINPRINT.DLL interprets journal files and raw files. ■ SFMSPRT.DLL supports Macintosh clients printing PostScript files. The Print Processor sends the document back to the spooler when it has completed its tasks.
WYSIWYG	What You See Is What You Get. This term is used to describe an application such as Word for Windows that displays a document as it will look when it is printed.
Print Router	Device that passes printer information from a workstation to the print server. The print router is used only if the workstation is printing to a

TABLE 9.1	Vocabulary for NT's Printer Subsystems (Continued)

Term	Description
Print Router (continued)	remote printer. The Print Router is made up of several files: ■ Print Servers: SPOOLSS.EXE, SPOOLSS.DLL, and WINSPOOL.DLL. ■ Client: WINSPOOL.DRV. The print router manages tracking local printers that have been connected to a remote printer and provides support for downloading the drivers from a server to the local workstation.
GDI Server	Graphics Device Interface server
Printer Driver	A file or set of files that provide some type of print services for a particular printer. Printer drivers are also used by NT to provide WYSIWYG support for applications. Printer drivers can be stored on the NT print server and are not needed on each NT workstation or server that uses the remote printer. Printer drivers are composed of three files: ■ Graphics driver such as PSCRIPT.DLL ■ Printer interface driver such as PSCRPTUI.DLL ■ Configuration file or minidriver
Configuration File	A file used as part of the printer driver such as Adobe PostScript (PPD) file.
Printer Graphics	The portion of the printer driver that handles rendering the print Driver output and managing the process. It is called from GDI Server.
Printer Interface Driver	The portion of the printer driver that contains the user interface and manages configuration of the printer. It is called from the client side of the printer router.
Minidriver	Usually contains printer information and not code, except in some instances. PostScript minidrivers are Adobe PostScript (PPD) files.
Remote Printer	A printer on another system on the LAN or WAN. You must connect to a remote printer before you can use it on your local system.
Spooler	Runs on each NT system (both client and server) and manages the entire printing process. Client and server spoolers communicate directly with each other in the background. The spooler works with the print system components such as drivers and the router and with the physical printer.
Print Monitor	Found on each printer device to manage it. NT includes the following print monitors: ■ LOCALMON.DLL supports LPT and COM ports, remote print shares, and named pipes. ■ HPMON.DLL supports HP laserjets that connect through network interfaces. ■ SFMON.DLL is included with NT Server and provides support for AppleTalk clients.

TABLE 9.1	Vocabulary for NT's Printer Subsystems (Continued)
Term	**Description**
	Developers and others can write their own print monitor for managing specific printers.
	The print monitor provides the direct interface to a printer. It opens and closes the port, monitors the status, and writes the data to the port. It can also provide real status information because it does not report that a job is complete until the printer actually finishes printing.
Printer Port	A physical port that is used for a printer, such as COM1:, LPT2: or logical port (\\Server\Printer).
Forms Database	Database that contains information on all forms used by the printers on a server. The database is managed by the spooler.
Print Provider	Another software component that NT uses between the spooler and the print device. NT includes several print providers: ■ LOACALSPL.DLL ■ WIN32SPL.DLL ■ LMSPOOL.DLL

A printer can be used as soon as it is created and the print device is available. The printer name is the most visible part of the printing process that will be seen by the end user. Printer names show up in applications, Print Manager, and the NET USE command.

You can link multiple print devices to a single printer. This feature is useful for setting up pools of printers that have the same capabilities. You can also point multiple printers to one print device. This is useful when you need to control certain aspects of a print device where some users have access to certain features and other users have full access. See "Using Multiple Printers Connected to One Print Device" and "Printer Pools."

Print Manager

Print Manager, the heart of the user interface to the NT printing system, is an enhanced version of the program we have grown to know and love in Windows 3.x.

The NT version of Print Manager provides tools for viewing printers, managing documents, installing and removing printers, and setting security on printers. Print Manager also provides the tools to connect to network printers, share printers over the network, to disconnect network printers, and to cancel shares on printers.

The layout of Print Manager is convenient. It has a menu bar for providing quick access to often-used functions, a menu bar to provide access to all functions, and a nice MDI layout of the windows Print Manager uses, as seen in Figure 9.1.

Each printer has its own window for its status and the documents that are currently scheduled to print on the printer. When you minimize the window of a printer, it becomes an icon at the bottom of the Print Manager window. For each printer, the minimized icons show you the type of printer, the name, and whether it is shared or not. Icons also represent servers that you have remotely attached to for administration purposes. There is also a separate window that shows all printers connected to the server. Figure 9.2 shows Print Manager (for NT version 3.51, which very similar to NT 4.0) with several icons and windows. Notice how quickly you can get to any printer or server by clicking a window or double-clicking an icon.

The balance of this chapter focuses on a number of different tasks that relate to printing and NT. All these tasks involve Print Manager in one form or another. You can find more information on Print Manager in the NT or NT Server documentation and in the NT Resource Kits.

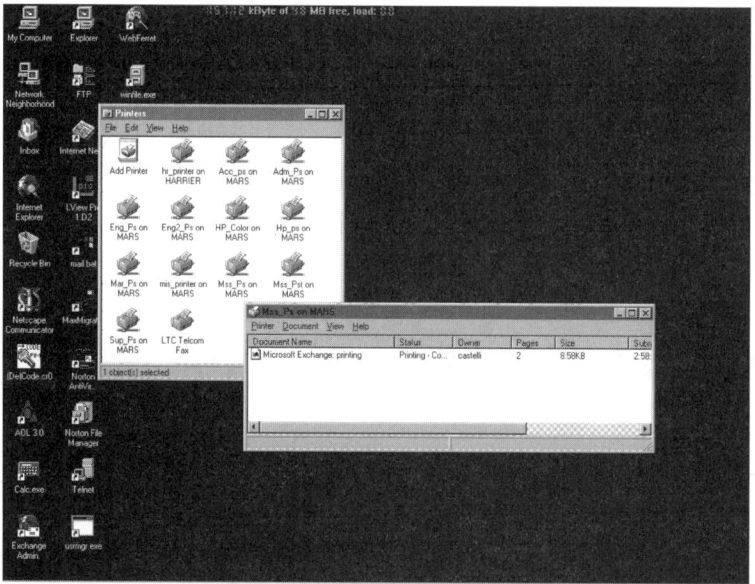

FIGURE 9.1 Managing printers through the Printer Manager interface of NT 4.0.

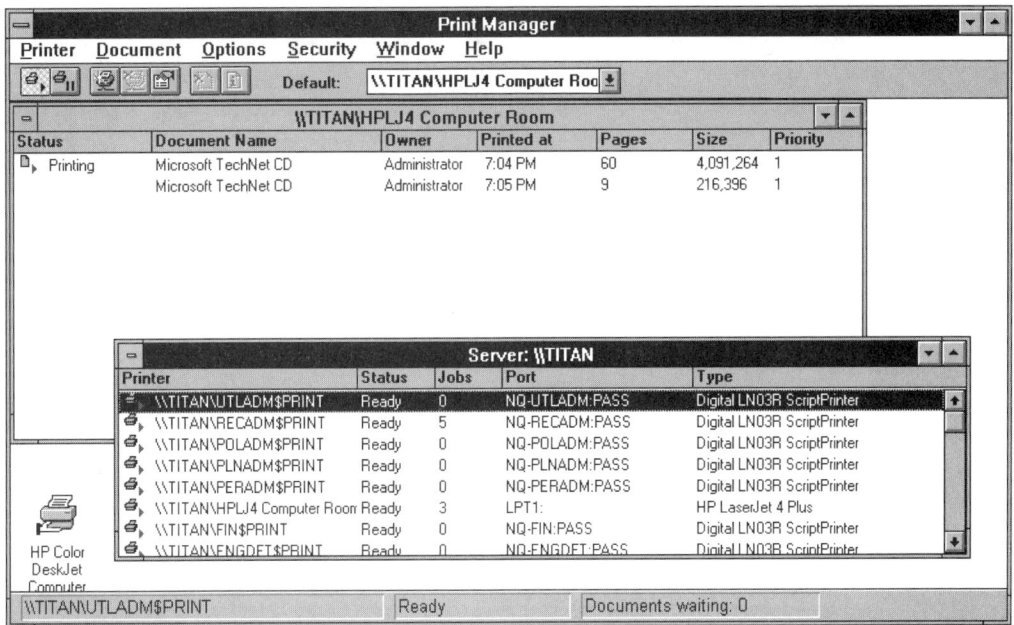

Status	Document Name	Owner	Printed at	Pages	Size	Priority
Printing	Microsoft TechNet CD	Administrator	7:04 PM	60	4,091,264	1
	Microsoft TechNet CD	Administrator	7:05 PM	9	216,396	1

Server: \\TITAN

Printer	Status	Jobs	Port	Type
\\TITAN\UTLADM$PRINT	Ready	0	NQ-UTLADM:PASS	Digital LN03R ScriptPrinter
\\TITAN\RECADM$PRINT	Ready	5	NQ-RECADM:PASS	Digital LN03R ScriptPrinter
\\TITAN\POLADM$PRINT	Ready	0	NQ-POLADM:PASS	Digital LN03R ScriptPrinter
\\TITAN\PLNADM$PRINT	Ready	0	NQ-PLNADM:PASS	Digital LN03R ScriptPrinter
\\TITAN\PERADM$PRINT	Ready	0	NQ-PERADM:PASS	Digital LN03R ScriptPrinter
\\TITAN\HPLJ4 Computer Room	Ready	3	LPT1:	HP LaserJet 4 Plus
\\TITAN\FIN$PRINT	Ready	0	NQ-FIN:PASS	Digital LN03R ScriptPrinter
\\TITAN\ENGDET$PRINT	Ready	0	NQ-ENGDET:PASS	Digital LN03R ScriptPrinter

\\TITAN\UTLADM$PRINT   Ready   Documents waiting: 0

FIGURE 9.2 The layout of Print Manager (NT 3.51) enables quick access to all of its functions.

Printer Security

NT allows you to assign security permissions to printers to control many different aspects of printer operation and maintenance. Security for printing may not sound like a big deal until you consider printers like check or invoice printers that stay loaded with a particular form. Setting permissions on these printers is a handy way to control access to this type of printer.

The security features are also nice for controlling who can manage a printer and the documents that have been sent to the printer.

Table 9.2 lists special categories of access for printer users and administrators that are controlled through Print Manager.

By default, a user must be a member of the Administrators, Print Operators, or Server Operators group to create a printer. Users must also have write access to the DRIVERS directory if they are printing from an NT system and the printer requires a new driver to download to the system.

NT enables you to audit your printers in the same manner as other objects. You can track the following events:

- Printing documents
- Changing job settings for documents
- Moving, pausing, restarting, and deleting documents

TABLE 9.2	Categories of Access Through Print Manager
Permission	**Description**
Full Control	Gives a user complete control and access to a printer. Administrators, power users, server operators, and print operators have full control permission by default. (NT Server does not have a Power User group.)
Manage Documents	Provides a user with the ability to change anything related to all documents for a Printer. The creator owner of a printer has Manage Documents permission by default.
Print	Allows a user to submit jobs to a printer. The Everyone group has Print permission.
No Access	Prohibits all access to a printer. This permission must be explicitly assigned to a user or group.

- Sharing a printer
- Changing printer properties
- Deleting a printer
- Changing printer permissions
- Taking ownership

Auditing must be enabled for a given printer in Print Manager. Before you enable auditing for a printer, you must turn on auditing in User Manager. The following steps walk you through setting up an audit on a printer.

Configuring Auditing a Printer:

1. Start Print Manager.
2. Select the printer to audit.
3. Select Auditing from the Security menu.
4. Choose the auditing properties for the groups and users you wish to audit, and set the appropriate audit events.

Table 9.3 lists the events that can be audited and the possible actions reported by the events.

All audited events are trapped in the Security event log. Event Viewer is used to review the audited events and event details.

Installing and Configuring Printers

Print Manager is used to create a new printer or modify an existing printer. As mentioned in "Architecture," you do not need to install a remote printer

Event	Actions Reported
TABLE 9.3 Printer Events That Can Be Audited	
Print	Printing of documents to the printer
Full Control	Changing job settings, pausing, restarting, moving, and deleting documents, sharing a printer, and changing printer properties
Delete	Deleting a printer
Change Permissions	Changing permissions for a printer
Take Ownership	Taking ownership of a printer

on NT if it is managed by another NT system. You can simply connect to the printer using Print Manager, and NT will use the driver on the server.

Installing a printer in NT 4.0, just like in Windows 95, is very easy. There are actually two ways to do it: Plug and Play printer detection, and using the Printer Wizard.

The plug and play method is used for Plug and Play printers. NT 4.0 will automatically detect the printer at installation time or during the boot process. The system will prompt you for the appropriate driver files if they are not resident in the NT directory.

As for the Printer Wizard, NT 4.0 provides a wizard (as shown in Figure 9.3) that walks you through the printer installation process.

Using 4.0's Printer Installation Wizard:

1. Click Start, select Settings, then Printers.
2. Double-click the Add icon to install a new printer.
3. Follow the instructions of the Printer Wizard.

The following outline covers the basic steps for installing a printer in NT 3.51. Other sections in the chapter discuss how to configure various aspects of the printer such as sharing the printer after it is installed or configuring the ports that a printer uses.

Installing a Printer in NT 3.51:

1. Select Create Printer from the Printer menu. Enter a name for the printer. The printer name will show up everywhere the printer is shown, so make sure it is descriptive. You may want to use a name such as Accounting Laserjet IV or Laserjet IV—Accounting instead of just the department name. The name can be from 1 to 32 characters long.

2. Select a driver for the printer. You may have to use a generic driver for your printer if it is not listed (such as an HP Laserjet driver for HP compatibles) or use a driver supplied from another source.

3. Enter a description for the printer. This description appears when network users browse the printers on the network. You can use the description to provide additional information about the printer.

4. Select a destination for the printer in the Print to: box. You can select a local port (that is, LPT1: or COM2:), a file, or a network address or enter a local port that is not listed. If you are installing a network interface printer, see page 386.

5. Share the printer if necessary. You can click Share This Printer on the Network box and share the printer as part of the installation process. Simply click the box and enter a share name and a location for the printer. The Location information shows up in the Connect to Printer dialog box whenever a user browses printers on the network.

6. Enter the location of the NT distribution files if necessary. This step is required only if NT needs to install a driver that is not already installed on the system.

7. Assign any special features for the printer.

As soon as the printer is created, you can either use it on the local system or share it over the network.

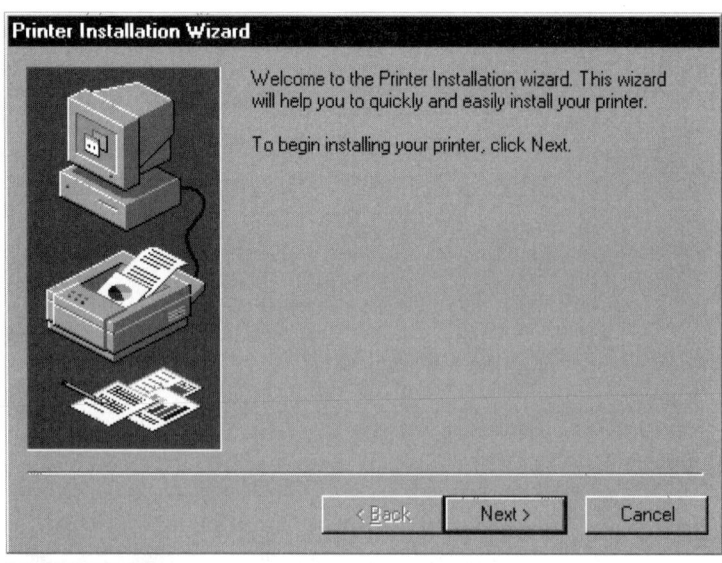

FIGURE 9.3   NT 4.0's Printer Installation Wizard makes it simple to install printers.

Changing Printer Properties

Printer properties control the operation of many aspects of the NT printing system. The properties control everything from the driver used for the printer to changing the port from which the printer is accessed.

Installing and Changing Drivers

Printer drivers are only one of the properties that you may wish to install or change for a printer. You may purchase an updated driver for your printer or possibly install a second driver for a printer if your system has mixed RISC and x86 NT systems.

RISC systems must have a driver installed for each type of RISC system installed on the network. Each different RISC system, such as a DEC Alpha or MIPS system, has a different binary architecture and requires a separate driver. If your network has different RISC systems, then you must have the correct driver for each RISC system loaded either on the RISC system or on the server. Placing multiple drivers on the server is the best way to handle them, because you will have a central place to maintain all your drivers.

When you install the drivers on the server, each system downloads the appropriate driver for its processor.

Configuring a printer in Windows NT 4.0 is much simpler than in NT 3.51. All printer configuration is consolidated onto a single property sheet for the printer that can be accessed from the Printers folder. As shown in Figure 9.4, the property sheet contains all printer parameters, such as the printer port (or network path) to which the printer is connected, the paper options for the printer, the fonts built in to the printer, and device options specific to the printer model.

Furthermore, to simplify printer configuration, NT 4.0 supports bidirectional communications between compatible printers and printer ports. With this functionality, NT 4.0 can actually query the characteristics and configuration options directly from the printer and can automatically configure the printer driver to exactly match the configuration of the printer, including the amount of memory, the paper options, and the fonts installed in the printer.

Installing Printer Drivers in NT 3.51:

1. Start Print Manager, and select the printer you wish to modify.
2. Select Properties from the toolbar or the Printer menu.
3. Select Other in the Driver box.
4. Specify the location for the driver. This should be the location of the driver and the PRINTER.INF file. You may have different locations for these files on your network if you have different types of systems installed.
5. Select the new driver from the list.

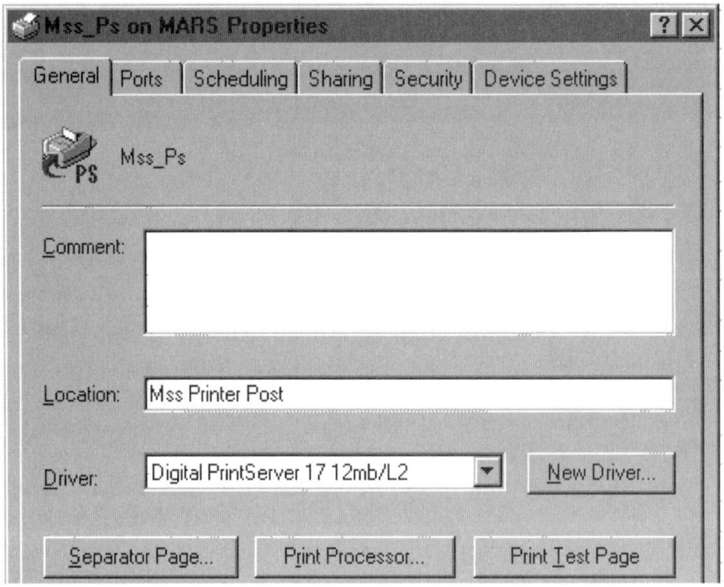

FIGURE 9.4 The Printer Property Sheet of NT 4.0.

Once you have completed these steps, Print Manager installs the driver on your system.

Other Properties

You can change many other properties besides the printer driver with the Printer Properties command. Printer properties can be accessed from the toolbar and the Printer menu. You must be logged on as an administrator, server operator, or print operator to change a printer's properties.

The Printer Properties dialog box is the same dialog box you saw in the Install Printer process. Using this dialog box, you can change any of the properties that were set during installation. This section focuses on changing properties that are specific to the Printer Properties dialog box. For properties such as sharing a printer, see the next section in this chapter.

The Printer Properties dialog box provides access to a number of other functions, which are listed in Table 9.4.

Sharing and Unsharing a Printer

You can share a printer when it is installed by clicking the Sharing tab (or Share This Printer on the Network check box during the installation process

TABLE 9.4	Buttons on the Printer Properties Dialog Box
Button	**Description**
Setup	The Setup button displays a Printer Setup dialog box that is specific to your particular printer. This dialog box usually looks somewhat similar to the Windows 3.x Printer Setup dialog boxes for the same printer.
Details	The Details button displays the Printer Details dialog box for the selected printer. This dialog box allows you to set available hours, separator file to be used, additional ports for the printer, priority, and other configuration options. It also provides access to the Job Defaults dialog box for choosing default orientation, forms, and other options.
Settings	The Settings button provides access to particular hardware settings for the port used by the printer.

of NT 3.51) under the properties options of the printer you selected in Printers, under Settings, as shown in Figure 9.5. The check box for the NT 3.51 version is located on the Printer Properties dialog box and can be accessed after installation by selecting the Printer Properties command from the toolbar or the Printer menu.

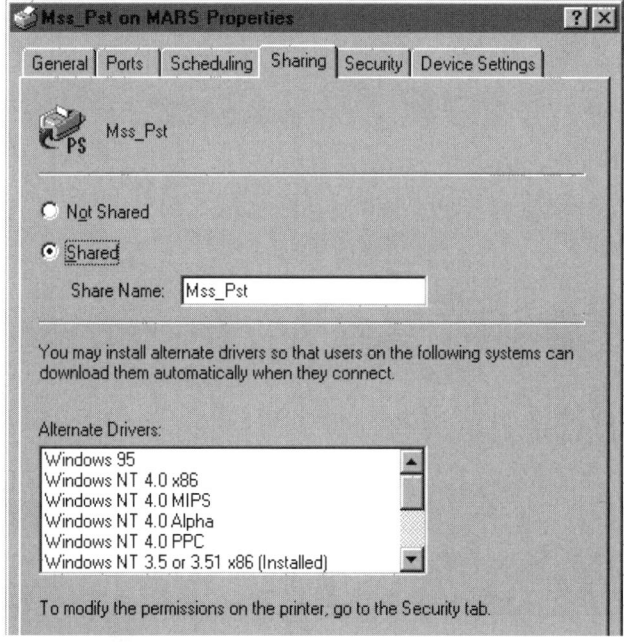

FIGURE 9.5 Sharing a printer through the Properties box on NT 4.0.

After you have clicked the Shared radio button (or check box on NT 3.51), simply fill in the Share Name (and optionally the location in NT 3.51), as shown in Figure 9.6. You may also want to change the description, because this field will be displayed in the Connect to Printer dialog box in the Printer Information area. The Location field also shows up in the Connect to Printer dialog box, along with the printer name and the name of the driver.

NT 3.51 and Windows for Workgroups workstations use the printer name to connect to printers on NT systems. The printer name can be up to 32 characters in length.

Use care in choosing the Share Name if you have any DOS-based clients on your network. They can only see and connect to a share name that is 12 characters within the 8.3 file name format. The default Share Name is the name of the printer. A default share name is automatically constructed by Print Manager and truncated to a format that DOS systems can recognize.

Sharing a Printer (Print Manager) on NT 3.51:

1. Start Print Manager.

2. Select the printer to share.

3. Select Properties from the Printer menu.

4. Click the Share check box.

5. Change other properties as needed.

6. Close the dialog box.

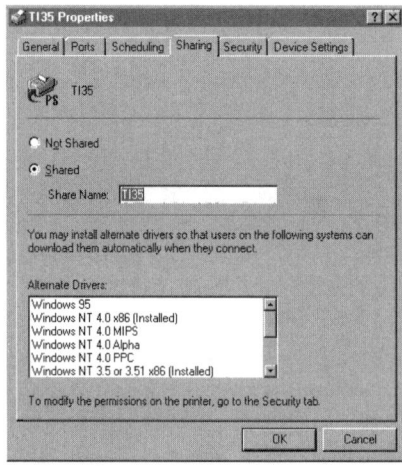

FIGURE 9.6 Giving a share name to the printer you are sharing.

Deleting Printers

It is very easy to delete a printer in NT 4.0. Figure 9.7 illustrates this process.

> **Delete a printer in NT 4.0:**
>
> 1. Select Settings.
> 2. Click Printers.
> 3. Select the printer you want to delete.
> 4. Click the right button of your mouse, and select Delete.

In Windows NT 3.51, you can delete a printer with either Print Manager or RegEdit, which can also be used as an alternative in NT 4.0. Considering the limitations on NT 3.51 compared to NT 4.0, notice how much shorter the steps are by using Print Manager. Print Manager is also much less hazardous to the health of your NT system than RegEdit is.

If you are running NT 3.51, the easiest way to delete a printer is by using Print Manager.

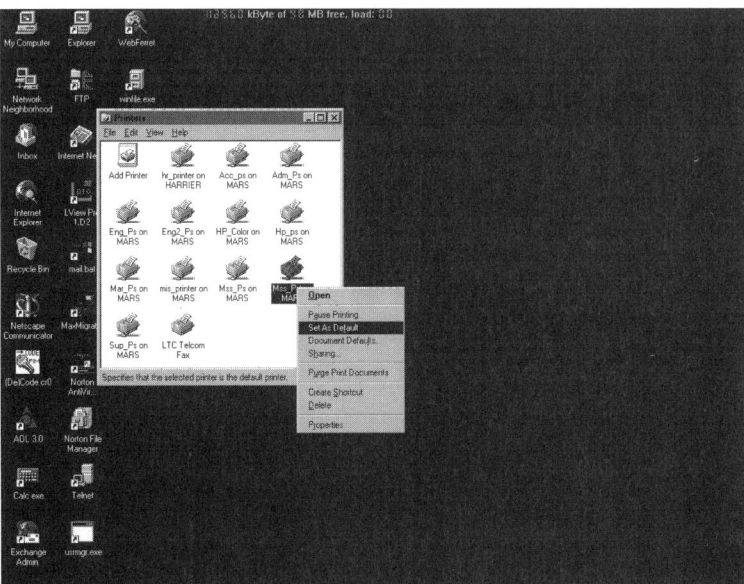

FIGURE 9.7 Deleting printers in NT 4.0 is done by clicking the right mouse button after selecting the printer to be deleted.

Deleting a Printer (Print Manager) in NT 3.51:

1.   Select the printer you wish to delete.
2.   Select the remove command from the toolbar or from the Printer menu.
3.   Answer Yes to the confirmation question. The Printer is gone.

Changes to printers and print shares are normally made with Print Manager, but there may be a time when you may need to delete a printer or print share manually when you are troubleshooting your system. The following procedure uses RegEdit to accomplish this task.

Deleting a Printer using RegEdit32 (for both NT 4.0 and 3.51):

1.   Search for all references to the printer or print share in the Registry under the following keys: HKEY_CURRENT_USER, HKEY_LOCAL_MACHINE, HKEY_USERS.
2.   Delete every reference to the printer or print share except the ones in the ControlSets other than CurrentControlSet.

These changes will not take effect until you log out and back in.

Connecting and Disconnecting to Printers

Using a printer that is connected to or managed by another system requires you to connect to the printer over the network. The Printer applet under Settings (NT 4.0), as well as the Print Manager of NT 3.51 can be used for this task, as well as a number of other applications. Many applications have a Network button located on the printer setup dialog box that enables you to perform the same connect operation as Print Manager. You can also call the WNetAddConnection and WNetCancelConnection API functions from a programming language such as C or VB.

For those using NT 3.51, here are the options provided by the standard NT 3.51 and client tools (such as Print Manager and the NET commands), although the same techniques work in many other applications.

The process of connecting to a remote printer in Print Manager is identical to connecting to a remote file service in File Manager.

Connecting to a Remote Printer (Print Manager):

1.   Start Print Manager.
2.   Select the Connect To Printer command from the toolbar or the Print menu. This command displays the Connect To Printer dialog box that lists most of the

workgroups, servers, and printers on your network. If you have servers on your network that do not support browsing, they are not listed. For instance, if you are running Pathworks for NT and have a Pathworks 4.2 or earlier server, you can connect to the printers managed by the Pathworks server, but the servers and printers do not show up in the browse list unless the Pathworks Naming service is installed.

3. Select a printer from the list. You may need to double-click a network or server to display the servers/printers in that group. The servers, printers, and networks each have their own icon. A plus sign (+) is displayed to the left of any item in the list that may be expanded.

4. Click OK.

The Print Information Box

A neat feature of the Connect To Printer dialog box is the information box at the bottom. This little box shows the description of the printer, the status, and the number of documents waiting for the printer. Let's use an example to describe how this information can be used:

It's four thirty on Friday and you need to print a 100-page proposal before you leave. Your department has two laser printers, and the department next door has four, one of which is a 16-ppm (page per minute) printer. Which printer should you send your document to? The easiest way to find out is to bring up the Connect To Printer dialog box and check its Print Information box. Simply click on each printer one at a time and note the printer's status and the number of documents waiting on that printer. Pick the one with 0 documents or the shortest list and the fastest output. You can send the job to the printer and then walk over in six minutes to make sure it has plenty of paper.

If you are connecting to a printer that is not shown on your list because its server cannot be browsed, or if you know the server and printer name, you can enter the printer information directly. In the Printer box at the top of the dialog box, enter the server and printer name in the following format:

\\Server\PrinterName

Once you have entered the server name and printer names, click OK.

You can disconnect from the remote printer by selecting the Disconnect Printer command from the toolbar or the Printer menu Remove Printer command. You can also remove a network printer to which you have connected by using the Remove Printer command when the printer is selected.

When you connect to a printer served by a non-NT system, NT will tell you that the server does not have a suitable printer driver available. You will be asked if you would like to pick one for your system to use; I call this a "polite user interface." Simply choose the correct printer from the list and click OK. If the server is an NT system, you will not go through this step because NT simply uses the printer driver on the server, unless the server does not have a suitable driver.

Using Multiple Printers Connected to One Print Device

You can create numerous printers and point them to one print device, which enables you to set different criteria, such as access times or priorities on each printer. The printers can be located on the same machine as the physical print device, or on other NT workstations or servers.

Multiple printers are convenient when you use a print device that can switch between PostScript and non-PostScript jobs. For these types of print devices, you should create one printer using a PostScript driver and another that uses the generic driver for the print device. This procedure enables you to send both types of jobs to the printer without the need to reconfigure it.

Printer Pools

A printer pool is a handy way to improve the throughput of your printing operations drastically. With the price of printers continuing to drop as the performance goes up, you can take three or four laser printers and attach them to an NT server and have one heck of a fast printer pool.

When you configure printers in a pool, the total throughput for the pool is the sum of the throughput for each printer. For instance, if you have three 8-ppm printers, your pool output should be approximately 24 ppm.

We use the term *approximately* because several factors have an impact on the performance of the pool. If you routinely send very long documents to a pool, your performance may be down. This decrease in performance would occur because each document would be sent to a specific printer. If you have four printers and only send three long documents to the pool, three of the printers will print the documents, and the fourth will be idle. If, on the other hand, you send 20 five- or ten-page documents, all the printers will fire up, and the load will be spread across them all.

Another thing that has an impact on the performance of your pool is the servers that manage the printers. If you use a Pentium with only 16MB of memory to handle several very fast (16-ppm) printers, you may bog down the server and slow the throughput to the printers. If, on the other hand, you put 32MB on the server, the printers should fly. NT is very sensitive to the amount of memory in the system—the more, the better.

Creating a printer pool in NT 4.0 is very easy. You just need to configure a printer to print to more than one destination.

Creating a printer pool in NT 4.0:

1. Physically attach all the printers to the server or the network. The printers can be attached to a single server, to multiple servers with shared connections, or as network devices.
2. Create a new printer with Add Printer from Printers.
3. Select the Ports tab and check the "Enable Printer Pooling" box.
4. Select and/or add port entries for each printer the pool will use.

Creating a Printer Pool on NT 3.51:

1. Physically attach all the printers to the server or the network. The printers can be attached to a single server, to multiple servers with shared connections, or as network devices.
2. Use Print Manager to create a single printer that points to all three printers.
3. Using Print Manager, point the printer to all the printer ports that will be used. Use Print Manager and select Printer Details. Then select the Print to Additional Ports option to select the ports that the print devices are attached to.

There are several things to keep in mind for printer pools:

- Make sure all print devices are of exactly the same type or capability. For instance, you could have LaserJet IVsi and LaserJet IV printers mixed in a pool, but not LaserJet IV and Epson printers.
- Any action on the printer takes effect on all print devices. These actions include changing properties and pausing the printer.
- Jobs are sent to the print devices in the order of how the print devices were added to the pool. Make sure that you add the fastest printer first, because it will be the most heavily used printer in the pool.
- You can mix the types of ports used for the print devices in a pool. For instance, you can have two locally attached print devices (LPT or COM) and two network print devices.
- All the print devices in the pool should be in close physical proximity. This arrangement reduces the effort required to find out where your document printed.

Figure 9.8 illustrates a printer pool with three identical laser printers.

Considerations for Special Printers

Special printers are available for many different tasks. Today we have network printers that connect directly to the network and are managed by NT, photo printers, color printers, label printers, and more. Many of these printers require special configurations so they can work correctly with NT.

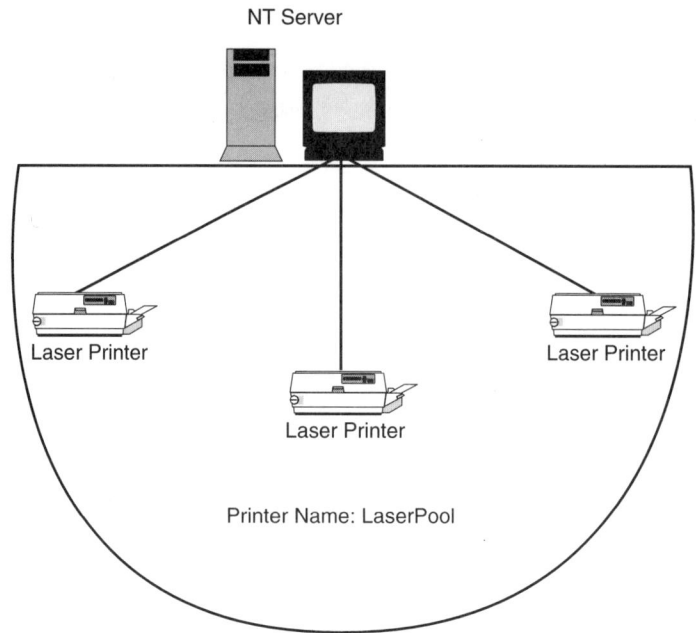

NT Server

Laser Printer

Laser Printer

Laser Printer

Printer Name: LaserPool

FIGURE 9.8 A printer named LaserPool that consists of three physical laser printers. Users see only one printer, named LaserPool.

Direct Network Interface Printers

Network interfaces for printers can free up resources on your server and improve your printing performance at the same time. Network interfaces generally plug into the special video port of HP Laserjet printers or into the parallel printer port, using a special network print server such as NetQue from Emulex. The difference in network printers normally is in their support for different protocols. For instance, the HP printer interfaces use DLC, whereas many others such as those from Emulex and Goldkey support TCP/IP, LAT, and other popular protocols.

Network interfaces reduce the need for special cables and ports because they can attach to the network just like a workstation or server. They also allow NT to manage the printer just as if it were directly attached to the NT server. Most network interfaces also improve the performance of your printer if it is a fast laser printer like the HP LaserjetIV si.

Another nice benefit of the network interface is the ability to manage the printer remotely if your printer and network interface support remote management. This feature should be coming to more and more printers in the future. Remote management usually gives you access to the printer over the network and enables you to check its status and issue commands to change its configuration.

DLC Printers

The network printer options from HP typically use DLC to talk to the printer. DLC is directly supported by NT and must be installed before you can configure a printer using this type of interface.

The limitation on total printers attached to a Windows NT Server print server should be determined by daily requirements for print throughput. Print throughput is determined by the processor capabilities. For example, a print server with approximately 64 MB RAM and a 486/66 or higher processor with a high throughput network card can support 25 to 30 DLC printers or 40 TCP/IP printers.

HP Laserjets with a DLC interface are easy to configure.

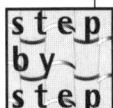

Configuring a Laserjet with a DLC Network Interface:

1. Decide which NT system will be the print server for the printer.
2. Install the DLC protocol in the Control Panel Network applet. Choose Add Software.
3. Use Print Manager to create a printer for the new device.
4. Select Network Port from the list and then HP or Other Network Port.
5. Configure the network address for the printer, and name the port.
6. Share the printer with a descriptive name. No other computer needs to have DLC installed to use the printer over the network.

TCP/IP Printers

The TCP/IP printing support of NT Server 3.51, especially with the NT 4.0 interface, is another one of those features that should make using printers on a network much easier. NT Server can manage a TCP/IP printer using the TCP/IP protocol on only the server that is used to control the printer. Other NT-compatible systems on the network can print on the printer using the same protocol they use for connecting to the NT server. Before installing a printer using TCP/IP, you must make sure that the TCP/IP printer support is installed.

Creating a TCP/IP Printer:

1. Make sure that the Microsoft TCP/IP printing service is running.
2. If in NT 3.51, create the printer using Print Manager (Click on Start, Settings and Printer, for NT 4.0).
3. In the Print To box choose Other, or click Add Printer and follow the instrustions, if in NT 4.0.
4. Choose LPT Port.

> 5. Enter the host address or name of the system providing the lpd (line printer daemon) service.
>
> 6. Enter the name of the printer on the system providing the lpd service. For instance, on Emulex printer servers, the default is PASSTHRU, whereas Goldkey print servers use HP_PRINTER.

Notice that step 5 can use the host IP address or the host name to define the printer destination. Using the actual name makes much more sense because it readily identifies the printer destination when you view the list. We carry this one step further and make the host name and the printer name almost the same. We simply prefix the host name with NJ for NetJet or something similar for your printer server. This step uniquely links the destination printer and print server name and eliminates many potential mistakes with mismatched printer destinations (IP address) and printers (printer name). Make sure that you can PING (see Chapter 4) a printer with its name before defining the printer. The print server IP address and name must be defined in the HOSTS file, WINS, or another method of name resolution.

PostScript Printer Characteristics

PostScript print devices require only slightly more care and feeding than generic print devices do. PostScript print devices process print jobs that consist of the PostScript language format in the print job. PostScript jobs are usually sent as ASCII files that are processed by the print device. PostScript print devices are normally much slower than other printers, taking what seems to be an eternity to print a file.

PostScript print devices also cause problems when you try to print non-PostScript files on them. These problems usually occur when you try to print an ASCII file from the NT DOS prompt, resulting in no printer output or an error on the printer. Likewise, when you send a PostScript file to a non-PostScript print device, you get a real mess. The print device usually starts printing lots of strange-looking codes on the device, prompting users to scream.

You should make sure that PostScript-specific drivers and configuration files are used for all PostScript printers. For instance, if you need a separator page, you must use the PSCRIPT.SEP file instead of the generic files.

Separator Pages

Separator pages are files that NT uses to separate documents that print on a printer. The files can contain codes that cause NT to print various types of information on the separator page identifying the user, file, print time, and so forth.

Each separator file uses a series of codes to determine the actions and text that is printed each time a document prints, as shown in Table 9.5.

TABLE 9.5	Separator Page Codes

Code	Description
/	Defines escape character for the file. Must be on the first line in the file. Make sure that this character does not conflict with other characters such as the \ used in file path names.
/B/M	Turns on printing double-width block characters. Turned off by a /U code.
/B/S	Turns on printing single-width block characters. Turned off by a /U code.
/D	Prints the print date for the job.
/E	Causes the printer to eject a page before printing the file. This is usually the last line in a separator file.
/Fpathname	Causes Print Manager to print the file pointed to by path name. You can change the contents of the separator page simply by changing this file.
/Hnn	Sends a hex code to the printer. The PCL.SEP file included with NT shows an example of using this code to send commands directly to the printer.
/I	Prints the job number for the print job.
/L*****	Prints the characters following /L until a new escape code is encountered.
/n	Skips the number of lines specified by n.
/N	Prints the user name of the user submitting the print job.
/T	Prints the time the job printed. Useful with /D.
/U	Turns off printing block characters.
/W	Allows you to change the separator page width. The default is 80 with a maximum of 256.

NT comes with several default separator files:

- PCL.SEP causes a printer to use switch to PCL mode.
- PSCRIPT.SEP causes a printer to use PostScript mode.
- PSLANMAN.SEP ejects a page before each document that prints.

You can specify only one separator page at a time per printer. The current separator page can be changed at any time. The Printer Details dialog box in Print Manager is used to change the current separator page. You can access Printer Details by first selecting Properties from the Printer menu and then clicking the Details button.

Simply enter the name of the separator page file in the Separator File box, and click OK. You can also select a separator page file by using the ... button next to the box. Separator pages are normally stored in the \WINNT35\SYSTEM32 directory.

Be sure to test the separator page after you have made the preceding changes by printing any file on the printer.

The best approach to building separator page files is to copy the standard NT file that most closely matches the printer you will use. For instance, for a Laserjet using PCL, choose the PCL.SEP page file and copy it to a new name. Change the file using Notepad or some other ASCII editor, and test.

Printer Messages

NT automatically sends a message to the user who has submitted a print job, notifying him or her of the status of a print job when it completes. This feature is handy for network users who are normally located at some distance from the physical print device. Figures 9.9 and 9.10 show what typical messages look like on NT 3.51 and NT 4.0, respectively.

This message can be displayed on systems that pick up messages from the NT Messenger service. NT systems do this automatically, but Windows for Workgroups may not. The solution is to start WinPopUp in the Windows for Workgroups client.

Starting WinPopUp on Windows for Workgroups Clients:

1. Start Control Panel on the Windows for Workgroups client.
2. Start the Network applet.
3. Click the Startup button.
4. Click the Enable WinPopUp check box.
5. Click OK.

WinPopUp starts the next time Windows restarts. You can also start WinPopUp directly by starting WINPOPUP.EXE in the Windows directory. Make sure that you do not close WinPopUp, or you will disable messaging.

You can install WinPopUp over the network for remote users. Simply edit the WIN.INI file, and place WinPopUp in the Load= line:

```
Load=Winpopup.exe
```

Specifying WINPOPUP.EXE on the Load= line starts WinPopUp as an icon each time Windows starts. You could automate the task by using SMS or another tool to update the user's WIN.INI file automatically the next time the user logs on.

Printing from an NT System to a Remote NT Printer

NT clients printing on remote printers controlled by other NT systems is a dream environment. An NT system does not normally need a driver installed for a remote printer as long as that printer is managed by another NT system.

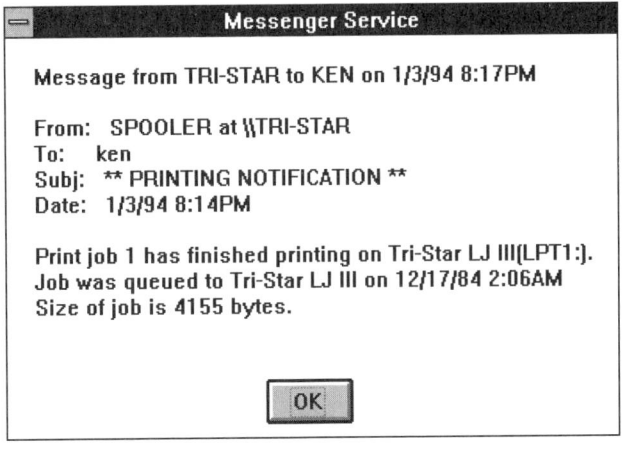

FIGURE 9.9 A message triggered when a print job is completed in NT 3.51.

When a user connects to a remote printer from an NT workstation or server, the spooler determines which printer driver is needed and then copies the driver to the DRIVERS directory of the user's system. If the spooler determines that the driver already exists but is an older version than the one on the server, it automatically updates the driver with the new version. The user must have write permission to the DRIVERS directory if he or she is using a remote printer.

The exception to this rule occurs when the driver already exists on the NT system from which the user is trying to connect. In this case, the connect operation works even if the spooler is not able to replace the driver, because there already is a compatible driver installed. NT in this instance automatically

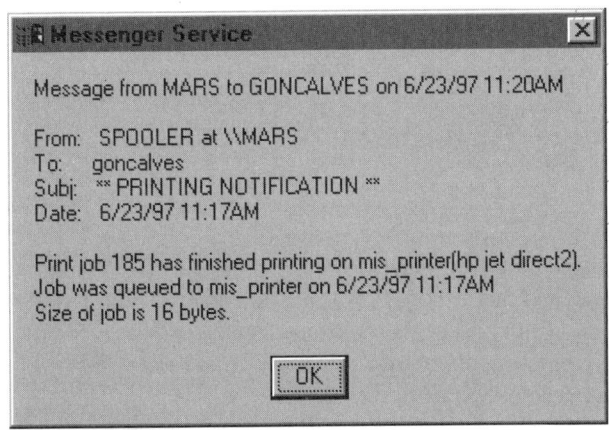

FIGURE 9.10 The Messenger Service box in NT 4.0 as it displays when a print job is completed.

uses the driver on the system managing the printer by downloading it into memory on the local system for the duration of the printing requirements.

You may run into problems with NT clients printing to printers that are managed by NT systems running on different architectures. For instance, an Intel client prints to a printer managed by an Alpha NT Server. In this scenario, for the client to be able to use the driver, the NT system managing the printer must have drivers for both systems available.

Installing a Nonnative Print Driver on a Server (NT 3.51):

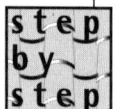

1. From a remote system (not the system managing the printer), log on the domain with an Administrative account.
2. Start Print Manager.
3. Choose Server Viewer from the Printer menu.
4. Select the server that manages the printer for which you wish to install the driver.
5. Select the first printer for which you need to install a driver.
6. Choose Properties from the Printer menu.
7. Enter the location for the printer drivers.
8. Repeat steps 5 and 6 for each printer that needs drivers for the architecture of the system from which you are currently logged on.

Installing a Nonnative Print Driver on a Server (NT 4):

1. Open the Printer Folder and open the Properties for the printer.
2. Click the Sharing. . .tab.
3. Select the operating system for which you need the driver.
4. Click OK to copy the driver.

Note: You will need the installation CD or other access to the printer driver for each OS type.

Printers on Non-NT Systems

Printing on non-NT print devices is slightly different from using an NT print device. A non-NT print device in this discussion is considered any printer that is attached to another system such as Windows for Workgroups or UNIX and is managed by that system. NT cannot use the printer driver from a non-NT system and must have a locally installed NT driver for the printer. NT prompts you to install on your system a driver that matches the target Printer.

This process works in the same fashion as printing on a Windows 3.x system. The printer you install on NT is simply connected to the print queue on the target system. You must be a member of the Administrators group to install a printer, because the driver must be into the Windows NT directory tree.

Using Printers from Network Clients

Microsoft network clients share the same basic printer connection interface via the NET commands. Windows systems add another interface via Print Manager or Windows 95.

Workgroup Add-On for MS-DOS and MS Client

The NET USE command is used to connect to printers from MS-DOS systems using the Workgroup Add-On for MS-DOS. The syntax is

```
NET USE port \\computername\sharename [password]
```

The following command illustrates how to use this command to attach to the LAS printer on the KENS server:

```
NET USE LPT1: \\KENS\LAS
```

Once this command is complete, the user can access this printer as LPT1. To disconnect from the printer on LPT1, enter the following command:

```
NET USE LPT1: /delete
```

Windows for Workgroups

Windows for Workgroups users can connect to printers on the domain quickly. Print Manager makes the connections in much the same way that File Manager makes file resource connections. The Printer applet in Control Panel can also be used to connect printers, as well as the Network button found on many Printer dialogs in applications.

Connecting to Network Printers with Print Manager:

1. Start Print Manager.
2. Select the printer you wish to connect.
3. Click the Connect button.
4. Choose the correct port from the device list.
5. Choose the network printer from the browse box, or enter the UNC name in the Path box.
6. Click OK.

Connecting to Network Printers with Control Panel:

1. Start Control Panel.
2. Double-click the Printers applet icon.
3. Select the printer you wish to connect.

---

4. Click the Connect button.

5. Select the port to connect from the list.

6. If the port is not already connected to the appropriate network printer, click the Network button.

7. Choose the correct port from the device list.

8. Choose the network printer from the browse box or enter the UNC name in the Path box.

9. Click OK.

10. Click OK on the Connect box.

11. Click Close.

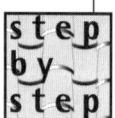

Connecting to Network Printers Using NET USE:

You can use the same command prompt approach as the Work Group Add-On for MS-DOS and MS Client.

1. Enter the proper NET USE command at the command prompt. The following example shows the successful completion of this command.

```
net use lpt2: \\ntas-tri-star\hp_lj_ii
```

The command completed successfully.

Newer applications also provide the ability to connect to network printers in the Printer Setup dialog box. This is usually indicated by a Network button on the dialog box. Click the button. The standard browse dialog box for connecting to printers should be displayed.

Windows 95

Windows 95 incorporates a totally new printing system compared to Windows for Workgroups. As mentioned previously, it is exactly the same as the NT 4.0 interface. The Printers folder (accessed from the Start menu, Settings option) contains icons for all the printers for a client and the Add Printer application. Add Printer is a wizard that walks you through the con-figuration of a printer. The Printers folder is shown in Figure 9.11.

The Printers folder is accessed from the Start menu and can optionally be placed on the desktop. You can also place any printer icon or the Add Printer application directly on the desktop.

Adding a Network Printer with Windows 95 or NT 4.0:

1. Open the Printers folder and start the Add Printer application.

2. Follow the prompts of the wizard.

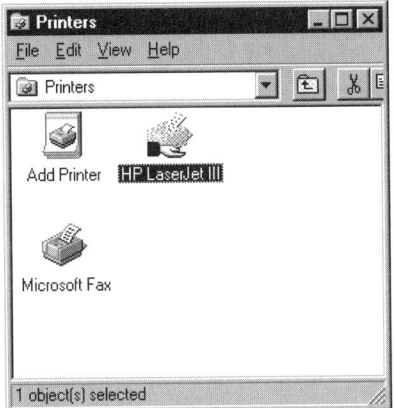

FIGURE 9.11 A sample Printer folder with only one printer and Microsoft Fax connection. Printers are created with the Add Printer application.

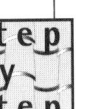

3. Specify Network Printer instead of Local Printer by highlighting the Network Printer button.

4. Enter the queue name (UNC), or click the Browse button to select the printer. Drill down with the mouse to select the printer from the browse list.

5. Answer the remaining prompts to complete the installation.

You can change a local printer to a network printer by using the Printer application for that printer and accessing the printer's properties. Windows 95 also lets you create printer ports, which are simply connections to network printers. A printer port does not require that a printer exist or be connected to the port when it is created. This is a big change over other versions of Windows, which required a specific printer be attached to a network port. Figure 9.12 illustrates the new interface for a printer in Windows 95.

Connecting to a Network Printer with Windows 95:

1. Start the Printer application for the printer you wish to connect to the network resource. Select the Properties option from the Printer menu. You can optionally simply right-click on the icon for the printer and select properties.

2. Click the Details tab.

3. Choose the port to use for the printer from the drop-down list. You can easily add a new connection by clicking the Add Port button and choosing Browse.

4. Click OK.

The Properties dialog box is shown in Figure 9.13.
The NET commands also work with Windows 95.

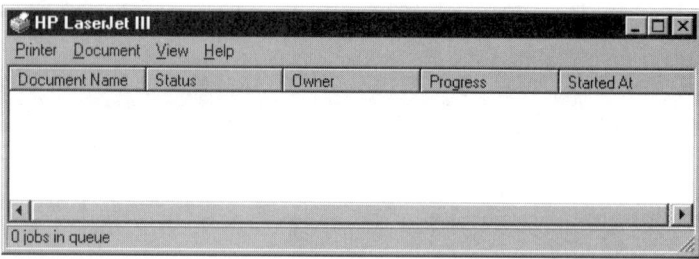

FIGURE 9.12 The Windows 95 Printer application has a nice clean interface. The Printer menu contains the Properties option for access to the detailed setup for the printer, including network connections.

Non-NT Print Servers

NT supports printing to non-NT print servers. You can print directly from NT and NT Server to a non-NT print server, as long as the correct network and printer protocols are in place. Your other non-NT client workstations such as Windows for Workgroups and Windows 95 can also print to these non-NT printers if the protocols are in place.

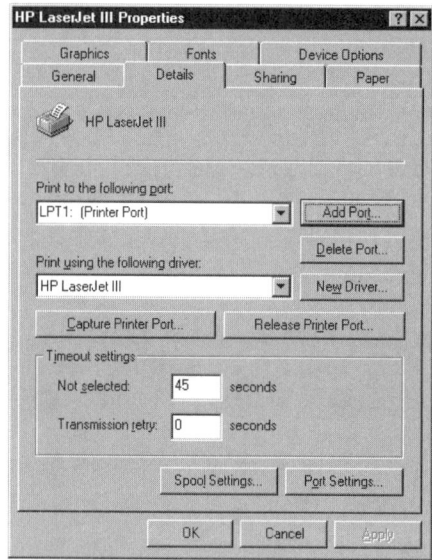

FIGURE 9.13 The Properties dialog box contains the network settings for a printer and most other printer-related settings. The network information is contained under the Details tab.

Windows for Workgroups

Windows 95 and Windows for Workgroups 3.11 are the preferred choice for non-NT computer-based print servers.

Windows for Workgroups handles printers well with Print Manager and with third-party tools such as the laser printer upgrades from LaserMaster Corporation.

The main drawback to using Windows 95 or Windows for Workgroups or any other system (except for NT) as a print server is that the operating system does not automatically share the printer drivers with NT. Windows for Workgroups uses a printer driver just like all Windows 3.x systems in that the driver must be installed and configured on the workstation before you can connect to and use a printer.

The steps for creating your Windows for Workgroups print server are deceptively simple.

Creating a Windows for Workgroups Print Server:

1. Connect the printer and configure Windows for Workgroups with the proper driver.
2. Share the printer with Print Manager.
3. Connect to the printer from remote workstations.

Workgroup Add-On for MS-DOS

The Workgroup Add-On for MS-DOS can be used as a low-cost print server on low-end DOS systems. We suggest using Workgroup Add-On for MS-DOS only for systems that do not run Windows well such as 386/25 or slower systems or systems with less than 4MB of memory. Systems that run Windows adequately should use Windows for Workgroups or Windows 95 as a print server.

The steps for creating your Workgroup Add-On for MS-DOS print server are easy and are almost exactly the same as the steps for Windows for Workgroups.

Creating a Workgroup Add-On for MS-DOS Print Server:

1. Connect the printer and configure Workgroup Add-On for MS-DOS with the proper driver.
2. Share the printer with NET SHARE.
3. Connect to the printer from remote workstations.

Once you have shared the printer, you can manage print jobs from the Workgroup Add-On from MS-DOS workstation. The command used for managing printers and displaying information about current print jobs is NET PRINT.

NET PRINT works with the current system and other systems. The syntax for displaying information about print jobs is

```
NET PRINT \\computername[\printername] | port
```

Entering NET PRINT with no options displays all printers on the current system and the respective print jobs for each. You can display the print queue for a remote system by entering

```
NET PRINT \\DOSPRT
```

This command displays all the print queues and associated print jobs for the system named DOSPRT. You can refine the output by entering the printer name after the computer name, as in the following example:

```
NET PRINT \\DOSPRT\PRTR1
```

The other option for displaying information is to use the port name for a local printer to display the associated print queue and print jobs. The following command displays the printers on LPT2:

```
NET PRINT LPT2:
```

The output of the command displays the name of the queue and the details of the print jobs. The details include both totals for all jobs for a queue and the individual job name, status, and size. The following command shows the command format:

```
NET PRINT LPT1:
```

and the resulting output:

```
Printer queues

Name      Job # Size  Status

-------------------------------

KENS Queue     2 Jobs        * Queue Active *
               102 231   Printing
               105 1022  Waiting
```

NET PRINT can also be used to manage your print queues. The syntax for the management options is

```
NET PRINT \\computername[\printername] | port
job# /pause -
| /resume | /delete
```

The options for this command (/pause, /resume, and /delete) cannot all be used at the same time. Table 9.6 explains these options.

TABLE 9.6	Net Print Options

Option	Description
/Pause	Suspends the print job specified with the command until /Resume or /Delete is entered.
/Resume	Causes a paused print job to continue.
/Delete	Deletes the specified print job.

The job number is entered after the printer specification. The next command shows how to delete job number 102 on the current system:

```
NET PRINT lpt1: 102 /delete
```

You can also specify a computer name if you wish to delete a print job on a remote system. The following command deletes job 102 on KENS:

```
NET PRINT \\KENS 102 /delete
```

Print job numbers are unique for a given system even if the system has multiple printers. These numbers allow you to specify only the computer name in a command related to print jobs.

```
NET PRINT \\DOSPRT\PRTR1

NET SHARE sharename=portname [/remark:"text"]
[/saveshare:no] [/full:password]
```

The syntax looks much more complex than it is. The following command shares the printer attached to LPT2: as DOTPRT and adds a comment:

```
NET SHARE DOTPRT=LPT2: /remark:"Kens office"
```

The following example performs the same share, except that it assigns the password MINE to the printer:

```
NET SHARE DOTPRT=LPT2: /remark:"Kens office"
/full:MINE
```

If you add a share password, you can restrict the printer to users who know the share password.

NET SHARE is also used to delete existing shares. The following command deletes the printer DOTPRT:

```
NET SHARE DOTPRT/delete
```

NetWare Printers

Did we say that correctly? What are NetWare printers doing in a chapter on NT Server printers? The NWLINK and NetWare Compatible Gateway provide access to both file and print services on NetWare servers. See Chapter 4 for information on installing the gateway, on sharing print and file resources on a NetWare server, and on sharing NetWare printers to NT Server clients.

Conclusion

This chapter has introduced you to the NT printing systems and to many of the thing you can do with it. You should also spend time with the Microsoft KnowledgeBase, found on either the Microsoft Web site (www .microsoft.com) or Microsoft TechNet. Both of these tools are invaluable for day-to-day use in managing an NT network printing solution.

The next chapter will take us into the world of disaster preparedness and management with NT. We take a look at topics such as RAID systems and tape backup solutions. There are also many new options that are coming out for NT, to assist you in keeping your servers and networks running and fixing them quickly when they fail.

Disaster Preparedness and Management

NT provides many different options for disaster preparedness. The most obvious are tape backup and some type of online backup for disk drives such as mirrored or duplexed drives. More sophisticated systems use RAID 5 to provide faster access to disk storage and fault tolerance.

Scenario 10.1:

You have just installed your NT Server and are looking at disaster preparedness options with some concern. Should you go with a tape backup, or forgo the tape backup because you have RAID 5? Should you use one of the traditional tape backup solutions, or go with one of the new options?

Scenario 10.2:

Your server dies on Friday at 5:01 P.M. Are you ready to tackle the job of getting it back up quickly, or will you spend Friday night staring at various configuration options?

What happens when a critical component such as a CPU or a memory chip goes out? This type of problem usually brings down a server regardless of what type of backup you have for the drives. Octopus Technologies provides a product called Octopus that provides real-time backup of selected files or directories to another server. Digital Equipment Corporation and AT&T, as well as Microsoft itself, are working on clustering technology for NT. Wolfpack, the clustering technology already in beta test by Microsoft, should allow NT to have two or more servers in a cluster providing improved performance and hot-swapover if a server goes down.

Other aspects of disaster preparedness are the mundane but critical things such as backup schedules and off-site storage of backup media. These items are often left over and fall by the wayside, but they can be the most critical part of the plan. Remember that the job is not complete until the paperwork is done.

This chapter introduces you to the backup strategies to use with NT. It is vital to understand the various options that Microsoft and other vendors provide you for preparing for the worst. The worst will come at some time, as indicated by Murphy's Law: If you are ready, it's an inconvenience. If you aren't, then you're in trouble!

Maintaining Tape Devices

NT supports a variety of different tape devices for backup. Before you start a backup on an NT tape device, you must install the tape device in the system and configure NT. Once this is completed, you can use the device with the NT Backup program.

NT supports several different tape devices out of the box. Hardware vendors that offer new products should also provide drivers if the current drivers don't work with their products. You may be able to use the generic option "4 millimeter DAT drive" for different drives of this type. I have successfully used this option with drives from Conner (MS2000DAT) and Digital Equipment (TLZ06 and the TLZ07).

DAT and DLT drives are our favorite option because of their high capacity and fast performance over older drives. The new DLT drives from some vendors offer extremely high capacity in a small package.

To add a tape device on NT 4.0 is much simpler then with NT 3.51. Figure 10.1 shows a screenshot of the Tape Devices applet in Control Panel.

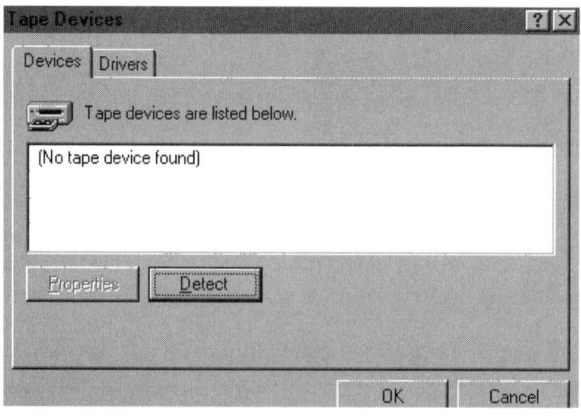

FIGURE 10.1 The Tape Device configuration box.

Adding a Tape Device on NT 4.0:

1.   From the Start button, click Setting, then Control Panel.
2.   Click the Tape Devices icon.
3.   Click the Detect button (NT will attempt to detect your backup drive).
4.   If necessary, click the Drivers tab to change your backup driver.

Adding a Tape Device on NT 3.51:

1.   Start the NT setup program.
2.   Select Add/Remove Tape Devices from the Options menu.
3.   Select your drive from the list or select the Other (requires a disk from a hardware manufacturer) option, which enables you to load a driver that is not listed.
4.   Once you have selected your tape device from the list, click the Install button to complete loading the driver.
5.   Once the tape device is loaded, you must restart NT before the change takes effect.

Another option for maintaining tape devices if you are using NT 3.51 is to use the Tape Devices applet from the NT Resource Kit in Control Panel. This applet is designed to perform one task only, and that is to make life easier for managing tape devices under NT. It is very useful for many tasks. For instance, one of us had removed a Colorado Memory Systems floppy tape from an NT system, and all of a sudden the SCSI tape drive quit working. I tried to reinstall using Setup and checked the devices on the system, among other things, but to no avail. Then I fired up the Tape Devices applet, selected the tape drive, and clicked Setup. Tape Devices informed me that as soon as I started the 4-mm dat service, the device would be ready. When I clicked the Start button, the drive was ready.

Tape devices can also be used to check the status of your tape device. Figures 10.2 through 10.4 illustrate the interface of the applet in NT 3.51 and show off its features.

Tape Devices is a handy tool to have around for managing tape devices.

Adding a Tape Drive with Tape Devices:

1.   Start the Tape Device applet in Control Panel.
2.   Select the tape drive to install. If the correct drive is not listed, make sure it is attached to the system and turned on, and then click the Rescan button.
3.   Click the Setup button.

4. Click the Add button to display the list of available drivers.

5. Select the correct driver from the list.

6. Complete the prompts for installing the new driver. You will probably have to reboot the system to recognize the new driver.

Removing a Tape Drive with Tape Devices:

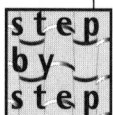

1. Start the Tape Device applet in Control Panel.

2. Select the tape drive to remove.

3. Click the Setup button.

4. Click the Remove button.

5. Complete the prompts to remove the driver.

Stopping a Tape Drive with Tape Devices:

1. Start the Tape Device applet in Control Panel.

2. Select the tape drive to stop.

3. Click the Setup button.

4. Select the driver to stop and click the Stop button.

With NT 4.0, the process is similar, but as you can see in Figure 10.5 and 10.6, the interface is a little different.

After NT is restarted, the new tape device will be visible to NT. Using the Backup program, you can select Hardware Setup from the Operations menu to verify that the new device is loaded. Selecting Hardware Setup displays a dialog box that should list the new drive. If the drive is not visible as the current selection in the list, drop the list by clicking on the Down arrow, and you should see the new drive. If not, there was most likely a problem in configuring the new device with Setup. In this case, go to Control Panel by

FIGURE 10.2 The Tape Devices dialog box showing one tape drive loaded.

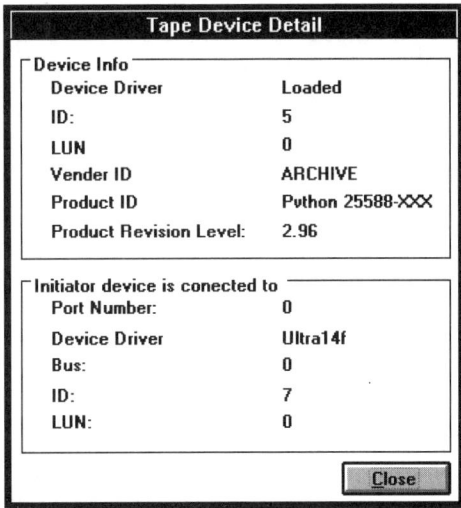

FIGURE 10.3 The Tape Device Detail dialog box
showing the current status of the device,
the SCSI port used for the device, and
details for the controller to which the device is attached.

clicking Start, selecting Settings, and then clicking Control Panel, and select
the Tape Devices applet. Click on the Driver tab and verify that the tape
driver was loaded, as shown in Figure 10.7.

If the tape device is not there, add it manually by clicking over the Add
button, as shown in Figure 10.8.

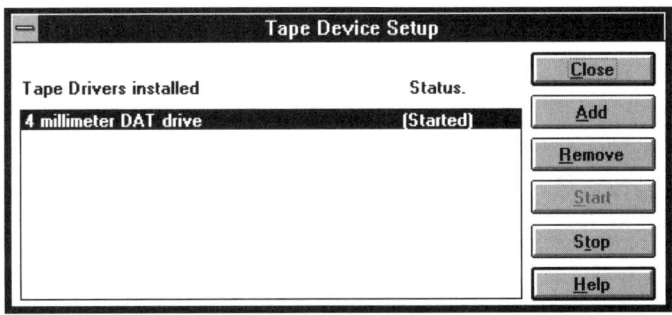

FIGURE 10.4 The Tape Device Setup dialog box is used to
add or remove a driver for a tape drive. You
can also start and stop the drive from this
dialog box.

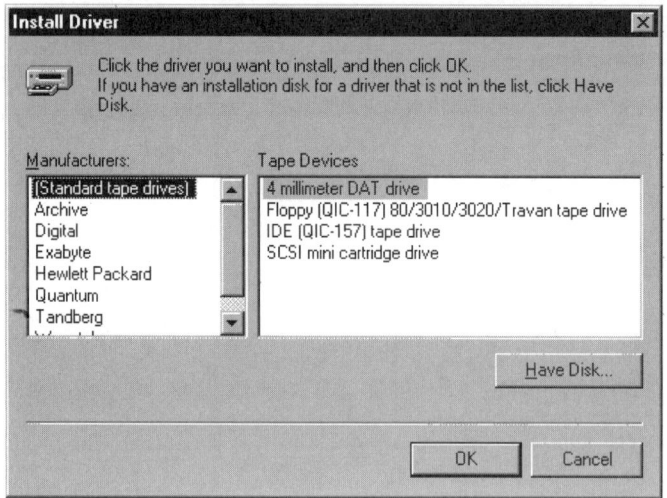

FIGURE 10.5 Installing a new device driver in NT 4.0.

FIGURE 10.6 Rescanning tape devices in NT 4.0.

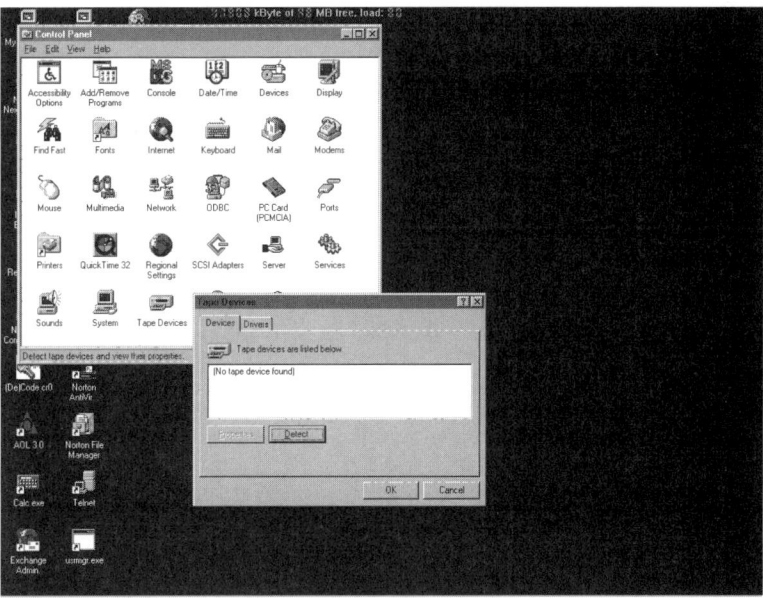

FIGURE 10.7 Verifying that the tape drive is loaded on NT 4.0 through the Tape Devices applet.

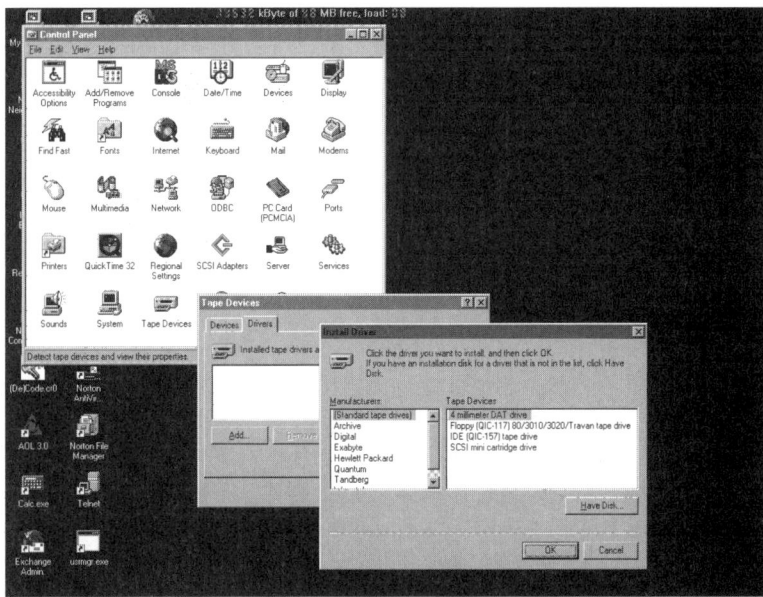

FIGURE 10.8 Manually adding a tape driver at the Tape Devices applet of NT 4.0.

Setting Up a Successful Backup Strategy

When you set up backup strategies, always keep Murphy's Law in mind: "Whatever can go wrong, WILL go wrong." This means:

- If you have a backup policy implemented for your network, a disaster will surely strike, and there will be no way for you to recover your data and applications.
- If you don't have a regular backup schedule in place, when disaster strikes, you will need to recover data exactly from the day(s) when your backup didn't run (or when you didn't think it was necessary!).
- If you always use the same batch of tapes to perform your backups, the tape will wear out exactly on the day when you need it to recover your CEO's personal files!

You think we're kidding? Everyone involved with computers, and especially with backup routines, has gone through one or more of these experiences. Believe it! Accidents happen, from a component that fails, to user error, to natural causes (floods, earthquakes, and other fun things). Therefore, you must have in place a reliable backup-and-recovery policy.

Much of your plan will concern the backup software and the hardware you're using, which will be discussed in more detail throughout this chapter. Everyone tells you how important it is to make backups, but often explicit guidelines are hard to find.

Generally speaking, we can have two types of backup: 1) the system backup (a backup of the operating system) and 2) the applications (files that only you, the administrator, should be allowed to change) and the user backup (a backup of the users' files). It is important that you treat system backups differently from the user backups.

System Backups

System backups are important because they can greatly minimize the effort required during recovery, in case of a crash, when you're trying to get the system up and running again. However, you don't want to spend most of your time making sure backup is running; there is much more to watch for when you're managing an NT network. The key to backing up effectively is to back up only what is absolutely necessary to enable speedy recovery when disaster strikes.

Let's assume that:

- Your system is fairly stable.
- Being a responsible administrator, you keep an updated copy of the repair disk.
- You did a full system's backup once you finished configuring your server.

Because we're assuming that your system is stable (if not, make sure it is!), let's take a look at what is likely to change on NT. One way your system will change is if you add new programs (software that didn't come as part of your NT distribution set).

When you install new software, be organized and keep any new programs separate from those on the distribution. Create directories and subdirectories in your drive in order to effectively separate and distinguish the new applications you're loading in your server. The major advantage of doing this is that you can easily see which programs you can restore from your distribution, and which programs you need to restore from elsewhere.

Another thing you are likely to change is the configuration files (registry, groups, systems setting) and users profiles. Many times, NT will "invisibly"' edit some of these files for you, based on your responses to certain questions, but often you have to edit them yourself.

A lot of the important files live in the /system32 directory. Depending on your setup, there are likely to be many others as well. Of course, some programs will use files in other places, but most of the basic NT systems files are configured under \\system32 and \\system directories.

Therefore, it is important to keep track of what changes you've made, so that, should disaster strike, you can get them back easily. The best way to do this is to make a note of all the modifications you make to the system (get yourself a log notebook and leave it next to your server), no matter how trivial they seem at the time, and always to update your repair disk.

User Backups

User backups are different from system backups, in that a user's files are liable to change frequently. It will almost certainly be impossible for you to have up-to-the-minute backups of a given user's file space. However, there are products that can do that.

In backing up user files, you are offering your users a virtual safety net—reasonably recent copies of their files they can fall back on if they do something silly (DEL *.* instead of DEL *.tmp—it does happen!), or if the hard disk fails.

User backups will have to be done much more frequently than system backups, most often daily. One useful feature of many backup programs is the ability to backup only files that have changed after a certain date (the last time you did a backup, for example). This can drastically reduce the amount of work in a user backup, because a user is likely to be working on only a small number of files at a given time. You can combine occasional full backups of your user space with more frequent incremental backups.

While it is possible to use floppy disks for your backups, each disk can only hold a small amount of data. Many programs allow a backup to span several disks, but this means that you have to be there to change them while the backup is taking place. If you only have a small system with few users, then this might be feasible, but often it isn't. Magnetic or digital tapes are probably a better choice, simply because of their higher capacity.

Both NT 4.0 and NT 3.51 support a wide range of tape drives. The price of tape drives has fallen quite dramatically, and they are now a realistic option for many. Alternately, your NT server might be on the same network as another machine with a tape drive. NT can also access tapes on remote machines.

You should look after whatever media you choose. Your backup is there for when things go wrong, so it is important that you can rely on it. You should always verify your backups; an unverified backup is worse than no backup at all.

You should also keep more than one set of backups. A popular strategy is based on the "grandfather-father-son" idea. You have three sets of backups; the last one (the son), the one before that (the father), and the one before that (the grandfather). When you do your next backup, you copy over the grandfather, so the son becomes the father, the father becomes the grandfather, and the grandfather is replaced with a new son. The advantage of this strategy is that should one of the sets fail, you at least have something to fall back on, but you don't have to make more than one backup at a time.

The next piece of advice might sound strange at first: Always keep at least one backup well away from your machine, preferably in a completely different building. In case of fire in the building, you can still recover the data once you have a new server ready to go.

The data on your computer make up its most valuable and irreplaceable component, so treat it with care.

Tape Backup Programs

There are many backup options available for NT. As NT has grown in market share, the vendors that supported NetWare and other platforms have now moved their products to NT. That's good news for the NT systems manager, as the backup program included with NT is severely lacking in robustness.

NT's Backup Program

NT's backup program works well enough, but it is not our favorite. Both the graphical interface and the command prompt method are very slow when they are used with a floppy interface tape (such as those from Colorado Memory Systems)—and we do mean slow. Neither of the programs uses any compression on the tape, so the backup tapes are limited in how much they can back up.

The capability of the NT Backup program is also somewhat limited. Backup does not have the ability to store catalogs or predefined backup sets. Other parts of the interface are also rather rudimentary compared to the Central Point or Norton backup programs for Windows 3.x. Arcada Software (formerly Conner Systems, now acquired by Seagate) developed the program for Microsoft and markets a more powerful backup program, Backup Exec. See "Backup Exec" Server.

Many vendors such as Cheyenne and others have moved their backup offerings to NT. These new offerings provide options that are required for most production NT systems. Scheduled backups, catalogs, shared tape drives across multiple systems, and other options make these programs a must-have.

You should also note that Windows 95 includes backup agents for Backup EXEC but not for the standard backup program. Windows 95 also includes an agent for the Cheyenne backup program for NT.

NT BACKUP (GRAPHICAL METHOD)

The NT backup program is easy to use for casual backups and for restoring files. Make sure that your tape device is installed and configured for NT (see "Maintaining Tape Devices" above)

We suggest running a test of the tape device to make sure that it works correctly before proceeding too far. Perform a backup of just a few directories to the device, and make sure that you have Verify After Backup checked.

The backup program is composed of three windows and a menu across the top. Table 10.1 describes the various windows.

Backup creates a separate save set for each volume that is backed up.

TABLE 10.1 Backup Program Windows

Window	Description
File	Contains a list of the directories and files on the currently selected drive. The directories and/or files selected for backup have the check box to the left of the name checked.
Drives	Shows the drives on the local system and any current network connections.
Tapes	Is normally minimized when you start backup, and shows the current tape in the tape drive. The tape and creation date are shown on the left, and the drive and other information are shown on the right.

The requirement to use a formatted tape poses a potential problem when you perform a backup that spans several tapes and there is no formatted tape available. Backup rejects the new tape until it has been formatted, and you can't format it until the backup is complete. The only solution is to use a formatted tape or abort the backup and restart it after you have formatted the tape.

You will be forced to erase a tape before you use it when you use a tape for the first time with backup.

Erasing a Tape (Backup—Graphical Method):

1. Place the tape to be erased in the drive.
2. Select the Erase Tape option on the Operations menu.

Performing a Backup (Backup—Graphical Method):

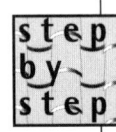

1. Select the files to back up.
2. Place a tape in the tape drive.
3. Select the Backup option either from the Operations menu or the Backup icon.
4. Complete the Backup Information dialog box, and click OK.

Backup takes over and performs its tasks without interruption.

The Backup Information dialog box appears after you have instructed backup to begin the Backup operation. The backup occurs when you click the Backup icon or select Backup from the Operations menu. Table 10.2 contains the options and parameters displayed on the Backup Information dialog box.

NT BACKUP (COMMAND PROMPT)

The problem with the graphical Backup program is its lack of automation. The NTBackup program can be also accessed from the command prompt. Running NTBackup from the command line is better than the graphical method for setting up automated operations from a batch file. NTBackup is also useful in conjunction with the NT Scheduler's AT command.

NTBackup's command-line options provide many of the same features as the graphical format, but they are much more useful for backup operations because NTBackup can be used to automate the operations.

NTBackup solves this somewhat by using the familiar command-line interface and a variety of switches to control its operation. This is the syntax for the command. Note that BACKUP is the operation name and is the only valid operation.

```
NTBACKUP BACKUP [pathname(s) options]
```

pathname(s) Describes the path(s) that the command will back up. The pathname is specified by listing the path(s), separated by spaces after the word BACKUP.

options Specifies exactly how the backup operation will be performed. The options allowed are the same as those for the graphical backup command, but they use switches to select the option.

TABLE 10.2 Backup Information Dialog Box Options

Option	Description
Current Tape	Displays the current tape name, if the tape has been used before.
Creation Date	Displays the date the original backup set was created or the date when it was last replaced.
Owner	The owner of the tape, which will be the user account name of the individual making the first backup to the tape.
Tape Name	Contains the name of the tape. The name can be 1 to 32 characters in length.
Append or Replace	The Operation box contains two options. Append instructs NT Backup to append the save set(s) to the tape. Replace instructs NT Backup to overwrite the contents of the tape. When Replace is specified and more than one backup set is required (for instance for multiple path names), NT Backup overwrites the tape with the first save set and then appends the balance of the save sets to the tape.
Verify	Causes NT Backup to verify the contents of the backup sets created. The verification process is performed in a second pass through the tape after the backup files are created.
Backup Local Registry	Causes NT Backup to back up the Registry information on the system running NT Backup. See the section on using RDisk in Chapter 6 for more information on protecting the Registry backups on multiple systems.
Restrict Access to Owner or Administrator	Restricts access to the owner of the tape and a user with administrator privileges.
Drive Name	Displays the name of the drive backed up on the current save set.
Description	Enables you to add a description to your backup save set. Specifies the description text in the appropriate box.

TABLE 10.2	Backup Information Dialog Box Options (Continued)

Option	Description
Backup Type	Specifies the type of backup operation. Allowable options are:
	Normal Specifies that a normal (full) backup be performed and that each file be marked as backed up.
	Copy Performs a normal backup but will not mark the files as backed up.
	Incremental Backs up all files that are marked as modified on the path specified. Files processed are marked as backed up.
	Differential Performs an incremental backup but does not mark the files.
	Daily Causes all files modified today to be backed up. The files processed will not be backed up.
Log File	Specifies the file name for the log file. The ... button beside the Log File box can be clicked to display a dialog box, to select an existing log file.
Full Detail	Instructs Backup to write the full details of each operation to the log file, including the file names and directories processed in the backup.
Summary Only	Can be used to cause the log file to contain only exceptions and major operations, drastically reducing the size of the file and making it much easier to spot errors in the backup process.
Don't Log	Instructs Backup to not log any information.

Table 10.3 lists each option. For full details on the options, see "NT Backup (Graphical Method)," above.

Now that we have covered the gory details of syntax for this command, let's see how this command can be used to our advantage.

```
NTBACKUP BACKUP C:\ /D "Backup Number 1" /B /L -
"c:\BackupLog" /E /T NORMAL
```

Note that this command is continued on two lines for clarity only. The entire command must be on a single line, whether it is executed at the DOS prompt or in a batch program.

Using NTBackup with the NT Scheduler

The NT Scheduler service is powerful and easy to use. Chapter 3, "Server Configuration and Management," has details on configuring the Scheduler service. One important distinction for the service is important when it is used to drive the NT Backup command: If the Scheduler is used with NT Backup,

TABLE 10.3	NT Backup Command Line Options

Option	Description
blank or /A	The mode option uses a blank or /A. /A instructs NTBackup to append the save set(s) to the tape. If /A is not specified, NTBackup overwrites the contents of the tape. When /A is not specified and more than one backup set is required (for instance for multiple path names), NTBackup overwrites the tape with the first save set and then appends the balance of the save sets to the tape.
/V	The verify option is specified with /V and causes NTBackup to verify the contents of the backup sets created. The verification process is performed in a second pass through the tape after the backup files are created.
/R	Restricts access to the owner of the resources backed up and a user with administrator privileges.
/D "text"	Allows you to add a description to your backup save set. Specifies the description text after the /D and a space. The text should be enclosed in quotes.
/B	Causes NT Backup to back up the Registry information on the system running NTBackup.
/T option	Specifies the type of backup operation. Allowable options are
	Normal — Specifies that a normal (full) backup be performed and that each file be marked as backed up.
	Copy — Performs a normal backup but does not mark the files as backed up.
	Incremental — Backs up all files that are marked as modified on the path specified. Files processed are marked as backed up.
	Differential — Performs an Incremental backup but does not mark the files.
	Daily — Causes all files modified today to be backed up. The files processed are not backed up.
/L "filename"	/L is used to specify the file name for the log file. Place the file name in quotes, and insert a space between /L and the name.
/E	/E can be used to cause the log file to contain only exceptions and major operations.

then the account used by the Scheduler must be a member of the Backup Operators group.

This change can be made by running User Manager and placing the account for the Scheduler in the Backup Operators group. Make sure that you also provide for the account to be used on all servers in the domain.

We recommend using a batch program to contain the actual NT Backup command(s) that is used by the Scheduler. A batch program makes it easy to manage the command syntax and properly debug the process. You can even include the entire syntax for the Scheduler and the backup process in the batch program. You may want to create a Visual Basic program that sets up the entire process each time NT boots.

Using the Scheduler with a Backup Batch Program:

1. Create a batch program with your backup commands (BACKUPNORM is used in this example).
2. Place the batch program in a directory that is on the path in order for it to be located by NT.
3. Set up the schedule by executing the AT command, as in the following example:

```
AT 03:00 /every:M,T,W,TH,F BACKUPNORM
```

Other Backup Options

The backup program included in NT is somewhat limited in its capabilities. For instance, Backup can't save different backup configurations. If you want to back up several different directory structures from one disk and then back up several other directories from another disk, except that for the second disk you want to skip several subdirectories under one directory while still backing up other directories under the same main directory this is easy to define with the graphical backup program, but you can't save the settings. To accomplish the same thing with the NT backup command, you need to develop several different commands and place them in a batch file.

Another backup option adds more capabilities to the backup process and makes it a lot easier—the Arcada Backup Exec Server.

ARCADA BACKUP EXEC SERVER

Arcada Software is the company that developed the NT Backup program. Arcada is the same company that used to be called Maynard, then Conner Systems; it has been acquired by Seagate. Backup Exec is an enhanced version of the NT Backup program and fills in many of the holes.

This product packs lots of features that are a must for network managers. Backup Exec enables you to create backup selections that specify the disk and/or directories to back up. Selections can contain both local and network selections. Once a selection has been created, you can use it inter-actively or within a backup job. You can create jobs for different backup types or days, then schedule the jobs to run at predefined times, using the graphical scheduler that comes with Backup Exec. It takes only a matter of minutes to set up a new selection and schedule a job to run it every day or only on certain days. Backup Exec also works with Microsoft Mail to send notification of completed backups automatically.

Many other options enable you to tweak and configure the operation of Backup Exec and your backup jobs.

AutoLoader is an optional module that works with many different tape drives with loaders. One of us has used this tool with a Digital Equipment TLZ06 and TLZ07 tape drive with a 12-tape loader. Installing both Backup Exec and AutoLoader took only a few minutes. Configuring the AutoLoader module took a little longer, but it was still accomplished in less than one hour.

Backup Exec also comes with an easy-to-use Scheduler that makes setting up routine backups painless. You can schedule one-at-a-time backups or routine backups that occur on certain days of the week. It is also easy to set up named backup jobs that back up certain files and systems that are run on different schedules. Figure 10.9 shows Backup Exec Loader's setup, and Figures 10.10 through 10.12 show sequential screens of Backup Exec for NT 4.0 when the Scheduler is set up.

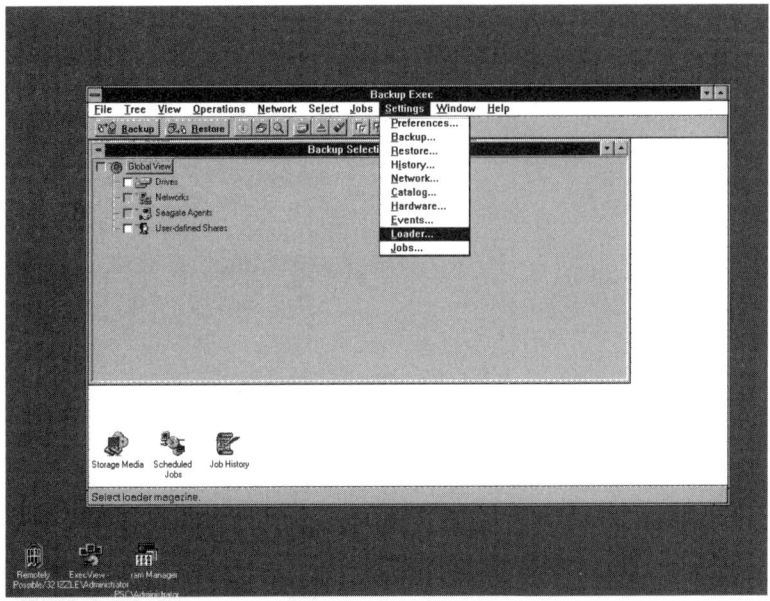

FIGURE 10.9 Backup Exec Job Launcher with a daily backup ready to run.

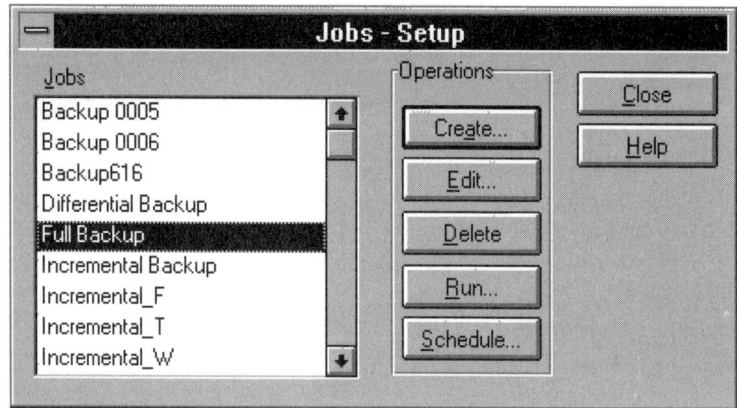

FIGURE 10.10 Arcada's Backup Exec Full Backup Scheduler setup.

Picking the Files to Back Up

One of the things most often overlooked in the design of a network is the file system. There are steps you can take in designing an easy-to-use file system that will simplify your backup procedures. There is a structure for your file system that has been proven by many managers and

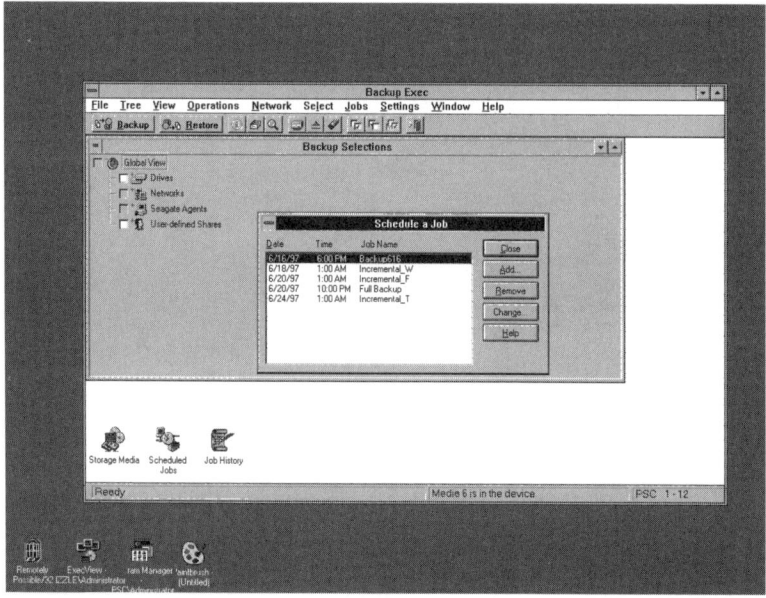

FIGURE 10.11 Scheduling a job in Backup Exec.

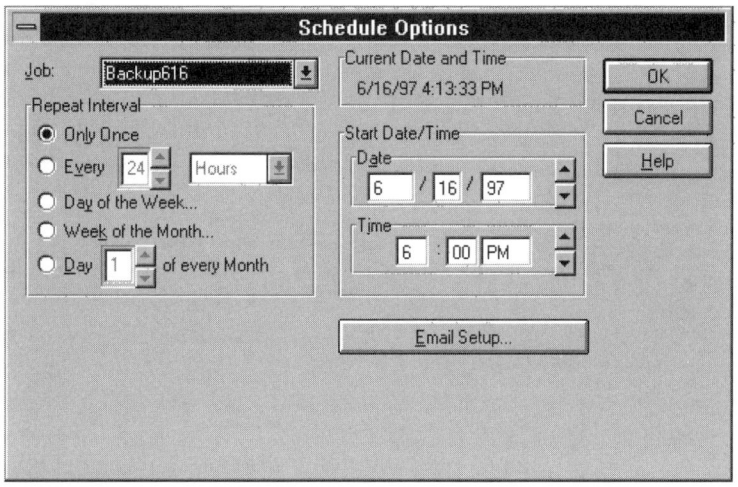

FIGURE 10.12 Job Scheduler window of Backup Exec.

users over the years. It is not only easy to back up; it's quite easy to use and manage.

DATA FILES

Data files are the most critical items to back up on a network. Your directory structure can play a critical part in making this task very simple or very difficult. We like to have only one or two directories off the root directory of a drive that actually hold the data directories and files. This approach enables us to pick only one directory tree to back up. The top level directories we use are

DATA

USERS

The backup process is simple; backing up these two directory trees gets all the data on the system. This structure also works well if you may also have a database manager such as SQL Server or other types of files that cannot be directly backed up.

Systems that are running a database such as SQL Server most likely have a separate directory for the database backup files. Backups for high-performance databases such as SQL Server typically use a special backup function of the database to perform an online backup to disk. The backup files placed on disk are backed up with the normal backup program. You must make sure that the database backup completes before the scheduled backup of the system starts because open files are not backed up.

REGISTRY

The Registry can pose an interesting problem for backups because it contains all the configuration information for the NT system. Backup programs that are designed specifically for NT should be able to back up the Registry with no problems. Some programs have a check box that must be checked so that the Registry files can participate in the backup.

REGBACK AND REGREST (NT RESOURCE KIT) • Another way to back up only the Registry files is to use the REBACK.EXE program to back up the Registry on all your systems to a common server. With the Registry files for all systems on a server, you can update a system very quickly if you have a problem. This program also makes sure that all your Registry information is backed up as long as the REGBACK program is run every day.

REGBACK can back up all the Registry hives or only certain hives. It also works when the hives are open and, in fact, only backs up Registry hives that are open. Other hives that are closed must be copied using File Manager or XCOPY. The account used to run REGBACK must have SetBackupPrivilege to execute this program.

You should always use REGBACK to back up the Registry to a hard disk directory. Running REGBACK targeted to a floppy disk is a recipe for disaster; the program fails if the floppy disk runs out of space. REGBACK also does not overwrite existing files, so make sure that you have deleted any backup files from the target directory.

The DOS Errorlevel variable is set to 0 if REGBACK does not encounter any errors. Errorlevel is set to 1 if the program encounters a hive that must be manually backed up, and it is 2 for any other errors.

The format for REGBACK is

```
REGBACK [directory]
```

       directory   Directory name to place backup in.

The following command backs up all open Registry hives:

```
REGBACK K:\BACKUP\CONFIG\THISERV
```

This command backs up the Registry to the K:\BACKUP\CONFIG\THISERV directory. Replace the last directory entry (THISERV) with a unique ID for the server you are backing up. Note that you can use the full server name for the file name if you are using NTFS or have extended names turned on for FAT drives.

REGREST is used to restore a backup made with REGBACK. This command works just like REGBACK in reverse:

```
REGREST backupfile savefile
```

backupfile   Specifies the file name of the Registry backup to restore.

savefile   Specifies the name of a file to save the current Registry file in before the replacement is made.

Other Files

There may be other files that you have missed in planning your backup strategy, unless you are backing up the entire drive each night. These are several types of files that could be important. Review this list, and research what other files or directories should be added to the list.

- WINS and DHCP database files
- WINNT and all subdirectories
- HOSTS, LMHOSTS, and other similar files if used
- Batch program directory or directories
- Directory containing user profiles
- NETLOGON shared directory
- SMS data directories

Backup Tapes

NT backups can span multiple tapes, creating a possible problem with tape management. The tapes in a backup set must always be in numbered order and in the sequence they are used. A backup set should always be kept together. Most managers also create a unique number for each tape set, allowing a set to be reconstructed if it is mixed up with other tapes.

One handy feature of some newly affordable technology provides us with auto loader tape drives. Many auto loaders use inexpensive magazines (less than $100) to hold the tapes. These magazines make a great caddie for storing the backup tapes and for automatically keeping them in order. Simply use a different magazine for each day's backup and label the magazine for the day. The tapes within the magazine should be labeled as to their position within the magazine. Using this technique, you might have a total of 20 magazines (five each week of the month) or more. Even with this many magazines, this is a cost-effective and practical solution.

It is possible to restore and list files from a backup set that has a missing tape by using the /MISSINGTAPE switch to start the backup program.

Restoring the System Files (Registry)

You can restore the NT boot volume if you have a backup copy. This process usually requires that NT first be reinstalled and then booted before you can access the backup tapes.

Restoring the NT System Files from Tape:

1. Boot the system with NT. You may have to install a new copy of NT to accomplish this.

2. Restore the SYSTEM32\CONFIG directory and all Registry files. If you are using a third-party backup product, you will probably have to reinstall the backup product before you can restore anything from the backup tapes.

3. Reboot the system.

4. Restore the entire backup of the NT volume except for the Registry files.

5. Reboot the system.

The system information should now be completely restored and operable. At this point, you can restore the remaining files from the backup tapes.

You can minimize the difficulty of reinstalling NT during a backup. One way is to use a mirrored disk or duplexed disk for the system and boot volume(s). This disk prevents the system disk from failing and causing a reinstall of NT. The other step is to keep an automated installation setup handy on more than one server. This backup enables you to reinstall very quickly over the network if there is a need. Using the SETUPMGR program from the NT Resource Kit, you can build automated answer files for each server, which saves lots of time in an emergency (see Chapter 2). You can always reinstall from CD, but this process takes longer as you answer all the prompts of a generic installation.

Restoring the NT System Files from Disk:

1. Boot the system with NT. You may have to install a new copy of NT to accomplish this.

2. Restore the SYSTEM32\CONFIG directory and all Registry files using REGREST. If you used a utility such as File Manager or Xcopy to back up any nonopen files, you should reverse the procedure to reinstall these files.

3. Reboot the system.

4. Restore the entire backup of the NT volume, except for the Registry files.

5. Reboot the system.

The system information should now be completely restored and operable. At this point, you can restore the remaining files from the backup tapes.

Backing Up Network Systems

You can back up resources on other systems from an NT 4.0 workstation or server. These other systems can include any resource that is accessible from the NT system. For instance, if you have Pathworks for Windows NT installed, you can back up resources on a Pathworks server during your NT backup session. Similarly, if you have access to Windows 95, Windows for Workgroups, or NetWare resources, they can be included in the backup as well.

Real-Time Backup of Server

Real-time backup of an NT system involves many different things. These range from backing up user files when they are accessed 24 hours a day to backing up a SQL Server or Oracle database when it is used 24 hours a day, seven days a week.

The need for this type of real-time backup becomes more and more critical as NT runs mission critical systems these days. We work with many organizations that have been relying on NT for production systems for several years. They are looking to clustering and other technologies as a way to add more flexible support to their NT network.

Octopus

Octopus from Octopus Technologies provides real-time backup to any data on your NT server. Candidates for Octopus backup are user data files, database files, mail system files, and any other critical files that change routinely. This list covers the most important features of Octopus:

- Operates in real time, capturing file I/O as it happens
- Mirrors actual file operations, without full file compares or copies
- Mirrors files and directories, rather than entire disks, partitions, or volume sets
- Uses store-and-forward, with no absolute requirements for connectivity or timing
- Recovers from lost connections or blocked files;Mirrors over the network to anywhere NetBIOS can connect
- Permits mirroring to multiple sites
- Protects files online
- Processes automatically, with no manual intervention
- Stores in the file system, with no special format
- Efficient for CPU, disk, and network resources
- Does not hold up application processing for its operations
- Transparent to the applications and to the users

PROBLEMS WITH TAPE BACKUP

Tape backup is a great tool with one major problem: Every tape backup system that we have used requires that all files backed up are closed. This presents problems for several types of files:

- Many database files are usually open 24 hours a day for production operations.
  - Most mail systems also run 24 hours a day.
- Users almost never exit all applications before leaving the office. You can force users to log off by using the log-on time feature of NT and automatically logging users off. What happens to users who must work during the backup period?

These types of systems are prime candidates for Octopus, which performs the backup as the file activity occurs and does not require the files to be closed.

OFF-SITE BACKUP WITH OCTOPUS

Octopus can also be used to back up files to an off-site location. This feature is useful if you have a high-speed connection to the off-site location that is not highly used during normal operations. This situation is ideal for Octopus, because it provides hot off-site backup, providing almost total disaster preparedness.

You may be in a better position to use the off-site backup than you think. If your system has separate buildings that are connected by a WAN, you may be able to run a separate segment that can be used for backup. The new segment provides high throughput for the backup operation and can serve as a backup segment for disaster recovery.

Real-Time Fault Tolerance with Clusters

As mentioned at the start of this chapter, Microsoft, Digital, AT&T, and other vendors are working on clustering or other fault-tolerance software for NT Server. A true clustering system allows you to group several servers that are seen as one by the network. Generally a cluster is known by an alias that relates to the entire cluster. For instance, if your cluster is known by the alias MYCLUSTER, you could connect to a shared directory using the UNC name:

```
\\MYCLUSTER\sharename
```

The cluster shares access to the drives, so that any server in the cluster can provide access to the resource to satisfy a request, providing load balancing and fault tolerance.

The best example of clustering with legacy systems is Digital's VMS cluster software. A VMS cluster is fault-tolerant and spreads the load across the cluster. The drawback to a VMS cluster is the large amount of overhead associated with running the cluster.

Digital has developed cluster software for NT that is based on its long track record with successful cluster systems on VMS. The first release of the product should include fault tolerance and load-balancing features for most applications, except for client/server databases. Cluster management for a client/server database requires more sophisticated software in the cluster system and will most likely not be available soon. Watch *ENT, Windows NT Magazine* and other publications for further developments on Clusters for Windows NT, Microsoft Cluster Server.

Microsoft Cluster Server provides a clustering technology that keeps server-based applications highly available, regardless of individual component failures. The application is already in beta and should soon be released.

Generally speaking, Microsoft Cluster Server is the clustering solution for computers running Windows NT Server developed by Microsoft. Version 1.0 supports clusters of two, specially linked servers running Windows NT Server Version 4.0 with Service Pack 3 or later. If one server in a cluster fails or is taken offline, the other server takes over the failed servers operations. Network clients connect to cluster resources in the same way they would connect to any network server, so using clusters requires no additional training for end users. Clustering also enables load balancing: the distribution of processes across servers.

There are two main components of Microsoft Cluster Server: clustering software and Cluster Administrator.

The clustering software enables the two servers of a cluster to exchange specific types of messages. This software communicates the status, resources being run, and activity of each server to the other server. The clustering software has two chief features: the Cluster Service and the Resource Monitor. The Cluster Service runs on every cluster server and controls cluster activity, communication between cluster servers, and failure operations. The Resource Monitor facilitates communication between the Cluster Service and the network resources. Each server can run one or more Resource Monitors, depending on how the cluster is configured.

The Cluster Administrator is a graphical application that network administrators use to manage a cluster, such as for tasks listed under "Advantages of Clustering."

If you're running NT 4.0 Server (or workstation), you can run the Cluster Administrator, as long as you have Service Pack 3 loaded.

Advantages of Clustering

Microsoft Cluster Server clustering provides three main benefits:

■ **High availability of resources**–Client/server applications rely on the availability of network services. These services are provided by resources, which are defined in this context as any entity residing on a server that can be managed by clustering software and that provides a service to clients in a client/server environment. For example, a public file share, a Web server, and a database application can all be managed as resources.

■ **Scaleability**–Clusters are highly scaleable; CPU, I/O, storage, and application resources can be added incrementally to efficiently expand capacity. This translates to reliable access to system resources and data as well as to investment protection of both hardware and software resources. Clusters are affordable because they can be built with commodity hardware (high-volume components that are relatively inexpensive).

■ **Centralized administration**–In an ordinary server environment, you use various administrative tools to identify the servers on your network and to monitor their contents and activities. However, in the cluster environment, the administration of applications and services is centralized through the use of a single tool, Cluster Administrator. For example, you can use Cluster Administrator to manage services, manage file shares, manage directory replication, review the activities and failures of the computers in each cluster, determine which nodes are currently running specific applications and services, and manually take individual nodes offline for maintenance.

Microsoft Cluster Server was initially released as part of NT Server Enterprise Edition.

Power Backup and Monitoring Systems

Uninterruptible Power Supply (UPS) devices are viewed by many LAN managers as a necessity. We consider ourselves part of that group due to the benefits they provide in reducing not only hardware problems or lost data but also in the improvement in up-time of network servers. A UPS is the most viable type of power backup (its name implies that it is uninterruptible when power goes off).

Choosing a UPS can be a difficult proposition because of the many options available. This decision is best considered like many other system decisions—consider all other related options during the process. This means that you should consider which UPS monitoring programs are available for the system you choose and what other devices and features are supported by the system. You should consider whether or not the UPS is expandable and can be shared by several servers with smart connections to each server in case of a power problem.

APC Power Chute

American Power Conversion (APC) has many years of experience in power systems and has developed its hardware and software accordingly. The integrated nature of its products provides the system manager with a complete suite of power management tools. Adding products such as Measure-UPS and Share-UPS to a system running the Power Chute Plus monitoring software gives you the unique ability to monitor many different events that have an impact on the environment in which your system is running from both a local or remote location. The ability to monitor power quality as well as the UPS temperature with the standard Power Chute Plus software is especially helpful.

APC codeveloped the original UPS monitoring with Microsoft for the LAN Manager UPS program. Simple UPS monitoring has made its way into the NT product via the UPS applet in Control Panel. Power Chute Plus is a software product from APC that adds a new level of UPS power management and control for system administrators. APC has a number of other products that augment Power Chute Plus in controlling and monitoring the environment in which our systems run. These products run on NT, VMS, NetWare, and other systems.

The most important features of Power Chute Plus and its UPS interface follow:

- There is a safe system shutdown in case of extended power failures.
- UPS Testing and status checks run at every UPS startup and can be scheduled to run at different times automatically.
- Remote UPS management enables a manager to log on a server from anywhere and to check the UPS. An additional product called Call-UPS II enables remote out-of-band management.
- Another product called Measure-UPS enables you to add on to the standard power monitoring features of Power Chute Plus and monitor environmental factors such as temperature, humidity, smoke alarms, and fire alarms.
- FlexEvents is new to version 4.2 of Power Chute Plus and enables a manager to choose different actions for certain types of power events. For instance, Power Chute can run a program or send electronic mail when a certain event is triggered.

Power Chute Plus on NT includes not only the standard UPS information we are used to but also some nice graphics depicting the status of the UPS and the incoming power. Tools are available under the Diagnostics menu for setting up regular UPS testing and performing on-the-spot tests.

Share-UPS is a small hardware box that enables up to eight servers to be connected to one UPS. One server becomes the UPS manager running Power Chute Plus and attaching to the Share-UPS with the black cable, whereas the other servers all have a connection to the Share-UPS box using the standard NT UPS applet and the gray cable.

Using this technique, you can manage the UPS from one server or from the network and effectively control all your systems attached to it. No longer do you need one UPS for each server or maybe two servers. The Share-UPS also has a serial port for out-of-band management from a PC, a terminal, or a modem connection.

Conclusion

This chapter has introduced you to many different issues and technologies concerned with disaster preparedness for NT. There are many options available, and you must choose wisely. The future is bright in this area, as both such software vendors as Microsoft and the hardware vendors are working on many different solutions that will make our tasks simpler than they are today.

The next chapter will introduce you to number of options on tuning NT systems. A number of tools that are included with NT and that come from third parties provide tuning capabilities for NT. One thing is critical for all of them—you must understand the basics of how NT works before you can tune it.

Tuning NT Servers and Networks

NT performs many tuning operations during normal operations. It normally tunes itself sufficiently, except when it runs out of hardware resources, such as disk, memory, or processor. NT cannot tune itself to suit the way you wish to use the system or for particular applications. NT also has no way of determining when specific users are overloading the system, when a bad application has gone haywire, or when some particular subsystem such as the network is causing problems.

Scenario 11.1:

Its Friday at 5:01 and your boss calls: The organization's Web site seems to be really slow. Can you fix it before you head out to the beach this evening?

Scenario 11.2:

You just powered up your last server, and now you are the proud owner of a 10-node NT Server powerhouse farm. Now you have the power to handle all those user requests and to power those SQL Server databases. But, the thought lingers....How do I make sure the servers always run at the optimum performance level?

Performance tuning is part art and part science. NT provides a number of tools for monitoring performance in both the NT Server box and the NT

Resource Kit. This chapter focuses on a number of these tools and on ways to use them with NT and NT Server systems. This chapter goes into more detail on tuning than do most NT Workstation books (including Spencer's NT book from Cardinal Business Monitors), because we assume that you will be placing a much higher demand on the system by using it as a server. After all, that is why you are reading this book, right?

Along with the tools included with NT and the NT Resource Kit, this chapter also touches briefly on Systems Management Server and a little bit of Simple Network Management Protocol, using a couple of different tools.

NT Performance Monitoring System

The primary NT tool used for tuning is the Performance Monitoring System (PMS). The PMS (the acronym is ours) includes the NT Performance Monitor and the various parts of NT and other systems that maintain the objects and counters used for tuning.

The PMS provides a nice view of many parts of the NT system, and it was built to extend this support to NT applications. The NT Resource Kit also includes a program that can be used to add your own objects to the PMS database (LODCTR).

Objects and Counters

The PMS system uses objects and counters to track the performance of particular parts of the system. The term *object* refers to any distinguishable entity in the system. A good example of PMS objects is the objects associated with the physical disks in your system.

Along with the objects, NT maintains counters for each part of an object that is tracked. The counters are usually broken down into percentages, discrete counts, or readings over time to provide useful information to system managers.

The Physical Disk object contains counters that relate to the total physical disk. If you have a disk that is partitioned into two logical disks, when you look at the Physical Disk object, you will see the activity for the disk as a whole, which includes both logical disks. If you look at the Logical Disk object, you will see the counters for a specific logical disk partition. You will find both types of counters useful in managing your system.

Instances are used to track multiple occurrences of a type of object. For example, you may have a system with two disk drives. When you look at the Physical Disk counters, you will see two copies of the counters, one for instance 0 and one for instance 1. You will also see multiple instances for processors with systems that use two or more CPUs.

Objects may be added to a system by any program that is installed on the system. Systems that ship with NT Server may also include additional counters for specific processors (such as the DEC Alpha or Intel Pentium chips). You may also install new hardware with new counters that are loaded when you install the driver for the device. Table 11.1 lists the core objects that are included on all NT systems.

Some instances have a parent instance that is used to identify the aggregate information for all instances. Examples of objects with parents are the Logical Disk (Physical Disk) object and the Thread Object (Process).

Objects are referenced by first specifying the object and then the counter:

```
Object:Counter
```

Multiple instances are expressed as you would an index to an array in a programming language:

```
Object:Counter[instance name]
```

Some instances are mortal because they exist only during the time the entity they report on exists. For instance, a process instance exists only when the process is actually running on the system. Mortal instances can be added to a chart only during the time they exist. Performance Monitor records data for the instance every time it is checked while the instance is alive, once the instance has been added to a chart. Whenever the mortal instance dies, the counter drops to 0 and picks up counting when the instance starts again.

TABLE 11.1	NT System Core Performance Object
Object	**Tracks**
Cache	File system cache.
Logical Disk	Counters related to the logical disk systems, such as partitions and space usage.
Memory	System memory (RAM).
Objects	Certain parts of system software.
Paging File	Virtual memory paging files.
Physical Disk	Counters related to the physical disk systems.
Process	Running programs.
Processor	System processor (CPU).
Redirector	File system redirector used to redirect file system requests to other systems.
System	Common counters to all system hardware and software.
Thread	Running threads.

Producing a List of Performance Monitor Counters

CTRLIST (NT Resource Kit) is used to produce a text file containing the Performance Monitor objects and counters. The information in the file includes the Explain text for each item. The file is useful for reviewing the objects and counters for a better understanding and for searching with a text editor like Notepad. You could also easily import the resulting file into an Access database for ease of use. The syntax for its use follows:

```
ctrlist > counters.txt
```

Performance Monitor

Performance Monitor is one tool with which you should become very familiar. It is great for tracking system performance and for sending alerts to a particular user and/or computer when a particular condition occurs.

As shown in Table 11.2, Performance Monitor has four different views.

For more information on the details of using Performance Monitor, consult your NT documentation, my book *A Practical Guide to Windows NT*, or Marshall Brain's book *Using Windows NT*.

Performance Monitor can monitor only one instance of a program at a time. If you need to monitor multiple instances of the same program, you should make a copy of the EXE file with a different name, and execute both programs. Performance Monitor also cannot track multiple instances of a 16-bit Windows program in the 3.1 release of NT and NTAS because all 16-bit Windows programs run in a single NT Virtual DOS Machine (NTVDM).

Performance Monitor can monitor objects from one or more computers at a time. Each item you place on a chart or report, for instance, can be from a different system. You must have the Access This Computer From The Network option enabled to place objects from other systems on a Performance Monitor display.

TABLE 11.2 Performance Monitor Views

Display Name	Description
Chart	Provides a nice graphical display. You can select between a line graph or histogram.
Report	Displays the counters in a simple report format. The values are displayed separately for each server.
Log	Displays the objects that are tracked in the log. You can also use the Add to Log dialog box from this view to add objects to the log.
Alert	Displays the current alerts. The Add dialog box can be used in this view to add new alerts.

You should be conscious of the performance hit that occurs when Performance Monitor is used to monitor lots of data from remote systems. The overhead on the monitored machine will be very low, but the network traffic and the load on the monitoring machine will be higher. The NT Resource Kit points out that you can actually measure the added Performance Monitor overhead by running another copy of Performance Monitor and watching the load on the monitoring system.

While Performance Monitor can monitor multiple systems at the same time, the data retrieved from the different systems will never be completely synchronized. This lack of synchronization occurs because of the differences in timing from the different systems and the varying network traffic when the counters are reported. Most of the time, the synchronization is not crucial because you are looking at representative numbers, as far as timing is concerned.

Before using Performance Monitor to monitor disk performance, you must enable disk performance measurement. Disk measurement is disabled by default because it consumes some amount of overhead. The following statement turns on disk performance monitoring:

```
DISKPERF -Y
```

Before the disk counters show up, the system must be rebooted. You can also run this command on a remote system by specifying the system name after the command:

```
DISKPERF -Y \\SYSNAME
```

Turning on disk counters places a performance penalty on your system, but it is minor on all but the slowest systems. Pentium and faster systems with good performing disk systems should not see a hit if disk counters are enabled all the time.

The Processor Queue counter is another important counter that has a hidden secret. Before the Processor Queue counter is activated, you must select at least one thread for monitoring. Once the Performance Monitor is collecting data for the thread, the Processor Queue shows the length of the queue by counting the number of threads waiting to execute.

Another little trick to use with Performance Monitor is to create different settings files and then create icons that start Performance Monitor with the settings file. This is accomplished by placing the settings file name on the command line after the command to start Performance Monitor. You can also start Performance Monitor with the AT command in this manner.

The NT Resource Kit gives several options for measuring remote statistics:

- Collect data at less frequent intervals.
- Reduce the number of objects that are monitored.

- Carefully choose which objects to monitor (The Thread object is the most expensive, with the Process object ranking second).
- Run multiple copies of Performance Monitor that each monitor only one type of object.

General Performance Monitor Tips

Performance Monitor is a powerful and easy-to-use tool. Figure 11.1 shows Performance Monitor and the Chart view. The far-left button on the toolbar is depressed. The other buttons are for Alerts, Log file, and Reports. The other buttons on the toolbar are Add to dialog, Modify Counter Parameters, Remove Counter from View, Update Counters Now, Add Bookmark to Log, and Display View Parameters for the Current View.

PMS perfoms and operates the same way in NT 3.51 and 4.0. The Add to dialog box is used to add a counter to the current Performance Monitor view. The Add to button on the toolbar displays the Add to dialog box. This dialog box is specific to the particular view you are currently using. Figure 11.2 shows the Add to Alert dialog box.

The Add dialog boxes allow you to select a different computer for each counter you add. Click the "..." button next to the computer name to display the Select Computer dialog box shown in Figure 11.3.

Setting Alerts with Performance Monitor

You should use Alerts to provide an ongoing proactive check on your system(s). Performance Monitor is used for setting Alerts via the Alert view.

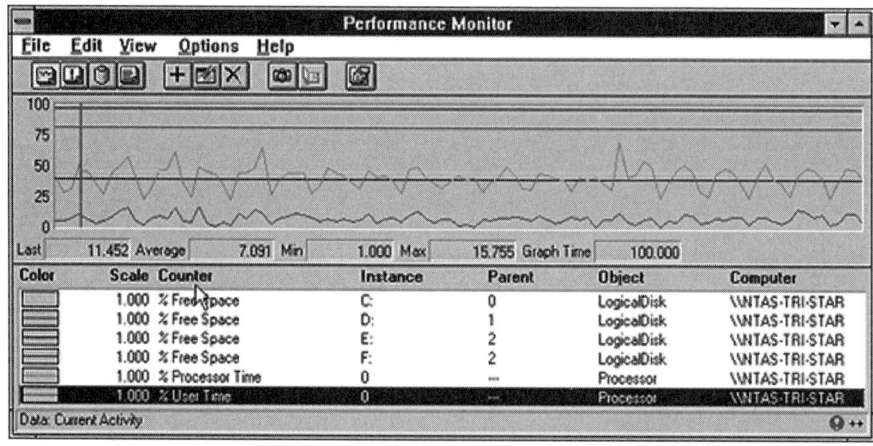

FIGURE 11.1 The Chart view is the default when Performance Monitor starts.

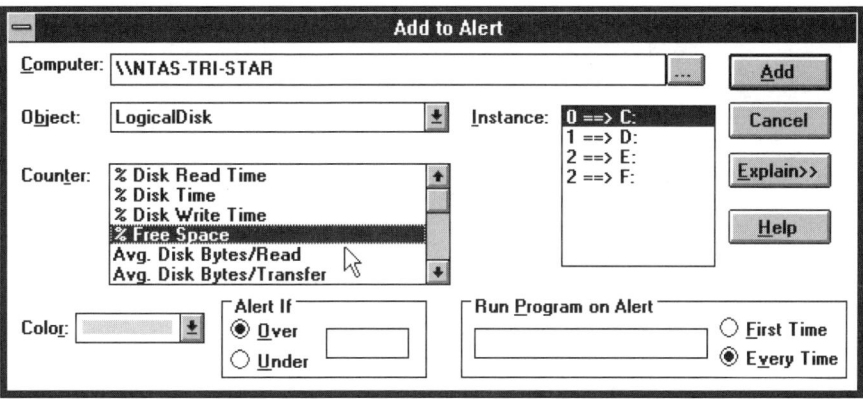

FIGURE 11.2 The Add dialog box is used to add a counter to a view. The dialog box is basically the same for all views, except for specific view options, such as the Run Program on Alert box shown here. Other dialog boxes have additional options or fewer options.

Alerts are useful; they can send a network message to a user or computer and/or run a program when an Alert occurs.

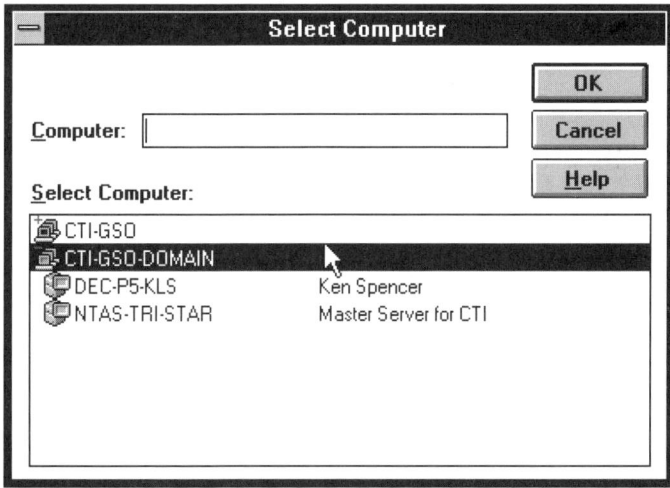

FIGURE 11.3 The Select Computer dialog box provides a quick method of selecting another system for a counter. Click the system to monitor and then click OK, or double-click the computer name.

Alerts must be chosen carefully, because they can generate a lot of overhead and can be a pain to the users and managers who receive the alerts. We usually use the 80/20 rule for choosing alerts: You can get approximately 80 percent of the benefits from monitoring only 20 percent of the values. We also like to start by selecting the values to catch only the worst offenders, and then tighten the alerts as performance improves.

We also suggest monitoring certain values over longer periods of time. You may want to have several copies of Performance Monitor running with different settings files for different types of alerts. For instance, such things as disk space can probably be done once a day. Others, such as paging rate or disk I/O, must be monitored on a more frequent basis when the load is occurring on the system.

You should be aware of two things when you send alert messages over the network: If the user who is to receive the alert message is logged in to multiple systems with the same account, the alert messages are received only by the system that the user logged in on. Alerts can also be irritating if you have a large number of alerts that send messages to users each time they are triggered.

Alerts can also be sent to an arbitrary name across the network. You can create the name by using the NET NAME command on any NT system. This command creates an arbitrary name on the computer that allows the computer to receive any messages sent to the name. The format for using the command is

```
NET NAME newname
```

Another intriguing thing about the Performance Monitor alert view is its ability to run a program when an alert occurs. This alert can be useful for triggering many different actions. What happens when your system periodically fills a disk with many temporary files? You can create an alert on disk space so that when it hits a certain percentage, the alert runs a program to delete or move some of the temporary files. Another possible candidate for this type of action is triggering an alert on a database to archive information when the database reaches a certain size. Figure 11.4 shows the Performance Monitor Alert View.

Performance Monitor can also run an alert only when a specific alert occurs. This is quite handy when you wish to monitor a specific counter and trigger a program when a certain condition occurs. The First Time button can be used to run the program on the first alert and ignore the program on subsequent alerts.

See the section on the DATALOG program from the NT Resource Kit later in this chapter for information on running Alert functions as a service.

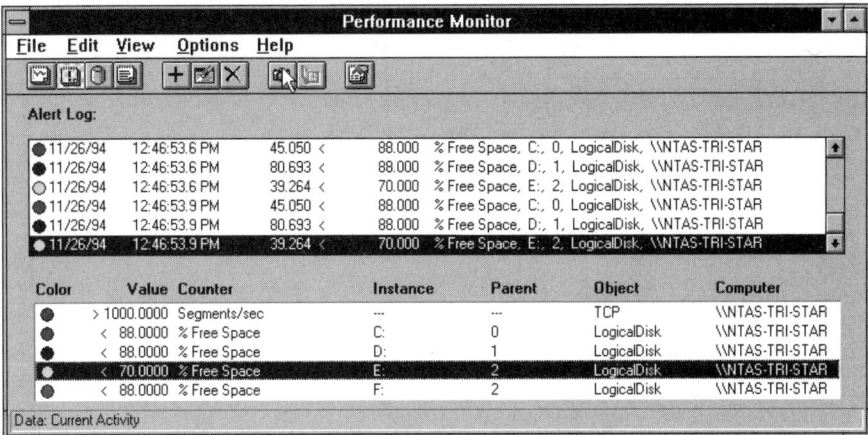

FIGURE 11.4 The Performance Monitor dialog box with the Alert view showing. Notice how many alerts have been triggered on a shortage of drive space.

Running a Program on a Specific Alert with Performance Monitor:

1. Click the Add or Modify button on the toolbar.

2. Choose the object to monitor.

3. Enter the alert condition in the text box.

4. Enter the name of the program to run when the alert occurs. Be sure to include the full path to the program.

5. Click the First Time to run the program only the first time the alert occurs, or click the Every Time button to run the program each time the alert occurs.

6. Close the dialog box.

NT Resource Kit

In addition to Performance Monitor shipped with NT, the NT Resource Kit contains several tools for monitoring the performance of your system. Table 11.3 shows these tools.

Automating Performance Monitor with DataLog (NT Resource Kit)

The NT Resource Kit is the new DataLog service version of Performance Monitor. DataLog provides support for the alert and logging features of Performance Monitor. Also included with DataLog is the Monitor utility to

TABLE 11.3	NT Resource Kit Tools for Monitoring Performance
Program	**Description**
DATALOG	A service version of Performance Monitor, implementing the Alert and Logging functions.
PERFMTR	Monitors systems performance numbers during the execution of a program. Different presentation views are selectable when PERFMTR starts.
PMON	Useful for monitoring a large number of memory statistics. Displays the same data available in Performance Monitor, but in a tailored form.
PVIEWER	Nice tool for reviewing processes. Similar to PMON in that most of the data are available in Performance Monitor but presented in a different manner.
WPERF	Another tool that is similar to Performance Monitor but displays its information in a different format.
TLIST	Used to display a list of all running processes and their process ID.

control the DATALOG service. You can start DataLog on the current NT system or on any other NT system over the network.

This is a great utility for monitoring performance. The best way to use this utility is to plan the items you wish to monitor, create a settings file with Performance Monitor, and then automatically start DataLog to perform the

Configuring DataLog:

1. Copy DATALOG.EXE to the system root directory (\WINNT35 \SYSTEM32). The settings file does not have to be in the system root directory.

2. Install DataLog using the Monitor command:

   ```
   monitor [servername] SETUP
   ```

   Replace [servername] with the name of the server to run DataLog. If you are installing DataLog on the current system, leave this blank.

3. Create a workspace settings file using Performance Monitor. Set the Alert and Log settings (include the Log name), but do not start the log. Save the settings file, using the Save Workspace option on the File menu.

4. Specify the settings file for DataLog to use:

   ```
   monitor [servername] filename
   ```

   Replace [servername] with the name of the server to run DataLog. If you are installing DataLog on the current system, leave this blank.

   Replace filename with the name of the settings file (that is, PHYSDISK.PMW or OVERVIEW.PMW). If you are specifying the settings file on a remote system, make sure the settings file is on that system, and specify the full path to the file.

tasks. DataLog runs as a service and does not have a user interface. DataLog places the results of any log activity in the log file specified by the settings file.

Starting DataLog:

1. Start DataLog with the command:

   ```
   monitor [servername] START
   ```

Stopping Datalog:

1. Stop DataLog with the command:

   ```
   monitor [servername] STOP
   ```

Once DataLog has created a log file, you can use Performance Monitor to review and manipulate the file. Simply open the file as you would any log file, and use the normal Performance Monitor features from there.

You can automate DataLog using the AT command to drive the scheduler service. Review the DATALOG.TXT file included with the NT Resource Kit for more information.

You can create some very large log files in a hurry with DataLog and Performance Monitor. You should use care when setting up these tools for logging and consider placing log files on a disk with lots of space. You should also consider setting up an automated routine to check for log files and delete them after a period, or to alert you to large and old files.

Monitoring Performance

Understanding the performance tuning tools is only part of the equation. You must also understand how NT works to some extent and have a good knowledge of troubleshooting techniques. We have found over the years that a good troubleshooting approach will enable us to fix things that we have no technical knowledge about. The approach itself guides us through finding out how something works, and then voilà, we find out what is wrong and fix it.

Bottlenecks and Other Problems

You may run into a vast number of problems using a network operating system such as NT Server, including bottlenecks in one portion of the system, problems with applications, or user problems.

A bottleneck typically occurs when your system begins to run out of a particular hardware or software resource. For instance, the system may swap a lot of data from RAM to the disk, causing the system to slow down for everyone using the system. When the amount of data swapped to disk becomes very high, the only resolution is to add more physical memory to the system, which will alleviate the bottleneck.

You also may experience a sort of bottleneck from an application program. A good example of a bad program is the EXTERNAL program for Microsoft Mail version 3.0 to 3.2. This program causes NT to experience a drastic drop in performance when EXTERNAL is running, even when the program is supposedly not doing anything. I suspect that this occurs because EXTERNAL expects to be running on a DOS system, which is by nature not multitasking. Under DOS, the only way for EXTERNAL to monitor the system is to continually loop. Performance Monitor is a great tool to use to look for exactly this kind of problem.

If you are using Microsoft Mail, get the NT version of External [called the Multitasking Transfer Agent (MTA)], and you will not experience these problems.

You should use care when you monitor your system's performance and make judgments on what to upgrade. We try to approach every problem using the Systems approach. This approach dictates that you must consider the entire system in any decision, not just the problem at hand. For instance, if the CPU is 100 percent utilized, your first guess is to move some of the load to another system or just add another processor. The proper response is to continue the investigation until you find out what is causing the 100 percent utilization. It could be a problem program or a particular piece of hardware that is creating the load.

Creating an Overview Performance Monitor Settings File

The Resource Kit suggests creating an overview settings file that provides a good glimpse of how your system is performing. This file should be called OVERVIEW.PMW or some such representative name and will save all the settings for your system overview. The objects and counters in Table 11.4 are good candidates for this file.

Steps for Tuning

NT automatically adjusts its configuration in response to workload changes. Some manual steps to augment this are discussed in this section. One major step that should be taken before any drastic tuning is to establish a benchmark

TABLE 11.4	Objects and Counters for Overview Setting File	

Object	Counter	Description
Processor	Percent Processor Time	Tracks percent of time that the processor is busy. This counter should go up as the load on the system increases and performance decreases unless some other factor besides the processor is causing the bottleneck.
	Percent Total Processor Time	The same as Percent Processor Time except that it combines the values for all processors in a multiprocessor.
	Processor Queue Length	Measures the backlog for your processor. This counter gives you a clue when a process(s) is hogging the processor.
Memory	Pages/second	Tracks the number of pages swapped to disk per second by the virtual memory system. When this counter gets consistently very high, your system is most likely running out of RAM.
Physical Disk	Percent Disk Time	Shows how busy the disk drive is. A separate instance should be monitored for each disk in the system. When this counter gets very high, it is an indicator that something such as paging or other high-disk usage is occurring.
NetBEUI	Bytes Total/second	Tracks the number of bytes per second sent and received over the NetBEUI interface and indicates when network traffic is high.
TCP/IP	Bytes Total/second	The same as the last one except it is for the TCP/IP interface.
Server	Bytes Total/second	Tracks the total bytes per second for the server.

of the system before the tuning takes place. The benchmark allows you to compare the performance of the system accurately after the tuning to the performance before the tuning.

Benchmarking a System Before Making Changes:

1. Record the current state of system with Performance Monitor.
2. Make changes.
3. Record the state of revised system with Performance Monitor under the same load conditions.

Here are some suggestions for improving server performance:

- Add lots of memory to NT servers. NT loves memory, especially when it gets busy. High-usage servers are a prime candidate for more RAM. If you are using NT Server Enterprise Edition, read the release notes and documentation if your server has over 100 MB of RAM.
- Use SMP servers in particular situations. Database servers running SQL Server or another similar client/server system improve substantially on an SMP platform. File and print services usually do not see the same measure of performance improvement using SMP. Use Microsoft Cluster Server to distribute the load over two servers.
- Distribute the server load in your network around, using several servers instead of one or two big ones. Many functions can be segregated to separate servers, to provide a big performance improvement and some degree of fault tolerance. These are several potential candidates:
  SMS
  Database Servers (that is, SQL Server)
  Primary Domain Controllers
  File and print servers
  Application servers
  WINS servers
  DNS servers
  DHCP servers
- Use the fastest CPU feasible. Incremental prices between different processor speeds are usually not extremely large these days.
- Create multiple-page files on different drives and controllers. Multiple files are more efficient, because each disk and controller can simultaneously process requests for information from the page files. Placing each page file on a different disk also shares the paging load, rather than having one file on a single disk carry all the load.
- Analyze the paging requirements for your system before you create the page files. NT expands page files as needed, but this is inefficient and can cause disk fragmentation. Creating a page file of the proper size performs much better.
  - Place the page file(s) on separate disks from the NT boot partition.
- Make sure the boot partition has plenty of free disk space (50MB or more). We have seen NT servers act strangely when disk space began to disappear (less than 10MB free). Connections would disappear, and the system would quit synchronizing with other BDCs, or the PDC, depending upon its role.
- Use high-performance disk drives. Drives that are 1GB or larger often have much higher performance rates than smaller drives do.
  - Use multiple high-performance disk controllers.
  - Use only PCI and EISA bus systems for disk controllers.
  - Create stripe sets with parity over multiple disks.

- Do not use any disks or controllers that would use the default ATDISK driver.
- Continuously analyze disk requirements and capacity.
- Continuously analyze memory requirements and capacity.
- Manage memory settings for the server.
- Match the network card bus (PCI, EISA, ISA) to the servers bus.
- Use high-performance network cards in the server.
- Spread the network load over multiple network adapters. Be sure to group the networks on an adapter logically, to make sure workstations can communicate with other workstations in the group.
- Use high-speed network components, such as 100BaseT, FDDI, and Ethernet switches.
- Select Maximize Throughput and Connections for the server and NetBEUI protocol. This option enables unlimited network connections and improves network performance. Be aware that network applications such as NetBEUI and the Server use nonpaged memory. This makes less nonpaged memory available to application programs.
- Use only one protocol if possible.

Monitoring and Controlling Server Usage

NT creates a session between a workstation and the server each time a user successfully connects to the server. The session validates the user's permissions and sets up the performance statistics for the session. You can track session usage statistics from any NT system and LAN Manager 2.x servers. Windows 95 also provides session statistics.

There are several ways to get a handle on server usage. One of the tools to use for this is the Server applet. Server shows you a current picture of the server; it does not store statistics over time. Even though it doesn't store statistics, it is a very good tool for checking the current status of your system and determining where the excessive load is coming from. For instance, maybe several users are copying their C drives to the server at the same time.

Quickly Checking on What Users Are Hitting Your System:

1. Start Server Manager.

2. Click the Users button.

3. Review the Connected users on your system. Note how many opens the users have, and notice the idle time for each user. The idle time will be very low (as in 0 or close to 0) if the user is actively using a resource. Select the user with the most opens and active time close to 0, and note the resources accessed by the user.

Now that you know who is using a resource, you can either use Performance Monitor to look at that particular resource, or you may have first used Performance Monitor, and determined which resource has the highest load.

If you know that a particular resource is heavily used, then you try to find out why.

Quickly Determining Who Is Using a Particular Resource:

1. Start Server Manager.
2. Click the Shares button.
3. Select the resource in question.
4. Review the bottom window, which will show all users connected to the resource. Pay attention to the In Use column. In Use indicates when a user has a file open on the resource (Yes). A No value indicates that the user has a connection to the resource but is not actively using the resource. A quick look down this list should show which users are placing the load on the resource.

The In Use button displays the Open Resources dialog box (shown in Figure 11.5), which is a quick way to check for users of currently open resources.

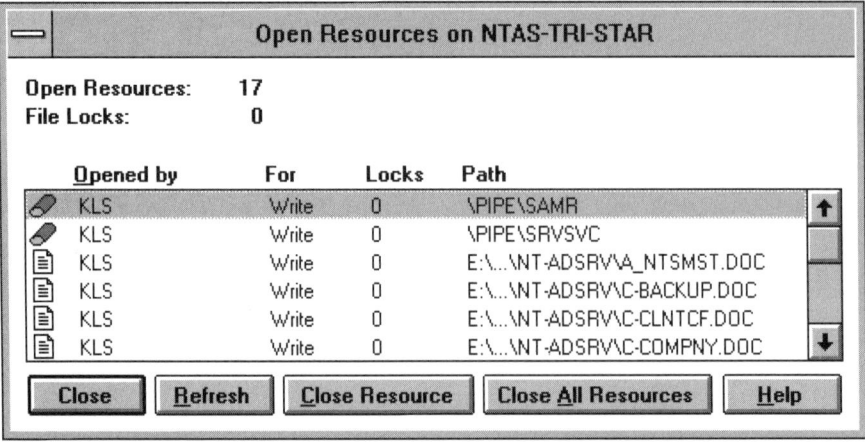

FIGURE 11.5 The Open Resources dialog box from Server Manager allows you to see who is using what resources, and to close a resource. You can display this dialog box by clicking the In Use button from the Server Properties dialog box.

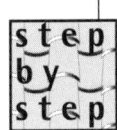

Quickly Checking Only Open Resources:

1. Start Server Manager.
2. Click the In Use button.
3. Review the list for resources and users in question.

Click the Refresh button once in a while, to update the display to current information.

Sometimes you will want to disconnect a user from a share, or to disconnect all users for a particular share. You can do this with the In Use button, but this would be time-consuming and would show only what files are in use. The easiest way to disconnect a user from a share is with the Shares button, which displays the dialog box shown in Figure 11.6.

Another tool for monitoring shared resources is Net Watch, which is described in Chapter 4. This tool is included in the NT Resource Kit and provides a nice graphical interface for monitoring shares. Server Manager is a more generic tool, providing access to numerous other options such as users on the system and files in use.

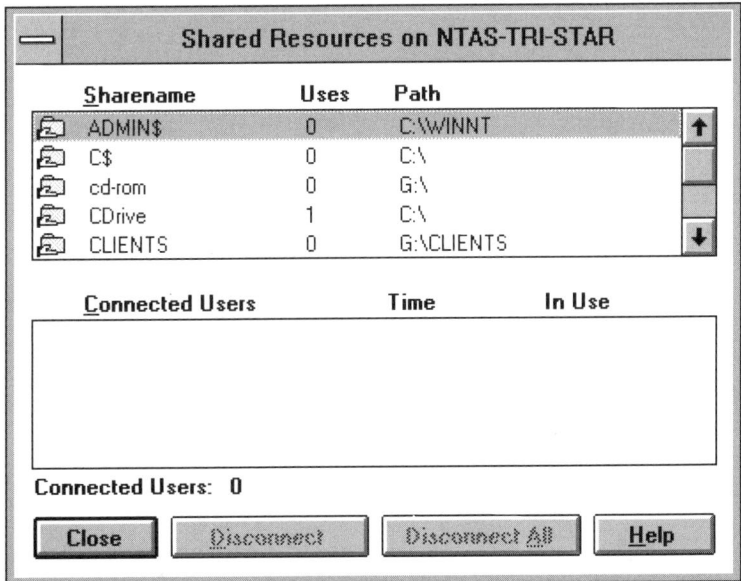

FIGURE 11.6   The Shared Resources dialog box shows the actual share name and the number of connections to that share. It also includes the path for the share.

Closing a Resource or Disconnecting a Share:

1. Start Server Manager.
2. Click the Shares button.
3. Select the share to close.
4. Click the Disconnect button, or click Disconnect All to disconnect all users from the share.

You can also use the Users dialog box to close a resource. This dialog box displays the users logged on the server and the shares to which they are connected.

Disconnecting a User with Server Manager:

1. Start Server Manager.
2. Click the In Use button.
3. Select the user to disconnect.
4. Click the Disconnect button, or click Disconnect All to disconnect all users.

Usually a systems manager must determine who is using a file when maintenance must be performed, or when for some reason there is a problem with a file. It is possible to determine whether there is a problem quickly, using File Manager. This feature is a great way to access this information, because you may well be using File Manager to perform the research regarding the file.

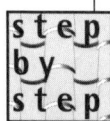

Quickly Determining Who Is Using a Particular File:

1. Start File Manager.
2. Click the file in question.
3. Press Alt+Enter, or select File/Properties to display the Properties dialog box.
4. Click the Open By button.

Server Manager can also show you who is using a file, although this will take a little longer if you have lots of files in use, as you must browse through the list to find the file.

Make sure that you have notified all users of a resource or the user you are going to disconnect before taking action to close the connection or resource. Failure to do so may cause loss of data or worse. Under severe circumstances you may have to take a close or disconnect action before a user is notified, but try to keep this to a minimum.

Determine Who Is Using a Particular File (Another Way):
1. Start Server Manager.
2. Click the In Use button.
3. Review the list for resources and users in question until you find the file you are looking for.

File use is also a good candidate for auditing. Auditing a file can show who is using the file and how often the file is opened and used. The DUMPEL program from the NT Resource Kit can be used in a batch file to dump the Event Log and to summarize information on audited resources.

Collecting Statistics with NET STATISTICS

Performance Monitor, the Server applet, Server Manager, Event Viewer, and several other programs display or collect statistics on NT. One command that is useful for reviewing server statistics is the NET STATISTICS command. NET STATISTICS (NET STATS) displays statistics that were captured over time. Tables 11.5 and 11.6 show items that are output by this command, and they provide a short explanation of each item.

Several pieces of information from NET STATISTICS are useful in managing your system. Notice that at a glance you can determine how many files have been accessed on the server or how many jobs have been spooled to the printer. Maybe you want to know how many sessions were accepted on the server versus how many were disconnected from time-outs or errors. The output also gives you a quick indication of the average response time.

This is a sample output from a lightly loaded system:

```
NET STATS SERVER
     Server Statistics for \\NTAS-TRI-STAR
     Statistics since 4/1/94 5:47PM
     Sessions accepted  1
     Sessions timed-out 0
     Sessions errored-out    3

     Kilobytes sent     83352
     Kilobytes received 41272
     Mean response time (msec) 0

     System errors      0
     Permission violations   0
```

```
Password violations       0


Files accessed       1714
Communication devices accessed  0
Print jobs spooled 0


Times buffers exhausted


 Big buffers 0
 Request buffers    0
The command completed successfully.
```

TABLE 11.5 Server Statistics

Item	Description
Server Statistics for \\NTAS-TRI-STAR	Indicates that this set of statistics is for a server, and the server name is \\NTAS-TRI-STAR.
Statistics since 4/1/94 5:47PM	Provides the starting date for the statistics.
Sessions accepted	Number of sessions that connected to the server.
Sessions timed-out	Number of sessions that timed-out and were automatically disconnected.
Sessions errored-out	Number of sessions that were disconnected because of an error.
Kilobytes sent	Number of kilobytes sent.
Kilobytes received	Number of kilobytes received.
Mean response time (msec)	The average server response time for responding to requests.
System errors	Number of system errors.
Permission violations	Number of times that a violation of some type of permission occurred.
Password violations	Number of times that a password violation occurred.
Files accessed	Number of files accessed.
Communication devices accessed	Number of times all communications devices were accessed.
Print jobs spooled	Number of print jobs spooled.
Times buffers exhausted	
Big buffers	Number of times that big memory buffers were exhausted.
Request buffers	Number of times that request buffers were exhausted.

TABLE 11.6	Workstation Statistics

Item	Description
Workstation Statistics for \\NTAS-TRI-STAR	Indicates that this set of statistics is for a workstation and that the workstation name is \\NTAS-TRI-STAR.
Statistics since 4/1/94 5:47PM	Provides the starting date for the statistics.
Server Message Blocks (SMBs) received	Number of SMBs received.
Bytes transmitted	Number of bytes transmitted.
Server Message Blocks (SMBs) transmitted	Number of SMBs received.
Read operations	Number of successful read operations.
Write operations	Number of successful write operations.
Raw reads denied	Number of failed read operations.
Raw writes denied	Number of failed write operations.
Connections made	Number of successful connections that were made from the workstation.
Reconnections made	Number of times reconnections were made from the workstation.
Server disconnects	Number of times the server disconnected resources connected by the workstation.
Hung sessions	Number sessions from the workstation were hung.
Failed sessions	Number of session connect attempts that failed.
Failed operations	Number of operations from the workstation to the server that failed.
Use count	Use count is related to the number of connections to a network resource. Each time you successfully connect, this counter increments, although not necessarily by one. Tests showed the counter changing from 3 to 5 for each new connection.
Failed use count	Shows the number of failed connections to a network resource.

Domains

Domains generally work, and they don't provide much management or maintenance. We have seen maintenance issues with domains only when a system manager has done something to create problems with the domain relationship or has changed the security settings on a part of the system causing an access problem that appears to be a domain problem.

DOMAIN MONITOR (DOMMON.EXE) (NT RESOURCE KIT)

Domain Monitor is a tool for monitoring the status of NT domains. It shows the status of a domain and its trusted domains, the PDC for each domain, and other useful information. Domain Monitor also allows you to disconnect and reconnect the connection to a trusted domain. Figure 11.7 shows the main Domain Monitor window.

Domain Monitor can provide details on the servers in a domain via the properties window. Double-click a domain name, or select Properties from the Domain menu to display the window in Figure 11.8. Notice the status of CTI01, which is a Backup Domain Controller that happens to be offline (because it is turned off).

Domain Monitor is also useful for checking the status of file replication between servers. See the RKTOOLS.HLP file or Domain Monitor help for more information.

The following sections overview some other tools to monitor or tune performance on NT 4.0.

DISK PROBE

This is a Windows NT sector editor (see Figure 11.9). This tool enables you to directly modify data on the local computer's hard drive. If you've ever used Norton's Disk Editor, you will understand very quickly what Disk Probe does. Data structures such as the Master Boot Record, partition tables, and partition boot sectors can be edited directly.

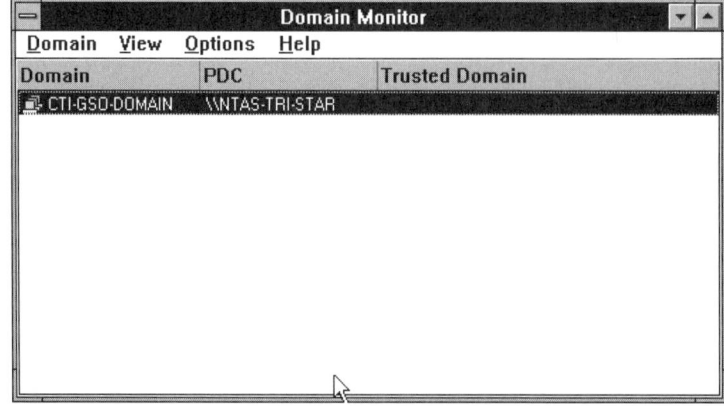

FIGURE 11.7 The main window for Domain Monitor, with one domain displayed. Notice that there is no trusted domain for CTI-GSO-DOMAIN at this time.

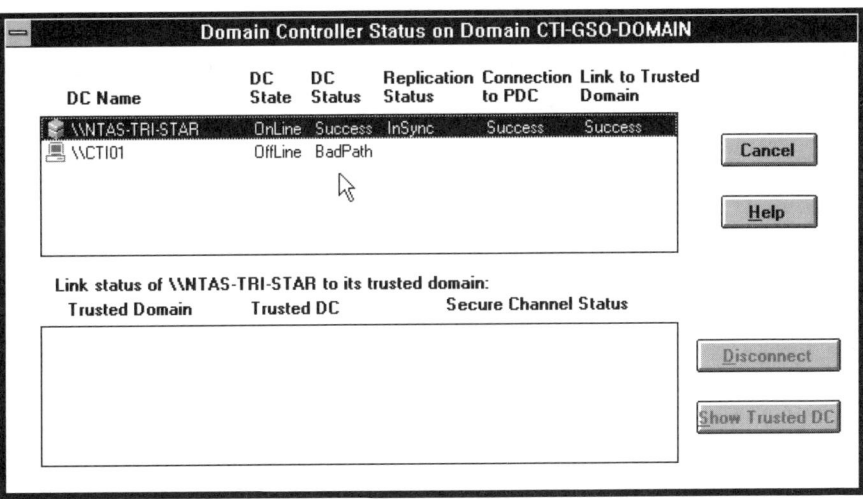

FIGURE 11.8 Properties window for Domain Monitor. Notice that Domain Monitor cannot find server CTI01.

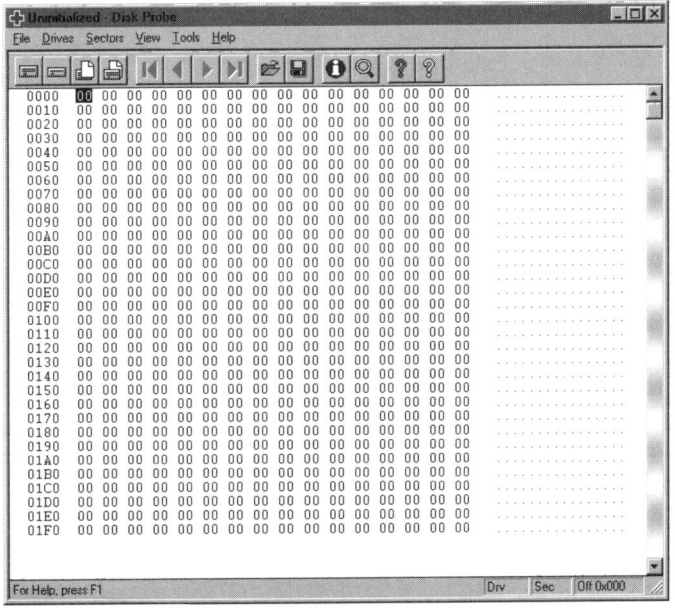

FIGURE 11.9 Disk Probe configuration screen.

FAULT TOLERANCE EDITOR

This tool enables you to edit disk and fault tolerance setting information directly to the registry. You must use it very carefully, especially if you have RAID configurations in your server, as any changes here could compromise your systems configuration. Figure 11.10 is a screen shot of the Fault Tolerance Editor tool.

PMON (NT RESOURCE KIT)

PMON.EXE displays resource usage by process. This information includes such things as the amount of CPU used, page faults, and thread count. The format for executing PMON is

```
pmon
```

If you have very many processes running on your system, the information quickly scrolls off the display. We usually run PMON with the following command:

```
pmon > PMONRUN.TXT
```

This command runs PMON and redirects the output to the specified text file. Pressing Ctrl+C aborts PMON and returns you to the command prompt. You can also run PMON like this from an icon and use the task list to abort the command when it has collected enough information. Use caution with this approach, because a run of 30 seconds or so can generate a 32K file.

The output from PMON looks like Figure 11.11.

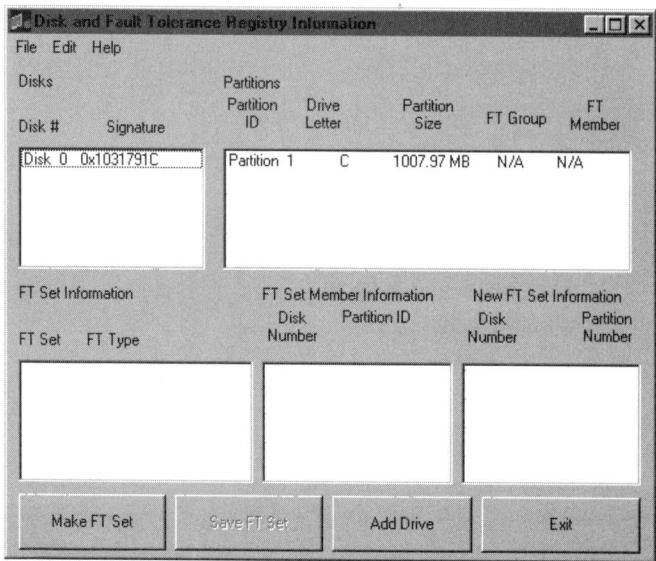

FIGURE 11.10   Disk and Fault Tolerance Registry Information.

```
                                       Command Prompt
              Mem   Mem     Page   Flts Commit    Usage    Pri Thd  Image
   %CPU CpuTime  Usage Diff  Faults Diff Charge NonP Page      Cnt  Name
                 1944    0  345277    0     0     0    0   0   1  File Cache
   100 17:44:38    16    0       0    0     0     0    0   0   1  Idle Process
     0  3:53:46    20    0    4942    0    32     0    1   8  27  System
     0  0:00:00     0    0     882    0   168     0    0  11   6  smss.exe
     0 391:04:54  3428    0  398685    0  4028     8   15  13  26  csrss.exe
     0  0:00:55    20    0   28098    0   400     9    6  13   3  winlogon.exe
     0  0:02:49   664    0  288177    0  1212   155   11   9  15  services.exe
     0  0:01:10   120    0  223193    0   784    18    6   9  13  lsass.exe
     0  0:05:53   280    0  256055    0   992   700    7   9   8  spoolss.exe
     0  0:00:00    20    0    2283    0   248     1    5  13   1  nddeagnt.exe
     0  0:01:18   268    0  127169    0  1028  2108    7   7  19  OCTO_SRV.EXE
     0  0:00:00     0    0     260    0   308    17    5   7   5  LOCATOR.EXE
     0  0:02:18   156    0   56010    0   396    33    6   7   3  snmp.exe
     0  0:01:32   120    0   11740    0   580  1795    6   7  11  FG_RECV.exe
     0  0:00:00     0    0     346    0   320   161    5   7   1  FG_RTR.exe
     0  0:00:07    64    0   52950    0   528   108    6   7  10  RPCSS.EXE
     0  0:00:56   308    0   12996    0   592     2    7  13   2  progman.exe
     0  1:30:28   304    0   61799    0  3424     3  138   7   5  ntvdm.exe
     0  0:00:00     0    0     283    0   220     1    4   7   1  CMD.exe
     0  0:00:00     0    0     647    0   668     2   70   7   3  OS2.exe
     0  2:10:54   120    0     490    0   512    10    8  24   6  OS2SRV.EXE
     0  0:00:00     0    0      60    0    88     0    0   8   1  os2ss.exe
     0 32:49:09   788    0 74827107    2   832     3   71   7   7  OS2.exe
     0  0:00:00     0    0     655    0   300     1    5   7   3  scm.exe
     0  0:00:00     0    0     491    0   300     1    4   8   4  psxss.exe
     0  0:01:31  1416    0   15437    0   624     2    7   7   3  WINFILE.EXE
     0  0:00:00    20    0    1224    0   276     9    4   7   4  AtSvc.Exe
     0  0:00:01   120    0     569    0   328     1    5   7   5  PRINTMAN.EXE
     0  0:00:00   844    0     233    0   224     1    5   9   1  CMD.exe
     0  0:00:27  1400    0     664    0   888     1   10   9   3  ntvdm.exe
     0  0:00:00   336   24     170   16   272     0    4  13   1  PMON.EXE
```

FIGURE 11.11   PMON's output provides a glimpse of the resource usage at any point in time.

PVIEWER (NT RESOURCE KIT)

Process Viewer (PVIEWER.EXE) is a cool little utility for checking out the processes on your system. PVIEW can not only view information on the various processes, but can kill a process once you've determined who the hog is. PVIEWER can also look at a process running on another NT system over the network. The syntax for executing the command is

pviewer

The Pviewer interface is pure simplicity, as is shown in Figure 11.12.

Due to its simplicity, the syntax of PVIEWER is straightforward. If you have any questions, see the RKTOOLS.HLP file in the NT Resource Kit directory.

Killing a Process with Pview:

1. Start Pviewer.
2. Select the process to kill from the top list box.
3. Click the Kill Process button.
4. Clicking the Memory button will provide lots of detail on the memory usage of the selected process.

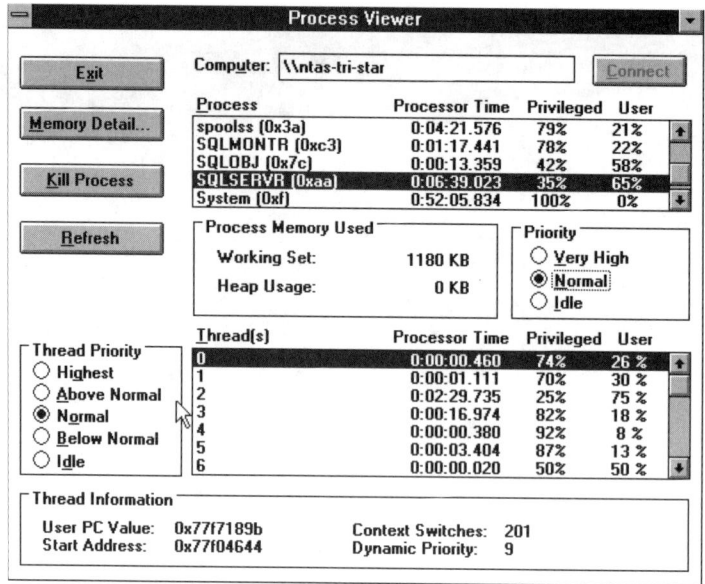

FIGURE 11.12 PVIEWER has a simple interface. Processes are shown in the top window, and the threads for the selected process are shown in the lower window. Click on a new process to display its threads.

QSLICE (NT RESOURCE KIT)

QSlice is another of those magical tools included with the NT Resource Kit. QSlice takes a quick slice of the processes at very short intervals and displays the results on a bar graph. This tool looks like magic, as the performance of your system unfolds before your eyes. Figure 11.13 shows the simple interface for QSlice.

This tool enables you to get a quick handle on your systems performance when you suspect that a process is going nuts or taking over. Double-click a process, and QSlice displays details on the threads for the process.

HP OPENVIEW (HEWLETT PACKARD)

HP OpenView is available in both Windows and UNIX versions. OpenView provides network diagramming capabilities and, most important, SNMP management tools. The Windows version does suffer when it is running on Windows 3.x or Windows for Workgroups 3.x or earlier. Running it on NT or Windows 95 should cause no resource problems.

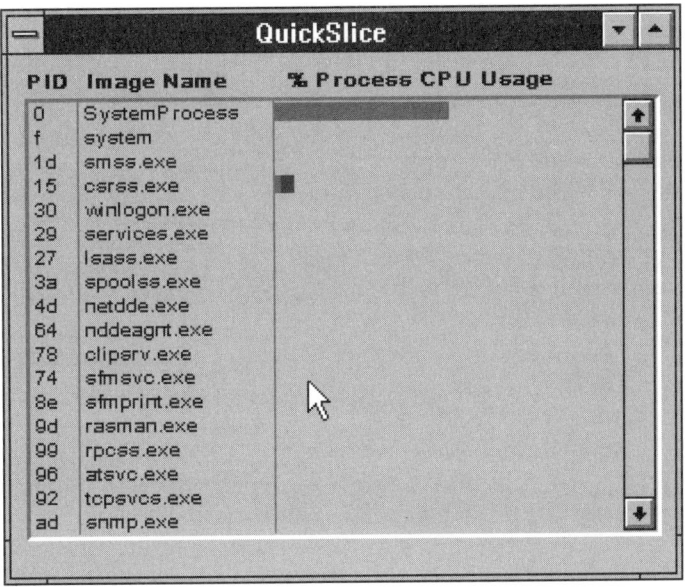

FIGURE 11.13 Notice how the System Process stands out in this example. This QSlice screen shot was taken when the system was idle, with almost no load.

The nicest feature of a tool like OpenView is the SNMP capability. SNMP gives you access to information about many different components on your network, including everything from NT Server to network devices such as routers and repeaters.

Add-on tools for many products enable you to actually manage the devices from OpenView. ChipCom has a product called On-Demand that integrates with OpenView and provides access directly to the ChipCom device. Using On-Demand, you can not only monitor devices but also set features on the device, such as disabling a port.

Microsoft Network Monitor

If you purchased either Microsoft Systems Management Server or Microsoft Back Office, you have a free sniffer, Network Monitor.

Network Monitor performs a number of different tasks:

- Captures frames (packets) from the network
- Captures frames remotely from an NT system and displays them on the local system
- Displays and searches captured frames
- Performs network loading by sending captured frames over the network
- Displays summary statistics of network performance

- Determines how many copies of Network Monitor are currently running
- Sets filters to determine which nodes and types of frames are monitored
- Sets display-only filters to restrict the display of captured data

Figure 11.14 shows the main window of Network monitor. It must be used on a system that supports "promiscuous mode," a state in which a network card detects all packets flowing over the network to which the card is attached. This is what allows Network Monitor to capture frames from all systems on the network. Check the documentation for your network card if you are not sure whether or not promiscuous mode is supported. The Network Monitor Capture window is shown in Figure 11.15.

This overview of Network Monitor is not meant to be an in-depth review but rather a glimpse of the product and how it can be used effectively in your network environment.

Network Monitor is useful if you spend the time to understand what normally happens on your network. This means understanding what type of traffic is normal, what a normal utilization looks like, and so forth. It is also useful to understand a little about what type of traffic is generated during certain operations.

For instance, if you know what happens when a Windows for Workgroups client performs a browse operation, you can quickly determine whether or not a user is having a problem by looking for those types of packets from that workstation.

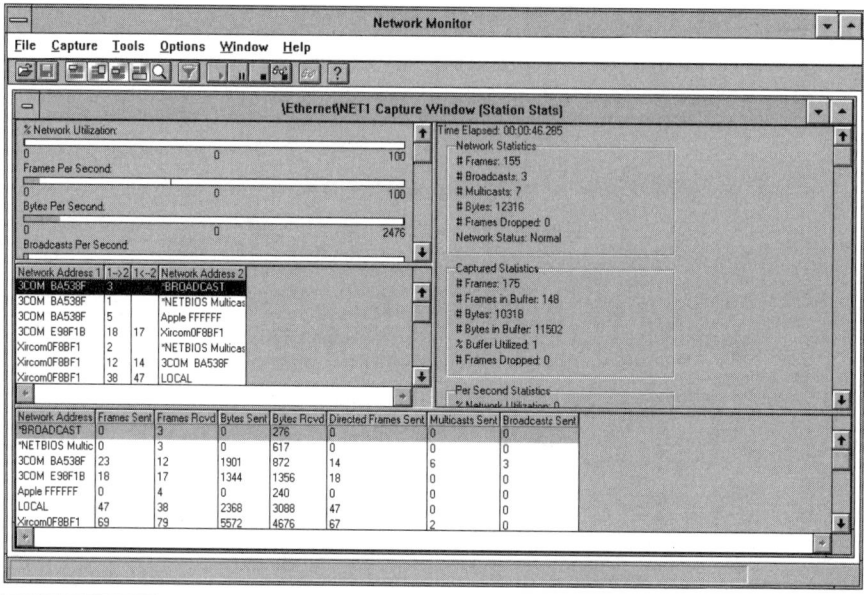

FIGURE 11.14 Network Monitor from Systems Management Server. Notice the great overview provided by the main form.

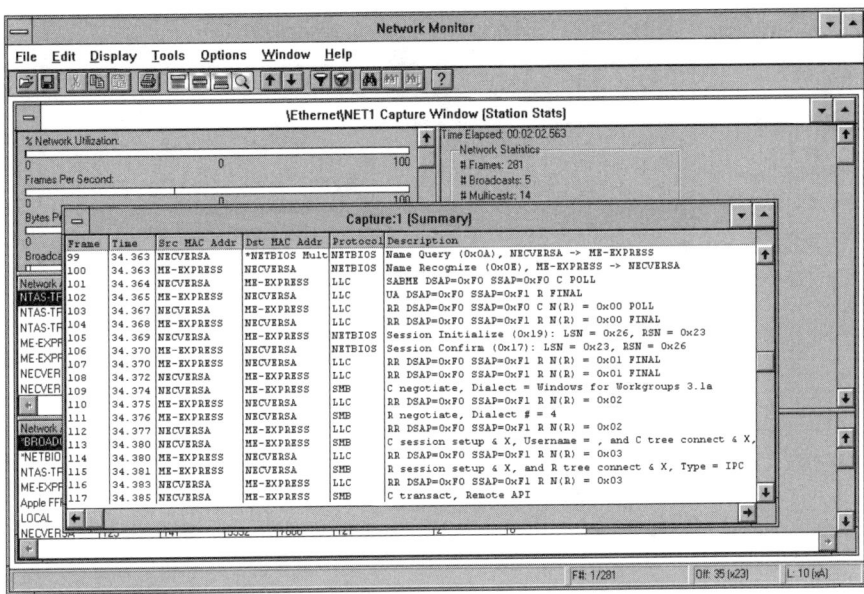

FIGURE 11.15 The Capture form shows all the frames captured by the Network Monitor.

The Network Monitor Capture Summary window is shown in Figure 11.16.

We have successfully used Network Monitor for a number of tasks in the first few months after installing it:

- Comparing the output of a home-grown SNMP monitor to that of OpenView for debugging
- Monitoring network utilization during moves from VMS to client/server systems
- Monitoring a PC that we thought had died while running a big task. Network Monitor showed us that I/O that was going on over the network proving the system was alive and well
- Performing research on exactly what happens to Windows for Workgroups and NT during normal and simulated operations like browsing and log-on

ADDRESS DATABASE

Before you use Network Monitor very much, you should build an address database that enables Network Monitor to display the name used to identify the system instead of the hexadecimal address associated with a frame. Network Monitor can store the names in a database for later use.

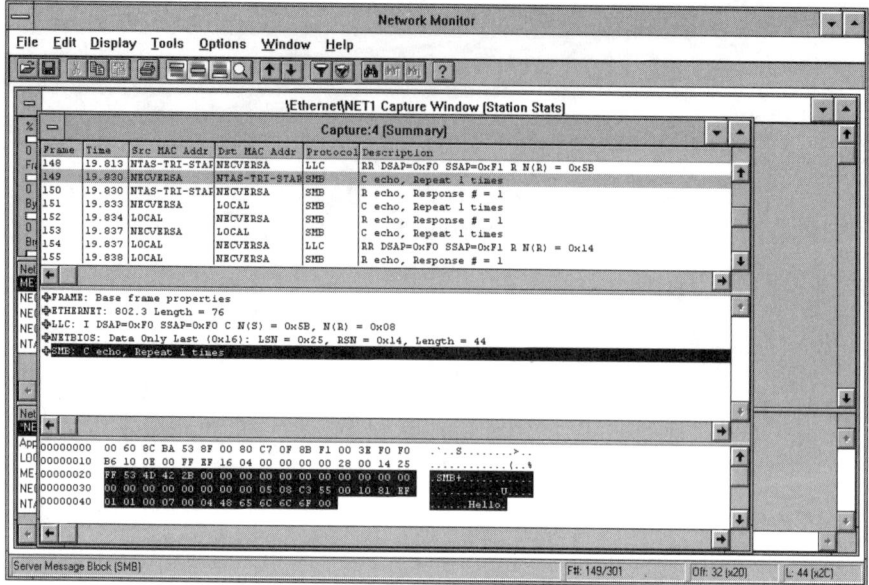

FIGURE 11.16 Capture form with the detail panes open. You can open the detail panes anytime by double-clicking a frame. The detail panes are synchronized with the selected frame.

Building an Address Database:

1. Start Network Monitor.
2. Choose Start from the Capture menu. Allow Network Monitor to run for some time (five minutes or more, for example) to collect frames.
3. Choose Stop from the Capture menu.
4. Choose Find Friendly Names from the Capture menu.
5. Click the OK button.
6. Choose the Addresses option from the Capture menu.
7. Click the Save button to save the names.

This database can be loaded later when you build a capture filter. Figure 11.17 shows a filtered view of captured packets.

USING NETWORK MONITOR

The easiest way to use Network Monitor when you have a problem is to fire it from SMS, which can provide many different displays of workstation information, including various queries sorted by user.

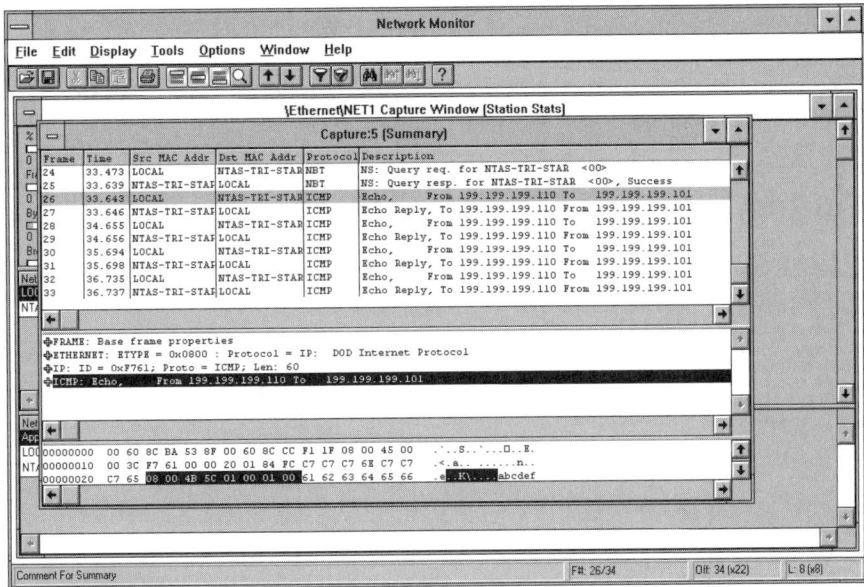

FIGURE 11.17 Capture window when we have applied filtering. The only frames allowed to show must use the IP, TCP/IP, or SNMP protocols.

Starting Network Monitor to Trace a Single Workstation or Server:

1. Start SMS Administrator.

2. Find the workstation or server you wish to monitor in a query or in any displayed list.

3. Double-click the workstation or server to display Properties window.

4. Scroll down the Properties list until you come to the Network Monitor icon.

5. Click the Network Monitor icon.

6. Click Start Network Monitor.

7. Click the Start Capture button once Network Monitor starts.

These steps enable you to quickly pinpoint the traffic from a particular system. You can also start Network Monitor by itself and set the filter options manually, which gives you the ability to monitor a selected group of systems at one time.

Network Monitor also adds two objects to the Performance Monitor database: Network Segment and Network Interface. These two objects contain a number of counters that provide detailed network statistics on various aspects of network performance. You should not use these counters for long periods of time on a server, because when they are activated, they place the network card into promiscuous mode. Promiscuous mode is not shut down until Performance Monitor exits, resulting in reduced performance over the network card. Always use these counters from an NT workstation or a noncritical server.

Tuning Specific NT Subsystems

Virtual Memory System

The NT Virtual Memory (VM) system uses a paging file(s) (PAGEFILE.SYS) to augment the physical memory of a system. The paging file in effect extends the memory of the system by allowing NT to move objects from memory to disk when it requires the memory for other tasks. The paging system is very effective, but it is much slower than physical memory (RAM). The counters for the Memory object in Table 11.7 are useful for monitoring the paging system within NT.

Table 11.8 lists several objects for the Paging File object that are useful to monitor.

You should be able to improve the performance of an NT system by splitting your paging files over multiple disk drives. This is accomplished by creating multiple page files on different disks. This is a good option if your

TABLE 11.7 Performance Monitor Memory Output Counters

Counter	Description
Commit Limit	Roughly the size of the physical memory of the system plus the paging file. The total is slightly less than the combination of these two because NT reserves a small amount of memory for itself.
Committed Bytes	The total amount of virtual memory committed at any point in time. When Committed Bytes approaches the Commit Limit, the system is running out of virtual memory, and the paging file must be extended.
Pool Nonpaged Bytes	Measures the amount of nonpaged memory in the system. When this value is greater than the physical memory of the system (4MB), the system will start thrashing, swapping memory back and forth to disk at a very fast rate. The only resolution to this problem is to add more physical memory to the system.
Pages Per Second	Measures the rate at which NT swaps memory to disk. The normal rate for this value is less than five pages per second. If the system begins to sustain a value of 10 or greater, the system is thrashing. You can lower the paging rate by adding physical memory to the system.

TABLE 11.8	Performance Monitor Paging File Objects
Counter	**Description**
Percent Usage	Shows the current percentage of a page file in use. If this counter nears 100%, the system is running out of paging space, and the page file should be manually expanded before it becomes full, to prevent automatic expansion. The page file should not be allowed to expand because it will become fragmented, and performance will really suffer.
Percent Peak Usage	Shows the peak percentage of a page files usage. If this counter nears 100%, the system is running out of paging space, and the page file should be expanded.

system has different disks attached to separate controllers or if the controller is able to process requests to each disk concurrently. Changes to the paging system are made in the Control Panel System applet.

Changing the Page File(s):

1. Start Control Panel.
2. Start the System applet.
3. Click the Virtual Memory button.
4. Choose the drive to create a paging file on.
5. Enter the size.
6. Click the Set button.
7. Repeat the process for each page file.

System Memory (RAM)

The shortest resource on most systems is RAM. This resource probably causes more grief than any resource other than disks. You should equip your servers with plenty of memory (32MB or more). In 1997 prices, you can add 32MB to your system for approximately $65. This is a small price to pay for the benefits it will bring in performance. We suggest that any server with more than 10 users should have 32MB or more of RAM.

You should be aware of one quirk with some Intel systems. Some systems use the memory above 16MB for caching parts of system ROM to improve performance. For instance, my Tri-Star system caches the ROM BIOS in the memory above 16MB. To install more than 16MB, you may need to disable caching of certain parts of the ROM in your system. Consult the technical manual for your system and/or the technical support department of your hardware vendor to determine how your system is set up.

ROM and BIOS caching should be turned off on all NT systems. NT does not use the BIOS for disk and screen operations, as does DOS. Turning off caching will free up memory that NT can use.

You can use WINMSD.EXE to monitor memory usage. The Memory display contains several bits of summary information on physical memory, paged memory, and the paging files. It also includes the Memory Load Index in the status bar at the bottom of the Memory window. The Memory Load Index provides an indication of memory utilization: 0 is no memory use, and 100 is full memory use.

Many servers that we have been implementing since late 1994 have used from 64MB to 640MB of RAM. This increase in RAM makes lots of sense because of its low cost, and it greatly improves the performance of the system. Table 11.9 shows two useful memory counters. Notice that the second counter is only for SQL servers.

You can come up with a fair approximation of additional memory requirements by using the Paging File: % Usage Max counter. This counter shows the amount of expansion the page file has incurred. The following formula uses this counter to determine how much memory to add to satisfy the memory demands to date.

```
New Memory = "Paging File: % Usage MAX * Page File Size
```

For example,

```
"Paging File: % Usage MAX = 20

Page File Size = 200MB

New Memory = 200 * 20
```

This example shows that we should add 40MB of memory to this server.

This very general approach should be used only as a starting point. Consider how applications use memory, when during the day memory is used (if only one application runs at 2:00 P.M. each day and consumes all the memory, move it to after hours), and any other parameters that may affect memory usage.

TABLE 11.9	Performance Monitor Counters for Selected Memory Options
Counter	**Description**
Memory: Available Bytes	Displays the amount of free physical memory. A reading that stays less than 1MB on NT Server indicates paging is occurring.
SQL Server: CacheHit Ratio	Displays how well the SQL Server cache is performing. If this counter is less than 80–90%, then more memory may improve the performance of SQL Server.

You should also consider increasing the secondary cache size any time that you add memory. Adding memory without increasing the secondary cache size could degrade processor performance because the hit rate from secondary cache would go down with more memory and the processor would be busier. This is a good example of why it is important to consider other than the most obvious factors before you make drastic changes.

Balancing the System Loading

The performance of the system should be balanced between network resources and system responsiveness for interactive users. We suggest setting the Tasking property to Foreground and Background Applications Equally Responsive for most NT Server systems, because the heaviest use of the system probably comes from network resource usage, which will be running as background tasks.

You can access the Tasking box dialog from the System applet in Control Panel, as is shown in Figure 11.18.

Configuring Priority Settings:

1. Start the Systems applet in Control Panel.
2. Click the Tasking button.
3. Click the Tasking option for your system.
4. Click OK.

The second step in balancing the system loading is to determine how your system is used. Table 11.10 shows the settings for the Memory Optimization dialog box for the Server in Network applet.

TABLE 11.10 Memory Optimization Dialog Box Settings

Setting	Type of Server Usage
Minimize Memory Used	Interactive with minor file and print server usage (up to 10 network users).
Balance	General usage with some file and print server usage (up to 64 network users).
Maximize Throughput for File Sharing	File and print server (greater than 64 network users). This is the default setting for NT Server.
Maximize Throughput Network Applications	Primary Application Server and some File and Print server usage (64 or for more network users). Application access to memory has priority over file cache access. Use this option for systems primarily running SQL Server, Systems Management Server, and Exchange Server.

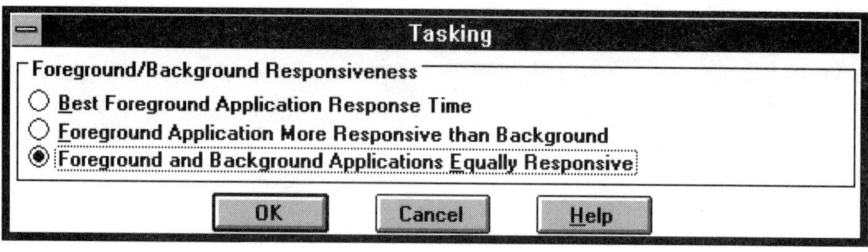

FIGURE 11.18 The Tasking dialog box controls how NT sets priority for different types of applications.

Configuring Server Memory Usage:

1. Start the Network applet in Control Panel.
2. Double-click the Server in the Network Software and Adapter Cards box.
3. Click the Optimization option for your system.
4. Click OK.

Network Performance

When your system seems to be experiencing performance problems, you can take several steps. The NT network system provides quite a number of counters that track various aspects of performance. It is always important to remember when you tune or troubleshoot a network that not only the network counters but also the counters involving the server must be monitored, because the two are inseparable. Table 11.11 contains a set of objects that are good candidates for a network settings file. These objects track both network settings and several settings for the server that have an impact on the network. Use Performance Monitor and/or Network Monitor to check the areas shown in Table 11.11.

A tremendous number of counters are available for network-related functions. Table 11.12 lists several counters that you should monitor.

There are a number of ways that you can improve network performance. Many of these are covered in other parts of this book but are mentioned briefly here for completeness.

- Match network controllers to the fastest bus on your system. Use PCI or EISA controllers instead of ISA. This should improve a high interrupt/second reading.
- Add memory to relieve Pool Paged Failures and Pool Nonpaged Failures.
- Use faster network cards in the server. New technologies such as the 3Com Parallel Tasking controller tend to off-load the CPU in servers.

TABLE 11.11 Potential Problem Areas	
Area to Check	**Suggest Solution**
Server workload	If the server workload is different on multiple servers, consider redistributing the load over all the servers.
Paging	If a system is paging at a high rate, it is probably running out of physical memory. The only solution is to change the load on the system or to add more memory.
Disk saturation	Disk saturation can result from many causes, including adding too many users or intensive applications reading and writing to an already heavily used disk. The normal resolution to this problem is to get a faster disk/controller or spread the application over several disks. Implementing a RAID 5 disk subsystem is an ideal candidate for this type of environment.
Network saturation	Network saturation occurs when your system has reached the capacity of the network or network card(s) in the system. The solution is to switch to a faster card or network system or to split the network. Splitting the network involves creating several physical networks with routers or adding additional network cards to the system and splitting the network across the additional cards.

- Faster networks such as 100BaseT and FDDI can relieve network bottlenecks. Make sure that you match your network segments to use fast network technologies on the same segment.
- Network switches can provide high performance on the same network by providing dedicated segments to users and servers.
- If transport (NetBEUI, TCP/IP): Bytes Total/second approaches the maximum transfer rate for your network, it indicates a saturation of that network segment. The saturation point is usually much less than the rated throughput for the network. Ethernet is reputed to max out at around 1.2MB/sec, even though Ethernet is rated at 10MB/sec. When you think that the network is approaching the saturation point, you can segment the network using a router, multiple network cards in the server, or a network switch. You can also combine some of these methods.

Network Monitor (included with SMS) provides a number of additional statistics for Performance Monitor and lots of additional features from its own interface. See "Network Monitor (Microsoft)," earlier in this chapter. Let's look at some things we may want to do with the results of inquiries with Network Monitor.

- Sort the Network Monitor Broadcasts Multicasts column in the Station Statistics pane (the bottom pane) to find the source of a broadcast storm. Rates of over 100 per second should be investigated. If the source is a PC, replace the network card. If the source is a router, check out the features for tuning the router.

■ Monitor % Network Utilization for increasing trends. When this counter starts approaching 40 percent or higher, the network will most likely start slowing down significantly. The use of faster media (cable), network cards, switches, and combining routers can improve network performance dramatically.

CPU

The question "How do you tune a system to improve CPU performance?" has been the all-time question for networks. Most networks do not place a

TABLE 11.12 Performance Monitor Counters for Network-Related Functions

Object Name	Short Description	Description
NetBEUI: Bytes Total/second	Number of bytes per second sent and received over the NetBEUI interface.	This counter indicates when network traffic is high. It includes only data bytes that were sent or received. Overhead for the protocol is not counted.
TCP/IP: Bytes Total/second		This counter is the same as the last one except that it is for the TCP/IP interface.
Server: Bytes Total/second	Total bytes per second for the server.	A steadily increasing value indicates an increasing load on the server.
Work Item Shortages	How many shortages of work item storage space are occurring.	An increasing value indicates that the server is overloaded and does not have enough SMB storage space, indicating a bottleneck at the server service.
Context Block Queue Time	How long a server request must wait in the server before it is processed.	This counter is one of the best parameters to use to detect a busy server. Watch for this value to increase as client load increases. If it averages greater than 50 (msec), it indicates that the server service is the bottleneck.
Context Blocks Queued/second	Rate at which context blocks must be placed on the queue.	It should increase as more client traffic changes and the context block queue time goes up.
Pool Paged Failures and Pool Nonpaged Failures	How often NT ran out of page and nonpaged memory.	Any value greater than 0 normally indicates a shortage of physical memory.
System: Total Interrupts/second	Total number of interrupts per second that occurred on the processor.	When this value is high for a given system, the processor may be heading toward saturation.

tremendous load on the CPU because they are offering mainly file and print services. NT can place much more stress on the CPU because of the wide variety of tasks NT can perform.

Most of the tuning options for improving or removing a CPU bottleneck require some investigation and a commonsense approach. If you have developed your network with solid and upgradeable servers, used multiple servers to spread the network load, and have some control over your applications, you are in good shape for this type of approach. Table 11.13 contains notes on several counters that should be monitored to try to determine what is causing the load on the CPU.

After checking these counters, you can do a number of things to improve the CPU utilization of your system.

- If a hardware device is generating excessive interrupts, upgrade the device, use a PCI network or disk controller instead of an ISA device, or use an intelligent communications controller.
- Add an additional processor to the system with the bottleneck. This option is especially helpful for application servers or for any system that has multiple threads contributing to the bottleneck.
- Upgrade the secondary cache.
- Use PVIEW to lower the priority of a process. Use the START command to execute an application and add one of the priority options: /low, /normal, or /high.

Disk Subsystems

The disk subsystems in network servers have traditionally presented a bottleneck at one point or another. Faster systems and faster disk devices have alleviated this problem to some degree, but the disk system is still one of the most important elements of any server.

TABLE 11.13 Performance Monitor Counters for Determining CPU Loads

Object Name	Short Description	Description
Processor: % Processor Time	% of time that a processor is performing useful work.	When this counter approaches 100%, you may be experiencing a processor bottleneck. The next step is to determine "what" or "who" is causing the problem.
Processor: Interrupts/second	Number of device interrupts per second.	When this counter hits 1000 or over, you should check the efficiency of hardware I/O devices (disk controllers, network cards, any other system devices).
System: System Calls/second	Number of calls to NT system service routines per second.	If Processor: Interrupts/second is greater than System: Calls/second, a hardware device may be triggering the excessive interrupts.

The Physical Disk object is the primary indicator for monitoring disk activity. Table 11.14 contains several counters and notes that should be routinely evaluated on all servers.

You can do quite a number of things to improve disk performance:

- Spread the disk load over multiple disks. Place the NT boot partition and the paging file(s) on different disks. Place user data on separate disks or a stripe set.
- Use NTFS instead of FAT or HPFS.
- Choose new disk drives with the lowest possible seek time.
- Match disk controllers to the fastest bus on your system. Use PCI or EISA controllers instead of ISA.
- Use a defragmentation utility (such as Disk Keeper) to reduce disk fragmentation.
- Disable short-file-name generation on NTFS partitions.
- Use a RAID 5 hardware controller for data disks. The more drives the better.
- Use mirrored or duplexed disks if you are not using the ATDISK driver, and your disk controller can perform asynchronous I/O. NT performs alternating reads on mirrored and duplexed disks to improve performance.
- Add memory to improve cache performance.
- Upgrade to a faster controller. Fast SCSI-2 (10MB/sec throughput), SCSI-2 (5MB/sec), ESDI (3MB/sec), IDE (2.5MB/sec).

Conclusion

So now you are a tuning expert. We have shown you many of the tools that you can use with NT. If you are a serious NT manager, then you also want to read many parts of the NT Resource Kit. You must understand Registry parameters, application performance, how applications work together, how databases work, and what load different applications such as WINS and DNS place on a server. The Microsoft Knowledgebase, which goes hand in hand with the NT Resource Kit, is also a must-have for the NT manager.

TABLE 11.14	Performance Monitor Counters for Routine Evaluation	
Object Name	**Short Description**	**Description**
Physical Disk: % Disk Time	% of time the disk is busy.	A reading near 100% indicates a physical disk as the bottleneck.
Physical Disk: Disk Queue Length	Number of pending disk I/O requests.	A number greater than 2 indicates that requests for disk services are backing up.

Chapter 12 examines NT security. You will learn how to secure files and other objects, and generally how to use the NT security tools. You will also learn some tips on managing user accounts and passwords to effectively secure your network.

Security

NT security was designed into the system from the beginning. The target for the NT security system was to obtain a C-2 rating. The security system is very thorough and applies to all objects in the system. The security controls of NT 4.0 even carry to objects such as accessing pixels on the screen during a screen copy.

Scenario 12.1:

You manage a large network, and you are planning to deploy NT in various configurations. How do you decide what the security settings will be? How do you set it up?

Scenario 12.2:

Your organization has just deployed NT on the Internet, and now you are wondering what this does to your security. How do we find the most granular level of control over an object? How do we make sure users have a trusted log-on connection?

This chapter delves into the NT security system and related matters and provides some useful suggestions to help you use the security system in a manner appropriate for your network. What is appropriate depends entirely upon your environment and requirements. Most networks require use of only the standard NT user account and password system, in combination with setting permissions on certain objects. This type of network is the focus of this chapter. If your system requires very strict security requirements such as a C2 rating, you should take the concepts from this chapter, thoroughly read and understand the NT 4.0 Resource Kit, especially the section dealing with C2 security, and consult other information resources, and then apply your knowledge to your network.

Microsoft has been working on C2 certification for the NT platform since 1991. In July of 1995, Microsoft first met the C2 Orange Book listing of the base operating system with NT 3.5 (with Service Pack 3).

You should know that the National Computer Security Center (NCSC) also recognized NT as meeting two B-level features:

- **B2 Trusted Path**–The Trusted Path functionality prevents Trojan Horse programs from intercepting username and password information during initial logging on.
- **B2 Trusted Facility Management**–With the Trusted Facility Management functionality, Windows NT supports separate account roles for operator and administrator functions, as NT provides separate administrative roles for Administrators, users tasked with backups, users tasked with administrating printers, privileged Power Users, and Users.

As of summer 1997, Microsoft was evaluating NT 4.0 to obtain the rating of C2 in a homogeneous networked environment. The NCSC publication "Trusted Network Interpretation," also called the "Red Book," serves as an interpretation of the Orange Book, as it applies to networking for this evaluation.

The typical NCSC security evaluation cycle takes longer than the product release cycle of Windows NT. No significant changes have been made to the Windows NT security model from version 3.5 to versions 3.51 and 4.0.

Microsoft is also conducting similar efforts in the United Kingdom and Germany, through the Information Technology Security Evaluation Criteria (ITSEC). ITSEC has similar evaluation process for C2 as in the United States. In 1996, the NT version 3.51 (in a homogeneous network environment) completed its first ITSEC evaluation. Microsoft is seeking a C2 rating for NT 3.51 with an assurance rating of E3. In an ITSEC evaluation, the assurance rating given to a product indicates the level of analysis and supporting documentation used in developing the product. The greater the assurance rating, the higher the assurance. An E3 rating is typically mapped to the level of analysis performed in a "B" level evaluation.

According to the document "Security Considerations and C2 Security Rating," (TechNet, June 1997), the NT Final Evaluation Report of the NCSC security evaluators indicates: "One of the major initial design goals for Windows NT was to assure C2-level security through an integral, uniform protection mechanism. All system resources are treated as objects, and thus a single security 'gate' can be the protection component that all users must pass through to acquire system resources." The same report concluded: "This results in much greater assurance that the system meets the applicable security criteria, because a single security mechanism is easier to understand and to verify then multiple *ad hoc* mechanisms. When security is not an absolute requirement of the initial design, it is virtually impossible through later add-ons to provide the kind of uniform treatment to diverse system resources that Windows NT provides."

For additional information on the security design of NT, check Microsoft Windows NT 3.5 *Guidelines for Security, Audit, and Control,* published by Microsoft Press, and the Microsoft Web Server.

Nevertheless, NT security will always be tested as malicious codes and unscrupulous individuals will always try to crack into it. In March of 1997, for example, Windows NT suffered one of its major attacks in history: A remote user, connected to a server, was able to break the encrypted information of NT, including all the users passwords on the registry, converting them into text!

This chapter discusses the security of NT, its strengths and weaknesses, and what can be done to prevent break-ins or enhance the level of security at your site.

Validation of Log-ons

A log-on process validates every log-on request from a user to an NT server. The local log-on process manages interactive log-ons through the system console, including display of the initial log-on dialog box.

The log-on screen is the first evidence of NT's commitment to security. On NT, you must press CTRL+ALT+DEL (CAD) to log-on the system. If you did this in DOS, you would reboot the system. The same principle is used with NT. When you log-on NT after the CAD sequence, you're actually booting into NT's virtual machine (VM). The security system of NT actually creates an access token for you, composed of your username, group, and related information, all listed in your profile when your account was created.

This log-on Secure Attention Sequence identifies and authenticates you with the NT system. Another security check that is executed behind the scenes when you press CTRL+ALT+DEL when booting on NT is the verification that no Trojan Horse programs are present in the system. NT also enables you, as an administrator, to audit all security events and user actions. The User Manager enables you to specify which events (log-on or file access, for example) will be monitored. All audited information is stored in the Event Log, which can be viewed using the Event Viewer, as shown in Figure 12.1.

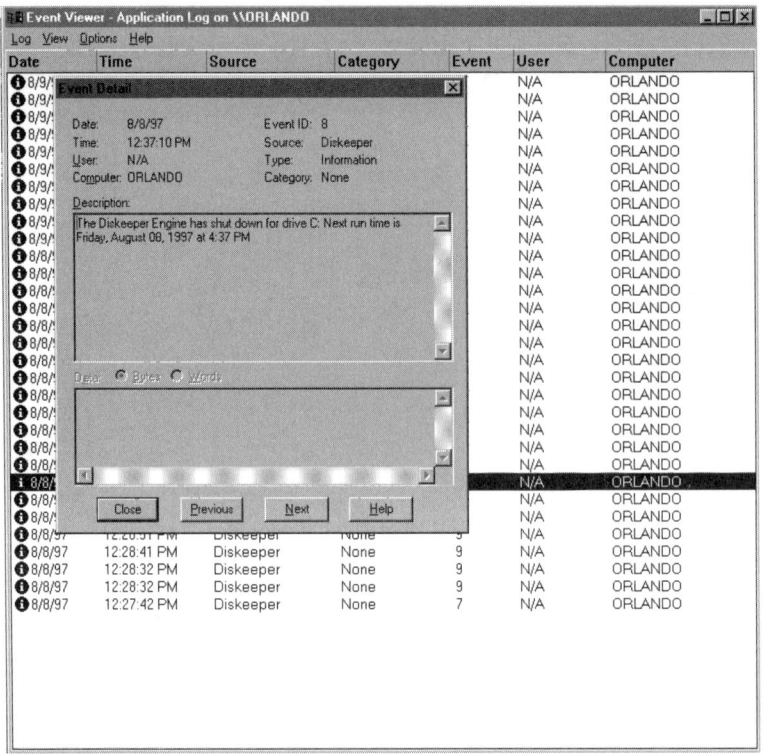

FIGURE 12.1 Event Viewer allows audited information on NT to be viewed at glance and details.

A remote log-on process similarly handles validation of users that request a log-on over the network.

Once a user is logged on, if any log-on script is specified for the user, it is executed.

Users can access resources on an NT server when they are not logged into a domain. You can accomplish this log-on by simply connecting to the server resource from File Manager or another application and specifying a correct user name and password when you are prompted. Any log-on script that is assigned to an account is *not executed* when connections are made in this manner. Standard NT permissions still apply to all access to an NT resource, and they prevent access to a resource from an unauthorized user.

To be more specific, here it is what happens when you invoke a log-on on NT:

- The log-on dialog box appears on the screen.
- You enter your username and password, then click OK or press ENTER.
- The Security Account Manager (SAM) checks the security database to determine whether or not the username and password you entered are valid.

- If the account is valid, the security subsystem creates an access token and sends it to the Winlogon process.
- Winlogon then calls the Win32 subsystem, which in turn presents to you a positive response through a new process, the Explorer-based one.

Figure 12.2 shows a summary of the log-on process.

Security Account Manager (SAM)

The Security Account Manager maintains the security accounts database (which includes users). This database contains all information for user accounts and groups. The database is stored in the SAM and SAM.LOG files in the \WINNT35\SYSTEM32\CONFIG directory.

SAM not only maintains the user accounts database, but it also provides the SID (security identifier) for user validation services when this is requested by the Local Security Authority at log-on. If you ever delete a users' account,

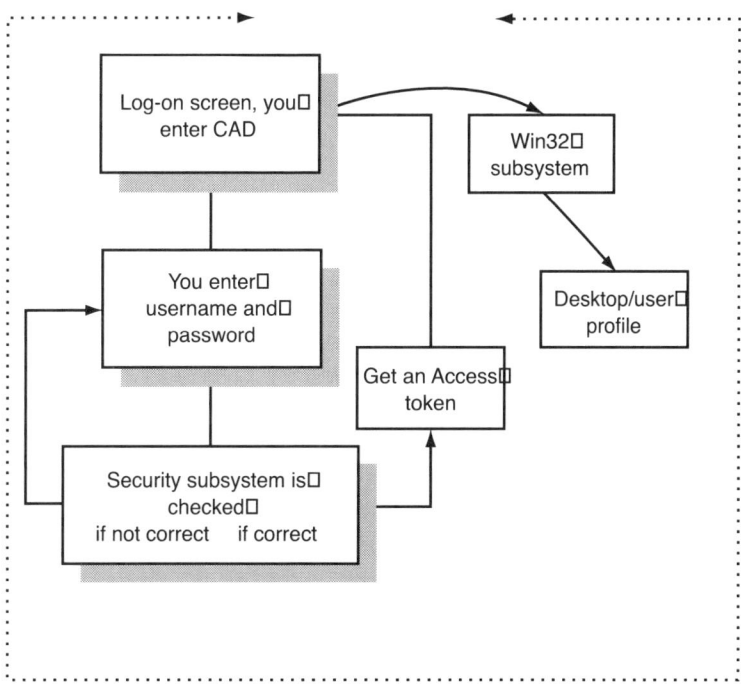

The Log-on Process on NT

FIGURE 12.2 Log-on process executed by the NT security subsystem at user's log-on.

the SID is never used again, even if you use that account name again, as all SIDs are unique.

In the incident described at the beginning of this chapter, the SAM database was cracked, and the authors of the script used to crack the database, Jeremy Allison and Yobie Benjamin, posted the script on the Internet. A lot of people already have access to it, which makes a lot of administrators nervous.

There are actually two basic types of SAMs, one stored locally on your computer, and the other one stored on the Primary Domain Controller (PDC), which is also replicated to the Backup Domain Controller (BDC), if it exists.

Although SAMs and many other services on NT can be threatened, the fact that NT is such a high-level security product doesn't make it unbreakable. No software is unbreakable! Even though the code developed by Allison and Benjamin was designed to be used on migrations of NT users to UNIX, it does allow anyone to see all the passwords registered and stored on NT, which until now was impossible.

With this code available on the Internet, anyone with malicious intentions can attack an NT server. At least all the ingredients are there, available on the Internet, although you must have the administrator's password in order to execute the script. But any nerd teenager with a PC and a modem can access an NT network, not via RAS or log-on attacks—as you already saw throughout this book, it would be almost impossible to accomplish— but through a Trojan Horse! It wouldn't be difficult to bundle a series of applets together, embed it into an executable file, and send via e-mail as an attachment to a user inside the network. You just need to make sure to motivate the user to execute the applet, which nowadays is not so difficult. Once inside the network, this applet could be instructed to run the code developed by Allison and Benjamin and then e-mail the file back to the hacker. This is possible in theory, but we haven't yet heard of NT's SAMs break-ins other than in labs.

Security Reference Monitor (SRM)

The access validation code is enforced by the SRM, which protects resources and objects from being hacked. SRM also is responsible for all the access validation and audit policy enforcement in the Local Security Authority (LSA). The SRM is a sort of law/security enforcement agent for NT. This is possible because every object has an access control list (ACL). These ACLs consist of access control entries (ACE) that all have a SID and an action policy to the object. Every time you attempt to access an object, the SRM checks your SID against an ACE list. If there is not a security match, the task is terminated.

Discretionary Access Controls (DACL)

DACLs enable you, as the network administrator, to control which users can or cannot connect to a resource or perform an action. Figure 12.3 shows an example where the floppy drive A can have its access controlled. You can determine who can and who cannot access it.

Security and RAS

The primary way to dial into an NT Server or NT network is to use the Remote Access Service (RAS). RAS is covered in detail in Chapter 4. The security impact of RAS access to the network is consistent with the general security of NT.

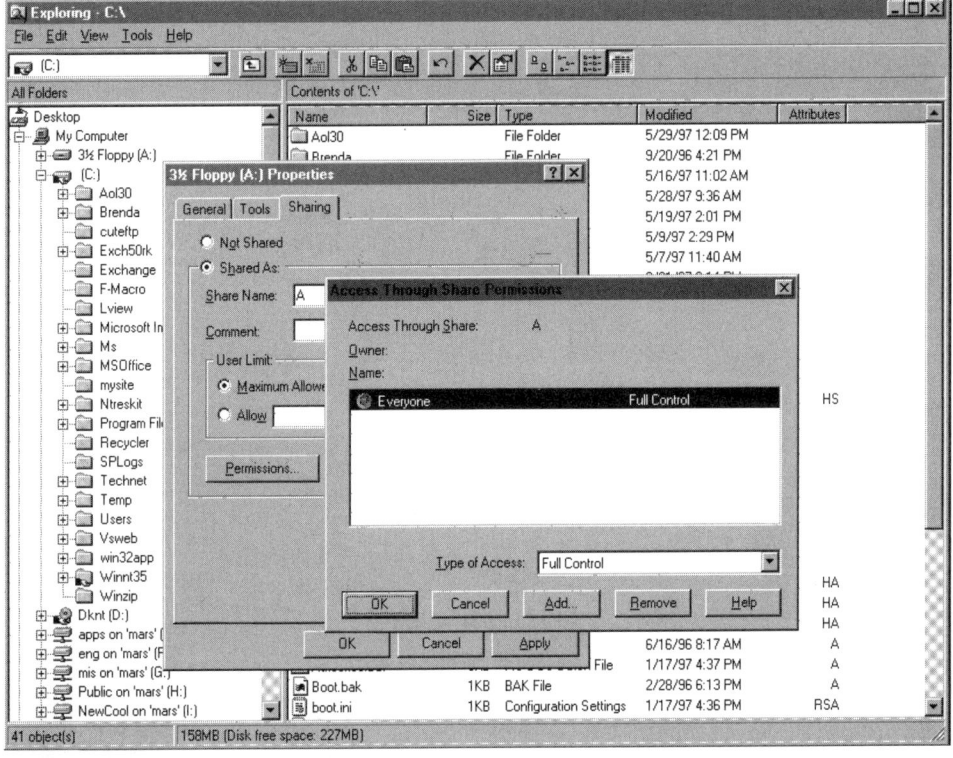

FIGURE 12.3 Clicking the Permissions button in the Sharing tab of the Properties dialog box opens the Access Through Share Permissions dialog box, which enables you to set the permissions for the chosen drive.

Before a user gets access to the network with RAS, the user must be validated. All user passwords and the authentication procedure are encrypted before they are sent over a phone line. This protects access to the network from snooping without a proper validation of the user account and password.

Once the user has accessed RAS server, you can further manage their access using standard NT tools and RAS tools. Table 12.1 lists several ways to control RAS access and describes and the tools necessary to perform the task.

RAS in NT 4.0 (as well as in NT 3.5 and 3.51) provides data encryption, which protects data being transmitted over the wires and ensures secure dial-up communications. NT provides data encryption using, the RSA Data Security Incorporated RC4 algorithm.

With NT 4.0, you can also take advantage of RAS, using Multi-Link PPP connections. You can combine the bandwidth of two or more physical communications links to increase your remote access bandwidth and throughput, using RAS Multi-link. RAS Multi-link lets you easily combine analog modem paths, ISDN paths, and even mixed analog and digital communications links on both your client and server PC.

TABLE 12.1   Remote Access Server Security Access Controls

Type of Access	Tool	Description
Network	Network Applet	You can enable or restrict network access can by binding the protocols that allow access to the network to the appropriate adapter. For instance, if TCP/IP is bound to an adapter, the RAS users can access all services that can be accessed through TCP/IP. This setting is global for all users.
All Access	RAS Administrator	You can disable or enable access through RAS by starting the RAS Administrator and choosing the proper option from the Computer menu. To temporarily stop RAS, select Pause from the Computer menu.
Callback	RAS Administrator	Setting the callback parameters for a user triggers RAS to dial the user back after the user has been authenticated. The callback number can be set by the administrator, or the user can be prompted to enter the callback phone number. The default is no callback.
User Access	RAS Administrator	Access for each user must be set, using the RAS Administrator program. This program allows you to enable or disable access by account and to configure callback for a particular account.

An important feature also present in RAS/NT 4.0 is its ability to restart file copying in case of a connection failure. RAS automatically begins re-transferring a file upon reconnection whenever your RAS connection has been lost. Nevertheless, if your connection has been idle for too long, RAS now has a new feature that will automatically disconnect you from the server. You or the administrator can specify the amount of time before this feature is activated. Another new feature with RAS for NT 4.0 is the ability for secure Internet transmissions using the new Point to Point Tunneling Protocol (PPTP) technology. PPTP allows remote users to access their network via the Internet through RAS. PPTP is fully integrated with NT 4.0 RAS, which also supports multiprotocol virtual private networks (VPNs). By using the Internet as a transferring mechanism, you will be able to save a lot of money on 800 services and long-distance calls.

You and your users can access your protected network by dialing into your Internet Service Provider (ISP) or connecting directly to the Internet. You can use modems, ISDN cards, and so forth to gain access to your network, with the benefit that all your data is encrypted by SSL. PPTP is compatible with IP, IPX, NetBEUI, and other mainstream protocols.

Access to Server Administrative Functions

For starters, only NT systems can fully administrate other NT or NT Server systems. Some applications and application environments are exceptions to this rule. SQL Server, for instance, comes with utilities for administering the SQL Server system from MS-DOS systems. NT Server also includes client tools mentioned earlier for managing certain parts of NT (see Chapter 7 for more information on these tools).

You should consider removing utilities such as RegEdt32 and RegEdit from NT systems that are not authorized to maintain NT servers and workstations. You can also prevent access to the utilities if they are located on an NTFS volume by denying access to all users except administrators.

Permissions

Permissions are used by NT to control everything from file and print services to entries in the NT Registry. Permissions are activated in the application that controls the object. For instance, permissions that control access to files are set in File Manager. Print Manager sets permissions for print services, and RegEdt32 sets permissions for Registry entries.

NT sets permissions on files and directories for NTFS volumes only. FAT and HPFS (for NT 3.51 only) file systems do not support the NT security scheme for files and directories. You can, however, set permissions on shares for these file systems, as well as NTFS file systems. SFM supports security because you must use NTFS for Macintosh volumes.

The NTFS file system uses a concept called an Access Control List (ACL) to manage permissions on an object. The ACL is attached to an object when you first define a permission on the object. Each time you change or add a new permission on the object, an entry called an Access Control Entry (ACE) is added in the ACL for the object. The ACE identifies the type of permission and the user or group ID assigned the permission.

As discussed earlier, when a user tries to access an object, NT reads the ACL for the object to determine the user's access. NT makes only one pass through the list and stops when it reaches the end of the list or reads an ACE with "deny access" as the permission. Deny access overrides all other permissions on an object. All other NTFS permissions are cumulative for access to an object. For instance, if a user has certain permissions granted directly and other permissions granted through a group to which the user belongs, the permissions accumulate, giving the user the total individual and group permissions. The only exception is "deny access," which overrides all other permissions, denying the user access to the object.

Files are "owned" by users. The user who owns a file can grant or deny access to the object at will. Permissions can be placed on an NTFS object by the owner of the object. A user with administrator rights can take ownership of an object and then give others rights to the object, but an audit trail is created for all changes if auditing is turned on for the object.

You can also protect such system functions on an NT system as setting the system time, shutting down the system, and formatting the hard disk, using User Rights.

Securing NT System Files

Because NT supports permissions only on NTFS volumes, you should create your boot partition on an NTFS volume. This means that you can use the NT security system to protect important files such as those in the Registry. The use of an NTFS boot partition also prevents anyone from booting the system with a DOS floppy disk and gain access to any NT files. You should review the "Server Management" section of Chapter 2 on providing backups and alternate boot methods for NT systems using an NTFS partition for the boot drive, because you will not be able to access the NT system files from DOS if the system fails to boot NT.

RISC systems are a bit of a problem because you can't make the boot partition anything but a FAT partition, but this is somewhat simplified; you can't boot a RISC system from a floppy DOS drive, and the only way you can get to a FAT partition on the RISC system is from NT or possibly from a DOS emulator running under UNIX. You can and should make the FAT partition around 6MB, and place the NT system files on an NTFS disk drive.

Securing Floppy Disk Drives on a Server

If your NT system is not locked inside a room, you may need to use Floppy Lock from the NT Resource Kit to restrict access. This program enables you to lock the floppy drive to prevent someone other than an administrator from using it.

When you install the Floppy Lock service on a system, make sure the path name on the INSTSRV command includes the complete path to the file, including the file name.

Installing Floppy Lock:

1. Copy the Floppy Lock program (FLOPLOCK.EXE) to a hard disk.

2. Execute the following command:

```
INSTSRV FloppyLocker D:\RESKIT40\FLOPLOCK.EXE
```

You can change the name FloppyLocker to any descriptive name of your choosing, as long as it is a legal name for a service.

Once Floppy Lock is installed, you must configure the service to start automatically.

Configuring the Floppy Lock Service:

1. Start the Services applet in Control Panel.

2. Select the FloppyLocker service, and click Configure.

3. Enter the account name for the service to use (for example, an account in the Administrator group) and the password for the account.

4. Reboot the system.

Once you have performed the installation and configuration steps, the floppy drive(s) on the server are locked to everyone except for an administrator. Note that this procedure works only as long as NT is running. If your system can be rebooted with another operating system (DOS or UNIX), someone may be able to obtain access to the system. A user gaining access in this manner will still not be able to access any files if you are using NTFS. The user could conceivably reinstall NT and gain access to the files, unless the files are protected, using NTFS security.

You can disable Floppy Lock by stopping the service with Server Manager or Control Panel. Once Floppy Lock is disabled, the floppy drives work normally until the system reboots. To remove Floppy Lock permanently, set the Floppy Lock service to disabled.

File Deletions

NT does not support recovering deleted files on any of its disk partitions (NTFS, FAT, and HPFS in case of NT 3.51). This restriction is a direct result of the C2 security features of NT, because under C2, the ability to recover a deleted file is considered a security breach. Most third-party utilities and other tools are also restricted from recovering files, but Executive Software, the makers of Diskeeper, does have a utility to restore files on NTFS partitions, which comes with Diskeeper for NT 4.0.

Computer Accounts

NT and NT Server systems that belong to a domain must have an account for the computer on the domain. Computer accounts are usually created automatically by NT or NT Server during the installation process. Server Manager can be used to view, add, or delete a computer account.

Passwords for the computer accounts are changed regularly by the Net Logon service. The password change occurs on both the PDC and a workstation or server at the same time, to keep the passwords in sync. The passwords must match on the domain and the workstation to allow a successful log-on into the domain from the workstation.

Before reinstalling NT Server or Workstation, use Server Manager to delete the computer account for the domain before you begin the reinstallation.

Domains and Trust Accounts

Domains can ensure that users have only one account to log on from anywhere in the enterprise. The trusted domain concept facilitates managing the accounts, because a user from one domain can access resources on another. This concept can also cause security problems, because an administrator of a domain can give anyone access to a trusting domain by adding the user to a group that has permission to access resources on the trusting domain. The permissions can be granted explicitly to the group, or the group can be added to a local group, either of which has the same effect of opening up access to the domain.

Guest Accounts

NT Workstation systems have a default Guest account enabled at installation. NT Server installs a Guest account but flags the account as disabled by default. Enabling the account allows unrestricted access to resources available to the account unless the account is protected with a password. Guest accounts should be used with care; many hackers normally look for Guest accounts on target systems. Leaving the Guest account disabled prevents any access through the account.

Integrating NT with some other networks such as Pathworks 5.x and later may require the use of a Guest account. In these environments, make sure that you tightly control the services accessible through the account.

Auditing

NT can audit certain resources, events, and users. The auditing facility provides a powerful tool for monitoring and administering a system. This tool is especially useful on systems that have tight security requirements or have problem users who tinker where they shouldn't. Auditing is also useful when it is used judiciously to monitor your system and make sure that the things you have put in place are working as they should. For instance, you may want to monitor system startup and shutdown requests to make sure that no one but administrators are performing this task.

Auditing is turned on in User Manager. Specific resources are set to be audited using either File Manager (or Explorer) or Print Manager (or Printer).

Rights

User rights is one of the ultimate controlling mechanisms of NT. User rights work by giving the user the right or ability to perform a task. For instance, accessing a system over the network is a right that is by default assigned to the groups Administrators and Everyone, allowing all users to access the system over the network. Conversely, the right to log on the server locally (via the system console) is given only to the Account Operators, Administrators, Backup Operators, Print Operators, and Server Operators groups, preventing everyone who is not in one of these groups from logging on from the system console.

These two examples of user rights illustrate how powerful the concept can be for controlling the system. NT automatically sets the defaults for rights to certain groups, thus setting up standard account control from a standard installation.

User rights are divided into two categories:

- Normal user rights, such as logging on over the network or performing backups
- Advanced user rights, such as allowing a user to act as part of the operating system or debug programs

Modifying User Rights:

1. Start User Manager.
2. Select the User Rights option from the Policies menu.
3. Select the Right to modify from the drop-down list. Click the Show Advanced User Rights check box to add advanced user rights to the list.
4. Add or remove users to the right by clicking the Add or Remove button.
5. Close the dialog box by clicking OK.

Table 12.2 describes some rights that you may want to change to restrict access to a specific server. Careful management of your user rights can ease your security management task.

SNMP and Security

Simple Network Management Protocol (SNMP) uses the SNMP protocol to open up access to certain parameters of NT to any system that can be accessed, including almost any system that runs TCP/IP, because of the widespread availability of SNMP tools and management systems.

You can control access to NT over SNMP by shutting off access to certain group names called Communities. NT can also restrict access over SNMP by IP address, effectively shutting down SNMP management, except from certain host systems.

Controlling SNMP Access:

1. Start the Network applet in Control Panel.
2. Double-click SNMP service in the Installed Network Software list.
3. Click the Security button.
4. Enter any community names to restrict access from in the top box. Enter the allowable IP addresses in the lower box. Be sure to delete the Public community name, as this is the default used by most systems.
5. Close the Network applet.

TABLE 12.2	Useful Rights to Change to Restrict Access
Type of Restriction	**User Right to Modify and Default Group(s)**
Prevent access to a system over the network	**Access this computer from network.** Granted to administrators and everyone by default.
Perform backups	**Right to back up files and directories.** Granted to administrators, backup operators, and server operators by default.
Perform restores of files and directories	**Restore files and directories.** Granted to administrators, backup operators, and server operators by default.
Boost process priorities	**Increase scheduling priority.** Granted to administrators by default.
Perform a remote shutdown	**Force shutdown from a remote system.** Granted to administrators and server operators by default.
Log on as a service	**Log on as a service.** Granted to none by default. This SMS service is granted this right during installation.
Traverse directory trees	**Bypass traverse checking.** Granted to everyone by default. This right allows a user to move around in directory trees. Denying this right to a user stops a user from moving from the current directory.
Prevent manipulation of the Audit and Security log	**Manage auditing and security log.** Granted to administrators by default.
Take ownership of files and objects	**Take ownership of files or other objects.** Granted to administrators by default.

Passwords

NT Server and NT Workstation store both an NT and a LAN Manager version of a password for user accounts. The LAN Manager passwords are not case-sensitive, whereas the NT passwords are. Both SFM and RAS always use the LAN Manager version of the password.

NT's Password validation is case-sensitive with a couple of exceptions. Case-sensitivity works as long as the machine you are trying to access and the one you are accessing from uses NT Challenge Response. If the machine from which you are accessing is not running NT, then passwords become case-insensitive.

This validation is further complicated if you use a NT Challenge Response machine to change your password with the NET PASSWORD command. Once the password has been changed from the non-NT system, the password is treated as case-insensitive from that point on.

Password Tips

Passwords are trouble. The average user has to contend with many passwords today: one or more for the bank account, one for the garage door, one for the security system, one for the network, another for the mini-computer or mainframe, and another for the mail system. It is no wonder that users complain when system managers ask them to have another password or two or maybe three.

Passwords are best used like many other things in life: Keep them simple. Many systems today use passwords that change every 30 or 90 days and that must be of a certain length. Many systems also allow you to force the user to use a password that hasn't been used in the last X months. NT works with all of these schemes, but using them may complicate the users' lives to the point that they blow your whole security scheme by writing down their passwords or coming up with a scheme that is easy to figure out.

A user can change to a blank password at any time, even if password history is turned on and he or she used a blank password before. This occurs because NT does not store blank passwords in the history file. You can work around this by specifying a minimum password length of one or more characters in the Password Policy.

NT does not cache passwords for persistent connections to share-level services, as Windows for Workgroups does. This means that NT prompts you for each password-protected connection to a share-level service when you log on.

Windows for Workgroups clients and their cousins, such as the Workgroup Add-On for MS-DOS and the MS Client, share a potential hole into the network. When a user enters a blank password for a password list and that user is the default user for the system, the user is logged on when the system boots. This approach is convenient, but problem-laden. If the user has logged in to a domain and the password for the domain account is cached in the password list (PWL), the user will be logged in next time with no prompting. This is a useful feature for systems such as a DOS box used to run EXTERNAL for Microsoft Mail, but it can be a real headache for any other type of interactive account. Make sure that you use the configuration utility for Windows for Workgroups ("ADMINCFG," see Chapter 7) to prevent blank passwords.

Changing Passwords

There are several ways to change passwords on a domain. You can accomplish this from Windows for Workgroups by using the network applet in Control Panel, clicking the Startup button, and then clicking the

Password button to display the Change Domain Password dialog box, shown in Figure 12.4.

Changing your password via the password button on the initial dialog box of the Network applet changes only the password for the password list for your user name, not the domain.

One of us has created a change password program for Windows for Workgroups in Visual Basic that calls both the Windows for Workgroups and domain password dialog boxes. The program uses these two API calls:

```
i = I_ChangePassword(Me.hWnd)

i = I_ChangeCachePassword(Me.hWnd)
```

I_ChangePassword changes the domain password, whereas I_ChangeCachePassword changes the Windows for Workgroups password list (.PWL) password. Of course, you must use the Declare statement to define the calls before they can be used. These two functions and many others are defined in the Windows for Workgroups Software Development Kit (SDK). The NT and Windows 95 SDKs define Win32 functions within the Windows 32 API.

Passwords can be changed using tools within NT when you log on interactively or use one of the NT tools over the network. User Manager can be used to change your own or anyone else's password. Simply select the user and access the Properties dialog box.

The Windows NT Security dialog box provides a Change Password button that can also be used. Simply press Ctrl+Alt+Del, and then click the Change Password button.

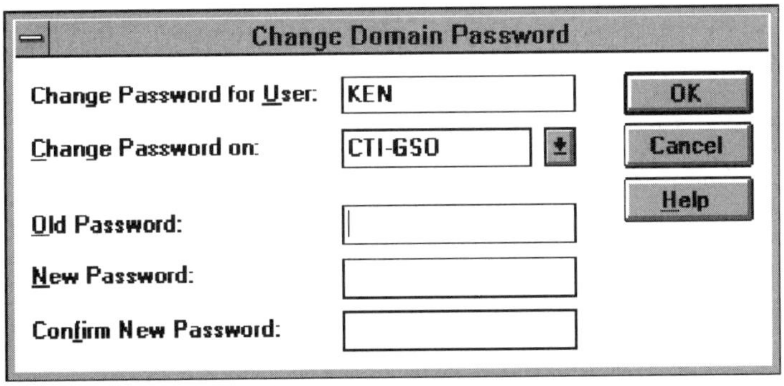

FIGURE 12.4 The Change Domain Password dialog box from the Network applet in Windows for Workgroups 3.11, simplifying access for users who want to change their password on the domain.

Log-on Restrictions

There are a number of restrictions that you can place on users to affect where and when they can log on to a domain. You can also display messages to the users before they log on. All of these techniques are useful in controlling access to your highly guarded asset, the Network.

Warning Messages at Logon

You can create a special caption and notice for a special dialog box that is displayed before users log on, after they press the Crtl+Alt+Del key sequence. These values are entered via RegEdit32 in LegalNoticeCaption and LegalNoticeText located under the key:

```
SOFTWARE\MicrosoftWindow NT\Currnet version\Winlogon
```

Restricting Access to Certain Programs

You should restrict access to programs on both the servers and workstations on your network to which you do not want users to have access. User Manager is a good example of such a program. A user who can access User Manager but is not a power user or administrator can still create a mess on the network by entering new local groups and user accounts. Even though the user could not add any permissions to the user accounts, they would still clutter up the account database and cause confusion for your managers.

The easiest way to restrict users' access is by not letting them know the program is there. Place programs that everyone should not have in Personal Program Manager groups for administrators, or lock up access to the servers. Remember also to protect the Windows 3.x versions, although these programs are not quite as destructive as the same tools running on NT because they require the user to enter the administrator password as the program runs.

Automatic NT Log-off

The NT Resource Kit includes the WINEXIT.SCR program, which is an automatic log-off screen saver. When the time-out period expires and the screen saver starts, users have a limited number of seconds to prevent the system from logging them off.

WinExit is a handy tool for secure environments or any time you need a little extra caution for NT workstation or server systems. Servers that are not in locked rooms, or sensitive users' NT workstations, are good examples of places where this tool is handy.

Setting Up WINEXIT.SCR on the NT 4.0 Environment:

1. Locate the WINEXIT.SCR file on the resource kit.
2. Copy this file to your \WINNT\SYSTEM32 directory.
3. Click the right button of your mouse anywhere on the screen.
4. Select Properties, then select Screen Saver tab.
5. Select the Logoff screen saver and configure it as you wish.

Be careful with this utility. Although it is very handy, this will close all the applications open at the time, and all unsaved data will be lost.

Installing the Logoff (WinExit) Screen Saver on a NT 3.51:

1. Copy the WINEXIT.SCR file from the resource kit directory to the \WINNT35\SYSTEM32 directory.
2. Start the Desktop applet in Control Panel.
3. In the Screen Saver list, choose the Logoff Screen Saver option. The NT Resource Kit documentation incorrectly shows the name as Windows Exit. In future versions, either the name or the documentation could change.
4. Set the delay time value in the delay box.
5. Click the Setup button.
6. Force Logoff setting: Checking this box causes the screen saver to shut down all applications without giving the user the opportunity to save any unsaved data. This box must be set to cause a totally unrestricted log-off, but it can cause a loss of data if users do not save frequently. Use caution.
7. Enter the delay time before the user is logged off in the Time To Logoff box. This is the actual amount of time in seconds the user has to cancel a log-off when the screen saver starts. Values can be between 0 and 999 seconds.
8. Enter the message to display for the Logoff dialog box in the Logoff Message box. The message can be up to 255 characters.
9. Test the screen saver.

This is another of those little tools that brings mainframe power to the desktop and server. Remember the time function on most larger systems that forces a user out after a certain period of inactivity?

When the Logoff screen saver activates, it will beep and display its Logoff dialog box with the countdown timer until the value reaches 0. When the timer reaches 0, the log-off process is initiated.

The user can abort the log-off by moving the mouse over the dialog box or pressing any key.

Using Profiles for Restricting Users

User profiles are handy for restricting users that log on from NT systems. A profile can restrict users to certain groups and not others, disable commands in Program Manager, and set other privileges for the user. Profiles can be established as defaults for new users and can be specified on a per user or per group basis. For instance, everyone in a certain department could have one profile, and another department would have another profile. Chapter 5, "User Management," contains more information on how to set up and manage profiles.

You should also explore the use of profiles with Windows 95. The profiles allow you to easily control access to workstation features for different users, regardless of where they log on.

Starting a Screen Saver Before Log-on

NT can start a screen saver before a user logs in. This feature hides the log-on prompt, but it can be used for amusement. You can also use it to show the name of the server in the banner of the screen saver. Displaying the server name on the screen saver is nice if you have a bank of servers or use a switch to move the monitor/keyboard/mouse across systems. In this way, whenever the switch changes systems, the monitor displays the server name using the screen server, whether or not a user is logged on.

Configuring NT to Start a Screen Saver Before a User Logs On:

1. Run RegEdit32.
2. Select HKEY_USERS.
3. Select the key \DEFAULT\Control Panel\Desktop.
4. Select ScreenSaveActive.
5. Choose String from the Edit menu.
6. Enter the value 1 and click OK.
7. Select SCRNSAVE.EXE from the parameter list.
8. Choose String from the Edit menu.
9. Enter the name of the desired screen.
10. Select ScreenSaveTimeOut from the parameter list.
11. Choose String from the Edit menu.
12. Enter the time-out value before the screen saver starts.

These changes take effect the next time you reboot NT. When a user fails to log on within the time-out of the screen saver, the screen saver starts.

Finding a User's Permissions with PERMS.EXE (ResKit)

There should be a way to check on the permissions assigned to an individual or group for a directory or file. Thankfully there are a couple of ways to accomplish this using File Manager (or Explorer) or PERMS (included with the NT Resource Kit). File Manager (or Explorer) is the easiest to use for normal operations because of the standard point-and-click interface. PERMS is useful when you wish to execute a command from the command line or a batch file. It is also useful to capture the permissions to a file for later use. For instance, you could create a batch file that checked permissions on a number of directories or files, and then collect them in a file.

PERMS.EXE can be used to display a user's access permissions for one or more files. PERMS.EXE can be used on the local system or against a remote system. You can also specify wildcards for the path. PERMS has the following format:

```
PERMS [domainname\|computername\]username path
[/i] [/s]
```

domain	Specifies the domain to check. Defaults to the current domain if a domain name is not specified.
computername	Specifies the computer name for a remote system. Defaults to the current system if no computer name is specified.
username	Specifies the user name to check.
path	The wildcard characters * and ? are supported.
/i	Assumes that the specified user is logged on locally at the system the check is to be performed on. /I causes PERMS to treat the user as a member of the Interactive group, not the Network group, which is the default.
/s	This switch displays permissions on files within all subdirectories. The /s switch is useful for displaying the permissions for an entire directory tree.

The PERMS command is ideal for a maintenance utility to check security for all users. Using the NET USER, you can obtain a list of all users. Using VB or another programming language, you can read the output of NET USERS and then construct a batch file to run PERMS selectively for each user, looking at the root directory and all subdirectories of each disk on the server. Taking the output of all the PERMS commands and combining them into one file gives you a list of all permissions on all directories for all users. Sort the file in different manners, and you have a nice security database for research.

Hidden Shares

NT systems automatically create a hidden administrative share for every drive on an NT system. The share name is the drive letter plus a $, such as C$. These shares can be connected to only by users with administrative access or backup operator access.

You can use a dollar sign ($) as the last character in the share name, to create a hidden share. Users can connect to the share but will not see the share name using the browse features of any system browsing the network. This technique works on Windows for Workgroups, Windows 95, NT, NT Server, and the Workgroup Add-On for MS-DOS systems. Any Microsoft network that can share resources can hide them from browsing by adding a $ to the end of the name. Don't forget that you can create a hidden share for a printer, for example, the one loaded with invoices or checks.

Client Security Issues

There are also a number of things you can do to improve security on client workstations. This technique can help you to keep unauthorized users out of PCs to which they should not have access, and it allows only the right users into your network.

Windows for Workgroups

ADMINCFG is a tool that can tighten security on a Windows for Workgroups system. ADMINCFG can set parameters for passwords and control shares. This program uses a security file that cannot be manipulated by the user. Support is also provided for maintaining the file on a network share. See Chapter 7 for more details.

Windows 95

Windows 95 is the second secure desktop system of the WOSA family, following NT Workstation. Windows 95 includes pass-through security, which takes the user name and password information from the client log-on process and performs the validation on the network server. With pass-through security, the user is trapped at the Logon dialog box until he or she successfully logs on the network. This type of security denies the user access to any system resources on either the desktop, network, or server.

Pass-through security derives another big benefit from using the server user name and password. When pass-through security is used with user-level security, access to your local shares on a Windows 95 system are also validated by using the network user names and passwords. This centralization of the security database is a great management enhancement for network managers.

Pass-through security is automatically enabled when you choose to participate in either a Windows NT or NetWare network during installation.

Windows 95 also includes user-level security, which provides the controls for a systems manager to make sure that unauthorized users do not have access to a system or make changes to setup information. Managers can also control resources available to specific users from a server. User-level security can also work in conjunction with pass-through security. User-level security must be explicitly enabled, because share-level security is enabled by default during installation.

Windows 95 includes a Registry database that is similar to the NT Registry. The Registry houses most of the information that we normally have seen in INI and other setup files on Windows 3.x networks. The Registry provides a secure storage center that cannot be accessed with a simple editor.

Windows 95 includes a version of RegEdit (REGEDIT.EXE) that must be used to manually change the Registry. RegEdit can access the local Registry or the Registry of a remote system.

Proxies With NT—Catapult, the Proxy Server

Microsoft Proxy Server was developed with the same level of security as packet filtering routers and firewalls are. Microsoft submitted its proxy product to a variety of security tests, including penetration attacks by Coopers & Lybrand's Information Technology Security Services, IP Spoofing, SATAN, and ISS tests. This level of security is not typically found in other proxy servers on the market, except for Process Software's (http://www .process.com) proxy, Purveyor, which is adopted by Digital's AltaVista search engine.

MS Proxy Server also provides support for the Web environment. The Web Proxy server supports both HTTP Basic authentication, which transmits passwords in clear text and NT C2 encrypted authentication. Among its features are:

- **Site Filtering**–Enables you to selectively permit or deny sites access to your site.
- **Access Control**–Enables you to set permissions per protocol for users and groups distinctively, per protocol in both the Web Proxy and WinSock Proxy components.
- **Logging to Text & ODBC Database**–Extensive logs are generated that can be processed by text parsers or database queries providing a detailed audit trail.
- **SSL Tunneling**–Support of SSL tunneling for encrypted connections, among other things.

Microsoft Proxy Server fully supports the multivendor ISAPI (developed by Process Software and Microsoft) Filter specification, enabling third parties to write value-enhancing add-ons to the Proxy server. For more information, check the URL `http://microsoft.com/proxy/default.asp`.

Conclusion

NT is a highly secure operating system. As it is designed for C2 security levels, NT provides the tools and features you need to secure your specific network. Out of the box, NT is just like any other system—insecure. Only you can take the steps to create the right user accounts, groups, and set the ACLs and so forth that you need to secure your system.

Listing of Products and Companies Mentioned

American Power Conversion

American Power Conversion (APC) produces a wide variety of products for managing and monitoring power issues and computer systems. The following are a few of its current products:

Power Chute Plus software for NT
Measure-UPS
Call-UPS
Share-UPS
Smart-UPS
Back-UPS
Matrix-UPS

APC can be reached at
132 Fairgrounds Road
P.O. Box 278
West Kingston, RI 02892
800-800-4APC
401-789-3180 fax

Arcada Systems (Now Owned by Seagate)

Arcada produces Backup Exec and AutoLoader for Backup Exec. These tools are designed to automate backup tasks in an NT environment.

> Arcada can be reached at
> Seagate
> 37 Skyline Drive, Suite 1101
> Lake Mary, FL 32746
> 1-800-3ARCADA

DigiBoard

DigiBoard produces a wide line of fast serial and other communication products. DigiBoard can be reached at 800-344-4273.

Consensys Corporation

Consensys makes the ChiliPorts high-speed communication products for NT and the new SMTP Mail product for NT and Microsoft Mail. Consensys can be reached at 905-940-2900.

Black Box

Black Box provides all types of cable and network products, including switching products for multiple servers using one CRT/keyboard/mouse.

> Black Box can be reached at
> P.O. Box 12800
> Pittsburgh, PA 15241
> 412-746-5500

Digital Equipment Corporation

Digital has a number of products for NT:

Pathworks for NT
X-Windows products
Alpha servers

Digital can be reached at 800-DIGITAL.

Executive Software

Executive Software markets several NT products, including Diskeeper for NT and Diskeeper for NT Server. Executive Software can be reached at 800-829-4357.

Intergraph

Intergraph has released a number of NT products, including products for

NFS connectivity
X-Windows
Workstations and servers

Intergraph can be reached at 205-730-6112.

Microsoft

Microsoft provides Windows NT, Windows for Workgroups, Windows 95, Systems Management Server, and so forth. Microsoft can be reached at 800-426-9400.

NetManage

NetManage has released NFS products for NT. NetManage can be reached at 408-973-7171.

Network Technologies

Network Technologies provides a number of switching and network products. It makes great switches for RGB-type monitors, including those used on Alpha and other RISC systems. Network Technologies can be reached at 800-RGB-TECH.

Octopus Technologies

Octopus for Windows NT provides System Fault Tolerance (SFT) to NT systems. Octopus Technologies can be reached at 215-822-8075.

Prentice Hall Technical Reference

Prentice Hall Technical Reference (PTR) is a division of Prentice Hall and is the publisher of the Managing the Enterprise with Microsoft BackOffice series, which includes:

NT Server: Management and Control
Systems Management Server
SQL Server
Exchange Server

Prentice Hall can be reached at
    Prentice Hall—PTR
    One Lake Street
    Upper Saddle River, NJ 07458
    `http://www.prenhall.com`

Glossary of Terms and Definitions

access permission   A rule associated with an object (usually a directory, file, or printer) to regulate which users can have access to the object and in what manner. Also known as *user right*.

access privileges   Permissions set by Macintosh users that allow them to view and make changes to folders on a server. By setting access privileges (called *permissions* when set on the computer running Windows NT Server), you control which Macintoshes can use folders in a volume. Services for Macintosh translates access privileges set by Macintosh users to the equivalent Windows NT permissions.

account lockout   A Windows NT Server security feature that locks a user account if a number of failed log-on attempts occur within a specified amount of time, based on account policy lockout settings. (Locked accounts cannot log on.)

account policy   Controls the way passwords must be used by all user accounts of a domain, or of an individual computer. Specifics include minimum password length, how often a user must change his or her password, and how often users can reuse old passwords. Account policy can be set for all user accounts in a domain when a domain is administered, and for all user accounts of a single workstation or member server when you administer a computer.

account domain   A domain that exists for the purpose of managing the user account and security database for a number of other domains. See Chapter 3.

ActiveX   A technology and set of programming tools from Microsoft for building interactivity with users into Web pages and application programs.

ActiveX includes what Microsoft used to call Object Linking and Embedding (OLE), among other things.

ASP (Active Server Page) An HTML page that includes one or more scripts or programs that are processed on the Web server before they are sent to the user.

ADSL Asymmetric Digital Subscriber Line.

agent In SNMP, agent information consists of comments about the user, the physical location of the computer, and the types of service to report, based on the computer's configuration. See also *SNMP*.

AltaVista The most popular search engine on the Internet. It has indexed the contents of over 31 million Web pages found on 476,000 servers. It has also indexed four million articles from 14,000 Usenet news groups. In early May 1997, AltaVista reported nearly 30 million accesses each weekday.

ANSI American National Standards Institute.

API Application Programming Interface, which is provided by many vendors for an interface into applications. NT and Windows 95 support the Win32 API, while Windows 3.1 and 3.11 support the Win16 API. Other APIs, such as MAPI, are available for products such as mail or various applications.

applet On the Web, the term is often *Java applet*. But applets existed before the Java programming language arrived. They're simply "little application programs" that are usually built in to an operating system or a larger application program. The built-in writing and drawing programs that come with Windows are sometimes called applets.

ARC menu Menu system used on RISC systems to change system parameters.

ASCII American Standard Code for Information Interchange. In ASCII data, one character is equivalent to one byte of memory.

ATAPI AT Attachment Packet Interface is an interface between your computer and attached CD-ROM drives and tape backup drives. Most of today's PC computers use the standard IDE (Integrated Drive Electronics) interface to address hard disk drives. ATAPI provides the additional commands you need for controlling a CD-ROM player or tape backup, so that your computer can use the IDE interface and controllers to control these newer device types.

AT Command Any of various commands issued to a modem for setting parameters, such as protocol usage, connections speeds, and so forth. The AT comes from *attention*, AT is usually entered immediately before any other commands/settings to first get the "attention" of the modem, telling it that it's about to receive commands.

audit policy   For the servers of a domain or for an individual computer, defines the type of security events that will be logged.

BDC   Backup Domain Controller, used for an NT server that maintains a copy of the account and security database.

bit   A binary digit—1 or 0, reflecting the use of a binary numbering system (only two digits)—used because the computer recognizes either of two states: ON or OFF. 8 bits make up one byte.

binding   A process that establishes the communication channel between a protocol driver (for example, TCP/IP) and a network card.

Bootstrap Protocol (BOOTP)   An TCP/IP network protocol, defined by RFC 951 and RFC 1542, used to configure systems. DHCP is an extension of BOOTP. See also *DHCP*.

browse list   A list kept by the master browser of all the servers and domains on the network. This list is available to any workstation on the network requesting it.

byte   A byte is a unit of measurement for computer data. In terms of ASCII, one character is equivalent to one byte. Each character you're reading is a single byte. Binary data contains special information within it that may make it take up more space than the ASCII version of the same data.

cache   This can be a piece of computer hardware in the form of DRAM, or it can be an allocation of hard drive storage space. Its purpose is to write and/or retrieve the same data, repeatedly. Because cache memory is faster than the computer system's SRAM, operations are completed much more quickly, especially if the data is repeated.

caching   In DNS name resolution, *caching* refers to a local cache where information about the DNS domain name space is kept. Whenever a resolver request arrives, the local name server checks both its static information and the cache for the name to IP address mapping. See also *DNS*.

Cairo   Code name used for NT 5.0 or something close.

CBCP   Callback Control Protocol, which negotiates callback information with a remote client.

CHAP   Challenge Handshake Authentication Protocol, a protocol used by Microsoft RAS to negotiate the most secure form of encrypted authentication supported by both server and client.

CGI   Common Gateway Interface.

Chicago   Code name used for Windows 95.

complete trust domain   A domain model that specifies how domains are managed. See Chapter 3.

computer Browser service   Maintains an up-to-date list of computers, and provides the list to applications when it is requested to do so. Provides the computer lists displayed in the Network Neighborhood, Select Computer, and Select Domain dialog boxes; and (for Windows NT Server only) in the Server Manager window.

DACL   Discretionary access control list. See *SACL*.

daemon   A networking program that runs in the background.

Daytona   Code name used for NT 3.5.

DCD   Data Carrier Detect, which tracks the presence of a data carrier. It is used to indicate when a line condition exists between a modem or other serial device and the computer.

DCOM   Distributed Component Object Model. Use the DCOM Configuration tool to integrate client/server applications across multiple computers. DCOM can also be used to integrate robust Web browser applications.

DCE   Data Communications Equipment (modems, for instance).

DHCP   Dynamic Host Configuration Protocol, an RFC (1533, 1534, 1541, 1542) for a TCP/IP management protocol. Microsoft has included tools for managing both TCP/IP clients and servers in Windows 95, NT, and the Windows for Workgroups (via the new TCP/IP drivers).

directory   A container for other directories or files.

directory replicator service   Replicates directories, and the files in those directories, between computers.

disabled user account   A user account that does not permit log-ons. The account appears in the user account list of the User Manager or User Manager for Domains window and can be reenabled at any time. See also *User Account*.

DLC   Data Link Control. This is a protocol used to communicate with IBM mainframes and printers such as the Laserjet 4si that attach directly to the network.

DLL   Dynamic-link library. An operating system feature that allows executable routines (generally serving a specific function or set of functions) to be stored separately as files with DLL extensions and to be loaded only when they are needed by the program that calls them.

DMI   Desktop Management Interface, the proposed management interface from the Desktop Management Task Force.

DNS   Domain Name Service, which translates computer names to IP addresses for TCP/IP networks.

domain   A grouping of NT servers and other servers in a network.

domain database   The user account and security database for a domain.

domain name   On the Internet, an alphanumeric name given to a computer attached to the Internet, for example, "www.process.com". Domain names are used to represent IP addresses on the Internet because the names are typically much easier to remember than the IP address. Some examples :

com–commercial

edu–education (mostly four-year colleges and universities in the United States)

gov–U.S. federal government

int–organizations established by international treaties

mil–U.S. military

net–network provider

org–miscellaneous organizations

uk–example country code (ISO-3166), in this case representing the United Kingdom

DTE   Data Terminal Equipment.

DTR   Data Terminal Ready, which indicates when a line condition exists between a modem or other serial device and the computer. The DTR line is used to signal a particular condition, for example, when the telephone line has been hung up.

DWORD   A data type composed of hexadecimal data with a maximum allotted space of four bytes.

EISA   Extended Industry Standard Architecture, which defines the successor bus for the PC to replace the original ISA bus.

environment variable   A named memory location that is accessible from programs or DOS batch programs. A typical example is TEMP, which usually contains the location for temporary files.

Event Log Service   Records events in the system, security, and application logs. Event Log Service is located in Event Viewer.

Explorer   Microsoft Windows NT Explorer is a program that enables you to view and manage the files and folders on your computer and make network connections to other shared resources, such as a hard disk on a server. Windows NT Explorer replaces Program Manager and File Manger, which were programs available in earlier versions of Windows NT. Program Manager and File Manager are still available, and they can be started in the same way you start other Windows-based programs.

Extranet   A collaborative network that uses Internet technology to link businesses with its suppliers, customers, or other businesses that share common goals. The term has been used by Jim Barksdale and Mark Andreessen of Netscape Communications to describe software that facilitates intercompany relationship

fault tolerance   Ensures data integrity when hardware failures occur. In Windows NT, fault tolerance is provided by the FTDISK.SYS driver. In Disk

Administrator, fault tolerance is provided using mirror sets, stripe sets with parity, and volume sets.

FIFO   Fast Input / Fast Output—usually refers to the capabilities of certain data buffers, like UART chips.

file fork   One of two subfiles of a Macintosh file. When Macintosh files are stored on a computer running Windows NT Server, each fork is stored as a separate file. Each fork can be independently opened by Macintosh users.

file replication service   A Windows NT service that allows specified file(s) to be replicated to remote systems, ensuring that copies on each system are kept in synchronization. The system that maintains the master copy is called the exporter, and the systems that receive updates are known as importers.

file sharing   The ability for a Windows NT computer to share parts (or all) of its local file system(s) with remote computers. An administrator creates share points by using either the file sharing command in My Computer or Windows NT Explorer or by using the net share command from the command prompt.

folder   A directory that is accessible from Macintosh clients in Services for Macintosh.

FTP   File Transfer Protocol, which provides a method to transfer files from one system to another. NT includes an FTP program.

gateway   A system (computer or dedicated device) that moves data from one network to another.

global account   For Windows NT Server, a normal user account in a user's domain. Most user accounts are global accounts. If there are multiple domains in the network, it is best if each user in the network has only one user account, in only one domain, and each user's access to other domains is accomplished through the establishment of domain trust relationships. See also *local account*.

global group   A group that is accessible across domains. Global groups can be included in local groups.

group account   A collection of user accounts. Giving a user account membership in a group gives that user all the rights and permissions granted to the group. See also *user account*; *local account*.

GUI   Graphical User Interface, a graphical operating environment that resides on a command-line-based operating system. Examples: GEOS, MS Windows 3.x, X-Windows

Hardware Compatibility List (HCL)   The Windows NT Hardware Compatibility List lists the devices supported by Windows NT. The latest version of the HCL can be downloaded from the Microsoft Web Page (www.microsoft.com) on the Internet.

home directory   A directory that serves as the user's default log-on directory and primary location for the user's files.

host   A network node in the UNIX or TCP/IP world. For instance, a PC and a server are both considered hosts.

HOSTS file   A local text file in the same format as the 4.3 Berkeley Software Distribution (BSD) UNIX \etc\hosts file. This file maps host names to IP addresses. In Windows NT, this file is stored in the \systemroot\ System32\Drivers\Etc directory.

HTTP   HyperText Transport Protocol, a protocol for retrieving multiple data-types on the Internet via the WWW and the many hypertext (HTML) files containing embedded links to other files (see RFC-2068).

IAB   Internet Architecture Board.

IETF   Internet Engineering Task Force

IGMP   Internet Group Management Protocol, used by workgroup software products and supported by Microsoft TCP/IP.

IIS   Microsoft's Internet Information Server, a tool for identifying your computer as an Internet server.

Internet   The virtual network of interconnected systems around the world. An internet is also a network segment on a TCP/IP network.

Internet control message protocol (ICMP)   A maintenance protocol in the TCP/IP suite, required in every TCP/IP implementation, that allows two nodes on an IP network to share IP status and error information. ICMP is used by the ping utility to determine the readability of a remote system.

Internet router   A device that connects networks and directs network information to other networks, usually choosing the most efficient route through other routers.

Internet Society   An international nonprofit organization, based in Reston, Virginia, and founded in 1992, that acts as a guide and conscience for the workings of the Internet. The Internet Society supports the Internet Architecture Board (IAB), which supervises technical and other issues. Among the IAB's activities is the Internet Engineering Task Force (IETF), which oversees the evolution of TCP/IP. The Internet Society has a Web site at `http://www.isoc.org`. You can also link directly to the IETF. Individuals and organizations are invited to become members and to be involved with the activities of the Internet Society.

interprocess communication (IPC)   The ability, provided by a multitasking operating system, of one task or process to exchange data with another. Common IPC methods include pipes, semaphores, shared memory, queues, signals, and mailboxes. See also *named pipes*; *queue*.

IP address   An address used to uniquely identify every TCP/IP network and node.

IPC   Inter-Process Communication. IPC defines a communication process between two processes.

IPX/SPX   The Internetwork Packet Exchange protocol, which is standard on Novell NetWare networks.

ISDN   Integrated Services Digital Network. ISDN is a newer telephone technology that has been slowly growing in popularity since the mid-1980s. It can provide speed and access advantages as it becomes available in more locations.

LCP   Link Control Protoco.

LMHOSTS file   A local text file that maps IP addresses to the computer names of Windows NT networking computers outside the local subnet. In Windows NT, this file is stored in the \systemroot \System32\Drivers\Etc directory.

local account   For Windows NT Server, a user account provided in a domain for a user whose global account is not in a trusted domain. Not required where trust relationships exist between domains. See also *global account*; *user account*.

local group   Local groups are the groups created on an NT or NT Server. Local groups cannot be used by trusted domains. See *global groups*.

local guest log-on   Takes effect when a user logs on interactively at a computer running Window NT Workstation, or at a member server running Windows NT Server, and specifies Guest as the user name in the Logon Information dialog box.

LPC   Local Procedure Call, a localized method of RPC used by NT in many of its programs. It is, at its simplest, one program calling routines in another program in the same system.

LSAPI   Licensing Services Application Programming Interface provides routines for controlling software licensing.

management information base (MIB)   A set of objects that represent various types of information about a device, used by SNMP to manage devices. Because different network-management services are used for different types of devices or protocols, each service has its own set of objects. The entire set of objects that any service or protocol uses is referred to as its MIB. See also *SNMP*.

MAPI   Messaging Application Programming Interface, the Microsoft interface into its messaging and mail systems.

master domain   A domain model that specifies how domains are managed. See Chapter 3.

MDI   Multiple document interface. MDI provides an application with the ability to have multiple windows contained within a master parent window.

When the child windows are minimized, they become icons at the bottom of the parent.

Memphis   Codename for the yet-to-be-released new version of Windows 95, also called Windows 98.

mirror set   A fully redundant or shadow copy of data. A mirror set provides an identical twin for a selected disk; all data written to the primary disk is also written to the shadow or mirror disk. This enables you to have instant access to another disk with a redundant copy of the information on a failed disk. Mirror sets provide fault tolerance. See also *fault tolerance*.

multiple master domain   A domain model that specifies how domains are managed. See Chapter 3.

multiprotocol routing (MPR)   Enables routing over IP and IPX networks by connecting LANs or by connecting LANS to WANs.

MUP   Multiple UNC Provider, a component of the NT network subsystem.

name server   A computer running DNS.

named pipes   A system interface that programs use to communicate between different systems.

NAS   Network Access Server, a device that provides access to a network, generally by allowing users to dial into it much in the same way that a modem allows access into an individual computer.

NBF   NetBEUI protocol driver for NT.

NBT   NetBIOS over TCP/IP. This module provides NetBIOS naming over TCP/IP for interpretability with systems and applications using NetBIOS.

NCP   NetWare Core Protocol. NetWare uses NCP, and it runs over NWLINK in an NT environment.

NDIS   Network Device Interface Specification.

NetBEUI   NetBIOS Extended User Interface. NetBEUI is the transport protocol used by Microsoft and other networks.

NetBIOS   Network Basic Input Output System. NetBIOS has been in use by many networks for quite a while. See *NetBEUI* and *NBF*.

network file system (NFS)   A service for distributed computing systems that provides a distributed file system, eliminating the need for keeping multiple copies of files on separate computers.

NIC   Network Interface Card.

NNTP   Network News Transfer Protocol.

nonpaged memory   Memory that cannot be paged to disk. See also *paging file*.

NT   Short name for Windows NT.

NTFS NT File System. The NTFS is new with NT and NT Server. It includes support for long file names, transaction logging, directory and file security, and other new features.

NTS Short name for NT Server.

NTS/E Short name for NT Server Enterprise.

NTW Short name for NT Workstation.

NWCS NetWare Compatible Service. NWCS runs over NWLINK and provides NT workstations and servers with NetWare client functionality for attaching to NetWare servers.

NWLINK The NetWare Link transport protocol is Microsoft's NDIS compliant version of IPX/SPX.

object Anything that can be thought of as a single entity such as a file, printer, or Registry entry.

one-way trust relationship One domain (the trusting domain) trusts the domain controllers in the other domain (the trusted domain) to authenticate user accounts from the trusted domain to use resources in the trusting domain.

orphan A member of a mirror set or a stripe set with parity that has failed in a severe manner, such as a loss of power or a complete head crash. When this happens, the fault-tolerance driver determines that it can no longer use the orphaned member and directs all new reads and writes to the remaining members of the fault-tolerance volume. See also *fault tolerance.*

OpenView A network management package from Hewlett-Packard.

paging file A special file on a PC's hard disk. With virtual memory under Windows NT, some of the program code and other information is kept in RAM, while other information is temporarily swapped into virtual memory. When that information is required again, Windows NT pulls it back into RAM and, if necessary, swaps other information to virtual memory. Also called a swap file.

parity Redundant information that is associated with a block of information. In Windows NT Server, *stripe sets with parity* means that there is one additional parity stripe per row. Therefore, you must use at least three disks, rather than two, to allow for this extra parity information.

PCI Peripheral Component Interconnect, which defines a new bus architecture for systems. It was developed by Intel.

PDC Primary Domain Controller. PDC is the NT Server that maintains the master copy of the account and security database.

Point-to-Point Tunneling Protocol (PPTP) PPTP is a new networking technology that supports multiprotocol virtual private networks (VPNs), enabling remote users to access corporate networks securely across the

Internet by dialing into an Internet service provider (ISP) or by connecting directly to the Internet.

print spooler   A collection of dynamic link libraries (DLLs) that receive, process, schedule, and distribute documents.

profile   Tracks the personal configuration information for a particular user. The profile editor can be used to create profiles for single users or groups of users and to control the user changes to configuration data and other options.

protocol   Defines the rules controlling how a network device such as a server or workstation will communicate with other network devices. Examples are TCP/IP and IPX/SPX.

proxy   A computer that listens to name query broadcasts and responds for those names not on the local subnet. The proxy communicates with the name server to resolve names and then caches them for a time period.

queue   In Windows NT terminology, a queue is a group of documents waiting to be printed. (In NetWare and OS/2 environments, queues are the primary software interface between the application and print device; users submit documents to a queue. However, with Windows NT, the printer is that interface—the document is sent to a printer, not a queue.)

RAID   Redundant Array of Inexpensive Disk, which defines a range of disk management and striping techniques.

RAS   Remote Access Server, which provides remote access to NT networks.

registry   The NT database that holds configuration, user, and security information for the system. The registry files are normally located in the \WINNT35 \SYSTEM32\CONFIG directory.

registry size limit (RSL)   The total amount of space that can be consumed by registry data (hives) is restricted by the registry size limit, which is a kind of universal maximum for registry space that prevents an application form filling the paged pool with registry data. See also *paging file*.

RIP   Routing Information Protocol.

roaming user profiles   Are enabled when an administrator enters a user profile path into the user account. The first time the user logs off, the local user profile is copied to that location. Thereafter, the server copy of the user profile is downloaded each time the user logs on (if it is more current than the local copy) and is updated each time the user logs off.

router   A system (computer or dedicated device) that moves traffic from one network to another. A router is an intelligent device that can make decisions about what packets it moves from one network to another.

RPC   Remote Process Communication between two or more processes and Remote Procedure Call of subprograms. RPC is used mainly when a program on one system calls a subroutine in a program on another system over the network.

RPI   Rockwell Protocol Interface.

SACL   System access control list. In Windows NT programming, a data structure that consists of smaller data structures called access control elements (ACE). SACL is used in Windows NT security.

SAM   Security Accounts Manager. SAM is the manager of all the security stuff in NT and NT Server.

SAP   In the Windows environment, SAP is an acronym for Service Advertising Protocol, a service that broadcasts shared files, directories, and printers categorized first by domain or workgroup and then by server name.

scavenging   Cleaning up the WINS database.

security ID   A unique name that identifies a logged-on user to the security system. Security IDs (SIDs) can identify one user, or a group of users.

server   Any system in a network that provides (serves) services to other systems on the network. This can be an NT Server or an NT desktop system that shares files or simply a print server that manages a few printers.

SFM   Services for Macintosh that run under NT Server.

SFT   System Fault Tolerance, a technique for shadowing a server, thus making the server immune to a single point of failure. SFT is not supported under NT—yet.

SGML   Standard Generalized Markup Language.

SID   Security ID. SID is a unique ID created by NT for every user account that logs on to an NT system.

SLED   Single large expensive disk.

SLIP   Serial Line Internet Protocol.

SMB   Server Message Block, a high-level protocol used when two Microsoft systems communicate over a network. SMB commands are imbedded in transport protocols such as TCP/IP or NetBEUI.

SMS   Systems Management Server, the network management software from Microsoft.

SMTP   Simple Mail Transfer Protocol, a protocol for sending e-mail across the Internet.

SNMP   Simple Network Management Protocol, a protocol used by some computer networks that allows for administration of that network by a computer connected, remotely (for example, by modem).

spooling   A process on a server in which print documents are stored on a disk until a printing device is ready to process them. A spooler accepts each document from each client, stores it, then sends it to a printing device when it is ready.

sockets   A method of network communications that are more portable than Named Pipes or Mail Slots. NT supports them over TCP/IP only.

SQL   Structured Query Language. SQL is a standard tool for accessing a relational database.

static routing   Static routing limits you to fixed routing tables, as opposed to dynamically updating the routing tables.

subkey   A key within a key. Subkeys are analogous to subdirectories in the registry hierarchy. Keys and subkeys are similar to the section heading in .ini files; however subkeys can carry out functions. See also registry.

system default profile   In Windows NT Server, the user profile that is loaded when Windows NT is running and no user is logged on. When the Begin Logon dialog box is visible, the system default profile is loaded. See also *user profiles*.

system log   Contains events logged by the Windows NT components. For example, the failure of a driver or other system component to load during startup is recorded in the system log. Use Event Viewer to view the system log.

TAPI   Telephony Application Programming Interface, used by programs to make data/fax/voice calls, including the Windows NT applets HyperTerminal, Dial-up Networking, Phone Dialer, and other Win32 communications applications written for Windows NT.

Task list   A window that shows all running applications and their status. View the Task list in the Applications tab in Task Manager.

Task Manager   Task Manager enables you to start, end, or run applications, end processes (either an application, application component, or system process), and view CPU and memory use data.

TCP/IP   Transmission Control Protocol/Internet Protocol. TCP/IP is a transport protocol that was developed by the Defense Advanced Research Projects Agency in the 1970s.

TDI   Transport Device Interface. The TDI is used by the LAN Manager service to talk to the network protocols.

thread   Threads are objects within processes that run program instructions. They allow concurrent operations within a process and enable one process to run different parts of its program on different processors simultaneously.

trusted domain   A domain that is allowed by another domain to access resources on that domain.

trusting domain   A domain that allows another domain to access resources on its network.

trust relationship   Trust relationships are links between domains that enable pass-through authentication, in which a trusting domain honors the log-on authentications of a trusted domain. With trust relationships, a user who has only one user account in one domain can potentially access the entire network. User accounts and global groups defined in a trusted domain can be given rights and resource permissions in a trusting domain, even though those accounts don't exist in the trusting domain's directory database.

two-way trust relationship   Each domain trusts user accounts in the other domain to use its resources. Users can log on from computers in either domain to the domain that contains their account.

UNC   Universal Naming Convention or Uniform Naming Convention, which defines the format for a consistent network connection to a shared resource.

URL   Uniform Resource Locator, the protocol, address, and/or file for whatever you happen to be viewing at any given time on the Web.

user account   A user's access to NT. Each user account is assigned a unique user name and user ID.

user profiles   Profiles that store information and restrictions about user accounts.

virtual memory (virtual storage)   Virtual (or logical) memory is a concept that, when implemented by a computer and its operating system, allows programmers to use a very large range of memory or storage addresses for stored data. The computing system maps the programmer's virtual addresses to real hardware storage addresses. Usually, the programmer is freed from having to be concerned about the availability of data storage.

volume password   A password that is assigned to a Macintosh volume when it is created.

volume   A disk volume (partition) in Services for Macintosh.

VPN   Virtual private network, a remote LAN that can be accessed through the Internet using the new PPTP. See also *Point-to-Point Tunneling Protocol (PPTP)*.

WFWSYS.CFG   Security configuration file for Windows for Workgroups 3.11.

WINMSD   The Windows NT version of the Microsoft Diagnostic utility.

WINS   Windows Internetwork Naming Service, which maintains the name database for a Windows NT TCP/IP network.

Win32s   Win32s is a Microsoft upgrade to the Windows 3.1 and Windows for Workgroups 3.1 operating systems, which run 16-bit applications, to allow them to run some 32-bit applications. If you have Windows 3.1 or Windows for Workgroups 3.1 and don't yet want to install Windows 95 (which is designed for 32-bit applications), you can download Win32s and install it so that certain 32-bit applications will run.

WinSockets   A network programming interface that allows systems to communicate with other systems.

Winsock 2 (Windows 2 sockets)   Like Winsock, Winsock 2 is a programming interface and the supporting program that handles input/output requests for Internet applications in a Windows operating system. It's called Winsock because it's an adaptation for Windows of the Berkeley UNIX sockets interface. Sockets is a particular convention for connecting with and exchanging data between two program processes. Winsock 2 is a 32-bit version of Winsock.

WNet   Windows Network Interface functions stored in the MRP.DLL.

WOSA   Windows Open Services Architecture from Microsoft, defines how operating systems, networks, databases, electronic mail, and applications interface.

WOW   Win16 on Win32. The translation of Windows 3.1-based application calls to standard mode for RISC-based computers and 386 enhanced mode for x86-based computers.

ZAK   Microsoft's Zero Administration Kit tools to provide near to zero administration and support to NT and Windows 95 workstations on a NT-based network

Contacting
the Authors

Ken Spencer can be contacted at:

32x Corporation
Greensboro, NC
910–632–1430
910–632–8924 FAX
KenSpencer@32x.com

Marcus Goncalves can be reached at:

VIBES-Virtual Business Educational Services
Southborough, MA
goncalves@process.com
http://members.aol.com/goncalvesv

About the CD-ROM

This is a list of the tools you will find on the CD that accompanies this book. Make sure to read any documentation and "readme" files that come with these tools. Most of them are evaluation versions and have expiration dates as indicated. Others are shareware, and we strongly recommend that you sponsor the developers and send in your registration fee, should you decide to use the tool for a longer period of time. Enjoy!

NTMUM

This is a beta version of an excellent tool. Among other things, NTMUM can:

1. Create multiple users from a text file
2. Create a user file
3. Make users members of groups
4. Create a home directory for each user
5. Dump user info from a server
6. Create groups from a text file
7. Dump groups info from a server
8. Add/remove multiple users/groups to the ACL of multiple files/folders
9. Share/unshare multiple files/folders

You can check for the latest version of this tool at the following URL:

`ftp://humserv2.hum.gu.se/pub/WindowsNT/NTMUM/BETA.`

If you have any questions, please contact Anders Wahlin at Anders.Wahlin@hum.gu.se

BlackBoard Lock

This program automatically loads at startup and will help prevent other users from using your computer. If the password isn't correctly typed in by the third time, windows restarts. When you first run the program, select EDIT, SET_PASSWORD and pick a password (case-sensitive). When the password is correctly typed in, the program closes, and you can use windows.

Installing Win95 or NT 4.x:

1. Click START.
2. RUN setup.

Installing Win 3.x (with Win32x drivers) or Win NT 3.x:

1. Click FILE.
2. RUN setup.

If you plan to use this software after 30 days, we ask you to register it. The registration varies from $10 to $20. For the latest version, you can visit `http://www.concentric.net/~laserjet`, e-mail `dalin@aol.com`, or mail:

Blackboard Software
P.O. Box 745494
Arvada, CO 80006-5494

Web Trend (30-day Evaluation Copy)

This is a statistics, Marketing, and Traffic Reporting for Web Servers from Software, Inc.

WebTrends is a 32-bit Windows application compatible with Windows NT 3.51, 4.0, and Windows 95. You can install WebTrends on your Web server system or on any other system that has a mapped drive or FTP or HTTP access to your log files.

WebTrends will analyze the log files created by your Web servers and provide you with invaluable information about your World Wide Web site and the users that access it. WebTrends is compatible with log files created by ANY Web server (Microsoft IIS, Apache, CERN, NCSA, O'Reilly, Lotus Domino, Oracle, Open Market, NetWare, and so forth).

Reports generated by WebTrends include statistical information as well as colorful graphs that show trends, usage, market share, and much more. Reports can be generated as HTML files that can be viewed by any browser on your local system or remotely from anywhere on the Internet with any browser. You can also create the reports in Microsoft Word, Excel, Text, and Comma Delimited formats.

DistStat (15-day Evaluation Copy)

DistStat is a common log analyzer that can distribute usage statistics to a number of different recipients. Each recipient can receive statistics only on the site they would be interested in, with a comparison against the statistics of the server as a whole. This application is geared toward a Web server that hosts many different Web sites, and gives the Web server administrator the ability to provide periodic usage statistics on each site located on their machine.

You will find an Alpha and an Intel version of this tool in the DistStat directory. Please note that this is an evaluation copy only. When you fill out the following form, you are granted a 15-day license period to evaluate DistStat. This eval copy has only one limitation: DistStat will not save caching information, forcing all log files to be parsed in their entirety on every run.

Before You Begin

Before you begin installing iPerForm, check to make sure your machine has a valid domain name. This is rarely a problem, but it can cause iPerForm to not run properly. You must have a valid domain name, and the machine name must be registered as that domain name, and if you are multihoming, the very first IP address in the list of addresses to which the machine responds must be the IP address to which the domain name points to. In most cases, there won't be a problem, but it's always a good idea to make sure up front.

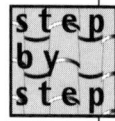

Manually Checking Your Domain Name Under WinNT 3.51:

1. Open Control Panel.
2. Select Network, then TCP/IP Protocol.
3. Choose Configure, then DNS.

Use iperform_config.exe to find out whether or not there are any potential problems with your setup.

The top of the DNS Configuration dialog should have the machine name listed under "Host Name," and your subdomain under "Domain Name." For example, our Web server's name is WWW, and our subdomain is RTIS.COM. On the Internet, you would access our machine as WWW.RTIS.COM. So, in the DNS configuration dialog box, we would enter WWW for "Host Name" and RTIS.COM for "Domain Name."

If you have not registered a domain name, or do not have one set up for your machine, you should enter the IP address and machine name in your HOSTS file, which is in the `\winnt35\system32\drivers\etc` directory. If you have no HOSTS file, just create one using any text editor. It should contain the following line:

```
xxx.xxx.xxx.xxx        aaaaa.aaaa.aaaa.com
```

Here "xxx.xxx.xxx.xxx" is the IP address, and "aaaaa.aaaa.aaaa.com" is the domain name.

CodeSafe for Win95/NT V3.0 Version

CodeSafe is a tool that enables you to protect your application programs, including executable files (.EXE) and Dynamic Link Libraries (.DLL), from being cracked or run without your permission. Thus, CodeSafe acts as:

- **Anti_Cracker**–The main aspiration of Codesafe is to make difficult for crackers to crack your applications. CodeSafe can protect your code and/or resource from being cracked. If you are a developer, you may have some critical code you want to protect.

■ **Password Protection**–You can also use this program to password protect your applications.

■ **Compression Utility**–Codesafe can be used as a compression tool.

If you wish to contact the developer, here is his address (available until JULY 1998):

> Zhang Dehua
> Room 403 Building 25th
> Tsinghua University
> Beijing, 100084
> People's Republic of China

Internet e-mail:

```
gleamd@usa.net
```

HomePage:

```
http://www.geocities.com/SiliconValley/Park/90
                    31/
```

Installing Diskeeper Lite:

1. From Windows NT Explorer or File Manager, double-click on SETUP.EXE in the directory where this README.TXT file resides.

2. Read the information displayed in the Setup Installation Wizard boxes, and click the Next button as appropriate.

3. In the Choose Destination Location dialog box, either accept the default installation location, or click the Browse button to specify a different disk and/or directory. If you specify a directory that does not exist, the setup program will create it for you.

4. Click the Next button after specifying a disk and directory, or to accept the default installation location.

5. After a short period of copying files, the installation is complete.

Diskeeper Lite for NT 4.0

Diskeeper defragment your NT partitions for better performance.

Commander: A File Utility Tool

Commander is a file utility tool similar to Norton Commander. This is a shareware, so if you feel that you benefit from this program in any way, we ask you to register it.

The registered users benefits to FREE UPDATES. Read the readme file in its directory for more details.

Dustman File Cleaner

Dustman scans your system for and automatically removes unneeded and otherwise burdensome files (such as old backup files and temporary files) that clutter your hard disk or network file server.

Dustman scans based on user-defined directory and file specifications (using wildcards or regular expressions) and deletes or recycles files based on user-defined aging criteria. Dustman also allows the use of expiration dates and retention periods as part of file names. Requires Windows 95 or Windows NT 4.0 or higher.

DUSTMN20.EXE is a self-extracting, self-installing ZIP file. To install Dustman, run DUSTMN20.EXE, which will extract itself to a temporary directory and then launch the setup program.

If you encounter problems with installation, or want more information, please contact Arcana Development at 71210.2524@compuserve.com.

INDEX

A

Access control, 494
Access control entities (ACE), 476, 480
Access control list (ACL), 476, 480
Access Controls. *See* Discretionary Access Controls
Account lockout, 251-252
Account duplication, 242
Account Lockout parameters, 252
Account Policy form, 251
Account Policy option, 272
Account restriction, 254
Account templates, 246-247
Accounts, operations, 246
ACE. *See* Access control entities
ACL. *See* Access control list
ActiveX objects, 10
Add-on cards, 230
Address database, 457-458
ADMINCFG.EXE. *See* Administration configuration program
Administration. *See* Centralized administration
Administration configuration program (ADMINCFG.EXE), 325, 327-330, 486, 492
Administrative alerts, 106
Administrative assistants, 3
Administrative options, 327
Administrative Tools group, 157
Administrative-type programs, 54
Administrative-type tasks, 353
Agents, 315
Alert view, 434
Alerts, 434-437. *See also* System alerts
setting. *See* Performance monitor
Alpha, 19, 23, 60, 114, 377. *See also* Digital Equipment Corporation
Alpha 4100, 118
Alpha 8100, 118
Alpha AXP, 32-37
Alpha computer, 29
Alpha files, 36
Alpha NT Server, 392
Alpha processors, 62
Alpha system, 17, 33, 36, 86, 116, 119
ALPHA.BIN, 262
Alpha-DEC, 18
AlphaServer 1000, 116
AlphaServer 2000, 32, 34, 116
AlphaServer 4000, 123
AlphaServer 8000, 123
American Power Conversion (APC), 495
Power Chute, 427-428

AMP. *See* Amphenol Interconnect Products
Amphenol Interconnect Products (AMP), 126
APC. *See* American Power Conversion
API. *See* Application Programs Interface
Appendices, 495-522
Apple LaserWriters, 346
AppleShare UAM, 351
AppleShare volume, 349
Applet File System, 302
AppleTalk, 166-167, 311
protocol, configuring, 355-356
workstations, 359
Application programs, 101
Application Programs Interface (API), 6, 11, 487. *See also* CryptoAPI; Win32 API
function. *See* Network API functions
Application records events, 101
Application-level protocols, 11
Applications, 80-81
stopping. *See* Servers
Appstation mode, 341
ARC menu, 32
starting, 34
ARCINST, 23, 26
Arcada Backup Exec Server, 416-418
Arcada Software, 411
Arcada Systems, 395-496
Architecture, 368-371. *See also* Domain architecture; Public-key security architecture; RISC architecture; Video architecture
ArcNet cards, 49
ArpCacheLife, 120
ArpTRSingleRoute, 120
Arrays. *See* Storage arrays
ASCII file, 147, 388
AT command, 61, 254, 412
AT functionality, 83
ATDT, 226
Audit events, 101
Auditing, 483
AuditPol.Exe, 60
Authors, 515
AUTOEXEC.BAT, 260, 331
Autoloader, 417
Automatic logon configuration. *See* Windows NT Server
Automatic NT logoff, 488-489
Auto-run CD, 28

B

B2 Trusted Facility Management, 472
B2 Trusted Path, 472
Back Office, 199
Back-end server, 12
BackOffice, 7-8, 23
BACKUP, 413, 414
Backup domain controller (BDC), 19-20, 24, 42, 50, 193, 194, 198, 202, 204, 205, 294, 442, 450
logging, 207
promotion, 206-207
Backup Exec, 411
Back-up information, 79
Backup Operators, 235
Backup Operators group, 415
Backup options, 416-418
Backup programs. *See* Tape backup programs; Windows NT backup programs
Backup strategy, setup, 408-410
Backup tapes, 421
Backups. *See* Network systems; Power backup; System backups; User backups; Windows NT backup
file selection, 418-421
Batch file IF commands, 63-64
Batch files, 73, 104
Batch programs, 61-64, 102
BDC. *See* Backup domain controller
BIOS, 28, 462. *See also* NetBIOS; ROM BIOS
Black Box, 95, 127, 496
Black screen, 107
BlackBoard Lock, 518
b-node computer, 146
Boot disk. *See* Installation boot disk
Boot option. *See* Clients; VGA boot option
adding, 109-110
BOOT.INI file, 34
BOOT.INI options, 109-111. *See also* Hardware devices; UPS
Bottlenecks, 439-440, 467
Broadcast Name Resolution, 144
Browse-master, 89
Browsemaster, 181
Browser Monitor, 182
Browsers, monitoring, 182-183
Browsing. *See* Domains
configuring, 180-183
functions. *See* Windows for Workgroups
BrowStat, 182
Built-in expansion factor, 116

Built-in maintenance processor, 116
BUS architecture, 118, 119

C

C/C++, 15, 86, 382. *See also*
    Visual C++
C2 Orange Book, 472
C2 requirement, 277
C2-level security, 50, 272, 472
C-2 rating, 471
Cabling, 126–127
Cache, 115–121
Caching. *See* Controllers; Drives
    controller, 118
CACLS, 101
Captured printers, 365
Catapult, 493–494
CDFS, 276
CD-ROM, 23, 31, 32, 35, 73, 88, 276,
    304–307, 316, 517–522. *See also*
    Unsupported CD-ROM
    drive, 343
        adding, 128–129
CD-ROM (X86), 32
Central Point backup programs, 411
Central Processing Unit (CPU), 123,
    401, 423, 426, 430, 452, 464,
    466–467
Centralized administration, 426
Certificate Authorities, 12
Certificate revocation list (CRL), 15
Certificate Services (CS), 15
Character-based setup, 46
Cheyenne backup program, 411
ChiliPort, 222
ChipCom, 455
CHKDSK, usage. *See* Problem finding
Choice command, 63
Clearing house, 13
Cleartext password. *See* Macintosh
    Cleartext password
Client authentication, 15
Client configuration. *See* Windows
    NT client configuration
Client Configuration Data, 259
Client directory, sharing, 306–307
Client management. *See* Windows
    NT client management
Client participation
    logon scripts usage, 259–265
    startup scripts usage, 259–265
Client security, issues, 492–493
Client Service for NetWare (CSNW),
    163, 164
Client software, 331
    stopping, 334
Client tools. *See* Windows NT 4.0
    server
    usage, 304–306

Clients. *See* Macintosh clients;
    Windows NT 4.0 server
    common features, 311–313
    configuring, 310–335
    network events, tracking, 339–340
    remote boot option, 335
CLIENTS directory, 309
Client/server applications, 426
Client/server complexity, 28
Client/server databases, 425
Client/server systems, 457
ClipBook, 184
Cluster Administrator, 425
Clustering, advantages, 425–426
Clusters, real-time fault tolerance,
    424–425
CMD.EXE, 61
CodeSafe (Win95/NT V3.0 version),
    520–521
Colorado Memory systems, 403, 410
COM1, 128, 230
COM2, 128, 226, 230
COM3, 230
COM4, 230
COM port, 110, 111, 232
    number, 128
Combination modes, 145
Comma-delimited file, 245
Command interpreter, 61
Command prompt. *See* Windows NT
    backup
    operations, 61–64
COMMAND.COM, 61
Commander, 522
Command-line domain, 60
Command-line options, 412
Commercial Internet System, 8
COMPACT
    usage. *See* Directories; Files
    utility, 292
Companies, list, 495–498
Compaq, 86
COMPAQ INSIGHT Manager, 124
Compaq Proliant, 124
Compaq Prosignia, 124
Complete trust model, 197–198
CompuServe, 129, 230, 231
Computer accounts, 482
Computer names, 201, 211, 312–313
Computer Profile Setup (CPS),
    42–45, 50
Computer profile setup installation,
    42–45
Computer Technologies, Inc., 245
CONFIG.SYS, 260
Configuration issues, 119–121
Connect Network Drive, 187
Conner MS2000DAT, 402
Conner Systems, 411, 416

Consensys Corporation, 496
Control panel, 83, 87, 106, 119, 129,
    150, 168, 174, 201, 203, 226, 229,
    236, 254, 322, 336, 402, 405. *See*
    also Network Control Panel
Control Panel Ports applet, 128
Controllers, 117–119. *See also*
    Network controllers;
    Rendundant Array of
    Inexpensive Disks; Small
    Computer Systems Interface
    caching, 118
CONVERT command, 347
Counters, 430–431. *See also*
    Performance monitor
CPS. *See* Computer Profile Setup
CPU. *See* Central Processing Unit
CRL. *See* Certificate revocation list
CryptoAPI, 14, 15
CS. *See* Certificate Services
CSNW. *See* Client Service for
    NetWare
CSV, 245
CTI, 259
CTI-NT SERVER, 291
CTRLIST, 432
Custom setup, comparison. *See*
    Default/custom setup

D

DACL. *See* Discretionary Access
    Controls
DAT, 21
DAT drives, 402
Data Carrier Detect (DCD), 229
Data directories, 285, 292, 419
Data files, 419
Data Link Control (DLC), 135, 162,
    386, 387
    interface, 162, 387
    printers, 387
Data Set Ready (DSR), 229
Database. *See* Address database;
    Internet databases; Intranet
    databases; ODBC database;
    Registry database
Database server, 114
DataLog, 439
    service, 437
    usage. *See* Performance monitor
DATALOG program, 436
DATALOG service, 438
DATALOG.TXT, 439
DB Server, 95
DCD. *See* Data Carrier Detect
DCOM. *See* Distributed Component
    Object Model
DDE data, 315

DDN-NIC. *See* Defense Data
    Network-Network Information
    Center
DEBUG option, 109
DEC. *See* Digital Equipment
    Corporation
DECnet, 136, 137, 310
DECnet networks, 168
Default user name, disabling, 252
Default variables, 263-264
Default/custom setup, comparison,
    28-29
DEFAULTS.INF file, 44
DefaultTTL, 120
Defense Data Network-Network
    Information Center
    (DDN-NIC), 139
Definitions. *See* Device definitions;
    Terms/definitions
Defragmentation. *See* Disk
    defragmentation
Dell, 122, 124
Device definitions, 34-35
Device drivers, 81-82
DFS, 282, 283
DHCP. *See* Dynamic Host
    Configuration Protocol
Dial-up networking application, 231
DigiBoard, 222, 496
    adapter, 226
DigiStat, 519-520
Digital Alpha, 60
Digital Equipment Corporation
    (DEC), 18, 23, 86, 122-124, 126,
    181, 213, 377, 401, 402, 496
    Alpha, 123, 431
Digital Prioris models, 123
Digital StorageWorks, 128
Direct network interface
    printers, 386
Directories. *See* Client directory; Data
    directories; Home directory;
    Macintosh users; USERS
    directory
    compressing, 291-293
    sharing, 286-289
    uncompressing, COMPACT
        usage, 292
Directory properties, 364
Directory Service Manager for
    NetWare (DSMN), 166
Directory structures, 283-291
Disappearing icons, 361
Disaster management, 401-428
    summary, 428
Disaster preparedness, 401-428
    summary, 428
Discretionary Access Controls
    (DACL), 477

Disk Administrator, 70, 71, 73, 74, 77,
    96, 118
Disk configuration information,
    saving, 74
Disk controllers. *See* Peripheral
    Component Interconnect
Disk defragmentation, 300
Disk drives, 117-119, 124-125. *See
    also* Floppy disk drives; Logical
    disk drives; Physical disk drives
    physical access, 81
Disk duplexing, 75
Disk fault tolerance, 75-81
Disk mirroring, 75
Disk Operating System (DOS), 2, 26,
    122, 126, 276, 277, 279, 306, 440,
    473, 481. *See also* MS-DOS; RIP
    DOS
    batch language, 63, 90
    boot disk, 308
    clients, 265
    directory tree, 360
    extension, 280
    floppy disk, 364, 480
    language, 131
    machines, 310
    network products, 177
    prompt, 41, 72, 73, 226, 239, 240,
        299, 328
    systems, 35-37, 71, 363, 380, 397
    users, 360, 362
    utilities, 246
Disk probe, 450-451
Disk recovery
    hardware solutions, 79-80
    NT Software Solutions usage,
        78-79
Disk striping, 75
Disk subsystems, 86, 467-468
Disk systems, 68-81, 124-125
    management, 68
Diskeeper, 482
Diskeeper Lite (NT 4.0), 521
Diskeeper LiteTM, 300
Disks. *See* Floppy disks; Small
    Computer Systems Interface;
    Unformatted disks
    adding, 80
DistStat, 519-520
Distributed Component Object
    Model (DCOM), 3, 16
Distributed Password Authentication
    (DPA), 10
DLC. *See* Data Link Control
DLLs, 286
DLT drives, 402
DNS. *See* Domain Name System
Domain account database, 212, 250
Domain Admins, 267

Domain architecture, 198
Domain controllers, 12, 84. *See also*
    Backup domain controller;
    Primary domain controller
    synchronizing, 204-206
Domain Guests, 267
Domain Logon, 337
Domain models, 195-199. *See also*
    Master domain model; Multiple
    master domain model; Single
    domain model
Domain monitor, 450
Domain Name, 324
Domain Name System (DNS), 121,
    145, 146
    server, 4, 150, 442
Domain names, 21, 200, 312
Domain password, changing,
    333-334
Domain security, 204
Domain user account, 242-254
Domain Users, 267
    groups, 235
Domains, 8-9, 199-203, 449-454,
    482. *See also* TRUSTED domains
    browsing, 181-182
    changing, server usage, 204
    logging on, 337-339
    management, tips, 201
    NTWs, adding, 335-337
    overview, 192-194
    RAS fit, 222-223
    User Manager, 97, 209, 215, 254
DontAddDefaultGateway, 120
DOS. *See* Disk Operating System
DOS Errorlevel variable, 420
DOS-based clients, 380
DOS/Windows/Windows, 260-261
DPA. *See* Distributed Password
    Authentication
Drive failure, 78
Drive letter assignation. *See* Volumes
Drive letters, 68, 71
Drives. *See* Disk drives; Logical drive
    adding. *See* CD-ROM
    caching, 118
Drivers, 23. *See also* Device drivers;
    Printer drivers
DRIVERS directory, 373, 391
DriveSpace, 291
Drop folders, 361
DRVLIB directory, 28
DSMN. *See* Directory Service for
    NetWare
DSR. *See* Data Set Ready
DumpEL, 102-103
DUMPEL program, 447
Duplexing. *See* Disk duplexing
Duplicate NT systems files, 297

Dustman File Cleaner, 522
Dynamic Host Configuration
    Protocol (DHCP), 137, 141, 148,
    152, 171, 176, 177, 421
    clients, 142
    configuration checking,
        IPCONFIG usage, 178-180
    DHCP/BOOTP relay agent, 142
    enabling, 174-177
    lease, 180
    manager, 134
    Manager, 175
    server, 142, 143, 153, 154, 174,
        175, 442
    systems. *See also* Non-DHCP
        systems

E

ECHO command, 62
ECU. *See* Extended Industry Standard
    Architecture
ECU-EISA Configuration Utility, 119
EDIT, 62
Edit menus, 66
EDO RAM, 124
EISA. *See* Extended Industry Standard
    Architecture
E-mail server, 8
Emergency Repair disk, 108
Emulex, 386
EnableSecurityFilters, 121
End volume sets, 71
Enterprise Edition, 7
Enterprise Server, 4
Error recovery, 106
EtherLink III, 49
Ethernet, 135, 166, 167, 211, 218,
    346, 465
EtherTalk, 166-167
Event ID, 103. *See also* Suspect
    event ID
Event Log, 89, 272, 339, 473. *See also*
    Security
Event logging, 99-107
    overview, 101
Event Viewer, 88, 89, 96, 97, 101-102,
    149, 374
Event Viewer System log, 78
EVENTVWR.EXE, 96
Exchange Server 5.0, 8
EXE files, 263, 286
Executable programs, 285-286
Executive Software, 300, 496
Export server, 232, 233
Extended Industry Standard
    Architecture (EISA), 442, 443
    Configuration Utility (ECU), 35
    controllers, 464, 468
Extended partitions, 69

Extended password
    management, 327
EXTERNAL program, 440

F

/f, 112
FAT. *See* File Allocation Table
Fault management software, 116
Fault tolerance. *See* Clusters
    editor, 452
FDDI, 211, 346, 443, 465
FDISK, 70
FIFO-enabled parameters, 128
File, 327
File access. *See* 32-bit file access
File Allocation Table (FAT), 25, 276,
    281-282, 468, 479, 482
    designation, 257
    disk, 36, 293
    drive, 235
    file systems, 291
    names, 61
    partition, 2, 70, 71, 276, 277,
        480, 481
    partition/NTFS, conversion, 80
    volume, 347, 364
File deletions, 482
File Manager, 66, 72, 97, 98, 236, 257,
    267, 279, 289-292, 305, 382, 393,
    446, 474, 483, 491
File menus, 66
File permissions, 362-364
File and Print Services for NetWare
    (FPNW), 165
File selection. *See* Backups
File Server, 95, 114, 346
File server access. *See* Macintosh
    clients
File systems, 275-302
    converting, 291-300
    issues. *See* Macintosh
    overview, 276-277
    summary, 302
File utility (tool), 521
Files. *See* Data files; Macintosh files
    compression, 291-293
        COMPACT usage, 292
    replication, 232-235
    uncompressing, 292
        COMPACT usage, 292-293
FileWise.Exe, 60
FloatBar, 259
FLOATBAR, 262-263
Floppy disk drives, securing,
    481-482
Floppy disks, 31, 37, 294. *See also*
    Disk Operating System
Floppy interface tape, 410
Floppy Lock service, 481, 482

Folder permissions, 362-364
    setting, 363
Folders. *See* Drop folders
FORFILES.EXE, 104
FORMAT, 347
FORMAT command, 68, 72
FPNW. *See* File and Print Services for
    NetWare
Fragmentation, 300
FrontPage 1.1, 4
FT Registry Information Editor,
    104-105
FTEDIT.EXE, 104-105
FTP server, 301
Fuzzy monitor, 114

G

Gateway Service for NetWare
    (GSNW), 163, 165, 217
Gateway services. *See* NetWare
Gateways, 140-141
General Protection Fault (GPF), 7,
    107
General-purpose servers, 115
Global groups, 266, 267, 348
Glossary. *See* Terms/definitions
Goldkey, 386
GPF. *See* General Protection Fault
Grandfather-father-son idea, 410
Group names, 199-201
Group profiles, 256
Groups, 265-271, 348. *See also*
    Global groups; Local groups;
    Special groups
    managing, 267-271
GSNW. *See* Gateway Service for
    NetWare
Guest accounts, 242, 483
    access, 229-230
GUI equivalent, 239
GUI interface, 113
GUI tool, 182, 246
GUI utility, 104
GUI-based setup, 46

H

HAL.DLL, 32
Hardware, changing, 128-129
Hardware Compatibility List (HCL),
    21, 221
Hardware configuration, 21-23
Hardware devices, BOOT.INI
    options, 110-111
Hardware notes, 121-129
Hardware problems, 122
    prevention, 122-123
Hardware RAID controller, 69
Hardware RAID options, 77

Hardware RAID solutions, 77, 125
Hardware recommendations, 123
Hardware requirements. *See* Remote
   Access Service
Hardware Setup, 404
Hardware solutions, usage. *See* Disk
   recovery
HCL. *See* Hardware Compatibility List
Hewlett-Packard (HP), 49, 124,
   454–455
   LaserJet printers, 386
Hidden shares, 492
High Performance File System
   (HPFS), 61, 235, 276, 282–283,
   291, 347, 468, 479, 482. *See also*
   Windows NT 3.51
Hive, 64. *See also* SYSTEM hive
HKEY_LOCAL_MACHINE key, 65
Home directories, 264–265, 284
HOSTS files, 145–148, 154, 178, 421.
   See also LMHOSTS files
Hot spare, 80
Hot-swap method, 79
Hot-swap systems, 125
HP. *See* Hewlett-Packard
HP OPENVIEW, 454–455
HPFS. *See* High Performance File
   System; Windows NT 3.51
HTML, 15
HTTP. *See* HyperText Transfer
   Protocol
HyperText Transfer Protocol (HTTP),
   15, 301
   Basic authentication, 493
HyperTerminal, 3

I

I386, 43, 60
I386-Intel version, 18
Icons. *See* Disappearing icons
Icontec, 127
IF commands, 62. *See also* Batch file
   IF commands
IgnorePushBitOnReceives, 121
IIS. *See* Internet Information Server
Import server, 232
IMPORT/SCRIPTS directory, 258
Individual profiles, 256
.INF. *See* Information
Information (.INF) file, 45
Information SuperHighway, 168
Information Technology Security
   Evaluation Criteria (ITSEC), 472
Informational messages, 112
INI files, 73, 94
Input/Output (I/O), 86, 423, 426, 457
Input/Output (I/O)
   configurations, 20
Input/Output (I/O) load, 81

Insert options, 106
Installation, 37. *See also* Computer
   profile setup installation;
   Network-based installation;
   Standard installation
Installation boot disk
   making, 307–308
   usage, 308–309
Installation media, Windows NT
   handling, 26–27
Intel, 18, 49, 116
Intel Pentium, 431
Intel processors, 43, 62
Intel systems, 123
Intel-based 486 DX2-66, 304
Intel-based computer, 29
   Windows NT installation, 30
Intergraph, 497
Internal ID, 200
Internet browsers, 10–11
Internet conferences, 230
Internet databases, 7
Internet Explorer, 15
Internet Information Server (IIS), 3,
   4, 7, 11, 15
Internet Protocol (IP), 138, 388
   address, 140, 142, 143, 150–152,
      171. *See also* Static IP address
   address mappings, 146
   network, 139
   protocols, 459
   routers, 140–141
   subnet broadcasts, 146
Internet Security Framework
   (ISF), 14
Internet security/privacy, 14
Internet server services, 301
Internet Service Providers (ISPs), 8
Intranet databases, 7
Inventory, 235
I/O. *See* Input/Output
IP. *See* Internet Protocol;
   Transmission Control
   Protocol/Internet Protocol
IPC$, usage. *See* System connection
IPCONFIG, usage. *See* DHCP
   configuration checking
IPX, 221
IPX protocols, 2
IPX/SPX, 135, 162–166, 168
   protocol stack, 165
IRQ, 20, 113, 128, 226, 230
IS managers, 341
ISA, 443, 464, 468
ISA device, 467
ISDN adapters, 221
ISDN servers, 228
ISDN support, 222
ISF. *See* Internet Security Framework

ISPs. *See* Internet Service Providers
ITSEC. *See* Information Technology
   Security Evaluation Criteria

J

Java, 15

K

KDC. *See* Key Distribution Center
Kerberos, 8
   definition, 12–16
Kerberos (version 5), 10
Kerberos SSP, 13
Kerberos ticket (TGT), 13
Kernel Profiler, 105–106
KERNPROF.EXE, 105
Key Distribution Center (KDC),
   12–14
Keyboard, multiple server usage, 114
KILL, 111

L

LABEL, 72, 73
LAN. *See* Local Area Network
LAN Manager 2.x servers, 213
LAN Manager client software, 310
LAN Manager OS/2 network
   clients, 304
Language networks. *See* Mixed
   language networks
LapLink, 50
LaserJet, 385
   printers. *See* Hewlett-Packard
LaserPool, 386
LaserWriter, 364, 365. *See also* Apple
   LaserWriter
Last-shared connections, 264
LAT, 386
LDAP, 15
LMHOSTS files, 145–148, 154,
   178, 421
Local Area Network (LAN), 4, 120,
   136, 258
   Manager, 283
   Manager Domain, 323
   manager servers, 192
   Manager systems, 237
   managers, 426
Local groups, 265–271
LocalTalk, 346
Lockout. *See* Account lockout
   period, 251–252
LODCTR, 430
Log file, 106
   name, 103
Logical disk, 76, 431
Logical disk drives, 68
Logical drive, 71

Logon configuration. *See* Windows NT Server
Logon dialog box, 252
Logon Hours, 248–250
Logon methods. *See* Macintosh users
Logon restrictions, 488
Logon scripts, 255, 258–265, 337, 339, 474. *See also* Systems Management Server; Workgroups logon scripts
  examples, 260–262
  tips, 264
  usage. *See* Client participation
Logon time expiration, 249–251
Logon times, control, 248–251
Logon wallpaper, changing. *See* Windows NT Server
LOGONOFF.EXE, 337
Logons, 490–491
  validation, 473–475
  warning messages, 488
Low-priority threads, 86
LPT, 385
LPT1, 393

M

Mac, 364
MacFile, 358
MacFile applet, 356
MacFile menu, 361, 363
Macintosh, services (Services for Macintosh / SFM), 166, 276, 311, 345–365, 485
  administration, 354–359
  components, 346–349
  configuring, 350
  file system issues, 360–364
  files, 354
  installing, 349–354
  MAC-NT, 276
  printing, 364–365
  removing, 349–354
  requirements, 346–347
  security, 347–348
  summary, 365
  workstation programs, installing, 350–353
Macintosh Cleartext password, 348
Macintosh clients, file server access, 349
Macintosh files, 361–362
  copying, 364
Macintosh network, 355, 365
Macintosh network topologies, services, 346
Macintosh path lengths, 360
Macintosh router, 355
Macintosh systems, requirements, 347

Macintosh users
  administering, 356–359
  logon methods, 347–348
  shared directories availability, 360–361
MACVOL, 360, 361
Mandatory profiles, 256
Master domain model, 196. *See also* Multiple master domain model
MaxForwardBufferMemory, 120
MaxForwardPending, 120
MaxNumForwardPackets, 120
MaxUserPort, 121
Maynard, 416
MCWS. *See* Microsoft Compatible Workstation Service
MDI layout, 372
Memory, 116–117
  optimization, 464
  options, 226
  utilization, optimization. *See* Servers
MEMORY.DMP, 107
Merge UAS option, 215
Message ID, 112
Messages. *See* Logons; Printer messages
  sending. *See* Users
Microsoft, 497, 455–460
Microsoft Compatible Workstation Service (MCWS), 163
Microsoft Diagnostics (WINMSD), 22, 112–113
Microsoft Down Load service, 296
Microsoft Excel, 285
Microsoft Knowledge Base, 208, 213
Microsoft Knowledgebase, 122
Microsoft Membership System (MMS), 10, 12
Microsoft Product Support, 122
Microsoft Professional Developers Conference, 16
Microsoft Word, 194, 280, 285
Migrate menu option, 74
Migration, 6
MIPS processors, 62
MIPS systems, 115, 377
MIPS Technologies, 19, 60
Mirror sets, creating, 77
Mirror volume, 79
Mirroring. *See* Disk mirroring
Mixed language networks, 212–213
MMS. *See* Microsoft Membership System
Modem pools, 221
Modems, 225–226
Modes. *See* Appstation mode; Combination modes; Taskstation mode

Monitor. *See* Network monitor
  multiple server usage, 114
Monitoring systems, 426–428
Mouse, multiple server usage, 114
MPR. *See* MultiProtocol Router
MS Client, workgroup add-on, 330–335, 393
  installation, 330
MS-DOS, 20, 24, 25, 70, 109, 256, 281, 291, 304, 479
  client software, 309
  clients, 235
  network boot disk, 343
  workstations, 330
MS-DOS, Workgroup Add-On, 259, 289, 290, 310, 329–335, 393, 397–399, 486, 492
  installation, 330
  logging off, 332
  logging on, 331–332
  usage, 331–332
MS-DOS-based terminal program, 231
Multi-homed computer, 150, 151, 174
Multi-link PPP connections, 478
Multi-platform operating system, 18
Multiple master domain model, 196–197
Multi-processor computer, 105
MultiProtocol Router (MPR), 121
Multi-Protocol routing, 4
MUSRMGR.EXE, 96

N

Name. *See* Computer names; Default user name; Domain names; Group names; User name; Workgroup name
Name resolution, 144–145. *See also* TCP/IP name resolution
National Computer Security Center (NCSC), 472
NBF. *See* NetBEUI Frame
NBT. *See* NetBIOS over TCP/IP
NC. *See* Network Computer
NCA. *See* Network Client Administrator
NCP. *See* NetWare Core Protocol
NCR chip set, 23
NCSC. *See* National Computer Security Center
NDS, 4
NET ACCOUNTS, 237
  command, 251
NET commands, 48, 227, 245, 382, 393
NET CONFIG, 236–237
  command, 235
Net DDE, 327
NET LOGOFF, 332

NET LOGON, 331, 332
Net Logon service, 206
NET NAME, 436
NET PASSWORD, 333, 485
NET PRINT, 333, 334, 398, 399
NET programs, 235-237
NET SEND, 239
Net Share, 287
NET SHARE, 288, 335, 399
Net Start, 227
NET START, 331
NET STATISTICS, usage. *See* Statistics
    collection
NET TIME, 334. *See also* Network
    time synchronization
NET USE, 260, 289-291, 309, 334
    command, 290, 371
NET USER, 491
NET VIEW, 236, 335
Net Watch, 191, 445
Net2Com, 231-232
NetBEUI. *See* NetBIOS Extended User
    Interface
NetBEUI Frame (NBF), 137
NetBIOS, 121, 137, 162, 180, 423
    name cache, 146
    service, 232
NetBIOS Extended User Interface
    (NetBEUI), 19, 120, 121,
    135-138, 159, 216, 310, 443, 465
    protocol, 218, 443
NetBIOS name server. *See* Windows
    Internet Name Service
NetBIOS over TCP/IP (NBT), 147,
    150, 151
    systems, 144, 145
NetBT, 121, 146
NetDDE, 82
NetDom.Exe, 60
NET.EXE, 235
NetJet, 388
NetLogon, 82
    services, 12
NETLOGON, 258, 259
    shared directory, 421
NetManage, 497
NetStart, 83
Netware 2.0a, 258
NetWare 3.12, 2
NetWare 3.x, 193
NetWare 4, 4
NetWare, 123, 162-166, 283
    gateway services, 216-218
    migration tools, 6
    printers, 399-400
    protocols, 221
    resources, 423
    servers, 164, 217, 218, 315
    utilities, 216

NetWare Core Protocol (NCP), 163.
    See also Novell NetWare Core
    Protocol
NetWare Loadable Modules
    (NLMs), 163
NetWatch, 191
Network adapters, 174
Network administration group,
    134-135
Network Administrative Tools, 174
Network API functions, 184
Network applet, 168, 170, 201, 218,
    226, 229, 322
Network cards, 46, 117
    disabling, 120
Network Client Administrator (NCA),
    134, 305-308
Network clients, printers usage,
    393-396
Network components, binding,
    218-219
Network Computer (NC), 303
Network configuration, 133-240. *See
    also* Zero Administration Kit
    summary, 240
Network connections control,
    profiles usage, 257-258
Network Control Panel, 163
Network controllers, 23-24
Network events, tracking. *See* Clients
Network ID, 139, 140
Network Interface Cards (NICs), 20,
    150, 211-212
Network management 133-240
    summary, 240
Network Monitor, 235, 455-460, 465
    usage, 458-460
Network performance, 464-466
Network providers, search order
    setting, 218
Network resources, 260
    connecting, 334
    viewing, 335
Network servers, designing, 210
Network setup, unattended answer
    file usage, 38-49
Network subsystems, 86
Network systems, backup, 422-423
Network Technologies, 95, 114, 497
Network time synchronization, NET
    TIME usage, 237-238
Network topologies, 135, 201. *See
    also* Macintosh network
    topologies
Network-based installation, 36-37
Networks
    applet, 336
    coexistence. *See* Windows NT
        Server/Networks

NICs. *See* Network Interface Cards
NLMs. *See* NetWare Loadable
    Modules
Node addresses. *See* TCP/IP node
    addresses
Non-DHCP systems, 153
Non-paged pool (NPP), 284
Non-PostScript jobs, 384
Non-PostScript printers, 364
Non-NT machine, 485
Non-NT print servers, 396-400
Non-NT systems, 383
    printers, 392
Norton backup programs, 411
Norton Disk Editor, 450
Novell NetWare Core
    Protocol, 163
NPP. *See* Non-paged pool
nslookup, 121
NT 3.51. *See* Windows NT 3.51
NT 4.0. *See* Windows NT 4.0
NT 5.0. *See* Windows NT 5.0
NT Server. *See* Windows NT Server;
    Windows NT Server 4.0
NT Time/TimeServ,
    synchronization, 238
NT Workstation. *See* Windows NT
    Workstation
NTAS, 432
NTBackup, usage. *See* Windows NT
    Scheduler
NTCD, 304
NTCONFIG, 49
NTDS. *See* Windows NT Directory
    Service
NTFS. *See* File Allocation Table;
    Windows NT File System
NTFSP, 62
NTLM. *See* Windows NT LAN
    Manager
NTLOGON, 259, 262-263. *See also*
    Windows NTLOGON scripts
    program, 265
NTMUM, 517-518
NTS. *See* Windows NT Server
NTVDM. *See* Windows NT Virtual
    DOS Machine
NTW. *See* Windows NT Workstations
NWLINK, 2, 135, 162-166
    protocol, 216

O

Objects, 430-431
Octopus, 401, 423-424
    usage. *See* Off-site backup
Octopus Technologies, 497
OCX, 286
ODBC database, 494
Off-site backup, Octopus usage, 424

OLE objects, 315
Open Resources, 444
OPENVIEW. *See* HP OPENVIEW
Operating system (OS), 20, 68, 101, 339, 408. *See also* Multi-platform operating system
   Windows NT installation, 24
Oracle database, 423
OS. *See* Operating system
OS/2, 24, 282
OS/2 clients, 262
OS/2 External/Dispatch utilities, 94
OS/2 network clients. *See* LAN Manager OS/2 network clients
OS/2 RAS servers, 231
OS/2 servers, 315
   password change, 271
   replication, 235
OS/2 subsystem, 94
OS/2 users, 276
OSF/1, 34
OSLOADER.EXE, 32
Output file name, 103
Overview performance monitor settings file, creation, 440

P

PAGEFILE.SYS, 460
Pages. *See* Separator pages
Paging files, 119
   sizing, 119–120
Parameters. *See* Router parameters
   passing, 62–63
Parity data, 79
Parity error, 107
Partitions, 69–70. *See also* Extended partitions; FAT partition; Virgin partition; Windows NT File System
   creating, 70–71
   deleting, 70–71
   formatting, 71–72
Password list (PWL), 201, 486, 487
   extension, 332
Passwords, 313–314, 485–487. *See also* Volume passwords
   changing, 486–487. *See also* Domain password management. *See* Extended password management tips, 486
Patches, problems, 296
Pathworks 5.x, 181, 213–216, 245
PC AnyWhere, 51
PcAnyWhere, 47
PCI. *See* Peripheral Component Interconnect
PCL, 390

PCT. *See* Private Communication Technology; Secure Socket Layer/Private Communication Technology
PDC. *See* Primary domain controller
Per Server licensing, 68
PERFMON.EXE, 96
Performance. *See* Network performance
   hardware issues, 129
   system design, 114–121
Performance Monitor, 93, 96, 98, 111, 129, 432–434
   alerts, setting, 434–437
   automation, DataLog usage, 437–439
   counters, 69
     list production, 432–434
   settings file creation. *See* Overview performance monitor settings file
   tips, 434
Performance monitoring, 439–460
   system. *See* Windows NT performance monitoring system
Peripheral Component Interconnect (PCI), 442, 443, 464
   bus, 118
   disk controllers, 116, 467
   network, 467
Permissions, 479–480. *See also* File permissions; Folder permissions
   assignation. *See* Users
   usage. *See* Users
Per-processor profile objects, 105
PERMS.EXE, usage. *See* Users
PerSeat license, 39
PersistentRoutes, 121
Physical disk, 431
Physical disk drives, 69–70
PID. *See* Process ID
PING, 141, 149, 152, 388
   command, 144
   connections verification, 177–178
Plug and Play printers, 375
PMON, 452–453
PMS. *See* Windows NT Performance Monitoring System
POINTER.INF, 26
Point-To-Point (PPP), 221
   connections. *See* Multi-Link PPP connections
Point-To-Point Tunneling Protocol (PPTP), 121
   technology, 479
POLEDIT.EXE, 340
Pool Paged Failures, 464
Pop-up interface, 289

Ports applet, 226
PostScript file, 365
PostScript jobs, 384. *See also* Non-PostScript jobs
PostScript mode, 389
PostScript printers, 364. *See also* Non-PostScript printers
   characteristics, 388
Power backup, 426–428
Power Chute. *See* American Power Conversion
Power PC systems, 116
PowerPC (PPC), 2, 19, 60
   systems, 119
PPC. *See* PowerPC
PPP. *See* Point-To-Point
PPTP. *See* Point-To-Point Tunneling Protocol
PPTPTFiltering, 121
PPTPTcpMaxData Retransmissions, 121
Preferences, 264
Prentice Hall, 199
   Technical Reference, 497–498
Price/performance ratio, 124
Primary domain controller (PDC), 20, 24, 31, 42, 50, 193–194, 202, 204–207, 256, 294, 442, 450, 482
   stopping, 207
Print, 327
Print information box, 383–384
Print Manager, 257, 368, 371–373, 381, 382, 483. *See also* Windows NT Server
Print Server, 346
Print servers, 114. *See also* Non-NT print servers
Printer applet, 393
Printer characteristics. *See* PostScript printer characteristics
Printer drivers
   changing, 377–378
   installing, 377–378
Printer management, 367–400
   conclusion, 400
Printer messages, 390
Printer pools, 384–385
Printer properties, 379
   changing, 377–378
Printer security, 373–374
Printer use, 367–400
   conclusion, 400
Printers. *See* Captured printers; Data Link Control; Direct network interface printers; NetWare; Non-NT systems; Remote NT printer; TCP/IP printers
   configuring, 374–376
   connecting, 382–383

considerations, 385-388
deleting, 381-382
disconnecting, 382-383
installing, 374-376
sharing, 378-380
unsharing, 378-380
usage, 384. *See also* Network
clients
Printing, 333-334. *See also*
Macintosh; Windows NT system
Private Communication Technology
(PCT), 15. *See also* Secure Socket
Layer/Private Communication
Technology
Problem finding, CHKDSK usage,
299-300
Process ID (PID), 111, 112
Processor (256K), 115-121
Processor Queue, 433
Processor subsystem, 86
Products, list, 495-498
Profiler. *See* Kernel Profiler
Profiles. *See* Group profiles;
Individual profiles; Mandatory
profiles; User profiles
assigning, 257-258
creating, 257-258
problems, 255-256
storage, 258
types, 256
usage. *See* Network connections
control; Users
Program INI files, 201
Program Manager, 97, 134-135,
328, 490
groups, 255
Programname, 112
Programs, access restriction, 488
Protocols, 135-167
changing, 168-177
choice, 120-121, 168
installing, 168-177
overview, 171-177
Proxy Server, 7, 493-494
Public-key certificates, 12
Public-key cryptography, 15
Public-key protocols, 11
Public-key security
architecture, 14
Public-key-based protocols, 10-12
PVIEW, 111, 467
PVIEWER, 453-454
PWL. *See* Password list
PWL files, 318, 319

Q

QSLICE, 454

R

RAID. *See* Redundant Array of
Inexpensive Disks
RAM. *See* Read Access Memory
RAS. *See* Remote Access Service
RawIpAllowedProtocols, 121
Rdisk, 109
RDISK form, 295
RDISK.EXE, 294, 295
Read Access Memory (RAM), 2, 6, 28,
86, 117, 118, 120, 122, 129, 304,
343, 347, 440, 442, 460-463. *See
also* EDO RAM
Real-time backup. *See* Servers
Real-time fault tolerance. *See* Clusters
Recycle Bin, 277
Redundant Array of Inexpensive
Disks (RAID), 75-80
array, 80, 125
configuration, 71, 452
controllers, 35. *See also* Hardware
RAID controller
implementations, 71
options. *See* Hardware RAID
options
RAID 1, 78, 79
RAID 5, 68, 75, 77-79, 118, 279,
401, 468
solutions. *See* Hardware RAID
solutions
systems, 78, 80, 118-119
REGBACK, 420-421
RegEdit, 382
usage. *See* Registry editing
REGEDIT.EXE, 314, 493
Regedit32, 488
REGEDT32, 64, 90, 95, 479
usage. *See* Registry editing
Regedt32.exe, 47
REGEDT32.EXE, 128
Reg.Exe, 60
Registry, 45, 74, 89, 108, 314-315,
420, 421-422, 493. *See also*
Windows 95
Registry database, 64-67
Registry editing
RegEdit usage, 65-66
REGEDT32 usage, 65-66
RegKey usage, 66-67
Registry editors, 93
Registry files. *See* Windows NT
Registry files
Registry size, 202-203
Registry Size Limit, 202
RegKey, usage. *See* Registry editing
REGKEY.EXE, 90
REGREST, 420-422

Remote Access Service (RAS), 6, 28,
96, 131, 219-231, 304,
476-479, 485
Administrator, 224
configuration, 221-223
design, 221-223
fit. *See* Domains
hardware configuration, 225-226
hardware requirements, 221-222
installing, 223-224
interaction. *See* Windows 95;
Windows for Workgroups 3.11
Monitor, 224
pausing, 226-227
permissions, 224
assignation. *See* Users
phonebook, management,
228-229
servers, 223, 228. *See also* OS/2
RAS servers
access, 229-230
service, 227
starting, 226-227
stopping, 226-227
system, management, 224-229
Remote boot option. *See* Clients
Remote Call Procedure (RPC), 10, 15,
82, 162
Remote NT printer, 390-392
Repair disk, 293-296
problems, 294, 296
updating, 294-296
REPAIR information, 108
Replication, 234-235. *See also* Files;
OS/2 servers; Windows NT
server
Request For Comments (RFCs), 137,
142, 144
ResKit, 491-492
Resource sharing, disabling, 327
Resources
availability, 426
sharing, 335
RFCs. *See* Request For Comments
Rights, 483-484
RIP DOS, 304
RISC, 116
RISC architecture, 124
RISC option, 28
RISC platform, 19
RISC system, 26, 33, 34, 42, 70, 114,
115, 123, 163, 377, 480
RISC-based computer, 29
RKTOOLS.HLP, 450, 453
RMTSHARE.EXE, 288
ROM, 462
ROM BIOS, 70, 461
Routers. *See* Internet Protocol

Routing. *See* Multi-Protocol Routing
Routing parameters, 355-356
RPC. *See* Remote Procedure Call
RS-232 interface, 222
RSA, 8

S

SAM. *See* Security Account Manager
Scalability, 426
SCANDISK, 277
Scenarios, 1, 17, 53, 133, 241, 275,
    303, 345, 367, 401, 429, 471
Screen saver, starting, 490-491
Scripts. *See* Client participation;
    Logon scripts; SQL scripts;
    Startup scripts; Systems
    Management Server; Windows
    NTLOGON scripts; Workgroups
    logon scripts
SCSI. *See* Small Computer Systems
    Interface
SDK. *See* Software Development Kit
Seagate, 411, 416, 495-496
Search order, setting. *See* Network
    providers
Secure Socket Layer (SSL), 15
    tunneling, 494
Secure Socket Layer/Private
    Communication Technology
    (SSL/PCT), 11
    protocols, 14
Security, 471-494. *See also* C2-level
    security; Client security; Domain
    security; Macintosh; Printer
    security; Volume-level security;
    Windows NT Security
    checklist, 271-272, 301-302
    considerations. *See* Windows
        NT 4.0
    event log, 374
    records security, 101
    settings, 359
    summary, 494
Security Account Manager (SAM),
    474-476
    database, 194, 202
Security ID (SID), 50, 253, 476
Security Reference Monitor
    (SRM), 476
Security Support Provider Interface
    (SSPI), 11
Selection filters, 102
Separator pages, 388-390
Serial communications, 128
Serial Line Internet Protocol
    (SLIP), 221
Server access. *See* Macintosh clients
Server administrative functions,
    access, 479

Server applet, 236
Server authentication, 12
Server configuration, 53-131
    automation, 47-49
    summary, 131
Server management, 53-131
    summary, 131
Server Manager, 96, 97, 150, 186, 192,
    288, 336, 482
Server Message Block (SMB),
    159-161
    protocol, 163
Server name, 103
Server Operators, 373
Server requirements. *See* Zero
    Administration Kit
Server tools, installation, 309-310
Server types, 115
Server usage
    controlling, 443-447
    monitoring, 443-447
Server-related options, 192
Servers, 199-201. *See also* File
    Server; LAN Manager 2.x servers;
    Network servers; Non-NT print
    servers; OS/2 RAS servers; Site
    Server; Systems management
    server; Transaction Server;
    Windows Internet Naming
    System; Windows NT Advanced
    Server; Windows NT Server 4.0;
    Windows NT servers
    access. *See* Remote Access Service
    application, stopping, 111-112
    automatic restart configuration,
        106-107
    memory utilization,
        optimization, 219
    real-time backup, 423-426
    replication. *See* OS/2 servers;
        Windows NT server
    starting, 88-89
    stopping, 89-93
    usage. *See* Domains; Keyboard;
        Monitor; Mouse
Server-specific access
    information, 12
Services, 82-86. *See also* Macintosh
    applet, 254
    management, 82-86
Services for Macintosh. *See*
    Macintosh
SETUP.EXE, 330
SETUPMGR program, 422
SETUPMGR.EXE, 38
SFM. *See* Macintosh
Shared directories, 186. *See also*
    Macintosh users

Shared directory, 307. *See also*
    NETLOGON
Shared resources, 184-192
    monitoring. *See* Windows NT
        3.51; Windows NT 4.0
Shares, 184-190. *See also* Hidden
    shares
Shell command, 94
SHELL line, 95
SHELL32.DLL, 297
SHH extension, 309
Shutdown command, 90
SHUTDOWN.BAT, 90, 92, 93
SHUTDOWN.EXE, 92
SID. *See* Security ID
Silicon Graphics, 19
SIMMS, 117
Simple Network Management
    Protocol (SNMP), 124, 136,
    484-485
    agent, 340
    capability, 455
    compliant systems, 54, 136
    data, 315
    management, 454-455
        tools, 454
    monitor, 457
    protocols, 459
Single domain model, 195
Single Large Expensive Disk
    (SLED), 75
Site filtering, 494
Site Server, 7
SLED. *See* Single Large Expensive
    Disk
SLIP. *See* Serial Line Internet Protocol
Small Business Server, 4
Small Computer Systems Interface
    (SCSI), 34, 468
    cables, 126
    chain, 69
    controllers, 46, 49
        problems, 23-27
    devices, 125-128
        connecting, 127-128
    disks, problems, 23-27
    drive ID, 23
    drives, 126
    hard drives, 23
    ID, 128
    number, 35, 125
    SCSICDRM, 128
    tape drive, 403
SMB. *See* Server Message Block
SMP. *See* Symmetrical MultiProcessor
SMS. *See* Systems Management Server
SMS.INI, 260
SMSLS.BAT, 262
SNA networks, 168

SNA server, 6-8, 148, 162, 221
SNMP. *See* Simple Network Management Protocol
Software Development Kit (SDK), 487
Software metering, 235
Special groups, 266-267
Specialty servers, 115
SpyWorks 5.0, 86
SQL scripts, 73
SQL server databases, 429
SQL servers, 4, 7, 23, 81, 83, 199, 221, 239, 419, 423, 442, 479
SRM. *See* Security Reference Monitor
SRVANY.EXE, 85
SRVMGR.EXE, 96
SrvMon.Exe, 60
SRVTOOLS directory, 309
SSL. *See* Secure Socket Layer
SSL/PCT. *See* Secure Socket Layer/Private Communication Technology
SSPI. *See* Security Support Provider Interface
Standard installation, 29
completion, 29-37
Startup scripts, usage. *See* Client participation
Static addresses, 153-154
Static IP address, 174
Static TCP/IP nodes, 134
Statistics collection, NET STATISTICS usage, 447-449
Storage arrays, 124-125
Stripe sets, 80-81
creating, 77-78
Subnet ID, 140
Subnet mark, 21
Subnet mask, 140
Subsystems. *See* Disk subsystems
Suspect event ID, 103
Symmetrical MultiProcessor (SMP), 117, 123, 124
configurations, 86-87
servers, 442
SysCon, 258
SYSDIFF.EXE, 45
SYSMON.EXE, 340
SYSTEM32 directory, 26, 97, 113, 297
SYSTEM32 subdirectory, 44
System, technical support, 129-131
System alerts, 98-99
System backups, 408-409
System connection, IPC$ usage, 96
System default, 256
System design. *See* Performance
System files. *See* Duplicate NT system files; Windows NT system files

repair, 108-109
replacing, 297-299
restoring, 421-422
SYSTEM hive, 105
System loading, balancing, 463-464
System log, 106
System memory, 460-463
System monitor, 340
System Policy Editor, 340
System records events, 101
System Recovery, 106
System resources, access limitation, 230
SYSTEM.DAT, 314
SYSTEM.INI, 181, 252, 317-319
Systems Management Server (SMS), 22, 54, 62, 82, 83, 114, 199, 458, 465
data directories, 421
database, 313
inventory agent, 235
logon script, 262

T

3Com, 49
32-bit file access, 325-327
Tape backup
problems, 424
programs, 410-422
Tape devices
applet, 402, 403, 405
maintenance, 402-407
TAPI. *See* Telephony Application Programming Interface
Task Manager, 3, 111
Taskstation mode, 341
TCP. *See* Transmission Control Protocol
TCP/IP. *See* Transmission Control Protocol/Internet Protocol
TcpTimedWaitDelay, 121
TechNet, 20, 39, 153, 222, 472
CD, 122, 127, 140
notes, 11
Telephony Application Programming Interface (TAPI), 3
Telnet, 135
Terminal, 135
Terminators, 127
Terms/definitions, glossary, 499-513
Text logging, 494
TGT. *See* Kerberos ticket
Third-party controls, 286
Third-party provider, 46
Third-party systems, 101
Third-party tools, 22
Thread object, 431, 434
Threads. *See* Low-priority threads; Top-priority threads

Time synchronization. *See* Network time synchronization
Time-outs, 447
TimeServ, synchronization. *See* NT Time/TimeServ
TLIST, 111, 112
Token Ring, 211, 218, 346
Topologies. *See* Macintosh network topologies; Network topologies
Top-priority threads, 86
Transaction Server, 7
Transitive trust, 12
Transitive trusting relationships, 10-12
Translate.Exe, 60
Transmission Control Protocol (TCP), 138
Transmission Control Protocol/Internet Protocol (TCP/IP), 42, 103, 120, 131, 137-159, 168, 170, 171, 174, 177, 218, 343, 386, 465, 484
addresses, 21, 141, 143-145, 148, 153, 154, 178, 179
configuring, 171-173
devices, 135
diagnostic utilities, 180
interface bindings, 151
management, 158
functioning process. *See* Windows NT 3.51
name resolution, 145-148
network systems, 177
node addresses, 139-140
nodes. *See* Static TCP/IP nodes
options, 159
parameters, 309
printers, 387-388
printing, 121
protocols, 2, 120, 138, 150, 221, 459
service, 149
stack, 120
troubleshooting programs, 177-180
utilities, 137
overview, 158-159
Trust accounts, 482
Trust model. *See* Complete trust model
Trust relationships, 195, 197, 207-210, 234
creation, 209-210
usage, 208-210
TRUSTED domains, 284
Trusting relationships. *See* Transitive trusting relationships

Tuning, 440-443. *See also* Windows NT networks;Windows NT servers;Windows NT subsystems
TYPE command, 104

U

UAM, 348, 351-353. *See also* AppleShare UAM
UAM Volume, 350, 353
UdpAllowerPorts, 121
Unattended answer file, usage. *See* Network setup
UNC. *See* Universal Naming Convention
Unformatted disks, 24
UNICODE, 212, 280, 360
   character, 360, 361
Uniform Resource Locator (URL), 19, 34, 60, 283, 344, 494
Uninterruptible Power Supply (UPS)
   applet, 428
   BOOT.INI options, 110-111
   devices, 426
   manager, 427
   signal line, 110
   subsystem, 98
United States National Computer Security Center, 50
Universal Naming Convention (UNC), 184, 395
   designation, 257
   name, 265, 424
UNIX, 24, 135, 145, 154, 392, 454, 476, 480, 481
   systems, 141
Unsupported CD-ROM, 35-36
Update programs, 264
UPS. *See* Uninterruptible Power Supply
URL. *See* Uniform Resource Locator
User accounts, 196, 199-201, 210, 254. *See also* Domain user account
   copying, 242-246
   creating, 242-246
   deleting, 242-246
   disabling, 253
   modifying, 242-246
   renaming, 253
   sorting, 247-248
User backups, 409-410
User default, 256
User management, 241-273
   summary, 272-273
User Manager, 244, 246, 265, 272, 347, 415, 473, 483. *See also* Domains
User name, 313-314. *See also* Default user name

User Profile Editor, 255, 257
User profiles, 254-258, 315
USER.DAT, 314
USER.INI, 262
Users. *See* Macintosh users
   adding, 245-246
   forcing off, 249-251
   logon control. *See* Workstations
   message sending, 238-240
   permissions finding, PERMS.EXE usage, 491-492
   RAS permissions assignation, 224
   restriction, profiles usage, 490
USERS directory, 265, 284
USRMGR.EXE, 96
USRTOGRP.EXE, 270

V

VAX, 136
VB. *See* Visual Basic
VB-DOS program, 260, 261
VBX files, 286
Vendor-supplied program, 35
Very Large Memory (VLM), 123, 124
VGA boot option, 129
VGA switches, 114
Video architecture, 3
Video cards, 21
Video display, adding, 129
Video systems, 117
Virgin partition, 25, 26
Virtual Memory (VM), 119, 203, 473
   system, 460-461
Virtual Private Networks (VPNs), 479
Visual Basic (VB), 86, 263, 382, 487
Visual Basic (VB) programs, 94, 238, 259, 416
Visual Basic (VB) Script, 15
Visual C++, 263
VLM. *See* Very Large Memory
VM. *See* Virtual Memory
VMS, 24, 33, 34, 145, 154, 457
VMS cluster, 424, 425
VMS installations, 90
VMS user list, 245
Volume. *See* Mirror volume
Volume choice. *See* Windows NT system files
Volume passwords, 363-364
Volume sets. *See* End volume sets
Volume-level access, 302
Volume-level security, 301-302
Volumes, 69-70. *See also* File Allocation Table
   drive letter assignment, 73-74

labeling, 72-73
VPNs. *See* Virtual Private Networks
VREDIR.386, 98, 180, 325

W

WaitFor.Exe, 60
WAN. *See* Wide Area Network
Web browsers, 11
Web page, 368
Web servers, 426
Web Trend, 518-519
Welcome dialog box, 89
WFW. *See* Windows for Workgroups
Wide Area Network (WAN), 120, 136, 424
   ports, 140
Wildcard option, 113
Win16 tools, 98
Win32 API, 97
Win32 functions, 487
Win32 subsystem, 475
Win32 system, 11
WINDISK.EXE, 96
Windows 3.x, 26, 112, 275, 367, 371, 397, 411, 454
   client, 83
   systems, management, 97-98
Windows 95, 6, 7, 20, 36, 63, 112, 123, 237, 240, 275, 281, 282, 290, 310, 311, 314, 335, 337-340, 367, 368, 375, 394-397, 454, 492-493
   client, 83, 256
   graphical interface, 3
   interface, 29, 31
   RAS interaction, 230-231
   registry, 314
Windows 95 systems, management, 97-98
Windows API, 313
Windows environments, choice, 6-7
Windows Internet Name Service (WINS), 137, 141, 144, 150, 421
   configuration, 178
   database, 148
   Manager, 156
   NetBIOS name server, 146
   options. *See* Windows NT 3.51
   server, 143, 144, 148, 150, 151, 155-157, 178, 442
   system, 155
Windows Internet Naming System, 134, 148-152
   manager, 134-135
   servers
      configuring, 153-158
      planning, 152-153
Windows NT
   batchcommands, 259
   boot volume, 421

booting, 34
handling. *See* Installation media
installation. *See* Intel-based
    computer
    upgrading, 49
    messages, 112
    protocols, 177
    reinstallation, 47
Windows NT 3.5, changes, 1–16
    summary, 16
Windows NT 3.51
    advent, 2
    High Performance File System
        (HPFS), 25, 28, 80, 281–283
    NT Resource Kit, 42–45
    shared resources, monitoring,
        191–192
    TCP/IP management, functioning
        process, 141–143
    upgrading, 46–47
    WINS options, 154–158
Windows NT 4.0, 2–6
    Deployment Tools, 50
    features, 28
    installation, 19. *See* Operating
        system
        security considerations, 49–50
    installation information, 20–21
    installation options, 19–20
    shared resources, monitoring,
        191–192
Windows NT 4.0 Resource Kit,
    104–106, 272
Windows NT 4.0 Server
    client tools, 304–310
    clients, 304–310
Windows NT 4.0 SYSDIFF.EXE, 45–46
Windows NT 5.0, 8–12, 272
Windows NT Advanced Server, 2
Windows NT backup, 411–414
    command prompt, 412–414
    graphical method, 411–412
    usage. *See* Windows NT Scheduler
Windows NT backup programs,
    410–414
Windows NT client configuration,
    303–344
    summary, 344
Windows NT client management,
    303–344
    summary, 344
Windows NT components,
    removal, 88
Windows NT Directory Service
    (NTDS), 283
Windows NT directory tree, 392
Windows NT File Server, conversion.
    See FAT partition/NTFS
Windows NT file types, 277–278

Windows NT File System (NTFS), 25,
    37, 61, 80, 276, 279–283, 341,
    363, 468, 482
    attributes, 364
    characters, 361, 362
    directories, 363
    disk drive, 481
    file names, 362
    file systems, 480
    files, 280, 281, 363, 364
    name, 281
    NTFS.SYS file, 298
    partitions, 72, 284, 293, 297,
        301, 346
    permissions, 362
    security, 301, 481
    system, 235
    users, 362
    volume, 97, 347, 349, 479, 480
Windows NT LAN Manager
    (NTLM), 10
    authentication, 15, 16
    security provider, 12
Windows NT logoff. *See* Automatic
    NT logoff
Windows NT networks, tuning,
    429–469
    summary, 468–469
Windows NT Performance
    Monitoring System (PMS),
    430–439
Windows NT Registry files, 47
Windows NT Resource Kit, 26, 38,
    66–67, 85, 90, 102–103, 111, 134,
    138, 144, 150, 153, 191, 231, 238,
    245, 270, 288, 372, 420–421, 430,
    432, 433, 437–439, 450, 452–454.
    See also Windows NT 3.51;
    Windows NT 4.0 Resource Kit
    choices, display, 63
    program usage, 60
    utilities, introduction, 54–60
Windows NT Scheduler, 254
    NTBackup usage, 414–416
Windows NT Security, 89
Windows NT Server (NTS), 2, 6, 17,
    42, 211
    automatic logon configuration,
        93–95
    logon wallpaper, changing, 95
    name, 21
    Print Manager, 97
    replication, 235
Windows NT Server 4.0, 7
Windows NT Server 4.0 installation,
    17–51
    methods, 27–29
    process, overview, 29–37
    summary, 51

tips, 18–23
    upgrading, 42–45
Windows NT Server 4.0 license
    management, 68
Windows NT Server resources,
    289–291
Windows NT servers
    adding, 203–204
    removing, 203–204
    tuning, 429–469
        summary, 468–469
Windows NT Server/Networks,
    coexistence, 213–219
Windows NT Software Solutions,
    usage. *See* Disk recovery
Windows NT subsystems, tuning,
    460–468
Windows NT system. *See* Non-NT
    systems
    printing, 390–392
Windows NT system files, 72. *See
    also* Duplicate NT system files
    securing, 480–481
    volume choice, 24–26
Windows NT Virtual DOS Machine
    (NTVDM), 432
Windows NT Workstations (NTW), 2,
    6, 7, 17, 18, 42, 48, 50, 304, 311,
    313–314, 335, 337
    adding, 203–203. *See also*
        Domains
    management, 96–97
    removing, 203–204
    tool, 96
Windows NTLOGON scripts,
    263–264
Windows Setup, 81
Windows for Workgroups (WFW),
    20, 63, 123, 181, 229, 230, 237,
    240, 248, 252, 256, 265, 289, 290,
    310, 312, 315–330, 337, 338, 390,
    392–394, 397, 423, 487, 492
    browsing functions, 325
    configuring, 317–325
    installation, 316–317
    workstations, 136, 242, 328
    WFWSYS.CFG, 325, 327–330
Windows for Workgroups 3.11, 182,
    231, 339, 310, 325, 339
    RAS interaction, 230–231
WINEXIT.SCR program, 488
WIN.INI, 260, 390
WinLogon single-logon
    architecture, 12
WinPopUp, 313, 325, 390
WINPOPUP.EXE, 390
WINMSD. *See* Microsoft Diagnostics
WINMSD.EXE, 113, 462
WINNT, 29, 35–39, 49, 62, 107, 421

WINNT /B, 20
WINNT boot directory, 294
WINNT boot drive, 60
WINNT command, 36
WINNT forum, 231
WINNT32, 29, 32, 35–38, 42, 49
    procedures, 35
WINNT32 /B, 20
WINNT32 file, 19
WINNT-based setup, 42
WINPOPUP.EXE, 240
WINS. *See* Windows Internet Name
    Service
Winsleuth Gold, 22
Wolfpack, 425, 426
Workgroup add-on. *See* MS Client;
    MS-DOS

Workgroup name, 311–312
Workgroups logon scripts, 260–261
Workstation programs. *See* Macintosh
Workstation requirements. *See* Zero
    Administration Kit
Workstations. *See* Windows NT
    Workstations; Windows for
    Workgroups
    logging in, 271
    user logon control, 248
Workstation-style monitors, 114
World Wide Web, 301
WOSA family, 492
WFWSYS.CFG file, managing,
    328–330

X

X.25, 228
X86, 37. *See also* CD-ROM
X86.BIN, 262
Xcopy, 50

Z

Zero Administration Kit (ZAK),
    341–344
    network configuration, 343
    requirements, 343–344
    server requirements, 343
    system requirements, 343–344
    usage, 342
    workstation requirements, 343

Bringing Technology Into Focus

Learn from the Experts

32X Corporation offers high quality public and private seminars on Microsoft products. Our public seminars are taught at locations throughout North America—see our web site (www.32x.com) for a location near you. Our private seminars can be scheduled at your convenience at your location. Both public and private seminars are packed with tips and information on getting the most out of the technology.

We offer these fast paced seminars:

Introducing Visual InterDev
Developing Dynamic HTML and Channels for Internet Explorer 4.0
Introduction to NT Server
NT Troubleshooting
Introduction to Visual Basic 5.0
Web Development with Visual Basic 5.0
NT Development with Visual Basic 5.0
Real World Java

Check out our web site for information on our seminars. We are adding new seminars on an on-going basis.

Private On-site Seminars

Experience the power of our seminars in the convenient setting of your own organization. Our instructors can deliver the same high-impact seminars in your training facility. Seminars in this format can be scheduled for classes of 15 and up. The smaller on-site classes provide a perfect opportunity for your personnel to interact with the instructor and get personalized feedback on active projects.

On-site seminars are available in either 2-day or 3-day formats. The 3-day format includes hands-on exercises throughout the course whereby the students work through examples with the instructor's guidance. This is an excellent mechanism for getting development teams up to speed quickly.

Created and Taught by Recognized Experts

Our seminars are created and taught by recognized industry experts. Ken Spencer and our other instructors contribute regularly to trade periodicals and newsgroups and are also featured speakers at major industry conferences such as Microsoft TechEd, VBITS, Microsoft Developer Days and Windows NT Intranet Solutions. We've written the book on the technologies we teach—literally. Each seminar was developed by the author of a leading book on that technology. For example, our Visual InterDev seminar was developed by Ken Miller and Ken Spencer, who co-authored "Inside Visual InterDev", by Microsoft Press.

Visit hyperlink http://www.32x.com for more details, including instructor bios.

32X Corporation
6000 Spanish Oak Dr.
Greensboro, NC 27409
800.417.1766

LICENSE AGREEMENT AND LIMITED WARRANTY

Read the following terms and conditions carefully before opening this software package. This legal document is an agreement between you and Prentice-Hall, Inc. (the "Company"). by opening this sealed software package, you are agreeing to be bound by these terms and conditions. If you do not agree with these terms and conditions, do not open the software package. Promptly return the unopened software package and all accompanying items to the place you obtained them for a full refund of any sums you have paid.

1. GRANT OF LICENSE: In consideration of your payment of the license fee, which is part of the price you paid for this product, and your agreement to abide by the terms and conditions of this Agreement, the Company grants to you a nonexclusive right to use and display the copy of the enclosed software program (hereinafter the "SOFTWARE") on a single computer (i.e., with a single CPU) at a single location so long as you comply with the terms of this Agreement. The Company reserves all rights not expressly granted to you under this Agreement.

2. OWNERSHIP OF SOFTWARE: You own only the magnetic or physical media (the enclosed disks) on which the SOFTWARE is recorded or fixed, but the Company retains all the rights, title, and ownership to the SOFTWARE recorded on the original disk copy(ies) and all subsequent copies of the SOFTWARE, regardless of the form or media on which the original or other copies may exist. This license is not a sale of the original SOFTWARE or any copy to you.

3. COPY RESTRICTIONS: This SOFTWARE and the accompanying printed materials and user manual (the "Documentation") are the subject of copyright. You may not copy the Documentation or the SOFTWARE, except that you may make a single copy of the SOFTWARE for backup or archival purposes only. You may be held legally responsible for any copying or copyright infringement which is caused or encouraged by your failure to abide by the terms of this restriction.

4. USE RESTRICTIONS: You may not network the SOFTWARE or otherwise use it on more than one computer or computer terminal at the same time. You may physically transfer the SOFTWARE from one computer to another provided that the SOFTWARE is used on only one computer at a time. You may not distribute copies of the SOFTWARE or Documentation to others. You may not reverse engineer, disassemble, decompile, modify, adapt, translate, or create derivative works based on the SOFTWARE or the Documentation without the prior written consent of the Company.

5. TRANSFER RESTRICTIONS: The enclosed SOFTWARE is licensed only to you and may not be transferred to any one else without the prior written consent of the Company. Any unauthorized transfer of the SOFTWARE shall result in the immediate termination of this Agreement.

6. TERMINATION: This license is effective until terminated. This license will terminate automatically without notice from the Company and become null and void if you fail to comply with any provisions or limitations of this license. Upon termination, you shall destroy the Documentation and all copies of the SOFTWARE. All provisions of this Agreement as to warranties, limitation of liability, remedies or damages, and our ownership rights shall survive termination.

7. MISCELLANEOUS: This Agreement shall be construed in accordance with the laws of the United States of America and the State of New York and shall benefit the Company, its affiliates, and assignees.

8. LIMITED WARRANTY AND DISCLAIMER OF WARRANTY: The Company warrants that the SOFTWARE, when properly used in accordance with the Documentation, will operate in substantial conformity with the description of the SOFTWARE set forth in the Documentation. The Company does not warrant that the SOFTWARE will meet your requirements or that the operation of the SOFTWARE will be uninterrupted or error-free. The Company warrants that the media on which the SOFTWARE is delivered shall be free from defects in materials and workmanship under normal use for a period of thirty (30) days from the date of your purchase. Your only remedy and the Company's only obligation under these limited warranties is, at the Company's option, return of the warranted item for a refund of any amounts paid by you or replacement of the item. Any replacement of SOFTWARE or media under the warranties shall not extend the original warranty period. The limited warranty set forth above shall not apply to any SOFTWARE which the Company determines in good faith has been subject to misuse, neglect, improper installation, repair, alteration, or damage by you. EXCEPT FOR THE EXPRESSED WARRANTIES SET FORTH ABOVE, THE COMPANY DISCLAIMS ALL WARRANTIES, EXPRESS OR IMPLIED, INCLUDING WITHOUT LIMITATION, THE IMPLIED WARRANTIES OF MERCHANTABILITY AND FITNESS FOR A PARTICULAR PURPOSE. EXCEPT FOR THE EXPRESS WARRANTY SET FORTH ABOVE, THE COMPANY DOES NOT WARRANT, GUARANTEE, OR MAKE ANY REPRESENTATION REGARDING THE USE OR THE RESULTS OF THE USE OF THE SOFTWARE IN TERMS OF ITS CORRECTNESS, ACCURACY, RELIABILITY, CURRENTNESS, OR OTHERWISE.

In no event, shall the Company or its employees, agents, suppliers, or contractors be liable for any incidental, indirect, special, or consequential damages arising out of or in connection with the license granted under this Agreement, or for loss of use, loss of data, loss of income or profit, or other losses, sustained as a result of injury to any person, or loss of or damage to property, or claims of third parties, even if the Company or an authorized representative of the Company has been advised of the possibility of such damages. In no event shall liability of the Company for damages with respect to the software exceed the amounts actually paid by you, if any, for the software.

Some jurisdictions do not allow the limitation of implied warranties or liability for incidental, indirect, special, or consequential damages, so the above limitations may not always apply. The warranties in this Agreement give you specific legal rights and you may also have other rights which vary in accordance with local law.

Acknowledgement

You acknowledge that you have read this Agreement, understand it, and agree to be bound by its terms and conditions. You also agree that this Agreement is the complete and exclusive statement of the Agreement between you and the Company and supersedes all proposals or prior agreements, oral, or written, and any other communications between you and the Company or any representative of the company relating to the subject matter of this Agreement.

Should you have any questions concerning this Agreement or if you wish to contact the Company for any reason, please contact in writing at the address below.

Robin Short
Prentice Hall PTR
One Lake Street
Upper Saddle River, New Jersey 07458